Lecture Notes in Computer Science 1369

Edited by G. Goos, J. Hartmanis and J. van Leeuwen

Springer
Berlin
Heidelberg
New York
Barcelona
Budapest
Hong Kong
London
Milan
Paris
Singapore
Tokyo

Sophie Cluet   Rick Hull (Eds.)

Database
Programming Languages

6th International Workshop, DBPL-6
Estes Park, Colorado, USA, August 18-20, 1997
Proceedings

 Springer

Series Editors

Gerhard Goos, Karlsruhe University, Germany
Juris Hartmanis, Cornell University, NY, USA
Jan van Leeuwen, Utrecht University, The Netherlands

Volume Editors

Sophie Cluet
Projet VERSO, Bat. 11
F-78153 Le Chesnay Cedex, France
E-mail: Sophie.Cluet@inria.fr

Rick Hull
Bell Labs, Lucent Technologies
600 Mountain Ave., Murray Hill, NJ 07974, USA
E-mail: hull@research.bell-labs.com

Cataloging-in-Publication data applied for

Die Deutsche Bibliothek - CIP-Einheitsaufnahme

Database programming languages : 6th international workshop ;
proceedings / DBPL-6, Estes Park, Colorado, USA, August 18 - 20,
1997. Sophie Cluet ; Rick Hull (ed.). - Berlin ; Heidelberg ; New
York ; Barcelona ; Budapest ; Hong Kong ; London ; Milan ; Paris ;
Singapore ; Tokyo : Springer, 1998
    (Lecture notes in computer science ; 1369)
    ISBN 3-540-64823-2

CR Subject Classification (1991): H.2.3, H.2, D.3, F.3, I.2.2

ISSN 0302-9743
ISBN 3-540-64823-2 Springer-Verlag Berlin Heidelberg New York

© Springer-Verlag Berlin Heidelberg 1998
Printed in Germany

Typesetting: Camera-ready by author
SPIN 10631879   06/3142 – 5 4 3 2 1 0   Printed on acid-free paper

Editors' Foreword

The Sixth International Workshop on Database Programming Languages (DBPL-6) took place in Estes Park, Colorado, August 18—20, 1997. The DBPL series of workshops focuses on the interaction of theory and practice in the design and development of database programming languages. This sixth meeting continued in the tradition of its predecessors in Roscoff, Finistère (September 1987), Salishan, Oregon (June 1989), Nafplion, Argolida (August 1991), Manhattan, New York (August 1993), and Gubbio, Umbria (August 1995).

The workshop was organized as a mixture of invited speakers, semi-formal presentations of papers, a panel, and discussions. DBPL-6 was a good illustration of the dynamism of our community. Traditional themes were well represented, and many interesting papers on new areas such as cooperative work, spatial applications, and string or textual databases were presented.

This volume contains papers based on the two invited presentations, a paper summarizing the panel discussion, and papers based on the technical presentations at the workshop. A short overview of the invited talks, the technical papers, and the panel now follows.

The two invited talks focused on two highly active fields within database programming languages.

- Jan Paredaens, from the University of Antwerp, gave a thorough survey on the developments in constraint databases and their application to spatial databases. He also presented new research on a model and query language for spatial databases that is based on Euclidian geometry.
- Philip Wadler, from Bell Labs, Lucent Technologies, outlined important principles from functional programming languages and emphasized how these languages have impacted the database and programming languages communities. He also presented an overview of the Pizza Language, an extension of Java that incorporates parametric polymorphism, higher-order functions, and algebraic data types.

The technical program of the workshop consisted of 20 papers, selected from a field of 40 submissions. These papers were formally reviewed and revised before inclusion in this volume. The program was broken into eight sessions, which are now described.

Spatial Databases

The issue of spatial databases has always been central to the field of Geographic Information Systems. The development of Constraint Query Languages by Kanellakis, Kuper, and Revesz in 1990 has generated new interest in this area, because the paradigm offers rich but tractable query languages for spatial data. In addition to the invited talk by J. Paredaens, two technical papers were presented in this area of using constraint query languages to access spatial data.

- S. Grumbach, P. Rigaux, M. Scholl, and L. Segoufin describe the system DEDALE, arguably the first substantial prototype system to support constraint query languages. The system is built on the O_2 DBMS, and provides a platform for studying one of the fundamental issues in constraint query languages, namely, query optimization.
- B. Kuijpers presents new theoretical results on monotonic transformations of spatial data. An elegant non-collapsing hierarchy of families of monotonic queries is developed, beginning with pointwise transformations, then transformations expressible in terms of pairs of points, up to transformations expressible using a countably or even an uncountably infinite number of points. At the finite levels of the hierarchy, equivalence of monotonic calculus queries is decidable.

Typing

In the design of programming languages a fundamental objective is to develop languages that support static type checking. This has been an elusive goal for object-oriented languages, and for languages that support persistence. The two papers in this session develop promising new approaches for providing static type checking for such languages

- S. Alagić develops a new approach for typing in object-oriented programming languages. The traditional approach to subtypes in these languages, where methods of a subtype have a covariant/contravariant relationship to methods of the parent type, is typically inappropriate in application. Alagić develops a new approach to guaranteeing type safety that is based on matching rather than inheritance. The system uses temporal logic to be able to reason about the runtime binding of variables.
- R. Connor focuses on developing an approach to typing for languages that support persistence. It is typical in such languages that the persistent store holds objects having type "any", and that injection and extraction functions are provided for converting objects from their type to "any" and back. The traditional approach to typing in this context is based on universally quantified types; Connor shows that using existentially quantified types is feasible and more appropriate.

Query Languages for New Applications

An important component of a database system is its query language, which enables substantial independence between the logical and physical representations of data. This independence makes it easier to write programs that are not invalidated by data reorganization. As database systems and applications evolve, so must query languages. This session includes three interesting papers on the subject. The first two reflect the increased interest in the database community for Web-related topics. The third concerns database versions, a topic central to many new applications such as software engineering or computer-aided design.

- A. Bonner and G. Mecca propose a new language for querying strings based on the coupling of Datalog with generalized transducers.

- M. Fernandez, L. Popa, and D. Suciu show how one can efficiently support queries on poorly structured data, e.g., the data found in the World Wide Web.
- T. Abdessalem and G. Jomier propose a model and query language for multi-version databases. The language permits queries against versions in a manner that is largely independent of the history of how the versions were created.

Views

Database views provide a mechanism for accessing a single data set structured in a variety of different ways. Research on database views continues to flourish, because of the challenges of new data models and new applications. The three papers in this session are representative of advances currently being made in this area.

- Z. Lacroix, C. Delobel, and P. Brèche study views in object-oriented database models. The continuing challenge here is that the model of views used in the relational model does not naturally generalize to include object identifiers (OIDs), because mechanisms are needed to create new OIDs. In the approach developed in this paper, the created OIDs are structured. This permits a given OID to be included in multiple classes (e.g., a base class and one or more view classes), and makes it possible to trace how a view OID came into being.
- A. Kawaguchi, D. Lieuwen, I. Mumick, and K. Ross introduce an algorithm for the incremental maintenance of views defined over nested relations. (These also arise as complex values in object-oriented databases). The algorithm has been implemented, and a performance analysis is presented.
- L. Libkin and L. Wong study the issue of supporting incremental maintenance of recursive views over a relational database. A broad class of questions here is: if auxiliary relations are permitted, can an update against the base relations be converted into an update against the recursive view using only non-recursive queries against the base and auxiliary relations. This paper explores the use of a nested relational language and of aggregate queries in this context. An important result here states that materialized views based on commonly arising recursive queries can be incrementally maintained using auxiliary relations and aggregate queries.

Expressive Power

A central topic in database research has been the formal study of the expressive power of query languages. Classical results here include the equivalence of the relational algebra and calculus, the fact that the relational algebra cannot express transitive closure, the development of "complete" query languages that capture all computable and generic database transformations over various data models, and establishing formal connections between the expressive power of query languages with complexity classes. Three papers in the workshop addressed fundamental topics in this area.

- C. Beeri, T. Milo, and P. Ta-Shma present a very fundamental study on the notion of generic languages. Speaking loosely, a language is said to be "generic" if it is invariant under isomorphisms over the underlying domain. It is common to restrict attention to isomorphisms that preserve a finite set of constants, or that preserve properties of certain types (e.g., arithmetic properties of the integers). This paper goes in the opposite direction, and identifies query languages whose queries are invariant under all mappings, including many-to-many mappings.

- L. Libkin and L. Wong consider the folklore result that the relational algebra, extended to include aggregate operations, cannot express transitive closure. The paper provides a complete proof of this result, using the formulation of the nested relational algebra based on structural recursion.
- M. Cadoli, L. Palopoli, and M. Lenzerini study the expressive power of query languages built up from Datalog and description logics. These hybrid languages support an interesting synergy between knowledge representation and conventional query languages. The work explores different ways that expressive power results can be stated in this domain, and then provides characterizations of the expressive power of representative hybrid languages.

Aggregate Queries

Decision making often relies on the ability to analyze large amounts of data corresponding to past or present experiences. For some years now, the database community has been very active in that field and notably in providing tools for on-line analytic processing (OLAP). OLAP applications offer two interesting challenges: they require an efficient treatment of aggregate queries and the ability to view the same data according to a broad variety of groupings across different categories. This session contains two papers:

- A. Poulovassilis and C. Small present a formal model for optimizing aggregate queries. An important aspect of this model is its generality: it can support most database query languages.
- L. Cabibbo and R. Torlone introduce a calculus for capturing queries on multi-dimensional data, thus providing a formal understanding of applications that usually rely on *ad hoc* extensions of SQL.

Cooperative Work

Emerging applications such as electronic commerce and cooperative authoring have increased interest of the database community in workflow management and business processes control. This is not surprising, since these applications entail sophisticated management of persistent data and some sort of transaction management. This session addresses the issue from two different perspectives:

- F. Faase, S. Even, R. de By, and P. Apers present a language allowing to integrate organizational and transactional aspects of cooperative activities. The paper is a good illustration of what database researchers, with their expertise in declarative languages and transaction-based activities, can do to improve the programming environment and paradigms used for workflow management applications.

- F. Matthes proposes an architecture based on agents and the Action Workflow model of Winograd and Flores, to allow distributed systems to coordinate their activities through *business conversations*. Persistent programming languages are shown to be adequate tools for the implementation of such an architecture.

Transactions

Transactions are at the core of database technology. Among the various factors that keep this field very active is the everlasting need for better flexibility and efficiency. This session addresses these two issues.

- A. Bonner proposes a Datalog language enhanced with the ability to specify and combine simple transactional units. This language offers the flexibility required by emerging cooperative applications.
- D. Spelt and H. Balsters propose a tool, based on a theorem prover, that permits compile-time checking for constraints that may be violated by a transaction in an object-oriented environment. This reduces the need for run-time checking and thus works for more efficiency.
- G. Amato, F. Giannotti, and G. Mainetto also address the efficiency problem by providing the means to check transactional programs statically. Specifically, they propose a method to deal with a new concurrency control protocol called multigranularity locking.

The Panel, moderated by Dave Maier from the Oregon Graduate Center, focused on the use of Meta-Data for Database Interoperation. The participants were Sophie Cluet (INRIA), Richard Connor (University of Glasgow), Rick Hull (Bell Labs, Lucent Technologies), Florian Matthes (University of Hamburg), and Dan Suciu (AT&T Research Labs).

DBPL-6 was co-chaired by Sophie Cluet and Rick Hull. Marcia Derr was the organizing chair. The Program Committee members were:

C. Beeri (Hebrew U.)	L. Cabibbo (U. Roma)
S. Cluet (INRIA)	R. Connor (U. St. Andrews)
S. Davidson (U. Penn)	M. Derr (U S West)
D. DeWitt (U. Wisconsin)	G. Dong (U. Melbourne)
M. Gyssens (U. Limburg)	R. Hull (Bell Labs)
A. Mendelzon (U. Toronto)	G. Moerkotte (U. Mannheim)
J. Schmidt (U. Hamburg)	V. Vianu (UCSD)
L. Wong (ISS)	

The committee wishes to thank James Bailey, Anthony Bonner, Ti-Pin Chang, Mike Doherty, Avigdor Gal, Stéphane Grumbach, Bart Kuijpers, George Mihaila, Tova Milo, Rainer Mueller, Rodolphe Nassif, Claudia Niederee, Wolfgang Scheufele, Gerald Schroeder, David Toman, Jan Van den Bussche, and Jens Wahlen for their help in refereeing submissions to the workshop.

The organizers are extremely grateful for the financial support given by INRIA, Bell Labs, and NSF.

X

The organizers also thank Mike Doherty for preparing the informal version of the proceedings that was distributed at the workshop. Finally, thanks go to Laura Vidal, for her assistance with local arrangements and accounting.

Sophie Cluet and Rick Hull
DBPL-6 Co-Chairs

May 1998

Table of Contents

Views

Expressive Power

Aggregate Queries

Cooperative Work

Transactions

Euclid, Tarski, and Engeler Encompassed

(Preliminary Report)

Jan Paredaens,[1] Bart Kuijpers,[1] Gabriel Kuper,[2]* and Luc Vandeurzen[3]

[1] University of Antwerp (UIA), Dept. Math. & Computer Sci.,
Universiteitsplein 1, B-2610 Antwerp, Belgium
Email: {pareda, kuijpers}@uia.ua.ac.be
[2] Bell Laboratories, 700 Mountain Avenue, Murray Hill, NJ 07974, USA
Email: kuper@lucent.com
[3] University of Limburg (LUC), Dept. WNI
B-3590 Diepenbeek, Belgium
Email: lvdeurze@luc.ac.be

Abstract. The research presented in this paper is situated in the framework of constraint databases that was introduced by Kanellakis, Kuper, and Revesz in their seminal paper of 1990. In this area, databases and query languages are defined using real polynomial constraints. As a consequence of a classical result by Tarski, first-order queries in the constraint database model are effectively computable, and their result is within the constraint model.

In practical applications, for reasons of efficiency, this model is implemented with only *linear* polynomial constraints. Here, we also have a closure property: linear queries evaluated on linear databases yield linear databases. The limitation to linear polynomial constraints has severe implications on the expressive power of the query language, however. Indeed, the constraint database model has its most important applications in the field of spatial databases and, with only linear polynomials, the data modeling capabilities are limited and queries important for spatial applications that involve Euclidean distance are no longer expressible.

The aim of this paper is to identify a class of two-dimensional constraint databases and a query language within the constraint model that go beyond the linear model. Furthermore, this language should allow the expression of queries concerning distance. Hereto, we seek inspiration in the Euclidean constructions, i.e., constructions by ruler and compass. In the course of reaching our goal, we have studied three languages for ruler-and-compass constructions.

Firstly, we present a programming language. We show that this programming language captures exactly the ruler and compass constructions that are also expressible in the first-order constraint language with arbitrary polynomial constraints. If our programming language is extended with a **while** operator, we obtain a language that is complete for all ruler-and-compass constructions in the plane, using techniques of Engeler.

* Research conducted while the author was at the Université Libre de Bruxelles. His work was supported by the ULB and the FNRS.

Secondly, we transform this programming language into a query language for a constraint database model. We show that the full expressive power of this query language is that of the first-order language with arbitrary polynomial constraints. It is therefore too powerful for our purposes. Thirdly, we consider a safe fragment of this language. Safe queries have the property that they map finite point relations to finite point relations that are constructible from the former.

The latter language is the key ingredient in the formulation of our main result. We prove a closure property for the class of constraint databases consisting of those planar figures that can be described by means of constraints that use linear polynomials and polynomials that represent circles. Based on our notion of safe queries, mentioned above, we define a query language on this class of databases. When the attention is restricted to finite databases, this language captures exactly the ruler-and-compass constructions.

We also compare the expressive power of the different languages mentioned above.

1 Introduction and motivation

Kanellakis, Kuper, and Revesz [23] introduced the framework of *constraint databases* which provides a rather general model for spatial databases [25]. Spatial database systems [1, 6, 9, 19, 28] are concerned with the representation and manipulation of data that have a geometrical or topological interpretation. In the context of the constraint model, a spatial database, although conceptually viewed as a possibly infinite set of points in the real space, is represented as a finite union of systems of polynomial equations and inequalities. For example, the spatial database consisting of the set of points on the northern hemisphere together with the points on the equator of the unit sphere in the three-dimensional space $\mathbf{R}^3$ can be represented by the formula $x^2 + y^2 + z^2 = 1 \wedge z \geq 0$. The set $\{(x,y) \mid (y-x^2)(x^2-y+1/2) > 0\}$ of points in the real plane lying strictly above the parabola $y = x^2$ and strictly below the parabola $y = x^2 + 1/2$ is an example of a two-dimensional database in the constraint model. In mathematical terms, these sets are called *semi-algebraic*. For an overview of their properties, we refer to [5].

Several languages to query databases in the constraint model have been proposed and studied. A simple query language is obtained by extending the relational calculus with polynomial inequalities [25]. This language is usually referred to as FO + poly. The query deciding whether the two-dimensional database S is a straight line, for instance, can be expressed in this language by the sentence

$$(\exists a)(\exists b)(\exists c)(\neg(a = 0 \wedge b = 0) \wedge ((\forall x)(\forall y)(S(x,y) \leftrightarrow ax + by + c = 0))).$$

Although variables in such expressions range over the real numbers, queries expressed in this calculus can still be computed effectively, and we have the closure property that says that an FO + poly query, when evaluated on a spatial database in the constraint model, yields a spatial database in the constraint model.

These properties are direct consequences of a quantifier elimination procedure for the first-order theory of real closed fields that was given by Tarski [29].

This quantifier elimination procedure is computationally very expensive, however. For an algorithmic description of quantifier elimination and an analysis of its complexity, we refer to [7] and [27]. The implementation of a query evaluation procedure based on quantifier elimination, which is double-exponential, seems therefore infeasible for real spatial database applications. In existing implementations of the constraint model (see the work of Grumbach et al. [13, 14, 16]), the constraints are restricted to *linear* polynomial constraints. The sets definable in this restricted model are called *semi-linear*. It is argued that linear polynomial constraints provide a sufficiently general framework for spatial database applications [16, 30]. Indeed, in geographical information systems, which is one of the main application areas for spatial databases, linear approximations are used to model geometrical objects (for an overview of this field since the early 90's we refer to [1, 6, 9, 19, 28]).

When we extend the relational calculus with linear polynomial inequalities, we obtain an effective language with the closure property as above, but this time with respect to linear databases. We refer to this language as FO + lin, and, so, we have the property that an FO + lin query evaluated on a linear constraint database yields a linear constraint database. There exists an "easier" way to eliminate quantifiers in the linear case, usually referred to as Fourier's method (see, e.g., [22, 24]), but it is not more efficient than the elimination procedure for FO + poly. There is however a slight gain in data complexity: Grumbach et al. have shown that the data complexity for FO + lin is NC^1 while it is NC for FO + poly [17]. Another, more significant, advantage of the linear model is the existence of numerous efficient algorithms for geometrical operations [26].

These complexity issues are not our main concern, however. There are a number of serious disadvantages of the restriction to linear polynomial constraints and these mainly concern the limited expressive power of the query language FO + lin. The expressive power of the language FO + lin has been extensively studied (see, e.g., [3, 4, 15, 18, 30, 31] and references therein). Of all the limitations of FO + lin we mention that this language is incapable of expressing queries that involve Euclidean distance, betweenness and collinearity. A query like "Return all cities in Belgium that are further than 100 km away from Brussels" is however a query that is of importance in spatial database applications.

The aim of this paper is to overcome these limitations for two-dimensional spatial databases in the constraint model.

We note that languages whose expressive power on semi-linear databases is strictly between that of FO + lin and FO + poly have already been studied. Gyssens, Vandeurzen, and Van Gucht [30, 31] have shown that, even though FO + lin extended with a primitive for collinearity yields a language with the complete expressive power of FO + poly, a "careful" extension with a collinearity operator yields a language whose expressive power is strictly between that of FO + lin and that of FO + poly on semi-linear databases. This extension does not allow the expression of queries involving distance, however.

We will identify a query language that is strictly more powerful than FO + lin on linear databases and less powerful than FO + poly and that allows the expression of queries concerning distance, betweenness, and collinearity. We also identify a class of two-dimensional constraint databases on which this language is closed. Because queries concerning distance are expressible in this language, it is also possible to define data by means of distance. The class of constraint databases we propose is a strict superclass of the class of linear databases. Its elements are describable by means of polynomial equalities and inequalities that involve linear polynomials and polynomials that define circles. We will call these databases *semi-circular*.

To accomplish this goal, we have turned, for inspiration, to the *Euclidean constructions*, i.e., the constructions by ruler and compass that we know from high-school geometry. These constructions were first described in the 4th century B.C. by Euclid of Alexandria in the thirteen books of his *Elements* [12, 20]. Of the 465 propositions to be found in these volumes only 60 are concerned with ruler-and-compass constructions. Most of these constructions belong to the mathematical folklore and are known to all of us. "Construct the perpendicular from a given point on a given line" or "construct a regular pentagon" are well-known examples. Since the 19th century, we also know that a certain number of constructions are *not* performable by ruler and compass, e.g., the trisection of an arbitrary angle or the squaring of the circle are impossible. For a 20th century description of these constructions and of the main results concerning them, we refer to [21].

In the course of reaching our goal, we have defined and studied three languages for ruler-and-compass constructions.

Firstly, we introduce a programming language that describes Euclidean constructions. We will refer to this procedural language as EuPl. Engeler [10, 11] has studied a similar programming language in the 60's. Engeler's language, however, contains a while-loop and therefore goes beyond FO + poly. Another difference with our language concerns a choice-statement that we have included in EuPl. This statement corresponds to choosing arbitrary points in the plane, something that is also done in constructions with ruler and compass on paper. We show that EuPl captures exactly the ruler-and-compass constructions that are expressible in FO + poly. It turns out that the choice-statement, at least for deterministic programs, can be omitted. We also prove a number of useful decidability properties of EuPl programs: equivalence and satisfiability of EuPl programs are decidable; it is decidable whether a program is deterministic.

Secondly, we transform the programming language EuPl into a query language for a constraint database model, called EuQl. This calculus can express non-constructible queries. In fact, we show that the expressive power of EuQl is the same as that of FO + poly. It is therefore too powerful for our purposes.

Thirdly, we have studied a *safe* fragment of EuQl, whose queries are all constructible. In particular, a SafeEuQl query returns constructible finite point relations from given finite point relations.

SafeEuQl is the key ingredient in our query language for semi-circular databases. SafeEuQl and FO + poly cannot be compared straightforwardly, however. Since the former works on finite databases, we let it work on intentional representations of semi-circular databases. We give FO + poly-definable mappings from one representation to the other.

Finally, we compare the expressive power of our languages with the expressive powers of FO + poly and FO + lin.

This paper is organized as follows. In the next section, we define FO + poly and FO + lin as data modeling tools and query languages. In Section 3, we introduce the class of the semi-circular databases and describe a complete and lossless representation of them by means of finite databases. We devote the next three sections to the study of the three languages for ruler-and-compass constructions: EuPl, EuQl, and SafeEuQl. The query language for semi-circular databases is given in Section 7, where we show that it is closed and compare its expressive power with those of FO + lin and FO + poly.

2   Constraint-based database models

In this section, we provide the necessary background for the polynomial and linear database models. We explain the notions of query in the context of these database models. We formally define two natural query languages, FO + poly and FO + lin, for the polynomial and the linear database model, respectively. Since the linear database model is a sub-model of the polynomial database model, we start with the latter.

We denote the set of the real numbers by $\mathbf{R}$.

2.1   The polynomial database model

First, we define a *polynomial formula* as a well-formed first-order logic formula in the theory of the real numbers (i.e., over $(+, \times, <, 0, 1)$). In other words, a polynomial formula is built with the logical connectives $\wedge$, $\vee$, and $\neg$ and the quantifiers $\exists$ and $\forall$ from atomic formulas of the form $p(x_1, \ldots, x_n) > 0$, where $p(x_1, \ldots, x_n)$ is a polynomial with integer coefficients and real variables $x_1, \ldots, x_n$.

Every polynomial formula $\varphi(x_1, \ldots, x_n)$ with n free variables $x_1, \ldots, x_n$ defines a point set

$$\{(x_1, \ldots, x_n) \in \mathbf{R}^n \mid \varphi(x_1, \ldots, x_n)\}$$

in the n-dimensional Euclidean space $\mathbf{R}^n$ in the standard manner. Point sets defined by a polynomial formula are called *semi-algebraic sets*. We will also refer to them as *semi-algebraic relations*, since they can be seen as n-ary relations over the real numbers.

We remark that, by the quantifier-elimination theorem of Tarski [29], it is always possible to represent a semi-algebraic set by a quantifier-free formula. The same theorem also guarantees the decidability of the equivalence of two polynomial formulas.

A *polynomial database* is a finite set of *semi-algebraic relations*. Relations and databases can be represented finitely in this model by means of the corresponding polynomial formulas.

Example 1. Figure 1 shows an example of a binary semi-algebraic relation which is represented by the formula

$$x^2/25 + y^2/16 \leq 1 \wedge x^2 + 4x + y^2 - 2y \geq -4$$
$$\wedge\, x^2 - 4x + y^2 - 2y \geq -4 \wedge (x^2 + y^2 - 2y \neq 8 \vee y > -1).$$

Fig. 1. Example of a semi-algebraic relation.

A query in the polynomial database model is defined as a mapping of m-tuples of semi-algebraic relations to a semi-algebraic relation, which (i) must be computable; and, (ii) must satisfy certain genericity conditions which are discussed at length by Paredaens, Van den Bussche, and Van Gucht [25].

The most natural query language for the polynomial data model is the relational calculus augmented with polynomial inequalities, i.e., the first-order language which contains as atomic formulas polynomial inequalities and formulas of the form $R_i(y_1, \ldots, y_n)$, where R_i ($i = 1, \ldots, m$) are semi-algebraic relation names for the input parameters of the query, and $y_1, \ldots, y_n$ are real variables. In the literature, this query language is commonly referred to as FO + poly.

Example 2. The FO + poly formula

$$R(x,y) \wedge (\forall \varepsilon)(\varepsilon \leq 0 \vee (\exists v)(\exists w)(\neg R(v,w) \wedge (x - v)^2 + (y - w)^2 < \varepsilon))$$

has x and y as free variables. For a given binary semi-algebraic relation R, it computes the set of points with coordinates (x, y) that belong to the intersection of R and its topological border.

Tarski's quantifier-elimination procedure ensures that every FO + poly query is effectively computable and yields a polynomial database as result [23].

2.2 The linear database model

Polynomial formulas built from atomic formulas that contain only linear polynomials are called *linear formulas*. Point sets defined by linear formulas are called *semi-linear sets* or *semi-linear relations*.

We remark that there is also a quantifier elimination property for the linear model: for any linear formula that contains quantifiers, there is an equivalent quantifier-free linear formula. There is a conceptually easy algorithm, usually referred to as Fourier's method, to eliminate quantifiers in the linear model (this method is described in [22, 24]).

A *linear database* is a finite set of *semi-linear relations*. Relations and databases can be represented finitely in this model by means of the corresponding linear formulas.

Example 3. The binary semi-linear relation depicted in Figure 2 is described by the formula

$$x - 3 \leq 0 \wedge x + 3 \geq 0 \wedge y - 3 \leq 0 \wedge y + 3 \geq 0$$
$$\wedge \ \neg(x - 2 \leq 0 \wedge x - 1 \geq 0 \wedge y - 2 \leq 0 \wedge y - 1 \geq 0)$$
$$\wedge \ \neg(x + 1 \leq 0 \wedge x + 2 \geq 0 \wedge y - 2 \leq 0 \wedge y - 1 \geq 0)$$
$$\wedge \ \neg(x \geq -2 \wedge x \leq 0 \wedge 2y + x + 4 = 0)$$
$$\wedge \ \neg(x \geq 0 \wedge x \leq 2 \wedge y - x + 4 = 0).$$

Fig. 2. Example of a semi-linear relation.

As in the polynomial model, queries in the linear model are defined as mappings from m-tuples of semi-linear relations to a semi-linear relation. A very appealing query language for the semi-linear data model, called FO + lin, is obtained by restricting the polynomial formulas in FO + poly to contain only linear polynomials. Using algebraic computation techniques for the elimination of variables, one can see that the result of every FO + lin query is a semi-linear relation [22, 24].

Example 4. The FO + lin formula

$$R(x,y) \wedge (\forall \varepsilon)(\varepsilon \leq 0 \vee (\exists v)(\exists w)(\neg R(v,w) \wedge x - \varepsilon < v < x + \varepsilon \wedge y - \varepsilon < w < y + \varepsilon))$$

has two free variables: x and y. For a given binary semi-linear relation R, it computes the set of points with coordinates (x, y) that belong to the intersection of R and its topological border. In fact, this formula is equivalent to the one in Example 2. It makes use of a different metric to compute the topological border, however. It should be clear that not every FO + poly formula has an equivalent FO + lin formula.

3 Semi-circular relations and a complete and lossless encoding

In this section, we describe a class of planar relations in the constraint model that can be described by polynomial inequalities that involve linear polynomials and polynomials that describe circles. We also give a way to encode these relations as finite relations of points: this representation will be used later on.

Definition 1. We call a subset of $\mathbf{R}^2$ an *semi-circular set* or *semi-circular relation* if and only if it can be defined as a Boolean combination of sets of the form

$$\{(x,y) \mid ax + by + c \geq 0\},$$

or

$$\{(x,y) \mid (x-a)^2 + (y-b)^2 \geq c^2\},$$

with a, b, and c real algebraic numbers.

As far as planar figures are concerned, the class of semi-circular relations clearly contains the class of semi-linear relations.

Example 5. Figure 3 (a) shows an example of a semi-circular relation. It is the set

$$\{(x,y) \mid x^2 + y^2 \leq 1 \vee (y = 0 \wedge 1 \leq x < 2) \vee (x > 2 \wedge \neg y = 0)\}.$$

Given such an semi-circular database, we can then consider the figure consisting of all sets $\{(x,y) \mid p(x,y) = 0\}$ for each $p(x,y)$ in the definition of the semi-circular relation.

For the semi-circular relation of Figure 3 (a), these sets are shown in part (b) of Figure 3 and they are defined by the equations $x^2 + y^2 - 1 = 0$, $y = 0$, $x - 1 = 0$, and $x - 2 = 0$. We refer to these lines and circles as the *carrier* of the semi-circular relation. The carrier of Figure 3 (b) partitions the plane $\mathbf{R}^2$ into 21 classes, each of which belongs entirely to the semi-circular relation or to its complement. Representatives $p_1, \ldots, p_{21}$ of each of these classes are shown in Figure 3. We can therefore represent a semi-circular relation R by a finite database that consists of three relations, L, P and C, as follows:

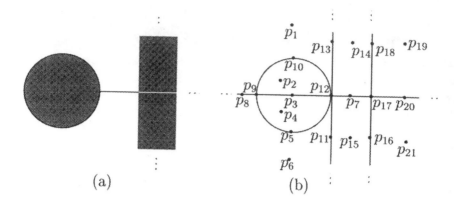

Fig. 3. A semi-circular relation (a) and its carrier (b).

- L contains, for each line in the carrier of R, a pair of its points;
- C contains, for each circle in the carrier of R, its center and one of its points;
- P contains a representative of each class in the partition induced by the carrier of R, that belongs to R.

L and C are binary relations of points in the plane. P is a unary relation of points.

We will refer to such a finite representation of a semi-circular relation as an *intensional LPC-representation*. Clearly, a semi-circular relation can have more than one intensional LPC-representation.

For the semi-circular database of Figure 3 (a) we get the following finite representation: L consists of the tuples (p_7, p_8), (p_{11}, p_{12}), and (p_{16}, p_{17}); C consists of one single tuple (p_3, p_5); and P consists of the points p_9, p_{10}, p_2, p_3, p_4, p_5, p_{12}, p_7, p_{19}, and p_{21}.

We remark that an intensional LPC-representation of a semi-circular relation is lossless in the sense that it contains enough information to reconstruct the semi-circular relation it represents.

4   The language EuPl

We start by defining a language EuPl, for expressing Euclidean constructions. In this language, we have one basic type $\langle \text{var} \rangle$ that ranges over points in the plane. Lines are represented by pairs of points, and circles by triples, where (p_1, p_2, p_3) represents the circle with center p_1 and radius equal to the distance between p_2 and p_3.

The boolean conditions in EuPl are formed, using the standard propositional connectives, out of the following:

1. **defined**($\langle$var$\rangle$);
2. $\langle$var$\rangle$ = $\langle$var$\rangle$;
3. $\langle$var$\rangle$ **is on line** ($\langle$var$\rangle$, $\langle$var$\rangle$);
4. $\langle$var$\rangle$ **is on circle** ($\langle$var$\rangle$, $\langle$var$\rangle$, $\langle$var$\rangle$);
5. $\langle$var$\rangle$ **is in circle** ($\langle$var$\rangle$, $\langle$var$\rangle$, $\langle$var$\rangle$);
6. $\langle$var$\rangle$ **is on the same side as** $\langle$var$\rangle$ **of line** ($\langle$var$\rangle$, $\langle$var$\rangle$);
7. **l-order** ($\langle$var$\rangle$, $\langle$var$\rangle$, $\langle$var$\rangle$);
8. **c-order** ($\langle$var$\rangle$, $\langle$var$\rangle$, $\langle$var$\rangle$, $\langle$var$\rangle$).

The first condition means that the variable in question is already defined. The meanings of the next 5 conditions should be clear. The predicate **l-order** (p_1, p_2, p_3) (line-order) means that all 3 points are on the same line, and that p_2 is between p_1 and p_3. The predicate **c-order** (p_1, p_2, p_3, p_4) (circle-order) means that all 4 points are on the same circle, in the same order in the clockwise or counter-clockwise direction.

The expressions in EuPl include the following operations that compute the intersection point(s) of 2 objects (line/line, line/circle and circle/circle):

1. **l-l-crossing** ($\langle$var$\rangle$, $\langle$var$\rangle$, $\langle$var$\rangle$, $\langle$var$\rangle$);
2. **l-c-crossing** ($\langle$var$\rangle$, $\langle$var$\rangle$, $\langle$var$\rangle$, $\langle$var$\rangle$, $\langle$var$\rangle$);
3. **c-c-crossing** ($\langle$var$\rangle$, $\langle$var$\rangle$, $\langle$var$\rangle$, $\langle$var$\rangle$, $\langle$var$\rangle$, $\langle$var$\rangle$).

The language EuPl is largely a standard procedural programming language, without iteration, using these primitives. The one nonstandard feature is a non-deterministic choice operator, whose syntax is

choose $\langle$var$\rangle$ **such that** $\langle$condition$\rangle$

We illustrate the usage of the language by several examples.

Example 6. Our first example is to construct the intersection of the perpendicular to a given line from a given point p (p not on that line) with the given line. It is illustrated in Figure 4.

multifunction perp(p, p_1, p_2) = (p_5);
begin ;
choose q **such that** **not** (q **is on the same side as** p **of line** (p_1, p_2));
    r, s := **l-c-crossing** (p_1, p_2, p, p, q);
    p_3, p_4 := **c-c-crossing** (r, r, p, s, s, p);
    p_5 := **l-l-crossing** (p_1, p_2, p_3, p_4);
end

Our second example shows how to construct an arbitrary point on an ellipse (note that the entire ellipse is not constructible with ruler and compass).

Example 7. Given the collinear points a, b, p, and q, with $d(a, p) = d(b, q)$, p between a and q, and q between p and b, we can construct an arbitrary point r' on the ellipse through a and b with foci p and q (see Figure 5), as follows:

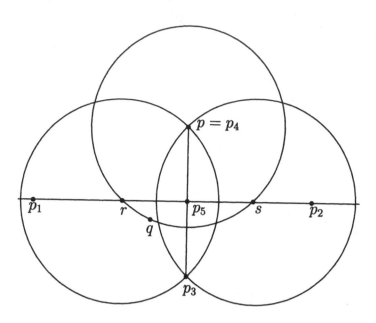

Fig. 4. Construction of the perpendicular.

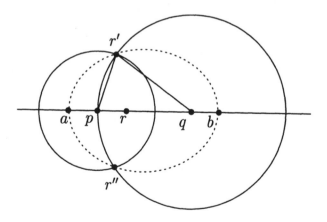

Fig. 5. Construction of a point on an ellipse.

multifunction put-ellipse$(a, b, p, q) = (r')$;
begin ;
choose r **such that l-order** (a, r, b);
    $r', r'' :=$ **c-c-crossing** (p, a, r, q, b, r);
end

In EuPl, a line is represented by 2 points, and a circle by 3 points. A given line has many different representations, and the natural question to ask is whether the result of a EuPl program depends on the representation of the input or not.

The answer is that the result could depend on the representation: for a very simple example, consider the program that takes as input a line, represented by the pair (p_1, p_2), and results in p_1. In fact, the question as we have just posed it, is not yet meaningful, as the input to a EuPl program is merely a tuple of points, with no semantics attached. If we add such semantics, i.e., we specify which points represent points/lines/circles, we can then show that, while we can write programs whose result depends on the representation, we can at least tell whether a program is a good one, i.e., whose result is representation independent (as are our two examples above).

Theorem 2. *It is decidable whether the result of a EuPl program depends on the representation of its inputs or not.* □

From the definition of the EuPl language, it follows that:

Theorem 3. *All EuPl multifunctions are constructible with ruler and compass.* □

The converse is not strictly true. Our language essentially models *first-order* ruler-and-compass constructions[4]. For an example of a non-first order ruler-and-compass construction, consider the following example.

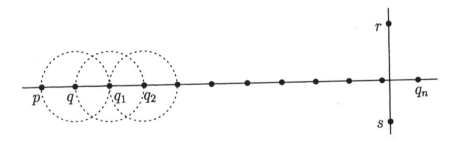

Fig. 6. Non first-order construction.

Example 8. Let p, q, r, and s be four points as shown in Figure 6. Consider the following construction: first construct the point q_1 on the line through p and q such that $d(q_1, q) = d(q, p)$ and q_1 closer than q to the line through r and s than q. Then we repeat this construction until we get to the other side of the line through r and s, and the result is the first point to the right of the vertical line (q_n with $n = 10$ in Figure 6). The computation of this point requires a while-loop, and it can be proved that it cannot be done by a EuPl program.

Previous languages based on Euclidean geometry, such as [10, 11], have included such a **while** constructor, and the first-order nature of EuPl—motivated

---

[4] As all geometric constructions in Euclid [12] are first-order, we could claim that our language does indeed model Euclidean geometry.

by our interest in query languages for databases—is what distinguished EuPl from languages such as Engeler's.

We now turn our attention to the role of the choice operator in EuPl. In Example 6, the result of the program is independent of the choice made by the choice operator, and this is true for the classic Euclidean constructions as well as for all other "reasonable" EuPl programs. An important result (which follows from Tarski's result [29] on the decidability of the theory of real closed fields) is that the question whether the result of a program depends on the choices made by the **choose** operator is decidable.

Theorem 4. *It is decidable whether the result of a* EuPl *program depends on the choices made by* **choose** *operators.*   □

Furthermore, it turns out that the necessity of having choice operators in EuPl is related to the absence of a notion of unity. If we add such a notion, encoded as two fixed, distinguished, points, we can dispense with the choice operator.

Theorem 5. *If the database contains two fixed, distinguished, points p_0 and p_1, then every deterministic* EuPl *program is equivalent to a program without the* **choose** *operator.*   □

For the rest of this paper, we shall assume that we always have two such fixed points, and we shall not use the **choose** operator any more.

We conclude with a number of useful properties of EuPl programs.

Theorem 6. *Equivalence and satisfiability are decidable properties of* EuPl *programs.*   □

5   The language EuQl

We now wish to define a database query language for Euclidean geometry. We start with our first attempt, EuQl, at defining such a language. In essence, EuQl is a query-language equivalent of EuPl. Contrary to EuPl however, EuQl is a declarative language. For example, the crossing-point operators will be provided under the form of predicates rather than assignment statements.

The relations in what follow are point relations. R_i, of arity m_i, is an m_i-ary point relation, i.e., an $2m_i$-ary relation over the reals. The instances are those that are definable in the polynomial constraint model.

A EuQl query over a schema $R_1, \ldots R_n$ has the form

$$Q(R_1, \ldots, R_n) = \{(v_1, \ldots, v_m) \mid \varphi(R_1, \ldots, R_n, v_1, \ldots, v_m)\},$$

where φ is a standard first-order language with equality, database predicates, and the following special primitives:

1. ⟨var⟩ **is on line** (⟨var⟩, ⟨var⟩);
2. ⟨var⟩ **is on circle** (⟨var⟩, ⟨var⟩, ⟨var⟩);
3. ⟨var⟩ **is in circle** (⟨var⟩, ⟨var⟩, ⟨var⟩);
4. ⟨var⟩ **is on the same side as** ⟨var⟩ **of line** (⟨var⟩, ⟨var⟩);
5. **l-order** (⟨var⟩, ⟨var⟩, ⟨var⟩);
6. **c-order** (⟨var⟩, ⟨var⟩, ⟨var⟩, ⟨var⟩);
7. ⟨var⟩ **is l-l-crossing point of** (⟨var⟩, ⟨var⟩, ⟨var⟩, ⟨var⟩);
8. ⟨var⟩ **is l-c-crossing point of** (⟨var⟩, ⟨var⟩, ⟨var⟩, ⟨var⟩, ⟨var⟩);
9. ⟨var⟩ **is c-c-crossing point of** (⟨var⟩, ⟨var⟩, ⟨var⟩, ⟨var⟩, ⟨var⟩, ⟨var⟩).

The semantics of EuQl is defined as a function

$$S(Q) : \mathcal{R}_1 \times \cdots \times \mathcal{R}_n \to \mathcal{R},$$

where $\mathcal{R}_i$ is the type of relation R_i and $\mathcal{R}$ the type of the result of Q. The interpretations of variables, logical connectives, etc., are standard. The special predicates are interpreted as follows:

1. $S(v_1$ **is on line** $(v_2, v_3))(r_1, \ldots, r_n)$ is the set of those tuples of points for which a_{v_2} and a_{v_3} are distinct, and a_{v_1}, a_{v_2} and a_{v_3} are collinear.
2. $S(v_1$ **is on circle** $(v_2, v_3, v_4))(r_1, \ldots, r_n)$ is the set of such tuples, where a_{v_1} is on the circle with center a_{v_2} and radius $d(a_{v_3}, a_{v_4})$, where a_{v_3} and a_{v_4} are distinct.
3. $S(v_1$ **is in circle** $(v_2, v_3, v_4))(r_1, \ldots, r_n)$ is the set of such tuples where a_{v_1} is in the interior of the circle with center a_{v_2} and radius $d(a_{v_3}, a_{v_4})$, where a_{v_3} and a_{v_4} are distinct.
4. $S(v_1$ **is on the same side as** v_2 **of line** $(v_3, v_4))(r_1, \ldots, r_n)$ is the set of such tuples where a_{v_1} is on the same side as a_{v_2} of the line (a_{v_3}, a_{v_4}), where a_{v_3} and a_{v_4} are distinct, and a_{v_2}, a_{v_3} and a_{v_4} are not collinear.
5. $S(\text{l-order}(v_1, v_2, v_3))(r_1, \ldots, r_n)$ is the set of such tuples for which a_{v_1}, a_{v_2}, and a_{v_3} are distinct and collinear, and a_{v_1} lies between a_{v_2} and a_{v_3}.
6. $S(\text{c-order}(v_1, v_2, v_3, v_4))(r_1, \ldots, r_n)$ is the set of such tuples for which a_{v_1}, a_{v_2}, a_{v_3} and a_{v_4} are distinct and lie on the same circle, in this order (either clockwise or counter-clockwise).
7. $S(v_1$ **is l-l-crossing point of** $(v_2, v_3, v_4, v_5))(r_1, \ldots, r_n)$ is the set of such tuples for which a_{v_2} and a_{v_3} are distinct, a_{v_4} and a_{v_5} are distinct, and the lines (a_{v_2}, a_{v_3}) and (a_{v_4}, a_{v_5}) are distinct, non-parallel, and intersect at a_{v_1}.
8. $S(v_1$ **is l-c-crossing point of** $(v_2, v_3, v_4, v_5, v_6))(r_1, \ldots, r_n)$ is the set of such tuples for which a_{v_2} and a_{v_3} are distinct, a_{v_5} and a_{v_6} are distinct, and a_{v_1} is a crossing point of the line (a_{v_2}, a_{v_3}) and the circle $(a_{v_4}, a_{v_5}, a_{v_6})$.
9. $S(v_1$ **is c-c-crossing point of** $(v_2, v_3, v_4, v_5, v_6, v_7))(r_1, \ldots, r_n)$ is the set of such tuples for which a_{v_3} and a_{v_4} are distinct, a_{v_6} and a_{v_7} are distinct, and a_{v_1} is a crossing point of the two circles $(a_{v_2}, a_{v_3}, a_{v_4})$ and $(a_{v_5}, a_{v_6}, a_{v_7})$.

Example 9. Given a binary relation R that consists of pairs of points, return the unary relation with the midpoints of each tuple of R.

$\{(p) \mid (\exists p_1)(\exists p_2)((R(p_1, p_2) \land p_1 = p_2 \land p = p_1) \lor$

$\quad (R(p_1, p_2) \land \neg(p_1 = p_2) \land p$ **is on line** $(p_1, p_2) \land$

$\quad (\exists p_3)(\exists p_4)((p_3$ **is on circle** $(p_1, p_1, p_2) \land$

$\quad\quad (p_3$ **is on circle** $(p_2, p_2, p_1)) \land$

$\quad\quad (p_4$ **is on circle** $(p_1, p_1, p_2)) \land$

$\quad\quad (p_4$ **is on circle** $(p_2, p_2, p_1)) \land$

$\quad\quad \neg(p_3 = p_4) \land p$ **is on line** $(p_3, p_4)))$

$\quad)\}.$

The problem with EuQI is that it is too powerful. To illustrate this, we now show that in EuQI we can construct an ellipse. In EuPI we could only construct a single, arbitrary, point of an ellipse. The construction itself is quite similar to the EuPI construction, with the difference due to the fact that first-order quantifiers essentially allow us to iterate over choice operators.

Example 10. Given a 4-ary relation of points, for each tuple t, return the ellipse with foci t_1 and t_2, and major axis equal to $d(t_3, t_4)$.

$\{(p) \mid (\exists t_1)(\exists t_2)(\exists t_3)(\exists t_4)(\exists q)$

$\quad ((R(t_1, t_2, t_3, t_4) \land t_2$ **is in circle** $(t_1, t_3, t_4) \land \neg(t_3 = t_4) \land$

$\quad$ **l-order** $(t_3, q, t_4) \land p$ **is on circle** $(t_1, t_3, q) \land p$ **is on circle** $(t_2, t_4, q))$

$\quad \lor$

$\quad (R(t_1, t_2, t_3, t_4) \land t_2$ **is on circle** $(t_1, t_3, t_4) \land \neg(t_3 = t_4) \land$

$\quad$ **l-order** $(t_3, q, t_4) \land p$ **is on circle** $(t_1, t_3, q) \land p$ **is on circle** (t_2, t_4, q)

$\quad))\}.$

As this example shows, EuQI is too powerful a language for capturing only those queries that are expressible as ruler-and-compass constructions. A similar construction can be used to express the query that trisects a given angle. Either construction shows the following:

Theorem 7. *The language* EuQI *expresses queries that are not constructible in Euclidean geometry.*
$\qquad\qquad\qquad\qquad\qquad\qquad\qquad\qquad\qquad\qquad\qquad\qquad\qquad\qquad$ □

While this result shows that EuQI does not match the intuition behind its design, one might still hope that it would still serve as a language between FO + lin and FO + poly, even if it is no longer clear what, intuitively, can be expressed in this language. However, this is not the case:

Theorem 8. *The language* EuQI *has the same expressive power as* FO + poly.
$\qquad\qquad\qquad\qquad\qquad\qquad\qquad\qquad\qquad\qquad\qquad\qquad\qquad\qquad$ □

As a consequence, EuQI cannot have the closure property on semi-circular relations. In order to obtain the language we are looking for, we will need to restrict EuQI in an appropriate way.

6 The language SafeEuQl

We now study a subset of the EuQl queries, the SafeEuQl queries. They satisfy a syntactically defined *safety* condition. We show that SafeEuQl can only express constructible queries.

Let R be a relation with attributes of type point. Denote the set of safe variables of an expression φ, with φ in safe-range normal form [2], by $Sv(\varphi)$. The set $Sv(\varphi)$ then is defined as follows:

- $Sv(R(v_1, \ldots, v_p))$ equals $\{v_1, \ldots, v_p\}$;
- for any of the special EuQl primitives φ, $Sv(\varphi)$ equals the empty set;
- $Sv((\exists v)\varphi)$ equals $Sv(\varphi) - \{v\}$;
- $Sv(\neg \varphi)$ equals the empty set;
- $Sv(\varphi_1 \wedge \varphi_2)$ equals the smallest set S such that the following closure properties hold:
  - if φ_i is the expression "$v_1 = v_2$" with v_1 or v_2 in S, then both v_1 and v_2 are in S;
  - if φ_i is the expression "v_1 **is l-l-crossing point of** (v_2, v_3, v_4, v_5)" and the variables $v_2, \ldots, v_5$ are in S, then v_1 is in S;
  - if φ_i is the expression "v_1 **is l-c-crossing point of** $(v_2, v_3, v_4, v_5, v_6)$" and the variables $v_2, \ldots, v_6$ are in S, then v_1 is in S;
  - if φ_i is the expression "v_1 **is c-c-crossing point of** $(v_2, v_3, v_4, v_5, v_6, v_7)$" and the variables $v_2, \ldots, v_7$ are in S, then v_1 is in S; and
  - $Sv(\varphi_1) \cup Sv(\varphi_2)$ is a subset of S;
- $Sv(\varphi_1 \vee \varphi_2)$ equals $Sv(\varphi_1) \cap Sv(\varphi_2)$.

Definition 9. An EuQl query $\{(v_1, \ldots, v_n) \mid \varphi(R_1, \ldots, R_m, v_1, \ldots, v_n)\}$, where φ is in conjunctive normal form, is called *safe* if (i) for each EuQl-term of φ of the form $(\exists v)\psi$, $v \in Sv(\psi)$ holds, and (ii) every free variable v_i of φ is in $Sv(\varphi)$.

Example 11. Consider again the query which computes the midpoints of all tuples of a binary relation R. This query can be expressed with a safe EuQl query as follows:

$$\{(p) \mid (\exists p_1)(\exists p_2)(p_1 = p_2 \wedge R(p_1, p_2) \wedge p = p_1) \vee$$
$$(\exists p_1)(\exists p_2)(\exists p_3)(\exists p_4)(\neg(p_1 = p_2) \wedge \neg(p_3 = p_4) \wedge R(p_1, p_2) \wedge$$
$$p_3 \text{ is c-c-crossing point of } (p_1, p_1, p_2, p_2, p_1, p_2) \wedge$$
$$p_4 \text{ is c-c-crossing point of } (p_1, p_1, p_2, p_2, p_1, p_2) \wedge$$
$$p \text{ is l-l-crossing point of } (p_1, p_2, p_3, p_4))\}.$$

The variables p_1 and p_2 are safe in both parts of the disjunction because of the EuQl term $R(p_1, p_2)$. The variables p_3 and p_4 in the second part of the disjunction are safe since they are the two intersection points of circles defined in terms of the safe variables p_1 and p_2. Finally, p is safe because it denotes the intersection point of two lines defined by safe variables.

To illustrate that safety of an EuQl query is a purely syntactical requirement, consider the query that computes the midpoint of two points as given in Example 9. This time, the formula is not safe because p_3, p_4 and p are unsafe.

The set of all EuQl queries which are safe defines a query language which we shall call SafeEuQl. We have the following closure property for SafeEuQl:

Theorem 10. *A SafeEuQl query applied to a finite database yields a finite database which can be constructed by ruler and compass from the input.* □

7   The main results

In this section, we define two query languages which are closed on semi-circular relations. The first, Φ_{circ}, captures those geometrical constructions that can be described by ruler and compass. The second captures all FO + poly expressible queries that map semi-circular relations to semi-circular relations.

Finally, we state a number of results concerning the expressive power of the different query languages.

In this section, we use the following convention: R_{poly} refers to a 2-dimensional semi-algebraic relation, R_{circ} refers to a semi-circular relation, and R_{lin} refers to a 2-dimensional semi-linear relation.

7.1   The query language Φ_{circ}

In this subsection, we define Φ_{circ}. First, we need two lemmas.

Lemma 11. *There exists an FO + poly query $Q_{R_{circ} \to (L,P,C)}$ that maps every semi-circular relation to an intentional LPC-representation thereof.*

Proof. (Sketch) Let R_{circ} be a semi-circular relation. It can be shown that there is an FO + poly query that computes the Whitney-stratification of a semi-circular relation (for semi-linear relations this was shown by Dumortier et al. in [8]). To compute the finite (L, P, C) database from the Whitney-stratification, we first compute what Dumortier et al. [8] call the "significant points" in the Whitney-stratification of R_{circ}. It can be shown that these significant points contain enough information to allow the computation of an intentional representation of R_{circ}. □

Lemma 12. *There exists an FO + poly query $Q_{(L,P,C) \to R_{circ}}$ that maps every intentional LPC-representation of a semi-circular relation to the semi-circular relation it represents.*

Proof. (Sketch) The query $Q_{(L,P,C) \to R_{circ}}$ is straightforwardly expressible in the language FO + poly as follows. The elements q of the relation P can: belong to no line in L and no circle in C; belong to one line of L and to no circle in C; belong to one circle in C and no line in L; or belong to more than one line or circle in L and C. For instance, for all elements q of P that are not on any line of L or on any circle of C, the intersection of the set of points in the plane that are on the same side as q of each line in L, on the one hand, with the set of points that are on the same side as q of each circle in C, on the other hand, is added to the result. The other cases can be treated similarly. □

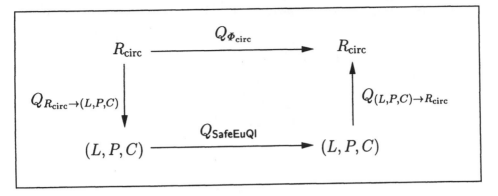

Fig. 7. The query language Φ_{circ} is closed on semi-circular relations.

Definition 13. We say that a query Q, that maps semi-circular relations to semi-circular relations, belongs to the language Φ_{circ} if it is a composition of the form

$$Q_{(L,P,C)\rightarrow R_{circ}} \circ Q_{\mathsf{SafeEuQl}} \circ Q_{R_{circ}\rightarrow (L,P,C)},$$

with Q_{SafeEuQl} a $\mathsf{SafeEuQl}$ query (see Figure 7).

$Q_{(L,P,C)\rightarrow R_{circ}}$ and $Q_{R_{circ}\rightarrow (L,P,C)}$, are syntactically well-defined, so are the $\mathsf{SafeEuQl}$ queries. It would be desirable, however, to find a more elegant syntactic definition of Φ_{circ}.

The language Φ_{circ} has the closure property on the class of semi-circular relations. This is illustrated in Figure 7.

We thus have a syntactically defined subclass of FO + poly that is closed on semi-circular relations.

7.2 On semi-circular relations Φ_{circ} is more expressive than FO + lin

As discussed in Section 3 and Lemma 11, every semi-linear relation can be intensionally represented as a finite LPC-database. It should be noted that for semi-linear relations there always exists a representation with an empty C relation. We will show that every FO + lin query on semi-linear relations can be simulated in $\mathsf{SafeEuQl}$ on the intensional level.

This is shown in more detail in Figure 8 and stated more precisely in

Theorem 14. *There exist FO + poly queries* $Q_{R_{lin}\rightarrow (L,P,C)} : R_{lin} \mapsto (L,P,C)$ *and* $Q_{(L,P,C)\rightarrow R_{lin}} : (L,P,C) \mapsto R_{lin}$ *such that, for every FO + lin query* $Q_{lin} : R_{lin} \mapsto R_{lin}$, *there exists a* $\mathsf{SafeEuQl}$ *query* $Q_{\mathsf{SafeEuQl}} : (L,P,C) \mapsto (L,P,C)$ *such that*

$$Q_{lin} = Q_{(L,P,C)\rightarrow R_{lin}} \circ Q_{\mathsf{SafeEuQl}} \circ Q_{R_{lin}\rightarrow (L,P,C)}.$$

□

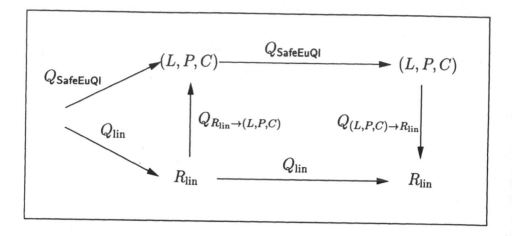

Fig. 8. Any FO + lin query on semi-linear relations can be simulated in SafeEuQl on the intensional level. The two arrows at the left denote the property that any semi-linear relation can be defined in the language FO + lin and that any (L, P, C) database can be defined in SafeEuQl.

7.3 On semi-circular relations the language FO + poly is more expressive than Φ_{circ}

Definition 15. We denote the set of FO + poly queries that map semi-circular relations to semi-circular relations by FO + $\text{poly}_{\text{circ}}$.

Φ_{circ} is a strict subset of FO + $\text{poly}_{\text{circ}}$:

Theorem 16. (Figure 9) *For every SafeEuQl query* $Q_{\text{SafeEuQl}} : (L, P, C) \mapsto (L, P, C)$, *there exists an* FO + $\text{poly}_{\text{circ}}$ *query* $Q_{\text{circ}} : R_{\text{circ}} \mapsto R_{\text{circ}}$ *such that*

$$Q_{\text{SafeEuQl}} = Q_{R_{\text{circ}} \to (L,P,C)} \circ Q_{\text{circ}} \circ Q_{(L,P,C) \to R_{\text{circ}}},$$

but not conversely.

Proof. (Sketch) The first part is similar to previous proofs.

For the second part, consider the query that maps a semi-circular relation consisting of a line segment $[q, r]$ and a point p (illustrated in Figure 10) that is not collinear with q and r to that relation augmented with two line segments ps and pt such that the angles $\angle pqs$, $\angle pst$, and $\angle ptr$ are equal. This query is expressible in FO + poly. Since the query maps every semi-circular relation to a semi-circular relation, it belongs to FO + $\text{poly}_{\text{circ}}$. It is not expressible in Φ_{circ}, however, since the trisection of an angle with ruler and compass cannot be done, and is therefore not expressible in SafeEuQl. □

In addition, any FO + $\text{poly}_{\text{circ}}$ query on semi-circular databases can be simulated in FO + poly:

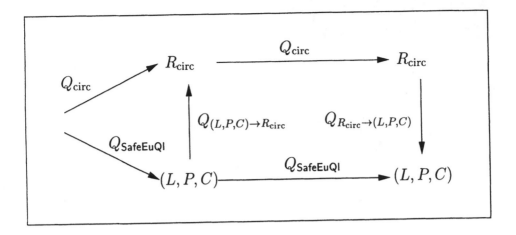

Fig. 9. The query languages Φ_{circ} and $\mathsf{FO} + \mathsf{poly}_{circ}$. Again, the arrows at the left denote which relations and databases can be defined in the respective languages.

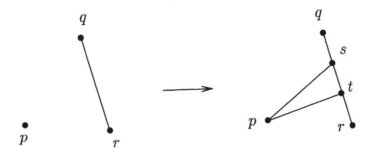

Fig. 10. The trisection query.

Theorem 17. *There exist* $\mathsf{FO} + \mathsf{poly}$ *queries* $Q_{R_{circ} \to R_{poly}} : R_{circ} \mapsto R_{poly}$ *and* $Q_{R_{poly} \to R_{circ}} : R_{poly} \mapsto R_{circ}$ *such that for every* $\mathsf{FO} + \mathsf{poly}_{circ}$ *query* $Q_{circ} : R_{circ} \mapsto R_{circ}$ *there exists an* $\mathsf{FO} + \mathsf{poly}$ *query* $Q_{poly} : R_{poly} \mapsto R_{poly}$ *such that*

$$Q_{circ} = Q_{R_{poly} \to R_{circ}} \circ Q_{poly} \circ Q_{R_{circ} \to R_{poly}}.$$

□

7.4 Conclusion

Figure 12 summarizes the results of the previous subsections. We review the expressive power of the languages we discussed.

- On the bottom level of Figure 12, we have $\mathsf{FO} + \mathsf{lin}$ as a query language on semi-linear relations. We recall that queries concerning Euclidean distance

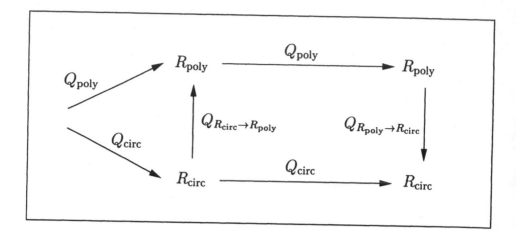

Fig. 11. Simulation of an FO + poly$_{circ}$ query by an FO + poly query.

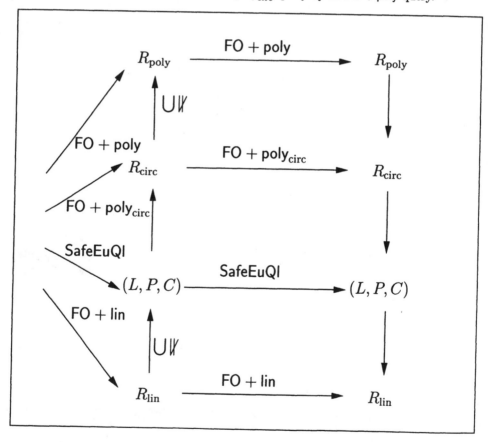

Fig. 12. Comparison of the different query languages.

are not expressible in this language. Not only does the data model only allows for semi-linear relations, but, moreover, there are FO + poly queries mapping semi-linear relations to semi-linear relations that are not expressible in FO + lin. The transformation of a relation into its convex hull is an example [31].

- On the next level, we have more expressive power on (the intensional representation of) semi-linear relations. We can also express queries that involve Euclidean distance. The data model also supports a class of relations wider than the semi-linear ones. All queries expressible in SafeEuQl are constructible. So, the trisection of a given angle, for instance, is *not* expressible in SafeEuQl.
- In FO + poly$_{circ}$, we gain expressive power compared to the previous level. On this level, the trisection of a angle is expressible. On the other hand, FO + poly$_{circ}$ is strictly less expressive than FO + poly on semi-circular relations. We can, e.g., not express the construction of an ellipse in FO + poly$_{circ}$.
- On the top level, we have FO + poly.

Acknowledgments

The authors wish to thank Marc Gyssens and Jan Van den Bussche whose comments considerably improved the presentation of the paper.

References

1. D. Abel and B.C. Ooi, editors. *Proceedings of the 3rd International Symposium on Spatial Databases*, volume 692 of *Lecture Notes in Computer Science*, Berlin, 1993. Springer-Verlag.
2. S. Abiteboul, R. Hull, and V. Vianu. *Foundations of Databases*. Addison Wesley, 1995.
3. F. Afrati, T. Andronikos, and T. Kavalieros. On the expressiveness of first-order constraint languages. In G. Kuper and M. Wallace, editors, *Proceedings of the 1st Workshop on Constraint Databases and their Applications*, volume 1034 of *Lecture Notes in Computer Science*, pages 22–39, Berlin, 1995. Springer-Verlag.
4. F. Afrati, S. Cosmadakis, S. Grumbach, and G. Kuper. Linear versus polynomial constraints in database query languages. In A. Borning, editor, *Proceedings of the 2nd International Workshop on Principles and Practice of Constraint Programming*, volume 874 of *Lecture Notes in Computer Science*, pages 181–192, Berlin, 1994. Springer-Verlag.
5. J. Bochnak, M. Coste, and M.F. Roy. *Géométrie Algébrique Réelle*. Springer-Verlag, Berlin, 1987.
6. A. Buchmann, editor. *Proceedings of the 1st International Symposium on Spatial Databases*, volume 409 of *Lecture Notes in Computer Science*, Berlin, 1989. Springer-Verlag.
7. G.E. Collins. Quantifier elimination for real closed fields by cylindrical algebraic decomposition. In H. Brakhage, editor, *Automata Theory and Formal Languages*, volume 33 of *Lecture Notes in Computer Science*, pages 134–183, Berlin, 1975. Springer-Verlag.

8. F. Dumortier, M. Gyssens, L. Vandeurzen, and D. Van Gucht. On the decidability of semi-linearity for semi-algebraic sets and its implications for spatial databases. In *Proceedings of the 16th ACM SIGACT-SIGMOD-SIGART Symposium on Principles of Database Systems*, pages 68–77, New York, 1997. ACM Press.

9. M.J. Egenhofer and J.R. Herring, editors. *Proceedings of the 4th International Symposium on Spatial Databases*, volume 951 of *Lecture Notes in Computer Science*, Berlin, 1995. Springer-Verlag.

10. E. Engeler. Remarks on the theory of geometrical constructions. In A. Dold and B. Echraun, editors, *The Syntax and Semantics of Infinitary Languages*, volume 72 of *Lecture Notes in Matemathics*, pages 64–76, Berlin, 1968. Springer-Verlag.

11. E. Engeler. *Foundations of Mathematics*. Springer-Verlag, Berlin, 1992.

12. Euclid. *Euclides Elementorum Geometricorum Lib. XV*. Basileae: Apud Iohannem Hervagium, 1537.

13. S. Grumbach. Implementing linear constraint databases. In V. Gaede, A. Brodsky, O. Günther, D. Srivastava, V. Vianu, and M. Wallace, editors, *Proceedings of the 2nd Workshop on Constraint Databases and Applications*, volume 1191 of *Lecture Notes in Computer Science*, pages 105–115, Berlin, 1997. Springer-Verlag.

14. S. Grumbach, P. Rigaux, M. Scholl, and L. Segoufin. Dedale, a spatial constraint database. In this volume.

15. S. Grumbach and J. Su. Finitely representable databases. In *Proceedings of the 13th ACM SIGACT-SIGMOD-SIGART Symposium on Principles of Database Systems*, pages 289–300, New York, 1994. ACM Press.

16. S. Grumbach and J. Su. Towards practical constraint databases. In *Proceedings of the 15th ACM SIGACT-SIGMOD-SIGART Symposium on Principles of Database Systems*, pages 28–39, New York, 1996. ACM Press.

17. S. Grumbach and J. Su. Queries with arithmetical constraints. *Theoretical Computer Science*, 173(1):151–181, 1997.

18. S. Grumbach, J. Su, and C. Tollu. Linear constraint query languages: Expressive power and complexity. In D. Leivant, editor, *Proceedings of the Logic and Computational Complexity Workshop*, volume 960 of *Lecture Notes in Computer Science*, pages 426–446. Springer-Verlag, 1994.

19. O. Günther and H.-J. Schek, editors. *Proceedings of the 2nd International Symposium on Spatial Databases*, volume 525 of *Lecture Notes in Computer Science*, Berlin, 1991. Springer-Verlag.

20. T. Heath. *The thirteen books of Euclid's Elements*. Dover, New York, 1956.

21. D. Hilbert. *Grundlagen der Geometrie*. Springer-Verlag, Berlin, 1930.

22. J.E. Hopcroft and J.D Ullman. *Introduction to Automata Theory, Languages, and Computation*. Addison-Wesley, Reading, Massachusetts, 1979.

23. P.C. Kanellakis, G.M. Kuper, and P.Z. Revesz. Constraint query languages. *Journal of Computer and System Sciences*, 51:26–52, 1995.

24. J. L. Lassez. Querying constraints. In *Proceedings of the 9th ACM SIGACT-SIGMOD-SIGART Symposium on Principles of Database Systems*, pages 288–298, New York, 1990. ACM Press.

25. J. Paredaens, J. Van den Bussche, and D. Van Gucht. Towards a theory of spatial database queries. In *Proceedings of the 13th ACM SIGACT-SIGMOD-SIGART Symposium on Principles of Database Systems*, pages 279–288, New York, 1994. ACM Press.

26. M.F. Preparata and M.I. Shamos. *Computational Geometry*. Springer-Verlag, New York, 1985.

27. J. Renegar. On the computational complexity and geometry of the first-order theory of the reals. *Journal of Symbolic Computation*, 13:255–352, 1989.

28. M. Scholl and A. Voisard, editors. *Proceedings of the 5th International Symposium on Spatial Databases*, volume 1262 of *Lecture Notes in Computer Science*, Berlin, 1997. Springer-Verlag.

29. A. Tarski. *A Decision Method for Elementary Algebra and Geometry*. University of California Press, Berkeley, 1951.

30. L. Vandeurzen, M. Gyssens, and D. Van Gucht. On the desirability and limitations of linear spatial query languages. In M.J. Egenhofer and J.R. Herring, editors, *Proceedings of the 4th International Symposium on Spatial Databases*, volume 951 of *Lecture Notes in Computer Science*, pages 14–28, Berlin, 1995. Springer-Verlag.

31. L. Vandeurzen, M. Gyssens, and D. Van Gucht. On query languages for linear queries definable with polynomial constraints. In E.C. Freuder, editor, *Proceedings of the 2nd International Conference on Principles and Practice of Constraint Programming*, volume 1118 of *Lecture Notes in Computer Science*, pages 468–481, Berlin, 1996. Springer-Verlag.

Functional Programming: An Angry Half-Dozen*

Philip Wadler[1]

Bell Labs, Lucent Technologies, USA (wadler@research.bell-labs.com)

"Have you used it in anger yet?"

The time is a dozen years ago, the place is Oxford, and my fellow postdoc has just scrutinized my new bike. He's admired the chrome, checked the gears, noted the Kryptonite lock. Now he wants to know if I've used it to serious purpose. Gleaming chrome is well and good, but will it run you through the woods?

"Have you used it in anger yet?"

Having read the title of this column, you may have just asked the same question, though perhaps in different words. You've scrutinized functional languages. You've admired the elegance of lambda calculus, checked the benchmarks from the compilers, noted the security provided by strong typing. Now you want to know if they have been used to serious purpose. Mathematical elegance is well and good, but will it run that mission-critical system?

Here are a half-dozen examplars of functional programs used in anger. Many, but not all, involve databases in a central way.

0   Compilers

This one's a freebie. I won't count it toward the six, as it is the obvious and incestuous example of functional languages used in anger.

Most compilers for functional languages are implemented in the language they compile. The Standard ML of New Jersey compiler (SML/NJ) is about 130K lines of Standard ML. The Glasgow Haskell compiler is about 90K lines of Haskell. Caml, another dialect of ML, is implemented in Caml. Erlang is implemented in Erlang, and some versions of Scheme in Scheme. The British firms Abstract Hardware Limited and Harlequin both market commercial ML compilers, each bootstrapped in ML.

In some corners, functional languages bear a reputation for gross inefficiency, but this reputation is out of date. Code quality ranges from a shade better than C to an order of magnitude worse, with the typical case hovering at a factor of two or so slower. One example is the Pseudoknot benchmark, based on an application that uses backtracking search to determine three-dimensional protein structure. A large number of functional languages were benchmarked against this program, the best running two to three times slower than the equivalent C [?].

The functional community splits into two camps. Lazy languages evaluate arguments on demand, and so require highly disciplined use of side effects; strict languages evaluate arguments eagerly, but make it easier to exploit side effects. Haskell, Miranda, and Clean are lazy; Standard ML, Caml, Erlang, and Scheme

---
* A version of this article also appears in SIGPLAN Notices.

are strict. Over the past few years there has been remarkable convergence between the two communities, and the Pseudoknot tests show lazy and strict languages have comparable performance.

Most functional languages now provide some means of interworking with programs written in C or other imperative languages. This is straightforward in a strict language, but figuring out how to integrate such side effects into a lazy language has been one of the key advances of recent years. Profiling systems for functional languages have also improved vastly over the last few years, and the usual code-measure-improve cycle is now routinely applied to improve the time and space behaviour of functional programs. However, there are still few good debuggers for functional languages.

1 HOL and Isabelle

Hewlett-Packard's Runway multiprocessor bus underlies the architecture of the HP 9000 line of servers and multiprocessors. Hewlett-Packard applied the HOL (Higher-Order Logic) theorem prover to verify liveness properties of the arbitration protocols in Runway. Verification was achieved by a hybrid of theorem-proving in HOL and model-checking in SMV. This approach uncovered errors that had not been revealed by several months of simulation [?].

The Defence Science and Technology Organisation, a branch of the Department of Defence in Salisbury, South Australia, is applying the Isabelle theorem prover to verify arming conditions for missile decoys. A graphical front-end has been added to Isabelle for this purpose, humorously called DOVE (Design-Oriented Verification and Evaluation) [?].

Both HOL and Isabelle are implemented in Standard ML. Standard ML is a descendant of ML, the metalanguage of the groundbreaking LCF theorem prover, which is in turn an ancestor of both HOL and Isabelle. This circle reflects the intertwined history of theorem provers and functional languages [?, ?, ?].

ML/LCF exploited two central features of functional languages, higher-order functions and types. A proof tactic was a function taking a goal formula to be proved and returning a list of subgoals paired with a justification. A justification, in turn, was a function from proofs of the subgoals to a proof of the goal. A tactical was a function that combined small tactics into larger tactics. The type system was a great boon in managing the resulting nesting of functions that return functions that accept functions. Further, the type discipline ensured soundness, since the only way to create a value of type *Theorem* was by applying a given set of functions, each corresponding to an inference rule. The type system Milner devised for ML remains a cornerstone of work in functional languages.

HOL and Isabelle are just two of the many theorem provers that draw on the ideas developed in LCF, just as Standard ML is only one of the many languages that draw on the ideas developed in ML. Among others, Coq is implemented in Caml, Veritas in Miranda, Yarrow in Haskell, and Alf, Elf, and Lego in Standard ML again. An upcoming issue of the *Journal of Functional Programming* is devoted to the interplay between functional languages and theorem provers.

2 Erlang

Ericsson's Mobility Server is marketed in twelve countries. Among other things, it controls some mobile phones for the European Parliament in Strasbourg. The Mobility Server is the first of a range of Ericsson products implemented using Erlang, a functional language designed by Ericsson for telecommunications applications [?].

Ericsson has a separate division, Erlang Systems, that handles marketing, training, and consulting for Erlang. Over one thousand Ericsson employees have attended Erlang course and over five hundred are currenly involved in product development using Erlang. The Mobility Server contains hundreds of thousands of lines of Erlang code, and products written in Erlang have earned Ericsson millions of kronor

You might guess Erlang stands for "Ericsson Language", but actually it is named for A. K. Erlang, a Danish mathematician who also lent his name to a unit of bandwidth. (A phone system designed to bear 0.33 erlang will work even if one-third of its phones are in use at the same time.)

Erlang is dynamically typed in the same sense as Lisp, Scheme, or Smalltalk, which makes it one of the few modern languages to eschew ML's heritage of static typing. The basic data types are integers (with arbitrary precision, so overflow is not a problem), floats, atoms, tuples, lists, and process identifiers.

Primitives allow one to spawn a process, send a message to a process, or receive a message. Any data value may be sent as a message, and processes may be located on any machine. Erlang uses compression techniques to minimise the bandwidth required to transmit a value. Thus it is both trivial and efficient to send, say, a tree from one machine to another. Compare this with the work required in a language such as C, C++, or Java, where one must separately establish a connection, serialise the tree for transmission, and apply compression. To support robust systems, one process can register to receive a message if another process fails.

Ever since Guy Steele's pioneering work on Scheme, tail-calls have been a mainstay of functional languages, and they are put to good use in Erlang. A server in Erlang is typically written as a small function, with arguments representing the state of the server. The function body receives a message, performs the computation it requests, sends back the result, and makes a tail-call with parameters representing the new state. Finite state machines are easily represented: just have one function for each state, with state transitions represented by tail calls. The daunting tasks of changing running code on the fly is solved by a surprisingly simple use of higher-order functions and tail-calls: just design the server to receive a message containing a new function for the server, which is applied with a tail-call; a new variable can be added to the server state by a tail-call to a function with an added parameter.

Functional programmers often claim that the use of higher-order functions promotes reuse. The classic examples are the *map* and *fold* functions, which encapsulate common forms of list traversal, and just need to be instantiated with an action to perform for each element. Most, but not quite all, list processing can be easily expressed in terms of these functions. The Erlang experience suggests this notion of reuse scales up to support concurrent client-server architectures. A set of libraries encapsulate common server requirements, and just need to be instantiated with the action to be performed for each request. Most, but not quite all, required servers can be easily expressed in terms of these libraries.

Erlang bears a striking resemblance to another modern phenomenon, Java. Like Java, Erlang (along with all other functional languages) uses heap allocation and garbage collection, and ensures safe execution that never corrupts memory. Like Java, Erlang comes with a library that provides functionality independent of a particular operating system. Like Java, Erlang compiles to a virtual machine, ensuring portability across a wide range of architectures. And like Java, Erlang achieved its first success based on interpreters for the virtual machine, with faster compilers coming along later.

Erlang succeeded not just because it was a good language design, but because its designers took the right steps to promote its growth. They evolved the language in tandem with its applications, worked closely with developers, and provided documentation, courses, hot-lines, and consultants. A foreign-language interface was essential to allow interworking with existing software in C. Users were often attracted to Erlang by the availability of tools and packages, such as the ASN.1 interface compiler and the Mnesia real-time distributed database, both implemented entirely in Erlang.

3 Pdiff

If you've ever made a phone call in the US, you've probably used a Lucent 5ESS phone switch. Each 5ESS contains an embedded, relational database to maintain information about customers, features such as call waiting, rates, network topology, and so on. The database is complex, containing nearly a thousand relations. There are tens of thousands of consistency constraints (also called *population rules*) that the data must satisfy [?].

As new features are added to the switch, new transactions are required to update the corresponding data, say to register a customer for call waiting. Each transaction should be *safe* in that it should leave the database in a consistent state. Ensuring safety was difficult and error prone, especially since the constaints were embedded in C programs that audit the database for consistency, and transactions were performed by other C programs.

The first step was to introduce PRL (Population Rule Language) to describe constraints and transactions. This marked a vast improvement over the use of C, but left the problem of determining for each transaction what conditions must be satisfied to ensure safety.

The next step was to introduce Pdiff (PRL differentiator). The input to Pdiff is the safety constraint for the database and an unsafe transaction, both written in PRL. Pdiff computes what condition must hold in advance of the transaction to ensure the database is consistent afterward. (This is similar to Dijkstra's computation of the weakest precondition that must hold in advance of a command to ensure a given predicate holds afterward.) Additional steps simplify this condition on the assumption that the database is consistent before the transaction. The output is a safe transaction in PRL, which checks all the necessary constraints.

Pdiff consists of about 30K lines of code written in Standard ML, written by researchers at Bell Labs. Pdiff improves the quality and reliability of switches, reduces the time to deploy new features, and has saved Lucent millions of dollars in development costs.

The Pdiff history points out some of the problems of using a functional language in practice. The 5ESS team considered using Standard ML to write the PRL compiler, but since Standard ML wasn't available for their machine (an Amdahl), they used C++ instead. When the time came to hand off maintenance of Pdiff to the 5ESS staff, no internal candidate could be found for the role. Developers prefer to have C++ or Java on their resume, and balk at languages perceived as "weird". Eventually a physicist looking to change fields was hired for the purpose.

4 CPL/Kleisli

In April 1993, a workshop organised by the US Department of Energy considered the database requirements of the Human Genome Project. An appendix of the workshop report listed twelve queries that would be difficult or impossible to answer with current database systems, because they require combining information from two or more databases in disparate formats [?].

All twelve of these queries have been answered using CPL/Kleisli. CPL (Collection Programming Language) is a high-level language for formulating queries. Kleisli, the system that implements CPL, translates CPL into SQL for querying relational databases, or runs the queries against data in ASN.1, ACE, or other formats. CPL/Kleisli is in active use at the Philadelphia Center for Chromosome 22 and at the BioInformatics Centre of the Institute for Systems Science in Singapore [?].

Functional programming plays two roles here: CPL is a functional language, and Kleisli is written in Standard ML. The basic data types of CPL are sets, bags, lists, and records. The first three of these may be processed using a comprehension notation familiar to mathematicians and functional programmers. For instance, a mathematician may write $\{x^2 \mid x \in Nat, x < 10\}$ for the set of squares of natural numbers less than ten. Similarly, the CPL query

```
{ [ Name = p.Name, Mgr = d.Mgr ] |
  \p <- Emp, \d <- Dept,
  p.DNum = d.DNum }
```

returns a set of records pairing employees with their managers. The comprehension notation is reminiscent of SQL, where one may write

```
SELECT Name = p.Name, Mgr = d.Mgr
```

```
FROM Emp p, Dept d
WHERE p.DNum = d.DNum
```

for the same query. But CPL allows sets, bags, lists, and records to be arbitrarily nested, whereas SQL can only process "flat" relations, consisting of sets of records. The extra nesting in CPL helps one formulate queries for databases that don't fit the relational model.

A standard technique in functional programming is to apply mathematical laws to transform an elegant but inefficient program into an efficient equivalent. This technique is applied to good effect in CPL/Kleisli. The standard laws for transforming comprehensions can be viewed as generalising well-known optimisations for relational algebra. For instance, a CPL query may depend on two relational databases held on different servers. The Kleisli optimiser will transform this into two SQL queries to be sent to the servers (performing as much work as possible locally at the server), and a remaining CPL program at the query site to combine the results. Lazy evaluation and concurrency allow SQL computation at the database sites and CPL processing at the query site to overlap.

CPL/Kleisli also exploits record subtyping. In the example above, Emp represents employees by a set of records. Each record must contain a Name and DNum field, but may contain other fields as well. The type system that permits this flexibility and the technique for implementing it efficiently were both adopted directly from research in the functional community.

5   Natural Expert

Every flight through Orly and Roissy airports in Paris is processed by an expert system called Ivanhoe, which generates invoices and explanations for the services used. Ivanhoe is written in Natural Expert, an expert system shell, formerly marketed by the German firm Software AG [?].

Polygram in France controls about one-third of the European market for CDs and cassettes. The Colisage expert system plans packing schedules to minimise empty space and routes to minimise numbers of stops (somewhat like simultaneously solving the Bin Packing and Traveling Salesman problems). Colisage was originally written in a production rule system called GURU, but was ported to Natural Expert when the GURU version proved hard to maintain. Polygram praised the Natural Expert system as shorter and easier to maintain.

Dozens of other applications have been programmed in Natural Expert, including a management support system, a system for assessing bank loans, a tool to plan hospital menus, and a natural-language front end to a database.

Natural Expert integrates an entity-attribute database management system with NEL (Natural Expert Language), a higher-order, statically typed, lazy functional language, roughly similar to Haskell.

One of the selling points of Natural Expert is its user environment. The database is used not only to manipulate user data, but also to store the NEL program itself, which is structured as a number of rules. The database records what rules refer to what other rules, aiding program maintenance. A simple hyper-text facility lets the reader jump from use of a rule or attribute to its definition.

The result returned from a database access is typically a list of entity indexes. Lazy evaluation processes entities one at a time, reducing the amount of store required. This is important, because Natural Expert runs on mainframes. One might expect a mainframe to provide more resources than a personal computer, but Natural Expert typically uses only 80K for the heap, and even then some clients complain it is too large.

Traditionally, lazy languages disallow side effects, because the order in which the effects occur would be difficult to predict. NEL, however, permits one use of side effects, a primitive that prints a given question on a terminal and returns the answer typed by the user. Questions are printed in an arbitrary order, but that's no problem for this domain. More importantly, thanks to lazy evaluation, a question is asked only if it's relevant to the task at hand. Expert systems people call this "backwards chaining".

Training is key to industrial use of any system. Natural Expert is taught in a one-week course, which includes polymorphic types and higher-order functions. Typically, students grumble about all the compile-time error messages generated by the unfamiliar type system, but are pleased to discover that once a program passes the compiler it often runs correctly on the first try. Nonetheless, clients still point to lack of familiarity with functional languages as a bar to wider acceptance.

Although many of the applications built with Natural Expert are successful and in current use, sales of the system generated insufficient revenue, and Software AG has dropped it as a product.

6 Ensemble

Ensemble is a library of protocols that can be used to quickly build distributed applications. Ensemble is in daily use at Cornell to coordinate sharing of keys in a secure network, and to support a distributed CD audio storage and playback service. A number of commercial concerns have begun projects with Ensemble, including BBN, Lockheed Martin, and Microsoft [?].

Ensemble protocol stacks typically have ten or more layers. Highly-layered stacks are flexible, but can be inefficient. Ensemble avoids these inefficiencies by a series of optimisations. The protocol designer segments the code in each the layer, marking common cases. It is a simple matter (currently performed by hand, but easily automated) to trace which segments execute together, and collect these into optimised *trace handlers*. They also cache information to minimise header size and reorder computations to preserve latency. The result is a win-win architecture, offering both modularity and performance.

Ensemble is written entirely in Objective Caml, a dialect of ML. Ensemble beats the performance of its predecessor, Horus, by a wide margin, even though

Horus is written in C. To quote the designers, "The use of ML does mean that our current implementation of Ensemble is somewhat slower than it could be, but this has been more than made up for by the ability to rapidly experiment with structural changes, and thereby increase performance through improved design rather than through long hours of hand-coding the entire system in C."

The designers took care to restrict the use of features of ML they deemed expensive. Higher-order functions are used only in stylised ways that can be compiled efficiently. Exception handling and garbage-collected objects are avoided in the trace handlers. To squeeze the most out of Ensemble, a final step is to translate the trace handlers (which constitute only a small part of the code) into C by hand. This achieves a further improvement of about a factor of two.

A related effort is the Fox Project at Carnegie-Mellon University, which first demonstrated that systems software can be written in functional languages. You can access the FoxNet Web Server at `foxnet.cs.cmu.edu`. The HTTPD server, the TCP/IP stack, and everything down to the driver protocol is implemented in the Fox variant of Standard ML [?].

While the Fox Project has done excellent work, Ensemble makes a more convincing case for functional programming: FoxNet was created by researchers primarily interested in languages, while Ensemble was created by researchers primarily interested in networking.

7   Conclusions

So there you have it, six instances of functional languages used *in anger*. Or rather more than six, depending on how you count.

Prolog and other logic programming languages find many of their strongest applications in connection with databases, and the same appears to be true of functional languages. CPL/Kleisli is a database language. Natural Expert is sold in tandem with a database management system. Erlang provides a comprehension syntax for accessing the Mnesia database, similar CPL/Kleisli. Pdiff maintains database transactions.

Perhaps some disclaimers are in order. I'm one of the designers of Haskell. Glasgow Haskell is due to my former colleagues, SML/NJ is due to my current colleagues, HOL is largely due to another former colleague, and Pdiff is due to other current colleagues. I consulted for Ericsson on the design of a type system for Erlang. CPL/Kleisli is partly based on my research into comprehensions. So I may be biased.

The list of applications given here is far from exhaustive. I've omitted Microsoft's Fran animation library for Haskell [?], Lufthansa's combination of a simple functional language with partial evaluation to speed up crew scheduling [?], Hewlett Packard's ECDL network control language, the Lolita natural language understanding system, and Mitre's speech recognition system, to name a few. Some of these are listed at the Real-World Applications of Functional Programming web page [?]. If you know of other applications that belong, please do write.

References

1. Joe Armstrong. The development of Erlang. *ACM SIGPLAN International Conference on Functional Programming*, June 1997; *SIGPLAN Notices* 32(8):196–203, August 1997. Also see the Erlang page:
   http://www.erlang.se
2. Lennart Augustsson. Partial evaluation in aircraft crew planning. *ACM SIGPLAN Symposium on Partial Evaluation and Semantics-Based Program Manipulation*, June 1997; *SIGPLAN Notices* 32(12):127–136, December 1997.
3. Edoardo Biagioni, Robert Harper, Peter Lee, and Brian G. Milnes. Signatures for a network protocol stack: A systems application of Standard ML. *ACM Conference on Lisp and Functional Programming*, 1994. Also see the Fox Project page:
   http://foxnet.cs.cmu.edu
4. P. Buneman, S. B. Davidson, K. Hart, C. Overton, and L. Wong. A Data Transformation System for Biological Data Sources. *Proceedings of 21st International Conference on Very Large Data Bases*, Zurich, Switzerland, September 1995. Also see the Kleisli page and the twelve queries:
   http://sdmc.iss.nus.sg/kleisli/
   MoreInfo.html,misc/doe-queries.html
5. P. Buneman, L. Libkin, D. Suciu, V. Tannen, and L. Wong. Comprehension Syntax. *ACM SIGMOD Record* 23(1):87-96, March 1994. (Invited paper.)
6. Albert J. Camilleri. A hybrid approach to verifying liveness in a symmetric multiprocessor. *10'th International Conference on Theorem Proving in Higher-Order Logics*, Elsa Gunter and Amy Felty, editors, Murray Hill, New Jersey, August 1997. Lecture Notes in Computer Science 1275, Springer Verlag, 1997.
7. Sandra Corrico, Bryan Ewbank, Tim Griffin, John Meale, and Howard Trickey. A tool for developing safe and efficient database transactions. *XV International Switching Symposium of the World Telecommunications Congress*, pages 173–177, April 1995.
8. Robert J. Robbins, Editor. Report of the Invitational DOE Workshop on Genome Informatics, 26–27 April 1993.
   http://www.bis.med.jhmi.edu/Dan/DOE/
   whitepaper/contents.html
9. Conal Elliot and Paul Hudak. Functional reactive animation. *ACM SIGPLAN International Conference on Functional Programming*, June 1997; *SIGPLAN Notices* 32(8):196–203, August 1997.
10. M. J. Gordon and T. F. Melham, editors. *Introduction to HOL: A theorem proving environment for higher-order logic.* Cambridge University Press, 1993. Also see the HOL page:
    http://www.dcs.glasgow.ac.uk/tfm/ fmt/hol.html
11. M. Gordon, R. Milner, and C. Wadsworth. *Edinburgh LCF.* Lecture Notes in Computer Science, Vol. 78, Springer-Verlag, 1979.
12. Pieter Hartel, *et al.* Benchmarking implementations of functional languages with 'Pseudoknot', a float-intensive benchmark. *Journal of Functional Programming*, 6(4):621–656, July 1996.
13. Mark Hayden and Robbert vanRenesse. Optimizing Layered Communication Protocols. *Symposium on High Performance Distributed Computing*, Portlan, Oregon, August 1997. Also see the Ensemble page:
    http://simon.cs.cornell.edu/Info/ Projects/Ensemble/

34

14. Jonathon Hogg and Philip Wadler. Real-world applications of functional programming.
    http://www.dcs.gla.ac.uk/fp/realworld/
15. Nigel W. O. Hutchison, Ute Neuhaus, Manfred Schmidt-Schauss, and Cordy Hall. Natural Expert: a commercial functional programming environment. *Journal of Functional Programming*, 7(2):163–182, March 1997.
16. M. A. Ozols, K. A. Eastaughffe, and A. Cant. DOVE: Design Oriented Verification and Evaluation. *Proceedings of AMAST 97*, M. Johnson, editor, Sydney, Australia. Lecture Notes in Computer Science 1349, Springer Verlag, 1997.
17. Lawrence C. Paulson. *Isabelle: A Generic Theorem Prover*. Springer-Verlag LNCS 828, 1994. Also see the Isabelle page:
    http://www.cl.cam.ac.uk/Research/ HVG/Isabelle/

Panel Session:
Metadata for Database Interoperation

Sophie Cluet[1], Richard Connor[2], Rick Hull[3], David Maier[4], Florian Matthes[5]
and Dan Suciu[6]

[1] INRIA, France (Sophie.Cluet@infria.fr)
[2] Glasgow University, Scotland (richard@dcs.gla.ac.uk)
[3] Bell Labs, USA (hull@research.bell-labs.com)
[4] Oregon Graduate Institute, USA (maier@cs.ogi.edu)
[5] Technical University of Hamburg-Harburg, Germany (f.matthes@tu-harburg.de)
[6] AT&T, USA (suciu@research.att.com)

The panelists approached the panel topic from complementary perspectives (metadata and query optimization, metadata and semi-structured databases, liberal type systems and metadata, data description languages for ontologies, process knowledge as metadata). Each of the panelists was given five minutes time for a personal position statement.

This text summarizes the results of these presentations and the lively open discussion after the individual presentations. The structure for this synopsis of the main panel results on the use of metadata for database interoperation was designed jointly by the panelists at the workshop in an informal evening session.

Data, Code and Process Metadata: The focus of current metadata research is on purely structural aspects of *data*. Software engineers are also concerned with metadata describing *code* interfaces as a basis for systems interoperability (via APIs, remote method invocation, object request brokers, etc.). Additionally, metadata on cooperative *processes* which describe the goal-oriented and long-term interaction between multiple human and/or software agents may be relevant to go beyond the current "read-only" integration of heterogeneous information systems.

Data First vs. Schema First: Classical information systems are designed and operated by an enterprise based on an analysis of the information needs of an organization or an organizational unit as a whole. The database schema is designed *before* information is collected and queried and the metadata often serves as a means to enforce business rules and policies, i.e. to disallow data, code or processes that do not fit the corporate metadata.

On the other hand, individuals within an enterprise are collecting and querying (less structured or implicitly structured) information that serves their individual information needs (addresses, calendar items, notes, spreadsheets, ...). Cooperative work between these individuals requires metadata to be "discovered" or to be made explicit *after* data has been collected.

Guiding vs. Controlling Metadata: It seems to be necessary to distinguish between (at least) two kinds of metadata: Metadata to be consumed by *humans* and metadata to be processed automatically by *programs*. While humans utilize metadata to guide their use of the data being described and are capable of handling exceptions in an "intelligent" way, software agents need a much more strict separation between (preferably immutable) metadata controlling their behavior and the primary data to be processed.

This classification based on information consumers may also help to identify suitable metadata description languages and models. Similar to the situation in traditional (relational) databases, it may be necessary to support both perspectives simultaneously and effectively. For example, today's databases store both, fuzzy but expressive diagrams, comments, memos for humans and an exact conceptual, logical and physical schema which is utilized for database management.

Description logics as a stylized subset of first order logic with decidable inference rules seems to be an interesting candidate for the description of controlling metadata which goes beyond classical relational or object-oriented database models.

Multiple Types: A recurring theme in metadata research is the use of multiple types to describe the structure of data collections. Instead of having a single type describing all instances, it may be useful to have a minimal structure (shared by all instances) as well as a maximal structure (e.g., the set of attributes defined at least by a single instance), or even statistical information about the number of instances that possess a certain attribute. It should be noted that this meta information may change on any update of the database.

Structural vs. Quality Metadata: The interoperation between various databases makes it necessary to be explicit about the quality (the reliability, the precision) of the data at hand. For example, it may be necessary to have information on possible round-off errors, or on the timeliness of a particular data source. Alternatively, it may be desirable to express precedence rules between multiple data sources based on their relative reliability or performance. This quality metadata is to be considered an orthogonal issue to structural or functional information provided by classical data models.

The design and evaluation of a metadata model should be very explicit about the two following underlying assumptions:

$O(N)$ **vs.** $O(N^2)$ **Architecture:** An interoperation of N databases can either be achieved by $O(N)$ mappings to a common integrated model assuming a single "standard" semantics (e.g., a domain-specific ontology or a reference data model), or by N^2 bilateral mappings between pairs of databases that mutually agree on a common semantics only for those entities that are involved in a cross-database workflow. Large-scale integration efforts (the human genome project, a world patent database, world trade directories, ...) typically are based on $O(N)$ architectures. On the other hand, $O(N^2)$ architectures make it possible to attribute the integration cost to an identifiable common business activity and are therefore often adopted if interoperation occurs between two autonomous business partners.

Intended Use: While guiding metadata (see above) is mainly declarative in nature, the models and languages used to express controlling metadata have to be tailored to the specific intended integration task at hand. For example, the optimization of a single user query against multiple databases requires a metadata representation that differs substantially from the information needed by an automatic mediator generator. As another example, take a tool which performs automatic quality assurance to validate updates that occur in a cluster of multiple related databases. Again, other forms of metadata are required in this specific scenario.

Workflow definitions can be understood as a very restricted form of meta data spanning multiple data collections, since for each business case (query, update, insertion, deletion, ...) there has to be an explicit imperative "procedure" to validate and propagate changes in the underlying data collections.

Acknowledgements

This work has been funded by a joint EC/US collaboration agreement between the NSF and the EC Working Group *Pastel*.

DEDALE, A Spatial Constraint Database*

Stéphane Grumbach[1], Philippe Rigaux[2], Michel Scholl[1,2], and Luc Segoufin[1]

[1] INRIA, Rocquencourt BP 105, F-78153 Le Chesnay, France —
{Stephane.Grumbach,Michel.Scholl,Luc.Segoufin}@inria.fr
[2] Cedric/CNAM, 292 rue St Martin, F-75141 Paris Cedex 03, France —
{scholl,rigaux}@cnam.fr

Abstract. This paper presents a first prototype of a constraint database for spatial information, DEDALE. Implemented on top of the O_2 DBMS, data is stored in an object-oriented framework, with spatial data represented using linear constraints over a dense domain. The query language is the standard OQL, with special functions for constraint solving and geometric operations.

A simple geographical application from the French Institute for Geography, IGN, is running on DEDALE. The data initially in vector mode was loaded into the database after a translation to constraint representation. Although it is too early to speak of performance since not all operations have been optimized yet, our experience with DEDALE demonstrates already the advantages of the constraint approach for spatial manipulation.

1   Introduction

General purpose database management systems (DBMS) are not well-suited for new applications that involve multidimensional data. This is due to the structural complexity of multidimensional data, which requires new querying facilities, and specific indexing techniques [LJF94,VG96], not provided by most existing DBMS.

The amount of spatial information is growing extremely rapidly. The manipulation of such information is one of the very important challenges of database technology [Gue94]. To satisfy the need, different systems have been developed for various subareas related to multidimensional data. Among them, Geographical Information Systems (GIS) constitute a large field of interest [ABC93,EH95].

Most systems devoted to the manipulation of geographic data are based on an architecture coupled with a relational DBMS, but dedicated to geographic information with special purpose tools for manipulating spatial data. This is the case of one of the most prominent systems for geographic information, namely ARC/INFO [Mor89]. Although these systems have been widely used for more than a decade, it is clear that the lack of integration between spatial data processing and standard data management is rather not desirable. Among various limitations, there is no high level query facility: In order to reach a high level of performance, the user has to be an expert in the system and use low level

---

* Work supported in part by TMR project Chorochronos.

efficient primitives. There has been a large number of proposals in the literature [Gue94] for integrating spatial features with other traditional thematic alphanumeric features of geographic objects in a single framework. However, because of the complexity of spatial data and the variety of GIS applications, there has not been a common agreement on a satisfactory model for representing geographic data. Moreover for applications dealing with data of dimension higher than 2 (geology, spatio-temporal applications, etc.), there is a crucial lack of models and query languages.

GISs use two alternative modes for the representation of geometric objects. In the *raster* mode, data consists of an unstructured bitmap which renders the detection of geometric objects (lines, zones, etc.) difficult. The *vector* format is commonly used, whether segment-based or point-based, to provide a structured representation of the geometric objects, in terms of polylines and polygons, defined by the list of their vertices or alternatively a list of segments.

The constraint database model introduced by Kanellakis, Kuper and Revesz [KKR90], turns out to be a good candidate for a sounder representation of spatial data. Linear constraint databases have been extensively studied recently, because of their potential application to geographical databases [VGV95]. One of the most promising features of constraint databases is their declarative query language based on first-order logic, and the existence of equivalent algebras, leading to a procedural expression of queries which offer potential for optimization. Indeed one of the drawbacks of the models proposed in the literature for representing and manipulating geographic information is that there is little framework for describing the semantics of the operations necessary for optimization.

The tight correspondence between the vector mode representation of GISs and the linear constraint framework is remarkable. There is an easy translation from one to the other. The main difference between the two representations is that in the linear constraint framework the objects are modeled as collections of simple convex polygons, while in the vector model, the polygons can be non-convex. There are efficient algorithms to perform polygon convexification. Moreover, most algorithms are both simpler and more efficient on convex polygons. The constraint representation simplifies the programmer's work, and might result in an increased efficiency.

While most GIS data models are not extensible, one of the nice features of the constraint model is the ability to handle more than 2 dimensions. This should be particularly useful for representing information in earth science applications.

Two families of algebras where defined for manipulating constraint relations: first, algebras that correspond exactly to the traditional relational algebra, and whose semantics is defined with respect to the effect of the usual algebraic operators on infinite relations [GST94,PVV94], and second, algebras that apply on special encoding for relations and generalized tuples [KG94]. We follow the first trend in the present approach.

The complexity of linear first-order queries was shown to be in NC^1 [GS97]. The expressive power of first-order logic with linear constraints has been broadly investigated [GST94,PVV95,GS97]. This language turns out to be rather restricted, in a way similar to the case of finite relations: For example, transitive closure and topological connectivity cannot be expressed in this language.

In this paper, we describe the first version of a prototype of a linear constraint database, DEDALE, and a simple geographical application. To the best of our knowledge, this is the first attempt to implement such a system. The C^3 system [BS97] differs strongly from DEDALE. It relies on a constraint calculus instead of an algebra, and the implementation is done on top of ObjectStore. Moreover, the application range as well as the prototypical queries are distinct.

The application is based on data from the French National Geographic Institute, IGN. It contains, for the Orange county in Provence [May90], some typical data as commonly found in GISs, such as ground occupancy, roads, powerlines, rivers, etc.

In the present setting, the data is modeled in an object-oriented framework. Essentially, spatial objects have an identifier, *thematic* attributes, and a spatial attribute expressed as a constraint relation. Therefore two limitations of the pure constraint model are overcomed. First spatial objects can be manipulated as first class citizens, by means of their identifier. In pure constraint models, the quantification is only over numbers, and not sets. The necessity to consider sets of points in the space explicitly has been addressed in particular in [GS95,PSV96]. The second restriction results from the rather limited expressive power of first-order linear queries in this context. Functions such as measures of distances for instance cannot be expressed since they are not linear. In DEDALE, they are expressed in the general purpose standard query language OQL [Cat94].

The paper is organized as follows. In the next section, we present the architecture of DEDALE and the current state of the implementation. The algebra for linear constraint relations is then presented in Section 3. In Section 4, we describe the geographical application, explain the data representation, and give examples of queries involving spatial operations. The main algorithms used in DEDALE for constraint solving, geometry, and query evaluation are described and analyzed in Section 5. The last section presents our ongoing work and perspectives.

2 Architecture of DEDALE

In this section, we present our architectural choices and the current state of implementation of the prototype. DEDALE has been implemented on top of the O_2 Database Management System (DBMS) [BDK92]. The architecture is forecast to deal with n-dimensional data. Present algorithms for implementing algebraic operations in the n-dimensional case are not yet optimal though.

To prove the feasibility of our approach, we have focused for the first version of the current prototype on 2-dimensional data and chosen a simple geographic application illustrating the features of DEDALE, described in Section 4. The implementation of the algebraic operations presented in the appendix is rather efficient. However in this first setting query processing is not yet fully optimized. Figure 1 illustrates the architecture of DEDALE. It consists of the following components:

1. A Graphical User Interface (GUI).

2. The DEDALE processor composed of the following modules: (i) the lexical and syntactical analyzer of an algebraic query which requires the access to the data dictionary stored in the O_2 database, (ii) the query optimizer which transforms an algebraic expression into an optimal execution plan. It relies on the existence of indices for a fast data access. It generates OQL queries calling functions of (iii) the *constraint solving engine*.

3. The O_2 DBMS providing OQL for querying the database.

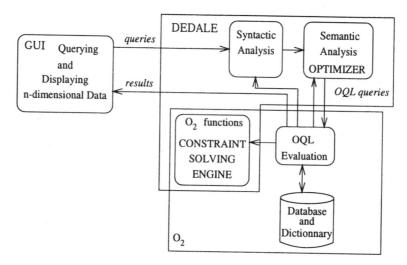

Fig. 1. Architecture of DEDALE

The GUI allows to query the database with query parameters such as points or rectangles, and to display query results including maps and other thematic data. The standard query language OQL is used for querying the database. The spatial data is dealt with through a constraint solving engine. It has been designed as a set of constraint solving operations, implemented as O_2 functions written in C. Since O_2 functions in the above set can be called in an OQL query, this design allows to mix constraint solving operations with classical query evaluation. However, the problem of query optimization is only partially addressed in the current prototype. Only spatial data has been implemented by constraints and O_2 functions, implementing algebraic operations on constraint relations representing convex objects in the 2D plane, are used in the body of OQL queries.

We might have chosen to implement descriptive attributes by (single equality) constraints as well, and chosen, as a query language on these relations, the operations of the algebra as defined below. Instead, for simplicity in this first implementation, we chose to rely on the existence of the O_2 data model (and the query language OQL) for the representation (and query) of thematic attributes, restricting the use of the constraint model and associated algebra to the representation of the geometry and for solving spatial predicates and operators.

3 Constraint algebra

We present in this section the algebra for linear constraint databases, which it equivalent to first-order logic. We consider the classical algebra introduced by Codd for finite relations [Cod70], in the case of infinite relations, that is that the operators apply to any relation, finite or infinite. We define a *symbolic algebra*, with operators applying to the finite representations of the possibly infinite sets, and whose effects on the finite representation corresponds exactly to the operations on the infinite relations.

The symbolic algebra consists of the following operations: Cartesian product, $\times$, projection, π, union, $\cup$, set difference, $-$, and rename, ρ. The algebra operations are performed on sets of generalized tuples, i.e. on quantifier-free formulas in *disjunctive normal form*.

Suppose R is an n-ary relation represented by a quantifier-free formula, φ, of the form:

$$\varphi \equiv \bigvee_{i=1}^{k} \bigwedge_{j=1}^{\ell_i} \varphi_{i,j}$$

where the $\varphi_{i,j}$'s are atomic formulas (simple linear constraints with integer coefficients using equality or inequalities predicates). Then, we also denote the representation φ as a collection of generalized tuples t_i in the set notation:

$$\left\{ t_i \mid 1 \leqslant i \leqslant k, \, t_i = \bigwedge_{j=1}^{\ell_i} \varphi_{i,j} \right\}$$

We now describe the effect of symbolic operators on sets of generalized tuples. Let R_1 and R_2 be two relations, and respectively e_1 and e_2 be sets of generalized tuples defining them.

1. $R_1 \times R_2 = \{ t_1 \wedge t_2 \mid t_1 \in e_1, t_2 \in e_2 \}$.
2. $\pi_{\overline{x}} R_1 = \{ \pi_{\overline{x}} t \mid t \in e_1 \}$,
   where

$$\pi_{\overline{x}} t = \bigwedge_{1 \leqslant k \leqslant K, 1 \leqslant \ell \leqslant L} b^k \overline{x} - b_0^k \leqslant a_0^\ell - a^\ell \overline{x} \wedge \bigwedge_{1 \leqslant i \leqslant I} c^i \overline{x} \leqslant c_0^i.$$

is given by the Fourier-Motzkin Elimination method [Sch86] from a tuple t defining a polyhedron $P(\overline{x}, y) \subseteq \mathbb{Q}^{n+1}$ described by the inequalities (once the coefficients of y have been normalized):

$$\begin{cases} a^\ell \overline{x} + y \leqslant a_0^\ell & \text{for } \ell = 1, \dots, L \\ b^k \overline{x} - y \leqslant b_0^k & \text{for } k = 1, \dots, K \\ c^i \overline{x} \leqslant c_0^i & \text{for } i = 1, \dots, I \end{cases}$$

where $\overline{x}$ ranges over $\mathbb{Q}^n$, and y over $\mathbb{Q}$.

3. $R_1 \cup R_2 = e_1 \cup e_2$.
4. $R_1 - R_2 = \{t_1 \wedge t_2 \mid t_1 \in e_1, t_2 \in (e_2)^c\}$,
   where e^c is the set of tuples or disjuncts of a DNF formula corresponding to $\neg e$.

The symbolic operations defined above are well defined in the sense that their effect on the intensional definition of sets correspond exactly to the semantics of the corresponding relational operators from the relational algebra over the possibly infinite extension of the sets. The relational intersection, join and selection are definable with the symbolic Cartesian product. The variable sets are different in these three operations. For the Cartesian product, the variables of the two relations are disjoint, they are similar in the case of the intersection, and with a non empty intersection in the case of the join and the selection.

The behavior of symbolic operators implies computation at different levels of the formulae. The representation in DNF has various imbricated structural levels: the disjunction, the conjunctions, the predicates of the atomic constraints, and the parameters of the constraints. Union has an effect only at the upper level of the disjunction. Cartesian product has an effect at the level of the intersections. Set difference has an effect at all levels till the predicates of the constraints, which can be inversed. Finally, projection has an effect at all levels including the parameters, and implies some numerical computation.

It was shown in [GST94] that the algebra $\text{ALG}_{\mathcal{L}}$ is equivalent to first-order logic over the class of linear constraint databases. The proof is quite similar to that of the equivalence of the classical relational algebra and calculus over finite structures. The combination of selection and Cartesian product can yield complicated forms of selections.

The data complexity of linear constraint queries has first been investigated in [KKR90], where it was shown more generally that polynomial constraint queries had NC data complexity. In the linear case, the complexity is actually of NC^1 [GS97]. It has also been shown in [GST94] that the data complexity of linear constraint queries restricted to k-bounded classes of linear constraint inputs is in AC^0 (a class of linear constraint relations is k-bounded if each individual linear constraint appearing in a tuple of a relation contains at most k occurrences of the addition symbol, and only integer parameters).

Section 5.3 describes the current implementation in DEDALE of the algebraic operators. Each operator checks its input's bounding boxes first and, if needed, applies different algorithms depending on the dimension. For example, in dimension 2, projection is easily obtained by projecting the bounding box on the corresponding axis, negation uses techniques from cell decomposition, etc. (See Section 5.3 for more details). All algebraic operations correspond to pure symbolic constraint manipulation. Only an operation called *normalization*, which puts tuples in a normal form described in the following section, actually evaluates the query, i.e. checks for tuple or relation satisfiability. Normalization can be postponed until the end of the execution plan, which is not necessarily optimal. Choosing in the execution plan when to execute normalization remains a research issue. A worst case analysis has been studied in [GL95].

4 A geographic application implemented with DEDALE

In this section, we present the application that is running on DEDALE. We first consider the geographic objects, and then give a sample of queries, using successively the algebra and its implementation with OQL and the constraint solving operations.

The experiment uses a dataset provided by the French *Institut Géographique National* (IGN) and extracted from their "Base de données topographique" [BDT91]. Geographic entities are samples of features commonly found in GIS: *Ground occupancy* (denoted *GO* in the following), *Roads, Powerlines, Rivers, Water Points, Buildings* and *Tracks*.

In conventional 2-dimensional Geographic Information Systems (GIS), each geographic entity is represented by *descriptive* alphanumeric attributes (thematic attributes), such as the ground type and the owner's name for ground occupancy, and by a geometric attribute representing the location on earth as well as the geometry of the entity. This attribute usually is in a *vector* format.

It is noteworthy that most of the time, the geometry is not convex. A road, for instance, is spatially represented as a list of consecutive segments (a *polyline*). Polygons usually are *simple* but not convex.

Each geometric object must then be split into convex components in order to satisfy the constraint model requirement that each tuple be a conjunction of linear constraints: therefore each geographic object is associated with a set of generalized tuples with the same descriptive attribute values.

We chose the following O_2 schema for implementing geographic objects. (For illustration we only give a schema for *GO*. A similar schema can be given for *Roads*, etc). Each geographic object is represented by some descriptive attributes followed by a geometric attribute of type *Relation* (a generalized relation) representing the set of its convex components: each generalized tuple has two attributes (x and y coordinates in the plane).

class *GO*
tuple [*No:* **integer**,
       ground-type: **string**,
       owner: **string**,
       geometry : Relation]

The sample database has the following characteristics: the main O_2 file is 30MB. The number of instances for each entity ranges from 20 (*waterpoints*) to 600 (*buildings*). The *GO* collection contains 307 parcels which represent the most complex spatial objects: the average parcel is a simple polygon with 80 vertices, some parcels having up to 300 vertices.

4.1 Constraint representation of spatial data

Before giving some examples of queries, let us look at the representation of constraints in O_2. Generalized relations are implemented according to the following schema:

type *Relation*		**type** *Tuple*	
tuple [*mbb: Rectangle,*		**tuple** [*mbb: Rectangle,*	
tuples : **set** *(Tuple)*]		*constraints* : **list** *(Constraint),*	
		geo-type : **GEO-TYPE**	
		normal : **Boolean**]	

where **GEO-TYPE** = {*Point, Segment, Polygon, Unknown*}, *Constraint* is defined below.

The schema is a straightforward implementation of the generalized relational model, as presented in Section 3. The following information, mostly intended to speed up the evaluation process, have been added to the schema:

1. A first step towards optimization is achieved by associating with each tuple its *minimal bounding box* (*mbb*) defined as the tuple (($\min_1$, $\min_2$,..., $\min_n$), ($\max_1$, $\max_2$, ..., $\max_n$)) of points in the n-dimensional space with minimal (maximal) coordinates satisfying the constraints. Using *mbb*'s in query evaluation is very common: it allows a first fast filtering step. The relation's *mbb* is also added. It is defined as the *mbb* of the *mbb*'s of its tuples.

2. The *normal* attribute is a **Boolean** set to "true" if the tuple is in *normal form*, defined as follows:

   (a) There does not exist any couple of redundant constraints in the list *constraints*. For instance, $x < 5$ and $x < 1$ cannot belong to the same normalized tuple.

   (b) There does not exist any couple of inconsistent constraints in *constraints*. For instance, $x > 5$ and $x < 1$ cannot belong to the same normalized tuple. It follows that a normalized non-empty tuple is always satisfiable.

   (c) Although not central to the normalization, the **list** constructor implies that the constraints are in a given order, important for displaying polygons: graphical devices rely on a point based representation of polygons (an ordered sequence of polygon vertices). The conversion constraints to point representation is of course faster (linear in the number of polygon vertices) if the constraints are in the right order.

3. While constraints are not typed in our data model, typing might be useful in the context of geographical databases. In particular in 2-dimensional geographical databases, a tuple is either a point, a polyline, or a polygon. In our prototype, this typing information will only be used for display purposes: data has to be displayed using graphical devices which make the usual distinction between points, lines and polygons.

Attribute *geo-type* gives the geometric type of the object to be represented by the tuple. Since a conjunction of constraints defines a convex object, this type can be either a *Point*, a line *Segment* or a convex *Polygon*. An *mbb* can be defined on any segment or polygon.

Unbounded objects (for instance a half straight line, or an infinite triangle defined by two intersecting half-planes) do not have any *mbb*. They are assigned the *Unknown* type. The *mbb* attribute is not relevant in this case.

It remains to define the type *Constraint*. Any constraint is of the form:

$$a_1x_1 + a_2x_2 \ldots + a_kx_k \ op \ b$$

where k is the arity (or dimension) of the relation, x_i is the variable associated with the A_i attribute, each a_i and b are rational and op belongs to **OP** $\{=, <, \leqslant, \geqslant, >\}$. Therefore a constraint is implemented as

type *Constraint*
tuple [*constants:* **list** (rational)
      op : **OP**]

where the vector of constraints *constants* is a list of $k + 1$ rationals.

    This concludes the logical schema related to constraints representation. However, in the current implementation, a more physical implementation has been used: instead of using the **list** constructor for storing the constraints of a tuple, we consider a constraint as a binary object and represent the tuple's constraints as an array of bytes. This allows an efficient clustering of constraints which are always to be read together, and avoids the penalty of indirections in the O_2 **list** constructor.

4.2 Mapping non-convex objects to a constraint-based representation

Mapping non-convex objects to a constraint-based representation (a generalized relation) is necessary at least for data loading since data in the outside world is available in the vector format. The conversion is trivial for points, which are represented by two constraints of the form $x = a \wedge y = b$. Things are a bit more complex for polylines and polygons.

Polylines: A polyline is an ordered collection of connected segments whose point-based representation is a list of points $< P_1, P_2, \ldots, P_n >$. A segment P_iP_{i+1} can be represented by a tuple of the form $x_{min} \leqslant x \leqslant x_{max} \wedge y_{min} \leqslant y \leqslant y_{max} \wedge a_1x + a_2y + b = 0$, a conjunction of 5 constraints: one for the equation of the line collinear to the segment, and 4 for the bounding box.[1]

Polygons: A point-based representation of a polygon is also a list of points $< P_1, P_2, \ldots, P_n >$ describing the boundary as a polyline, adding a last segment P_nP_1 since the boundary is closed. If a polygon is not convex, it must be partitioned into convex components. This is done in two steps: first the simple polygon is triangulated in $n - 2$ triangles, second we merge adjacent triangles whose union is still convex in order to obtain a smaller number of convex components.

A tuple is created for each resulting convex polygon: the boundary is scanned in counterclockwise order, and for each edge e the constraint $a_1x + a_2y \leqslant b$ representing the half-plane located to the side of e is appended to the *constraints* attribute of the tuple.

---

[1] This is not optimal since a segment can be described by 3 constraints. However the bounding box is already stored as part of the tuple.

It is worth noting that each tuple thereby inserted in the database is normalized: there are no redundant nor inconsistent constraint. In addition, the order of the constraints in a *Polygon* tuple is also the order of the segments along the boundary of the convex polygon. Thanks to this order obtained through the **list** constructor in the *Tuple* type, the vector representation can be computed back by a simple scan.

4.3 Examples of queries

To illustrate the power of the constraint approach and the functionalities of the current prototype, a sample of queries is given below, expressed in OQL as implemented in the prototype on objects whose schema was given in the previous subsection. The implementation of the constraint solving functions used is presented in Section 5. Formally, they rely on the algebra presented in the previous section. The entry points to the O_2 database (O_2 **names**) used are *GO, Roads, Waterpoints, Cities* and *Buildings*.

- Display the part of roads which is inside the rectangle @*rectangle* drawn on the screen.

> **select**   *SELECT(r.geometry, @rectangle)*
> **from**   *r* in *Roads*
> **where**   *SATISFY (SELECT(r.geometry, @rectangle))*

This query computes, for those roads that overlap the rectangle, the part inside the rectangle (*SELECT* call in clause **select**). *SELECT* (which implements the algebraic selection using the symbolic operator cross product) takes as inputs the set of convex tuples (*r.geometry*) representing the geometry of *r* and the @*rectangle* constraints. *SATISFY* is true if the result of *SELECT* is non empty.
- *No* of the forests crossed by a road.

> **select**   *o.No*
> **from**   *o* in *GO, r* in *Roads*
> **where**   *o.ground-type = "forest"*
> **and**   *SATISFY (INTERSECTION(o.geometry, r.geometry))*

The join between a forest geometry and a road geometry is performed by the *INTERSECTION* function (implementing algebraic operator *INTERSECTION*). *SATISFY* is true if the result of *INTERSECTION* is non empty.
- *No* of the forests crossed by a road inside the rectangle @*rectangle*?

> **select**   *o.No*
> **from**   *o* in *GO, r* in *Roads*
> **where**   *SATISFY (SELECT(INTERSECTION(o.geometry,*
>   *r.geometry),*
>   @*rectangle))*
> **and**   *o.ground-type = "forest"*

This query consists of a join between *Roads* and *GO*, which yields forests crossed by roads, and a selection which keeps that part of the previous result inside the user-defined rectangle.

Note that the order of operations in the OQL expression, intersection first, followed by selection, is not necessarily optimal.

– Waterpoints south of Orange.

select   *w.No*
from   *w* **in** *WaterPoints, c* **in** *Cities*
where   *c.City-name="Orange"*
and   *SATISFY(SELECT(JOIN(JOIN(w,PROJECT(c.geometry,x)),*
                                       RENAME(PROJECT(c.geometry,y),
                                              $y \rightarrow y')),$
                    $y < y'))$

The inner join keeps the waterpoints whose abscissa is inside "Orange" abscissas range. The second join keeps those whose ordinate is smaller than the ordinate of at least one point in "Orange".

Finally the following query uses the algebraic difference as defined in Section 3 and denoted *DIFF*.

– Buildings surrounded by a forest.

In the OQL expression below, the "**where** *SATISFY*" clause selects the buildings included in and intersecting forests, while the "**and** ¬" clause selects the buildings intersecting or outside forests.

select   *b*
from   *b* **in** *Buildings, f* **in** *GO*
where   *SATISFY (INTERSECTION(f.geometry,b.geometry))*
and   ¬*SATISFY (INTERSECTION(NOT(f.geometry),(b.geometry)))*
and   *f.ground-type = "forest"*

All the queries commonly found in spatial database applications (*clipping, windowing, point-in-polygon, map overlay*, etc.), as well as some less common requests can be expressed in DEDALE using the small set of operations above.

Figure 2 illustrates the GUI of DEDALE. The top-left window allows to enter OQL queries as shown above. The results obtained during a querying session can be displayed in several maps, each showing a subset of the whole data retrieved from the database [PR95]. MAP0 in Figure 2 contains several kinds of geographical objects (ground occupancy, roads, waterpoints). MAP1 displays a subset of MAP0: only objects of *GO* are selected, and only the part of the parcels included in a given rectangle referred to by $1. MAP1 is the result of a query expressed as explained previously.

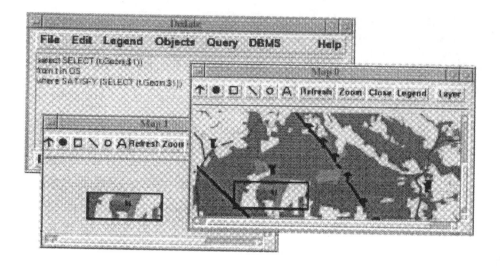

Fig. 2. Interactive querying with DEDALE

5 Constraint solving and geometric algorithms

In this section, we describe the current implementation of DEDALE. The presentation is bottom-up: we begin with *geometric operations* that are used in *constraint manipulation primitives*, which in turn are the basis to evaluate the *algebraic operators* of Section 3. The section ends up with a short discussion on the query evaluation strategy currently implemented in DEDALE.

5.1 Geometric operations

The first goal of these operations is to interface DEDALE with the outside world, both for *data loading* since geographical data is usually provided in vector mode, and for *data display* using graphical softwares which rely on a vector representation.

Data loading (function *ToConstraint*)
The function *ToConstraint* transforms a point-based representation towards its equivalent constraint representation. The conversion is trivial for points and simple for lines (see Subsection 4.2) but deserves some further explanations for polygons.

Many algorithms have been designed for polygon partition, mostly for polygon triangulation [GJPT78,FM84,TvW88,Cha91,Sei91]. However, triangulation results in a large possibly prohibitive number of convex components in the partition. Given a polygon with n vertices, the number of triangles in the partition is $n - 2$. Thus, we would like to minimize the number of convex elements in the partition. There exists an algorithm proposed in [Kei85] which gives the optimal number of convex components. Unfortunately, in addition to being rather complex, the algorithm time complexity is large: $O(r^2 n \log n)$ where r is the number of "notches".[2] Hence, we preferred to implement an algorithm suboptimal in terms of the number of components, but simple to implement and running in linear time [HM83].

The algorithm takes as input a set of triangles obtained by triangulation,[3] together with the adjacency graph produced by the former triangulation algorithm, a binary tree representing adjacent triangles. This tree is scanned bottom up: one first tests whether the union of triangle t_1 with another adjacent triangle t_2 is convex. If yes one keeps scanning the tree up and merging a convex polygon with adjacent triangles until the object is no longer convex. The process is then repeated with another leaf if any.

The algorithm is linear in the number of vertices of the initial polygon. As a result, we get a set of convex polygons whose number of elements, as shown in [HM83], is never worse than four times the optimal.

Table 1 gives some statistics on the convex partitioning of the polygons of the *GO* collection. There are 307 simple polygons, with an average of 80.87 vertices per polygon. The partitioning yields 10 457 convex components with an average number of vertices of 4.46. The average number of "notches" is a measure of the "non-convexity" of the polygon: 41.23% of the vertices are notches.

Avg(vertices) (SP)	% of notches	Avg(convex/notches)	Avg(vertices) (CC)
80	41.23	0.95	4.46

Table 1: Convex partitioning statistics[4]

If r is the number of notches, the optimal number of components is in $[\lceil \frac{r}{2} \rceil + 1, r + 1]$ [CD85]. Table 1 shows that we get almost r (0.95) in spite of the algorithm sub-optimality. This proves the efficiency of our implementation, but the large ratio (approximately 30) between the number of convex polygons and the number of simple polygons illustrates the need for an efficient representation of constraints (generalized tuples).

Data display (function *ToVector*)

The function *ToVector* takes as input a *normalized* tuple and delivers the corresponding vector representation. As shown in Subsection 4.2, the design of a normalized tuple makes this operation quite easy.

Half-Plane Intersection

The third geometric operation, *Half-Plane Intersection*, denoted *HPI*, optimizes 2-dimensional constraint solving. Given a set of half-planes, this operation computes the associated convex polygon. We implemented the algorithm

---

[2] A notch is a vertex such that the internal angle is larger than π.
[3] The triangulation algorithm implemented here is the "greedy" $O(n^2)$ algorithm described in [O'R94].
[4] SP stands for simple polygons, and CC for convex components.

of [PS85] which is optimal and whose time complexity is $O(n \log n)$ where n denotes the number of half-planes.

5.2 Constraint manipulation

Tuple *normalization* is central to the implementation of the algebra. Normalization eliminates redundancy. If the resulting set is empty, then the tuple is unsatisfiable. The normalization algorithm works as follows: first the constraints are scanned in order to count the number of constraints with operator *equal*. Except for degenerated cases, this number indicates the type of the result: if it is larger than 2, the tuple is non satisfiable; if it is equal to 2, the constraint represents a point, 1 a linear object and 0 means that every constraint defines a half-plane, in which case *half-plane intersection* computes a convex polygon which is converted into constraints.

The algorithm is given below[5]: CEQ denotes the subset of $t.constraints$ such that op is '=' (straight lines), CNE is $t.constraints - CEQ$ (half-planes). The MBB function computes the bounding box of any point-based geometric object.

Function *NORMALIZE*
Input: *a tuple t*
Output: *a normalized tuple t'*
begin
    $t'.constraints := \emptyset$; $t'.type := Unknown$; $t'.mbb := \emptyset$; $t'.normal := true$
    if $Card(CEQ) > 2$ **return** t' // *Unsatisfiable*
    else if $Card(CEQ) = 2$ **do** // *A point pt*
    begin
        Check that each constraint in CNE contains pt
        if *yes* **then**
            $t'.type := Point$
            $t'.constraints \leftarrow (x = pt.x \wedge y = pt.y)$
            $t'.mbb := MBB\ (pt)$
        else *return* t'
    endif
    else if $Card(CEQ) = 1$ **then** // *A segment*
    begin
        $t'.type := Segment$; $t'.mbb := MBB(HPI(CNE))$
        $t'.constraints \leftarrow CEQ + ToConstraints(MBB(HPI(CNE)))$
    endif
    else if $Card(CEQ) = 0$ **then** // *A convex polygon*
    begin
        $t'.type := Polygon$; $t'.mbb := MBB(HPI(CNE))$
        $t'.constraint := ToConstraint(HPI\ (t.constraints))$
    endif
return t'
end

---

[5] Note that to simplify its description, we assume that the input does not contain any degenerated case such as two constraints representing parallel straight lines, or unbounded objects.

At the relation level, two other functions are useful for constraint solving. The first one *SATISFY*, Boolean, is set to true if the generalized relation argument is non empty. *SATISFY* simply scans the tuples of the relation, normalizes each tuple and returns "true" as soon as it finds a satisfiable tuple. The second function, *OVERLAP* takes as input two relations, R_1 and R_2, and performs a nested loop over both collections of tuples, taking the conjunction of each pair of tuples. A simple optimization is possible in order to eliminate some empty tuples: two tuples are concatenated only if the intersection of their respective bounding boxes is non empty. This algorithm works in the general n-dimensional case, and is currently implemented for 2-dimensional data.

Function *OVERLAP*
Input: *two relations, r_1 and r_2*
Output: *a relation r_3*
begin
    if $r_1.mbb \cap r_2.mbb \neq \emptyset$ **then**
    begin
       for each t_1 *in* r_1 **do**
       begin
          for each t_2 *in* r_2 **do**
          begin
             if $t_1.mbb \cap t_2.mbb \neq \emptyset$ **then**
             begin
               Create a new tuple t
               $t.normal := false$; $t.type := Unknown$; $t.mbb := t_1.mbb \cap t_2.mbb$
               $t.constraints := t_1.constraints \wedge t_2.constraints$
               Insert t in $r_3.tuples$; $r_3.mbb := R_3.mbb \cap t_3.mbb$
             endif
          enddo
       enddo
    endif
  return r_3
end

Note that the tuples of the resulting relation are not normalized: some constraints in a tuple might be redundant or inconsistent.

5.3 Implementation of the algebraic operators

We now describe the current implementation of the algebraic operators. Recall that the constraint-based representation is restricted to generalized relations of arity 2 for geometric data. At the physical level, we consider various operations not distinguished at the logical level. This is the case of join, intersection, and selection, which can all be expressed at the logical level by a Cartesian product.

Projection, π

$r = \pi_{\bar{x}}(r_1)$ is defined as the relation whose tuples are the projection of each tuple of r_1 on the $\bar{x}$ axis. To compute the projection of a tuple in the general case, we use an algorithm based on the Fourier-Motzkin method.

However, when restricted to dimension 2 there is an easiest and fastest way to perform projection. First each tuple is normalized; during normalization, the tuple minimal bounding box (*mbb*) is computed; then the *mbb* is projected on the correct axis: this gives the result.

Join, ⋈

The join $r = r_1 \bowtie r_2$ is obtained by computing the conjunction of each tuple of r_1 with each tuple of r_2. The conjunction of two tuples is just the concatenation of their constraints. The resulting set is *not* normalized, i.e. checked for satisfiability and redundancies. In the 2-dimensional case, the join is implemented by a direct call to the above *OVERLAP* function.

Intersection, ∩

$r = r_1 \cap r_2$ is a special case of join. Here r_1 and r_2 are supposed to be defined on the same attributes. In the current implementation of DEDALE (2-dimensional data), the operator is implemented by a direct call to the *OVERLAP* primitive.

Union, ∪

$r = r_1 \cup r_2$ is defined as the set of tuples which belong either to r_1 or to r_2 and is simply implemented as the concatenation of the tuples lists from r_1 and r_2.

Selection, σ

$r = \sigma_F(r_1)$ is easy to implement since F is just a constraint which has to be added to each tuple of r_1. For 2-dimensional data, selection uses once more the $OVERLAP(r_1, r_2)$ primitive, r_2 being in that case the F singleton. Once again, r is not normalized: it might contain empty tuples.

Difference, −

$r = r_1 - r_2$ gives the set of points that are in r_1 but not in r_2. $r_2 = \bigvee \bigwedge c_{ij}^l$, therefore its negation is $\neg r_2 = \bigwedge \bigvee \neg c_{ij}^l$ which is a conjunctive normal form (CNF) formula. As $r = r_1 \cap \neg r_2$, computing r is transforming a CNF formula into a DNF one. This transformation is exponential in general. However when the dimension (arity) is fixed it is possible to compute r in polynomial time. For dimension 2, which is our case of interest here, it is possible to compute negation in time $O(n^3)$ where n is the number of constraints of r_1 and r_2. This algorithm is maybe not the best, but the technique of *cell decomposition* is interesting by itself and could be reused to compute the connectivity of a region for example. The idea is roughly to get a *cell decomposition* of the plane using the constraints of r_1 and r_2. Each constraint of r_1 or r_2 gives a line in the plane. All the lines partition the plane into *cells*. One can show that r_1 and r_2 are unions of such *cells* and therefore r is the union of the *cells* that are part of r_1 but not part of r_2. See Figure 3. The computation of the cells, together with the constraints defining it, can be done in time $O(n^2 \log n)$ where n is the number of constraints in r_1 and r_2. Then we just have to check whether a *cell* c belongs or not to a relation r_i. This can be done in time linear on the size of r_i ($O(n)$) because it is enough to check whether a point of c is in r_i. As there might be n^2 such cells, the overall computation time is $O(n^3)$.

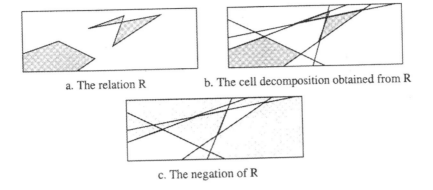

a. The relation R   b. The cell decomposition obtained from R

c. The negation of R

Fig. 3. negation

Function *DIFF*
Input: *two relations, r_1 and r_2*
Output: *a relation r*
begin
    First get the list of all the line equations in all constraints in all tuples of r_1 and r_2. Those lines partition the plane into cells which are convex areas. See fig 3 step 2. Compute the constraints defining the cells.
    for each cell c **do**
    begin
        if $c \subset r_1 \wedge c \not\subset r_2$ **then**
        begin
          Create a new tuple t
          $t.normal := true; t.type := Area; t.mbb := c.mbb$
          $t.constraints := c.constraints$
          Insert t in $r.tuples; r.mbb := r.mbb \cup c.mbb$
        endif
    enddo
end

Computing the cell decomposition is the hardest part. This can be done in time $O(n^2 \log n)$ where n is the number of lines involved using the following algorithm.

Assume that we are given a list L of lines in the plane. Let L_p be the list of all their intersecting points. A cell is then completely defined by any of its vertices with the corresponding *angular sector*. If all lines are sorted on their slope, all *angular sectors* of a given point p are defined by two successive lines intersecting at p. To compute the cell from this point we need to be able to go from one point of L_p to the next one in the same line. This can be easily done by sorting for all lines the intersection points with the other lines using their x, y coordinates. All cells have been computed when all *angular sectors* of each point have been used. During the computation of L_p it is possible to compute the list of *angular sectors* for each point. Each time a point is "used" for computing a cell we mark it as used. When they are all used, the corresponding point is removed from L_p. The 2 last operations are done by a function *visit(p)*. When L_p is empty, all cells have been computed.

Function *Linear Cell Decomposition*
Input: *a list of lines equations L*
Output: *a relation r which generalized tuples are precisely the cells*
begin
    1) *Sort lines using their slopes.*
    2) *Compute the intersecting points, together with their angular sectors.*
    3) *Sort the points in L_p*
    NewRelation(r) // *init a new relation*
    while $L_p \neq ()$ **do**
        NewTuple(t) // *init a new tuple*
        $(p, o) \in L_p$ // *get a point which has not been visited enough time,*
        $line_{beg} = first(p, o)$ // *get the corresponding line equationss,*
        $line_{cur} = second(p, o)$ // *which are used to define the first constraints.*
        Visit(p, o); *record that (p, o) was visited, remove p of L_p if needed.*
        AddConstraint($t, line_{beg}$);
        AddConstraint($t, line_{cur}$);
        while $line_{cur} \neq line_{beg}$ **do**
            get the next point in the current line.
            // *This is possible in constant time using the index computed*
            // *at step 2)*
            $(p, o) = Next(p, o)$;
            $line_{cur} = second(p, o)$;
            // *return the next line in order after $line_{cur}$ in (p, o).*
            AddConstraint($t, line_{cur}$) // *which is the one that will define*
            Visit(p, o);
        enddo
        AddTuple(r, t);
    enddo
end

Function *NOT*
    The complement operation, denoted $\neg$, is implemented by the function *NOT*. $r = \neg r_1 = \mathbf{R}^2 - r_1$ is a variant of difference: the cell decomposition is done using only the lines of the constraints of r_1. Then one just has to check whether a given cell is or not part of r_1.

5.4 Query evaluation

As shown previously, all the operators can be done by only symbolic manipulation: $\cup$ manipulates relations, $\times$ manipulate tuples, but none of them checks for tuple's or relation satisfiability. Hence, the actual evaluation of the query is delayed until a call to the *NORMALIZE* operation.

This suggests that choosing the right place in the execution plan to carry out the normalization process is an essential part of the query processing strategy. Such strategies were proposed in [GL95]. The current implementation of DEDALE uses the simplest one, *lazy evaluation*. Normalization is only performed once (except for projection), as the root operation of the query execution tree. This *lazy evaluation* was shown to be rather inefficient. Needless to say, we plan to experiment some more sophisticated evaluation strategies, and integrate them in the optimizer module.

6 Perspectives

The main challenge of such an implementation was to prove the feasibility of a constraint database approach for representing and querying geographic information. The theoretical advantages of the approach, widely addressed now in the literature are a sound mathematical foundation for spatial data representation which is extensible and the possibility of defining query languages based on the classical relational framework. In practice, the linear constraint model corresponds nicely to the vector mode representation of GIS in the sense that the same 2-dimensional data can be stored in both paradigms. The promising features are:

- A simple powerful model applicable to a large variety of geographical applications, with no limitation on data dimension.
- A high level declarative language for querying geographical information.
- The potential for optimization given by the algebra. We are currently integrating spatial indices already implemented with O_2 [SGR96].
- Simple expression of queries that are cumbersome to express and process with current GIS, such as interpolation of values, interdependent values, queries involving direction predicates (North-West of, etc.).
- A potential for parallel evaluation. The use of constraints clarifies indeed what operations can be parallelized. Moreover, parallel complexity results for some subclasses of the full algebra lead directly to parallel algorithms.

The constraint solving engine has been completely implemented. It could have been possible to reuse partly existing softwares for constraint solving from linear programming for instance. Because of the specificity of our needs, we started from scratch and developed much simpler algorithms and code. For the 2-dimensional case the implemented functions are rather efficient. But one of the advantages of the constraint modelization is that it is not restricted to bidimensional data. It is easy to extend the current version of DEDALE to handle higher dimensional data in a fully modular way. All the algorithms proposed in Section 5.3 are valid in the n-dimensional case, as long as there exists an algorithm for normalization. Clearly the implementation of some of these operators in the n-dimensional case deserves more efficient algorithms. Mapping n-dimensional data onto 2-dimensional output devices also deserves a specific study.

Thus our first objective is to test DEDALE against an application handling data with higher dimensions. We plan to investigate a spatio-temporal application involving moving objects, where both time and space are modeled with constraints.

Our second objective is a full optimization of queries expressed on constraints (module *optimizer* in Figure 1). It includes as a specific task the design of indexing for spatial data represented as constraints. But the main problem here is to translate general algebraic queries into an optimal execution plan. The current implementation handles thematic attributes (with OQL) separately from spatial data (O_2 functions for solving constraints). This leads only to partial optimization through OQL query evaluation which does not take into account the O_2 function semantics for the optimization. We plan to implement an independent query parser and optimizer fully devoted to an efficient evaluation of constraint-based queries. Note that, for efficiency reasons, the query evaluator is aware of the dimension of the objects manipulated and calls distinct algorithms for dimension 1, 2 or more.

Acknowledgments

The authors wish to warmly thank Zoé Lacroix and Gabi Kuper for the numerous discussions that oriented the choices made in the present prototype. We are also indebted to Stéphane Solé who implemented the intersection operator and to Guillaume Masson who provided the convexification statistics. Thanks also to Manolis Koubarakis for comments on a draft of the paper, and to Guido Moerkotte for very helpful discussions on the algebraic operators.

References

[ABC93] D. Abel and B.-C.Ooi, editors. *Proc. Intl. Symp. on Large Spatial Databases (SSD)*. LNCS No. 692. Springer-Verlag, 1993.

[BDK92] F. Bancilhon, C. Delobel, and P. Kanellakis, editors. *Building an Object-Oriented Database System: The Story of O_2*. Morgan Kaufmann, San Mateo, California, 1992.

[BDT91] La Base de Données Topographiques de l'I.G.N. Bulletin d'Information de l'I.G.N., No. 59, 1991.

[BS97] A. Brodsky and V.E. Segal. The c^3 constraint object-oriented database system: an overview. In *Constraint Databases and Applications, Proc. second international workshop on Constraint Databases Systems (CDB97)*, Lecture Notes in Computer Science, pages 134–159, 1997.

[Cat94] R.G.G. Cattell, editor. *The Object Database Standard ODMG-93*. Morgan Kaufmann, San Francisco, California, 1994.

[CD85]   B. Chazelle and D.P. Dobkin. Optimal Convex Decomposition. In G.T. Toussaint, editor, *Computational Geometry*, pages 63–133. North Holland, 1985.

[Cha91]   B. Chazelle. Triangulating a Simple Polygon in Linear Time. *Discrete and Computational Geometry*, 6:485–524, 1991.

[Cod70]   E.F. Codd. A relational model of data for large shared data banks. *Communications of ACM*, 13:6:377–387, 1970.

[EH95]   M.J. Egenhofer and J. Herring, editors. *Proc. Intl. Symp. on Large Spatial Databases (SSD)*. LNCS No. 951. Springer-Verlag, 1995.

[FM84]   A. Fournier and D.Y. Montuno. Triangulating simple polygons and equivalent problems. *ACM Transactions on Graphics*, 3:153–174, 1984.

[GJPT78]   M.R. Garey, D.S. Johnson, F.P. Preparata, and R.E. Tarjan. Triangulating a Simple Polygon. *Information Processing Letter*, 7(4):175–180, 1978.

[GL95]   S. Grumbach and Z. Lacroix. Computing queries on linear constraint databases. In *Fifth Int. Workshop on Database Programming Languages*, 1995.

[GS95]   S. Grumbach and J. Su. Dense order constraint databases. In *14th ACM Symp. on Principles of Database Systems*, pages 66–77, San Jose, May 1995.

[GS97]   S. Grumbach and J. Su. Queries with arithmetical constraints. *Theoretical Computer Science*, 173, 1997. Invited to a special issue.

[GST94]   S. Grumbach, J. Su, and C. Tollu. Linear constraint query languages: Expressive power and complexity. In D. Leivant, editor, *Logic and Computational Complexity*, Indianapolis, 1994. Springer Verlag. LNCS 960.

[Gue94]   R. Gueting. An Introduction to Spatial Database Systems. *The VLDB Journal*, 3(4), 1994.

[HM83]   S. Hertel and K. Mehlorn. Fast Triangulation of Simple Polygons. In *Proc. Intl. Conf. on Foundations of Computer Theory*, LNCS No. 158, pages 207–218. Springer-Verlag, 1983.

[Kei85]   J.M. Keil. Decomposing a Polygon into Simpler Components. *SIAM Journal of Computing*, 14(4):799–817, 1985.

[KG94]   P. Kanellakis and D. Goldin. Constraint programming and database query languages. In *Manuscript*, 1994.

[KKR90]   P. Kanellakis, G Kuper, and P. Revesz. Constraint query languages. In *Proc. 9th ACM Symp. on Principles of Database Systems*, pages 299–313, Nashville, 1990.

[LJF94]   K. Lin, H.V. Jagadish, and Christos Faloutsos. The tv-tree - an index for high-dimensional data. *VLDB Journal*, 1994.

[May90]   Peter Mayle. *A Year in Provence*. Knopf, New York, 1990.

[Mor89]   S. Morehouse. The Architecture of ARC/INFO. In *Proc. Intl. Symp. on Computer-Assisted Cartography (Auto-Carto 9)*, pages 266–277, 1989.

[O'R94]   J. O'Rourke. *Computational Geometry in C*. Cambridge University Press, 1994.

[PR95]   J.-P. Peloux and P. Rigaux. A Loosely Coupled Interface to an Object-Oriented Geographic Database. In *Proc. Intl. Conf. on Spatial Information Theory (COSIT)*, 1995.

[PS85]   F. Preparata and M. Shamos. *Computational Geometry: An Introduction*. Springer Verlag, 1985.

[PSV96]   C.H. Papadimitriou, D. Suciu, and V. Vianu. Topological queries in spatial databases. In *15th ACM Symp. on Principles of Database Systems*, Montréal, June 1996.

[PVV94] J. Paredaens, J. Van den Bussche, and D. Van Gucht. Towards a theory of spatial database queries. In *Proc. 13th ACM Symp. on Principles of Database Systems*, pages 279–288, 1994.

[PVV95] J. Paredaens, J. Van den Bussche, and D. Van Gucht. First-order queries on finite structures over the reals. In *Proceedings 10th IEEE Symposium on Logic in Computer Science.* IEEE Computer Society Press, 1995.

[Sch86] A. Schrijver. *Theory of Linear and Integer Programming.* Wiley, 1986.

[Sei91] R. Seidel. A Simple and Fast Incremental Randomized Algorithm for Computing Trapezoidal Decompositions and for Triangulating Polygons. *Computational Geometry*, 1(1), 1991.

[SGR96] M. Scholl, G. Grangeret, and X. Rehse. Point and window queries with linear spatial indices: An evaluation with O_2. Technical Report RRC-96-09; ftp://ftp.cnam.fr/pub/CNAM/cedric/tech_reports/RRC-96-09.ps.Z, Cedric Lab, CNAM, Paris, 1996.

[TvW88] R.E. Tarjan and C.J. van Wyk. An $O(n \log \log n)$ Time Algorithm for Triangulating a Simple Polygon. *SIAM Journal of Computing*, 17(1):143–178, 1988.

[VG96] V.Gaede and O. Guenther. Multidimensional Access Methods. Technical Report TR-96-043, ICSI, 1996.

[VGV95] L. Vandeurzen, M. Gyssens, and D. Van Gucht. On the desirability and limitations of linear spatial database models. In *Advances in Spatial Databases, 4th Int. Symp., SSD'95*, pages 14–28. Springer, 1995.

Degrees of Monotonicity
of Spatial Transformations

Bart Kuijpers

University of Antwerp*

Abstract. We consider spatial databases that can be defined in terms of polynomial inequalities, and we are interested in *monotonic transformations* of spatial databases.

We investigate a hierarchy of monotonicity classes of spatial transformations that is determined by the number of degrees of freedom of the transformations. The result of a monotonic transformation with k degrees of freedom on a spatial database is completely determined by its result on subsets of cardinality at most k of the spatial database. The result of a transformation in the largest class of the hierarchy on a spatial database is determined by its result on arbitrary large subsets of the database. The latter is the class of *all* the monotonic spatial transformations.

We give a sound and complete language for the monotonic spatial transformations that can be expressed in the relational calculus augmented with polynomial inequalities and that belong to a class with a finite number of degrees of freedom. In particular, we show that these transformations are finite unions of transformations that can be written in a particular conjunctive form. We also address the problem of finding sound and complete languages for monotonic transformations that are expressible in the calculus and have an infinite number of degrees of freedom. We show that Lyndon's theorem, which is known to fail in finite model theory, also fails in this setting: monotonic spatial transformations expressible in the calculus do *not* correspond to the transformations expressible by a positive formula.

We show that it is undecidable whether a query expressed in the relational calculus augmented with polynomial inequalities is a monotonic spatial transformation of a certain degree. On the other hand, various interesting properties (e.g., equivalence, genericity), which are undecidable for general spatial transformations expressible in the calculus, become decidable for monotonic spatial transformations of finite degree.

1 Introduction and summary

Spatial database systems [1, 7, 10, 11] are concerned with the representation and manipulation of data that have a geometrical or topological interpretation. The conceptual view of such a database is that of a possibly infinite set of points

* Address: UIA, Informatica, Universiteitsplein 1, B-2610 Antwerpen, Belgium. Email: `kuijpers@uia.ua.ac.be`

in the real space. The framework of *constraint databases*, introduced by Kanellakis, Kuper, and Revesz [15], provides an elegant and powerful model of spatial databases [20]. In this setting, a spatial database is represented as a Boolean combination of polynomial equalities and inequalities. For example, the spatial database consisting of the set of points on the northern hemisphere together with the points on the equator of the unit sphere in the three-dimensional space $\mathbf{R}^3$ can be represented by the formula $x^2+y^2+z^2 = 1 \wedge z \geq 0$. The set of points in the real plane lying strictly above the parabola $y = x^2$ and strictly below the parabola $y = x^2 + 1/2$ is another example of a spatial database. This database is depicted in Figure 1.

Fig. 1. A spatial database that consists of the points lying strictly between the parabola $y = x^2$ and the translated one $y = x^2 + 1/2$.

Several languages have been proposed to query and transform spatial databases in the constraint model. If, e.g., the relational calculus is extended with polynomial inequalities, a simple but effective query language is obtained [20]. The translation of a 2-dimensional spatial database S by the vector $(1, 2)$, for instance, can be expressed in this language by the formula

$$(\exists x')(\exists y')(S(x', y') \wedge x' + 1 = x \wedge y' + 2 = y). \qquad (*)$$

The free variables x and y of this formula are the coordinates of the points in the result of the transformation. Although their variables range over the real numbers, such calculus expressions can be computed effectively [6, 8, 22].

Also, various extensions of this calculus with recursion have been introduced and studied. In [15, 16, 17], a spatial version of Datalog has been studied. In [13], computationally complete languages for spatial database queries and transformations were studied.

In this paper, we are especially interested in *monotonic* transformations of spatial databases. A transformation is monotone if it yields increasing outputs on increasing inputs. This interest is motivated by classes of transformations that frequently occur in spatial database practice [1, 7, 10, 11]. The spatial transformation determined by the expression (∗) is monotone and it is exemplary for such a class. It works *pointwise* on the spatial data, i.e., its result on a spatial database is the union of the results of the transformation when applied to the individual points of the spatial database. Many other transformations, like rotations or projections, also satisfy this property. "Return the points within distance 1 from the input database" is another example of a pointwise spatial transformation. The result of these transformations is completely determined by their result on single points.

By adding one extra degree of freedom, we obtain a larger class of monotonic transformations whose results are determined by the results of the transformations on subsets with at most two elements. "Return the midpoints of each pair of different points in the input database" is a transformation with two degrees of freedom. It is not a pointwise transformation, however. The transformation of a spatial database into itself if its diameter is larger than 1 and into the empty set if it is not larger than 1 is another example.

Continuing in this way, every larger number of degrees of freedom gives rise to a larger class of monotonic transformations. The monotonic transformations with k degrees of freedom are exactly the transformations that are monotonic and that are completely determined by their result on sets of cardinality at most k. An example of a monotonic transformations with k degrees of freedom that is of practical importance is the transformation of a $(k-1)$-dimensional spatial database into its convex hull.

If the number of degrees of freedom is uncountably infinite, we obtain, as we will show, the set of *all* monotonic spatial transformations. We thus obtain a hierarchy of monotonicity classes of spatial transformations that is indexed by degrees of freedom (i.e., by cardinal numbers).

We syntactically describe sound and complete languages that capture the monotonic spatial transformations that are expressible in the relational calculus augmented with polynomial inequalities and that have a finite number of degrees of freedom. We show, more precisely, that these transformations are finite unions of transformations that can be written in a particular conjunctive form.

We also address the problem of finding sound and complete languages for monotonic transformations that are expressible in the calculus and that have an infinite (countable or uncountable) number of degrees of freedom. From model theory, Lyndon's theorem suggests that the set of transformations expressible by a *positive* calculus formula is likely to capture the set of all monotonic transformations expressible in the calculus. We show, however, that Lyndon's theorem, which is known to fail in finite model theory, also fails in our setting.

Finally, we show that it is undecidable whether a calculus formula expresses a monotonic spatial transformation of a certain degree. On the other hand, various interesting properties (e.g., equivalence, genericity), that are undecidable for general spatial database transformations, become decidable for monotonic spatial transformations that are expressible in the calculus and that have a finite **number of degrees of freedom.**

This paper is organized as follows. In Section 2, we give the definitions of spatial databases, spatial transformations and of monotonic transformations along with some basic properties of monotonic transformations. In Section 3, we present sound and complete languages for monotonic transformations of finite degree. In Section 4, we discuss complete languages for monotonic transformations of infinite degree. We give decidability and undecidability results in Section 5. We end the paper with a discussion in Section 6. We discuss alternative hierarchies of monotonicity classes and state some open problems concerning complete languages for monotonic transformations.

2 Definitions and preliminaries

In this section, we define spatial databases and spatial database transformations. Also, the notion of monotonic spatial transformation of degree k is defined and illustrated.

2.1 Spatial databases and spatial database transformations

$\mathbf{R}$ denotes the set of the real numbers. So, $\mathbf{R}^m$ is the corresponding m-dimensional space, where m is arbitrarily fixed.

Definition 1. A *spatial database* is a geometrical figure in $\mathbf{R}^m$ that can be defined as a Boolean combination of sets of the form $\{(x_1, \ldots, x_m) \mid p(x_1, \ldots, x_m) > 0\}$, where $p(x_1, \ldots, x_m)$ is a polynomial with integer coefficients in the real variables $x_1, \ldots, x_m$.[2]

The set $\{(x, y, z) \mid x^2 + y^2 + z^2 = 1 \wedge z \geq 0\}$, mentioned in the Introduction, is an example of a spatial database in $\mathbf{R}^3$. The polynomial equality $p = 0$ can be seen as an abbreviation for $\neg(p > 0) \wedge \neg(-p > 0)$. The set $\{(x, y) \mid (y - x^2)(x^2 - y + 1/2) > 0\}$, also mentioned in the Introduction, is a spatial database in $\mathbf{R}^2$.

Definition 2. A *spatial database transformation* (or just *transformation*) is a function that maps every spatial database to a spatial database.

In this paper, we will use the relational calculus augmented with polynomial inequalities, the *spatial calculus* for short, as a language to express transformations. In this language, the result of a transformation Q on an input spatial database S is of the form

$$Q(S) = \{(x_1, \ldots, x_m) \mid \varphi(x_1, \ldots, x_m, S)\},$$

---

[2] Often, a spatial database is defined as a n-tuple of such geometrical figures (see, e.g., [13, 20]). In order not to overload the notations further on, we have restricted ourselves to $n = 1$. The results of this paper carry over straightforwardly to the more general situation.

with φ a formula built from the atomic formulas $S(y_1,\ldots,y_m)$ and $p(z_1,\ldots,z_n) > 0$, the logical connectives $\neg$, $\wedge$, $\vee$ and the quantifiers $\forall$, $\exists$. Here, S is an m-ary relation name that represents the input spatial database and $p(z_1,\ldots,z_n)$ is a polynomial with integer coefficients and real variables $z_1,\ldots,z_n$.

Formula $(*)$ in the Introduction is an example of a spatial calculus formula that expresses a transformation in $\mathbf{R}^2$.

Further on, to economize on space and to improve readability, we will also use the vector notation in expressions. We use bold characters to denote vectors $\mathbf{x}$ in $\mathbf{R}^m$. Also, if $\mathbf{x} \in \mathbf{R}^m$, then we abbreviate, e.g., $(\exists x_1)\cdots(\exists x_m)(\varphi(x_1,\ldots,x_m))$ by $(\exists\mathbf{x})(\varphi(\mathbf{x}))$.

2.2 Monotonic transformations of degree k

Let $\mathbf{N}$ denote the set of the natural numbers and let $|S|$ denote the cardinality of the set S.

Definition 3. A transformation Q is called monotone if for all spatial databases S and S', $S \subseteq S'$ implies $Q(S) \subseteq Q(S')$.

It can easily be verified that Q is monotone if and only if

$$Q(S) = \bigcup_{S' \subseteq S} Q(S')$$

for all spatial databases S.

Definition 4. Let k be a cardinal number less than or equal to $|\mathbf{R}|$. A *monotonic spatial database transformation of degree k* is a spatial transformation that is monotone and that is completely determined by its result on sets of cardinality at most k.

We denote the set of all monotonic spatial database transformations of degree k by $\mathcal{M}^k$ and the set of all monotonic transformations by $\mathcal{M}$. Before giving examples and counterexamples of monotonic transformations of degree k, we give some of their basic properties, the proofs of which follow straightforwardly from the above observation and the subsequent examples.

Proposition 5. *Let k be a cardinal number less than or equal to $|\mathbf{R}|$.*

(a) A transformation Q belongs to $\mathcal{M}^k$ if and only if

$$Q(S) = \bigcup_{S' \subseteq S, |S'| \le k} Q(S')$$

for every spatial database S.
(b) We have that

$$\mathcal{M}^0 \subsetneq \mathcal{M}^1 \subsetneq \cdots \subsetneq \mathcal{M}^l \subsetneq \mathcal{M}^{l+1} \subsetneq \cdots \subsetneq \bigcup_{l\in\mathbf{N}} \mathcal{M}^l \subsetneq \mathcal{M}^{|\mathbf{N}|} \subsetneq \mathcal{M}^{|\mathbf{R}|} = \mathcal{M}.$$

(c) If the transformations Q_1 and Q_2 belong to $\mathcal{M}^k$, $k \geq 0$, then so does $Q_1 \cup Q_2$.

(d) The projection on a subspace $\mathbf{R}^n \subset \mathbf{R}^m$ belongs to $\mathcal{M}^1$. The selection of the points of a spatial database that belong to a fixed set $F \subset \mathbf{R}^m$ belongs to $\mathcal{M}^1$.

(e) If Q_1 and Q_2 belong to $\mathcal{M}$, then so does $Q_1 \circ Q_2$. If Q_1 belongs to $\mathcal{M}^1$ and Q_2 belongs to $\mathcal{M}^k$, $k \geq 0$, the $Q_1 \circ Q_2$ belongs to $\mathcal{M}^k$.

(f) There exist spatial transformations that are not monotone. □

Example 1. 1. $\mathcal{M}^0$ is the set of spatial transformations that map every spatial database to some fixed figure in $\mathbf{R}^m$. These transformations obviously also belong to every $\mathcal{M}^k$, $k \geq 0$.

2. Translations, isometries, similarities, affinities of spatial databases belong to $\mathcal{M}^1$, and hence to every $\mathcal{M}^k$, $k \geq 1$.

3. "Return $\mathbf{R}^m$ if the diameter of the database is larger than 1, else return the empty set" belongs to $\mathcal{M}^2$ but not to $\mathcal{M}^1$.

4. The transformation that returns $\mathbf{R}^m$ on an input that contains at least k points and the empty set in any other case, belongs to $\mathcal{M}^k$ but not to $\mathcal{M}^{k-1}$.

5. The transformation that maps a spatial database to its convex hull belongs to $\mathcal{M}^{m+1}$. Remark that here the degree depends on the dimension of the space $\mathbf{R}^m$ in which the database is embedded.

6. The transformation of a spatial database S into the empty set if $|S|$ is finite and into $\mathbf{R}^m$ if $|S|$ is infinite belongs to $\mathcal{M}^{|\mathbf{N}|}$ but not to $\bigcup_{k \in \mathbf{N}} \mathcal{M}^k$.

7. The transformation of a spatial database to its topological interior, is a monotonic transformation, but not monotone of any finite degree nor of infinitely countable degree.

8. The complement transformation $Q(S) = S^c$ is *not* monotone of any degree.

3 Sound and complete languages for monotonic transformations of finite degree

In this section, we give sound and complete languages for the monotonic transformations that have a finite number of degrees of freedom and that are expressible in the spatial calculus.

Theorem 6. *Let k be a natural number and let Q be a spatial database transformation that is expressible in the spatial calculus. The transformation Q belongs to $\mathcal{M}^k$ if and only if Q is equivalent to a finite union of monotonic transformations of degree k that are expressible by conjunctive formulas of the form*

$$\bigwedge_{i=1}^{n} p_i(\mathbf{y}) \, \theta_i \, 0,$$

or

$$(\exists \mathbf{x}_1) \cdots (\exists \mathbf{x}_k)(\bigwedge_{l=1}^{k} S(\mathbf{x}_l) \wedge \bigwedge_{i=1}^{n} p_i(\mathbf{y}, \mathbf{x}_1, \cdots, \mathbf{x}_k) \, \theta_i \, 0),$$

where p_i are polynomials with integer coefficients and $\theta_i \in \{\geq, >\}$.

Proof. (Sketch) It is an easy set-theoretical exercise to show that the given conjunctive formulas express monotonic transformations of degree k. The if-direction then follows immediately from (c) of Proposition 5.

For the only-if-direction, let Q be a transformation expressed by the spatial calculus formula φ, i.e., $Q(S) = \{\mathbf{y} \mid \varphi(\mathbf{y}, S)\}$. We first remark that the equality

$$Q(S) = \bigcup_{S' \subseteq S, |S'| \leq k} Q(S')$$

implies that $Q(S) = Q(\emptyset)$ if $k = 0$ and

$$Q(S) = Q(\emptyset) \cup \{\mathbf{y} \mid (\exists \mathbf{x}_1) \cdots (\exists \mathbf{x}_k)(\bigwedge_{l=1}^{k} S(\mathbf{x}_l) \wedge \varphi(\mathbf{y}, \{\mathbf{x}_1, \ldots, \mathbf{x}_k\}))\}$$

if $k > 0$.

$Q(\emptyset)$ is a fixed m-dimensional spatial database and is therefore, as mentioned in Section 2, a Boolean combination of sets of the form $\{\mathbf{y} \mid p(\mathbf{y}) > 0\}$. This Boolean combination can be written as a union of intersections of the form

$$\{\mathbf{y} \mid \bigwedge_{i=1}^{n} p_i(\mathbf{y}) \, \theta_i \, 0\},$$

with $\theta_i \in \{\geq, >\}$.

For what concerns the other set, $\varphi(\mathbf{y}, \{\mathbf{x}_1, \ldots, \mathbf{x}_k\})$ is a spatial calculus formula with free variables $\mathbf{y}, \mathbf{x}_1, \ldots, \mathbf{x}_k$. Tarski's quantifier elimination property for the theory of the field of real numbers (see, e.g., [6, 8, 22]) guarantees the existence of a quantifier-free spatial calculus formula $\psi(\mathbf{y}, \{\mathbf{x}_1, \ldots, \mathbf{x}_k\})$ that is equivalent to $\varphi(\mathbf{y}, \{\mathbf{x}_1, \ldots, \mathbf{x}_k\})$. We can write $\psi(\mathbf{y}, \{\mathbf{x}_1, \ldots, \mathbf{x}_k\})$ in disjunctive normal form as

$$\bigvee_{i=1}^{d} \bigwedge_{j=1}^{c_i} p_{ij}(\mathbf{y}, \mathbf{x}_1, \ldots, \mathbf{x}_k) \, \theta_{ij} \, 0,$$

with p_{ij} polynomials with integers coefficients and $\theta_{ij} \in \{\geq, >\}$. Using some well-known logical equivalences we then obtain that

$$Q(S) = Q(\emptyset) \cup \{\mathbf{y} \mid \bigvee_{i=1}^{d} ((\exists \mathbf{x}_1) \cdots (\exists \mathbf{x}_k)(\bigwedge_{l=1}^{k} S(\mathbf{x}_l) \wedge \bigwedge_{j=1}^{c_i} p_{ij}(\mathbf{y}, \mathbf{x}_1, \ldots, \mathbf{x}_k) \, \theta_{ij} \, 0))\}.$$

This completes the proof. □

To illustrate this result, we return to the convex hull. The convex hull of a spatial database S is the smallest convex database that contains S. Usually, the convex hull of $S \subset \mathbf{R}^m$ is given as

$$\{\mathbf{y} \mid (\exists \mathbf{x}_1) \cdots (\exists \mathbf{x}_{m+1})(\exists \lambda_1) \cdots (\exists \lambda_{m+1})(\bigwedge_{i=1}^{m+1} S(\mathbf{x}_i) \wedge \bigwedge_{i=1}^{m+1} \lambda_i \geq 0$$

$$\wedge \, \lambda_1 + \cdots + \lambda_{m+1} = 1 \wedge \mathbf{y} = \lambda_1 \mathbf{x}_1 + \cdots + \lambda_{m+1} \mathbf{x}_{m+1})\}.$$

However, as mentioned before, the m-dimensional convex hull belongs to $\mathcal{M}^{m+1}$. Hence, the theorem tells us that it must be possible to express this with less quantifiers, namely by the quantifier prefix $(\exists \mathbf{x}_1) \cdots (\exists \mathbf{x}_{m+1})$. Indeed, we can express the convex hull as

$$\{\mathbf{y} \mid (\exists \mathbf{x}_1) \cdots (\exists \mathbf{x}_{m+1})(\bigwedge_{i=1}^{m+1} S(\mathbf{x}_i) \wedge \mathrm{CH}(\mathbf{x}_1, \ldots, \mathbf{x}_{m+1}, \mathbf{y}))\},$$

where $\mathrm{CH}(\mathbf{x}_1, \ldots, \mathbf{x}_{m+1}, \mathbf{y})$ abbreviates the formula that expresses that, for every subset of m points from $\{\mathbf{x}_1, \ldots, \mathbf{x}_{m+1}\}$, the point $\mathbf{y}$ lies in the appropriate halfspace determined by that subset. This formula can be expressed without the use of quantifiers. The convex hull of a 1-dimensional database S is, e.g., given by

$$\{y \mid (\exists x_1)(\exists x_2)(S(x_1) \wedge S(x_2) \wedge x_1 \leq y \wedge y \leq x_2)\}.$$

The previous example illustrates how Theorem 6 can be used to write certain transformations in a more compact way. The main importance of Theorem 6, however, is that it provides a syntactic framework, by means of a normal form for calculus expressions, in which transformations are guaranteed to belong to $\mathcal{M}^k$. In other words, for every finite number k, Theorem 6 provides for a sound and complete language in which *only* transformations that belong to $\mathcal{M}^k$ can be written, but in which also *all* transformations of $\mathcal{M}^k$ expressible in the calculus, can be written.

4   Monotonic transformations of infinite degree

In this section, we search for sound and complete languages for monotonic transformations of infinite degree that are expressible in the spatial calculus.

It might seem that, since the spatial calculus is incapable of characterizing infinitely countable sets, there are no differences between different infinite degrees of monotonicity for transformations expressible in the calculus. The following proposition shows that this is not the case.

Proposition 7. *For transformations expressible in the spatial calculus, the following inclusions are strict:*

$$\bigcup_{k \in \mathbf{N}} \mathcal{M}^k \subsetneqq \mathcal{M}^{|\mathbf{N}|} \subsetneqq \mathcal{M}^{|\mathbf{R}|} = \mathcal{M}.$$

Clearly, there exist also transformations expressible in the spatial calculus that are not monotone.

Proof. The transformations in 6 and 7 of Example 1 are expressible in the calculus (see [20]). This proves the strictness of the two inclusions. The last transformation of Example 1 is expressible in the calculus. This proves the second claim.   □

Obviously, the union over $\mathbf{N}$ of the sound and complete languages for $\mathcal{M}^k$, as provided by Theorem 6, yields a sound and complete language for the spatial calculus transformations that belong to $\bigcup_{k \in \mathbf{N}} \mathcal{M}^k$. We therefore have

Theorem 8. *Let Q be a transformation that is expressible in the spatial calculus. The transformation Q belongs to $\bigcup_{k \in \mathbf{N}} \mathcal{M}^k$ if and only if Q is equivalent to a finite union of monotonic transformations of finite degree that are expressible by conjunctive formulas of the form*

$$\bigwedge_{i=1}^{n} p_i(\mathbf{y}) \, \theta_i \, 0,$$

or

$$(\exists \mathbf{x}_1) \cdots (\exists \mathbf{x}_k)(\bigwedge_{l=1}^{k} S(\mathbf{x}_l) \wedge \bigwedge_{i=1}^{n} p_i(\mathbf{y}, \mathbf{x}_1, \cdots, \mathbf{x}_k) \, \theta_i \, 0),$$

for some $k \in \mathbf{N} \setminus \{0\}$ and with p_i polynomials with integer coefficients and $\theta_i \in \{\geq, >\}$. □

We now turn our attention to $\mathcal{M}^{|\mathbf{N}|}$ and $\mathcal{M}^{|\mathbf{R}|}$. Here, the story is more complicated. From model theory, we know that first-order logic sentences that are preserved under homomorphisms, i.e., that are monotone, have a "positive" equivalent. This property is usually referred to as Lyndon's homomorphism theorem [3, 14]. Thus, it is a natural question to ask whether also every monotonic spatial transformation is expressible by a spatial calculus formula that is positive. More technically, we call a spatial calculus formula *positive* if every atomic subformula $S(y_1, \ldots, y_m)$ lies within the scope of an even number of negation symbols. We can easily prove by induction on the length of formulas that

Proposition 9. *A transformation that is expressed by a positive spatial calculus formula is monotone.* □

We can use the transformation of a spatial database into its topological interior as an illustration. Indeed, for 2-dimensional databases, for example, this transformation can be expressed by the positive formula

$$(\exists \varepsilon)(\forall x')(\forall y')(\varepsilon > 0 \wedge ((x - x')^2 + (y - y')^2 \geq \varepsilon \vee S(x', y'))).$$

Hence, it is monotone (as already observed before).

The converse of Proposition 9, on the other hand, is not obvious. Ajtai and Gurevich have shown that Lyndon's theorem fails when only finite models are considered [2].

We will show that Lyndon's theorem also fails in our setting:

Theorem 10. *There is a monotonic spatial transformation, expressible in the spatial calculus, that is not expressible by a positive spatial calculus formula.*

For a sketch of the proof we refer to the Appendix.
We conclude this section with one positive result:

Proposition 11. *A monotonic spatial transformation that is expressible by a quantifier-free spatial calculus formula is positively expressible in the spatial calculus.*

Proof. (Sketch) We first give the proof for 1-dimensional spatial transformations. Then we sketch how it can be generalized to higher dimensional transformations.

So, let $Q(S) = \{x \mid \varphi(x, S)\}$ be a 1-dimensional spatial transformation. $\varphi(x, S)$ can be written in disjunctive normal form as

$$(S(x) \wedge \pi_1(x)) \vee (\neg S(x) \wedge \pi_2(x)),$$

where $\pi_1(x)$ and $\pi_2(x)$ are Boolean combinations of polynomial inequalities. We can write this formula also as $\varphi_1(x, S) \vee \varphi_2(x, S) \vee \varphi_3(x, S)$, with

$$\varphi_1(x, S) = S(x) \wedge \pi_1(x) \wedge \neg\pi_2(x),$$

$$\varphi_2(x, S) = \neg S(x) \wedge \pi_2(x) \wedge \neg\pi_1(x), \text{ and}$$

$$\varphi_3(x, S) = \pi_1(x) \wedge \pi_2(x).$$

We now consider two cases. If $\varphi_2(x, S)$ is *false* for all $x \in \mathbf{R}$ and all spatial databases S, then $\varphi(x, S)$ is equivalent to $\varphi_1(x, S) \vee \varphi_3(x, S)$, and therefore positively expressible.

If, on the other hand, there exists a spatial database S_0 and $x_0 \in \mathbf{R}$, such that $\varphi_2(x_0, S_0)$ is *true*, we can easily show that $x_0 \in Q(S_0)$, but $x_0 \notin Q(S_0 \cup \{x_0\})$. Therefore, Q is not monotone. Thus the second case cannot occur. This completes the proof for the 1-dimensional case.

For the m-dimensional case, we also can write any quantifier-free formula $\varphi(x_1, \ldots, x_n, S)$ in disjunctive normal form with $2^{(m^m)}$ disjuncts, each of which is a conjunction of m^m conjuncts of the form $S(y_1, \ldots, y_n)$ or $\neg S(y_1, \ldots, y_n)$, with $y_i \in \{x_1, \ldots x_n\}$, and of a conjunct $\pi(x_1, \ldots x_n)$, which is a Boolean combination of polynomial inequalities. As in the 1-dimensional case, we can then split up the polynomial parts which results in additional disjuncts consisting of m^m, $m^m - 1, \ldots$ conjuncts that are disjoint with the longer disjuncts. We can then apply an argumentation, similar to the 1-dimensional case, that shows that no negation can occur. □

5 Undecidability and decidability results

In this section, we show that it is undecidable whether a spatial transformation expressible in the spatial calculus belongs to $\mathcal{M}^k$. We also show that many interesting properties of spatial transformations that are undecidable in general (see [20]) become decidable for monotonic transformations of finite degree, in contrast to our first result.

Theorem 12. *The following problems are undecidable:*

(a) Given a spatial transformation Q, tell whether Q is monotone, and

(b) For $k \in \mathbf{N}$ and a given spatial transformation Q, tell whether Q belongs to $\mathcal{M}^k$.

Proof. (Sketch) Statement (a) follows directly from the fact that it is undecidable whether a first-order sentence $\varphi(S)$ is monotone [12].

For (b) and $k = 0$, we observe that two spatial transformations $Q_1(S) = \{\mathbf{y} \mid \varphi_1(\mathbf{y}, S)\}$ and $Q_2(S) = \{\mathbf{y} \mid \varphi_2(\mathbf{y}, S)\}$ are equivalent if and only if $Q(S) = \{\mathbf{y} \mid \varphi_1(\mathbf{y}, S) \wedge \neg\varphi_2(\mathbf{y}, S)\}$ belongs to $\mathcal{M}^0$ and $Q(\emptyset) = \emptyset$. The latter condition is decidable. Since equivalence of spatial transformations is undecidable [20], it follows that membership of $\mathcal{M}^0$ is undecidable.

To prove the theorem for $k \in \mathbf{N} \setminus \{0\}$, we can use a reduction technique that was introduced in [20]. We sketch the proof for $k = 1$ in dimension 1. Other cases can be proved analogously.

It is well-known that the $\exists^*$-fragment of number theory is undecidable. Encode a natural number n by the 1-dimensional spatial database

$$\text{enc}(n) = \{0, 1, \ldots, n\}$$

and encode a vector of natural numbers $(n_1, \ldots, n_k)$ by the database

$$\text{enc}(n_1, \ldots, n_k) = \text{enc}(n_1) \cup (\text{enc}(n_2) + n_1 + 2) \cup \cdots \cup (\text{enc}(n_k) + n_1 + 2 + \cdots + n_{k-1} + 2).$$

The corresponding decoding is expressible in the spatial calculus. We can reduce the decision of the truth of a $\exists^*$-sentence $(\exists\mathbf{x})\psi(\mathbf{x})$ of number theory to deciding whether the transformation "if S encodes $\mathbf{x}$ and $\psi(\mathbf{x})$, return $\mathbf{R}$, else return the empty set" belongs to $\mathcal{M}^1$. $\qquad\square$

Many interesting properties of spatial transformations, such as equivalence of transformations, containment, and genericity are undecidable for transformations expressed in the spatial calculus (see [20]). For monotonic transformations of finite degree, many of these properties become decidable. As an illustration, we give

Theorem 13. Let k be a natural number. Let Q, Q_1 and Q_2 be spatial transformations that are expressible in the spatial calculus and that belong to $\mathcal{M}^k$. The following properties are decidable:

- Q_1 and Q_2 are equivalent,
- Q_1 is contained in Q_2,
- Q is generic,
- for every S, $Q(S)$ contains a line.

Proof. (Sketch) As an example, we give the proof for containment. Suppose that Q_1 and Q_2 are expressed by spatial calculus formulas φ_1 and φ_2. Q_1 is contained in Q_2 if for all databases S, $Q_1(S) \subseteq Q_2(S)$ holds. If Q_1 and Q_2 are in $\mathcal{M}^k$, this second-order condition is equivalent to $Q_1(\emptyset) \subseteq Q_2(\emptyset)$ and

$$(\forall\mathbf{x}_1) \cdots (\forall\mathbf{x}_k)(\forall\mathbf{y})(\varphi_1(\mathbf{y}, \{\mathbf{x}_1, \ldots \mathbf{x}_k\}) \to \varphi_2(\mathbf{y}, \{\mathbf{x}_1, \ldots \mathbf{x}_k\})).$$

Both are first-order sentences in the theory of the field of real numbers. From Tarski's quantifier elimination property it follows that this sentence can be decided (see, e.g., [6, 8, 22]).   □

6   Discussion

We end this paper with the discussion of two topics. First, we address the question of how unique the hierarchy described in this paper is. Secondly, we state some open problems concerning sound and complete languages for the class of all monotonic transformations.

6.1   Alternative hierarchies of monotonicity classes

In this paper, we have discussed a hierarchy of monotonicity classes of spatial transformations that is indexed by the degrees of freedom of spatial transformations, i.e., that is indexed by cardinal numbers. In our opinion, this hierarchy is a very natural one. It is, however, not the only possible one.

In the hierarchy proposed in this paper, the monotonic transformations have the form

$$Q(S) = \bigcup_{S' \subseteq S, |S'| \le k} Q(S')$$

where k is (in most cases) finite, i.e., the transformation is determined by its images on certain finite subsets.

However, we can also consider a hierarchy of monotonic transformations that are determined by their image on certain infinite subsets. We then obtain a hierarchy indexed by classes of infinite figures. We give an example of this and restrict our attention for a moment to the plane $\mathbf{R}^2$. Take, for instance, $\mathcal{P}_n$ to be the class of figures that are the convex hull of regular polygons of i sides with $i \le n$. Let $\mathcal{N}^n$ be the class of transformations of the form

$$Q(S) = \bigcup_{S' \subseteq S, S' \in \mathcal{P}_n} Q(S').$$

The elements of $\mathcal{N}^n$ are also monotone. They also form a hierarchy of monotonicity classes for increasing n: $\mathcal{N}^0 \subsetneq \mathcal{N}^1 \subsetneq \mathcal{N}^2 \subsetneq \cdots$.

For each $n \in \mathbf{N}$, we also obtain sound and complete languages, in the style of Theorem 6, that express exactly the transformations in $\mathcal{N}^n$ that are expressible in the spatial calculus. Indeed, in Theorem 6, we needed a finite number of quantifiers to quantify over subsets of the database of some finite cardinality. To quantify over polygonal subsets of the database, also a finite number of quantifiers suffice.

More results in the style of Theorem 6 are possible. We give one more example, interesting in its own. For transformations in $\mathbf{R}^m$, consider the class of monotonic spatial transformations that satisfy

$$Q(S) = \bigcup_{S' \subseteq S, S' \in \mathcal{B}_m} Q(S'),$$

where $\mathcal{B}_m$ is the class of m-dimensional open spheres with a radius $r \geq 0$. The transformation of a spatial database into its topological interior belongs to this class. Again, in the style of Theorem 6, we obtain that spatial transformations expressible in the spatial calculus belong to this class if and only if they are expressible as a finite union of spatial transformations expressible by formulas of the form

$$\bigwedge_{i=1}^{n} p_i(\mathbf{y}) \; \theta_i \; 0,$$

or

$$(\exists \mathbf{x})(\exists \varepsilon > 0)((\forall \mathbf{z})(d_m(\mathbf{x}, \mathbf{z}) < \varepsilon \rightarrow S(\mathbf{z})) \wedge \bigwedge_{i=1}^{n} p_i(\mathbf{x}, \mathbf{y}, \varepsilon) \; \theta_i \; 0),$$

where p_i are polynomials with integer coefficients and $\theta_i \in \{\geq, >\}$, where $d_m(\mathbf{x}, \mathbf{z})$ abbreviates the quadratic polynomial $\sum_{i=1}^{m}(x_i - z_i)^2$, and where $\mathbf{y}$ are the result vectors.

All the above formulas are positive in S. This proves, in an alternative way, that the transformation of a spatial database into its topological interior is monotone.

The examples given in this section show that other hierarchies are possible. Depending on the applications one has in mind one may be preferred to the other.

6.2 Is there a sound and complete language for all monotonic spatial calculus transformations?

In Section 4, we have searched for a sound and complete language for all spatial transformations expressible in the spatial calculus. The only likely candidate for such a language seems to be the set of *positive* spatial calculus formulas. Since Theorem 10 rules out this possibility, the search for a complete language seems a very difficult, if not impossible task.

The same problem remains for $\mathcal{M}^{|\mathbf{N}|}$. We therefore state the following:

Open problem 14. *Is there a sound and complete language that captures the transformations expressible in the spatial calculus*

- *that belong to $\mathcal{M}^{|\mathbf{R}|}$?*
- *that belong to $\mathcal{M}^{|\mathbf{N}|}$?*

The only positive result we can show in this context is that Lyndoms' theorem holds when the attention is restricted to spatial transformations expressible by a quantifier-free formula (see Proposition 11). Gurevich points out a number of other classes of first-order sentences for which Lyndon's theorem survives in the case of finite structures [12]. He mentions existential sentences, universal sentences, prenex sentences with prefix $\exists^n \forall$, and prenex sentences with prefix $\forall^n \exists$. Also in the context of the spatial calculus, these languages seem interesting candidates for further research.

Another interesting question is the following: although for spatial databases monotonic formulas cannot be translated into positive formulas, do the least fixed points of these two classes coincide?

Acknowledgments

The author is indebted to Jan Paredaens and Jan Van den Bussche for the collaborative research that has lead to several of the results discussed in this paper and to Stijn Dekeyser for proofreading earlier versions of the paper. The author also wishes to thank Marc Gyssens whose comments considerably improved the presentation of the paper.

References

1. D. Abel and B.C. Ooi, editors. *Advances in spatial databases—3rd Symposium SSD'93*, volume 692 of *Lecture Notes in Computer Science*, Springer-Verlag, 1993.
2. M. Ajtai and Y. Gurevich. Monotone versus Positive. *Journal of the Association for Computing Machinery*, Vol. 34, pages 1004–1015, October 1987.
3. J. Barwise, editor. *Handbook of Mathematical Logic*. North-Holland Publishing Company, Amsterdam, 1989.
4. M. Benedikt, G. Dong, L. Libkin, and L. Wong. Relational expressive power of constraint query languages. In *Proceedings 15th ACM Symposium on Principles of Database Systems (PODS'96)*, pages 1–16, ACM Press, 1996.
5. M. Benedikt and L. Libkin. Languages for Relational Databases over Interpreted Structures. In *Proceedings 16th ACM Symposium on Principles of Database Systems (PODS'97)*, pages 87–98, ACM Press, 1997.
6. J. Bochnak, M. Coste, and M.-F. Roy. *Géométrie algébrique réelle*. Springer-Verlag, 1987.
7. A. Buchmann, editor. *Design and implementation of large spatial databases—First Symposium SSD'89*, volume 409 of *Lecture Notes in Computer Science*. Springer-Verlag, 1989.
8. G.E. Collins. Quantifier elimination for real closed fields by cylindrical algebraic decomposition. In *Automata theory and formal languages*, volume 33 of *Lecture Notes in Computer Science*, pages 134–183, Springer-Verlag, 1975.
9. M. Coste. Ensembles semi-algébriques. In *Géometrie algébrique réelle et formes quadratiques*, volume 959 of *Lecture Notes in Mathematics*, pages 109–138, Springer-Verlag, 1982.
10. M.J. Egenhofer and J.R. Herring, editors. *Advances in Spatial Databases*, volume 951 of *Lecture Notes in Computer Science*, Springer-Verlag, 1995.
11. O. Gunther and H.-J. Schek, editors. *Advances in spatial databases—2nd Symposium SSD'91*, volume 525 of *Lecture Notes in Computer Science*. Springer-Verlag, 1991.
12. Y. Gurevich. Toward logic tailored for computational complexity. In *Computation and Proof Theory*, M. Richter et al., editors, volume 1104 of *Lecture Notes in Mathematics*, pages 175–216, Springer, 1984.
13. M. Gyssens, J. Van den Bussche, and D. Van Gucht. Complete geometrical query languages. In *Proceedings of the 16th ACM Symposium on Principles of Database Systems (PODS'97)*, pages 62–67, ACM Press, 1997.
14. W. Hodges. *Model Theory*. Cambridge University press, Cambridge, 1995.
15. P.C. Kanellakis, G.M. Kuper, and P.Z. Revesz. Constraint query languages. *Journal of Computer and System Sciences*, 51(1):26–52, August 1995.

16. B. Kuijpers, J. Paredaens, M. Smits, and J. Van den Bussche. Termination properties of spatial Datalog programs. In *Proceedings of "Logic in Databases" (LID'96)*, D. Pedreschi and C. Zaniolo, editors, volume 1154 of *Lecture Notes in Computer Science*, pages 101–116, Springer-Verlag, 1996.

17. B. Kuijpers and M. Smits. On expressing topological connectivity in spatial Datalog. In *Proceedings of the workshop Constraint Databases and Their Applications (CDB'97)*, V. Gaede, A. Brodsky, O. Gunter, D. Srivastava, V. Vianu, M. Wallace, editors, volume 1191 of *Lecture Notes in Computer Science*, pages 116–133, Springer-Verlag, 1997.

18. G. McColm. The dimension of the Negation of Transitive Closure. *The Journal of Symbolic Logic*, Vol. 60, Nr. 2, pages 392–414, June 1995.

19. L. Libkin. Personal communication. August 1997.

20. J. Paredaens, J. Van den Bussche, and D. Van Gucht. Towards a theory of spatial database queries. In *Proceedings of the 13th ACM Symposium on Principles of Database Systems (PODS'94)*, pages 279–28, ACM Press, 1994.

21. A. P. Stolboushkin. Finitely Monotone Properties. In *Proceedings of the Tenth Annual IEEE Symposium on Logic in Computer Science (LICS'95)*, pages 324–330, IEEE Computer Society Press, 1995.

22. A. Tarski. *A Decision Method for Elementary Algebra and Geometry*. University of California Press, 1951.

Appendix

In the following pages we sketch the proof of Theorem 10. Our proof is inspired by an alternative proof of the result of Ajtai and Gurevich that was given by Stolboushkin [21]. It uses a characterization of definability by positive first-order formulas by means of an Ehrenfeucht-Fraïssé-like game. This characterization was developed by Stolboushkin [21] and, independently, by McColm [18].

The spatial transformation Q that witnesses Theorem 10 actually is a transformation that works on two 2-dimensional spatial databases S and T. The transformation Q is expressed by a spatial calculus sentence $\varphi(S,T)$. This means that viewed as a spatial transformation, Q transforms the pair (S,T) either into $\emptyset$ or into $\mathbf{R}^2$. We now give a detailed description of $Q(S,T)$.

Let $\psi(S,T,y)$ be the formula $(\forall x)((T(x,y) \vee x = y) \to (\forall z)(S(z,x) \to (\forall u)((T(u,z) \vee u = z) \to (T(u,x) \wedge T(u,y)))))$.

Then $\varphi(S,T)$ is equivalent to the sentence

$$\varphi_0(S,T) \vee \varphi_1(S,T) \vee \varphi_2(S,T) \vee \varphi_3(S,T) \vee \varphi_4(S,T) \vee (\varphi_5(S,T) \wedge \varphi_6(S,T)),$$

with

$\varphi_0(S,T) = $ "S is infinite" $\vee$ "T is infinite";

$\varphi_1(S,T) = (\exists x)(\exists y)(S(x,y) \wedge S(y,x));$

$\varphi_2(S,T) = (\exists x)(\exists y)(T(x,y) \wedge T(y,x));$

$\varphi_3(S,T) = (\exists x)(\exists y)((\forall z)(\neg S(z,y) \wedge T(x,y));$

$\varphi_4(S,T) = (\exists x)(\exists z)((\forall y)(S(y,x) \rightarrow \psi(S,T,y)) \wedge T(z,x) \wedge (\forall y)(S(y,x) \rightarrow (\neg(T(z,y) \vee z = y))));$

$\varphi_5(S,T) = (\forall x)(\forall y)(S(x,y) \rightarrow T(x,y));$ and finally

$\varphi_6(S,T) = (\forall x)(\forall y)(\forall z)(T(x,y) \wedge T(y,z) \rightarrow T(x,z)).$

We remark that $\varphi_0(S,T)$ is expressible in the spatial calculus. For instance, "S is infinite" is expressed by the sentence $\neg(\forall x)(\forall y)(S(x,y) \rightarrow ((\exists \varepsilon > 0)(\forall x')(\forall y')(((x-x')^2 + (y-y)^2 < \varepsilon \wedge S(x',y')) \rightarrow (x = x' \wedge y = y')))$. For finite S and T, $\varphi_1(S,T) \vee \varphi_2(S,T) \vee \varphi_3(S,T) \vee \varphi_4(S,T) \vee (\varphi_5(S,T) \wedge \varphi_6(S,T))$ characterizes a class of structures that contains what Stolboushkin calls *grids* [21]. This sentence, however returns *false* on incomplete grids.

We now first show that $Q(S,T) = \{(x,y) \in \mathbf{R}^2 \mid \varphi(S,T)\}$ is monotone in T, i.e., that $T_1 \subseteq T_2$ implies that $Q(S,T_1) \subseteq Q(S,T_2)$.

Lemma 15. *The transformation $Q(S,T)$ is monotone in T.*

Proof. For finite S and T the lemma was proven in [21] (Lemma 4.4). For S or T infinite, $\varphi_0(S,T)$ guarantees monotonicity. □

In order to formulate the next results, we turn to some more precise terminology from logic. The transformation $Q(S,T)$, as given above, is expressed by a first-order sentence over the signature $\langle S,T,+,\times,<,0,1\rangle$. This sentence is, however, invariant under monotonic transformations of $\mathbf{R}$. From a collapse theorem on the expressiveness of first-order logic of the reals by Benedikt, Dong, Libkib, and Wong [4] (see also [5]) it follows that

Lemma 16. *The transformation $Q(S,T)$ can be expressed by a first-order sentence $\bar{\varphi}(S,T,<)$ over the signature $\langle S,T,<\rangle$.* □

We will now describe how a characterization of definability by positive first-order sentences by means of an Ehrenfeucht-Fraïssé-like game will lead us to the conclusion that $Q(S,T)$ is not expressible by a formula that is positive in T.[3] This characterization and these games are described in [18] and [21]. First, we will describe the games specialized to our situation (i.e., specialized to the

---

[3] A formula is positive in T if every subformula of the form $T(u,v)$ is in the scope of an even number of negation symbols.

signature $\langle S, T, < \rangle$). Next, we will specialize the characterization theorem of [18] and [21] to our setting.

The pebble game is played by two players, the Spoiler and the Duplicator, on two $\langle S, T, < \rangle$-structures $\mathcal{A} = (S^A, T^A, <^A)$ and $\mathcal{B} = (S^B, T^B, <^B)$. The underlying domain of these structures is $\mathbf{R}$. As usual, the Spoiler tries to distinguish between these structures, while the Duplicator tries to show that they are equivalent.

The game, which we will call the *positive game from $\mathcal{A}$ to $\mathcal{B}$ of depth n*, consists of n rounds in which n pebbles will be placed on elements $a_1, \ldots, a_n$ in $\mathcal{A}$ and n pebbles will be placed on elements $b_1, \ldots, b_n$ in $\mathcal{B}$. The ith round of the game consists of the Spoiler choosing one of the structures $\mathcal{A}$ and $\mathcal{B}$, placing a pebble on the domain of that structure, and the Duplicator placing a pebble in the domain of the other structure. After n rounds, for each round i ($i \leq n$), there are pebbles on a_i in $\mathcal{A}$ and on b_i in $\mathcal{B}$ respectively.

We say that the Duplicator wins the positive game from $\mathcal{A}$ to $\mathcal{B}$ of depth n if and only if after the n moves of the game the following four conditions are fulfilled

1. for all $i, j \leq n$, $a_i = a_j$ if and only if $b_i = b_j$;
2. for all $i, j \leq n$, $a_i < a_j$ if and only if $b_i < b_j$;
3. for all $i, j \leq n$, $S(a_i, a_j)$ if and only if $S(b_i, b_j)$;
4. for all $i, j \leq n$, $T(a_i, a_j)$ implies $T(b_i, b_j)$.

The following lemma is due to Stolboushkin [21] and McColm [18]. The converse is also in [21].

Lemma 17. *Let $\chi(S, T, <)$ be a first-order sentence of quantifier depth n over the signature $\langle S, T, < \rangle$ that is positive in T. If the Duplicator has a winning strategy for the positive game from structure $\mathcal{A} = (S^A, T^A, <^A)$ to structure $\mathcal{B} = (S^B, T^B, <^B)$ of depth n, then $\mathcal{A} \models \chi(S, T, <)$ implies that $\mathcal{B} \models \chi(S, T, <)$.*
□

We will now describe two $\langle S, T, < \rangle$-structures $\mathcal{A} = (S^A, T^A, <^A)$ and $\mathcal{B} = (S^B, T^B, <^B)$ such that the Duplicator has a winning strategy for the positive n-round game from $\mathcal{A}$ to $\mathcal{B}$. These structures are inspired by the finite grid structures described by Stolboushkin [21]. As mentioned before, the domain of both structures is $\mathbf{R}$. Both $<^A$ and $<^B$ are the natural order on the real line. S^A is the finite relation

$$\{(i \cdot 2^{n+2} + j, i \cdot 2^{n+2} + j + 1) \mid 0 \leq i < 2^{n+1} \text{ and } 1 \leq j < 2^{n+2}\} \cup$$
$$\{(i \cdot 2^{n+2} + j, (i+1) \cdot 2^{n+2} + j) \mid 0 \leq i < 2^{n+1} - 1 \text{ and } 1 \leq j \leq 2^{n+2}\}$$

and T^A is the transitive closure of S^A. S^B is the same finite relation as S^A and $T^B = T^A \setminus \{(2^{n+1}, 2^{n+1} \cdot (2^{n+2} - 1))\}$.

We have the following lemma:

Lemma 18. *The Duplicator has a winning strategy for the positive n-round game from $\mathcal{A}$ to $\mathcal{B}$.*

Proof. (Sketch) We omit the details of the proof, but point out that the structures $\mathcal{A} = (S^A, T^A, <^A)$ and $\mathcal{B} = (S^B, T^B, <^B)$ correspond for what concerns their S and T components to what Stolboushkin calls a grid and a reduced grid. However, these grids are placed in a particular way on the real line: the different rows of Stolboushkin's grids are placed one after the other on $\mathbf{R}$. The game strategy outlined in [21] can then be adapted to fit this situation. An additional complication is that the game in [21] is played on finite structures while our game is played on an infinite structure. $\square$

The next lemma follows directly from [21].

Lemma 19. *Let $\mathcal{A}$ and $\mathcal{B}$ be the structures described above. Let $\bar{\varphi}(S, T, <)$ be the first-order sentence that expresses $Q(S, T)$. Then $\mathcal{A} \models \bar{\varphi}(S, T, <)$ and $\mathcal{B} \not\models \bar{\varphi}(S, T, <)$.* $\square$

This proves that $\bar{\varphi}(S, T, <)$ is not positively expressible in T over the signature $\langle S, T, <\rangle$. Indeed, if $\bar{\varphi}(S, T, <)$ would be positively expressible in T, then, by Lemma 17, it should also evaluate to *true* on $\mathcal{B}$, which, according to Lemma 19, it does not.

To complete the proof of Theorem 10, it suffices to prove that

Lemma 20. *The formula $\bar{\varphi}(S, T, <)$ is not positively expressible in T over the signature $\langle S, T, +, \times, <, 0, 1\rangle$.*

Proof. (Sketch) Suppose that $\bar{\varphi}(S, T, <)$ is positively expressible in T over $\langle S, T, +, \times, <, 0, 1\rangle$, say by $\psi(S, T, +, \times, <, 0, 1)$. The formula $\psi(S, T, +, \times, <, 0, 1)$ is equivalent to "S is infinite" $\vee$ "T is infinite" $\vee$ $\bar{\psi}(S, T, +, \times, <, 0, 1)$, where the sentence $\bar{\psi}(S, T, +, \times, <, 0, 1)$ is $\psi(S, T, +, \times, <, 0, 1)$ but considered to work on finite databases. $\bar{\psi}(S, T, +, \times, <, 0, 1)$ is generic and therefore expressible over the signature $\langle S, T, <\rangle$ [5]. Libkin [19] has shown that it follows from results in [5] that $\bar{\psi}(0, 1, +, \times, <, 0, 1)$ is also positively expressible in T over the signature $\langle S, T, <\rangle$. Since "S is infinite" $\vee$ "T is infinite" can also be expressed in a positive way over $\langle S, T, <\rangle$, we obtain a contradiction. $\square$

Constrained Matching is Type Safe*

Suad Alagić

Department of Computer Science
Wichita State University
Wichita, KS 67260-0083, USA
e-mail: alagic@cs.twsu.edu

Abstract. Temporally constrained matching in a persistent and declarative object-oriented system is introduced as a semantic alternative to the existing approaches to the covariance/contravariance problem. While the existing object-oriented type systems are based on subtyping, F-bounded polymorphism and matching, this language system is based entirely on inheritance, which is identified with matching. The type of matching used in this paper relies on the temporal constraint system. We prove that this constrained matching guarantees type safe substitutability even in situations where matching alone would not. This is possible only because the underlying formal system is semantically much richer than the paradigms of type systems. Its temporal constraint system can capture subtleties that go far beyond the level of expressiveness of object-oriented type systems. The temporal nature of the language and its distinctive orthogonal model of persistence make this language system successful in handling a variety of non-trivial applications.
Keywords: Type systems, declarative programming, temporal logic, constraints, persistence.

1 Introduction

Object-oriented type systems are based on subtyping. But the core idea of the object-oriented paradigm is inheritance. In fact, subtyping is almost never what a programmer wants. Although the contravariant/covariant subtyping rule guarantees type safety with static type checking, it is counterintuitive in its contravariant part. It limits significantly the expressiveness of the language. This is why Eiffel [Mey92] and O2 [BDK92] adopt covariance sacrificing type safety in some situations.

Several notions have been proposed to represent specific situations where covariant inheritance is really what is needed. Two particularly important and related ideas are F-bounded polymorphism [CCH89] and matching [BSG95], [AC96]. But in F-bounded polymorphism all the intuition is lost. Matching is a related notion [AC96], but it is much easier to understand and explain in intuitive terms. Matching guarantees type safe substitutability if used properly

* This material is based upon work supported in part by the U.S. Army Research Office under grant no. DAAH04-96-1-0192.

in conjunction with bounded quantification, just like F-bounded polymorphism. But matching does not really solve the problem. It turns out that if one wants to guarantee type safe substitutability in all situations including assignments, subtyping is still needed [BSG95]. At the same time, a type system that integrates subtyping, matching and parametric polymorphism is complex even for a well-educated programmer [GM96].

On the formal side of the story things are not much better. The contravariant part of the subtyping rule is one of the reasons for many difficulties in developing a model theory for the object-oriented paradigm. In fact, such a full-fledged theory does not exist at the moment. Contravariance makes most type functions determined by parametric classes non-monotonic. Monotonicity (and in fact continuity) is required by well established theories of recursive types defined as suitable fixed points.

One of the reasons why type systems are not based on inheritance is that inheritance is a relationship between classes viewed as program modules. Subtyping is a relationship among class interfaces only. Because of this, the formal definition of subtyping is much easier. A formal definition of inheritance involves the whole language, which makes such a formal definition a formidable task. To our knowledge, no type system of a full-fledged object-oriented programming language is based on such a definition.

It would be nice to have an object-oriented system that is based on a single, and formally defined notion of inheritance. The type system should allow at least a limited form of covariance (required by binary methods) and yet programs should not fail at run-time due to type errors. In this paper we present such a language and its associated type system.

MyT is a declarative, temporal, strongly typed object-oriented language. In the type system of *MyT* inheritance is identified with matching. The notion of subtyping is completely abandoned in the type system. The temporal constraint system is used to prevent well-known anomalies related to covariance. The language has well-defined formal semantics developed as a follow-up to [AA97]. This last property has been an elusive goal for full-fledged procedural object-oriented programming languages.

An orthogonal model of persistence is also a key component of this language system. However, the model of persistence is really orthogonal to the problems discussed in this paper. Because of this, the model is explained very briefly. The underlying database-oriented architecture of *MyT* which includes optimization, access paths and access algorithms is described briefly in [Ala97a].

A crucial difference in comparison with other approaches to covariance is that other approaches try to solve the problem in the syntactic universe of type systems. We doubt that such a solution will ever be found. We consider the problem in a framework semantically much richer than the paradigms of object-oriented type systems. The paradigm is behavioral, based on a suitable temporal logic. Unlike type systems, this formal system is semantic, and a solution to the covariance problem becomes possible.

This paper presents illustrative examples (section 2), the core of the formal system based on constrained matching (section 3), and a proof of its type safety (section 4).

2 Constrained Matching

In this section we first introduce the constraint language and its underlying temporal paradigm. We then illustrate the covariance/contravariance problem as it appears in temporal classes. The constrained matching technique is explained in this section informally and compared with other approaches.

2.1 Semantic constraints

Our temporal paradigm is based on the notion of time, that is discrete and linear, extending infinitely to the future. The constraint language contains three temporal operators [AM87], [Bau92]. The operator *always* is denoted as $\Box$. If C is a constraint, then $\Box C$ is true in the current state iff C evaluates to true in all object states, starting with the current one. The operator *nexttime* is denoted as $\bigcirc$. The constraint $\bigcirc C$ is true in the current state iff the constraint C is true in the next object state. The operator *sometime* is denoted as $\Diamond$. $\Diamond C$ is true iff there exists a state, either the current one or a future one, in which C evaluates to true. The constraints are expressed by temporal Horn clauses. Standard Horn clauses have the form $A \leftarrow B_1, B_2, ..., B_n$, where A is the head, $B_1, B_2, ..., B_n$ is the body of the clause, $A, B_1, B_2, ..., B_n$ are atomic predicates, $\leftarrow$ denotes implication and comma denotes conjunction. Our constraint language, in addition, allows the three temporal operators to appear in temporal Horn-clauses.

There are restrictions on the usage of the temporal operators in the constraint language. The restrictions for the operator $\Box$ are that it may appear in the head of a clause only, or else it may apply to the entire clause. The operator $\Diamond$ may appear in bodies of temporal Horn clauses only. These rules limit the expressive power of the language, but at the same time they guarantee the existence of the execution model of the language, and its formal semantics [Bau92], [AA97]. In spite of its limitations, the language allows a wide variety of database oriented applications to be handled in a high-level, declarative manner.

The semantics of temporal constraints is determined according to the following rules with i=1,2,... standing for the i-th state:

- $s_i(B_1, B_2, ..., B_n) = \top$ iff $s_i(B_j) = \top$ for $j = 1, 2, ..., n$
- $s_i(H \leftarrow B) = \top$ iff $s_i(B) = \bot$ or $s_i(H) = \top$
- $s_i(\bigcirc A) = \top$ iff $s_{i+1}(A) = \top$
- $s_i(\bigcirc^{k+1} A) = \top$ iff $s_i(\bigcirc^k(\bigcirc A)) = \top$
- $s_i(\Box A)$ iff $s_k(A) = \top$ for all $k \geq i$
- $s_i(\Diamond A)$ iff $s_k(A) = \top$ for some $k \geq i$

Temporal constraints are illustrated below by a sample class specification in *MyT*:

Class TwoDPoint
Observers
x(Number), y(Number)
Mutators
move(Number)
Constructors
midPoint(MyType): MyType
Constraints
ForAll self,P2: MyType, X1,X2, Y1,Y2: Number:
$\Box$self.x(X1) $\leftarrow$ $\Diamond$self.x(X1),
$\Box$($\bigcirc$self.y(Y1.add(Y2)) $\leftarrow$ self.y(Y1), self.move(Y2)),
$\Box$(self.midPoint(P2).x(X1.add(X2).div(2)) $\leftarrow$ self.x(X1), P2.x(X2)),
$\Box$(self.midPoint(P2).y(Y1.add(Y2).div(2)) $\leftarrow$ self.y(Y1), P2.y(Y2))
End TwoDPoint.

The above example contains signatures for three types of messages that can be sent to a TwoDPoint object.

– *Observers* are atomic predicates (x and y in the above example) on the underlying object state. Whatever the representation of the object state may be, it is completely hidden from the users. State properties can be inspected only by sending observer messages.
– *Mutators* are external events (move in the above example). Mutator messages affect the underlying object state. The result type of both observers and mutators is Boolean, and it is thus omitted, as in the logic programming paradigm.
– *Constructors* of new objects are represented as functions (midPoint in the above example).
– The *constraints* specify the effect of mutator messages on the observers, as well as the observers of objects constructed by constructor messages.

Note that the constraint section of the TwoDPoint class states that the x coordinate is rigid, so that points can be moved only along the y coordinate axis. Separate explicit specification of mutators is a way of specifying frame axioms, which would require negation in the clause body. The underlying assumption is that if no mutators are executed, the object state is not changed, and thus its observers are unaffected.

2.2 Covariance-contravariance controversy

The classical TwoDPoint - ThreeDPoint problem will illustrate temporally constrained matching. Consider a class ThreeDPoint derived by inheritance from the class TwoDPoint:

Class ThreeDPoint
Inherits TwoDPoint
Observers
z(Number)
Constraints
ForAll self,P3: MyType, Z1,Z2: Number:
□self.z(Z1) ← ◇ self.z(Z1),
□(self.midPoint(P3).z(Z1.add(Z2).div(2)) ← self.z(Z1), P3.z(Z2))
End ThreeDPoint.

ThreeDPoint does not define a subtype of TwoDPoint. Let us denote sub-typing with the usual symbol <:, the signature of midPoint in TwoDPoint as midPoint(A2):B2 and the signature of midPoint in ThreeDPoint as mid-Point(A3):B3. According to the definition of subtyping, in order to have Three-DPoint <: TwoDPoint we must have A2 <: A3 (contravariance) and B3 <: B2 (covariance).

The signature of the method midPoint in the class TwoDPoint is effec-tively midPoint(TwoDPoint): TwoDPoint. The signature of midPoint in the class ThreeDPoint is effectively midPoint(ThreeDPoint): ThreeDPoint. The covariant part of the subtyping rule applies to the result types and it is satisfied. However, subtyping requires that the argument type of midPoint in the class TwoDPoint is a subtype of the argument type of this method in the class ThreeDPoint. This condition is not satisfied in the above perfectly natural example of a class Three-DPoint derived by inheritance from a class TwoDPoint. This is the contravariant, non-monotonic and counter intuitive part of the subtyping rule. Exactly the op-posite is true in the above sample classes.

If we allow substitution of an object of the class ThreeDPoint in place of an object of the class TwoDPoint, type safety cannot be guaranteed by static type checking. This applies to systems with single dispatch and dynamic binding.

Here is an example illustrating this problem. With P1,P2: TwoDPoint the expression P1.midPoint(P2) obviously satisfies the static type check. But at run time the receiver P1 may in fact be an object of a class derived by inheritance from TwoDPoint, such as ThreeDPoint. At the same time the run-time type of the argument object may naturally be equal to its compile-time type, which is TwoDPoint. Single dispatch will perform selection of the relevant method based on the run-time type of the receiver. This situation leads to a run-time failure due to a wrong type of the argument. Indeed, since the run-time type of the receiver object is ThreeDPoint, the relevant constraints are those specified in the class ThreeDPoint. But these constraints require the observer z, which the argument object does not have!

A really disturbing fact is that TwoDPoint does not have any subtypes! This fact is a clear indication of how counterintuitive subtyping is in the object-oriented paradigm. Notice that if we fix the interpretation of MyType, ThreeD-Point becomes a subtype of TwoDPoint. This is exactly the idea behind match-ing. Although ThreeDPoint is not a subtype of TwoDPoint, we say that Three-DPoint matches TwoDPoint. Messages that can be sent to objects of the class

TwoDPoint can also be sent to objects of the class ThreeDPoint. But type safety with static type checking is lost. In fact, matching works well with bounded type quantification and then it provides type safety [BSG95], [AC96].

2.3 Constrained matching

Constrained matching is a technique developed in this paper to address the type safety issue for matching. The technique has two essential components. The first one is the temporal constraint system that allows formal specification of additional conditions that cannot be expressed in a type system. These additional conditions prevent the anomalies. The other component is a more sophisticated run-time technique. The usual dynamic binding based on the receiver object is extended with inspecting run-time types of those arguments (multiple dispatch) whose compile-time type is *MyType*.

Consider now a class ThreeDPoint derived by constrained matching from the class TwoDPoint:

Class ThreeDPoint
Inherits TwoDPoint
Observers
z(Number)
Constructors
midPoint(TwoDPoint): MyType
Constraints
ForAll self,P3: MyType, P2: TwoDPoint, Z1,Z2: Number:
$\Box$self.z(Z1) $\leftarrow$ $\Diamond$ self.z(Z1),
$\Box$(self.midPoint(P2).z(Z1.div(2)) $\leftarrow$ self.z(Z1)),
$\Box$(self.midPoint(P3).z(Z1.add(Z2).div(2)) $\leftarrow$ self.z(Z1), P3.z(Z2))
End ThreeDPoint.

Subtyping requires that the argument type of the method midPoint in the class ThreeDPoint is a subtype of TwoDPoint. This effect is achieved in our formal system by an additional (overloaded) method signature midPoint(TwoDPoint): MyType and a constraint $\Box$(self.midPoint(P2).z(Z1.div(2)) $\leftarrow$ self.z(Z1)) for P2: TwoDPoint. This way the method midPoint in the class ThreeDPoint is defined both for the arguments of types ThreeDPoint and TwoDPoint. The usual bottom-up search for locating the relevant method definition starts with the run-time type of the receiver object. In our system it is augmented with inspection of the run-time types of the arguments (multiple dispatch). This way the correct method definition is always located. The formal proof is presented in section 4.

2.4 Other approaches

Temporally constrained matching can be compared with the approach proposed in [BC96]. The approach presented in [BC96] amounts to adding the signature midPoint(TwoDPoint): TwoDPoint to the ThreeDPoint class automatically by the compiler. But this automatic fix-up *does not solve the problem at all*, because it requires the signature of midPoint and its implementation to be identical to the one in TwoDPoint class. But that is not really what is needed. One would like midPoint in ThreeDPoint to be able to handle arguments of TwoDPoint class in spite of the perfectly natural covariant redefinition of its argument type. In addition, it should still produce the expected result, which is ThreeDPoint. This cannot be accomplished by automatic compiler-generated methods. In fact, the problem is a semantic one, and has to be dealt with in a semantic paradigm. A possible natural constraint is given explicitly in the above solution. In general, there may be many semantically valid options. The advantage of a declarative system is that the required semantics can be expressed formally, free from the details of procedural decomposition.

Other approaches are based on a more complex type system, which supports both subtyping and matching. Matching does not always guarantee type safe substitutability, subtyping does. The programmer has the choice to restrict MyType one way or the other [GM96]:

Class TwoDPoint(MyType <: TwoDPoint)

. . .

End TwoDPoint.

Since the type of MyType in TwoDPoint class is restricted to be a subtype of TwoDPoint (MyType <: TwoDPoint), the first definition of ThreeDPoint in section 2.1 will be rejected by the compiler. It would be accepted if the type constraint was MyType $\leq$ TwoDPoint, where we use $\leq$ to denote matching.

There are two problems with this approach. The first one is that the restriction on the type of MyType is given in the superclass. Thus whatever that restriction is, we must comply with it when deriving a subclass. Thus if the type constraint is MyType <: TwoDPoint as above, there is no way of using matching subsequently in classes derived from TwoDPoint. And that may be exactly what we want, as the ThreeDPoint class illustrates. The other problem is the complexity of a type system, which includes matching, subtyping and type quantification. Our type system is much simpler and it is based on a single notion which corresponds to identifying inheritance with matching. Subtyping is not used at all, and type safety is guaranteed by the temporal constraint system.

2.5 Monotonicity

A major controversy related to subtyping is that type functions determined by typical object types are not monotone with respect to subtyping.

Consider a type function $F : OBJECT \rightarrow OBJECT$ where $OBJECT$ denotes the collection of all object types:

$F(T)=$ OBJECT(T){x(Number): Boolean, y(Number): Boolean,
move(Number): Boolean,
midPoint(T): T}

Since the type parameter T appears both in the argument and in the result position of the method $midPoint$, we have $T_2 <: T_1 \not\Rightarrow F(T_2) <: F(T_1)$. Although $ThreeDPoint \not<: TwoDPoint$ for the same reasons, one can easily verify that $ThreeDPoint <: F(ThreeDPoint)$.

The last condition specifies the relationship between ThreeDPoint and TwoD-Point in a type system based on subtyping. This is precisely the idea behind F-bounded polymorphism [CCH89]. Such an awkward way of specifying a simple and natural relationship between ThreeDPoint and TwoDPoint indicates clearly the difficulties of object-oriented type systems based on subtyping. Matching [BSG95] was introduced in order to find a more natural specification of this relationship.

If we look at the collection of all types T such that $T <: F(T)$, then TwoD-Point is meant to have a distinctive property:

$$TwoDPoint <: F(TwoDPoint) \text{ and } F(TwoDPoint) <: TwoDPoint.$$

In other words, TwoDPoint is a fixed point of the type function F. This is hard to explain because F is not even monotone, let alone continuous with respect to subtyping. Well-established theories of recursive types require not just monotonicity, but even continuity.

Consider now the collection of object types OBJECT ordered by constrained matching. Now we have:

$$T_2 \leq T_1 \Rightarrow F(T_2) \leq F(T_1).$$

The collection of all types T such that $T \leq TwoDPoint$ is partially ordered by $\leq$. This collection has a terminal type, which is precisely TwoDPoint. It becomes easy to explain why TwoDPoint is defined as a fixed point of a type function F that is now monotone with respect to constrained matching.

The formal system presented in this paper has both class types and object types. Both are ordered by constrained matching denoted $\leq$. Class types contain the semantic part of the paradigm expressed by temporal constraints. A full-fledged model theory underlying the formal system presented in this paper has been developed as a follow-up to [AA97]. It is necessarily the topic of a separate paper.

We just mention briefly that we view a class C as a theory. This view is in the spirit of [Gog91]. The associated object type T of C is interpreted as a model of C, denoted $T \models C$. Let $C_2 \leq C_1$ for classes C_2 and C_1. When $MyType$ is used in C_1, the signatures and constraints inherited in C_2 from C_1 are transformed. Denote with $\mathcal{C}$ the set of constraints of a class C. Let $\mathcal{C}^* = \{P \mid T \models C \Rightarrow T \models P\}$. Now if $h : \mathcal{C}_1 \to \mathcal{C}_2$ is the transformation of constraints, constrained matching still has the property that $h(\mathcal{C}_1) \subseteq \mathcal{C}_2^*$. Observe that this holds only on condition that no redefinition of the constraints in $\mathcal{C}_1$ occur in $\mathcal{C}_2$. Only additional constraints are allowed. This way type safety is preserved and so is monotonicity. No object-oriented type system can provide this solution. The solution is simply beyond the universe of type systems.

3 Formal System

The formal system supports both class types and object types. The semantic part of the paradigm (temporal constraints) is naturally placed in class types. *This is a major difference in comparison with an object-oriented type system.* On the other hand, object types are in our type system based on signatures of method suits only, as usual.

3.1 Environments and persistence

In the formal system that follows, E denotes an environment. As usual, an environment is a collection of bindings. Identifiers in an environment may be bound to class types, object types and objects. If an environment contains a binding for an object type, the binding is recorded by a type expression of the form $OBJECT(MyType)R$. As in [Bru93] and [BCM93], $MyType$ denotes a bound variable that stands for the type itself. R is a record of method signatures. A binding of a class is recorded by a type expression of the form $CLASS(MyType)RC$, where C stands for a collection of temporal constraints. An environment also naturally contains the inheritance relationships among class types.

A statement of the form $E \vdash \top$ asserts that the environment E is well formed. An environment is well formed if it is constructed according to the rules specified in this section.

In MyT *Main* denotes the main environment. *Main* always contains a number of predefined bindings, such as those for classes *Any*, *Boolean*, *String* etc. In addition, embedded environments control hierarchical name spaces.

Any is the top class and *ANY* is the top object type, both with respect to the ordering $\leq$ defined below. Orthogonal persistence is accomplished by placing methods for making a class or an object persistent in these two classes. We believe that this is a novelty by itself and the most natural way of providing orthogonal persistence in an object-oriented language. However, the issue is really orthogonal to this paper, and it is elaborated in a separate one. For the sake of some completeness we present the specification of the class Any:

Class Any
Observers
same_as(Any),
persistent()
Mutators
persists(String),
Constructors
copy(): MyType
Constraints
ForAll self: MyType, S: String:
$\Box(\bigcirc\text{self.persistent}() \leftarrow \text{self.persists}(S))$
End Any.

The message *persists* promotes the receiver object to longevity and introduces a binding of the argument string to the receiver object in the currently valid (persistent) environment. For further explanations about this approach to persistence see [Ala97b].

3.2 Class types and object types

If *aClass* belongs to an environment E, then the class type of *aClass* can be derived from E. The fact that every class is implicitly derived from *Any* is reflected in the method suit and the constraint section of the class type of *aClass*.

$$\frac{E \vdash \top, \quad \textbf{Class } aClass\ R_a\ C_a\ \textbf{End} \in E}{E \vdash aClass : CLASS(MyType)\ R_{Any} \cup R_a\ C_{Any} \cup C_a}$$

Note that R_a contains only the signatures of the methods declared in *aClass*. R_a does not contain the signatures of the inherited methods. The same applies to the constraints C_a. This explains the usage of $\cup$ in the above rule. It also demonstrates a specific form of monotonicity underlying the overall paradigm.

A type expression $CLASS(MyType)\ R\ C$ defines a function $F : CLASS \rightarrow CLASS$ defined as $F(T) = CLASS(T)\ R[MyType/T]\ C[MyType/T]$ where $[MyType/T]$ denotes substitution of T for $MyType$ (see also section 2.5). $CLASS$ denotes the collection of all class types. The type of aClass, denote it as aClassType, is intended to be the least fixed point of F, so that we have $aClassType \cong F(aClassType)$. However, a major difference is that F is now monotone with respect to constrained matching.

The above rule generalizes as follows:

$$\frac{E \vdash \top, \quad \textbf{Class } bClass\ \textbf{Inherits } aClass\ R_b\ C_b\ \textbf{End} \in E}{E \vdash bClass : CLASS(MyType)\ R_{Any} \cup R_a\ \cup R_b\ C_{Any} \cup C_a \cup C_b}$$

The rules that follow specify how the method suit and the constraint section of a class type are constructed. Note that in particular we have:

$$\frac{Main \vdash \top}{Main \vdash Any : CLASS(MyType)\ R_{Any}\ C_{Any}}$$

$$\frac{Main \vdash \top}{Main \vdash ANY : OBJECT(MyType)\ R_{Any}}$$

where

$R_{Any} = \{same\_as(Any) : Boolean,\ persistent() : Boolean,\ persists(String) : Boolean,\ copy() : MyType\}$

$C_{Any} = \{\textbf{ForAll } self : MyType,\ S : String : \Box(\bigcirc self.persistent() \leftarrow self.persists(S))\}$

If an environment E contains a binding $a : aClass$, then the object type of a may be derived from E according to the following rule:

$$\frac{E \vdash \top, \quad E \vdash aClass : CLASS(MyType)\ R\ C, \quad a : aClass \in E}{E \vdash a : OBJECT(MyType)\ R}$$

The inheritance relationships among class types must be explicitly recorded in an environment. Checking acceptable inheritance relationships requires checking the method suits and the constraint sections of the classes involved in the relationship.

$$\frac{E \vdash \top, \quad \textbf{Class } bClass \textbf{ Inherits } aClass\ R_b\ C_b \textbf{ End} \in E}{E \vdash bClass \leq aClass}$$

The inheritance relationship among object types is based on the inheritance relationship of their corresponding classes.

$$\frac{E \vdash \top, \quad E \vdash CLASS(MyType)\ R_2\ C_2 \leq CLASS(MyType)\ R_1\ C_1}{E \vdash OBJECT(MyType)\ R_2 \leq OBJECT(MyType)\ R_1}$$

3.3 Inheritance ordering

The main environment always contains bindings for classes *Any* and *Boolean*:

$$\frac{Main \vdash \top}{Main \vdash Any \leq Any}$$

$$\frac{Main \vdash \top}{Main \vdash Boolean \leq Any}$$

Main will naturally contain other predefined classes. Managing name spaces and persistence requires the class *String*. Efficient handling of database applications (queries in particular), requires predefined collection classes, such as *Collection, Bag, Set* etc.

MyType denotes a class:

$$\frac{E \vdash \top}{E \vdash MyType \leq Any}$$

self denotes an object of *MyType*:

$$\frac{E \vdash \top, \quad E \vdash MyType : CLASS(MyType)\ R\ C}{E \vdash self : OBJECT(MyType)\ R}$$

The inheritance ordering is naturally reflexive and transitive:

$$\frac{E \vdash \top, \quad E \vdash aClass \leq Any}{E \vdash aClass \leq aClass}$$

$$E \vdash \top, \quad E \vdash cClass \leq Any, \quad E \vdash bClass \leq cClass, \quad E \vdash aClass \leq bClass$$
$$\overline{E \vdash aClass \leq cClass}$$

The rules that follow define the inheritance ordering of method suits viewed as sets of method signatures. Every method suit is derived by inheritance from the method suit R_{Any} of the class Any. The inheritance ordering of method suits is in fact the subset relation. *Thus the only redefinition of signatures that is allowed is based on the change of interpretation of MyType in a derived class.* This is precisely constrained matching as it applies to the type system.

$$E \vdash \top, \quad E \vdash R_1 \leq R_{Any}, \quad E \vdash R_2 \leq R_{Any}, \quad R_1 \subseteq R_2$$
$$\overline{E \vdash R_2 \leq R_1}$$

The following two rules are in fact an inductive definition of derivation of a valid method suit from the method suit R_{Any}.

$$E \vdash \top, \quad E \vdash C_i \leq Any, \text{ for } 1 \leq i \leq k, \quad E \vdash C \leq Any,$$
$$m \notin \{same\_as, persistent, persists, copy\}$$
$$\overline{E \vdash \{m(C_1, C_2, \ldots, C_k) : C\} \cup R_{Any} \leq R_{Any}}$$

$$E \vdash \top, \quad E \vdash \{m_1(C_{11}, \ldots, C_{1M1}) : C_1, \ldots, m_k(C_{k1}, \ldots, C_{kMk}) : C_k\} \leq R_{Any},$$
$$E \vdash C_{li} \leq Any, \text{ for } 1 \leq i \leq Ml, \quad E \vdash C_l \leq Any, \quad m_l \neq m_i \text{ for } 1 \leq i \leq k$$
$$E \vdash$$
$$\{m_1(C_{11}, \ldots, C_{1M1}) : C_1, \ldots, m_k(C_{k1}, \ldots, C_{kMk}) : C_k, m_l(C_{l1}, \ldots, C_{lMl}) :$$
$$C_l\} \leq R_{Any}$$

3.4 Messages

Consider first type checking a constructor message of the form $a.f(a_1, a_2, \ldots, a_n)$. This message is a term, and so is each of $a, a_1, a_2, \ldots, a_n$. The types of these terms are determined based on the types of variables that occur in these terms. These variables are bound variables of the relevant constraint section. The condition $E \cup \bigcup_{i=1}^{n} \{X_i : C_i\} \vdash a : OBJECT(MyType) \, R_a$ thus determines the type of the receiver object a, given the types of bound variables of the constraint section. Likewise, the condition $E \cup \bigcup_{i=1}^{n} \{X_i : C_i\} \vdash a_i : OBJECT(MyType) \, R_{ai}$ determines the type of the i-th argument given the types of bound variables of the constraint section.

Constrained matching comes into play in the remaining type checking conditions. We must make sure that the receiver object is equipped with a constructor method with a correct signature. This is expressed by the condition $E \vdash R_a \leq R_{Any} \cup \{f(C_1, C_2, \ldots, C_n) : C\}$. Note that $\leq$ denotes constrained matching. The type of the i-th actual argument in the message $a.f(a_1, a_2, \ldots, a_n)$ must be derived by constrained matching from the type the i-th formal parameter of f. This requirement is expressed by the condition $E \vdash R_{ai} \leq R_i$.

In determining the type of the result we must remember that $MyType$ stands for the type of the receiver object a. Because of this, in the type of the result of the message $a.f(a_1, a_2, \ldots, a_n)$, $MyType$ is replaced by $OBJECT(MyType) R_a$.

$$E \vdash \top,$$
$$E \cup \bigcup_{i=1}^{n} \{X_i : C_i\} \vdash a : OBJECT(MyType) R_a,$$
$$E \vdash R_a \leq R_{Any} \cup \{f(C_1, C_2, \ldots, C_n) : C\},$$
$$E \cup \bigcup_{i=1}^{n} \{X_i : C_i\} \vdash a_i : OBJECT(MyType) R_{ai},$$
$$E \vdash R_{ai} \leq R_i,$$

$$\overline{E \cup \bigcup_{i=1}^{n} \{X_i : C_i\} \vdash a.f(a_1, a_2, ..., a_n) :}$$
$$OBJECT(MyType) R_C[MyType/OBJECT(MyType) R_a]$$

Note that the type of the message $a.f(a_1, a_2, \ldots, a_n)$ is in the end determined on the basis of the given types of the bound variables of the relevant constraint section.

A subtle point in the above rule is that the body of the method implementing the message is not used in the type checking rule. The reason for this is that the constraints specify the observer predicates of the object constructed by a constructor message. Type checking method bodies thus comes up in the rule for type checking observer messages.

Consider now type checking of an observer message $a.p(a_1, a_2, ..., a_n)$. The conditions $E \cup \bigcup_{i=1}^{n} \{X_i : C_i\} \vdash a : C_a$, $E \vdash C_a \leq C$ and $E \vdash R_C \leq R_{Any} \cup \{p(C_1, C_2, \ldots, C_n) : Boolean\}$ guarantee that the receiver object is equipped with an observer with a correct signature. The conditions $E \cup \bigcup_{i=1}^{n} \{X_i : C_i\} \vdash a_i : C_{ai}$, $E \vdash C_{ai} \leq C_i$ guarantee that the types of the actual arguments are derived by constrained matching from the types of the corresponding formals.

We now have to recall that a message $a.p(a_1, a_2, ..., a_n)$ is in fact a call whose body is the body of the constraint with $a.p(a_1, a_2, ..., a_n)$ in its head. The proof rule given below considers a typical constraint of the form $\Box(\bigcirc a.p(a_1, a_2, \ldots, a_n) \leftarrow B)$, but other forms of constraints bring nothing new. The condition $E \vdash \forall(X_i : C_i)\Box(\bigcirc a.p(a_1, a_2, \ldots, a_n) \leftarrow B) \in \mathcal{C}_C$ makes sure that the receiver object a is equipped with a constraint with an observer $a.p(a_1, a_2, ..., a_n)$ in its head.

Asserting that a message is type correct will now be based on the assumption that the body of the associated constraint is type correct. Type checking of the body will be based on the assumption that $MyType$ stands for a type that is derived by constrained matching from the compile time type of the receiver object a, hence the condition $MyType \leq C_a$. If under this assumption we can conclude that the type of the body is $Boolean$, then we can conclude that the type of the observer message $a.p(a_1, a_2, ..., a_n)$ is also $Boolean$. All of this is expressed in the rule that follows:

$$E \vdash \top, \quad E \vdash C : CLASS(MyType)\, R_C C_C,$$
$$E \vdash R_C \leq R_{Any} \cup \{p(C_1, C_2, \ldots, C_n) : Boolean\},$$
$$E \vdash \forall(X_i : C_i)\Box(a.p(a_1, a_2, \ldots, a_n) \leftarrow B) \in \mathcal{C}_C,$$
$$E \cup \bigcup_{i=1}^n \{X_i : C_i\} \vdash a : C_a, \quad E \vdash Ca \leq C,$$
$$E \cup \bigcup_{i=1}^n \{X_i : C_i\} \vdash a_i : C_{ai}, \quad E \vdash C_{ai} \leq C_i,$$
$$\underline{E \cup \bigcup_{i=1}^n \{X_i : C_i\} \cup \{MyType \leq C_a\} \vdash B : Boolean,}$$
$$E \cup \bigcup_{i=1}^n \{X_i : C_i\} \vdash a.p(a_1, a_2, \ldots, a_n) : Boolean$$

3.5 Temporal constraints

Further rules for type checking temporal constraints present no difficulty and are given here only for the sake of completeness.

$$\frac{E \vdash \top, \quad E \vdash B_i : Boolean,\ 1 \leq i \leq n}{E \vdash B_1, B_2, \ldots, B_n : Boolean}$$

$$\frac{E \vdash \top, \quad E \vdash B : Boolean}{E \vdash \bigcirc B : Boolean}$$

$$\frac{E \vdash \top, \quad E \vdash B : Boolean}{E \vdash \Diamond B : Boolean}$$

$$\frac{E \vdash \top, \quad E \vdash B : Boolean, \quad E \vdash H : Boolean}{E \vdash H \leftarrow B : Boolean}$$

$$\frac{E \vdash \top, \quad E \vdash B : Boolean \quad E \vdash N : Boolean}{E \vdash \Box(N \leftarrow B) : Boolean}$$

Consider now type checking of the constraint section **ForAll** $X_1 : C_1, X_2 : C_2, \ldots, X_n : C_n : e$. In addition to the bindings that exist in an environment E, type checking the constraints e is carried out with additional bindings $X_i : C_i$ of bound variables X_i to classes C_i. This explains the assumption $E \cup \bigcup_{i=1}^n \{X_i : C_i\}$ where E must already contain bindings for the classes C_i, i.e., $C_i \leq Any$.

$$\frac{E \vdash \top, \quad E \vdash C_i \leq Any\ for\ i = 1, 2, \ldots, n, \quad E \cup \bigcup_{i=1}^n \{X_i : C_i\} \vdash e : Boolean}{E \vdash \textbf{ForAll}\ X_1 : C_1, X_2 : C_2, \ldots, X_n : C_n : e : Boolean}$$

4 Main result

Let **Class** aClass **Inherits** bClass $R_a\, C_a$ **End**. Constrained matching requires the following:

- If R_b contains a signature $f(C_1, C_2, \ldots, C_j, \ldots, C_n) : C$ with $C_j = MyType$ for some $j = 1, 2, \ldots, n$, then R_a contains a signature $f(C_1, C_2, \ldots, bClass, \ldots, C_n) : C$.

- Suppose that C_b contains an observer $a.p(a_1, a_2, \ldots, a_n)$ in the head of a constraint. If any of the terms $a, a_1, a_2, \ldots, a_n$ contains a constructor message with an argument of $MyType$, C_a must contain a corresponding constraint with the observer $a.p(a_1, a_2, \ldots, a_n)$ in the head, in which the type of this $MyType$ argument is replaced with $bClass$. Messages in the body of this constraint are restricted to method signatures without $MyType$. Extensions of the formal rules given in section 3 can capture these requirements explicitly.
- Search for the relevant constraints for executing a message sent to an object starts with the run-time type of the receiver. But in addition, the run time types of the arguments are also inspected (multiple dispatch) to locate the correct method signature. This is required only for the actual parameters whose corresponding formal parameters are declared to be of type $MyType$. If a matching signature is not found in the run-time type of the receiver, the search applies recursively to the immediate superclass.

Under the above conditions we can prove the following result.

Theorem *Temporally constrained matching is type safe.*

Proof. The proof proceeds by induction on the depth of the inheritance tree.

In the initial step we consider a class **Class** aClass R_a C_a **End** in an environment E in which the immediate superclass of $aClass$ is Any. We prove that messages with method signatures inherited from Any are type safe. This part of the proof is immediate because R_{Any} does not contain signatures with $MyType$ argument types.

The inductive hypothesis is that the environment E contains a class $bClass$ such that all messages with method signatures inherited in $bClass$ from its superclass are type safe.

In the inductive step we consider adding a class **Class** aClass **Inherits** bClass R_a C_a **End** to the environment E where $aClass$ is derived by constrained matching from $bClass$. Then we have to prove that all messages with method signatures inherited in $aClass$ from $bClass$ are type safe.

Consider a message $a.f(a_1, a_2, ..., a_n)$ where $f(C_1, C_2, ..., C_n) : C$ is a signature in R_b and the static type of a is $bClass$. The run-time type of a then may be either $bClass$ or $aClass$. The only case which requires careful consideration is the case in which the dynamic type of a is $aClass$. The search for the relevant set of constraints in this case starts with $aClass$.

If $C_j \neq MyType$ for $j = 1, 2, \ldots, n$, the search for the correct method signature necessarily goes back to $bClass$, since no redefinition of method signature occurs in $aClass$. Thus the correct set of constraints is located in $bClass$. These constraints will in general involve messages in their bodies with method signatures from $bClass$ or its superclass. By the inductive assumption these messages are type safe.

Consider now the case in which $C_j = MyType$ for some $j, 1 \leq j \leq n$. Then $aClass$ must contain a method signature $f(C_1, C_2, ..., C_{j-1}, bClass, C_{j+1}, ...Cn) : C$ together with the relevant constraints. The static check ensures that the run-time type of a_j is either *aClass* or *bClass*. If the run-time type of a_j is *aClass*, the relevant method signature is $f(C_1, C_2, ..., C_{j-1}, aClass, C_{j+1}, ..., C_n) : C$, otherwise it is $f(C_1, C_2, ..., C_{j-1}, bClass, C_{j+1}, ..., C_n) : C$. In either case the search which starts with *aClass* locates the relevant set of constraints. Messages that occur in the bodies of these constraints are type safe by the inductive hypothesis, and thus the message $a.f(a_1, a_2, ..., a_n)$ is type safe. This completes the proof.

Note that the above proof deals only with the inherited method signatures, as those are the only ones affected by the redefinition of signatures caused by constrained matching. *Any* is in our formal system defined in such a way that it contains no method signatures with *MyType* in the argument position. This way there are no particular constrained matching requirements for the classes derived directly from *Any*. Of course, the result type of the method *copy* is *MyType* and thus it is redefined when inherited. The associated additional constraints are thus required in all classes other than *Any*. But our technique obviously does not depend upon these particular and natural design decisions.

5 Comparisons with Related Research

In our opinion, searching for a solution for the covariance/contravariance controversy in a system with single dispatch and static type checking is futile. And it does not help either to claim that the problem is not real [Cas95].

We do not even try to solve the problem within the framework of an object-oriented type system alone. We look at the problem in a much richer paradigm, which is still formal. The paradigm is semantic, behavioral, and based on a temporal logic. In this paradigm the type constraint system is extended with temporal constraints. Problems that cannot be handled by the type system alone are delegated to the temporal constraint system. This is the main difference between our approach and the approaches based on F-bounded polymorphism [CHC90] and matching [BSG95]. The problem is of the semantic nature, and thus compiler generated additional methods [BC96] are hardly an acceptable solution.

One implication of the above approach is that the type system becomes considerably simpler. Contrary to a type system which supports subtyping, matching and type quantification [GM96], our type system is based on a single notion, which corresponds to identification of inheritance with constrained matching. Because of that, it becomes possible to define a type system that is based on inheritance rather than on subtyping. *This makes our formal system very different from the existing object-oriented type systems*, that typically do not rely on a *formally defined notion of inheritance*. And it is inheritance that is the core notion of the object-oriented paradigm, rather than subtyping.

A closely related *distinctive feature* in comparison with object-oriented type systems is the fact that *class types in our formal system include the semantic information expressed by temporal constraints*. To our knowledge, no object-oriented type system has this feature. All of this is possible because *MyT* is

94

a declarative language. In spite of its limitations, the language covers a wide variety of database-oriented nontrivial applications [Ala95], [Ala97a]. And in addition, it has a well-defined semantic model [AA97] and an execution model.

The technique obviously targets binary methods, which is where the covariance/contravariance problem comes up most frequently. Although the technique works in a general case, its leads to a significant increase of the number of the required constraints when there are more arguments whose type is declared as $MyType$. Scaling up is thus an issue.

Other logics have been proposed as a basis of the object-oriented paradigm, such as Horn-clause logic with equality ([GM87], [ASB94]) and its extensions, F-logic [KLW93], and the rewriting logic [Mes93]. Neither F-logic nor Horn-clause logic with equality can express properly state changes. A temporal logic based paradigm captures observable object state transitions, and allows specification of behavioral, event-oriented properties of objects. A temporal paradigm can also express assertions on sequences of object states. These advantages apply to a comparison with the rewriting logic [Mes93] and the dynamic logic [WJS94].

Our work also differs considerably from other temporal languages (such as [Fis94] and [FM94]) in its truly object-oriented nature that includes classes, messages, methods and inheritance. The proposed temporal languages, even when executable, are at best object-based as opposed to being object-oriented. Unlike the language system presented in this paper, other temporal languages are not based on an advanced object-oriented type system. On the implementation side, the underlying implementation architecture [Ala97a] differs dramatically from the implementation architectures of temporal languages.

The proof itself does not seem to depend critically on the fact that the underlying logic is temporal. However, it does depend on the clausal form of constraints.

MyT is a non-trivial language system. The language has an orthogonal model of persistence, very different from the models proposed so far for mainstream object-oriented languages. The model is high-level and frees the users from low-level details, which is naturally expected in a declarative paradigm. The underlying persistence implementation architecture is necessarily based on reachability. It is elaborated in a separate paper [Ala97a].

There are two obvious open problems to be considered in future research. One of them is how to apply the approach presented in this paper to a paradigm with multiple inheritance. The other issue is whether constrained matching is affected by extending the model with parametric polymorphism. An open question is also how general this technique is, as it has been developed in the framework of a declarative, logic based object-oriented language system.

Acknowledgment

I would like to thank Svetlana Kouznetsova for her comments on this paper.

References

[AM87] M. Abadi and Z. Manna, Temporal Logic Programming, Proceedings of Symposium on Logic Programming, IEEE Computer Society Press, pp. 4-16, 1987.

[AC96] M. Abadi and L. Cardelli, On Subtyping and Matching, Proceedings of ECOOP'96, *Lecture Notes in Computer Science*, Springer-Verlag, Vol. 1098, pp. 145-167, 1996.

[Ala97a] S. Alagić, A Temporal Constraint System for Object-Oriented Databases, Constraint Databases and Applications, Proceedings of CDB'97 and CP'96 Workshops, *Lecture Notes in Computer Science* Vol. 1191, pp. 208-218, Springer-Verlag, 1997.

[Ala97b] S. Alagić, The ODMG Object Model: Does it Make Sense? Proceedings of the OOPSLA '97 Conference, pp. 253-270, ACM, 1997.

[AA97] S. Alagić, M. Alagić, Order-Sorted Model Theory for Temporal Executable Specifications, *Theoretical Computer Science 179*, pp. 273-299, 1997.

[Ala95] S. Alagić, A Statically Typed, Temporal Object-Oriented Database Technology, *Transactions on Information and Systems*, IEICE, Vol. 78, pp. 1469-1476, 1995.

[ASB94] S. Alagić, R. Sunderraman and R. Bagai, Declarative Object-Oriented Programming: Inheritance, Subtyping and Prototyping, Proceedings of ECOOP '94, *Lecture Notes in Computer Science* Vol. 821, pp. 236-259, 1994.

[Ala94] S. Alagić, F-bounded Polymorphism for Database Programming Languages, Proceedings of the 2nd East-West Database Workshop, *Workshops in Computing*, pp. 125-137, Springer-Verlag, 1994.

[AM95] M. Atkinson and R. Morrison, Orthogonally Persistent Object Systems, *VLDB Journal*, 4, pp. 319-401, (1995).

[BDK92] F. Bancilhon, C. Delobel and P. Kanelakis (eds), *Implementing an Object-Oriented Database Management System: The Story of O2*, Morgan Kauffman, 1992.

[Bau92] M. Baudinet, A Simple Proof of the Completeness of Temporal Logic Programming, In: L. F. Del Cerro and M. Penttonen, *Intensional Logics for Programming*, Studies in Logic and Computation, 1 Clarendon Press, pp. 51 – 83, 1992.

[Bru93] K. Bruce, Safe Type Checking in a Statically Typed Object-Oriented Programming Language, Proceedings of the ACM Conference on Functional Programming, pp. 285-298, ACM 1993.

[BCM93] K. Bruce, J. Crabtree, T. P. Murtagh and R. van Gent, A. Dimock and R. Muller, Safe and Decidable Type Checking in an Object-Oriented Language, Proceedings of the OOPSLA Conference, pp. 29-46, 1993.

[BSG95] K. Bruce, A. Schuett, and R. van Gent, PolyTOIL: a Type-Safe Polymorphic Object Oriented Language, *Proceedings of ECOOP '95, Lecture Notes in Computer Science Vol. 952*, pp. 27-51, Springer-Verlag, 1996.

[BC96] J. Boyland and G Castagna, Type-Safe Compilation of Covariant Specialization: a Practical Case, Proceedings of ECOOP '96, *Lecture Notes in Computer Science*, Vol. 1098, pp. 3-25, Springer-Verlag, 1996.

[Cas95] G. Castagna, Covariance and Contravariance: Conflict Without a Cause, *ACM Transactions on Programming Languages and Systems*, Vol. 17 (3) pp. 431-447, 1995.

[CCH89] P. Canning, W. Cook, W. Hill, W. Olthoff and J.C. Mitchell, F-Bounded Polymorphism for Object-Oriented Programming, Proceedings of the ACM Conference on Functional Programming Languages and Computer Architecture, pp. 273-280, 1989.

[CHC90] W. R. Cook, W. L. Hill and P. S. Canning, Inheritance is not Subtyping, Proceedings of the ACM Conference on Principles of Programming Languages, pp. 125-135, 1990.

[Coo89] W. R. Cook, A Proposal for Making Eiffel Type Safe, *The Computer Journal*, Vol. 32, no. 4, pp. 305-311, 1989.

[GM96] A. Gawecki and F. Matthes, Integrating Subtyping, Matching and Type Quantification: A Practical Perspective, Proceedings of ECOOP '96, *Lecture Notes in Computer Science*, Vol. 1098, pp. 25-47, Springer-Verlag, 1996.

[Gog91] J. Goguen, Types as Theories, In: G.M. Reed, A. W. Roscoe and R.F. Wachter, *Topology and Category Theory in Computer Science*, pp. 357-390, Clarendon Press, 1991.

[GM87] J. Goguen and J. Meseguer, Unifying Functional, Object-Oriented and Relational Programming with Logical Semantics, In B. Shriver and P. Wegner, editors, *Research Directions in Object-Oriented Programming*, pp. 417- 477, MIT Press, 1987.

[Fis94] M. Fisher, A Survey of Concurrent METATEM – The Language and its Applications, Proceedings of the 2nd Temporal Logic Conference, *Lecture Notes in AI*, pp. 48-66, Springer-Verlag, 1994.

[FM94] J. L. Fiadeiro and T. Maibaum, Sometimes "Tomorrow" is " Sometime" Action Refinement in a Temporal Logic of Objects, Proc. of the 2nd International Temporal Logic Conference, *Lecture Notes in AI*, pp. 48-66, Springer-Verlag, 1994.

[KLW93] M. Kifer, G. Lausen, and J.Wu, Logical Foundation of Object-Oriented and Frame-Based Languages, Technical Report 93/06, Department of Computer Science, SUNY at Stony Brook, to appear in the Journal of the ACM.

[Kro87] F. Kroger, *Temporal Logic of Programs*, EATCS Monograph on Theoretical Computer Science, New York, Springer-Verlag, 1987.

[LW94] B. Liskov and J. M. Wing, A behavioral notion of subtyping, *ACM Transactions on Programming Languages and Systems*, 16, pp. 1811-1841, 1994.

[Mes93] J. Meseguer, Solving the Inheritance Anomaly in Concurrent Object-Oriented Programming, Proceedings of ECOOP '93, *Lecture Notes in Computer Science*, Vol. 707, pp. 220-246, 1993.

[Mey92] B. Meyer. *Eiffel: the Language*, Prentice-Hall, 1992.

[WJS94] R. Wieringa, W. de Jonge and P. Spruit., Roles and Dynamic Subclasses: A Modal Logic Approach, Proceedings of the ECOOP Conference, *Lecture Notes in Computer Science*, Vol. 821, pp. 33-59, 1994.

Existentially Quantified Procedures: A Mechanism for Abstracting Type in Dynamic Typing Constructs

Richard Connor

Department of Computing Science, University of Glasgow,
Glasgow G12 8QQ, Scotland

richard@dcs.gla.ac.uk

Abstract

Existential quantification of procedures is introduced as a mechanism for languages with dynamic typing. It allows abstraction over types whose representations require to be manipulated at run time. Universal quantification, the mechanism normally associated with procedural type abstraction, is shown to be unsuitable for this style of abstraction. For many such procedures only a single type specialisation is correct, hence the analogy with existential quantification from predicate logic. For any invocation of an existentially quantified procedure, the run-time system will require to maintain a single type representation for which the abstracted type stands. Existential quantification represents a class of *ad hoc* polymorphism, where operations over values of the abstracted type may behave differently according to the actual specialisation.

1. Introduction

This section gives the models of persistence and polymorphism assumed in the rest of the paper. Simple models are used, which do not necessarily provide an ideal programming language, but are instead chosen to simplify the context as far as possible. The paper goes on to show that an unacceptable interaction between these models exists, resulting in major run-time overheads due to the manipulation of run-time type information, and compomising the concept of polymorphism. It is shown how to easily restore pure polymorphism and avoid the run-time overhead, but at cost of reducing the useful expressive power of the language. This expressive power, and more, is then re-introduced using a new language concept, that of existentially quantified procedures.

The running text relies upon informal descriptions and examples; formal definitions of all the language constructs introduced are given in an appendix.

1.1. Models for persistence and dynamic typing

We assume a global, distributed persistent store with a single, flat namespace. Values placed in, and extracted from, the persistent store are represented as dynamically typed infinite unions, with injection required before a value is placed in the store, and projection required before an extracted value can be used. The essence of persistence in this model is that an extracted value can not be distinguished in terms of its semantics with the value which was placed there [ABC+83, ABM88].

The type *any* is used to represent the infinite union. There are two associated operations, injection and projection. Appendix 1 gives a formal model of these operations; for the moment we suffice with the example in Figure 1.1.

```
let fortyTwo = 42

let fortyTwoAsAny = inject( 42 )

let fortyTwoAgain = project fortyTwoAsAny as
                            x : int in x
```

Figure 1.1 : Dynamic typing example

In this example, the integer value denoted by *fortyTwo* is injected into the infinite union type. The type of the identifier *fortyTwoAsAny* is *any*, rather than *int*, and other than projection no operations are defined over it. To use this value as an integer again, it must be successfully projected, as happens in the final line of code. The projection statement takes a value of type *any* and introduces a new typed identifier for it (*x : int* in this case). The value of the whole statement is the expression after the keyword *in*. This expression may include the new identifier, which stands for the re-typed dynamic value. This operation is of course prone to failure if the dynamic value is of an inappropriate type.

This terse form of projection syntax is unforgiving for a real programming language, where some kind of alternative is normally provided in case of failure. It is also commonly possible to interrogate a value of type *any* to determine its more specific type. Neither of these are included here, to simplify the model and shorten the examples.

Having dealt with dynamic typing an equally simple model of persistence is introduced. There are two operators, *intern* and *extern*, operating within a single global namespace modelled as strings. Once again a more formal definition is given in Appendix 2, and an informal one here based on the example in Figure 1.2.

```
let fortyTwo = 42

extern( "fortyTwo", inject( fortyTwo ) )

let fortyTwoAgain = project intern( "fortyTwo" ) as
                            x : int in x
```

Figure 1.2 : Using the persistent namespace

The dynamically typed version of *fortyTwo* is exactly the same as in the last example. The difference is that here, the value is placed in the persistent namespace, with the name "fortyTwo". Having placed it there, using the *extern* operation, it can be fetched back using the *intern* operation, and then projected back to integer. Once again, this rather terse persistence interface is chosen to clarify the examples in the text.

1.2. The type substitution model of parametric polymorphism

Polymorphic procedures are defined as those whose behaviour is independent of some part of the type of their operands [Str67, CW85]. The most common model used to capture this concept is that of type substitution [Gir72, Rey74]. In this model, a polymorphic procedure is applied to a type argument to produce a monomorphic version, before being subsequently applied to a value of that type. This type application simply performs a textual substitution of actual for formal type parameters through the signature and body of the procedure.

It should be stressed that this is a reduction semantics model, rather than a suggestion for an implementation of polymorphism; one of the most appealing attributes of the model is that type application is never necessary, and may be factored out statically[1]. An example reduction according to the model is given in Figure 1.3.

```
let first = proc[ forall t ]( x, y : t → t ) ; x
    in first[ int ]( 3 , 4 )

=>    ( ( proc[ forall t ]( x, y : t → t ) ; x )
          [ int ] ) ( 3 , 4 )

=>    ( proc( x, y : int → int ) ; x ) ( 3 , 4 )

=>    3
```

Figure 1.3 : Type substitution reduction

The reason for introducing this model is that the major hypothesis of this paper is that such semantics are unsuitable for modelling parametric polymorphism in the presence of dynamic typing.

2. Problems with polymorphism and dynamic typing

There are two problems which result from the adoption of the type substitution model in a language with dynamic typing. These are a problem with efficient implementation, and a problem with the resulting language definition.

---

[1] This turns out to be true only in languages without dynamic typing!

Figure 2.1 shows a simple procedure which mixes the concepts. The procedure is an abstraction over the *inject* statement, taking an argument of any type and returning the same value re-typed as *any*. It is superficially reasonable; its meaning is clearly defined under the substitution model, and it shows the basis of a useful class of type abstraction. In implementation terms however there is a crucially important difference when compared with a system without dynamic typing: its correct implementation requires the specialising type information to be marshalled at an instance of its call, and passed through the calling mechanism. This information is required for the correct execution of the injection.

```
let injectQ = proc[ forall t ]( x : t → any )
     inject( x )
```

Figure 2.1 : Injection of a quantifier type variable

In itself this is not a major problem; the extra cost of passing the type information is minor compared to constructing it in the first place, so a number of calls to this procedure would not cost significantly more than executing in-line *inject* statements for each of the values involved. However we are interested in systems with first-class procedures, where persistent bindings are made to procedures whose source is not available within the same compilation unit. In this context there is in general no way of telling, from the context of a procedure call, whether the specialising type information is required to be passed or not. It must therefore always be passed except in those cases where it can be avoided as a specific optimisation. Therefore the cost of polymorphism in general, even in applications which do not use such abstractions, is likely to become unacceptable because of the amount of run-time type information it becomes necessary to maintain.

The other problem with the model in the presence of dynamic typing is better exemplified by Figure 2.2. This procedure represents an abstraction over the projection operator, and the use of the polymorphic form now looks quite bizarre. Although the procedure is typed as one applicable to all types, ranged over by t, in fact for any invocation only a single instance of t is correct. The type variable t appears in terms of the analogy with predicate logic to be more like an existential quantifier than a universal one.

```
let projectQ = proc[ forall t ]( x : any → t )
     project x as y : t in y
```

Figure 2.2 : Project of a quantifier type variable

Once again, however, the procedure has a clearly defined meaning under the type substitution model, and once again it represents a class of useful type abstraction. However, the procedure does not represent a universally quantified procedure as its behaviour is not independent of the abstracted type. In short, the system is not actually polymorphic, as indeed might already be suspected because of the requirement to pass run-time type information.

We can construct even odder looking examples, such as in Figure 2.3, by injecting a value of a quantified type variable and subsequently projecting it onto a manifest type.

```
let discoverQ = proc[ forall t ]( x : t → int )
       project inject( x ) as y : int in y
```

Figure 2.3 : Testing the type of a universal quantifier instance

Although the procedure is typed as polymorphic over *t*, it is in fact only meaningful where *t = int*. In general, it is possible to test for the actual instance of a quantifier type variable for a particular invocation. While the ability to test for the specific type of a value typed as *any* is quite reasonable, the ability to transfer the test to the abstracted type within a polymorphic procedure is less so. In any case, the model is clearly quite different from polymorphism and universal quantification, which it was originally intended to capture.

3. A first solution

The problems described above were first encountered during the initial implementation of the language Napier88 [MBC+94], believed to be the first implemented language to contain the combination of parametric polymorphism and dynamic typing [Con90]. The problem was solved by using a different model for polymorphism, which maintains purely polymorphic behaviour even for the examples given in the preceding section. The solution is now briefly presented; while preserving pure polymorphism and avoiding run-time type manipulation, it reduces expressive power. In the next section it is shown how this may be re-introduced by the new mechanism.

The solution is to restrict the type substitution model to the typing of procedure calls, and to use a new type introduction model for quantifier type variables within the procedure body. Essentially, universal quantifier type variables are represented by new unique types within a procedure body. These types are compatible only with other instances of the same quantifier; that is their equality is by name, rather than structural. The types have no operations defined over them, other than those defined on all types.

Statically this model makes no difference whatsoever to the typechecking of polymorphic procedures. The difference is apparent only when the procedure body contains either a dynamic injection or a dynamic projection statement which involves the quantifier variable type. In these cases a unique type representation is dynamically generated at the time of the procedure invocation. The representation is based upon the type variable within the context of that invocation, and its dynamic extent is therefore confined to the body of the procedure for that invocation. This means that there is no extra cost in the implementation of polymorphism for the majority of polymorphic procedures that do not contain dynamically typed operations, and there is no overhead in the procedure call mechanism.

If the three troublesome procedures of Figures 2.1, 2.2 and 2.3 are re-examined with respect to this model, their behaviour can be seen to be polymorphic, in that they have exactly the same behaviour irrespective of the type of the particular specialisation. This behaviour, however, is arguably not very useful; procedures 2.2 and 2.3 always fail (which is at least consistent!), and procedure 2.1 results in an infinite union value which can never be successfully projected.[2]

The alternative would have been simply to disallow injection and projection where the types involved contain a quantifier variable. However not only does this create an annoying restriction in the language design, it also prevents the use of injection and projection where they may be successful within the context of a single invocation, as is shown in Figure 3.1.

```
let injectAndProjectQ = proc[ forall t ]( x : t → t )
        project inject( x ) as y : t in y
```

Figure 3.1 : Projecting a locally injected universal quantifier instance

Essentially, dynamic typing may still be used within the scope of a procedure body, but any dynamically typed values that escape the scope of the procedure may not be successfully projected thereafter.

4. Introduction to existentially quantified procedures

It was observed earlier that the programming examples given were useful abstractions, even if they were not examples of polymorphism. We now revisit such abstractions, and show how they can be coded, but as a different concept. The concept is, as hinted earlier, that of existentially quantified procedures. It should perhaps be clarified that this term is coined directly by parallel analogy with propositional logic, and has no connexion with the Mitchell and Plotkin model of abstract types [MP88].

We motivate both the concept and the name of this abstraction by another example, shown in Figure 4.1, which involves the manipulation of dynamic types whose details are abstracted through a procedural interface. This example is actually motivated by complaints from Napier88 programmers who had tried to achieve similar abstraction through the use of parametric polymorphism. The meaning of the code should be intuitively clear, once a programmer understands the distinction from universal quantification.

---

[2]This is not true in integrated systems such as the St Andrews hyperprogramming environment [KBC+95, KCC+92], where source code can contain direct links, as well as textual references, to types and values. No textual type description that will match can ever be created, but the original type may be discovered by browsing and inserted into new projection code.

```
let usePersistentStore = proc[ exists t ]()
  project intern( "op" ) as f : proc( t → t ) in
    project intern( "data" ) as x : t in
      extern( "newdata", inject( f( x ) ) )
```

Figure 4.1 : An existentially quantified procedure

Notice first that the keyword *forall* which appeared in the examples of polymorphic procedures has been replaced by *exists*, denoting an existential quantification. The code of the procedure performs two projections of values brought in from the persistent store onto types using the existential quantifier variable. The values are a procedure, and a piece of data which the procedure can take as its argument. The procedure is applied to this data, and the result placed back in the persistent store.

The analogy with existential quantification should be clear. Given the intention of the code, the implicit assertions contained in the projection statements are that there exists a type, named locally as t, such that $op : proc(\, t \to t\,)$ and $data : t$. The type of $op(\, data\,)$ is therefore also t, and the type associated with *newdata* in the persistent store, after the successful completion of the procedure, should be the same as that of *data*.

For the procedure to operate as described, the actual representation of the type must be available to the run-time system to allow the projection and injection to be performed. In this example, the actual instance of the type is found by unification at the time of the first projection, rather than being specified by the programmer at the time of procedure call. Specialising type information is not a part of the syntax of existentially quantified procedure calls. As will be seen, this makes the model more complex, but increases its power of abstraction. For example, the abstraction in

Figure 4.1 itself is substantially less useful if an instantiation for t has to be specified at its call.

Before moving on to a fuller description of the model, the three earlier example procedures are briefly re-examined. Figure 4.2 repeats their code, with the universal quantifier replaced by an existential one. The details of typings and implementation are not yet under consideration, only the justification of their description as existentially quantified.

```
let injectQ = proc[ exists t ]( x : t → any )
  inject( x )

let projectQ = proc[ exists t ]( x : any → t )
  project x as y : t in y

let discoverQ = proc[ exists t ]( x : t → int )
  project inject( x ) as y : int in y
```

Figure 4.2 : Existentially quantified procedures

The procedure *injectQ* is not so clearly an example of the existential model; it is in fact universal, as it will operate correctly for any substitution of *t*. However this fits well with the logical analogy, as any condition which allows universal quantification trivially allows existential quantification also.

The procedure *projectQ* more clearly requires an existential model, as the procedure will execute correctly for only a single type. The interesting aspect of this procedure is that, although the unification of the type variable does not occur until during the execution of the procedure body, a value typed as the existential quantifier escapes this scope as the result type, posing an interesting typing problem.

The last procedure, *discoverQ*, also fits with the existential model, although less generally as it is only correct when the type *t* is *int*. In general, the discovery of this fact is beyond mechanical typechecking, and unification with a different type would be allowed at the procedure call resulting in a run-time error. Whenever more than a single unification might occur there is a possibility of run-time error; this is hardly surprising, however, as it can only occur at a dynamic projection operation. The general illustration of this procedure is that, unlike a universal quantifier, it is quite reasonable to dynamically discover the type of an existential quantifier during execution and perform different actions as a result.

5. Description of the model

To summarise the purpose of existential quantification of procedures, it is a mechanism for languages with dynamic typing which allows abstraction over types whose representations are required dynamically. It is useful for abstraction over types involved in infinite union injection and projection, and therefore persistent store access. For any invocation of an existentially quantified procedure, the run-time system will require to maintain a type representation of the instance of the abstracted type, hence the intuition of existential quantification : the abstraction is over a single type, rather than all types. Existential quantification represents a class of ad hoc polymorphism, where the operations over values of the type may behave differently according to the actual specialisation.

To set the framework for the description, the following syntax is introduced as a language extension:

T   ::=   ... | proc[exists t](T → T) | t

E   ::=   ... | proc[exists t](x : T → T) ; E | E(E)

The *t* in the type syntax represents the set of identifiers representing existential quantifiers, which should be distinguished from other type aliases. The procedure application in the expression syntax is included to emphasise the fact that the syntactic form of existential procedure application does not include an explicit type specialisation.

The run-time system requires to maintain a representation of the abstracted type, and this representation is determined by unification at the earliest possible dynamic opportunity. It is important to note that the only way to introduce a denotation whose type contains a quantifier variable is either as a procedure parameter or as the result of an infinite union projection; in either case, the type becomes resolved before the value can be manipulated[3]. This means any operation over such a value where an instance of the associated type representation is required, such as infinite union injection, is always well defined.

The range of expression available within the body of existentially quantified procedures is identical to that of universally quantified procedures, the only difference being in the interpretation of injection and projection operations. Thus the typing of the procedure introduction is identical, except that the type alias *t* in the type assignment is identified as a unique existential quantifier.

The typing of procedure application, however, is quite different. This is due to the fact that a specialising type is not part of the syntactic form, which as noted increases the expressive power of the construct at the cost of complicating the typing.

If the quantifier type variable appears in the parameter type, then unification is required to determine its specialisation. This is straightforward to perform mechanically. Unification is necessary both to determine the representation to be dynamically passed into the procedure, and to statically determine the result type if the quantifier variable occurs there also.

There is a further case which is less straightforward, when the quantifier variable appears in the result type but not in the argument type. An example of such a procedure was given earlier, and is repeated in Figure 5.1.

```
let projectQ = proc[ exists t ]( x : any → t )
    project x as y : t in y
```

Figure 5.1 : Quantifier variable appears in result type only

The difficulty is that a type, abstracted over by a quantifier variable, escapes the scope of this procedure, and there is no way of determining in the static context of the call what this type might be. The answer is to treat this escaping type as another existential quantifier type; the fact that it has no associated syntactic form does not matter. When the procedure is executed, the actual resolved type representation (again, there must be one if a value is available) can be passed back

---

[3]This is not the case if the language includes a value creation operator based on type, for example *new*; it may be desirable to define such operations only on resolved quantifier types. There is a minor complication also with some quasi-type dependent operations such as *createEmptyList*

out through the return mechanism and associated with the type representation in the local context. It is important to note that a new quantifier type is generated for each instance of a call, as successive calls to the even the same procedure may resolve to different type representations.

In the outer context, the result may be used in any of the ways a local existential quantifier may be used; it may be injected and placed in the persistent store, or projected onto a specific type representation[4].

6.   Programming Examples

To re-emphasise the motivation of abstracting over type in the context of persistent store access, some fuller examples of the uses of existential quantified procedures are given. The examples are given in an invented language, the details of which are largely unimportant except for the use of constructs explained above.

6.1.   Example 1 : automatic name generation for persistent values

Figure 6.1 illustrates simple abstraction over the type of a value that is to be placed in the persistent store, in association with some other computation for which a procedural abstraction is desirable. In this case automatically generated names are used, and the procedure returns the generated name used to store the argument.

```
let autoStore =
begin
     let init := 0

     proc[ exists t ]( x : t → string )
     begin
          init := init + 1
          let name = "value" ++ intToString( init )
          extern( name, inject( x ) )
          name
     end
end
```

Figure 6.1 : Abstracting over a persistent store placement

The example is a block expression, the result of the block being an existentially quantified procedure typed as *proc[exists t](t → string)*. A local variable *init* is first declared within the scope of the result procedure. The procedure code first increments this integer, then constructs a string based on its new value. The procedure argument is then stored using this new string, and the string is returned as the result.

---

[4]Projection is not defined over quantifier types, although this is a possibility. However it may be achieved by simply projecting the injected form of the value.

This is another example of a procedure that is in fact universally applicable. Giving the procedure an existential type, however, means that the actual type representation of the parameter type will be passed into the procedure.

6.2. Example 2 : abstracting over persistent store types

Figure 6.2 illustrates an example which was discovered impossible to write in the Napier88 system. In the persistent store a list of persistent type representations is maintained for administrative purposes. Various utilities are required over this list; the example shown determines how many types are currently stored.

```
let countTypeList = proc[ exists typeRep ]( → int )
project intern( "typeList" ) as
    types : list( typeRep ) in
begin
    let count := 0 ; let listPntr := types
    while not( isEmptyList( listPntr ) ) do
    begin
        count := count + 1
        listPntr := tail( listPntr )
    end
    count
end
```

Figure 6.2 : Abstraction over a projected type

This is a true existential example, as the procedure is correctly typed only for a single instantiation of *typeRep*. The actual type for *typeRep* is discovered at the projection statement, although in this example it is not required further. The rest of the procedure counts the number of elements in the list.

The utility of this abstraction is that the procedure can be both written and applied without any knowledge of the actual type of the list element. This means not only that the annoying task of placing unnecessary type information in the source can be avoided, but also that the same procedure can be used either if the element type evolves through the lifetime of the system, or if it happens to be an abstract type for which no syntactic form exists in the context.

6.3. Example 3 : delayed projection of a persistent value

This example shown in Figure 6.3 involves an anonymous quantifier, that is one that appears in a scope outside the procedure in which it was declared.

```
let fetchList = proc[ exists t ]( string loc →
                                            list( t ) )
     project intern( loc ) as x : list( t ) in x

let useList = proc()
begin
     let l = fetchList( "myList" )
     let x = head( l )
     extern( "myListHead", inject( x ) )

     let myInt = project inject( x ) as y : int in y

     !  the following assignment is not well typed
     !  x := head( fetchList( "myOtherList" ) )
end
```

Figure 6.3 : An anonymous quantifier

The type of *x* in procedure *useList* has no local syntactic form, but this is thought unlikely to cause a problem[5]. The compiler has enough information to plant code to keep a local copy of the type representation which is passed back from the application of *fetchList*, and this dynamic type representation is used in subsequent calls of injection and projection. Notice that a new quantifier type is generated, both statically and dynamically, for each call of the procedure *fetchList*.

6.4.   Example 4 : Constructing an abstract package

The last example again uses anonymous quantifiers, but this time the quantifier appears across a structure type signature, to give functionality similar to an abstract data type. Within the procedure *usePack*, the static typing is identical to that within an abstract *open* clause [MP88]. The type is qualitatively different, however, as it is possible to discover the implementation type.

---

[5]Syntax could easily be invented to provide such a form, such as that of the Mitchell and Plotkin *open* operator [MP88]. However this would seem to be an overkill in this context.

```
type pack[ t ] is structure( create : proc(  → t )
                             change : proc( t → t )
                             store  : proc( t ) )

let makePack = proc[ exists t ](  → pack[ t ] )
begin
     let aCreate = project intern( "aCreate" ) as
         cr : proc(  → t ) in cr
     let aChange = project intern( "aChange" ) as
         ch : proc( t → t ) in ch
     let aStore = proc( x : t )
         extern( "aResult", inject( x ) )

     pack[ t ]( aCreate , aChange , aStore )
end

let usePack = proc()
begin
     let thePack = makePack()
     ...
end
```

Figure 6.4 : Pseudo-abstract type formation

It can be seen from this example that the amount of run-time type manipulation that is required can be quite significant. Previous examples have required only the assignment of type graphs that may be constructed at compile time (this is especially easy in a persistent system [Con90, Cut92]), or the dynamic instantiation of a simple quantifier type representation. However the run-time system in this example must construct a representation of a relatively complex type of which the quantifier type is a component, requiring significantly more work.

7. Related work

The first languages to model persistence with dynamic typing in an otherwise statically typed context were Amber [Car85] and Napier88 [AM85, MBC+94]. Napier88 was the first language to implement the combination of dynamic typing and parametric polymorphism. The combination also occurs in descriptions of the languages Quest [Car89] and Tycoon [Mat95], but early implementations of these languages failed to allow the combination in practice. Some of the difficulties of the combination are documented in [Con90] and [ACP+95]. A full description of the implementation of the dynamic typechecking involved is given in [Con90], part of which appears in [CBC+90]. A more formal treatment of dynamic typing is given in [ACP+91], extended in [ACP+95].

[ACP+95] gives a treatment of the combination of dynamic typing and System F, a type substitution model of polymorphism. The authors note the potential difficulties with the efficiency of the implementation, but also show how some of the class of examples shown in this paper can be programmed. A language mechanism is introduced that allows the programming of some of the examples given here, notably 4.1 and 6.2 which can not be specified using a simple combination of the substitution model and dynamic typing. This expressivity is achieved by the introduction of an unspecialised type variable which becomes instantiated at run-time in a manner similar to that proposed here. The scoping rules associated with the variable prevent values with run-time inferred types from escaping into an outer context. Overall this treatment gives less expression than that proposed here whilst taking a general performance penalty over all uses of polymorphism.

The difficulties of the combination also became apparent to the designers of the Tycoon language, who solved the problem by adding a new keyword *dyn* in contexts where the run-time representation of the type is required to be passed at a polymorphic call, this acting as a signal to the compiler to muster the type representation and pass it at run-time. [LM97]. Polymorphic functions which use the *intern* and *extern* functionality require this keyword in the function header, otherwise they are rejected by the typechecker. This avoids the cost to polymorphism in general, but allows the expression only of example 6.1. For finer details of this mechanism the reader is referred to its designers, as the work is currently documented only in German and is thus inaccessible to this author.

The work described here bears only a little relation to Mitchell and Plotkin's description of abstract types as existentially quantified record types [MP88], as it only borrows the same analogy in a different context. The typing of the resulting quantifiers is substantially different. In particular the typing of an escaping quantifier type can not be handled in the same way.

It should be straightforward and interesting to extend the model to a bounded quantification model. This may be particularly appropriate with respect to abstractions over persistent store projection; however this has not yet been examined in detail and must be logged as future work.

8. References

[ABC83]   M.P. Atkinson, P. Bailey, K.J. Chisholm, W.P. Cockshott and R. Morrison "An Approach to Persistent Programming" The Computer Journal 26, 4 (1983) pp 360 - 365

[ABM88]   M.P. Atkinson, O.P. Buneman and R. Morrison "Binding and Typechecking in Database Programming Languages" Computer Journal 31, 2 (March 1988) pp 99 - 109

[ACP+91]   Martín Abadi, Luca Cardelli, Benjamin C. Pierce, and Gordon D. Plotkin. Dynamic typing in a statically-typed language. ACM Transactions on Programming Languages and Systems, 13(2):237-268, April 1991

[ACP+95]   Martín Abadi, Luca Cardelli, Benjamin C. Pierce, and Didier
             Rémy. Dynamic typing in polymorphic languages. Journal of
             Functional Programming, 5(1):111-130, January 1995

[AM85]   M.P. Atkinson and R. Morrison "Types, Bindings and Parameters
             in a Persistent Environment" In M.P. Atkinson, O.P. Buneman
             and R. Morrison (editors) "Data Types and Persistence", Springer -
             Verlag (1988) pp 1 - 24

[Car85]   Cardelli, L. "Amber" Tech. Report AT7T. Bell Labs. Murray Hill,
             U.S.A. (1985).

[Car89]   L. Cardelli "Typeful Programming" DEC SRC Technical Report
             No. 45 (May 1989)

[CBC+90]   Connor, R. C. H., Brown, A. B., Cutts, Q. I., Dearle, A.,
             Morrison, R. and Rosenberg, J. (1990) Type Equivalence
             Checking in Persistent Object Systems. In A. Dearle, G. M. Shaw
             and S. B. Zdonik (eds), *Implementing Persistent Object Bases,
             Principles and Practice*, pp. 151-164, Morgan Kaufmann,

[CM88]   L. Cardelli and D. McQueen "Persistence and Type Abstraction" In
             M.P. Atkinson, O.P. Buneman and R. Morrison (editors) "Data
             Types and Persistence", Springer - Verlag (1988) pp 31 - 41

[Con90]   Connor, R. C. H. (1990) Types and Polymorphism in Persistent
             Programming Systems. *Ph.D. Thesis,* University of St Andrews.

[Cut92]   Cutts, Q. I. (1992) Delivering the Benefits of Persistence to
             System Construction and Execution. *Ph.D. Thesis,* University of
             St Andrews.

[CW85]   Cardelli, L. and Wegner, P. (1985) On Understanding Types, Data
             Abstraction and Polymorphism. *ACM Computing Surveys,* **17**
             (4), 471-523.

[Gir72]   J.-Y. Girard "Une extension de l'interpretation de Gödel à l'analyse,
             et son application à l'élimination des coupure dans l'analyse et
             théorie des types" Proc. 2nd Scandinavian Logic Symposium (
             1972) pp 63 - 92

[KBC+95]   Kirby, G. N. C., Brown, A. L., Connor, R. C. H. *et al.* (1995)
             The Napier88 Standard Library Reference Manual Version 2.2.1.
             University of St Andrews.

[KCC+92]   Kirby, G. N. C., Connor, R. C. H., Cutts, Q. I., Dearle, A.,
             Farkas, A. M. and Morrison, R. (1992) Persistent Hyper-
             Programs. In A. Albano and R. Morrison (eds), *Persistent Object
             Systems,* pp. 86-106, Springer-Verlag

[LM97]   Bernd Larssen and Florian Matthes, private communication at the DBPL workshop.

[Mat95]   F. Matthes. Higher-Order Persistent Polymorphic Programming in Tycoon. In M.P. Atkinson, editor, Fully Integrated Data Environments. Springer-Verlag (to appear)

[MBC+94]   Morrison, R., Brown, A. L., Connor, R. C. H. *et al.* (1994) The Napier88 Reference Manual (Release 2.0). University of St Andrews.

[MP88]   J.C. Mitchell and G.D. Plotkin "Abstract Types have Existential Type" ACM ToPLaS 10, 3 (July 1988) pp. 470 - 502

[Rey74]   J.C. Reynolds "Towards a Theory of Type Structure" Proc. Paris Colloquium on Programming (1974) pp 408 - 425

[Str67]   C. Strachey "Fundamental Concepts in Programming Languages" Oxford University Press (1967)

9.   Appendix: formal models

The models are described as extensions. For each one, extensions to the type and expression syntax are given first, followed by type rules and a denotational semantics for the new syntactic constructs. Where necessary, metaoperations in the semantic context are described subsequently.

9.1. Dynamic typing

T   ::=   ... | any

E   ::=   ... | inject(E) | project E as x : T in E

$$\frac{\pi \vdash e : t}{\pi \vdash inject(\ e\ ) : any} \qquad \frac{\pi \vdash e_1 : any \qquad \pi\ ;\ x : t \vdash e_2 : t_1}{\pi \vdash project\ e_1\ as\ x : t\ in\ e_2 : t_1}$$

$[\![inject(\ e : t\ )]\!]_\emptyset = formDynamic([\![e]\!]_\emptyset, typeRep(\ t\ ))$

$[\![project\ e_1\ as\ x : t\ in\ e_2]\!]_\emptyset =$ if $typeEquiv(\ typeRep(\ t\ ), dTypeRep([\![e_1]\!]_\emptyset))$

then $[\![e_2]\!]_\emptyset\ ;\ x = dValRep([\![e_1]\!]_\emptyset)$

else fail

Semantic context:

$$dValRep(formDynamic(\text{val, trep})) \quad = \quad \text{val}$$

$$dTypeRep(formDynamic(\text{val, trep})) \quad = \quad \text{trep}$$

Examples of the functions *typeRep* and *typeEquiv* for a sophisticated polymorphic language are given in [Con90], and are too complex to repeat here. It should be noted, however, that in a persistent system the evaluation of *typeRep* can usually be completed at compilation time, and the value made available in the evaluation context.

9.2. Persistent naming and binding

$$E \quad ::= \quad \dots \mid \text{intern}(\ E\ ) \mid \text{extern}(\ E\ ,\ E\ )$$

$$\frac{\pi \vdash e : \text{string}}{\pi \vdash \text{intern}(\ e\ ) : \text{any}} \qquad \frac{\pi \vdash e_1 : \text{string} \qquad \pi \vdash e_2 : \text{any}}{\pi \vdash \text{extern}(\ e_1, e_2\ ) : \text{unit}}$$

$$[\![\text{intern}(\ e\ )]\!]_\emptyset \quad = \quad getFromPersistentStore([\![e]\!]_\emptyset)$$

$$[\![\text{extern}(\ e_1, e_2\ )]\!]_\emptyset \quad = \quad placeInPersistentStore([\![e_1]\!]_\emptyset, [\![e_2]\!]_\emptyset)$$

The funtions *getFromPersistentStore* and *placeInPersistentStore* simply represent abstractions of the code of a persistent object store suitable for the language under consideration. The implementation of these abstractions is of course a non-trivial task!

9.3. Universally quantified procedures - type substitution model

The typings in the next three sections rely upon the concept of a unique quantifier model. This is captured by a function *uniqueQ*, a function of no arguments which returns a type representation recognisable as a member of the set *quantifierRep*. For each invocation, *uniqueQ* returns a new unique type representation which is equivalent only with itself under the *typeEquiv* function. As explained in [Con90], when typechecking a persistent system the same *typeEquiv* function may be used for both static and dynamic checking, and calls to *uniqueQ* therefore occur in both type rules and semantics.

To avoid complication in the rules shown here, type alias bindings are included in the type assignment; the meaning is unambiguous as long as the same identifiers are not overloaded as types and values. In some of the examples, corresponding run-time type representations are similarly modelled in the run-time environment.

The syntax e[x ← f] is used to denote the substitution of the variable x by the expression f throughout the expression e.

T   ::=   ... | proc[forall t](T → T) | t

E   ::=   ... | proc[forall t](x : T → T) ; E | E[T](E)

$$\frac{\pi \; ; t = uniqueQ() \; ; x : t_1 \vdash e : t_2}{\pi \vdash proc[\ forall\ t\ ](\ x : t_1 \rightarrow t_2\ ) \; ; e : proc[\ forall\ t\ ](\ t_1 \rightarrow t_2\ )}$$

$$\frac{\pi \vdash e_1 : proc[\ forall\ t\ ](\ t_1 \rightarrow t_2\ ) \qquad \pi \vdash e_2 : t_1[\ t \leftarrow t_0\ ]}{\pi \vdash e_1[\ t_0\ ](\ e_2\ ) : t_2[\ t \leftarrow t_0\ ]}$$

$[\![$ proc[forall t](x : t_1 → t_2) ; e $]\!]_\emptyset$ = $formPolyClosure($ e, t, x, $\emptyset$)

$[\![$ $e_1[\ t_1\ ](\ e_2\ )$ $]\!]_\emptyset$ =

   let E1 = $[\![$ e1 $]\!]_\emptyset$ in

   $[\![$ $code($ E1 $)[$ $typeParam($ E1 $) \leftarrow t_1\ ]$ $]\!]$closure$($ E1 $)$; $param($ E1 $) = [\![$ e2 $]\!]_\emptyset$

Semantic context:

$code($ $formPolyClosure($ e, t, x, $\emptyset$)) = e

$typeParam($ $formPolyClosure($ e, t, x, $\emptyset$)) = t

$param($ $formPolyClosure($ e, t, x, $\emptyset$)) = x

$closure($ $formPolyClosure($ e, t, x, $\emptyset$)) = $\emptyset$

Note that, in terms of the dynamic typing constructs, this semantics introduces no complication to the *typeRep* and *typeEquiv* functions. It does mean, however, that the function *typeRep* can no longer always be evaluated at compilation time, as its type argument may not be manifest.

9.4.   Universally quantified procedures - Napier88 model

T   ::=   ... | proc[forall t](T → T) | t

E   ::=   ... | proc[forall t](x : T → T) ; E | E[T](E)

$$\frac{\pi \; ; \; t = uniqueQ() \; ; \; x : t_1 \vdash e : t_2}{\pi \vdash proc[\; forall\; t\;](\; x : t_1 \rightarrow t_2\;)\; ; \; e : proc[\; forall\; t\;](\; t_1 \rightarrow t_2\;)}$$

$$\frac{\pi \vdash e_1 : proc[\; forall\; t\;](\; t_1 \rightarrow t_2\;) \qquad \pi \vdash e_2 : t_1[\; t \leftarrow t_0\;]}{\pi \vdash e_1[\; t_0\;](\; e_2\;) : t_2[\; t \leftarrow t_0\;]}$$

$$[\![\; proc[\; forall\; t\;](\; x : t_1 \rightarrow t_2\;)\; ; \; e\;]\!]_\emptyset \qquad = \qquad formPolyClosure(\; e, t, x, \emptyset\;)$$

$$[\![\; e_1[\; t_1\;](\; e_2\;)\;]\!]_\emptyset =$$

let $E1 = [\![\; e_1\;]\!]_\emptyset$ in

$$[\![\; code(\; E1\;)\;]\!]_{closure(\; E1\;)}\; ; \; param(\; E1\;) = [\![\; e2\;]\!]_\emptyset\; ; \; typeParam(\; E1\;) = uniqueQ()$$

The static typing in this model is exacly the same as in the last, as is the meaning of a closure formation. The key difference is in the semantics of application, where the formal type parameter is not substituted before the evaluation of the procedure body. With respect to dynamic typing, this means that the *typeRep* function is interpreted over a formal parameter, typed as a member of *quantifierRep*, rather than a concrete type expression. As explained in the running text, the model used is to create a unique type representation at the procedure call, which here is placed in the dynamic environment named as the type variable itself. Notice that this is a different representation to that used for static typechecking, as a new representation is generated for each call of the procedure.

$$typeRep(\; t\;) \qquad = \qquad lookup(\; t\;), \text{ where } t \in quantifierRep$$

9.5. Existentially quantified procedures

T ::=   ... | proc[exists t]($T \rightarrow T$) | t

E ::=   ... | proc[exists t](x : $T \rightarrow T$) ; E | E(E)

As explained, static typing of existentially quantified procedure formation is once again the same:

$$\frac{\pi \; ; \; t = uniqueQ() \; ; \; x : t_1 \vdash e : t_2}{\pi \vdash proc[\; exists\; t\;](\; x : t_1 \rightarrow t_2\;)\; ; \; e : proc[\; exists\; t\;](\; t_1 \rightarrow t_2\;)}$$

Typing of the applications is different however, as specialisation type information is not provided. A type unification function is required, defined by

$$unify(\ t,\ t_1,\ t_2\ ) = S \text{ where } t_1 = t_2[\ t \leftarrow S\ ]$$

$$\frac{\pi \vdash e_1 : proc[\ exists\ t\ ](\ t_1 \rightarrow t_2\ ) \qquad \pi \vdash e_2 : t_1}{\pi \vdash e_1(\ e_2\ ) : t_2}$$

$$iff\ t\ not\_free\_in\ t_1\ ,\ t_2$$

$$\frac{\pi \vdash e_1 : proc[\ exists\ t\ ](\ t_1 \rightarrow t_2\ ) \qquad \pi \vdash e_2 : t_3 \qquad S = unify(\ t,\ t_3,\ t_2\ )}{\pi \vdash e_1(\ e_2\ ) : t_2[\ t \leftarrow S\ ]}$$

$$iff\ t\ free\_in\ t_1$$

$$\frac{\pi \vdash e_1 : proc[\ exists\ t\ ](\ t_1 \rightarrow t_2\ ) \qquad \pi \vdash e_2 : t_1}{\pi \vdash e_1(\ e_2\ ) : t_2[\ t \leftarrow uniqueQ()\ ]}$$

$$iff\ t\ not\_free\_in\ t_1,\ t\ free\_in\ t_2$$

$$[\![\ proc[\ exists\ t\ ](\ x : t_1 \rightarrow t_2\ ) ; e\ ]\!]_{\emptyset} \quad = \quad formPolyClosure(\ e,\ t,\ x,\ \emptyset\ )$$

If the existential quantifier appears free in the formal parameter, application is defined the same as for the type substitution model of parametric polymorphism:

$$[\![\ e_1 : proc[\ exists\ t\ ](\ t_1 \rightarrow t_2\ )(\ e_2 : t_3\ )\ ]\!]_{\emptyset} \quad =$$

let $E1 = [\![\ e_1\ ]\!]_{\emptyset}$ and $env1 = closure(\ E1\ )\ ;\ param(\ E1\ ) = [\![\ e_2\ ]\!]_{\emptyset}$ in

$$[\![\ code(\ E1\ )[\ typeParam(\ E1\ ) \leftarrow unify(\ t,\ t_3,\ t_2\ )\ ]\ ]\!]env1$$

Otherwise, it is defined as follows:

$$[\![\ e_1(\ e_2)\ ]\!]_{\emptyset} \quad =$$

let $E1 = [\![\ e_1\ ]\!]_{\emptyset}$ in

$$[\![\ code(\ E1\ )[\ typeParam(\ E1\ ) \leftarrow uniqueQ()\ ]\ ]\!]closure(\ E1\ )\ ;\ param(\ E1\ ) = [\![\ e_2\ ]\!]_{\emptyset}$$

The last requirement is to provide an alternative form of projection and injection semantics for cases where quantifier resolution is required. This requires a dynamic update to the type representation associated with the quantifier. To achieve this, we attach a location to the representation returned by *uniqueQ*, and the following functions:

$$isResolved(\ quantifierRep \rightarrow bool\ )$$

$$updateQRep(\ quantierRep,\ typeRep \rightarrow unit\ )$$

$$getQRep(\ quantifierRep \rightarrow typeRep\ )$$

isResolved returns *false* when applied to any instance of *quantifierRep* type until such time as *updateQRep* has been applied to it, after which it returns true. *getQRep* returns the type passed in by a previous call of *updateQRep*. This gives enough functionality for the first call to *typeEquiv* to perform the necessary dynamic resolution of that representation:

$$typeEquiv(\ t_1, t_2\ ) \quad = \quad (\ t_1 \in quantifierRep\ )$$

$$\text{if } isResolved(\ t_1\ )$$

$$\text{then } typeEquiv(\ getQRep(\ t_1\ ), t_2\ )$$

$$\text{else } \{\ updateQRep(\ t_1, t_2\ )\ ;\ true\ \}$$

$$typeRep(\ t\ ) \quad = \quad getQRep(\ lookup(\ t\ )\ ), \text{ where } t \in quantifierRep$$

Querying Sequence Databases with Transducers

Anthony J. Bonner[1] and Giansalvatore Mecca[2]

[1] University of Toronto – Department of Computer Science – Toronto, ON, Canada
http://www.cs.toronto.edu/~bonner

[2] D.I.F.A. – Università della Basilicata – via della Tecnica, 3 – 85100 Potenza, Italy
http://poincare.inf.uniroma3.it:8080/~mecca

Abstract. This paper develops a database query language called *Transducer Datalog* motivated by the needs of a new and emerging class of database applications. In these applications, such as text databases and genome databases, the storage and manipulation of long character sequences is a crucial feature. The issues involved in managing this kind of data are not addressed by traditional database systems, either in theory or in practice. To address these issues, in recent work, we introduced a new machine model called a *generalized sequence transducer*. These generalized transducers extend ordinary transducers by allowing them to invoke other transducers as "subroutines." This paper establishes the computational properties of Transducer Datalog, a query language based on this new machine model. In the process, we develop a hierarchy of time-complexity classes based on the Ackermann function. The lower levels of this hierarchy correspond to well-known complexity classes, such as polynomial time and hyper-exponential time. We establish a tight relationship between levels in this hierarchy and the depth of subroutine calls within Transducer Datalog programs. Finally, we show that Transducer Datalog programs of arbitrary depth express exactly the sequence functions computable in primitive-recursive time.

1 Introduction

This paper develops a database query language, called *Transducer Datalog*, motivated by the needs of a new and emerging class of database applications. In these applications, such as text databases and genome databases, the storage and manipulation of long sequences is a crucial feature [12, 10]. The issues involved in managing this kind of data are not addressed by traditional database systems, either in theory or in practice. In particular, traditional database query languages are poor at manipulating sequence data. This is because they treat data items as atomic entities without any internal structure. Thus, they cannot interrogate or manipulate the sequential structure of items such as documents, DNA sequences and protein sequences.

To address this limitation, sequence operations have been introduced into recent data models and query languages (e.g. [4, 7]). In many cases, however, the sequence operations are *ad hoc* and are not investigated in a theoretical framework. In other cases, (e.g. [17, 26]) the operations are designed for pattern extraction but not for sequence restructuring. Although pattern recognition is a fundamental feature of any language for querying sequences, sequence restructurings are equally important. For example, in genome databases, one frequently needs to concatenate sequences together, to splice out selected subsequences, and to compute the reverse of a sequence.

Introducing sequence operations into database query languages presents interesting theoretical challenges. For instance, the resulting query language should be *expressive* both in terms of pattern matching and sequence restructurings. At the same time, it should be *safe*; that is, a query should always return a finite answer and terminate in a finite amount of time. Unlike traditional databases, safety and finiteness of computations are major problems in sequence databases, since sequences can grow to arbitrary length, and the set of possible sequences is infinite, even when the underlying alphabet—or domain—is finite. This means that, unlike traditional database queries, sequence queries can end up in non-terminating computations.

To achieve expressiveness, database researchers have developed sequence query languages based on abstract machines, such as automata or *transducers*. Unfortunately, the resulting languages are unsafe, and to achieve safety, syntactic restrictions have been imposed, restrictions that severely limit expressiveness (*e.g.*, [11, 14]). To resolve these problems, we recently developed a query language for sequence data called *Transducer Datalog* [22, 6, 20], which extends classical Datalog [8] so that it can handle sequence data. A key element in Transducer Datalog is a new machine model called a *generalized sequence transducer*. Intuitively, a generalized transducer is a transducer that can invoke other transducers as "subroutines." These *subtransducers* can likewise invoke other transducers as sub-subroutines. Etc. Like ordinary transducers, generalized transducers always terminate. The result is a query language for sequence databases that is safe; moreover, because generalized transducers are more powerful than ordinary transducers, the query language has considerable expressive power, and its computational complexity can be tuned by restricting the transducers used in the language. These properties of the query language, which are a result of the computational properties of the generalized transducers, are studied in this paper.

By coupling a declarative query language, like Datalog, with a procedural model of computation, like generalized transducers, we have been able to develop a flexible paradigm for querying sequence databases. In Transducer Datalog, set-oriented database operations are easily expressed using a semantics based on Datalog, while powerful sequence manipulation procedures can be programmed using transducers. The language itself combines database query primitives with a powerful computational model for sequences, which is an important requirement for sequence databases. For example, in genome databases, because genome-technology is rapidly evolving, new sequence operations are constantly needed, operations that cannot be anticipated in advance. Genome databases thus need to combine a query language with arbitrary procedures for executing sequence operations [13]. Clearly, different models of computation could be embedded in the query language to achieve the same goal. However, unlike other models, generalized transducers are highly modular, and although very powerful, they preserve finiteness and allow one to tune the complexity of the language.

In previous work ([22, 6]), we established the complexity and expressibility of a simple class of generalized transducers, namely those with at most two levels of subtransducer calls. In this paper, we generalize and extend those results by characterizing the complexity of arbitrarily nested transducers. Section 3 first reviews the definition of generalized transducers. It then introduces a restriction called *controlled feedback*, and shows that this leads to an elegant characterization of the complexity and expressibility of generalized transducers in terms of the Ackermann function [2, 25].

Section 4 reviews the query language Transducer Datalog, which is obtained by enriching classical Datalog with interpreted function terms called *transducer terms*. This language allows a user to compose transducers and combine them into "networks," in which the output of one transducer is fed to the inputs of other transducers. The language is an extension of Horn logic and is capable of expressing *sequence queries*, *i.e.*, queries to databases containing sequences over a fixed alphabet. The expressive power of classical Datalog grows dramatically when transducers are added to it. We show, for instance, that Transducer Datalog with stratified negation is computationally complete for sequence databases. This completeness result extends our previous results on function expressibility [22, 6] to query expressibility.

Like classical Datalog, queries in Transducer Datalog can be recursive. However, in Transducer Datalog, the combination of recursion and transducers allows queries to be infinite and non-terminating. To guarantee finiteness and termination, we previously introduced a syntactic restriction called *safety*, in which recursion through transducer terms is not allowed [22, 6, 20]. Section 5 reviews the definition of safety, and then establishes several new expressibility results for safe programs. We show in particular that the complexity of a safe program depends on its *order*, *i.e.*, on the maximum depth to which transducers are invoked as subroutines. Formally, we first develop a hierarchy of time-complexity classes based on the Ackermann function [2, 25]. We then show that the lower levels of this hierarchy correspond to well-known complexity classes, such as PTIME and the *elementary functions* [24], i.e. hyper-exponential time. This extends the complexity results of our previous work [22, 6]. Finally, we show that safe programs of order k express exactly the sequence functions in the kth level of this hierarchy. As a corollary, we show that safe Transducer Datalog expresses exactly the sequence functions computable in primitive-recursive time.

The query completeness result and the characterization in terms of the Ackermann complexity hierarchy represent the main contributions of the paper. For space reasons, proofs are omitted and can be found in the full paper [5].

Note that the Ackermann hierarchy is somewhat similar to the *Grzegorczyk hierarchy* [16] of primitive recursive functions. However, the latter is based on a different set of initial functions and each level is obtained by closure with respect to substitution and bounded primitive recursion, instead of function composition.

In [18] a hierarchy of primitive recursive functions based on the Grzegorczyk hierarchy is presented to characterize the behavior of a family of finite automata. However, unlike the generalized transducers used here, the machines used in [18] are not finite state devices in the usual sense, since a "state" is essentially a counter, so a machine of this kind can have infinitely many states. In contrast, generalized transducers have a finite number of states.

Other characterizations of the primitive recursive functions have been presented in the literature. For instance, a characterization in terms of *loop programs* is developed in [23]. The complexity of loop programs is also based on a hierarchy of complexity classes; however, the latter is different from the Ackermann's hierarchy developed in this paper, since, for example, there is no level equivalent to PTIME.

2 Preliminary Definitions

This section provides technical definitions used in the rest of the paper, including *sequence database*, *sequence query* and *sequence function*.

Let Σ be a countable set of symbols, called the *alphabet*. Σ^* denotes the set of all possible sequences over Σ, including the *empty sequence*, ϵ. We now describe an extension of the relational model, in the spirit of [11, 14]. The model allows for tuples containing sequences of elements, instead of just constant symbols. A *relation* of arity k over Σ is a finite subset of the k-fold Cartesian product of Σ^* with itself. A *database* over Σ is a finite set of relations over Σ. We assign a distinct predicate symbol of appropriate arity to each relation in a database.

A *sequence query* is a partial mapping from the databases over Σ to the relations over Σ. Given a sequence query, Q, and a database, DB, Q(DB) is the result of evaluating Q over DB. Usually, a notion of *genericity* [9] is introduced for queries. The notion can be extended to sequence queries in a natural way. To do this, we consider permutations of alphabet symbols in Σ, that is, one-to-one mappings $\rho : \Sigma \to \Sigma$ of Σ onto itself; permutations can be extended in a natural way to strings in Σ^*, tuples of strings, relations and databases. We say that a sequence query Q is *generic* if, for each permutation ρ of alphabet symbols, Q commutes with ρ, that is, for every database DB such that Q is defined on DB, it is the case that: $Q(\rho(\text{DB})) = \rho(Q(\text{DB}))$. We say that a sequence query Q is *computable* [9] if it is generic and partial recursive.

A *sequence function* is a partial mapping from Σ^* to itself. Sequence functions can be thought of as queries from a database, $\{input(\sigma_{in})\}$, containing a single sequence tuple, to a relation, $\{output(\sigma_{out})\}$, containing a single sequence tuple. Thus, we say that a language, L, expresses a sequence function if it expresses the corresponding query. A sequence function f is *computable* if it is partial recursive. This paper focuses on sequence functions for which the alphabet, Σ, is finite. Of course, the domain of such functions may still be infinite; e.g., it may be all of Σ^*.

In this paper, we address the complexity of sequence functions, and the data complexity [28] of sequence queries. Given a sequence function, f, the *complexity* of f is defined in the usual way, as the complexity of computing $f(\sigma_{in})$, measured with respect to the length of the input sequence, σ_{in}. Given a sequence query, Q, a database, DB, and a suitable encoding of DB as a Turing machine tape, the *data complexity* of Q is the complexity of computing an encoding of $Q(\text{DB})$, measured with respect to the size of DB.

A language, L, is said to *express* a class C of sequence functions, if (i) each sequence function expressible in L has complexity in C, and conversely, (ii) each sequence function with complexity in C can be expressed in L. Likewise, we say that a language L *expresses* a class QC of queries if (i) each sequence query expressible in L has complexity in C, and conversely, (ii) each sequence query with complexity in C can be expressed in L.

3 Generalized Sequence Transducers

The notion of generalized sequence transducer was introduced in [22, 6, 20]. After reviewing the definition, this section introduces a restriction called *controlled feedback*, and shows that it leads to a characterization of the complexity of generalized transducers in terms of the Ackermann function [2, 25].

Ordinary *transducers* – i.e., finite state machines with n input lines and one output line – have very low complexity—essentially linear time. There are therefore many sequence restructurings that they cannot perform. To allow for more complex restructurings, we introduce a new computational device, which we call a *generalized sequence transducer*.

Intuitively, a generalized transducer is a transducer that can invoke another transducer as a subroutine. At each step of a computation, a generalized transducer must consume an input symbol, and may append a new symbol to its output, just like an ordinary transducer. In addition, at each step, a generalized transducer may transform its entire output sequence by sending it to another transducer, which we call a *subtransducer*. This process of invoking subtransducers may continue to many levels. Thus a subtransducer may transform its own output by invoking a sub-subtransducer, etc. Subtransducers are analogous to subroutine calls in programming languages, and to some extent, to oracle Turing machines of low complexity.

We shall actually define a hierarchy of transducers. $\mathcal{T}^k$ represents the set of generalized transducers that invoke subtransducers to a maximum depth of $k-1$; k is called the *order* of the transducer. $\mathcal{T}^1$ thus represents the set of ordinary transducers, which do not invoke any subtransducers. We define $\mathcal{T}^{k+1}$ in terms of $\mathcal{T}^k$, where $\mathcal{T}^0$ is the empty set. For convenience, we shall often refer to members of $\mathcal{T}^1$ as *base transducers*, and to any generalized sequence transducer simply as a transducer.

To formally define the notion of generalized sequence transducers, we use three special symbols, $\triangleleft$, $\rightarrow$ and $-$. $\triangleleft$ is an end-of-tape marker, and is the last symbol (rightmost) of every input tape. $\rightarrow$ and $-$ are commands for the input tape heads: $\rightarrow$ tells a tape head to move one symbol to the right (*i.e.*, to consume an input symbol); and $-$ tells a tape head to stay where it is. Although the following definition is for deterministic transducers, it can easily be generalized to allow nondeterministic computations. As such, it generalizes other transducer models proposed in the literature (for example, see [11, 27]).

A *generalized n-input sequence transducer* of *order k* (for $k > 0$) is a 4-tuple $\langle K, q_0, \Sigma, \delta \rangle$ where: *(1)* K is a finite set of elements, called *states*; *(2)* $q_0 \in K$ is a distinguished state, called the *initial state*; *(3)* Σ is a finite set of symbols, not including the special symbols, called the *alphabet*; *(4)* δ is a partial mapping from $K \times \{\Sigma \cup \{\triangleleft\}\}^n$ to $K \times \{-, \to\}^n \times \{\Sigma \cup \{\epsilon\} \cup T^{k-1}\}$, called the *transition function*. T^k consists of all generalized transducers of order at most k, for $k > 0$; $T^0 = \{\}$.

For each transition, $\delta(q, a_1, \ldots, a_n)$ of the form $\langle q', c_1, \ldots, c_n, \text{OUT} \rangle$, we impose three restrictions: *(i)* at least one of the c_i must be $\to$, *(ii)* if $a_i = \triangleleft$ then $c_i = -$, and *(iii)* if $\text{OUT} \in T^{k-1}$ then it must be an $n+1$-ary transducer. These restrictions have a simple interpretation. Restriction *(i)* says that at least one input symbol must be consumed at each step of a computation (c_i is a command to input head i). Restriction *(ii)* says that an input head cannot move past the end of its tape (a_i is the symbol below input head i). Restriction *(iii)* says that a subtransducer must have one more input than its calling transducer.

The computation of a generalized sequence transducer over input strings $\langle \sigma_1, \ldots, \sigma_n \rangle$ proceeds as follows. To start, the machine is in its initial state, q_0, each input head scans the first (*i.e.*, leftmost) symbol of its tape, and the output tape is empty. At each point of the computation, the internal state and the tape symbols below the input heads determine what transition to perform. If the internal state is q and the tape symbols are $a_1 \ldots a_n$, then the transition is $\delta(q, a_1, \ldots, a_n) = \langle q', c_1, \ldots, c_n, \text{OUT} \rangle$. This transition is carried out as follows:

- If OUT is a symbol in Σ, then it is appended to the output sequence; if $\text{OUT} = \epsilon$, then the output is unchanged. This takes constant time.
- If OUT represents a call to a transducer $T \in T^{k-1}$ then T is invoked as a subtransducer. In this case, the transducer suspends its computation, and the subtransducer begins. The subtransducer has $n+1$ inputs: a copy of each input of the calling transducer, plus a copy of its current output. When the subtransducer starts, its head scan the first symbol of the corresponding input tape, and the output tape is initialized to the empty sequence. The transfer of control and initialization of the subtransducer takes constant time. The subtransducer then consumes its inputs and produces an output sequence. When it is finished, the output of the subtransducer is copied to (overwrites) the output tape of the calling transducer. The overwriting takes constant time.
- The transducer "consumes" some input by moving at least one tape head one symbol to the right. This takes constant time.
- The transducer enters the next state, q', and resumes its computation. This takes constant time.

The transducer stops when every input tape has been completely consumed, that is, when every input head reads the symbol $\triangleleft$. Since transducers (and subtransducers) must consume all their input, the computation of every generalized transducer is guaranteed to terminate.

Finally, note that an n-ary transducer defines a *sequence mapping, T* : $(\Sigma^*)^n \to \Sigma^*$, where $T(\sigma_1, \ldots, \sigma_n)$ is the output of the transducer on inputs $\sigma_1, \ldots, \sigma_n$. Generalized transducers express a much wider class of mappings than ordinary transducers. For instance, they can compute outputs whose length is polynomial and even exponential in the input lengths, as illustrated in Example 1.

step	input	output	operation	new output
1	a bc◁	ϵ	invoke T_{append}	abc
2	a b c◁	abc	invoke T_{append}	abcabc
3	ab c ◁	abcabc	invoke T_{append}	abcabcabc

Fig. 1. Squaring the input.

This table illustrates the computation of transducer T_{square} from Example 1 on the input sequence abc. Each row of the table represents one step of the computation. The column labelled "input" shows the position of the input head just before the step, the column labelled "output" shows the contents of the output tape just before the step, and the column labelled "new output" shows the contents of the output tape just after the step. The column labelled "operation" describes what the step does. The table shows that at each step, T_{square} appends a copy of its input to its output by invoking the subtransducer T_{append}.

Example 1. [**Quadratic Output**] Let T_{square} be a generalized transducer with one input and one subtransducer. At each computation step, T_{square} appends a copy of its input to its output. After k steps, the output consists of k copies of the input concatenated together. At the end of the entire computation, the output has length n^2, where n is the length of the input. To append its input to its output, T_{square} invokes a subtransducer called T_{append} with two inputs. One input to T_{append} is the input to T_{square} and the other input is the output of T_{square}. T_{append} simply appends its two inputs. The output of T_{append} then becomes the output for T_{square}, overwriting the old output.

To illustrate the combined effect of transducer and subtransducer, let σ_{in} be the input to T_{square}. Just before the ith invocation of the subtransducer, one input to T_{append} is σ_{in} and the other input is $i-1$ copies of σ_{in} concatenated together. Thus, when T_{append} finishes this computation, its output is i copies of σ_{in} concatenated together. This behaviour is illustrated in Figure 1, in which the transducer input is abc, and the output is abcabcabc.

3.1   Controlled Feedback

In [22, 6], we established the complexity of generalized transducers of order 2 and 3. This paper extends those results to transducers of arbitrary order. To do this, we focus on a transducer model that is slightly more restrictive than the one described above, but which is identical to it for transducers of order 1 and 2.

In the generalized transducer model developed above, a subtransducer has access to all the input lines of the transducer that invoked it, plus a copy of its output line. A subtransducer thus has one more input than its parent. Consequently, suppose that transducer T_1 invokes T_2, which invokes T_3, which invokes... T_i, which invokes T_{i+1}. Then the input to transducer T_{i+1} consists of copies of all the inputs to T_1 plus all the outputs of $T_1, T_2, ..., T_i$. Thus, if T_1 has n inputs, then T_{i+1} has $n + i$ inputs, as illustrated in Figure 2(a).

To reduce the amount of feedback and simplify the computation, we now restrict the model. In the restricted transducer model, a subtransducer has access to the output line of the transducer that invoked it (its "parent"), but *not* the output lines of any higher transducers. Thus, the input to transducer T_{i+1} above includes the output of T_i, but *not* the outputs of $T_1, ..., T_{i-1}$. To formalize this idea, we provide each transducer with a single *distinguished input* line. When a transducer invokes a subtransducer, all non-distinguished inputs of the transducer become non-distinguished inputs of the subtransducer. In addition, the output of the transducer becomes the distinguished input of the subtransducer. In this way, all non-distinguished inputs are passed from a transducer to all its descendants, but the output is passed only to the transducer's immediate descendants (its "children"). We define the distinguished input to the top-level transducer to be the empty sequence.

Consequently, suppose that transducer T_1 invokes T_2, which invokes T_3, which invokes... T_i, where T_1 is the top-level transducer. Then, the non-distinguished inputs of each T_j are a copy of the non-distinguished inputs of T_1. In addition, the distinguished input of T_1 is empty, and the distinguished input of T_{j+1} is a copy of the output of T_j, for $1 \leq j < i$. Each transducer T_j thus has the *same* number of inputs. Moreover, since all output lines are initially empty, all distinguished input lines are initially empty too. These ideas are illustrated in Figure 2(b). Because this model restricts the amount of feedback from outputs to inputs within a generalized transducer, we refer to it as the model with *controlled feedback*.

In the following sections, we will always refer to transducers with controlled feedback. Note, however, that the distinction is significant only for transducers of order greater than 2, since for orders 1 and 2, the distinction is irrelevant.

3.2   Complexity of Generalized Transducers

We are now ready to establish two important results about the complexity of generalized sequence transducers. We shall see that the deterministic time complexity of a transducer is closely related to the *Ackermann function* [2, 25], also

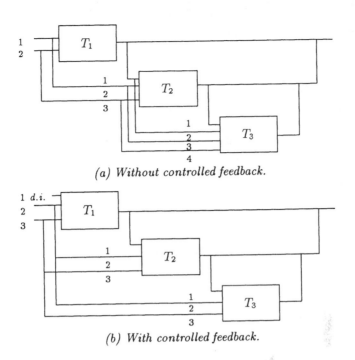

(a) Without controlled feedback.

(b) With controlled feedback.

Fig. 2. An order-3 transducer with and without controlled feedback. T_1 *is the top-level transducer,* T_2 *is a subtransducer of* T_1*, and* T_3 *is a sub-subtransducer. In (b), the distinguished input (d.i.) of* T_1 *is empty, by convention.*

called the *generalized exponential function*. This is a ternary function $\text{ACK}(k, x, y)$ such that:

$$\text{ACK}(1, x, y) = y + x,$$
$$\text{ACK}(2, x, y) = yx,$$
$$\text{ACK}(3, x, y) = y^x,$$
$$\dots$$

We call the first argument, k, the *level* of the function. For each level, $\text{ACK}(k, x, y)$ can be viewed as a function of two variables, x and y. Thus, the first levels of the function capture well known operations: level 1 is *addition*, level 2 is *multiplication*, and level 3 is *exponentiation*. Formally, the Ackermann function is defined using double induction, as follows:

Definition 1. (Ackermann's Function)[3] For $k, x, y \geq 0$,

---

[3] This definition is a minor variant of the definition given in [2]. In particular, $\text{ACK}(k, x, y)$ in our definition coincides with $\text{ACK}(k - 1, x, y)$ in the definition of [2].

$$
\begin{aligned}
\text{ACK}(0, x, y) &= 0, \\
\text{ACK}(1, 0, y) &= y, \\
\text{ACK}(1, x + 1, y) &= \text{ACK}(1, x, y) + 1, \\
\text{ACK}(2, 0, y) &= 0, \\
\text{ACK}(k, 0, y) &= 1, \quad \text{for all } k > 2, \\
\text{ACK}(k + 1, x + 1, y) &= \text{ACK}(k, \text{ACK}(k + 1, x, y), y), \quad \text{for all } k \geq 1.
\end{aligned}
$$

This paper uses mainly a one-argument version of the Ackermann function in which x is equal to y and the level, k, is fixed. We therefore define the following: $\text{ACK}_k(y) = \text{ACK}(k, y, y)$.

The following theorem provides an upper bound on the time complexity of generalized transducers with controlled feedback in terms of the Ackermann function.

Theorem 2. (Upper Complexity Bound) *Given a generalized transducer of order k, its running time (and output length) is $\text{ACK}_k(\mathcal{O}(n))$, where n is the sum of the input lengths.*

The next theorem shows that the relationship between generalized transducers and the Ackermann function is even closer. In particular, for each k, the function $\text{ACK}(k, x, y)$ can be computed by a generalized transducer of order k. This result is based on a unary encoding of integers. An integer n is thus encoded as a sequence of length n consisting of n occurrences of the same character, $\#$. We say that a transducer *computes* an integer function $v = f(w)$ if on input $\#^w$, of length w, it produces the output $\#^{f(w)}$, of length $f(w)$.

Theorem 3. (Computing Ackermann's Function) *For every integer $k \geq 1$, there is a generalized sequence transducer of order k with 2 inputs that computes $\text{ACK}(k, x, y)$. That is, for all inputs x, y with $x > 0$, the output of the transducer is $\text{ACK}(k, x, y)$.*

Theorem 3 shows that the upper bound in Theorem 2 is tight. These results will prove useful in the following sections.

4 Transducer Datalog

In [22, 6, 20], we developed a query language for sequence databases by incorporating generalized transducers into classical Datalog [8]. This language allows an application programmer to use the framework of classical Datalog to combine generalized transducers into *networks*, in which the output of one transducer can be fed to the inputs of other transducers. Such networks greatly increase the ability of Transducer Datalog to express database queries, as we shall see. This section first reviews the syntax and semantics of Transducer Datalog, and then shows that it is expressively complete for sequence database queries. Due to space limitations, we cannot present the formal semantics of Transducer Datalog here. Instead, we illustrate the semantics informally through examples. The interested reader is referred to [22, 6, 20] for details.

4.1 Syntax and Semantics

To invoke transducer computations from within a logical rule, we augment the syntax of classical Datalog (function-free Horn logic) with special interpreted function symbols, one symbol for each generalized sequence transducer. From these function symbols, we build function terms of the form $T(s_1, \ldots, s_n)$, called *transducer terms*. The term $T(s_1, \ldots, s_n)$ is interpreted as the output of transducer T on inputs $s_1, \ldots, s_n$. Transducer terms are allowed only in the heads of rules. The resulting language is called *Transducer Datalog*. Transducer Datalog uses generalized transducers to manipulate sequences in the language. For example, suppose we want to concatenate every pair of sequences X, Y in predicate q. The following Transducer Datalog program performs this task:

$$p(T_{append}(X, Y)) \leftarrow q(X, Y).$$

where T_{append} is a transducer that concatenates its two inputs. In Transducer Datalog, rules with transducer terms in the head are called *constructive* rules (or clauses), since they can construct new sequences during inference. We also say that a program in Transducer Datalog has *order* k if k is the maximum order of all transducers in the program. A program with no transducers, *i.e.* a classical Datalog program, has order 0.

The semantics of Transducer Datalog generalizes the semantics of classical Datalog. The main change is to extend the interpretation of terms to include transducer terms. To be more precise, the language of terms uses three countable, disjoint sets: a set of constant symbols, $a, b, c, \ldots$, called the *alphabet* and denoted Σ; a set of variables, $R, S, T, \ldots$, called *sequence variables* and denoted V_Σ; and a set of *function symbols*, $T_1, T_2, \ldots$, each with an associated arity. A constant sequence (or *sequence*, for short) is an element of Σ^*. From these sets, we construct the set of *sequence terms* (or *terms*, for short), as follows:

- each constant sequence in Σ^* is a term;
- each sequence variable in V_Σ is a term;
- given n terms $s_1, \ldots, s_n$ and a function symbol T of arity n, $T(s_1, \ldots, s_n)$ is a term, called a *transducer term*; we require that transducer terms not contain other transducer terms; thus, each argument s_i is either a constant sequence or a variable.

As in most logics, the language of formulas for *Transducer Datalog* also includes a countable set of predicate symbols, $p, q, r, \ldots$, each with an associated arity. If p is a predicate symbol of arity n, and $s_1, \ldots, s_n$ are sequence terms, then $p(s_1, \ldots, s_n)$ is an atom. Moreover, if s_1 and s_2 are sequence terms, then $s_1 = s_2$ and $s_1 \neq s_2$ are also atoms. From atoms, we build *facts* and *clauses* in the usual way [19]. A clause that contains a transducer term in its head is called a *constructive clause*. A Transducer Datalog *program* is a set of Transducer Datalog clauses. As usual, we require that each variable occurring in the head of a rule also occur in the body of the rule.

A substitution, θ, is a mapping that associates a sequence with each variable in V_Σ. Substitutions can be extended to mappings on sequence *terms* in a straightforward way. Because these terms are interpreted, the result of a substitution is a constant sequence. Formally, let θ be a substitution. θ is the identity function for each sequence in Σ^*. To extend θ to transducer terms, we define $\theta(T(s_1, \ldots, s_m))$ to be the output of transducer T on inputs $\theta(s_1), \ldots, \theta(s_m)$, where the symbols of each $\theta(s_i)$ are consumed from left to right.

The semantics of clauses is defined in terms of a least fixpoint theory. As in classical logic programming [19, 8], each Transducer Datalog program, P, and database, DB, has an associated operator, $T_{P,\text{DB}}$, that maps relational databases to relational databases. Each application of $T_{P,\text{DB}}$ may create new atoms, which may contain new sequences. We have shown that $T_{P,\text{DB}}$ is monotonic and continuous, and thus has a least fixpoint that can be computed in a bottom-up, iterative fashion [22, 6, 20].

If a Transducer Datalog program has recursion through transducer terms, then the least fixpoint of the program can be infinite. That is, as a result of evaluating transducer terms, new sequences can be computed; and because of recursion, the length of these sequences can be unbounded. In this case, we say that the semantics of P over DB is *infinite*; otherwise, we say it is *finite*.

A Transducer Datalog program can be thought of as a *network* of transducers, and vice-versa. This is because the *result* of a transducer term in one rule can be used as an *argument* for a transducer term in another rule. This corresponds to feeding the output of one transducer to an input of another transducer.

Below we give an example of sequence restructuring in Molecular Biology. It is naturally represented as a transducer network. By embedding this network in Transducer Datalog, an entire database of sequences can be restructured and queried.

Example 2. [**From DNA to RNA to Protein**] Two fundamental operations in Molecular Biology are the transcription of DNA into RNA, and the translation of RNA into protein. All three molecules in this process can be modelled as sequences. DNA molecules are modeled as sequences over the alphabet $\{a, c, g, t\}$, where each character represents a *nucleotide*. RNA molecules are modeled as sequences over the alphabet $\{a, c, g, u\}$, where each character represents a *ribonucleotide*. During transcription, each nucleotide in a DNA sequence is converted into a ribonucleotide in an RNA sequence according to the following rules:

> Each a becomes u.   Each c becomes g.
> Each g becomes c.   Each t becomes a.

For example, the DNA sequence $acgtacgt$ is transcribed into the RNA sequence $ugcaugca$.[4]

Protein molecules are modeled as sequences over a twenty-character alphabet, $\{A, R, N, D, C, Q, E, G, H, I, L, K, M, F, P, S, T, W, Y, V\}$, where each character represents an *amino acid*. To translate RNA into protein, ribonucleotides are grouped into triplets, called *codons*, such as $aug, acg, ggu, \ldots$[5] Each

---

[4] For simplicity, this example ignores biological complications such as intron splicing [29], even though it can be encoded in Transducer Datalog without difficulty.

[5] This grouping is analogous to the grouping of *bits* into *bytes* in computers.

codon is then translated into a single amino-acid. Different codons may have the same translation. For example, the codons *gau* and *gac* both translate to *aspartic acid*, denoted D in the twenty-letter alphabet. Thus, the RNA sequence *gaugacuuacac* is first grouped into a sequence of four codons, *gau/gac/uua/cac*, and then translated into a sequence of four amino acids, DDLH.[6]

The transformation of DNA into the corresponding protein is easily and naturally expressed using a Transducer Datalog program. Given a relation, *dna_seq*, containing DNA sequences, the following Transducer Datalog program associates a protein with each sequence.

$$rna\_seq(D, T_{transcribe}(D)) \leftarrow dna\_seq(D).$$
$$protein\_seq(D, T_{translate}(R)) \leftarrow rna\_seq(D, R).$$

The program implements a simple serial network which transforms DNA into RNA, and then RNA into protein. It uses two sequence transducers: (i) $T_{transcribe}$, in which the input is a DNA sequence, and the output is a RNA sequence; (ii) $T_{translate}$, in which the input is a RNA sequence, and the output is a protein sequence. Intuitively, the predicate $rna\_seq(D, R)$ means that D is a DNA sequence, and R is the corresponding RNA sequence. Likewise, the predicate $protein\_seq(D, P)$ means that D is a DNA sequence, and P is the corresponding protein sequence.

Although the Transducer Datalog program consists of only two rules, two features are worth noting: (*i*) all sequence restructurings performed by the program take place "inside" the transducers; and (*ii*) the program terminates for every database, since there is no recursion through construction of new sequences.

4.2   Expressive Power

Transducer Datalog has considerable power for manipulating sequences, and can express any computable sequence function [22]. However, although Transducer Datalog is function complete, it is not query complete, since it expresses only *monotonic* queries. Thus, like classical Datalog, it cannot express non-monotonic queries, even very simple ones, such as the difference of two database relations. To achieve query completeness, we must add some form of non-monotonicity to the language. We do this by allowing negated atoms in rule bodies, and interpreting negation as failure. To avoid the plethora of problems associated with recursion through negation, we restrict our attention to *stratified negation* [3, 8], which can be extended from classical Datalog to Transducer Datalog in a natural way. The following theorem is the main result about this language, which we call *stratified Transducer Datalog*.

Theorem 4.   (Completeness) *Stratified Transducer Datalog expresses all computable sequence queries.*

---

[6] For simplicity, this example ignores biological complications such as reading frames, ribosomal binding sites, and stop codons [29].

5 Safe Transducer Datalog

In [22, 6, 20], we introduced syntactic restrictions that define a sublanguage of Transducer Datalog called *safe Transducer Datalog*. The restrictions forbid recursion through transducer terms in a rather standard way [1], in order to guarantee that the transducer network corresponding to a Transducer Datalog program is acyclic. From a database perspective, safe Transducer Datalog programs are interesting because they are *finite*, *i.e.*, their least fixpoint is finite for every database [22, 6, 20], and can thus be materialized. This section reviews the definition of safe Transducer Datalog, and establishes results on its expressibility. Formally, we introduce a hierarchy of complexity classes based on the Ackermann function, and then we characterize the expressibility of natural fragments of safe Transducer Datalog in terms of this hierarchy. As a corollary, we show that safe Transducer Datalog expresses exactly the sequence functions computable in primitive-recursive time.

5.1 Safety

Let P be a Transducer Datalog program. We say that a predicate symbol p *depends* on predicate symbol q in program P if for some rule in P, p is the predicate symbol in the head and q is a predicate symbol in the body. If the rule is constructive, then p *depends constructively* on q. Now, let P be a Transducer Datalog program. The *predicate dependency graph* of P is a directed graph whose nodes are the predicate symbols in P. There is an edge from p to q in the graph if p depends on q in program P. The edge is *constructive* if p depends constructively on q. A *constructive cycle* is a cycle in the graph containing a constructive edge.

Definition 5. (Safe Programs) A Transducer Datalog program is *safe* if its predicate dependency graph does not contain any constructive cycles.

The program in Example 2 is safe since it is non-recursive, and thus its dependency graph contains no cycles.

5.2 The Ackermann Time Hierarchy

This section develops a hierarchy of time-complexity classes based on the Ackermann function. This hierarchy will be used in the next subsection to characterize the expressibility of Transducer Datalog programs. In particular, we shall see that programs of order k express exactly the sequence functions in the kth level of the hierarchy.

Our time-complexity classes are defined in terms of repeated function composition. Given a unary function $f(x)$, the *composition* of f with itself i times, denoted $f^{(i)}(x)$, is defined in the usual way: (i) $f^{(1)}(x) = f(x)$; (ii) $f^{(i+1)}(x) = f(f^{(i)}(x))$ for $i \geq 1$. By composing the level-k Ackermann function $\text{ACK}_k(y)$ with itself i times, we obtain a new function, $\text{ACK}_k^{(i)}(y)$. It is not hard to see that for each i, $\text{ACK}_2^{(i)}(y)$ is a polynomial in y, since $\text{ACK}_2(y) = y^2$, and $\text{ACK}_3^{(i)}(y)$ is a hyper exponential in y, since $\text{ACK}_3(y) = y^y$.

132

Definition 6. (Ackermann Time Hierarchy) For each $k \geq 0$, k-ACKTIME is the class of sequence functions computable in deterministic time $\text{ACK}_k^{(i)}(\mathcal{O}(n))$ for some i. That is:

$$k\text{-ACKTIME} = \bigcup_{i \geq 1} \text{DTIME}[\text{ACK}_k^{(i)}(\mathcal{O}(n))]$$

The *Ackermann time hierarchy* is the union of k-ACKTIME for all k:

$$\text{ACK-HIER} = \bigcup_{k \geq 0} k\text{-ACKTIME}$$

The Ackermann time hierarchy has close connections with well-known complexity and computability classes. For instance, it is not hard to see that (i) 2-ACKTIME is PTIME, and (ii) 3-ACKTIME is the class of *elementary sequence functions* [24], that is, the class of sequence functions computable in hyper-exponential time. In addition, the hierarchy is related to the classical notion of *primitive recursive function* [25]. Formally, let PR-TIME denote the class of sequence functions computable in primitive-recursive time. That is, PR-TIME $= \bigcup_{f \in \mathcal{PR}} \text{DTIME}[f(\mathcal{O}(n))]$, where $\mathcal{PR}$ is the set of primitive recursive functions. The Ackermann time hierarchy coincides with this time class; that is ACK-HIER $=$ PR-TIME. These relationships are summarized in Figure 3.

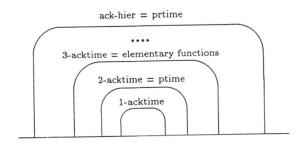

Fig. 3. The Ackermann's hierarchy of complexity classes

Note that the Ackermann hierarchy is somewhat similar to the *Grzegorczyk hierarchy* [16] of primitive recursive functions. However, the latter is based on a different set of initial functions and each level is obtained by closure with respect to substitution and bounded primitive recursion, instead of function composition.

5.3 Expressibility of Safe Programs

The following theorems establish expressibility results for safe Transducer Datalog programs in terms of the Ackermann time hierarchy. All theorems refer to the transducer model with controlled feedback.

Theorem 7. (Safe Programs of Order-k) *Safe Transducer Datalog programs of order k express exactly k-ACKTIME, for $k \geq 2$.*

Note that since 2-ACKTIME is PTIME, and 3-ACKTIME is the class of elementary sequence functions, Theorem 7 leads immediately to Corollaries 8 and 9, below. In [6], we show that Corollary 9 also holds for the unrestricted transducer model developed in Section 3, *i.e.*, the model *without* controlled feedback. The two transducer models are therefore equivalent for order 3. That is, in both models, acyclic transducer networks of order 3 express the same class of sequence functions. Finally, Theorem 7 also leads to Corollary 10, which gives a simple characterization of the expressive power of safe Transducer Datalog programs.

Corollary 8. (Safe Programs of Order-2) *Safe Transducer Datalog programs of order 2 express exactly* PTIME *[22].*

Corollary 9. (Safe Programs of Order-3) *Safe Transducer Datalog programs of order 3 express exactly the elementary sequence functions.*

Corollary 10. (Safe Programs of Arbitrary Order) *Safe Transducer Datalog programs express exactly* PR-TIME, *the class of sequence functions computable in primitive-recursive time.*

Corollary 10 is especially interesting, since it shows that the subtransducer mechanism greatly enhances the power of finite state transducers, taking them well beyond the linear time bound of basic transducers.

Acknowledgements: The authors would like to thank several people for their contributions: Steve Cook, Faith Fich and Charles Rackoff for fruitful discussions on the use of machines for computing sequence functions; and Paolo Atzeni and Victor Vianu for numerous comments and suggestions about the language. The first author was partially supported by an operating grant from the Natural Sciences and Engineering Research Council of Canada (NSERC), and the second author was partially supported by MURST and Consiglio Nazionale delle Ricerche (CNR).

References

1. S. Abiteboul and P. Kanellakis. Object identity as a query language primitive. In *ACM SIGMOD International Conf. on Management of Data*, pages 159–173, 1989.
2. W. Ackermann. Zum Hilbertschen Aufbau der reellen Zahlen. *Math. Annalen*, 99:118–133, 1928.
3. K. Apt, H. Blair, and A. Walker. Towards a theory of declarative knowledge. In J. Minker, editor, *Foundations of Deductive Databases and Logic Programming*, pages 89–148. Morgan Kauffman, Los Altos, 1988.
4. F. Bancilhon, S. Cluet, and C. Delobel. A query language for the O_2 object-oriented database system. In *Second Intern. Workshop on Database Programming Languages (DBPL'89)*, pages 122–138, 1989.

5. A. J. Bonner and G. Mecca. Querying string databases with Transducers. http://poincare.inf.uniroma3.it:8080, 1997.

6. A. J. Bonner and G. Mecca. Sequences, Datalog and Transducers. *Journal of Computing and System Sciences*, Special Issue on PODS'95, 1997. To Appear. http://poincare.inf.uniroma3.it:8080.

7. R. G. G. Cattel. *The Object Database Standard ODMG-93*. Morgan Kaufmann Publishers, San Francisco, CA, 1994.

8. S. Ceri, G. Gottlob, and L. Tanca. *Logic Programming and Data Bases*. Springer-Verlag, 1989.

9. A. K. Chandra and D. Harel. Computable queries for relational databases. *Journal of Computing and System Sciences*, 21:333–347, 1980.

10. Communications of the ACM. Special issue on the Human Genome project. vol. 34(11), November 1991.

11. S. Ginsburg and X. Wang. Pattern matching by RS-operations: towards a unified approach to querying sequence data. In *Eleventh ACM SIGACT SIGMOD SIGART Symp. on Principles of Database Systems (PODS'92)*, pages 293–300, 1992.

12. G. H. Gonnet. Text dominated databases: Theory, practice and experience. Tutorial presented at PODS, 1994.

13. N. Goodman. Research issues in Genome databases. Tutorial presented at PODS, 1995.

14. G. Grahne, M. Nykanen, and E. Ukkonen. Reasoning about strings in databases. In *Thirteenth ACM SIGMOD Intern. Symposium on Principles of Database Systems (PODS'94)*, pages 303–312, 1994.

15. S. Grumbach and T. Milo. An algebra for POMSETS. In *Fifth International Conference on Data Base Theory, (ICDT'95), Prague, Lecture Notes in Computer Science*, pages 191–207, 1995.

16. A. Grzegorczyk. Some classes of recursive functions. *Rozprawy Matematyczne*, 4, 1953. Instytut Matematyczne Polskiej Akademie Nauk, Warsaw.

17. C. Hegelsen and P. R. Sibbald. PALM – a pattern language for molecular biology. In *First Intern. Conference on Intelligent Systems for Molecular Biology*, pages 172–180, 1993.

18. V. A. Kozmidiadi. On a generalization of finite automata generating a hierarchy analogous to the A. Grzegorczyk's classification of the primitive recursive functions. *Problemi Kibernetiki*, 23:127–170, 1970.

19. J. W. Lloyd. *Foundations of Logic Programming*. Springer-Verlag, second edition, 1987.

20. G. Mecca. *From Datalog to Sequence Datalog: Languages and Techniques for Querying Sequence Databases*. PhD thesis, Università di Roma "La Sapienza", Dipartimento di Informatica e Sistemistica, 1996. http://poincare.inf.uniroma3.it:8080.

21. G. Mecca and A. J. Bonner. Finite query languages for sequence databases. In *Fifth Intern. Workshop on Database Programming Languages (DBPL'95), Gubbio, Italy*. electronic Workshops in Computing - Springer-Verlag, 1995. http://www.springer.co.uk/eWiC/Workshops/DBPL5.html.

22. G. Mecca and A. J. Bonner. Sequences, Datalog and Transducers. In *Fourteenth ACM SIGMOD Intern. Symposium on Principles of Database Systems (PODS'95), San Jose, California*, pages 23–35, 1995. http://poincare.inf.uniroma3.it:8080.

23. A. R. Meyer and D. M. Ritchie. Computational complexity and program structure. *I.B.M. Res. Rep.*, 1817, 1967.

24. C. H. Papadimitriou. *Computational Complexity*. Addison-Wesley, 1994.

25. H. Rogers, Jr. *Theory of recursive functions and effective computability*. MIT Press, Cambridge, Mass., 1987.

26. D. B. Searls. String Variable Grammars: a logic grammar formalism for dna sequences. Technical report, University of Pennsylvania, School of Medicine, 1993.

27. D. Stott Parker, E. Simon, and P. Valduriez. SVP – a model capturing sets, streams and parallelism. In *Eighteenth International Conference on Very Large Data Bases (VLDB'92), Vancouver, Canada*, pages 115–126, 1992.

28. M. Vardi. The complexity of relational query languages. In *Fourteenth ACM SIGACT Symp. on Theory of Computing*, pages 137–146, 1988.

29. J. D. Watson et al. *Molecular biology of the gene*. Benjamin and Cummings Publ. Co., Menlo Park, California, fourth edition, 1987.

A Structure-Based Approach
to Querying Semi-structured Data

Mary Fernandez[1] and Lucian Popa[2] and Dan Suciu[1]

[1] AT&T Labs — Research, Florham Park NJ 07932, USA
[2] University of Pennsylvania, Philadelphia PA 19104, USA

Abstract. Several researchers have considered integrating multiple unstructured, semi-structured, and structured data sources by modeling all sources as edge labeled graphs. Data in this model is self-describing and dynamically typed, and captures both schema and data information. The labels are arbitrary atomic values, such as strings, integers, reals, etc., and the integrated data graph is stored in a unique data repository, as a relation of *edges*. The relation is dynamically typed, i.e. each edge label is tagged with its type.
Although the unique, labeled graph repository is flexible, it looses all static type information, and results in severe efficiency penalties compared to querying structured databases, such as relational or object-oriented databases. In this paper we propose an alternative method of storing and querying semi-structured data, using *storage schemas*, which are closely related to recently introduced graph schemas [BDFS97]. A storage schema splits the graph's edges into several relations, some of which may have labels of known types (such as strings or integers) while others may be still dynamically typed. We show here that all positive queries in UnQL, a query language for semistructured data, can be translated into *conjunctive queries* against the relations in the storage schema. This result may be surprising, because UnQL is a powerful language, featuring regular path expressions, restructuring queries, joins, and unions. We use this technique in order to translate queries on the integrated, semi-structured data into queries on the external sources. In this setting the integrated semi-structured data is not materialized but virtual and the problem is to translate a query against the integrated view, possibly involving regular path expressions and restructuring, into queries which can be answered by the external sources. Here we use again the storage schema in order to split the graph into relations according to their sources. Any positive UnQL query is decomposed based on these relations and translated into queries on the external sources.

1 Introduction

Integration of unstructured and structured data sources is an active area of research. We are particularly interested in integrating the unstructured graphs of HTML pages with one or several structured (relational or object-oriented) databases, into a single web site. We do the integration by *modeling* all data sources as edge-labeled graphs. Such graphs are an appropriate model for integrating various types of data sources, because they can model unstructured data that have no fixed schema, semi-structured data whose schema imposes only weak constraints on the data, and structured data that have fixed schema. Both schema information and data are integrated into a single graph [PGMW95], which is self-describing and dynamically typed. The graphs' labels can be arbitrary atomic types, such as strings, integers, reals, etc., and the graph is stored in a common data repository in which each label is tagged with its type. Several query languages have been proposed for querying semi-structured data modeled as edge-labeled graphs: for example Lorel [QRS⁺95], UnQL [BDHS96a]. All of them allow some kind of recursion, typically in the form of regular path expressions, which serves two purposes: either to browse through a structured data source whose structure is unknown to the user, or to query a truly unstructured data source, such as the graph of a collection of HTML pages, which requires traversal of arbitrarily long paths.

Although we want to model various data sources as graphs, we do *not* want to materialize them as graphs, because materializing is prohibitively expensive and raises the problems of maintaining consistency between the original and materialized data. Moreover, we would like to have the external sources answer queries directly, by translating queries expressed against the integrated graph data into queries on the external sources. In general these queries are recursive, because they contain regular path expressions: when the sources have known structure, then recursive queries are typically unfolded into non-recursive ones. But when the sources are truly unstructured, then the recursion cannot be eliminated. For example, in our application of integrating HTML pages with relational databases we would like to translate such a query into a recursive query on the portion of the graph described by the HTML pages and into relational queries on the relational databases.

Representing a graph as a single relation, however, complicates the translation, because the relation has all type and source information stored dynamically, instead of statically. In this paper we propose a new method of storing and querying semi-structured data based on *storage schemas*, a concept related to recently introduced graph schemas [BDFS97]. A storage schema divides the semi-structured graph data into several relations, some of which contain statically typed, monomorphic edges and some of which remain dynamically typed. When the semi-structured data is virtual, then these relations are virtual as well, i.e. they are queries on the external sources. We show that this method is effective by proving that it can support the evaluation of queries in a semi-structured query language. For that we chose UnQL [BDHS96a], a query language powerful enough to support regular path expressions and restructurings. We show that any positive UnQL query Q can be evaluated as follows. Given a storage schema for the input graph data, we compute a new storage schema describing how Q's answer is stored. Each relation in the new storage schema is a conjunctive query on some of the relations of the input data graph. Thus, when the input relations are statically typed, so is the resulting storage schema and so are all conjunctive queries. Moreover, when the input storage schema is virtual, then the output storage schema contains queries which reach directly into the external sources, typically in the form of relational algebra (RA) queries. For relational external sources we go one step further and show how to extract the result from the output storage schema as a single SQL expression, in the process eliminating the recursion from the original query.

We begin in Section 2 with an extended example that illustrates the main ideas. In Section 3 we review the data model, graph schemas, and query language. We introduce storage schemas in Section 4, and state our main translation result in Section 5. We briefly describe the main ideas behind the translation in Section 6, and show two applications in Sections 7 and 8.

2 An Example

Consider the following UnQL query, which searches for an edge y with a label that contains the string *"Security"* and returns the surrounding structure:

Query Q1 : select $\{x \Rightarrow \{y \Rightarrow t\}\}$
             where $* \Rightarrow x \Rightarrow y \Rightarrow t$ in DB,
                  y matches *"Security"*

For example, on the graph database in Figure 1, the query returns the graph in Figure 2(a). UnQL actually produces the more complex graph in Figure 2(b), which includes *epsilon* (ε) *edges*. Intuitively, ε edges represent the edges in the source graph that are not part of the result and are eliminated from the result graph. Epsilon edges are important in the implementation of our translation technique, described later.

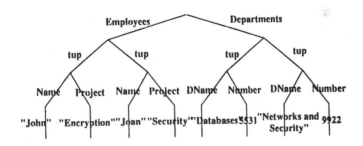

Fig. 1. Example graph database, DB_1.

Labeled graphs modeling semi-structured data are stored in two relations: a ternary relation, $E(Oid, Label, Oid)$, storing the edges, and a unary one, $Root(Oid)$, storing the root [PGMW95,AV97]. *Oid* is a graph node's unique identifier and *Label* is an edge label. Since atomic values can be of any type, e.g., *Int*, *String*, *Bool*, etc., *Label* must be their disjoint union, i.e., *Label* = *Int* $\cup$ *String* $\cup$ *Bool* $\cup \ldots$.

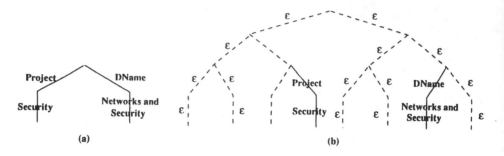

Fig. 2. Result of applying query $Q1$ to graph database, DB_1.

Given this untyped, relational representation, we could translate our example query into the Datalog program:

$$C(r) \quad : - \; Root(r)$$
$$C(n') \quad : - \; C(n), E(n, \_, n')$$
$$Answ(r, x, n') \quad : - \; Root(r), C(n), E(n, x, n'), E(n', y, n''),$$
$$\text{matches}\,(y, "Security")$$
$$Answ(n', y, n'') : - \; C(n), E(n, x, n'), E(n', y, n''), \text{matches}\,(y, "Security")$$

If we know, as we do in our example, that the data is a graph with bounded depth, we could unfold the Datalog program into the equivalent non-recursive program:

$$Answ(r, x, n') \quad : - \; Root(r), \qquad\qquad // \; \text{Unfolding 1}$$
$$E(r, x, n'), E(n', y, n''), \text{matches}\,(y, "Security")$$
$$Answ(n', y, n'') : - \; Root(r),$$
$$E(r, x, n'), E(n', y, n''), \text{matches}\,(y, "Security")$$
$$Answ(r, x, n') \quad : - \; Root(r), E(r, \_, n) \qquad // \; \text{Unfolding 2}$$
$$E(n, x, n'), E(n', y, n''), \text{matches}\,(y, "Security")$$
$$Answ(n', y, n'') : - \; Root(r), E(r, \_, n)$$
$$E(n, x, n'), E(n', y, n''), \text{matches}\,(y, "Security")$$
$$Answ(r, x, n') \quad : - \; Root(r), E(r, \_, n_1), E(n_1, \_, n), // \; \text{Unfolding 3}$$
$$E(n, x, n'), E(n', y, n''), \text{matches}\,(y, "Security")$$
$$Answ(r, y, n'') \quad : - \; Root(r), E(r, \_, n_1), E(n_1, \_, n),$$
$$E(n, x, n'), E(n', y, n''), \text{matches}\,(y, "Security")$$

For our example graph data, the first two unfoldings are vacuous, but without explicit knowledge on the graph's structure, they cannot be eliminated. Like the original recursive query, the non-recursive query does not preserve any type

Employees	
Name	Project
John	Encryption
Joan	Security

Departments	
DName	Number
Databases	5531
Networks and Security	9922

Fig. 3. Relational database.

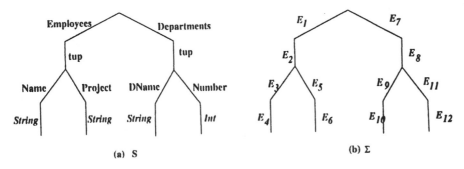

(a) S   (b) Σ

Fig. 4. (a) Graph schema, S, and (b) storage schema, Σ, for relational database in Figure 3.

information; for example, we cannot determine from the *Answ* rules in the third-level unfolding that x is always a string and that y can be a string or an integer.

We propose a technique for representing graph data that preserves the type and structure information associated with the source data. To illustrate, assume the external data source for Figure 1 is the relational database in Figure 3. Then we can describe the graph's structure using a *graph schema* [BDFS97]: for our example the graph schema S is in Figure 4 (a). It specifies that the data graph has two first-level edges labeled "Employees" and "Departments". Each second-level edge in the data graph is labeled "tup". Then, the third level edges are labeled with the strings "Name", "Project", "DName", or "Number" respectively. The first three are followed by edges labeled with strings, while the last is followed by edges labeled with integers. The graph schema is only intended to say what labels are allowed to occur in the graph database. It cannot prevent labels to be missing, nor does it say anything about unique v.s. multiple occurrences, see [BDFS97].

We push the concept of graph schema one step further and define a *storage schema*, to describe a specialized storage of the data graph. In our example, the corresponding storage schema is in Figure 4(b). Each of the 12 relations $E_1, \ldots, E_{12}$ stores a fragment of the original edge relation E, namely the graph fragment that contains those edges that "populate" the corresponding schema edge. While $E = E_1 \cup \ldots \cup E_{12}$, notice that the new edge relations are strongly typed, e.g., $E_1, \ldots, E_{11}$ have the type $(Oid, String, Oid)$, and E_{12} has the type (Oid, Int, Oid). The translation from the relational database $Employees(Name, Project)$, $Departments(DName, Number)$ to the storage schema is handled by a wrapper which computes the 12 relations E_i, each of which is a conjunctive query on *Employees* and *Departments*, see Section 7.

We show now how query $Q1$ can be evaluated in terms of the storage schema. A key observation is that the answer of a query can be also stored according to some storage schema. For example, Figure 5(a) depicts the graph schema for the result of applying $Q1$ to graphs that conform to the schema in Figure 4(a). Note that the query's result in Figure 2(b) conforms to the output schema in Figure 5(a). Figure 5(b) depicts the result's storage schema. Each of the 20 relations, Q_i, can be expressed as a conjunctive query over the input relations $E_1, \ldots, E_{12}$. Most of the queries depend on a single relation, some depend on two:

$$Q_3(n,x,n') \; :- \; E_3(n,x,n'), E_4(n',y,n''), \text{matches}\,(y,\text{"}Security\text{"})$$
$$Q_5(n,x,n') \; :- \; E_5(n,x,n'), E_6(n',y,n''), \text{matches}\,(y,\text{"}Security\text{"})$$
$$Q_9(n,x,n') \; :- \; E_9(n,x,n'), E_{10}(n',y,n''), \text{matches}\,(y,\text{"}Security\text{"})$$
$$Q_{11} \qquad\quad := \; \emptyset$$
$$Q_i(n',y,n'') :- \; E_i(n',y,n''), i = 4,6,10,12$$
$$Q_i(n,\varepsilon,n') \; :- \; E_i(n,\_,n'), i = 1,2,7,8$$
$$Q'_i(n,\varepsilon,n') \; :- \; E_i(n,\_,n'), i = 3,4,5,6,9,10,11,12$$

The type information preserved in the storage schema allows us to optimize

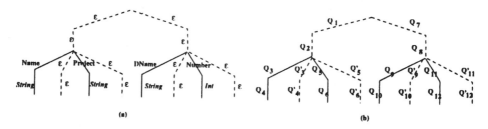

(a)   (b)

Fig. 5. (a) Graph schema, $S' = Q1(S)$, for result of query $Q1$. (b) Storage schema, $\Sigma' = \bar{Q}1(\Sigma)$, for query result.

queries that we could not optimize in the single edge relation representation. For example, we can simplify the query

$$Q_{11}(n,x,n') : -E_{11}(n,x,n'), E_{12}(n',y,n''), \text{matches}\,(y,\text{"}Security\text{"})$$

to $Q_{11} := \emptyset$, because we know that the y attribute in E_{12} is always an integer value and can never match a string value. Finally, we can push the queries Q_i to the external source, by composing the Q_i queries with the conjunctive queries E_i, which are defined in terms of the original *Employees* and *Departments* relations. Note that by separating a graph's edges according to a storage schema we can use the same oid's for distinct nodes in the resulting graph. For example the edges populating Q_4 and Q'_4 use the same oid's for their end nodes, but these oid's denote different nodes.

The main application of our technique is translating queries on an integrated, semi-structured information system into queries on the external sources. Other systems, such as Tsimmis [PGMU95,PGGMU95,PAGM96], address this problem. Tsimmis uses a datalog-like language, called MSL, to integrate data from heterogeneous information sources into a graph-like, semi-structured data model. A query against the integrated information source is then composed with the MSL query. When both queries are non-recursive, the resulting query can be efficiently "pushed to the sources". But their technique does not work with recursion. We address the same problem here, but allow recursion, which is indispensable in our application, because one of the data sources (the graph of HTML pages) is unstructured. For example, consider the data in Figure 6 (a), in which some HTML pages are integrated with the *Employees* relation from our previous example into a unique Web site. The bold edges denote the fragment of the data that is fetched from the relational database, other edges denote HTML hyper-links. The idea is that every employee page will have a link to a piece of information from *Employees* relation: for example Joan's page points to the *Employees* tuple with $Name = ``Joan''$. We shall explain in Section 8 how this integration is achieved. Suppose that we are evaluating the query $Q1$ above on this integrated data: "Security" edges may be found both in the HTML graph and the relational part of the data. We want to translate $Q1$ into a recursive query on the HTML graph and a relational query on the *Employee* relation. We show how to do this using storage schemas. First, the graph schema for this example is in Figure 6 (b) and the storage schema in (c). The latter says that the data consists of (1) a graph relation $E1$ holding all the HTML links, and (2) five virtual relations $E2, E3, \ldots, E6$ defined in terms of the *Employee* relation. $E3, \ldots, E6$ are conjunctive queries on *Employee*, while $E2$ does the matching between HTML links labeled with names and their corresponding entry in *Employees*. Applying our translation technique to $Q1$ and Σ_2 results in a storage schema[1] whose associated graph schema is S'_2 in Figure 6(d). We shall see in Section 8 how this storage schema helps us generating some relational queries on *Employees* and a recursive query on the HTML graph (corresponding to the ε loop on the top of Figure 6(d)).

3   Background

Data Model. We use the data model described in [BDHS96a,BDHS96b] for unstructured data. A *database* is a *rooted, edge-labeled graph*, with labels from an infinite universe $Label = Int \cup String \cup \ldots$ Only the part of the graph accessible from the root matters, but sometimes we store also unaccessible nodes and edges because removing them can be expensive. Each graph can be viewed as a *set* of label-graph pairs: $\{a_1 \Rightarrow t_1, \ldots, a_n \Rightarrow t_n\}$, where $a_1, \ldots, a_n \in Label$ and $t_1, \ldots, t_n$ are other graphs. For example, the databases in Figure 7 (a) and (b)

---

[1] The storage schema is depicted in Figure 13(a).

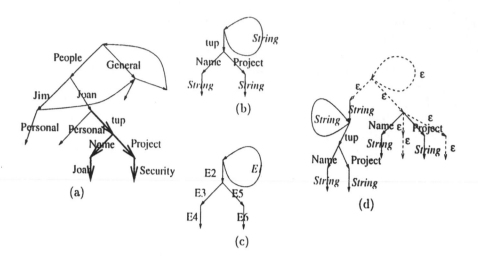

Fig. 6. (a) Integrated HTML and relational data graph, DB_2. (b) Database DB_2's graph schema, S_2. (c) Graph schema S_2's storage schema Σ_2. (d) Graph schema $S_2' = \bar{Q}1(S_2)$.

can be written as: $t = \{a \Rightarrow \{c, d \Rightarrow \{e\}\}, b \Rightarrow \{f\}\}$ and $t' = \{a \Rightarrow \{b\} \cup T\}$ where $T = \{c \Rightarrow T\}$ respectively. Since graphs are sets, we can define the *union* of two graphs $t \cup t'$ and the *empty* graph $\{\}$, which has one node and no edges. For t, t' above, $t \cup t' = \{a \Rightarrow \{c, d \Rightarrow \{e\}\}, b \Rightarrow \{f\}, a \Rightarrow \{b \cup T\}\}$ in Figure 7 (c). We shall use the special symbol ε to label "silent" or "empty" edges. An edge $x \overset{\varepsilon}{\to} y$ means that every label visible from node y is also visible from node x. That is, we may remove the ε edge, if for every edge $y \overset{a}{\to} z$ we introduce a new edge $x \overset{a}{\to} z$. The silent edges are just a convenient, concise notation. For example the union of the graphs in Figure 7 (a) and (b) can be represented as in (d). A formal treatment of how to remove ε-edges uses bisimulation [BDHS96a].

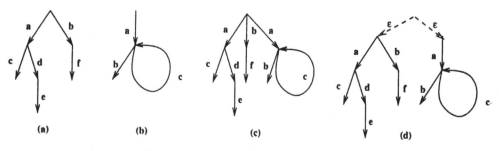

Fig. 7. Examples of rooted graphs.

144

Graph Schemas. In recent work we introduced *graph schemas* [BDFS97] for the purpose of query optimization. A graph schema is a graph with n nodes $s_1, \ldots, s_n$ called *states*, a designated *root* state s_1, and edges labeled with unary predicates over *Label*. Figure 4(a) represents a schema with 13 states. An edge with the constant label "Employees" denotes the predicate $l = $"Employees"; an edge with predicate label *String* denotes the predicate *isString(l)*.

Graph schemas recapture some of the structural and type information lost by unifying schema information and data in a single graph. Graph schemas, however, are more like *data guides* [Abi97] than like traditional database schemas, because they do not fully describe a graph's structure. For example, Figure 6(b) does not specify the structure of the graph above the "tup" edges.

Query Language. UnQL is a query language for querying and restructuring data modeled as rooted graphs. It is compositional and supports regular path expressions. A complete description appears elsewhere [BDHS96a]. UnQL is equivalent to UnCAL, a calculus in which the salient construct is a simple form of recursion on trees called *gext*: UnQL's regular path expressions and its more complex restructuring constructs can all be translated into this form of tree recursion. We will use UnCAL rather than UnQL to describe the evaluation technique based on storage schemas. UnCAL is revised in Appendix A. Here we briefly review it's salient construct, its recursion on trees.

UnCAL's *gext* construct allows us to define k mutually recursive functions, $g_1, \ldots, g_k$, as in Figure 8. Each function g_i returns the empty graph on the empty graph, $\{\}$, and commutes with union. On a singleton graph $\{l \Rightarrow t\}$, where l is an edge and t is a graph, it may call recursively any of the functions $g_1(t), \ldots, g_k(t)$ and combine their results into an expression F_i, which may also depend on l and t. Thus the functions are defined as if they were applied to trees only, and not to graphs with cycles. The important observation in [BDHS96a,BDHS96b] is that by imposing minor restrictions on the form of the expressions F_i we can guarantee that they are well defined on graphs with cycles too[2]. The expressions F_i may have other recursive functions defined inside. For example query $Q1$ of Section 2 can be expressed as a recursive function g, having another recursive function inside, see Figure 9.

$$g_1(\{\}) \stackrel{\text{def}}{=} \{\} \qquad \cdots \qquad g_k(\{\}) \stackrel{\text{def}}{=} \{\}$$
$$g_1(\{l \Rightarrow t\}) \stackrel{\text{def}}{=} F_1(l, t, g_1(t), \ldots, g_k(t)) \cdots g_k(\{l \Rightarrow t\}) \stackrel{\text{def}}{=} F_k(l, t, g_1(t), \ldots, g_k(t))$$
$$g_1(t \cup t') \stackrel{\text{def}}{=} g_1(t) \cup g_1(t') \qquad \cdots \qquad g_k(t \cup t') \stackrel{\text{def}}{=} g_k(t) \cup g_k(t')$$

Fig. 8. Defining k mutually recursive functions.

---
[2] We will use of this fact in the translation, Appendix A: there we define functions $f_1, \ldots, f_k$ by recursion on tree storage schemas (Figure 15), and argue that they are still well defined on storage schemas with cycles.

$$g(\{\}) \quad \overset{\text{def}}{=} \{\}$$

$$g(\{x \Rightarrow t\}) \overset{\text{def}}{=} \text{let } g'(\{\}) \quad \overset{\text{def}}{=} \{\}$$

$$g'(\{y \Rightarrow t'\}) \overset{\text{def}}{=} \text{if } (y \text{ matches "Security")} \text{ then } \{x \Rightarrow \{y \Rightarrow t'\}\}$$
$$\text{else } \{\}$$

$$g'(t'_1 \cup t'_2) \overset{\text{def}}{=} g'(t'_1) \cup g'(t'_2)$$
$$\text{in } g(t) \cup g'(t)$$

$$g(t_1 \cup t_2) \overset{\text{def}}{=} g(t_1) \cup g(t_2)$$

Fig. 9. Query $Q1$ of Section 2 expressed as a recursive function.

Conjunctive queries Conjunctive queries are extensively covered in textbooks, see for example [AHV95]. For the purpose of our paper, we need conjunctive queries in a different formalism, namely as a certain fragment of the comprehension syntax [BLS+94,Won94]. We call this formalism CONJ. It has two kinds of expressions: scalar and set expressions. Scalar expressions are $S ::= \langle S_1, \ldots, S_n \rangle \mid \pi_i(S) \mid z \mid a$, where $\langle \ldots \rangle$ constructs a tuple, $\pi_1, \pi_2, \ldots$ denote projections, z is a scalar variable, and $a \in Int \cup String \cup \ldots$ is a constant. The set expressions denote flat sets (we don't have nested sets) and are $E ::= \{S \mid C_1, \ldots, C_n\} \mid R_1 \mid \ldots \mid R_m$. Here $R_1, \ldots, R_m$ are relation names. The core of the comprehension syntax is the comprehension, $\{S \mid C_1, \ldots, C_n\}$: here each of C_i is either a *generator*, i.e., $z \in E$ with z a variable and E a set expression, or a *condition*, i.e., $S = S'$ or $S \neq S'$. For example, the expression $\{\langle \pi_1(z), \pi_2(z') \rangle \mid z \in R_1, z' \in R_2, \pi_2(z) = \pi_1(z')\}$ computes the join of R_1 and R_2. When convenient, we use pattern matching for shorthand, e.g., the join query can be written as $\{\langle x, y \rangle \mid \langle x, v \rangle \in R, \langle w, y \rangle \in R', v = w\}$.

Conjunctive queries are strongly typed. The scalar types are given by:

$$b ::= Int \mid String \mid \ldots \mid \varepsilon \qquad \text{(base types)}$$
$$s ::= b \mid (s_1 \times \ldots \times s_n)$$

We allow a special base type ε, with a single value, ε. In this paper, we distinguish between $s_1 \times (s_2 \times s_3)$ and $s_1 \times s_2 \times s_3$. We call *Unit* the empty cartesian product $(s_1 \times \ldots \times s_n$ with $n = 0)$; its only value is the empty tuple, $\langle \rangle$. A *set type* has the form $\{s\}$.

4 Storage Schemas

A *storage schema* is a rooted graph whose edges are labeled with conjunctive queries over some fixed, relational schema $R_1, \ldots, R_m$. We call its nodes *states*. Since storage schemas look like graph data, we use the same notation for them, e.g. $\{E \Rightarrow \{E'\}, E''\}$ etc. When we write the CONJ queries explicitly, we delimit them to help distinguish between the two languages. For example, $\{\boxed{\{\langle x, y, y\rangle \mid \langle x, y\rangle \in R\}} \Rightarrow \{\boxed{\{\langle z, z, z\rangle \mid z \in R'\}}\}\}$ denotes a storage schema with 3 states and two edges.

We require storage schemas to be well typed. More precisely, we say a storage schema Σ is well typed if there exists an assignment of set types to its states such that if some state has type $\{s\}$, then all incoming edges are labeled with CONJ expressions of type $\{s' \times b' \times s\}$, for some types s', b', and all outgoing edges have type $\{s \times b'' \times s''\}$, for some types b'', s''.

Storage schemas extend the graph schemas. The latter assign predicates to the edges, saying what types the edges in the data graph can be. The storage schema goes one step further and associates a ternary relation for each schema edge, in effect defining the set of all data edges populating the schema edge. The type can be recaptured from the type of the ternary relation: when an edge in the storage schema is labeled with a CONJ expression of type $\{s \times b \times s'\}$, then the predicate in the corresponding graph schema is $P(l) \stackrel{\text{def}}{=} l \in b$.

A storage schema Σ is intended to be a recipe for storing a data graph, namely by storing one ternary relation for each edge in Σ. Given an instance of the relational database $R_1, \ldots, R_m$, we can recover the data graph as follows. Let $s_1, \ldots, s_n$ be Σ's states, and let E_{ij} be the CONJ expression labeling the edge $s_i \to s_j$ (or $E_{ij} = \emptyset$ if there is no edge). Then the graph database DB has as edges the disjoint union of all E_{ij}'s: $E \stackrel{\text{def}}{=} \bigsqcup E_{ij}$. We use certain terminology to relate DB to the storage schema Σ. We say that an edge $e \in E_{ij}$ *populates* or *belongs to* the edge $s_i \to s_j$ in Σ. Similarly we say that a node $n \in \Pi_1(E_{ij})$ or $n \in \Pi_3(E_{ki})$ *belongs to* the state s_i. We explicitly allow the same value to denote different nodes if it belongs to different schema states. For example, assume that the schema states s_4 and s_6 have type *String* and that, say "abc" populates[3] both s_4 and s_6, then DB will have two nodes corresponding to two distinct copies of the string "abc": one belonging to s_4 the other to s_6. Finally DB's root is, by definition, the node $\langle \rangle$. That implies that Σ's root state, s_1, has type *Unit*. This can be always achieved, e.g. by adding an extra state and a ε edge in Σ.

We explicitly allow storage schemas to be populated by ε edges. That is, certain edges in Σ are labeled with CONJ expressions E_{ij} of type $\{s \times \varepsilon \times s'\}$, where ε is the atomic type containing the single value ε. For example the 12 edges $Q_1, Q_2, Q_3', Q_4', Q_5', Q_6', Q_7, Q_8, Q_9', Q_{10}', Q_{11}', Q_{12}'$ in the storage schema Σ of Figure 5 (b) are populated only by ε edges. If these edges form no cycle in the storage schema, then all ε-edges can be eliminated by a relational algebra query, by essentially computing joins. For example, for Σ above, the edges of the ε-free data graph are given by[4] $E = \Pi_{167}(Q_1 \bowtie Q_2 \bowtie Q_3) \cup \Pi_{167}(Q_1 \bowtie Q_2 \bowtie$

---

[3] That is, "abc" belongs both to $\bigcup_{j=1,n} \Pi_1(E_{4i}) \cup \bigcup_{k=1,n} \Pi_3(E_{k4})$ and to $\bigcup_{j=1,n} \Pi_1(E_{6i}) \cup \bigcup_{k=1,n} \Pi_3(E_{k6})$.

[4] To keep the example simple, we assume that the states in Σ are populated by disjoint sets of nodes.

$Q_5) \cup \Pi_{167}(Q_7 \bowtie Q_8 \bowtie Q_9) \cup \Pi_{167}(Q_7 \bowtie Q_8 \bowtie Q_5 11) \cup Q_4 \cup Q_6 \cup Q_{10} \cup Q_{12}$:
this constructs the data graph in Figure 2 (a). However when Σ has cycles of
ε-edges, then we need to compute transitive closure in order to produce a ε-free
data graph.

5   Main Result

Theorem 1. *Let Q be a positive UnQL query and Σ a storage schema. Then
there exists a storage schema Σ' over the same relational schema as Σ, which
can be effectively computed from Σ and Q, such that: for any instance of the
relational schema, if DB and DB' are the graph databases denoted by Σ and Σ'
respectively, then[5] $Q(DB) = DB'$. We denote Σ' with $\bar{Q}(\Sigma)$.*

The theorem says that we can evaluate the UnQL query Q by essentially
evaluating a collection of conjunctive queries. Namely first compute the resulting
storage schema Σ', based on Σ and Q. Then evaluate each conjunctive query
on the edges of Σ'. The result denotes a graph which is precisely $Q(DB)$. So
far there was no need to compute any recursive queries. However the resulting
graph, $Q(DB)$, typically contains lots of ε edges. If the ε-edges form no cycle
in Σ', then we can still eliminate them, as described in Section 4. Otherwise we
need to compute a recursive query.

In Section 6 we describe the main ideas underlying Theorem 1. Appendix A
describes the complete translation. The formal proof is deferred to the full version
of the paper.

6   Translating Positive UnQL Queries into Conjunctive
Queries

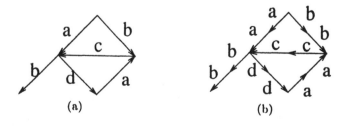

Fig. 10. (a) A graph database, DB. (b) $gext_Z(\lambda(l,t).(Z := \{l \Rightarrow \{l \Rightarrow Z\}\}))(DB)$

---

[5] Equality $Q(DB) = DB'$ should be read here as bisimulation [BDHS96a].

Translating recursive functions. Consider the UnCAL query $Q2(DB) = g_1(DB)$ where g_1 is:

$$g_1(\{\}) \overset{\text{def}}{=} \{\}$$

$$g_1(\{l \Rightarrow t\}) \overset{\text{def}}{=} \{l \Rightarrow \{l \Rightarrow g_1(t)\}\}$$

$$g_1(t_1 \cup t_2) \overset{\text{def}}{=} g_1(t_1) \cup g_1(t_2)$$

Formally it is written in UnCAL as $Q2(DB) = (gext_Z(\lambda(l,t).(Z := \{l \Rightarrow \{l \Rightarrow Z\}\}))))(DB)$. It copies the entire graph DB, doubling each edge (see Figure 10). Assume that the data is stored according to the storage schema in Figure 11 (a) and that the relation $E2$ is populated by the six edges in Figure 11(b), i.e., $E2 = \{\langle x,a,u\rangle, \langle x,b,v\rangle, \langle v,c,w\rangle, \langle z,d,w\rangle, \langle z,e,p\rangle, \langle z,f,q\rangle\}$. After applying $Q2$ to the input graph we expect each edge to be doubled (Figure 12(a)). This graph fragment has six new intermediate nodes, for which we have to "create" oid's in CONJ. The new nodes correspond to the six edges populating $E2$, so we name the new nodes after these edges: each new node is a triple of the form $\langle n,l,n'\rangle \in E2$. Now we have non-uniformly named nodes in this graph fragment: some are atomic values (like $x, y, z, u, \ldots$) while others are triples[6] (like $\langle x,a,u\rangle, \langle x,b,v\rangle, \ldots$). For uniformity, we replace this graph with another one, depicted in Figure 12(b), which adds some ε-edges. Here the "internal" nodes are uniformly named using triples, while "input-output" nodes have names from the old graph. We describe these intermediate results by the storage schema fragment in Figure 12(c), where $E2_{\text{in}}$ and $E2_{\text{out}}$ store the input and output ε-edges, and $E2'$ and $E2''$ store the internal edges. The expressions for these four relations are:

$$E2_{\text{in}} = \{\langle n, \varepsilon, \langle n,l,n'\rangle\rangle \mid \langle n,l,n'\rangle \in E2\}$$

$$E2_{\text{out}} = \{\langle\langle n,l,n'\rangle, \varepsilon, n'\rangle \mid \langle n,l,n'\rangle \in E2\}$$

$$E2' = E2'' = \{\langle\langle n,l,n'\rangle, l, \langle n,l,n'\rangle\rangle \mid \langle n,l,n'\rangle \in E2\}$$

Putting everything together, we derive the storage schema $\Sigma_3' = \bar{Q}2(\Sigma_3)$ in Figure 12(d).

Other constructs. We translate a union expression $e_1 \cup e_2$ by first translating e_1, e_2 to obtain the storage schemas Σ_1, Σ_2. The result storage schema will be $\{E \Rightarrow \Sigma_1, E \Rightarrow \Sigma_2\}$, where E is the following CONJ expression: $\{\langle\langle\rangle, \varepsilon, \langle\rangle\rangle\}$. Note that the resulting root in the data graph is $\langle\rangle$, and that this construct assumes that the roots of the data graphs denoted by Σ_1, Σ_2 are also $\langle\rangle$. A conditional if $l = l'$ then e_1 else e_2 is translated into: $\{E_1 \Rightarrow \Sigma_1, E_2 \Rightarrow \Sigma_2\}$, where E_1, E_2 are CONJ expressions denoting either ε-edges or the empty set. Namely: $E_1 = \{\langle\langle\rangle, \varepsilon, \langle\rangle\rangle \mid l = l'\}$, while $E_2 = \{\langle\langle\rangle, \varepsilon, \langle\rangle\rangle \mid l \neq l'\}$.

Implementation. We have implemented an UnCAL interpreter in ML and are currently implementing a translator. The core of the translator is the translation of *gext*: here the translator is described in terms of k recursive functions

---

[6] One can think of these triples as semantic oid's.

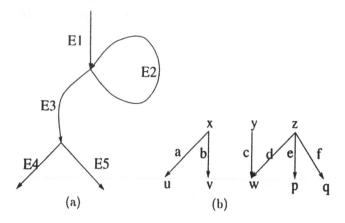

Fig. 11. (a) A storage schema, Σ_3, and (b) six edges populating $E2$.

$f_1, \ldots, f_k$, Figure 15. These functions have to traverse a storage schema Σ, which in general can be cyclic. We used here the crucial observation [BDHS96a,BDHS96b] that such recursive functions are well defined on cyclic graphs too. In the implementation we went one step further and realized that these recursive functions are an instance of $gext$, when given the right context. Namely let us denote the set of all data graphs by $Graph(Label)$, emphasizing that the graphs' edges are labeled with elements from $Label$. Then the set of storage schemas is $Graph(\text{CONJ})$, i.e., they are data graphs, but whose edges are labeled with expressions in CONJ. Similarly, $UnCAL(Label)$ denotes the set of UnCAL queries $Q : Graph(Label) \rightarrow Graph(Label)$. Now it makes sense to talk about the "query language" UnCAL(CONJ): a query in this language, $\bar{Q}$ maps an input storage schema Σ into some output storage schema $\Sigma' = \bar{Q}(\Sigma)$, i.e. $\bar{Q} : Graph(\text{CONJ}) \rightarrow Graph(\text{CONJ})$. The language UnCAL(CONJ) has the same primitives as UnCAL($Label$), including a $gext$ construct which allows us to define the functions $f_1, \ldots, f_k$ from Figure 15. In addition it has a set of external functions operating on the "labels", which are now CONJ expressions, which allow us to construct more complex CONJ expressions from simpler ones. In our implementation, we translate $Q \in UnCAL(Label)$ into $\bar{Q} \in UnCAL(\text{CONJ})$, such that the following diagram commutes:

$$
\begin{array}{ccc}
Graph(Label) & \xrightarrow{\;Q\;} & Graph(Label) \\
\scriptstyle{Denotes}\Big\uparrow & & \Big\uparrow\scriptstyle{Denotes} \\
Graph(\text{CONJ}) & \xrightarrow{\;\bar{Q}\;} & Graph(\text{CONJ})
\end{array}
\qquad (1)
$$

Optimizations. The CONJ expressions derived during the translation are highly redundant, but can be simplified dramatically by using the optimization rules

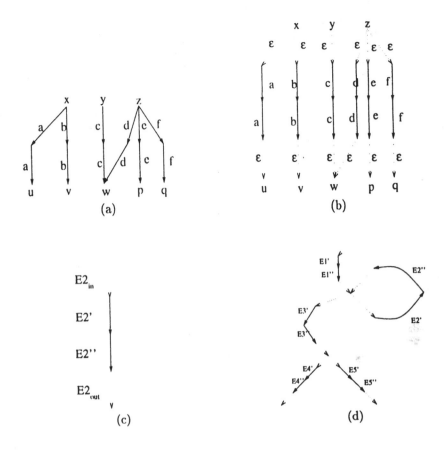

Fig. 12. (a) and (b) Result of "double-edge" query. (c) Result's storage schema for edge E_2. (d) Complete storage schema, $\Sigma_3' = \bar{Q}2(\Sigma_3)$.

in [Won94]. The most effective rule is "vertical loop fusion", which eliminates intermediate results. Also, many of the edge expressions have a constant label value in the second position, e.g., the E_3 in Figure 4(b) is of the form $\{\langle n, "Name", n'\rangle \mid \ldots\}$. When these expressions occur in conditionals generated by UnCAL expressions, they can often be reduced to empty sets.

We identified another rule, which we call *join elimination*, that can be applied when the result expression involves only one of the input relations; this is a novel rule, not mentioned among the optimization rules in [Won94]. The rule is:

$$\{x_1 \mid x_1 \in e, x_2 \in e, x_1 = x_2\} \to e$$

7 Applying UnQL queries to relational databases

There are several reasons why we would like to translate UnQL queries on relational databases into SQL. First, UnQL can easily express *browsing* queries, like "find all records containing the string 'Security' in the database". Our translation uses the source's relational schema to generate several SQL queries that can do the browsing. Second, this translation is a starting point for the more ambitious goal of pushing queries to multiple external sources that are components of an integrated, semi-structured database. We describe that problem in the next section. Third, the translation offers the base of an alternative proof that UnQL is a conservative extension of the relational algebra [BDHS96a].

In our translation of UnQL queries into SQL, we consider a relational database encoded as a tree data-graph (see Figure 1). Given an UnQL query Q, we search for an "equivalent" SQL query Q'. In UnQL, we can write queries returning nested sets, therefore there won't always find an equivalent SQL query. Even when the result is not nested, it may return a heterogeneous set, for example query $Q1$ in Section 2. In this case, although there is no equivalent SQL query, Q is equivalent to the union of several SQL queries, returning sets of different types.

Tree Schemas. Any relational schema can be represented as a tree with depth four. The corresponding storage schema is obtained as follows. We will refer to Figure 4(b), where the relational schema is *Employee* : {*String* × *String*}, *Departments* : {*String* × *Int*}:

1. The root state and the states at the first level are populated with the empty tuple $\langle\rangle$.

$$E_1 \stackrel{\text{def}}{=} \{\langle\langle\rangle, "Employees", \langle\rangle\rangle\}$$
$$E_7 \stackrel{\text{def}}{=} \{\langle\langle\rangle, "Departments", \langle\rangle\rangle\}$$

2. The nodes at the second level are populated with records from the corresponding relation. The CONJ expressions are fan-out subgraphs. In our example:

$$E_2 \stackrel{\text{def}}{=} \{\langle\langle\rangle, "tup", z\rangle \mid z \in Employees\}$$
$$E_8 \stackrel{\text{def}}{=} \{\langle\langle\rangle, "tup", z\rangle \mid z \in Departments\}$$

3. The attributes edges are "parallel" edges. In our example:

$$E_3 \stackrel{\text{def}}{=} \{\langle z, "Name", z\rangle \mid z \in Employees\}$$
$$E_9 \stackrel{\text{def}}{=} \{\langle z, "DName", z\rangle \mid z \in Departments\}$$
$$E_5 \stackrel{\text{def}}{=} \{\langle z, "Project", z\rangle \mid z \in Employees\}$$
$$E_{11} \stackrel{\text{def}}{=} \{\langle z, "Number", z\rangle \mid z \in Departments\}$$

4. Finally, the value edges are also parallel edges, but they contain the real data:

$$E_4 \overset{\text{def}}{=} \{\langle z, \pi_1(z), z\rangle \mid z \in Employees\}$$

$$E_{10} \overset{\text{def}}{=} \{\langle z, \pi_1(z), z\rangle \mid z \in Departments\}$$

$$E_6 \overset{\text{def}}{=} \{\langle z, \pi_2(z), z\rangle \mid z \in Employees\}$$

$$E_{12} \overset{\text{def}}{=} \{\langle z, \pi_2(z), z\rangle \mid z \in Departments\}$$

Given a relational database RDB and an UnQL query Q, our translation from UnQL to SQL has three steps. First, we construct the storage schema, Σ, associated with RDB as described above. Second, we translate Q into $\bar{Q}$ on schema Σ, as in Theorem 1, and obtain an output schema Σ'. Third, we reconstruct a relational type from Σ' and derive the SQL query. The last step is more difficult and we describe it in the rest of this section.

Set-edges. Given a storage schema Σ, we say that an edge labeled E is a *single-edge* if the functional dependency $n \rightarrow n'$ holds for the triples $(n, l, n') \in E$, otherwise it is a *set-edge*. For instance, the fan-out edges E_2 and E_8 in Figure 4(b) are set-edges, but all others are single-edges. The set-edges in a relational storage schema are always the "tup" edges. But in general, for a derived schema Σ', any edge could be a set edge. Rather than trying to derive a functional dependency from a conjunctive query, we compute the *set-edge* property during schema translation; we omit the details from this abstract. For example, we infer that the edges Q_2 and Q_8 in Figure 5(b) are set edges, while all others are single-edges. We have:

Proposition 2. *Let Σ be a tree storage schema. Then the data graph denoted by Σ is a tuple of flat sets and/or scalar values iff on each path from the root to some leaf in Σ there exists at most one set-edge. Otherwise, Σ denotes data graphs that are nested sets.*

Type reconstruction. After constructing Σ', we must construct valid record types for the output relations. We know that there is at most one set-edge on any path in Σ' from the root to the leaves. We divide all edges into *upper edges, set edges,* and *lower edges*: the latter are under some set edge. For example Q_1, Q_7 are the only upper edges in Figure 5(b). The reconstructed type is a tuple of sets and/or scalar values: paths through the upper edges correspond to positions in this tuple. Each set edge denotes a set, whose type we reconstruct as follows. Each lower edge may be labeled by an attribute (like "*Name*" or "*Project*") or by a base type (like *String* or *Int*). In the storage schemas corresponding to relational databases, we always find one attribute edge followed by exactly one value edge. But in general this is no longer the case, because attribute edges and value edges may be intermixed arbitrarily, forming any subtree. We generate a record type with as many fields as there are value edges and generate a field's attribute name by concatenating the labels along the path from the root of the subtree up to the edge. In addition, we generate a field of type *Unit* for each path from the root to a leaf that only contains edges that correspond to labels. For example, consider the following fragment of Σ':

$$E_1$$
$$E_2 \quad\quad E_3$$

where E_1, E_2, E_3 are sets of triples, E_1 corresponds to an attribute name A, E_2 corresponds to the base type *Int*, and E_3 to the attribute name B. The type reconstruction phase produces the record type $\langle A : Int, A\_B : Unit\rangle$.

Generating an RA query. To generate an RA query, we join the expressions that label the edges of storage schema. For Σ' above, the result expression is:

$$\{\langle A : x, A\_B : \langle\rangle\rangle \mid \langle n_1, A, n_1'\rangle \in E_1, \langle n_2, x, n_2'\rangle \in E_2,$$
$$\langle n_3, B, n_3'\rangle \in E_3, n_1' = n_2, n_1' = n_3\}$$

Conditionals. Conditionals introduce additional complexity. For every conditional, our translation of schemas produces two subtrees, corresponding to the two branches of the conditional, joined together by two epsilon edges. The first epsilon edge is labeled with a CONJ expression that produces a singleton set when the condition evaluates to true and the empty set when the condition evaluates to false, and vice-versa for the second epsilon edge. Suppose the condition evaluates to true. Then one of the two subtrees will contribute an empty set to the final result. If we apply the above join algorithm, we always get an empty set, which is incorrect. Instead, we choose either one of the sets produced by the two subtrees, depending on the result of the conditional by marking explicitly the edges that come from a conditional. Finally, subtrees in which all the edges are labeled epsilon are eliminated, because they don't correspond to real data.

8 Evaluating UnQL Queries in an Integrated System

The main application of our translation technique is the translation of recursive queries on semi-structured data into non-recursive queries on structured, external sources. We illustrate with the example at the end of Section 2. There we integrated a HTML graph with the *Employees* relation, and the corresponding storage schema Σ_2 is in Figure 6 (c). For $E3, E4, E5, E6$, we have similar definitions as for the storage schema in a relational database, see Section 7. $E1$ is given a priori and represents the HTML graph. The interesting part is $E2$, which is populated by edges that link the HTML graph with the relational database. Namely:

$$E2 \stackrel{\text{def}}{=} \{\langle n, "tup", z\rangle \mid \langle n, l, n'\rangle \in E1, z \in Employees, \pi_1(z) = l\}$$

Here l is the label on some hyper-link in the HTML graph, while $\pi_1(z)$ denotes the Name of $z \in Employees$. That is $E2$ will introduce a "tup" edge in the data graph from every HTML page n reachable by a hyper-link l whose label matches the name of some employee z. Note how the storage schema Σ_2 helps us keeping track of the source of the integrated data: the edges populating $E1$ are all HTML hyper-links, those populating $E3, \ldots, E6$ are all from the external source $Employees$, while the edges in $E2$ are making the connection, in effect performing the integration.

After applying query $Q1$, we obtain the storage schema in Figure 13(a). Some of its eighteen relations are defined as the conjunctive queries in Figure 13(b). The important fact to note here is that the external source, $Employees$, is still queried only with conjunctive queries. However, in order to eliminate the ε-edges from the resulting data we need to compute the transitive closure on the $Q1$ relation: this translates into a recursive query on the HTML graph ($E1$).

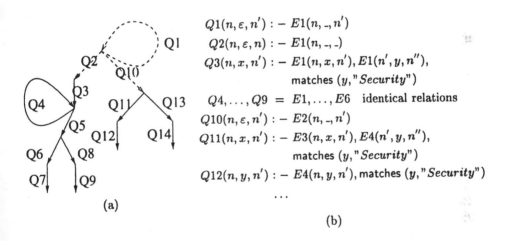

$$Q1(n, \varepsilon, n') : - E1(n, \_, n')$$
$$Q2(n, \varepsilon, n) : - E1(n, \_, \_)$$
$$Q3(n, x, n') : - E1(n, x, n'), E1(n', y, n''),$$
$$\text{matches}(y, "Security")$$
$$Q4, \ldots, Q9 = E1, \ldots, E6 \quad \text{identical relations}$$
$$Q10(n, \varepsilon, n') : - E2(n, \_, n')$$
$$Q11(n, x, n') : - E3(n, x, n'), E4(n', y, n''),$$
$$\text{matches}(y, "Security")$$
$$Q12(n, y, n') : - E4(n, y, n'), \text{matches}(y, "Security")$$
$$\cdots$$

(a)

(b)

Fig. 13. (a) Storage schema $\Sigma_2' = \bar{Q}1(\Sigma_2)$. (b) Definitions of Σ_2''s conjunctive queries.

9 Conclusions

We have described a technique for translating queries on semi-structured data into a collection of conjunctive queries. For that we have introduced the notion of storage schema, which is a technique allowing a semi-structured database to be stored as a collection of structured relations. Our main contribution consists in showing how storage schema can be used to translated queries on the semi-structured data into conjunctive queries on these structured relations. Some comments are in order:

1. We are currently working on an implementation of the translation in ML, in conjunction with an UnQL interpreter. We observed that our translation described in Appendix A sometimes introduces an unnecessary level of joins in the resulting conjunctive queries, when translating certain *gext* expressions. As a consequence join-free queries like $Q1$ of Section 2 end up being translated into three-way joins in CONJ. In future work we plan to optimize the translation to avoid generating unnecessary joins.

2. Languages designed for querying semi-structured data are useful also in querying structured data, because they allow us to write concisely browsing queries. We have extended our technique to translate browsing queries into collections of SQL queries. When given as input an UnQL query which is some SQL query Q, we expect the result of the translation to be Q itself (or a syntactically equivalent query). For this we need to implement the optimization described above, else the translated query will have additional, unnecessary joins.

3. Semi-structured data is particularly useful in integrating information sources with various data formats [PGMW95]. The main challenge in such a system is to develop techniques for translating queries on the integrated semi-structured data into queries on the original sources [PGGMU95,PAGM96]. In applications like web site management [FFK+97] one source — the graph of HTML pages — is still unstructured, which requires us to deal with recursive queries. We have briefly described here how storage schemas can address this problem.

References

[Abi97]   Serge Abiteboul. Querying semi-structured data. In *ICDT*, 1997.

[AHV95]   Serge Abiteboul, Richard Hull, and Victor Vianu. *Foundations of Databases*. Addison Wesley Publishing Co, 1995.

[AV97]   Serge Abiteboul and Victor Vianu. Queries and computation on the web. In *ICDT*, pages 262–275, Deplhi, Greece, 1997. Springer Verlag.

[BDFS97]   Peter Buneman, Susan Davidson, Mary Fernandez, and Dan Suciu. Adding structure to unstructured data. In *ICDT*, pages 336–350, Deplhi, Greece, 1997. Springer Verlag.

[BDHS96a]   Peter Buneman, Susan Davidson, Gerd Hillebrand, and Dan Suciu. A query language and optimization techniques for unstructured data. In *SIGMOD*, 1996.

[BDHS96b]   Peter Buneman, Susan Davidson, Gerd Hillebrand, and Dan Suciu. A query language and optimization techniques for unstructured data. Technical Report 96-09, University of Pennsylvania, Computer and Information Science Department, February 1996.

[BLS+94]   P. Buneman, L. Libkin, D. Suciu, V. Tannen, and L. Wong. Comprehension syntax. *SIGMOD Record*, 23(1):87–96, March 1994.

[FFK+97]   M. Fernandez, D. Florescu, J. Kang, A. Levy, and D. Suciu. STRUDEL - a web-site management system. In *SIGMOD*, Tucson, Arizona, May 1997.

[PAGM96]   Y. Papakonstantinou, S. Abiteboul, and H. Garcia-Molina. Object fusion in mediator systems. In *Proceedings of VLDB*, September 1996.

$$E ::= DB \mid t \mid \{\} \mid \{L \Rightarrow E\} \mid E_1 \cup E_2 \mid E_1 \, @_\mathcal{X} \, E_2 \mid \text{if } B \text{ then } E_1 \text{ else } E_2 \mid$$
$$X \mid (X_1 := E_1, \dots, X_m := E_m) \mid$$
$$gext_{\{Z_1 \dots Z_k\}}(\lambda(l,t).(Z_1 \stackrel{\text{def}}{=} E_1, \dots, Z_k \stackrel{\text{def}}{=} E_k))(E)$$
$$B ::= L_1 = L_2 \mid L_1 \neq L_2$$
$$L ::= l \mid a$$

Fig. 14. UnCAL's grammar.

[PGGMU95] Y. Papakonstantinou, A. Gupta, H. Garcia-Molina, and J. Ullman. A query translation scheme for rapid implementation of wrappers. In *Int'l Conf. on Deductive and Object-Oriented Databases*, 1995.

[PGMU95] Y. Papakonstantinou, H. Garcia-Molina, and J. Ullman. Medmaker: A mediation system based on declarative specifications. In *IEEE International Conference on Data Engineering*, pages 132–141, March 1995.

[PGMW95] Y. Papakonstantinou, H. Garcia-Molina, and J. Widom. Object exchange across heterogeneous information sources. In *IEEE International Conference on Data Engineering*, March 1995.

[QRS+95] D. Quass, A. Rajaraman, Y. Sagiv, J. Ullman, and J. Widom. Querying semistructure heterogeneous information. In *International Conference on Deductive and Object Oriented Databases*, 1995.

[Won94] Limsoon Wong. *Querying Nested Collections*. PhD thesis, Department of Computer and Information Science, University of Pennsylvania, Philadelphia, PA 19104, August 1994. Available as University of Pennsylvania IRCS Report 94-09.

A Translation of UnCAL into Conjunctive Queries

Review of UnCAL Before describing UnCAL we extend slightly our data model. First we consider an infinite set of *markers* to be given: we denote markers with $X, X_1, Y, Z, \dots$ For a set of markers $\mathcal{Y} = \{Y_1, \dots, Y_n\}$ we call a labeled graph *with outputs* $\mathcal{Y}$ a rooted, edge-labeled graph as before, in which some leaf nodes may be labeled with markers from $\mathcal{Y}$. For a set of markers $\mathcal{X} = \{X_1, \dots, X_m\}$, we call a labeled graph *with inputs* $\mathcal{X}$ an edge-labeled graph as before, which has m distinguished input nodes, associated to the m markers in $\mathcal{X}$, instead of a single root. Combining the two concepts we get labeled graphs with inputs $\mathcal{X}$ and outputs $\mathcal{Y}$. The rooted graphs considered before correspond to $\mathcal{X} = \{X_1\}$ and $\mathcal{Y} = \emptyset$.

The grammar in Figure 14 describes the positive fragment of UnCAL: it is the same language as in [BDHS96a], without the non-monotone operator *isempty*. DB denotes the input database, t is a tree variable, $\{\}$ produces the empty graph, $\{L \Rightarrow E\}$ produces a singleton graph, and $E_1 \cup E_2$ produces the union of two rooted graphs. The append operator, $E_1 \, @_\mathcal{X} \, E_2$, is the "vertical" equivalent of union: it is assumed that both E_1's outputs and E_2's inputs are $\mathcal{X} = \{X_1, \dots, X_m\}$.

$$f(\Sigma) \stackrel{\text{def}}{=} (Z_1 := f_1(\Sigma), \ldots, Z_k := f_k(\Sigma))$$

$$f_i(\{\}) \stackrel{\text{def}}{=} \{\}$$

$$f_i(\{E \Rightarrow \Sigma\}) \stackrel{\text{def}}{=} \{\boxed{\{\langle n, \varepsilon, \langle n, l, n' \rangle \rangle \mid \langle n, l, n' \rangle \in E\}} \Rightarrow Z\} \, @_z \quad // \text{ "In" part}$$

$$(Z := tr(\, e_i, z_{new}, (gen, z_{new} \in E),$$

$$(env, [\, l := \boxed{\pi_2(z_{new})}\,,$$

$$t := replicate(\Sigma, z_{new}, \boxed{z_{new} \in E}\,)]))))\, @_z$$

$$(Z_1 := \{\boxed{\{\langle\langle n, l, n' \rangle, \varepsilon, n' \rangle \mid \langle n, l, n' \rangle \in E\}} \Rightarrow Z_1\}, \quad // \text{ "Out"}$$

$$\cdots \qquad\qquad\qquad\qquad\qquad\qquad\qquad // \text{ part}$$

$$Z_k := \{\boxed{\{\langle\langle n, l, n' \rangle, \varepsilon, n' \rangle \mid \langle n, l, n' \rangle \in E\}} \Rightarrow Z_k\}),$$

$$f_i(\Sigma \cup \Sigma') \stackrel{\text{def}}{=} f_i(\Sigma) \cup f_i(\Sigma')$$

$$rep(E, z, gen) \stackrel{\text{def}}{=} \boxed{\{\langle\langle z, n \rangle, l, \langle z, n' \rangle\rangle \mid gen, \langle n, l, n' \rangle \in E\}}$$

$$replicate(\Sigma, z, gen) \stackrel{\text{def}}{=} map(\lambda(E).rep(E, z, gen))(\Sigma)$$

Fig. 15. Translation of *gext*.

Then the result is the graph E_1 in which each leaf marked X_i in E_1 is "replaced" by the input node X_i of E_2. if is a conditional: it can only compare for equality or inequality two label variables and/or constants. X is the same as the empty graph but with the unique node labeled as output X. $(X_1 := E_1, \ldots X_m := E_m)$ constructs a graph with inputs $\{X_1, \ldots, X_m\}$. Finally *gext* allows us to define k mutually recursive functions as in Figure 8. Namely $gext_z(\lambda(l, t).(Z_1 := E_1, \ldots, Z_k := E_k))(E)$ defines k recursive functions $g_1, \ldots, g_k$ as in Figure 8, in which each expression F_i is:

$$F_i(l, t, g_1(t), \ldots, g_k(t)) \stackrel{\text{def}}{=} E_i(l, t) \, @_z \, (Z_1 := g_1(t), \ldots, Z_k := g_k(t))$$

By imposing such restrictions on form of the recursive functions we can guarantee well definedness on cyclic graphs, see [BDHS96b]. For the purpose of this paper we define the meaning of the *gext* expression to be $g_1(E)$. For example, query $Q1$ of Section 2 is equivalent to the following *gext* expression:

$$gext_{X_1}(\lambda(x, t).(X_1 := X_1 \cup gext_{X_2}(\lambda(y, t').(X_2 := \text{if } (y \text{ matches } "Security")$$
$$\text{then } \{x \Rightarrow \{y \Rightarrow t'\}\}$$
$$\text{else } \{\}))(t)))(DB)$$

Translating queries with free variables Let us review how we compute $\Sigma' = gext(\lambda(l, t).(Z := e_1))(\Sigma)$. As illustrated in Section 6, we obtain Σ' by translating e_1 once for every edge labeled $E2$ in Σ. But the translation of e_1 cannot be a

UnCAL expression e	$\Sigma = tr(e, z, gen, env)$	Comments
DB	$replicate(DB, z, gen)$	*replicate* defined in Fig. 15
t	$env(t)$	
$\{\}$	$\{\}$	
$\{l \Rightarrow e_1\}$	$\{rep(\boxed{\{\langle\langle\rangle, env(l), \langle\rangle\rangle\}}, z, gen) \Rightarrow \Sigma_1\}$	*rep* defined in Fig. 15
$e_1 \cup e_2$	$\{rep(\boxed{\{\langle\langle\rangle, \varepsilon, \langle\rangle\rangle\}}, z, gen) \Rightarrow \Sigma_1,$ $rep(\boxed{\{\langle\langle\rangle, \varepsilon, \langle\rangle\rangle\}}, z, gen) \Rightarrow \Sigma_2\}$	
$e_1 \,@_{y_1}\, e_2$	$\Sigma_1 \,@_{y_1}\, \Sigma_2$	
if $l = l'$ then e_1 else e_2	$\{ rep(\boxed{\{\langle\langle\rangle, \varepsilon, \langle\rangle\rangle\}}, z,$ $\boxed{gen, (env(l) = env(l'))}) \Rightarrow \Sigma_1,$ $rep(\boxed{\{\langle\langle\rangle, \varepsilon, \langle\rangle\rangle\}}, z,$ $\boxed{gen, (env(l) \neq env(l'))}) \Rightarrow \Sigma_2\}$	
Y $(X_1 := e_1, \ldots, X_m := e_m)$	Y $(X_1 := \Sigma_1, \ldots X_m := \Sigma_m)$	
$gext_z(\lambda(l,t).(\ Z_1 := e_1,$ $\ldots,$ $Z_k := e_k))(e')$	$f(\Sigma')$	$\Sigma' = tr(e', z, gen, env)$; f defined in Figure 15

Fig. 16. Translation of UnCAL.

normal storage schema, because e_1 may refer to free variables, such as l and t. We handle free variables as follows. Consider a label variable l (it can be introduced only in a *gext* construct). Suppose l appears in e_1 as $\{l \Rightarrow \ldots\}$. Taken in isolation, this denotes a single edge, which we would construct as $E1 = \{\langle\langle\rangle, l, \langle\rangle\rangle\}$, but taken in context, that edge has to be replicated once for every element in the set denoted by $E2$. Hence, we actually generate the set $\{\langle z, \pi_2(z), z\rangle \mid z \in E2\}$. For an analogy, consider a subexpression $\{a \Rightarrow \ldots\}$ in e_1, where a is a label constant. In isolation, this should generate the CONJ expression $E1 = \{\langle\langle\rangle, a, \langle\rangle\rangle\}$, but in context, we have to replicate this edge once for every element in $E2$, so the correct expression is $\{\langle z, a, z\rangle \mid z \in E2\}$. We cannot collapse these identical edges into one, because they may lead to distinct subgraphs underneath. To translate an expression e_1 that refers to free variables, we need the additional information:

- The CONJ variable name, z.
- The scalar CONJ expression which replaces l, in our case $\pi_2(z)$. This requires an *environment*, which maps label variables to CONJ scalar expressions

and maps tree variables to storage schemas. It is denoted by $env = [l_1 :=$
$E_1, \ldots, l_n := E_n, t_1 := \Sigma_1, \ldots, t_m := \Sigma_m]$, and for a label variable l_i, $env(l_i)$
denotes its associated value, E_i, while for a tree variable t_j, $env(t_j)$ denotes
Σ_j. When a is a label constant, we define $env(a) = a$.

- The *generator* $z \in E2$. In general, a generator is a sequence $C_1, \ldots, C_n$ where
each C_i is either of the form $z \in E$, or a condition of the form $E = E'$ or
$E \neq E'$ (with E, E' scalar expressions). The latter are introduced by the
translation of if expressions.

The translation The translation function is described in Figures 16 and 15. Here
$tr(e, z, gen, env)$ takes a UnCAL expression e, a CONJ variable z, a generator
gen, and an environment env, and returns the storage schema Σ. The function
is recursive on the structure of e: whenever e has subexpressions $e_1, e_2, \ldots$, we
assume that $\Sigma_i = tr(e_i, z, gen, env)$, for $i = 1, 2, \ldots$ The translation begins with
$tr(e, z, \boxed{z \in \{\langle\rangle\}}, [])$, where $[]$ is the empty environment. The auxiliary function
$rep(E, z, gen)$ takes a CONJ expression E denoting a set of edges $\langle n, l, n'\rangle \in E$
and "replicates" them according to the generator gen (see Fig. 15). E may
actually have free variables bound by the generator, hence it is placed after gen in
Fig. 15. The function $replicate(\Sigma, z, gen)$ does this for an entire storage schema
Σ, by replacing every label E with $rep(E, z, gen)$: here $map(f)(\Sigma)$ returns a
storage schema Σ' isomorphic to Σ, in which every label E is replaced with
$f(E)$.

The only non-trivial part of tr is in the translation of a $gext(\ldots)(e')$ expression. As explained earlier, we translate e' to get Σ, then we translate the body
of $gext$ several times, once for every CONJ expression E occurring in Σ'. This
is done by the function f, described in Figure 15, which actually consists of a
number of recursive functions f_i, $i = 1, k$, where k is the number of markers in
$gext$. The role of the f_i is to traverse the storage schema Σ', process each expression E in Σ', and replace E with a storage schema consisting of three parts:
the "in" part, a translation of the body of $gext$, and the "out" part. It is in
the translation of the body where the generator and environment are expanded;
z_{new} is a fresh CONJ variable.

We extend the convention that the root of the data graph is the empty tuple,
$\langle\rangle$, to the following invariant: the translation $tr(\Sigma, z, gen, env)$ denotes a family
of data graphs, whose roots are $\{\langle z, \langle\rangle\rangle \mid gen\}$. Applied to the top translation,
we obtain as root $\langle\langle\rangle, \langle\rangle\rangle$, instead of the desired $\langle\rangle$: a minor post-processing is
necessary. We summarize here, and defer the proof to a full version of the paper:

Theorem 3. *Let Σ be a storage schema and e be some UnCAL expression.
Then (1) $\Sigma' = tr(e, z, \boxed{z \in \{\langle\rangle\}}, [])$ is type correct, and (2) whenever DB is a
data graph denoted by the storage schema Σ, and DB' is the result of computing
e, then the data-graph denoted by Σ' is bisimilar to e.*

VQL: A Query Language for Multiversion Databases

Talel Abdessalem and Geneviève Jomier

Université de Paris-Dauphine, Laboratoire LAMSADE,
F-75775 Paris Cedex, France

Abstract. In this paper VQL, a language devoted to querying data stored in multiversion databases, is proposed. A multiversion database represents several states of the modeled universe. A formal model of such a database is presented. VQL, which is based on a first order calculus, provides users with the ability of navigating through object versions, and through the states of the universe modeled by the multiversion database.

Keywords: query language, versions, multiversion database, database formal model.

1 Introduction

Numerous papers on versions, which have been appearing for twenty years, are mainly devoted to their representation in file systems and databases [22, 16, 7]. Only few papers deal with querying databases with versions. They may be grouped in two families.

The first one concerns query languages for temporal databases [26, 20, 27, 15, 24]. In such databases timestamps are associated with object versions, tuple versions or attribute versions. Timestamps may be either mono or multidimensional, based on validation time, transaction time or user-defined time. A temporal database represents as many states of the modeled universe as the number of determined time units. Query languages for temporal databases are founded on the semantics of time [25, 23, 20, 27]. Their characteristic feature is the exploitation of the total ordering of versions imposed by each temporal dimension. However, note that time is only one of multiple semantics which may be associated with versions. For instance, in design applications like CAD or CASE, versions may represent variants or alternative design choices. In such case version semantics is not related to time and version ordering is no more total.

A special case of this first family of papers is [4], where the query language IQL(2) is proposed as a unique formal support for querying distributed databases, objects with multiple roles, views and versions. We classify it as belonging to the first family, because of its concept of *context*. A context is identified and may be perceived as the place where an object or a value appears, for instance, a site in a distributed database. Such contexts are to some extent similar to the states of the modeled universe appearing in temporal databases.

In the second family of papers [7, 21], no special semantics is associated with object versioning. Object versions are implemented as objects and query languages are extended by some primitives which permit version manipulation. However, from the operational point of view, navigation in such a database containing object versions does not differ much from the navigation in a database without versions. As a consequence of the lack of versioning semantics, expressiveness of query languages is reduced and a big part of the potential of the information contained in the database cannot be used.

In this paper we propose a data model and a query language VQL for multiversion databases. The data model is an extension of the one proposed in [3] by version control which in turn is based on the Database Version approach [6]. The query language VQL is conceived as an extension of the IQL language proposed in [3]. VQL is the main contribution of this paper.

The paper is organized as follows. In Section 2 the main concepts of the Database Version approach are presented. In Section 3 a formal model of a multiversion database is proposed. This model is the basis of the query language VQL described in Section 4. In Section 5 VQL is compared with other languages proposed in the literature. Section 6 concludes the paper.

2 Database Version Approach

In this section the database version approach is presented from the user point of view. This description is limited to the concepts required to understand the remainder of this paper: database version (DBV), logical/physical object version and multiversion object.

Database Version. A conventional monoversion database (i.e. a database without versions) represents one state of the modeled universe. According to the database version approach, several states of the modeled universe are represented simultaneously in a *multiversion database*. Each state is called *database version* and denoted DBV (cf. Figure 1). A DBV has an identifier and contains one version, called a *logical version*, of each object of the modeled universe: thus objects are multiversion. A logical object version is similar to an object in a monoversion database: it has an identity and a value. The identifier of the logical version of an object o in a database version v is a couple (o, v). To represent the fact that an object does not exist in a DBV, its logical version contained in this DBV gets a special value $\perp$.

Logical/physical version. When several logical object versions have the same value, this value is stored only once, in a *physical version*. The version manager controls the association between logical and physical object versions. More details on the database version approach may be found in [6, 13].

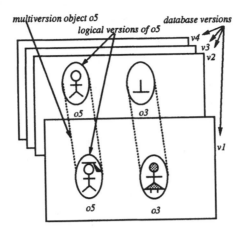

Fig. 1. A multiversion Database.

3   Data model

In this section the data model of a multiversion database is presented. It is an extension of the one proposed in [3] for the multiversion case.

3.1   Basic elements

We consider the following countably infinite and pairwise disjoint sets of atomic elements:

1. relation names $\{R_1, R_2, R_3, ...\}$,
2. class names $\{C_1, C_2, C_3, ...\}$,
3. attributes $\{A_1, A_2, A_3, ...\}$,
4. constants $D = \{d_1, d_2, d_3, ...\}$,
5. object identifiers (oids) $O = \{o_1, o_2, o_3, ...\}$,
6. DBV identifiers $V = \{v_1, v_2, v_3, ...\}$.

The product $O \times V$ denotes the set of logical object version identifiers (cf. Section 2).

Definition 1. The set of o-values, *O-Value*, is the smallest set containing $D \cup O$ and such that if $ov_1, ..., ov_k$ $(k \geq 0)$ are o-values then $[A_1 : ov_1, ..., A_k: ov_k]$ and $\{ov_1, ..., ov_k\}$ are o-values.

Throughout this exposition, the generic notation $[A_1 : ..., ..., A_k: ...]$, where $k \geq 0$, is used for a tuple formed using any k distinct attributes $A_1, ..., A_k$. Sets are represented using $\{\ \}$ symbols.

Definition 2. The set of v-values, *V-Value*, is the smallest set containing V and such that if $v_1, ..., v_k$ $(k \geq 0)$ are v-values then $[A_1 : v_1, ..., A_k: v_k]$ and $\{v_1, ..., v_k\}$ are v-values.

Definition 3. Let **R** be a finite set of relation names and **C** a finite set of class names.

1. **R** is composed of two disjoint subsets: **R** = **Rv** ∪ **Ro**, **Rv** for v-value relations, called *v-relations*, and **Ro** for o-value relations, called *o-relations*;
2. A *v-value assignment* for **Rv** is a function ρ_v: **Rv** ⟶ *V-Value* mapping each name in **Rv** to a v-value;
3. Let **V** = $\{v \mid v \in V$ and v is a component of $\rho_v(R_v)$, $R_v \in$ **Rv**$\}$. An *o-value assignment* for **Ro** is a partial function ρ_o mapping each couple (relation name in **Ro**, DBV identifier in **V**) to an o-value. ρ_o: **Ro** × **V** ⟶ *O-Value*;
4. An *oid assignment* for **C** is a function π: **C** ⟶ 2^O_{fin} mapping each name in **C** to a finite set of oids, such that if $C \neq C'$ then $\pi(C) \cap \pi(C') = \emptyset$, where $C, C' \in$ **C**.

Informally, in an object-oriented database, **C** is the set of all class names, **R** is the set of all persistent root names, and *O-Value* is the set of all oids and possible object values. In the multiversion case, a new kind of relations is introduced: the v-relations, which are composed of DBVs. The traditional relations, composed of o-values, are called o-relations.

Remark 4. From the language point of view, persistent roots are used as entry points to get information from the database. Implementation aspects are beyond the scope of this paper.

The assignment functions ρ_v and ρ_o allow getting relation values. An o-relation value may change from one DBV to another. When an o-relation R_o is not defined (does not exist) in a DBV v, its value $\rho_o(R_o, v)$ is $\{\}$ if R_o is of set type, otherwise $\rho_o(R_o, v)$ is undefined.

Remark 5. The oid assignment function π defined above is global to all DBVs: an object belongs to the same class in every DBV. This hypothesis simplifies type checking. For this reason, we assume that the type of objects and o-relations does not change from one DBV to another.

3.2 Syntax and semantics of types

The set of type expressions *Types* is defined as: *Types* = *types*(**C**) ∪ *types*(*DBV*), where *types*(**C**) denotes the set of type expressions associated with o-values and *types*(*DBV*) denotes the set of type expressions associated with v-values. Types associated with o-values are similar to the types used in monoversion databases.

Types associated with o-values. Let **C** be a set of class names and π an oid assignment for **C**. The set of type expressions *types*(**C**) is defined as follows:

$$\tau = \emptyset \mid D \mid C \mid [A_1 : \tau, \ldots, A_k : \tau] \mid \{\tau\} \mid (\tau \vee \tau) \mid (\tau \wedge \tau); \text{ where } \tau \in types(\mathbf{C}),$$
$$C \in \mathbf{C} \text{ and } k \geq 0.$$

Each type expression $\tau \in types(\mathbf{C})$ is given a set of o-values, denoted $\left[\!\left[\tau\right]\!\right]_\pi$, as its *interpretation*, in the following natural manner:

- $\left[\!\left[\emptyset\right]\!\right]_\pi = \emptyset$, $\left[\!\left[D\right]\!\right]_\pi = D$, $\left[\!\left[C\right]\!\right]_\pi = \pi(C)$, for each $C \in \mathbf{C}$;
- $\left[\!\left[(\tau_1 \vee \tau_2)\right]\!\right]_\pi = \left[\!\left[\tau_1\right]\!\right]_\pi \cup \left[\!\left[\tau_2\right]\!\right]_\pi$ and $\left[\!\left[(\tau_1 \wedge \tau_2)\right]\!\right]_\pi = \left[\!\left[\tau_1\right]\!\right]_\pi \cap \left[\!\left[\tau_2\right]\!\right]_\pi$;
- $\left[\!\left[\{\tau\}\right]\!\right]_\pi = \left\{\{ov_1,\ldots,ov_j\} \mid j \geq 0, \text{ and } ov_i \in \left[\!\left[\tau\right]\!\right]_\pi, i = 1,\ldots,j\right\}$;
- $\left[\!\left[[A_1 : \tau_1,\ldots,A_k : \tau_k]\right]\!\right]_\pi = \left\{[A_1 : ov_1,\ldots,A_k : ov_k] \mid ov_i \in \left[\!\left[\tau_i\right]\!\right]_\pi,\right.$
  $\left. i = 1,\ldots,k\right\}$.

Remark 6. The set of type expressions $types(\mathbf{C})$ is depending on the set of class names $\mathbf{C}$. This is due to the fact that class names are used as type expressions, to designate abstract types.

Types associated with v-values. The set of type expressions $types(DBV)$ is defined as follows:

$$\tau = dbv \mid \{\tau\} \mid [A_1 : \tau,\ldots,A_k : \tau]; \text{ where } \tau \in types(DBV) \text{ and } k \geq 0.$$

Each type expression $\tau \in types(DBV)$ is given a set of v-values, denoted $\left[\!\left[\tau\right]\!\right]$, as its *interpretation*, in the following manner:

- $\left[\!\left[dbv\right]\!\right] = V$;
- $\left[\!\left[\{\tau\}\right]\!\right] = \left\{\{v_1,\ldots,v_j\} \mid j \geq 0, \text{ and } v_i \in \left[\!\left[\tau\right]\!\right], i = 1,\ldots,j\right\}$;
- $\left[\!\left[[A_1 : \tau_1,\ldots,A_k : \tau_k]\right]\!\right] = \left\{[A_1 : v_1,\ldots,A_k : v_k] \mid v_i \in \left[\!\left[\tau_i\right]\!\right], i = 1,\ldots,k\right\}$.

3.3 Database schema and instance

Definition 7. A multiversion database schema is a quadruple $S = (\mathbf{Ro}, \mathbf{Rv}, \mathbf{C}, \mathbf{T})$, where $\mathbf{Ro}$ is a finite set of o-relation names; $\mathbf{Rv}$ is a finite set of v-relation names; $\mathbf{C}$ is a finite set of class names and $\mathbf{T}$ is a function from $\mathbf{Ro} \cup \mathbf{Rv} \cup \mathbf{C}$ to the set of type expressions $Types$.

Definition 8. Given a multiversion database schema $S = (\mathbf{Ro}, \mathbf{Rv}, \mathbf{C}, \mathbf{T})$, a multiversion instance I of S is a quadruple $I = (\rho_o, \rho_v, \pi, \nu)$, where ρ_o is an o-value assignment for $\mathbf{Ro}$; ρ_v is a v-value assignment for $\mathbf{Rv}$; π is an oid assignment for $\mathbf{C}$ and $\nu: \{\pi(C) \mid C \in \mathbf{C}\} \times \mathbf{V} \longrightarrow O\text{-}Value$ is a value assignment function, such that:

1. $\rho_o(R_o, v) \subseteq \left[\!\left[\mathbf{T}(R_o)\right]\!\right]_\pi$, for each $R_o \in \mathbf{Ro}$ and $v \in \mathbf{V}$;
2. $\rho_v(R_v) \subseteq \left[\!\left[\mathbf{T}(R_v)\right]\!\right]$ for each $R_v \in \mathbf{Rv}$;

3. $\nu(\pi(C), v) \subseteq \left[\!\left[\mathbf{T}(C)\right]\!\right]_\pi$, for each $C \in \mathbf{C}$ and $v \in \mathbf{V}$;

4. ν is total on $\pi(C) \times \mathbf{V}$, for each $C \in \mathbf{C}$ with $\mathbf{T}(C)=\{\tau\}$.

Let $I = (\rho_o, \rho_v, \pi, \nu)$ be an instance of schema $S = (\mathbf{Ro}, \mathbf{Rv}, \mathbf{C}, \mathbf{T})$. Each oid occurring in I (i.e. in the ranges of ρ_o, π and ν) belongs to some $\pi(C)$, where $C \in \mathbf{C}$. This follows from conditions (1) and (3) of the Definition 8 and from the semantics of types.

A *set valued* oid in I is an oid belonging to a class C, where $\mathbf{T}(C)=\{\tau\}$ for some $\tau \in types(\mathbf{C})$. Condition 4 of Definition 8 specifies that ν is total for set valued oids. We follow the convention that, given a DBV v, if for a set valued oid o there is no o-value $ov \in \nu(o, v)$ then $\nu(o, v) = \{\}$, and if for a non-set valued oid o there is no o-value $ov = \nu(o, v)$ then $\nu(o, v)$ is undefined.

In section 2 we specified that an object has a logical version and then a value in each DBV. This value may be $\perp$, meaning "doesn't exist", in some DBVs. Formally, $\perp$ is an empty set for set valued oids, and it is an undefined value for non-set valued oids.

Example 9. To illustrate the concepts set out in this section, let us consider the "imaginary family" multiversion database shown on figure 2. Three names of relations appear: *My_ parents* and *My_ friends* designate two o-relations and *My_ DBVs* designates a v-relation. For My_parents the o-relation value is the same in every DBV. For My_friend the o-relation value varies according to the DBV. In this example, each DBV represents the state of persons that are "close to me", at a given time. Time is represented as an attribute of the object named DBV_Desc (i.e. DBV descriptor). In each DBV, the value of this object describes the corresponding state of the modeled universe.

Database schema:
  $\mathbf{Ro} = \{My\_parents, My\_friends, DBV\_Desc\}$,
  $\mathbf{Rv} = \{My\_DBVs\}$,
  $\mathbf{C} = \{Person, Descriptor\}$ and
  $\mathbf{T}$ is defined by:
    class Person : [Name : string, City : string, Kids : {Person}],
    class Descriptor : [Date : integer, State : string]
    type My_parents : {Person}, *type* My_friends : {Person},
    type DBV_Desc : Descriptor, *type* My_DBVs : {dbv}.
Instance description (limited to the content of DBVs v_1 and v_2):
  $\pi(Person) = \{o_1, o_2, o_3, o_4, o_5, o_6\}$, $\pi(Descriptor) = \{o_7\}$
  $\rho_v(My\_DBVs) = \{v_1, v_2, v_3, v_4\}$
  DBV v_1:
  $\rho_o(My\_parents, v_1) = \{o_1, o_2\}$, $\rho_o(My\_friends, v_1) = \{o_4, o_5\}$, $\rho_o(DBV\_Desc, v_1) = o_7$,
  $\nu(o_1, v_1) = [Name : Ben, City : Paris, Kids : \{\}]$,
  $\nu(o_2, v_1) = [Name : Margareth, City : Paris, Kids : \{\}]$,
  $\nu(o_3, v_1)$ is undefined,
  $\nu(o_4, v_1) = [Name : Charles, City : Paris, Kids : \{\}]$,
  $\nu(o_5, v_1) = [Name : Moustapha, City : St Denis, Kids : \{\}]$,
  $\nu(o_6, v_1)$ is undefined,
  $\nu(o_7, v_1) = [Date : 1980, State : adolescence]$.
  DBV v_2:
  $\rho_o(My\_parents, v_2) = \{o_1, o_2\}$, $\rho_o(My\_friends, v_2) = \{o_3, o_4\}$, $\rho_o(DBV\_Desc, v_2) = o_7$,
  $\nu(o_1, v_2) = [Name : Ben, City : Marseille, Kids : \{\}]$,
  $\nu(o_2, v_2) = [Name : Margareth, City : Marseille, Kids : \{\}]$,
  $\nu(o_3, v_2) = [Name : Imen, City : Nice, Kids : \{\}]$,
  $\nu(o_4, v_2) = [Name : Charles, City : Paris, Kids : \{\}]$,
  $\nu(o_5, v_2) = [Name : Moustapha, City : St Denis, Kids : \{\}]$,
  $\nu(o_6, v_2)$ is undefined,
  $\nu(o_7, v_2) = [Date : 1990, State : university]$.

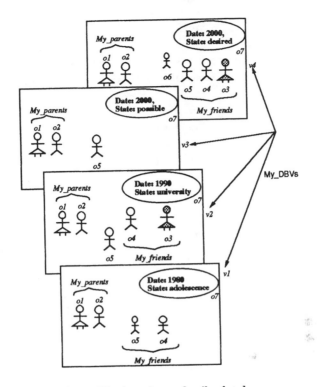

Fig. 2. The imaginary family database.

4 Query language

In this section a query language VQL, which is a first order calculus, is proposed. This calculus extends the proposals of [2, 4] to DBVs. From the language point of view, there are two main contributions of VQL: (1) specific terms to denote the modeled universe states (DBVs), and (2) a dereferencing operation taking into account the "DBV dimension". The first one enables user to specify the states of the modeled universe he/she wants to query. The second one makes it possible to keep the track of an object through DBVs, i.e. through different states of the modeled universe.

This section is organized as follows. In section 4.1, a complex value calculus integrating DBVs is proposed followed, in section 4.2, by some examples of queries explaining the use of VQL language. In section 4.3, the semantics of VQL queries is defined. In section 4.4, a navigation technique for multiversion databases is proposed. In section 4.5, the use of quantifiers over DBVs is analyzed and in section 4.6, the use of ⊥ values is described.

4.1 Calculus

Terms. There are two categories of terms: terms denoting v-values and terms denoting o-values.

- Terms denoting v-values (v-value terms)
  1. R_v, $R_v \in \mathbf{Rv}$;
  2. x_τ, where x is a variable of type $\tau \in types(DBV)$;
  3. projection $t.A$, where t is an v-value term of type tuple and A is an attribute name;
  4. constructed terms: tuples $[A_1 : t_1, \ldots, A_n : t_n]$ and sets $\{t_1, \ldots, t_n\}$, where $t_1, \ldots, t_n$ are v-value terms, $A_1, \ldots, A_n$ are attribute names and $n \geq 0$.
- Terms denoting o-values (o-value terms)
  1. d, d in D;
  2. $R_o(t)$, $R_o \in \mathbf{Ro}$ and t a v-value term of type dbv;
  3. x_τ, where x is a variable of type τ, $\tau \in types(\mathbf{C})$;
  4. projection $t.A$, where t is an o-value term of type tuple and A is an attribute name;
  5. *dereferencing* $*(t_1, t_2)$, where t_1 is an o-value term denoting an oid and t_2 a v-value term of type dbv;
  6. constructed terms: tuples $[A_1 : t_1, \ldots, A_n : t_n]$ and sets $\{t_1, \ldots, t_n\}$, where $t_1, \ldots, t_n$ are o-value terms, $A_1, \ldots, A_n$ are attribute names and $n \geq 0$.

Each variable has a type, and each value belongs to the interpretation of a type (cf. Definition 8). Therefore, each term has a type that can be determined easily. For example, the type of a tuple $[A_1 : t_1, ..., A_n : t_n]$, where $t_1, \ldots, t_n$ are terms of respective types $\tau_1, ..., \tau_n$, is $\tau = [A_1 : \tau_1, ..., A_n : \tau_n]$.

Formulas. Predicates $=$ and $\in$ applied to terms with the proper type restrictions yield *atomic formulas*: $t = t'$, $t \in t'$, with t and t' terms of compatible types. In addition, we define a new predicate $Undef()$. Applied to dereferencing terms, $Undef(*(t_1, t_2))$, where t_1 denotes an oid o and t_2 denotes a DBV v, indicates whether $\nu(o, v)$ is defined or not. The use of this predicate is extended to o-relation terms: $Undef(R_o(t_2))$, where R_o is an o-relation name, indicates whether $\rho_o(R_o, v)$ is defined or not. $Undef(*(t_1, t_2))$ and $Undef(R_o(t_2))$ are atomic formulas.

Formulas are obtained from atomic formulas by application of the connectives $\wedge$, $\vee$, $\neg$, and the quantifiers $\exists$ and $\forall$. If L_1 and L_2 are two formulas, then $L_1 \wedge L_2, L_1 \vee L_2, \neg L_1$, are formulas. If x_τ is a free variable of formula $L_1(x_\tau)$, then $\exists x_\tau (L_1(x_\tau))$ and $\forall x_\tau (L_1(x_\tau))$ are formulas.

Queries. A query on a multiversion database can be expressed in one of the following two ways:

- $\{ x \mid \varphi \}$, where φ is a formula and x the free variable of φ;
- $\{ (x, y) \mid \varphi \}$, where φ is a formula and x, y are the free variables of φ, x is of type $\tau \in types(\mathbf{C})$ and y is of type dbv.

The result of the first kind of queries is a selection of v-values or a selection of o-values. When a DBV is selected, implicitly, all the logical object versions it contains are selected. When an object is selected, implicitly, all its logical versions are selected.

The second kind of queries selects couples (o-value, DBV). The result of such a query is a multiversion instance, composed of the selected DBVs with the selected o-values. Let (o_1, v_1) and (o_2, v_2) be the result of a query. The output multiversion instance is therefore composed of two DBVs : v_1 and v_2. The only object existing in v_1 is o_1, and the only one existing in v_2 is o_2.

4.2 Examples of VQL queries

v-value selection. Consider the "imaginary family" database (cf. Example 9). The following query selects the DBV representing the year 1990.

$$Q_1 : \{ \ y \mid y \in \text{My\_DBVs} \land *(\text{DBV\_Desc}(y), y).\text{Date} = 1990 \ \}$$

The term DBV_Desc(y) denotes object o_7 for each y in My_DBVs. The dereferencing of this object *(DBV_Desc(y), y) allows the access to the value of o_7 in each of My_DBVs. Object o_7 is of tuple type, the projection on attribute Date allows to find out the corresponding year for each DBV. Only the DBV corresponding to 1990 is selected. The expression of query Q_1 in an OQL-like syntax [5, 18] is:

```
SELECT y
FROM   y in My_DBVs
WHERE  (DBV_Desc, y).Date = 1990
```

Here, the term DBV_Desc(y) has been simplified in DBV_Desc. This simplification is considered in the following, each time the designated o-relation does not vary from a DBV to another.

o-value selection. Let the DBV retrieved by query Q_1 be denoted Current_DBV. Query Q_2 retrieves the object representing "my friend Charles" in the "Current DBV".

$$Q_2 : \{ \ x \mid x \in \text{My\_friends}(\text{Current\_DBV}) \land *(x, \text{Current\_DBV}).\text{Name} = \text{``Charles''}\}$$

In an OQL-like syntax:

```
SELECT x
FROM   x in My_friends(Current_DBV)
WHERE  (x,Current_DBV).Name = "Charles"
```

Remark 10. A selection made in a fixed DBV is equivalent to the one in a monoversion database. For instance, if the current DBV is considered as a default DBV, query Q_2 can be written as follows:

```
SELECT x
FROM   x in My_friends
WHERE  x.Name = "Charles"
```

Couple (o-value, DBV) selection. The purpose of the (o-value, DBV) couple selection is to allow a user to know which DBV contains which o-value selected. The following query looks for "my friends" in the DBVs of 1980 and 1990. Each retrieved object is associated with the DBV in which it represents a "friend of mine".

$Q_3 : \{\ (x, y)\ |\ y \in$ `My_DBVs` $\qquad\qquad \wedge x \in$ `My_friends` $(y) \qquad\qquad \wedge$
$\qquad\qquad (*($`DBV_Desc`(y), $y)$.`Date=1980` $\vee\ *($`DBV_Desc`(y), $y)$.`Date=1990` $)\ \}$

In an OQL-like syntax:

```
SELECT (x, y)
FROM   y in My_DBVs, x in My_friends(y)
WHERE  (DBV_Desc, y).Date = 1980 or (DBV_Desc, y).Date = 1990
```

In this example, selected couples identify logical object versions. The selection is restricted to the DBVs of 1980 and 1990 (v_1 and v_2). The content of these DBVs is restricted to the logical versions of objects representing "my friends": o_4, o_5 in v_1 and o_3, o_4 in v_2, as presented in Figure 3.

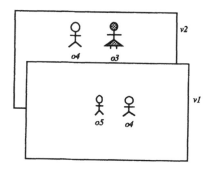

Fig. 3. Query Q_3 output.

4.3 Semantics

The notions presented in this section are staightforward extensions of those used for the semantics of IQL in [3]. They are slightly complicated by the use of DBVs in VQL. For the comprehension of VQL query semantics, we need to define projections of multiversion database schemas and instances. Let $S=(\mathbf{Ro}, \mathbf{Rv}, \mathbf{C}, \mathbf{T})$ be a multiversion database schema.

- A schema $S'= (\mathbf{Ro}', \mathbf{Rv}', \mathbf{C}', \mathbf{T}')$ is a *projection* of schema S if $\mathbf{Ro}' \subseteq \mathbf{Ro}$, $\mathbf{Rv}' \subseteq \mathbf{Rv}$, $\mathbf{C}' \subseteq \mathbf{C}$ and $\mathbf{T}'$ is the mapping of $\mathbf{T}$ on $\mathbf{Ro}' \cup \mathbf{Rv}' \cup \mathbf{C}'$.
- Given a multiversion instance $I = (\rho_o, \rho_v, \pi, \nu)$ of S, its projection on S', denoted $I[S']$, is defined as a mapping of ρ_o, ρ_v, π and ν on $\mathbf{Ro'}$, $\mathbf{Rv'}$ and $\mathbf{C'}$. $I[S']$ is an instance of S'.

A VQL query, denoted $\Gamma(S, S_{in}, S_{out})$, is composed of formulas over a schema S. Its semantics is a binary relation between multiversion instances. This relation, denoted γ, associates a multiversion instance over the *output schema* S_{out} to each instance over the *input schema* S_{in}, where S_{in} and S_{out} are two projections of S. Intuitively, S_{in} contains the names of the queried relations, the class names associated with the queried objects and the corresponding type association function, and S_{out} contains the names of the retrieved relations, the class names of the retrieved objects and the corresponding type function. The input of a query is a multiversion instance I over S_{in}, the computation of the query defines a multiversion instance J over S, and the output is $J[S_{out}]$.

Valuation. Given a multiversion instance $I = (\rho_o, \rho_v, \pi, \nu)$, the valuation of VQL queries is done using two disjoint functions: θ_v for *v-value valuation*, and θ_o for *o-value valuation*. θ_v is a partial function from variables y of type $\tau \in types(VBD)$ to *V-Value* such that: if $\theta_v\left(y\right)$ is defined, then $\theta_v\left(y\right) \in \left[\!\left[\tau\right]\!\right]$. A v-value valuation can be extended to v-value terms as follows:

$$\theta_v\left(R_v\right) = \rho_v(R_v);$$

$$\theta_v\left(t.A\right) = \theta_v\left(t\right).A;$$

$$\theta_v\left(\{t_1, \ldots, t_k\}\right) = \{\theta_v\left(t_1\right), \ldots, \theta_v\left(t_k\right)\},$$

$$\theta_v\left([A_1 : t_1, \ldots, A_k : t_k]\right) = [A_1 : \theta_v\left(t_1\right), \ldots, A_k : \theta_v\left(t_k\right)], \ k \geq 0.$$

An *o-value valuation function* θ_o is a partial function from variables x of type $\tau \in types(C)$ to o-values such that: if $\theta_o\left(x\right)$ is defined, then $\theta_o\left(x\right) \in \left[\!\left[\tau\right]\!\right]_\pi$. An o-value valuation can be extended to o-value terms as follows:

$$\theta_o\left(d\right) = d;$$

$$\theta_o\left(R_o(t)\right) = \rho_o(R_o, \theta_v\left(t\right));$$

$$\theta_o\left(t.A\right) = \theta_o\left(t\right).A;$$

$$\theta_o\left(*(t_1, t_2)\right) = \nu(\theta_o\left(t_1\right), \theta_v\left(t_2\right));$$

$$\theta_o\left(\{t_1, \ldots, t_k\}\right) = \{\theta_o\left(t_1\right), \ldots, \theta_o\left(t_k\right)\},$$

$$\theta_o\left([A_1 : t_1, \ldots, A_k : t_k]\right) = [A_1 : \theta_o\left(t_1\right), \ldots, A_k : \theta_o\left(t_k\right)], \ k \geq 0.$$

Satisfaction. Let I be a multiversion instance, θ_v a DBV valuation that must be defined on v-value terms t_1, t_2, and θ_o an o-value valuation that must be defined on o-value terms t_1', t_2'. The following rules allow to determine whether I *satisfies* ($\models$) a VQL query or not.

$$I \models t_1 \in t_2 \text{ if } \theta_v\left(t_1\right) \in \theta_v\left(t_2\right); \qquad I \models t_1' \in t_2' \text{ if } \theta_o\left(t_1'\right) \in \theta_o\left(t_2'\right);$$

$$I \models t_1 = t_2 \text{ if } \theta_v\left(t_1\right) = \theta_v\left(t_2\right); \qquad I \models t_1' = t_2' \text{ if } \theta_o\left(t_1'\right) = \theta_o\left(t_2'\right);$$

$$I \models \neg(t_1 \in t_2) \text{ if } \theta_v\left(t_1\right) \notin \theta_v\left(t_2\right); \quad I \models \neg(t_1' \in t_2') \text{ if } \theta_o\left(t_1'\right) \notin \theta_o\left(t_2'\right);$$

$$I \models \neg(t_2 = t_1) \text{ if } \theta_v\left(t_1\right) \neq \theta_v\left(t_2\right); \quad I \models \neg(t_2' = t_1') \text{ if } \theta_o\left(t_1'\right) \neq \theta_o\left(t_2'\right);$$

$$I \models Undef(*(t_1', t_1)) \text{ if } \nu(\theta_o\left(t_1'\right), \theta_v\left(t_1\right)) \text{ is undefined};$$

$$I \models \neg(Undef(t_1', t_1)) \text{ if } \nu(\theta_o\left(t_1'\right), \theta_v\left(t_1\right)) \text{ is defined};$$

$$I \models Undef(R_o(t_1)) \text{ if } \rho(R_o, \theta_v\left(t_1\right)) \text{ is undefined};$$

$$I \models \neg(Undef(R_o(t_1))) \text{ if } \rho(R_o, \theta_v\left(t_1\right)) \text{ is defined}.$$

In addition, let L_1, L_2 be two formulas. We say that:

$I \models L_1 \wedge L_1$ if $I \models L_1$ and $I \models L_2$; $\ I \models L_1 \vee L_2$ if $I \models L_1$ or $I \models L_2$;

$I \models \exists x_\tau(L_1(x_\tau)), \tau \in types(VBD)$, if it exists $v = \theta_v\left(x\right)$ such that $I \models L_1(v)$;

$I \models \exists x_\tau(L_1(x_\tau)), \tau \in types(C)$, if it exists $ov = \theta_o\left(x\right)$ such that $I \models L_1(ov)$;

$I \models \forall x_\tau(L_1(x_\tau)), \tau \in types(VBD)$, if for each $v = \theta_v\left(x\right)$, $I \models L_1(v)$;

$I \models \forall x_\tau(L_1(x_\tau)), \tau \in types(C)$, if for each $ov = \theta_o\left(x\right)$, $I \models L_1(ov)$;

$I \models \neg(L_1 \wedge L_1)$ if $I \models \neg L_1$ or $I \models \neg L_2$; $\ I \models \neg(L_1 \vee L_2)$ if $I \models \neg L_1$ and $I \models \neg L_2$;

$I \models \neg(\exists x_\tau(L_1(x_\tau)))$ if $I \models \forall x_\tau(\neg L_1(x_\tau))$; $\ I \models \neg(\forall x_\tau(L_1(x_\tau)))$ if $I \models \exists x_\tau(\neg L_1(x_\tau))$.

Example of valuation. Let's consider the query Q_2, presented in section 4.2 (cf. Page 9). I_{in} denotes the input instance of this query. The computation of Q_2 is done following the next valuation steps :

$I_{in} \models Q_2$ if $I_{in} \models x \in$ My_friends(Current_DBV) and

$\qquad\qquad I_{in} \models *(x, \text{Current\_DBV}).\text{Name} = \text{``Charles''}$

i.e., if $\quad I_{in} \models \theta_o\left(x\right) \in \theta_o\left(\text{My\_friends(Current\_DBV)}\right)$ and

$\qquad\qquad I_{in} \models \theta_o\left(*(x, \text{Current\_DBV}).\text{Name}\right) = \theta_o\left(\text{``Charles''}\right)$

i.e., if $\quad I_{in} \models \theta_o\left(x\right) \in \rho_o(\text{My\_friends}, \theta_v\left(\text{Current\_DBV}\right))$ and

$\qquad\qquad I_{in} \models \theta_o\left(*(x, \text{Current\_DBV})\right).\text{Name} = \text{``Charles''}$

i.e., if $\quad I_{in} \models \theta_o\left(x\right) \in \rho_o(\text{My\_friends}, \rho_v(\text{Current\_DBV}))$ and

$\qquad\qquad I_{in} \models \nu(\theta_o\left(x\right), \theta_v\left(\text{Current\_DBV}\right)).\text{Name} = \text{``Charles''}$

i.e., if $\quad I_{in} \models \theta_o\left(x\right) \in \rho_o(\text{ My\_friends, } v_2)$ $\qquad$ and

$\qquad I_{in} \models \nu(\theta_o\left(x\right), \rho_v(\text{Current\_DBV})).\text{Name} = \text{"Charles"}$

i.e., if (1) $I_{in} \models \theta_o\left(x\right) \in \{o_3, o_4\}$ $\qquad$ and

$\qquad$ (2) $I_{in} \models \nu(\theta_o\left(x\right), v_2).\text{Name} = \text{"Charles"}$

Query Q_2 looks for o-values $ov = \theta_o\left(x\right)$ such that (1) and (2) are satisfied. Instance I_{in} satisfies $\nu(o_4, v_2).\text{Name} = \text{"Charles"}$, but it does not satisfy $\nu(o_3, v_2).\text{Name}=\text{"Charles"}$. So, o_4 is the only object retrieved by Q_2, i.e. o_4 is the only oid occurring in Q_2 output instance.

Treatment of $\perp$ values. Let's imagine that object o_4 does not exist in DBV v_2, i.e. it has $\perp$ as a value in DBV v_2. Formally this means that $\nu(o_4, v_2)$ is undefined and, consequently, I_{in} doesn't satisfy $\nu(o_4, v_2).\text{Name} = \text{"Charles"}$.

4.4 Navigating through object versions

In a declarative language, a query states the required information and the path to reach it. In a monoversion database, a path goes through a finite sequence of objects/values [9, 8, 17]. In a multiversion database, a path may either be limited to one DBV only or it may go across DBVs (cf. Figure 4).

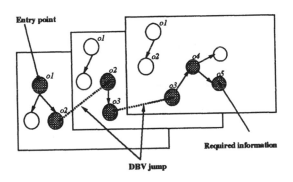

Fig. 4. A path going across several DBVs.

The dereferencing operation can be used to "jump" from one logical version of an object to another logical version of the same object, i.e. from one DBV to another. A path beginning in a DBV v_1 can continue in a DBV v_2, after an object dereferencing in v_2. So, a user may navigate in a multiversion database through a finite sequence of logical object versions/values, possibly contained in different DBVs.

Next example concerns paths across DBVs. We consider the "imaginary family" database with the following schema and instance additions.

```
class    Person : [Name : string, City : string, Kids : {Person}, Diploma : Certificate]
class    Certificate: [ Title: string, Institute : string]
type     My_best_friend : Person (My_best_friend ∈ Ro)
```

$\rho_o(My\_best\_friend, v_1) = o_5$
$\rho_o(My\_best\_friend, v_2) = o_4$
$\rho_o(My\_best\_friend, v_3)$ is undefined
$\rho_o(My\_best\_friend, v_4) = o_3$

$\nu(o_5, v_2) = [Name : Moustapha, City: St\ Denis, Kids : \{\}, Diploma : o_9]$
$\nu(o_9, v_2) = [\ Title: M.D.\ 93 - Computer\ Science, Institute: Univ.\ of\ St\ Denis\ ]$
$\nu(o_9, v_3)$ is undefined
$\nu(o_9, v_4) = [\ Title: M.D.\ 93 - DB\ and\ AI, Institute: Univ.\ of\ St\ Denis\ ]$

The title in 2000 of the diploma obtained in 1990 by the best friend I had in 1980 is required. Query Q_4 retrieves it. In this query, paths expressed by the term *(*(My_best_friend(t), z).Diploma, y).Title, go through three DBVs. Each path begins with the o-relation My_best_friend in the 1980 DBV, continues through the logical version of object o_5 in the 1990 DBV, then through the logical version of object o_9 in the 1990 DBV, and ends at a logical version of object o_9 in one the DBVs representing year 2000. This example shows that it is possible to select information contained in one DBV, starting from an entry point contained in another.

$Q_4 : \{\ (x,\ y)\ |\ y \in$ My_DBVs $\qquad \wedge$ *(DBV_Desc(y), y).Date = 2000 $\qquad \wedge$
$\qquad\qquad \exists z\ \exists t\ (\ z \in$ My_DBVs $\wedge$ *(DBV_Desc(z), z).Date = 1990 $\qquad \wedge$
$\qquad\qquad\qquad t \in$ My_DBVs $\wedge$ *(DBV_Desc(t), t).Date = 1980 $\qquad \wedge$
$\qquad\qquad\qquad x =$*(*(My_best_friend(t), z).Diploma, y).Title) }

In an OQL-like syntax:

```
SELECT (x, y)
FROM    y in My_DBVs, z in My_DBVs, t in My_DBVs
WHERE   (DBV_Desc, y).Date=2000 and (DBV_Desc, z).Date=1990 and
        (DBV_Desc, t).Date=1980 and
        x =*(*(My_best_friend(t), z).Diploma, y).Title
```

The valuation of variables t, z and y in query Q_4 gives :

$$\theta_v\left(t\right)\ =\ v_1, \theta_v\left(z\right) = v_2\ \ et\ \theta_v\left(y\right) \in \{v_3, v_4\}.$$

Consequently, two paths are explored:

(1) *(*(My_best_friend(v_1), v_2).Diploma, v_3).Title,
(2) *(*(My_best_friend(v_1), v_2).Diploma, v_4).Title.

Since $\nu(o_9, v_3)$ is undefined, the valuation of the first path, $\theta_o\left((1)\right)$, is undefined. Only the second path valuation returns a value for x : $\theta_o\left(x\right)=$"M.D. 93 - DB and AI".

4.5 Quantifying on DBVs

In VQL, the *quantification on v-values* is done in the same way as on objects or values (o-values). Quantification on v-values is usually associated with quantification on o-values. Query Q_5 is an example of association in the form $\{\ldots \mid \forall x \; \exists v \ldots\}$, where x designates an o-value and v a DBV. In this example, the value of v depends on that of x. Q_5 looks for "my friends" in 1990, whose all children own a PhD. Note that in each DBV only the diplomas obtained in the year corresponding to this DBV are represented.

Q_5 : {$(x,y) \mid y \in$ My_DBVs $\wedge x \in$ My_friends$(y) \wedge *$(DBV_Desc(y),y).Date=1990 $\wedge$
$\quad \forall t \; \exists z \; (t \in *(x, y)$.kids $\qquad \wedge z \in$ My_DBVs $\qquad\qquad \wedge$
$\qquad *(*(t,z)$.Diploma,z).Title = "PhD" $\qquad\qquad)$}

In an OQL-like syntax:

```
SELECT (x, y)
FROM   y in My_DBVs, x in My_friends(y)
WHERE  (DBV_Desc, y).Date = 1990 and for all t in (x, y).kids :
                 exists z in My_DBVs : ((t,z).Diploma, z).Title="PhD"
```

The PhD defense year is specific to each child. So, the DBV containing this information (PhD defense) depends on the child.

4.6 Using $\perp$ value

As mentioned in section 2, a logical version of an object o contained in a DBV v gets a special value $\perp$ to indicate that object o does not exist in DBV v. Formally, this value is {} for set valued oids and it is undefined for non-set valued oids. Value $\perp$ can be used as a selection criterion. For example, query Q_6 looks for the kids of "my friends" in 2000 that (the kids) are born after 1990, i.e. which are represented by objects having as a value $\perp$ in the DBV of 1990 and a value different from $\perp$ in one or both of the DBVs of 2000.

Q_6 : { $(x,y) \mid y \in$ My_DBVs $\qquad \wedge *$(DBV_Desc(y),y).Date=2000 $\wedge$
$\quad \exists t \; (t \in$ My_friends$(y) \wedge x \in *(t,y)$.Kids $\qquad\qquad \wedge$
$\qquad \exists z \; (z \in$ My_DBVs $\wedge *$(DBV_Desc(z),z).Date=1990 $\wedge$
$\qquad Undef(*(x,z)) \wedge \neg(Undef(*(x,y)))$ $\qquad)$ }

In an OQL-like syntax:

```
SELECT (x, y)
FROM   y in My_DBVs, t in My_friends(y), x ∈ *(t,y).Kids, z in My_DBVs,
WHERE  (DBV_Desc, y).Date = 2000 and (DBV_Desc, z).Date = 1990 and
       (x, z) = ⊥ and (x, y) != ⊥
```

5 Related work

In this section the main tools and languages proposed in the literature for querying databases with versions are analyzed. Two categories of propositions are successively presented: propositions based on version models, and propositions based on temporal models.

5.1 Version approaches

Most of version models proposed so far provide manipulation primitives in order
to create, read and update object versions [7, 16, 21, 22]. However, few papers
are concerned with querying databases with versions [22, 14]. Previous propositions are based on version models using the only concept of entity (or object)
versioning. The states of the modeled universe are not represented, giving raise
to consistency problems. The limits of these models are shown in [12].

Table 1 summarizes the previous contributions. The first column gives a paper
reference. The second column indicates whether a query language is proposed or
not. The next three columns give an idea on selection possibilities ("–" denotes
unmentioned operations). The fifth column concerns the keeping of the track of
an object through its versions, and the last column indicates whether a formal
support for a language is proposed or not.

version model	query language	object version selection	object selection	modeled universe states selection	object tracking	formal support
1	2	3	4	5	6	7
[7]	no	yes	–	no	–	no
[16]	no	mentioned	–	no	mentioned	no
[21]	no	yes	–	no	–	no
[22]	yes	yes	yes	no	–	no
[4]	yes	yes	no	yes	limited	yes
[14]	yes	yes	–	no	–	no
[27]	yes	yes	–	temporal model	–	no
[20]	yes	–	–	temporal model	–	no

Table 1. Version and temporal query tools

5.2 Temporal approaches

In temporal databases, data varying over time are time-stamped. Thus, implicitly, there are as many universe states represented in the database as there are
time units. The common point between temporal languages and VQL is that
they are devoted to databases representing simultaneously different states of the
modeled universe. However, temporal languages are mainly based on temporal
logic which is founded on the semantics and the specificity of time. A lot of
temporal query languages have been proposed in the literature [25, 23, 20, 27].
Most of them are devoted to relational databases [26, 25, 23]. Those devoted to
object-oriented databases may be separated in two categories: some of them,
like TOOSQL, TOSQL [19] or TMQL [15], carry on the work done for the relational model; others, like OODAPLEX, propose new querying facilities due to
object-oriented potential.

TOOSQL. This language [20] supports two time dimensions: valid time and transaction time, which appear on timestamps associated with attributes. Queries are realized using specific temporal constructs. For instance, the next query retrieves the third change of manager for Mary and the duration over which he/she was Mary's manager.

```
SELECT A.Manager.Nth(4), A.Manager.Nth(4).Duration(vt)
FROM   A: ADULT
WHERE  A.Name = "Mary"
```

Here, the Nth(4) operation returns the 4th manager of Mary. Duration(vt) is an operation defined on different time dimensions such as valid time (vt). In this example, it returns the length of the valid time interval during which the 4th manager of Mary didn't change. The FROM clause specifies that variable A ranges over class ADULT.

OODAPLEX. In contrast to the other temporal languages, OODAPLEX [27] proposes no special constructs. Queries that require special operators, like *when* or *shift*, in other languages can be formulated naturally in OODAPLEX, by allowing variables and quantifiers to range over time. In this sense, VQL propositions are similar to OODAPLEX ones: by allowing variables and quantifiers to range over v-values no special constructs are needed in VQL queries.

In OODAPLEX, a query is a function mapping objects to objects. Properties of objects, relationships among objects, and operations on objects are all uniformly modeled by functions, which are applied to objects. Time-varying properties, relationships, or behavior are modeled by functions that return other functions mapping time elements into snapshot values of the properties, as shown below.

```
function salary (e: employee ⟶
        f: ([valid_time: time, transaction_time: time] ⟶ s: money))
```

The following query salary$(e)(t_1, t_2)$ returns the employee e's salary at time t_1, as recorded by the database at time t_2. Time is treated as a first class object, and variables and quantifiers are allowed to range over time. For instance, the next query returns John's salary when he worked for the shoes department.

```
for each e in Extent(employee) where name(e) = 'John'
    for each t where name(dept(e)(t)) = 'Shoes'
            salary(e)(t)
    end
end
```

IQL(2). This model [4], issued from works on database languages, proposes a unique formal combining different features such as distributed databases, objects with several roles, versions and views. We classify it as belonging to the temporal approaches because of its concept of *context*. A context may be perceived as the place where an object or a value appears, for instance, a site in a distributed database. Such contexts are to some extend similar to the states of the modeled universe appearing in temporal databases. Two objects contained in different contexts may represent the same entity. An operator $\equiv$ is introduced in order to allow users to determine such objects. For instance, the following query looks for the phone number in Los Angeles context of an employee, called Mary, existing in the Paris context.

```
SELECT E'.phone
FROM   E in Emp(Paris), E' in Emp(LA)
WHERE  E ≡ E' and E.name = 'Mary'
```

Intuitively, the evaluation is the following. First the object representing employee Mary in the Paris context is selected from the persistent root Emp(Paris). Then, the equivalent object is selected from Emp(LA). However, if Mary is not considered as an employee in Los Angeles, the preceding query can't find her phone number. Moreover, if the user doesn't know to which persistent root is attached the object representing Mary in Los Angeles, querying Mary's phone number will be problematic.

6 Conclusion - Future work

In this paper we have proposed a formal query language VQL for multiversion databases. The DBV concept, corresponding to the modeled universe states, is integrated into both the underlying data model (cf. Section 3) and VQL formal support (cf. Section 4.1). This is done in order to allow users to query simultaneously object versions and the states of the modeled universe where these versions appear. The result is a straightforward language allowing users to easily formulate queries which may be complex. An implementation of VQL on top of a version manager corresponding to the DBV model is under development. Moreover, an implementation of VQL propositions on the versions manager of O_2 system, $O_2Version$, which is inspired from the DBV approach, is under study.

An important characteristic of VQL is its generality: different versioning semantics can be considered simultaneously. This semantics are associated with DBVs. For instance, in a CASE application where DBVs correspond to software configurations, DBVs may be associated with their creator, with their owner, with valid time, with hardware support, with software choices, etc. These versioning semantics can be combined and represented using the DBV descriptor (DBV_Desc, cf. Example 9). It is also possible to have many DBV descriptors, each one related to a specific versioning semantics or combining some of them.

From the language point of view, there are two main contributions of VQL: specific terms to denote the modeled universe states (DBVs), and a dereferencing operation taking into account the "DBV dimension". The first one enables users to specify the states of the modeled universe she/he wants to query. The second one makes it possible to keep the track of an object through DBVs, i.e. through different states of the modeled universe.

VQL is useful to several current work on multiversion databases such as constraint expression, view definition and querying in the case of a versioned schema. Constraints on a multiversion database may be "internal" to a DBV, as they may be applied on several DBVs [10]. For example, in the imaginary family multiversion database (cf. Example 9), the fact that My_parents denotes always the same objects, whatever is the DBV, is a constraint on several DBVs. Expressing such a constraint can be naturally done in VQL.

Queries on multiversion databases can be used for view definition, as queries on monoversion databases. A view may be used to restrict the vision of the user to some elements (o-values and/or DBVs) stored in the database. It may also be used to construct new elements, computed from the ones stored in the database. The output instance of query Q_3, described in Section 4.2, is an example of a view restrained to the logical object versions representing "my friends" in the DBV of 1980 and 1990 (cf. Figure 3).

To take into account schema versioning, VQL requires extensions to the data model described in Section 3, as well as an appropriate type checking technique.

Moreover, manipulation operations will be added to VQL, in order to develop a complete database programming language. These operations, presented in [11], enable a user to create and delete objects and DBVs, and make it possible to update object logical versions. Other advanced operations are also proposed to make it easier to merge the content of two DBVs, to update an object on several DBVs simultaneously, etc.

Finally, an implementation of the DBV model has been done on a relational system. In this case too, a manipulation language is required. A transposition of the concepts developed in VQL to the relational framework is proposed in [1].

References

1. T. Abdessalem. *Approche des versions et base de Données : représentation et interrogation des versions.* Ph.D. thesis, Paris-Dauphine University, France, 1997.
2. S. Abiteboul and C. Beeri. The power of languages for the manipulation of complex values. *VLDB Journal*, 4(4):727–794, Oct. 1995.
3. S. Abiteboul and P. C. Kanellakis. Object identity as a query language primitive. In *Proc. ACM SIGMOD Int. Conf.*, pp. 159–173, Portland, Oregon, 1989.
4. S. Abiteboul and C. Souza. IQL(2): A model with ubiquitous objects. In *5th Int. Workshop DBPL 95*, Gubbio, Italy, 1995.
5. F. Bancilhon, S. Cluet, and C. Delobel. A Query Language for O2. In *Bulding an Object-Oriented Database System*, pp. 234–277. Morgan Kaufmann, 1992.
6. W. Cellary and G. Jomier. Consistency of Versions in Object-Oriented Databases. In *Proc. 16th VLDB Conf.*, pp. 432–441, Brisbane, Australia, 1990.
7. H. T. Chou and W. Kim. A unifying framework for version control in a CAD environment. In *Proc. 12th Int. Conf. VLDB 86*, pp. 336–344, Kyoto, Japan, 1986.
8. V. Christophides, S. Abiteboul, S. Cluet, and M. Scholl. From structured documents to novel query facilities. In *Proc. ACM SIGMOD Conf.*, pp. 313–324, 1994.
9. V. Christophides, S. Cluet, and G. Moerkotte. Evaluating queries with generalized path expressions. In *Proc. ACM SIGMOD Conf.*, pp. 413–422, 1996.
10. A. Doucet, S. Gançarski, G. Jomier, and S. Monties. Maintien de la cohérence dans une base de données multiversion. In *Proc. BDA 96*, Cassis, France, 1996.

11. S. Gançarski. Versions et bases de données : modèle formel, supports de langage et d'interface-utilisateur. Ph.D. thesis, Paris-Sud University, France, 1994.

12. S. Gançarski and G. Jomier. Gestion des versions d'entités et de leur contexte : analyse et perspectives. *Ingénierie des Systèmes d'Information*, 3(6):677–711, 1995.

13. S. Gançarski and G. Jomier. Un Formalisme pour la Gestion de Versions d'Entité. In *Proc. BDA 94*, France, 1994.

14. G. Hubert. Les versions dans les bases de données orientées objet : modélisation et manipulation. Ph.D. thesis, Paul Sabatier University, Toulouse, France, 1997.

15. W. Käfer and H. Schöning. Realizing a temporal complex-object data model. In *Proc. ACM SIGMOD Conf.*, vol. 21(2) of *SIGMOD Record*, pp. 266–275, 1992.

16. R. H. Katz. Towards a unified framework for version modeling in engineering databases. *ACM Computing Surveys*, 22(4):375–408, December 1990.

17. M. Kifer, W. Kim, and Y. Sagiv. Querying object oriented databases. In *Proc. ACM SIGMOD Conf.*, vol. 21(2) of *SIGMOD Record*, pp. 393–402, 1992.

18. O2 Technology. *OQL User Manual, release 4.6*, 1996.

19. E. Rose and A. Segev. TOODM - A Temporal Object-Oriented Data Model with Temporal Constraints. In *Proc. 10th Int. Conf. ER 91*, 1991.

20. E. Rose and A. Segev. TOOSQL - A Temporal Object-Oriented Query Language. In *Proc. 12th Int. Conf. ER 93*, LNCS, pp. 122–136, Arlington, Texas, Dec. 1993.

21. E. Sciore. Multidimensional versioning for object–oriented databases. In *Proc. DOOD 91*, vol. 566 of *LNCS*, pp. 355–370, Berlin, Germany, Dec. 1991.

22. E. Sciore. Versioning and configuration management in an object-oriented data model. *VLDB Journal*, 3(1):77–106, Jan. 1994.

23. R. T. Snodgrass. An overview of the temporal query language TQuel. TR 92-22, University of Arizona, Aug. 1992.

24. R. T. Snodgrass. Temporal Object-Oriented Databases: A Critical Comparison. In *Modern Database Systems: the object model, interoperability and beyond*, pp. 386–408. Addison-Wesley, 1995.

25. R. T. Snodgrass, editor. *The TSQL2 Temporal Query Language*. Kluwer Academic, 1995.

26. A. U. Tansel, J. Clifford, S. Gadia, S. Jajodia, A. Segev, and R. T. Snodgrass, editors. *Temporal Databases: theory, design, and implementation*. Benjamin/Cummings, 1993.

27. G. T. J. Wuu and U. Dayal. A uniform model for temporal object-oriented databases. In *Proc. 8th ICDE*, pp. 584–593, Tempe, Arizona, 1992.

Object Views and Database Restructuring

Zoé Lacroix[*1] and Claude Delobel[**2] and Philippe Brèche[***3]

[1] University of Pennsylvania
[2] Université de Paris-Sud and INRIA
[3] INRIA

Abstract. We present a formal data model for views in Object DataBase Systems (ODBS) as a transformation mechanism for databases. Our model relaxes the usual constraint where an object belongs to a single class while using a generalization of *referent* and enables a deterministic creation of derived objects with *complex object identifiers*. We define an IQL-like language which enables the manipulation of such referents. The view-based transformation is achieved in two steps: an extension of the source instance followed by a projection of the extended instance. The extension and projection can be carried out using four object algebraic operators, namely *projection, join-specialization, join* and *generalization*, that specify both the virtual schema and its corresponding virtual instance. This simple algebra can express most of the view operators proposed in the literature and provides a real restructuring of the source schema and instance.

Keywords: object database systems, views, data model, object algebra, multiple-instantiation, database transformation.

1 Introduction

Database views are a well-known technique used by applications to customize shared data objects without affecting other applications. Views provide the user with the flexibility of defining objects derived from source ones that may evolve and play different roles over a period of time. New virtual schemas and instances are generated through view specifications and help to provide logical independence to data.

Various proposals in the relational database framework such as *Superviews* [Mot87] and its powerful operators, as well as in the object database one [AB91] and [Ber91,TYH+91,SS91,Run92,dSDA94,CKMS97], have been put forward but only very few of the latter ones are implemented. In the relational context, commercial databases successfully provide view mechanisms whereas none of the

[*] IRCS, University of Pennsylvania, Suite 400 A, 3401 Walnut Street, Philadelphia PA 19104, USA -- Work supported in part by NSF STC grant SBR-8920230 and partly done in the Verso project at INRIA.

[**] University of Paris XI, LRI, 91 405 Orsay Cedex, France – and Verso project in INRIA.

[***] Verso project– INRIA Rocquencourt BP. 105, 78 153 Le Chesnay Cedex, France

commercial object databases provides the user with any such mechanism. Some systems such as Pegasus [ADD+91], OPM [CKMS97] or a system supporting materialized views defined with ILOG [IIY90,Cha94] include view definition capabilities over object-based databases. To the best of our knowledge, the more advanced prototypes are MultiView/TSE [KR96] and O_2 Views [dS95a,dS95b]. But even these do not provide the flexibility and generality a user may expect from a view mechanism.

Very little has been said about a formal model for object views. Most of the literature focuses on the semantic aspect of object views (how to populate virtual classes) but no formal model that deals with syntax (how the virtual classes are inserted in the hierarchy) as well as semantics is proposed. Our view mechanism really structures the view. The main contribution of this paper is a formal model inspired by the work presented in [dS95a,dS95b], in line with IQL [AK89] and based on the data model in [AHV95] and O_2 [BDK92,LRV88]. We further extend these proposals with the construction of *complex referents* that can express multi-instantiation and, consequently new definitions for schema and instance. We propose a formal model for object views with an algebraic view-transformation language which provides restructuration of object databases.

It first seems natural to consider a view as a query, such as in the relational world [AB91,KKS92]. A language defining views in the object model has to deal with schemas as well as instances. We focus on views obtained from a source schema-instance by applying algebraic operators in two steps, a cascade of *extension* and *projection* transformations. These operators, *natural-join, join-specialization, union* and *projection*, allow the user to specify views. This algebra expresses most of the view operators proposed in [LS92,dS95b,CTR96,KR96] and in [CKMS97]. This functional approach allows one to define views from other view(s).

In the sequel, the main assumptions are that views are virtual (as opposed to materialized) and may be considered as queries (composed or not) applied against objects of a source database. Basically, in an algebraic perspective, virtual classes and objects are built up while combining object algebra operators. The virtual class is inserted in the class hierarchy and populated with respect to the source class(es) it derives from. Any attribute of the said virtual class is also *derived*, since it is defined as a query on the source. Therefore, the virtual instance is derived from a source schema and base. As opposed to [Ber91,Run92], schema evolution cannot be simulated in our context. In that scope, a view is "read only".

In our framework, a source schema-instance and its view have the following features: multiple-inheritance, O2-like overloading at the schema level, creation of new objects at the instance level, and multiple customized views. Classes are populated with *referents*, generalizing the ones introduced in [dS95b]. A referent is a pair (object identifier, class name), which enables us to relax the commonly adopted constraint of one object belonging to a unique class in which the object was created. Our Referent Model (RM) may also be used as a base for a Multiversion Data Model where an object may belong to several classes depending on the version.

Some models allow multi-instantiation [AdS95,Su91] but restrict the use of attribute names. In [AdS95], classes are populated with object identifiers (oids) and the value of an object depends on the context of the class it is seen in. The access of an attribute is considered as legal, if it is the attribute of only one class in one context. Similarly, the Referent Model generalizes the semantic data model presented in [Su91] where no attribute is shared by two classes and thus an object may belong to several classes. In the Referent Model, we allow classes to have common attributes, and there is no ambiguity in accessing an attribute, since it applies to a referent which specifies the object as well as the class (and its specific behavior). In [CML+96] as well as [AJ97], the model is restricted to the constraint that each object belongs to a unique class.

In the model presented here, object identifiers are generalized to *complex identifiers*. A complex identifier identifies a new object (imaginary object in [AB91]) as well as specifies the link from which the object is generated. In contrast to IQL [AK89], complex identifiers enable a deterministic assignment of new identifiers to derived objects. The explicit link between virtual and source objects, although invisible for a user, provides an efficient way of getting rid of possible duplicates during the query evaluation. In two different classes, two objects deriving from the same object(s) will have the same identifier. A complex oid can be seen as a Skolemized identifier [Mai86,KW89,KL89,KKS92] where the Skolem function does not depend on the class or its definition. A complex oid only depends on the oids of objects its derives from. Complex oids can also be used to *merge* objects with same value in a given class as in [CML+96]. Again, this ability of the Referent Model makes it a good candidate for restructuring several sources (as in data warehouse).

We propose RQL (Referent Query Language), an IQL-like language, to manipulate such referents. RQL expressions are used to answer queries, populate virtual classes and define virtual attributes. The four basic algebraic operators defining our views express the authorized transformations against the schema and the data. The algebra has a semantics (which defines the virtual schema as well as the virtual instance) by default, but virtual attributes and some filtering of the population of the defined virtual classes are expressible in RQL. Our algebra together with the referent model give the formal foundation that may be used to guarantee referential integrity constraints as well as key attributes on the view.

The rest of the paper is organized as follows. We motivate our work with an example given in Section 2 which is used and further developed in the ensuing sections. Section 3 introduces the object data model highlighting the notion of referent, and the possibility of multi-instantiation. We define the Referent Query Language (RQL) in Section 4. Section 5 introduces the basic object algebraic operators used (eventually combined) to create our views. Section 6 concludes on issues, and related work points to future work.

2 Motivating example

We present in this section the process of creating a schema and an instance. From now on, they are denoted as S for *source schema* and as I for *source instance*. The example records for each child in class Child, her/his first and last names, the set of her/his parents in class Adult and a school registration. An adult has both first and last names, an address, a spouse, a tennis partner and possibly a driving license. The schema corresponding to the previous specification is given in Figure 1.

```
                                class Adult
                                 public type tuple (
class Child                              first_name: string,
 public type tuple (                     last_name: string,
        first_name: string,              spouse: Adult,
        last_name: string,               address: Address,
        parents: set(Adult),             tennis_partner: Adult,
        school: boolean )                driving_license: boolean )
 end;                            end;
```

Fig. 1. The source schema S.

A view is specified using S and I to encompass the following information:

- class Child is imported[1] without the parents and the school registration (which are both hidden), as well as class Address.
- class Couple, derived from class Adult, has a name, an address and a set of children.
- class Driver is specialized from class Adult and is populated with adults having a driving license.
- class Person is the union of Adult and Child; it has both first and last names and an address.
- class Student, derived from Child, has both first and last names and an address (taken to be the parent's address, assuming that both parents live at the same address).
- class Team, derived from class Adult, has a pair of tennis partners.

Figure 2 represents the class hierarchies of the source schema S and of the view schema S'. Class Address is omitted. Newly created classes (*virtual classes*) are in grey whereas original classes (*source classes*) are in white.

---

[1] Classes which are not explicitly imported are implicitly masked in the view.

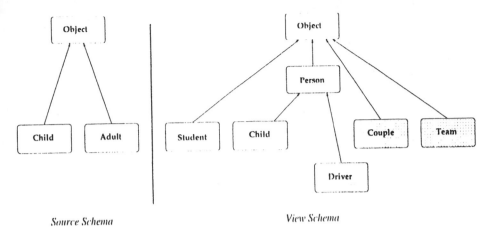

Source Schema   View Schema

Fig. 2. Class hierarchies of the source and view schemas.

3 Model

3.1 Syntax

We consider the set $\mathbf{C}=\{c_1, c_2, ...\}$ of class names (called *abstract class names* in [AHV95]), the set $\mathbf{V}=\{integer, string, float, boolean, char\}$ of value class names and the set $\mathbf{A}=\{a_1, a_2, ...\}$ of attribute names. $\mathbf{C}$, $\mathbf{V}$ and $\mathbf{A}$ are pairwise disjoint. Let $\mathbf{D}$ be an infinite set of constants from which value classes are populated. In the following, when there is no ambiguity, we do not distinguish classes and attributes from their names.

A *signature* is an expression $c \to \gamma(c')$ where c and c' are class names (only c' may be a value class name) and $\gamma(c')$ denotes either a class c' or a set of class $\{c'\}$. A *definition* of attribute a is a pair $(a, c \to \gamma(c'))$ where $c \to \gamma(c')$ is a signature. An attribute a is *defined* at c if there exists a definition of a at c. A *class hierarchy* is a 3-tuple $(C, \prec, \Delta)$ where C is a finite subset of $\mathbf{C}$, $\prec$ an acyclic binary relation on C (called the *sub-classing relationship* on C), and Δ a finite set of attribute definitions only at class names in C. For any $c, c' \in C$, $c \prec c'$ expresses that c is a subclass of c' or, equivalently, that c' is a superclass of c. The transitive closure of the sub-classing relationship $\prec$ on C is denoted by $\prec^*$ and $c \preceq^* c'$ is a notation for the disjunction $c \prec^* c'$ or $c = c'$. A set Δ of definitions is *unambiguous* if for each definition of a, and each $c \in C$ there is at most one definition of a at c. An attribute a is *overloaded* if there exists at least two definitions of a at two different classes along an inheritance path. An attribute a is *applicable* at c if it is defined at c or defined at some c' such that $c \prec^* c'$. Two definitions $(a, c_1 \to \gamma(c_1'))$ and $(a, c_2 \to \gamma(c_2'))$ of attribute a are *compatible* if $\gamma(c_1') = \{c_1'\}$ iff $\gamma(c_2') = \{c_2'\}$ and there exists c_0 such that $c_1' \prec^* c_0$ and $c_2' \prec^* c_0$ (ie. c_1' and c_2' have a common superclass). Δ obeys the *covariant* rule if for each overloaded $a \in \mathbf{A}$ and for each $c_1, c_2 \in C$ and $c_1', c_2' \in C \cup \mathbf{V}$, if $(a, c_1 \to \gamma(c_1'))$ and $(a, c_2 \to \gamma(c_2'))$ are in Δ such that $c_1 \preceq^* c_2$ then $\gamma(c_1') = \{c_1'\}$ iff $\gamma(c_2') = \{c_2'\}$ and $c_1' \preceq^* c_2'$. A class hierarchy $(C, \prec, \Delta)$ is *well-formed* if Δ is *unambiguous* and obeys the *covariant* rule. A schema describes the structure of the data stored in a database.

Definition 1. [Schema]
A *schema* is a 4-tuple $S = (A, C, \prec, \Delta)$, where A is a finite set of attribute names, and $(C, \prec, \Delta)$ is a well-formed hierarchy, such that all attribute names occurring in Δ are in A.

Methods are not considered to be part of the model since we are not interested in their possible side-effects in this paper. Methods were considered in an earlier version of the paper [LDB97] as relations between classes, though not distinguishable from attributes.

Example 2. According to Definition 1, the source schema S described in Figure 1 of Section 2 is a tuple $(A, C, \prec, \Delta)$. The set of attribute names is $A = \{$first_name, last_name, parents, school, spouse, address, tennis_partner, driving_license$\}$. The set C of class names is $\{$Child, Adult, Address$\}$. The class hierarchy $\prec$ is given in Figure 2, where an arrow from class c to class c' denotes $c \prec c'$. The set of attribute definitions is $\Delta = \{$ (first_name, Child $\to$ *string*), (last_name, Child $\to$ *string*), (parents, Child $\to$ $\{$Adult$\}$), (school, Child $\to$ *boolean*), (first_name, Adult $\to$ *string*), (last_name, Adult $\to$ *string*), (spouse, Adult $\to$ Adult), (address, Adult $\to$ Address), (tennis_partner, Adult $\to$ Adult), (driving_license, Adult $\to$ *boolean*) $\}$. The attributes in A are not overloaded.

3.2 Semantics

Traditionally, in object models such as [AHV95], objects are associated with only one class, the class where they are defined, have a unique identifier and their attributes are valued. An object **obj** is commonly a pair (**oid, val**), where **oid** is an object identifier (*oid*) and **val** its value (the value of all its attributes). The identity of an object is immutable during its life time when its value may change. The user only has access to values when the system is based on identity. In a class, two objects may have exactly the same values and updating may be an ambiguous task.

More difficulties even arise when the model allows an object to belong to two classes (not on an inheritance path). The same object may have different values (depending on the class it is seen in) over the same attributes. For example, two classes PersonFrance and PersonUSA with attributes *name* and *address* may have an object in common for which the value of attribute *address* is respectively an address in France and an address in the USA.

A newly created object has to be identified. Usually, it is either identified by an identifier picked out from an infinite set of available new identifiers which do not encode any information like in [AK89], or by an encoding of its value (*objectification*) as it is done in [AB91]. The former is purely based on identity. The latter seems to privilege values, but the encoded value is no longer used after creation of the object. In our data model, a new object is identified with an encoding of the identifiers of the source objects it derives from.

We propose a Referent Model which allows a deterministic identification of new objects as an *aggregate* of objects and relaxes the assumption where one object belongs to a unique class.

Virtual classes are derived from source or virtual (but already defined) ones. Virtual classes are populated with source objects or with new objects (*imaginary* in [AB91]) deriving from source ones when evaluating RQL expressions. The lack of an explicit link between identities may allow the creation of duplicates in a virtual class. In the example presented in Section 2, two classes `Couple` and `Team` derive from class `Adult`. A couple which is also a tennis pair may belong to both virtual classes. Suppose that later on, one wants to define class `Partnership` as a common superclass of class `Couple` and `Team`. If the couple *[claire,pierre]* is not identified the same way as the team *[claire,pierre]*, then the pair *[claire,pierre]* will be duplicated in class `Partnership`. The duplication is only relative to the real world where the couple *[claire,pierre]* coincides with the team *[claire,pierre]*. But, on the other hand, both the couple and the team derive from the same objects and we believe, in this sense, must have the same identity.

In our model, a virtual object is identified by an explicit encoding of the identifiers of the objects it derives from. We extend the set of usual *atomic* object identifiers $O = \{o_1, o_2, ...\}$ to *complex* ones of the form $o_1 \wedge ... \wedge o_n$. Intuitively, a new object is identified by $o_1 \wedge o_2$ if it derives from the objects respectively identified by o_1 and o_2. Both the couple and the team *[claire,pierre]* are identified by $o_4 \wedge o_5$ (see Example 6). The set of all identifiers, atomic and complex ones, is denoted by $\hat{O}$ and defined by the following grammar.

Definition 3. [Identifiers]
The set $\hat{O}$ of all identifiers is the set of o such that $o ::= i \mid o \wedge o$, where i ranges over elements of O.

Note that $o_1 \wedge ... \wedge o_n$ only denotes the result of the application of an encoding function to $o_1, ..., o_n$, which is associative $((o_1 \wedge o_2) \wedge o_3 = o_1 \wedge (o_2 \wedge o_3))$, commutative $(o_1 \wedge o_2 = o_2 \wedge o_1)$ and invertible. The encoding function is not known by the user (who cannot distinguish, when asking a query, complex oids from atomic ones either). A complex oid may be seen as a Skolemization of several atomic ones [Mai86,KW89,KL89,KKS92], but the same encoding function is used for all creation of complex identifiers. The Skolemization does not depend on the virtual class or its definition. As a result couple *[claire,pierre]* will be identified with the same oid as team *[claire,pierre]*.

We now consider the concept of *object referent*, previously introduced in [dS95b], which extends the ODBS data model to a Referent Model (RM). Since we relax the assumption where each object belongs to a unique class, we have to choose a way to access objects. In the Referent Model, we choose to access objects through their oid and the class we want to see them in. A referent is a pair $\langle o, c \rangle$, where $o \in \hat{O}$ and $c \in C$. Classes are populated with referents. Therefore attributes apply to referents. Referents are not mutable and identify objects just like object identifiers in the traditional model. In particular, a referent points to an object *as it is seen* and *as it behaves* in a given class. The object is still uniquely identified by its oid, but the same object can belong to several different classes and have different values and behaviors. This is a form of *multiple instantiation*, as opposed to the concept of single instantiation, according to which an object is an instance of one and only one single class. In [AdS95] an object may be seen in different contexts of a class and the notion of referent is implicit (it appears when the value assignment is defined since the value of an object may depend on the context). In the Referent Model, we extend the referents introduced in [dS95b] to referents defined with complex identifiers.

Definition 4. [Referents]

The set **R** of referents is the set of r such that $r ::= \langle o, c \rangle$, where $o \in \hat{O}$ and $c \in C$.

A referent $\langle o, c \rangle$ is *atomic* if o is an atomic oid, otherwise, it is *complex*. In the Referent Model, classes are populated with referents.

Definition 5. [Class population]

Let $(A, C, \prec, \Delta)$ be a schema.

A *referent assignment* $\pi : C \to 2^{\mathbf{R}}$ associates to each class name in C a finite set of referents such that for each $o \in \hat{O}$ and $c, c' \in C$, if $\langle o, c' \rangle \in \pi(c)$ then $c' = c$, that is two populations associated to two different classes are disjoint. In addition, subclass extensions are subsumed by superclass extensions: for all $c, c' \in C$, if $c \prec^* c'$ then for all $\langle o, c \rangle \in \pi(c)$, $\langle o, c' \rangle \in \pi(c')$.

A *constant assignment* $\nu : V \to 2^{\mathbf{D}}$ associates to each value class name in **V** a set of constants such that for each $v, v' \in \mathbf{V}$, if $v \neq v'$, then $\nu(v) \cap \nu(v') = \emptyset$.

Class	Object and its value
Child	$(\langle o_1, \text{Child} \rangle$, [Martine, Dupont, $\{\langle o_4, \text{Adult} \rangle, \langle o_5, \text{Adult} \rangle\}$, *true*]),
	$(\langle o_2, \text{Child} \rangle$, [Paul, Dupont, $\{\langle o_4, \text{Adult} \rangle, \langle o_5, \text{Adult} \rangle\}$, *false*]),
	$(\langle o_3, \text{Child} \rangle$, [Léon, Fontaine, $\{\langle o_6, \text{Adult} \rangle, \langle o_7, \text{Adult} \rangle\}$, *true*])
Adult	$(\langle o_4, \text{Adult} \rangle$, [Claire, Dupont, $\langle o_5, \text{Adult} \rangle$, $\langle o_{a1}, \text{Address} \rangle$, $\langle o_5, \text{Adult} \rangle$, *true*]),
	$(\langle o_5, \text{Adult} \rangle$, [Pierre, Dupont, $\langle o_4, \text{Adult} \rangle$, $\langle o_{a1}, \text{Address} \rangle$, $\langle o_4, \text{Adult} \rangle$, *true*]),
	$(\langle o_6, \text{Adult} \rangle$, [Hélène, Fontaine, $\langle o_7, \text{Adult} \rangle$, $\langle o_{a2}, \text{Address} \rangle$, *nil*, *true*]),
	$(\langle o_7, \text{Adult} \rangle$, [Bertrand, Fontaine, $\langle o_6, \text{Adult} \rangle$, $\langle o_{a2}, \text{Address} \rangle$, $\langle o_8, \text{Adult} \rangle$, *false*])
	$(\langle o_8, \text{Adult} \rangle$, [Michel, Puits, *nil*, $\langle o_{a3}, \text{Address} \rangle$, $\langle o_7, \text{Adult} \rangle$, *false*])

Fig. 3. The instance I of the source schema S.

Example 6. The source instance I of schema S given in Section 2 is fully described in Figure 3. Each class is populated with atomic referents. The corresponding virtual instance is given in Figure 4.

Objects *martine* and *léon*, respectively identified by o_1 and o_3, belong to Child as well as Student which are not on an inheritance path. Virtual classes Couple and Team are populated with complex referents deriving from objects of class Adult. They have the object *[claire,pierre]* identified by $o_4 \wedge o_5$ in common.

Class	Virtual Object and its value
Child	$(\langle o_1,\text{Child}\rangle,$ [Martine, Dupont]), $(\langle o_2,\text{Child}\rangle,$ [Paul, Dupont]), $(\langle o_3,\text{Child}\rangle,$ [Léon, Fontaine])
Student	$(\langle o_1,\text{Student}\rangle,$ [Martine, Dupont, $\langle o_{a1},\text{Address}\rangle$]), $(\langle o_3,\text{Student}\rangle,$ [Léon, Fontaine, $\langle o_{a2},\text{Address}\rangle$])
Couple	$(\langle o_4 \wedge o_5,\text{Couple}\rangle,$ [Dupont, $\langle o_{a1},\text{Address}\rangle$, $\{\langle o_1, \text{Child}\rangle, \langle o_2, \text{Child}\rangle\}$]), $(\langle o_6 \wedge o_7,\text{Couple}\rangle,$ [Fontaine, $\langle o_{a2},\text{Address}\rangle$, $\{\langle o_3, \text{Child}\rangle\}$])
Team	$(\langle o_4 \wedge o_5,\text{Team}\rangle,$ [{Dupont, Dupont}]), $(\langle o_7 \wedge o_8,\text{Team}\rangle,$ [{Fontaine, Puits}])
Person	$(\langle o_1,\text{Person}\rangle,$ [Martine, Dupont, $\langle o_{a1},\text{Address}\rangle$]), $(\langle o_2,\text{Person}\rangle,$ [Paul, Dupont, $\langle o_{a1},\text{Address}\rangle$]), $(\langle o_3,\text{Person}\rangle,$ [Léon, Fontaine, $\langle o_{a2},\text{Address}\rangle$]), $(\langle o_4,\text{Person}\rangle,$ [Claire, Dupont, $\langle o_{a1},\text{Address}\rangle$]), $(\langle o_5,\text{Person}\rangle,$ [Pierre, Dupont, $\langle o_{a1},\text{Address}\rangle$]), $(\langle o_6,\text{Person}\rangle,$ [Hélène, Fontaine, $\langle o_{a2},\text{Address}\rangle$]), $(\langle o_7,\text{Person}\rangle,$ [Bertrand, Fontaine, $\langle o_{a2},\text{Address}\rangle$]), $(\langle o_8,\text{Person}\rangle,$ [Michel, Puits, $\langle o_{a3},\text{Address}\rangle$])
Driver	$(\langle o_4,\text{Driver}\rangle,$ [Claire, Dupont, $\langle o_{a1},\text{Address}\rangle$]), $(\langle o_5,\text{Driver}\rangle,$ [Pierre, Dupont, $\langle o_{a1},\text{Address}\rangle$]), $(\langle o_6,\text{Driver}\rangle,$ [Hélène, Fontaine, $\langle o_{a2},\text{Address}\rangle$])

Fig. 4. The instance I' of the view schema S'.

We now introduce an attribute assignment μ which is a function mapping definitions of Δ to functions.

Definition 7. [Attribute assignment]

Let $(A, C, \prec, \Delta)$ be a schema. An *attribute assignment* μ is a function μ that associates to a definition in Δ, a function from $\mathbf{R}$ to either $\mathbf{R}$, $\mathbf{D}$, $2^{\mathbf{R}}$ or $2^{\mathbf{D}}$ such that:

- to abstract classes:
  1. if $d = (a, c \to c')$ then $\mu(d) \in \pi(c')^{\pi(c)}$;
  2. if $d = (a, c \to \{c'\})$ then $\mu(d) \in (2^{\pi(c')})^{\pi(c)}$;
- to value classes:
  1. if $d = (a, c \to v)$ then $\mu(d) \in \nu(v)^{\pi(c)}$;
  2. if $d = (a, c \to \{v\})$ then $\mu(d) \in (2^{\nu(v)})^{\pi(c)}$;

We use a *path expression* to denote for $d = (a, c \to \gamma(c))$ and $\langle o, c \rangle \in \pi(c)$,

$$\mu(d)(\langle o, c \rangle) = \langle o, c \rangle.a$$

In addition, μ must satisfy the following condition:

- if $d = (a, c_1 \to \gamma(c_1'))$ and $d' = (a, c_2 \to \gamma(c_2'))$, and $c_1 \prec^* c_2$ then for all $o \in \hat{O}$, if $\langle o, c_1 \rangle \in \pi(c_1)$ then $\langle o, c_1 \rangle.a = \langle o, c_2 \rangle.a$.

The latter insures the consistency of attribute assignment with overloaded attributes on an inheritance path.

A total function is assigned to each attribute name. As illustrated in Figure 3, when the value of attribute a of signature $c \to c'$ (resp. $c \to \{c'\}$) is not known on object o, then $\langle o, c \rangle.a = nil$ (resp. $\langle o, c \rangle.a = \{\}$).

Example 8. In the schema S of Section 2, the function assignment of attribute *first_name* of definition (*first_name*, Child $\to$ *string*) simply is the following: $\{(\langle o_1, \text{Child} \rangle, \text{Martine}), (\langle o_2, \text{Child} \rangle, \text{Paul}), (\langle o_3, \text{Child} \rangle, \text{Léon})\}$.

We can now define an *instance* (or *base*) of a schema.

Definition 9. [Instance of a schema]
An *instance* I of a schema $S = (A, C, \prec, \Delta)$ is a triple (π, μ, ν) where π, μ and ν are respectively a referent, a function and a constant assignment. The set of all instances of the schema S is denoted by $inst(S)$.

An object **obj** is now a pair (**ref**, [**val**]), where **ref** is a referent $\langle o, c \rangle$ and **val** is the value of all attributes applicable at c.

Example 10. The instance I of schema S of Section 2 is described in Figure 3. One can see that an object is now a pair (referent, value).

4 RQL: a query language to manipulate referents

We define RQL, the referent query language, a IQL-like language. Since the traditional concept of object identifier has been extended to referent, RQL is essentially the same as IQL but it manipulates referents. In our model, referents and classes have a type. The syntax and the semantics of the types are defined as follows with our notations. The set of type expressions, denoted **T**, is given by the following abstract grammar. **T** is the set of τ such that: $\tau = \emptyset \mid v \mid c \mid \{v\} \mid \{c\}$, where v and c respectively range over **V** and **C**.

The semantics of types is given with respect to referent and constant assignments (resp. π and ν). For all $v \in \mathbf{V}$ and $c \in \mathbf{C}$, $[\![\emptyset]\!] = \emptyset$; $[\![v]\!]_\nu = \nu(v)$; $[\![c]\!]_\pi = \pi(c)$ and finite setting is standard. The subtyping relationship is defined with respect to the subclassing relationship the usual way.

RQL is the set of expressions that are finite sets of rules defined from terms, literals, and heads as follows. The constants of the value classes are omitted for simplification in the variables. We suppose that there exists a a countable number of variables x and, for each type τ in $\mathbf{T}$, a countable number of variables x^τ of type τ.

Referent-terms The *referent-terms* are defined as follows ($n \geq 1$).

- x^τ, a variable of type τ, is a referent-term of type τ.
- $\langle x, c \rangle$, where x is a variable, is a referent-term of type c.
- $\langle x_1 \wedge \ldots \wedge x_n, c \rangle$, where the x_i's are variables, is a referent term of type c.

Terms The *terms* are defined as follows ($n \geq 1$).

- t, a referent-term of type τ, is a term of type τ.
- $t.a$, where t is a referent-term of type c, and $(a, c \to \gamma(c')) \in \Delta$, is a term of type $\gamma(c')$.
- $\{t_1, \ldots, t_n\}$, where t_i $(1 \leq i \leq n)$ is a term of type τ, is a term of type $\{\tau\}$.

Heads The *heads* are defined as follows.

- $\{t\}$, where t is a term, is a head.
- $c(t)$, where t is a referent-term of type c, is a head.

Literals The *literals* are defined as follows.

- $t_1 = t_2$ and $t_1 \neq t_2$, where t_1 and t_2 are terms of the same type, are literals.
- $t_1 \in t_2$ and $t_1 \notin t_2$, where t_1 and t_2 are respectively terms of type τ and of type $\{\tau\}$, are literals.

Rules A *rule* is an expression of the form $L \longleftarrow L_1, \ldots, L_k$ ($k \geq 0$), where L is either a head or a literal, and $L_1, \ldots, L_k$ are literals.

We relax in L_i the constraint over the type in the classical way with respect to the subtyping relationship.

Rules of the form $\{t\} \longleftarrow L_1, \ldots, L_k$ are used to express queries. As usual, when there is no ambiguity, a variable x^τ of type τ is simply denoted by x.

Example 11. The query *"First name of children"* is expressed in RQL by:

$$\{x.first\_name\} \longleftarrow \text{Child}(x)$$

Rules of the form $c(t) \longleftarrow L_1, \ldots, L_k$ are used to express constraints on the population of the virtual class c.

Example 12. The class Driver is populated with objects in class Adult that have a driving license. The query *"Adults who have a driving license"* constraints the population of class Driver (in the sense that not all the population of class Adult is in Driver) and is expressed in RQL by:

$$\text{Driver}(\langle x, \text{Driver}\rangle) \longleftarrow \text{Adult}(\langle x, \text{Adult}\rangle), \langle x, \text{Adult}\rangle.driving\_license = true$$

Rules of the form $x.a = y \longleftarrow L_1, \ldots, L_k$ (resp. $y \in x.a \longleftarrow L_1, \ldots, L_k$) are used to define virtual attributes. The usual type checking on the body of the RQL rule gives the signature $c \to c'$ (resp. $c \to \{c'\}$), of the defined attribute.

Example 13. Virtual class `Couple` has attribute *children* of signature `Couple` $\to$ `{Child}` defined by the following RQL expression.

$$y \in x.children \longleftarrow \text{Couple}(x), x = \langle z_1 \wedge z_2, \text{Couple}\rangle, \text{Child}(y), z_1 \in y.parents$$

Such a definition is of signature `Couple` $\to$ `{Child}`, since (i) it is of the form $y \in x.a$ (which implies that the signature is of the form $c \to \{c'\}$), and (ii) y is of type `Child` and x of type `Couple`.

We did not include among the terms the constants for simplification. They can be added easily with their classical operators. Moreover, we did not consider nested or fixed-point definitions as in IQL since the algebra proposed in the paper is not extended to operators based on these abilities of the language. In future work, operators such as *powerset* may be introduced in the algebra.

5   An algebra to express view-transformations

In [AK89], Abiteboul and Kannelakis introduce the notion of *projection* to express db-transformations, later extended by the notion of *extension* in [dS95b]. Conceptually, a db-transformation $\subseteq inst(S) \times inst(S')$ is performed in two successive steps: an extension from S (source schema) and a projection to S' (view schema). These steps express the relationships between the two schemas S and S' of a db-transformation. Intuitively, an *extension* consists in defining a schema ES (*extended-schema*) extending the source-schema with new classes, attributes and/or methods, when a *projection* consists in hiding classes, attributes and/or methods from the extended-schema to obtain S'. Since a db-transformation is seen as a query, it is a subset of $inst(S) \times inst(S')$ where S and S' are two given schemas. The class of view-transformations is a subclass of db-transformations, where the schema S' itself is *derived* from S. The virtual classes in S' are explicitly *derived* from the classes in S. If class c' derives from c, then the population of c' also derives from the population of c (c' is populated with objects from the population of c). It follows that the view-transformation must satisfy some constraints with regards to the derivation. For example, if c_1 is a subclass of c_2 in the source schema, if c_1' and c_2' are virtual classes deriving respectively from c_1 and c_2, then to guaranty the consistency of any population of the virtual classes, it should not be possible that c_2' is a subclass of c_1'.

We propose an algebra of four operators *join-specialization*, *join*, *generalization* and *projection* to express view-transformations. The first three express the extension of the schema and instance, whereas the last one expresses the projection of the schema and instance. A *rename* operator used to rename class and/or attribute names (with new names) could also easily extend the algebra. Its semantics is obvious and we do not consider it in this work.

The following sections give the definition of the operators and detail how we come up with the new classes (virtual classes) in the view, extending and projecting the source schema (see Figure 2) and instance (see Figure 3) of Section 2.

5.1 Extension

An *extension-expression* is a list $[e_1, \ldots, e_m]$ of *extension-instructions* as shown in the table on the right, where $n \geq 1$, $c', c_1, \ldots, c_n$ are class names (not value class names), and P a list of parameters.

Extension-instructions
$c' \Leftarrow \text{Join}_P(c_1, \ldots, c_n)$
$c' \Leftarrow \text{Generalization}_P(c_1, \ldots, c_n)$
$c' \Leftarrow \text{Join-Specialization}_P(c_1, \ldots, c_n)$

The semantics of each instruction of the algebra is made precise by an optional list of parameters P (RQL queries) containing a definition of the population and/or definitions of attributes. *Virtual attributes* (new attributes defined in the parameters of an extension-instruction) are computed with RQL definitions.

Definition 14. [Parameters of an extension instruction]
The list of parameters P of c' is of the form $[q; q_1; \ldots; q_m]$, where $q, q_1, \ldots, q_m$ are RQL expressions such that:

- q is of the form $c'(t) \longleftarrow L_1, \ldots, L_p$, where t is a referent term of type c',
- q_j is either of the form $x = t.a \longleftarrow L_1, \ldots, L_p$ or $x \in t.a \longleftarrow L_1, \ldots, L_p$ where t is a referent term of type c'.

In the sequel, A_P will denote the set of attribute names defined in the heads of rules of parameters in P.

The *extended schema ES* and its *extended instance EI* are defined by applying the extension-expression $[e_1, \ldots, e_m]$, where $e_1, \ldots, e_m$ are extension-instructions, to the source schema S and instance I such that $(S_0, I_0) = (S, I)$ and for all i such that $1 \leq i \leq m$, $(S_i, I_i) = e_i(S_{i-1}, I_{i-1})$, and $(ES, EI) = (S_m, I_m)$.

An extension instruction e is applicable to a schema $S_i = (A_i, C_i, \prec_i, \Delta_i)$ if:

- class is not already defined (i.e. $c' \notin C_i$);
- classes $c_1, \ldots, c_n$ are already defined (i.e. $c_1, \ldots, c_n \in C_i$);
- each a occuring in a body of q or q_j in P is in A_i;
- each c occuring in the body of q in P is in C_i;
- each c occuring in a body of q_j in P is in $C_i \cup \{c'\}$;
- all definitions of any common (applicable to at least two classes in the c_j's) attribute name a occuring in the parameters P are pairwise *compatible*

Example 15. The parameters necessary to define class Student consist of a query selecting from class Child the objects such that attribute *school* is true, and three queries defining respectively attributes *first_name*, *last_name* and *address* at Student. Formally class Student is defined with:

$P_S=$ [Student($\langle x,$ Student$\rangle$)) ← Child($\langle x,$ Child$\rangle$)),

$\quad\quad\quad\quad\quad\quad\quad\quad\quad\quad\quad\quad\quad\quad\quad\quad$ $\langle x,$ Child$\rangle.school = true;$

$\quad y = \langle x,$ Student$\rangle.first\_name$ ← $y = \langle x,$ Child$\rangle.first\_name;$

$\quad y = \langle x,$ Student$\rangle.last\_name$ ← $y = \langle x,$ Child$\rangle.last\_name;$

$\quad y = \langle x,$ Student$\rangle.address$ ← $z \in \langle x,$ Child$\rangle.parents,$

$\quad\quad\quad\quad\quad\quad\quad\quad\quad\quad\quad\quad\quad\quad\quad\quad$ $y = z.address]$

Note that the problem of verifying the semantic constraint that an attribute is single-valued when defined by a rule of head $y = x.a$ is not investigated in this paper (regarding this question see [AH88]). Another semantic constraint (inclusion dependency) satisfied by an attribute a of signature $c \to \gamma(c')$ if for each object o in class c, $\langle o, c \rangle.a$ results in objects that are actually in the population of class c' is not considered in this work either. These classes of constraints will be studied in a future work.

Example 16. The extended schema illustrated in Figure 5 is obtained by the following extension expression:

[Student ⇐ Join$_{P_S}$(Child),
Couple ⇐ Join$_{P_C}$(Adult, Adult),
Team ⇐ Join$_{P_T}$(Adult, Adult),
Person ⇐ Generalization$_{P_P}$(Child, Adult),
Driver ⇐ Join-Specialization$_{P_D}$(Adult)]

The parameters are detailed in Example 15 and in the sequel.

$P_C=$ [Couple($\langle x \wedge y,$ Couple$\rangle$)) ← Adult($\langle x,$ Adult$\rangle$)),

$\quad\quad\quad\quad\quad\quad\quad\quad\quad\quad\quad\quad\quad\quad\quad\quad$ Adult($\langle y,$ Adult$\rangle$)),

$\quad\quad\quad\quad\quad\quad\quad\quad\quad\quad\quad\quad\quad\quad\quad\quad$ $\langle x,$ Adult$\rangle.spouse = \langle y,$ Adult$\rangle;$

$\quad y = \langle y_1 \wedge y_2,$ Couple$\rangle.name$ ← $y = \langle y_1,$ Adult$\rangle.last\_name;$

$\quad y = \langle y_1 \wedge y_2,$ Couple$\rangle.address$ ← $y = \langle y_1,$ Adult$\rangle.address;$

$\quad x \in \langle y_1 \wedge y_2,$ Couple$\rangle.children$ ← Child(x),

$\quad\quad\quad\quad\quad\quad\quad\quad\quad\quad\quad\quad\quad\quad\quad\quad$ $y_1 \in x.parents]$

$P_T=$ [Team($\langle x \wedge y,$ Team$\rangle$)) ← Adult($\langle x,$ Adult$\rangle$)), $x' = \langle x,$ Adult$\rangle,$

$\quad\quad\quad\quad\quad\quad\quad\quad\quad\quad\quad\quad\quad\quad\quad\quad$ Adult($\langle y,$ Adult$\rangle$)), $y' = \langle y,$ Adult$\rangle,$

$\quad\quad\quad\quad\quad\quad\quad\quad\quad\quad\quad\quad\quad\quad\quad\quad$ $x'.tennis\_partner = y';$

$\quad x \in \langle y_1 \wedge y_2,$ Team$\rangle.players$ ← Adult(y_1),

$\quad\quad\quad\quad\quad\quad\quad\quad\quad\quad\quad\quad\quad\quad\quad\quad$ $y_1.last\_name = x]$

$P_P=$ [$y = \langle x,$ Person$\rangle.first\_name$ ← $y = \langle x,$ Child$\rangle.first\_name;$

$\quad y = \langle x,$ Person$\rangle.first\_name$ ← $y = \langle x,$ Adult$\rangle.first\_name;$

$\quad y = \langle x,$ Person$\rangle.last\_name$ ← $y = \langle x,$ Child$\rangle.last\_name;$

$\quad y = \langle x,$ Person$\rangle.last\_name$ ← $y = \langle x,$ Adult$\rangle.last\_name;$

$\quad y = \langle x,$ Person$\rangle.address$ ← $z \in \langle x,$ Child$\rangle.parents,$

$\quad\quad\quad\quad\quad\quad\quad\quad\quad\quad\quad\quad\quad\quad\quad\quad$ $y = z.address;$

$\quad y = \langle x,$ Person$\rangle.address$ ← $y = \langle x,$ Adult$\rangle.address]$

194

$P_D=[\texttt{Driver}(\langle x,\texttt{Driver}\rangle) \longleftarrow \texttt{Adult}(\langle x,\texttt{Adult}\rangle),$
$\langle x,\texttt{Adult}\rangle.driving\_license = true]$

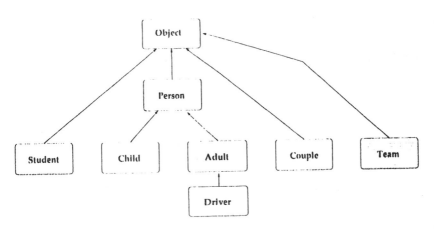

Fig. 5. Class hierarchy of the extended schema *ES*.

Join The *join* consists in either copying a class as a subclass of the root class (when applying to only one class) or creating new objects (*imaginary* objects in [AB91]) as *aggregates* of source objects. A virtual class which is a join of classes is a subclass of the root class (Object in Figure 5) of the class hierarchy.

The expression $c' \Leftarrow \text{Join}_P(c_1,\ldots,c_p)$ is applicable to instance I_i if for all $1 \leq j,k \leq p$, and all $\langle o_j,c_j\rangle \in \pi_i(c_j)$ and $\langle o_k,c_k\rangle \in \pi_i(c_k)$, then $\langle o_j,c_j\rangle.a = \langle o_k,c_k\rangle.a$.

The latter condition guaranties the unambiguity of the definition of attributes at the virtual class. For example, if one wants to define attribute *name* at **Team** with the following RQL query:

$$y = \langle y_1 \wedge y_2, \texttt{Team}\rangle.name \longleftarrow y = \langle y_1, \texttt{Adult}\rangle.last\_name$$

the definition of attribute *name* would be ambiguous since it may happen that $\langle y_1,\texttt{Adult}\rangle.last\_name \neq \langle y_2,\texttt{Adult}\rangle.last\_name$ for some $\langle y_1\wedge y_2,\texttt{Team}\rangle \in \pi(\texttt{Team})$ ($y_1 \wedge y_2$ and $y_2 \wedge y_1$ identify the same object).

In this paper, we suppose that the virtual Join classes are defined through a one-to-one relationship between objects. For example, a couple corresponds to two individuals related by a one-to-one relationship (attribute *spouse*). The problem of verifying such a constraint as well as the problem of defining a virtual Join class with respect to a many-to-many relationship will be addressed in a future work. The impact of the semantics of the Join on the schema is the following.

$c' \Leftarrow \text{Join}_P(c_1,\ldots,c_p),\ (p \geq 1)$	
A_{i+1}	$A_{i+1} = A_i \cup A_P$
C_{i+1}	$C_{i+1} = C_i \cup \{c'\}$
$\prec_{i+1}$	$\prec_{i+1} = \prec_i$
Δ_{i+1}	$\Delta_{i+1} = \Delta_i \cup \{(a, c' \to \gamma(c)) \mid c' \to \gamma(c) \text{ is the signature of } a \in A_P\}$

The virtual class Student is a filtered copy of source class Child. It is populated with referents $\langle o, \text{Student} \rangle$ such that $\langle o, \text{Child} \rangle$ is in $\pi(\text{Child})$ and $\langle o, \text{Child} \rangle.school = true$ (as expressed in the parameters). As shown in Figure 4, virtual classes Couple and Team are populated with new objects, aggregates of two objects of source class Adult.

More formally, the impact of the Join operator on the instance is the following.

population	$\pi_{i+1}(c') = q(I_i) \cap \{\langle o_1 \wedge \ldots \wedge o_n, c' \rangle \mid \langle o_j, c_j \rangle \in \pi_i(c_j)\}$
function	$\mu_{i+1}\big|_{\Delta_i} = \mu_i$
	$\forall d_j = (a_j, c' \to \gamma(c))$ defined by $q_j \in P$, $\mu_{i+1}(d_j) = q_j$

Generalization A *generalization* defines a virtual class as a superclass of the source classes it generalizes and as a subclass of all common superclasses (or of Object, when there is any). The expression $c' \Leftarrow \text{Generalization}_P(c_1,\ldots,c_p)$ is applicable to instance I_i if all $\langle o_j, c_j \rangle \in \pi(c_j)$ and $\langle o_k, c_k \rangle \in \pi(c_k)$, then $\langle o_j, c_j \rangle.a = \langle o_k, c_k \rangle.a$. Moreover, all queries in the parameters P define new attributes a (such that $a \notin A_i$) at c'. Its semantics is the following.

$c' \Leftarrow \text{Generalization}_P(c_1,\ldots,c_p),\ (p \geq 1)$	
A_{i+1}	$A_{i+1} = A_i \cup A_P$
C_{i+1}	$C_{i+1} = C_i \cup \{c'\}$
$\prec_{i+1}$	$\forall j,\ c_j \prec_{i+1} c'$ and for all c such that $\forall j,\ c_j \prec_i c$, then $c' \prec_{i+1} c$
Δ_{i+1}	$\Delta_{i+1} = \Delta_i \cup \{(a, c' \to \gamma(c)) \mid c' \to \gamma(c) \text{ is the signature of } a \in A_P\}$

Virtual class Person is a generalization of class Child and Adult. It is populated with objects of the form $\langle o, \text{Person} \rangle$ where either $\langle o, \text{Child} \rangle \in \pi(\text{Child})$ or $\langle o, \text{Adult} \rangle \in \pi(\text{Adult})$ (see Figure 4 in Section 3.2).

population	$\pi_{i+1}(c') = \{\langle o_j, c' \rangle \mid \langle o_j, c_j \rangle \in \pi_i(c_j)\}$
function	$\mu_{i+1}\big|_{\Delta_i} = \mu_i$
	$\forall d_j = (a_j, c' \to \gamma(c))$ defined by $q_j \in P$, $\mu_{i+1}(d_j) = q_j$

Note that if an object is identified by o belongs to at least two of the classes c_1 to c_n, then it is seen only once in c'.

Join-specialization A virtual class may be the *join-specialization* of classes. It is a subclass of all classes that it specializes. A restriction of the population and the definition of new attributes is possible. The expression $c' \Leftarrow \text{Join-Specialization}_P(c_1,\ldots,c_p)$ is applicable to schema S_i if the attributes defined in the parameters are not in A_j. Its evaluation has the following consequence on the schema.

$c' \Leftarrow$ Join-Specialization$_P(c_1, \ldots, c_p)$, $(p \geq 1)$	
A_{i+1}	$A_{i+1} = A_i \cup A_P$
C_{i+1}	$C_{i+1} = C_i \cup \{c'\}$
$\prec_{i+1}$	$\forall j \; c' \prec_{i+1} c_j$
Δ_{i+1}	$\Delta_{i+1} = \Delta_i \cup \{(a, c' \to \gamma(c)) \mid c' \to \gamma(c) \text{ is the signature of } a \in A_P\}$

The impact of the instruction on the instance is described in the following table.

population	$\pi_{i+1}(c') = q(I_i) \cap \{\langle o, c' \rangle \mid \langle o, c_j \rangle \in \pi_i(c_j)$ and
	$\forall j \forall k \forall a$ applicable at c_j and $c_k \langle o, c_j \rangle.a = \langle o, c_k \rangle.a$
function	$\forall d_j = (n_j, c' \to \gamma(c)) \in P$, $\mu_{i+1}(d_j) = q_j$

In an earlier version of the paper [LDB97], the *join-specialization* has the functionality of a *merge* operator. A *merge* operator consists in identifying objects (using complex identifiers) with same value in a virtual class. When restructuring different sources in a single object view, a merge operator would identify objects having different identities (given by different systems for example) but the same value. Such an operator is introduced in [CML+96]. For example, two sources Person1 and Person2 may be merged as a common subclass Person where an object $\langle o_1, \text{Person1} \rangle$ in class Person1, having the same value on all common attributes of classes Person1 and Person2 as object $\langle o_2, \text{Person2} \rangle$ in class Person2 will be uniquely identified in class Person by $\langle o_1 \wedge o_2, \text{Person} \rangle$. The *merge* operator will be studied together with *key-attributes* in future work.

5.2 Projection

Intuitively, the projection step consists in hiding information: hiding classes and attributes. A projection expression is a list of *projection instructions* of the form Projection$_P(c)$, where P is a list of attribute definitions $[d_1, \ldots, d_m]$, and $c \in EC$. All definitions where class c occurs as well as all definitions $d_1, \ldots, d_m$ in P are removed from Δ. The expression Projection$_P(c)$ is always applicable to schema S_i and its semantics is the following.

Projection$_P(c)$	
C_{i+1}	$C_{i+1} = C_i - \{c\}$
$\prec_{i+1}$	$\forall j \; \forall k$ if $c_j \prec_i c$ and $c \prec_i c_k$ then $c_j \prec_{i+1} c_k$
Δ_{i+1}	$\Delta_{i+1} = \Delta_i - [\{d \mid d \in P\} \cup \{(a, c \to \gamma(c')) \mid (a, c \to \gamma(c')) \in \Delta_i\}$
	$\cup \{(a, c' \to \gamma(c)) \mid (a, c' \to \gamma(c)) \in \Delta_i\}]$

When no class name is made precise in the projection-instruction, Projection$_P()$, only the set of definitions is affected: $\Delta_{i+1} = \Delta_i - \{d \mid d \in P\}$. In this paper, we do not address the problem of redefining attributes or methods of definition of the form $(n, c' \to \gamma(c))$ when the class c is hidden. The projection operator could also easily support the following. For each definition of the form $(n, c \to \gamma(c'))$

$(c' \neq c)$, for each c'' subclass of c, if there is no definition of n applicable at c'', then $(n, c'' \to \gamma(c'))$ is added to Δ. Regarding this topic, other strategies and models for schema evolution are discussed in [BW95,AH87].

Example 17. The view-schema given in Figure 2 is the result of the projection of class Adult. The population of Adult is still visible in class Person as well as Driver. On the other hand, most of attributes of class Driver (namely *spouse*, *tennis_partner* and *driving_license*) were applicable but not defined at Driver. As a result of the projection, they are no longer applicable at Driver (see Figure 4 in Section 3.2). The only attributes applicable at Driver are those defined at Person.

6 Conclusion

Issues: This paper introduces a formal data model for object views which is a continuation of the work presented in [AK89,AB91,dSDA94,dS95a]. The Referent Model is based on the notion of complex referent (generalizing the ones proposed in [dS95b]). A referent allows us to address an object in one of the possibly several different classes it may belong to. The view is obtained from the source database using four simple algebraic operators which define the schema as well as the instance (using RQL). Together, these operators constitute an approach with two conceptual steps: an extension followed by a projection of a source base [AK89,dSDA94,dS95a]. After a projection, only necessary classes (type closure) and objects are retained. In that sense, the transformation is a *restructuring* of the source schema and instance. In our framework, we cannot create information that is not derived and disallow typical schema-database updates. Note that the four algebraic operators (modulo renaming) enable the same kinds of change as the ones from [KR96] or COOL in COCOON [LS92]. Our model has the following main features:

1. The identification of an object in a target database (a view) always enables the retrieval of "components" via referents.
2. The use of complex oids enables us to consider new objects (join on various classes of different kinds, see Couple) as aggregates of source objects.
3. Referents enable multi-instantiation.
4. An algebra which really structures the view, is completed by a query language, RQL, which allows us to address referents populating the classes.
5. The mechanism of view transformation may be applied several times resulting in the possibility of building a view upon other views.

Related work: In Kuno and Rudensteiner [KR96], building a view extends a source schema-instance, the *global* schema, adding the newly created virtual class in the same class hierarchy. Additional intermediate classes are also inserted for classification purposes. As opposed to our model, there is only an extension phase. One may hide a class or properties in a class but it always leads to new class creation(s). The source schema is not restructured in that sense. As a consequence, over time, a large number of classes and underlying object instances decreases the performances of the system and makes consistent view removal necessary [CTR96]. Regarding the objects, object slicing technique [KRR95] is used: a *conceptual object* (a kind of abstract object) is made up of several *objects of implementation*. This makes data updates easier. The drawback is to multiply the objects of implementation, duplicating them in all the subclasses of a class, while our view classes are populated by extension.

In Souza [dS95b], the source schema is transformed in a target schema, importing all the classes necessary to the derivation clause. In O_2 Views the virtual classes are not classified but simply created in a flat hierarchy under the root class. In the model, the structuring of the target schema is not explicitly part of the view definition mechanism [dS95b].

Perspectives: Interesting classes of semantic constraints could be studied to guaranty consistent definitions of views. When defining a new attribute in the parameters of an extension-instruction, one may wish to verify that an attribute a of signature $c \to \gamma(c')$ is single-valued when defined by a rule of head $y = x.a$ and, that for each object o in class c, $\langle o, c \rangle . a$ results in objects that are actually in the population of class c' (inclusion dependency constraints). In [AH88] it is shown that for relational algebra functional dependency single-valuedness is undecidable, but syntactic conditions can be developed to ensure single-valuedness. It is open for the views in RDM whether single-valuedness is decidable.

We can address the problem of querying the view. The naive evaluation of a query on the view consists in first defining the whole view, and second, in evaluating the query on the resulting view. We can do better. Suppose that S and S' are respectively a source and a view schema. For any query Q, if I and I' are respectively an instance of S and S', for all expressions e' of Q on the view, there should exist an *equivalent* expression e on the source, that is such that $e(I) = e'(I')$. In order to optimize the evaluation, we have to propose a translation t of expressions of queries in RQL, based on the algebraic definition of the view. This translation can be formalized and results in only defining the part of the view that is necessary to evaluate the query.

The algebra can be extended to more sophisticated operators such as *merge* or *powerset*. The semantics of the *merge* operator can be based on the use of complex oids to uniquely identify several objects (with different identifiers) that have the same value in a given class. This technique may be of interest when considering different data sources (data warehousing) together with a notion of *key-attribute* that will be investigated in future work.

We also propose the notion of referent as a good candidate to extend the data model for object versions presented in [AJ97]. Indeed, in [AJ97] an object is associated with a unique class and is seen or hidden in the class depending on the version. Then the object *martine* cannot be an instance of class Child in a version and instance of class Adult in another version. The use of referents would give more flexibility to the model allowing an object to be seen in different classes depending of the version.

Knowing what subclass of view-transformations these views capture would be of interest. This could be a matter of giving a constraint on the target schema w.r.t. the source schema. If the constraint is satisfied, there exists an expression in the algebra that allows the definition of this view. This formalizes the notion of *View-Derivation* pointed out in [dS95b].

Note that in [Aa94], OQL is specified to allow objects construction with declarations having the form

`Select Couple(name:x.name,address:y.address) From ... Where ...`

where class `Couple` is assumed to be already created. An extension of OQL should cover this topic, creating "real" virtual classes.

Finally, we made some choices regarding the semantics of our four algebraic operators. They could be also extended to provide additional flexibility to the view designers (for instance sophisticated mechanism for class hiding).

Acknowledgment Cassio Souza dos Santos is thanked for getting the authors valuable comments on this data model and for discussions on views and O_2 Views. Peter Buneman, Val Tannen and Susan Davidson are also thanked for valuable suggestions. The authors wish to thank the anonymous reviewers and Rick Hull (our attentive DBPL shepherd) for their feedback.

References

[Aa94]   T. Atwood and al. *The Object Database Standard: ODMG - 94*. Morgan Kaufmann, San Francisco, 1994.

[AB91]   S. Abiteboul and A. Bonner. Objects and views. In *SIGMOD'91 Conference Proceedings, Int. Conf. on Management of Data*, San Francisco, California, March 1991. ACM Press.

[ADD+91] R. Ahmed, P. DeSmedt, W. Du, W. Kent, M. Ketabchi, W. Litwin, A. Rafii, and M. C. Shan. Pegasus heterogeneous multidatabase system. *IEEE Computer*, December 1991.

[AdS95]   S. Abiteboul and C. Souza dos Santos. IQL(2): A Model with Ubiquitous Objects. In *Proceedings of the Intl. Workshop on Database Programming Languages - DBPL'95*, Gubio, Italy, September 1995. Springer Verlag.

[AH87]   S. Abiteboul and R. Hull. IFO: A Formal Semantic Database Model. *ACM Trans. on Database Systems*, 12(4):525–565, 1987.

[AH88]   S. Abiteboul and R. Hull. Data Functions, Datalog and Negation. In *Proc. ACM SIGMOD Symp. on the Management of Data*, pages 143–153, 1988.

[AHV95]   S. Abiteboul, R. Hull, and V. Vianu. *Foundations of Databases*. Addison-Wesley, 1995.

[AJ97]   T. Abdessalem and G. Jomier. Vql: A query language for multiversion databases. In *Proc. of Intl. Workshop on Database Programming Languages*, August 1997.

[AK89]   S. Abiteboul and P. Kanellakis. Object identity as a query language primitive. In *ACM SIGMOD Symposium on the management of Data*, pages 159–173, Portland Oregon USA, June 1989.

[BDK92]   F. Bancilhon, C. Delobel, and P. Kanellakis, editors. *Building an Object-Oriented Database System — The Story of O_2*. Morgan Kaufmann, San Mateo, California, 1992.

[Ber91]   E. Bertino. A View Mechanism for Object-Oriented Databases. In *Intl. Conference on Extending Data Base Technology*, pages 136–151, Vienna, March 1991.

[BW95]   P. Brèche and M. Wörner. How to remove a class in an object database system. In *In Proceedings of the 2nd International Conference on Applications of Databases, ADB '95*, San José, California, December 1995.

[CH95]   T.-P. Chang and R. Hull. Using witness generators to support bi-directional update between object-based databases. In *Proc. ACM Symp. on Principles of Database Systems*, pages 196–207, 1995.

[Cha94]   T.-P. Chang. *On Incremental Update Propagation Between Object-Based Databases*. PhD thesis, University of Southern California, Los Angeles, CA, 1994.

[CKMS97] I.A. Chen, A.S. Kosky, V.M. Markowitz, and E. Szeto. Constructing and maintaining scientific database views. In *In Proceedings of the 9th Conference on Scientific and Statistical Database Management*, August 1997.

[CML$^+$96] I. Chen, V. Markowitz, S. Letovsky, P. Li, and K. Fasman. Version management for scientific databases. In *Proc. of Intl. Conf. on Extending Data Base Technology*, 1996.

[CTR96]   V. Crestana-Taube and E.A. Rundensteiner. Consistent View Removal in Transparent Schema Evolution Systems. *6th Int. Workshop on Research Issues on Data Engineering, Interoperability of Non-traditional Database Systems, RIDE'96, IEEE*, February 1996.

[dS95a]   C. Souza dos Santos. Design and Implementation of Object-Oriented Views. In N. Revell and A.Min. Tjoa, editors, *Proc. of the 6th International Conference on Database and Expert Systems Applications*, number 978 in LNCS, London, England, September 1995. Springer Verlag.

[dS95b]   C. Souza dos Santos. *Un Mécanisme de Vues pour les systèmes de Gestion de Bases de Données Objet*. PhD thesis, Université de Paris Sud - Centre d'Orsay, Paris, France, November 1995.

[dSDA94] C. Souza dos Santos, C. Delobel, and S. Abiteboul. Virtual Schemas and Bases. In *Proceedings of the International Conference on Extending Database Technology*, March 1994.

[HY90]   R. Hull and M. Yoshikawa. ILOG: Declarative Creation and Manipulation of Object Identifiers (Extended Abstract). In *Proc. of Intl. Conf. on Very Large Data Bases*, pages 455–468, 1990.

[HY91]   R. Hull and M. Yoshikawa. On the equivalence of database restructurings involving object identifiers. In *Proc. ACM Symp. on Principles of Database Systems*, pages 328–340, 1991.

[KKS92]   M. Kifer, W. Kim, and Y. Sagiv. Querying Object-Oriented Databases. In *Proc. ACM SIGMOD Symp. on the Management of Data*, 1992.

[KL89]   M. Kifer and G. Lausen. F-logic: A higher-order language for reasoning about objects. In *Proc. ACM SIGMOD Symp. on the Management of Data*, 1989.

[KR96]   H.A. Kuno and E.A. Rundensteiner. The MultiView OODB View System: Design and Implementation. *Journal of Theory and Practice of Object Systems (TAPOS). Special Issue on Subjectivity in Object-Oriented Systems*, 1996.

[KRR95]   H.A. Kuno, Y-G. Ra, and E.A. Rundensteiner. Object-Slicing: A Flexible Object Representation and Its Evaluation. Technical Report CSE-TR-241-95, University of Michigan, Electrical Engineering and Computer Science Dept, University of Michigan, Ann Arbor, April 1995.

[KW89]   M. Kifer and J. Wu. A Logic for Object-Oriented Logic Programming
           (Maier's O-Logic Revisited). In *Proc. ACM Symp. on Principles of Database
           Systems*, 1989.
[LDB97]   Z. Lacroix, C. Delobel, and Ph. Brèche. Object Views derived from Algebraic
           Operators. In *Proceedings of the French conference on Databases: Base de
           Données Avancées*, September 1997. to appear in Journal Ingénieurie des
           Systèmes d'Information.
[LRV88]   C. Lécluse, P. Richard, and F. Vélez. O_2, an Object–Oriented data model.
           In *Proceeding ACM SIGMOD, Chicago IL*, June 1988.
[LS92]   C. Laasch and M. H. Scholl. Generic Update Operations Keeping Object-
           Oriented Databases Consistent. In *Proc. 2nd GI-Workshop on Information
           Systems and Artificial Intelligence*. Springer, February 1992.
[Mai86]   D. Maier. A logic for objects. In *Workshop on Foundations of Deductive
           Databases and Logic Programming*, pages 6 26, Washington, D.C., August
           1986.
[Mot87]   A. Motro. Superviews: Virtual Integration of Multiple Databases. *IEEE
           Transactions on Software Engineering*, 13(7):785–798, July 1987.
[Run92]   E.A. Rundensteiner. Multi View: A Methodology for supporting Multiple
           View Schemata in Object-Oriented Databases. In *Proceedings of the 18th
           International Conference on Very Large Databases*, pages 187–198, Vancou-
           ver, Canada, August 1992. Morgan Kaufmann.
[SS91]   M.E. Scholl and H.-J. Schek. Supporting views in object-oriented databases.
           *IEEE Database Engineering Bulletin. Special Issue on Foundations of
           Object-Oriented Database Systems*, 2(14):43 47, June 1991.
[Su91]   J. Su. Dynamic constraints and object migration. In *Proc. of Intl. Conf. on
           Very Large Data Bases*, pages 233 242, 1991.
[TYH+91]   K. Tsuda, K. Yamamoto, M. Hirakawa, M. Tanaka, and T. Ichikawa.
           MORE: An Object-Oriented Data Model with Facility for Changing Ob-
           ject Structures. *IEEE Transactions on Knowledge and Data Engineering*,
           3(4):444–460, December 1991.

Implementing Incremental View Maintenance in Nested Data Models

Akira Kawaguchi[1] **Daniel Lieuwen**[2]
Inderpal Mumick[3] **Kenneth Ross**[1]

[1] Columbia University, {akira,kar}@cs.columbia.edu
[2] Bell Laboratories/Lucent Technologies, lieuwen@research.bell-labs.com
[3] Savera Systems (work performed at AT&T Laboratories), mumick@savera.com

Abstract. Previous research on materialized views has primarily been in the context of flat relational databases—materialized views defined in terms of one or more flat relations. This paper discusses a broader class of view definitions—materialized views defined over a nested data model such as the nested relational model or an object-oriented data model. An attribute of a tuple deriving the view can be a reference (*i.e.*, a pointer) to a nested relation, with arbitrary levels of nesting possible. The extended capability of this nested data model, together with materialized views, simplifies data modeling and gives more flexibility.

Simple extensions of standard view maintenance techniques to the nested model would do too much work for maintenance: a change in a nested set would re-process the entire nested set, not just the changed parts. We show how existing incremental maintenance algorithms can be extended to maintain the views without performing this additional work.

We describe the implementation of these techniques in the **SWORD** interface to the Ode database system. The implementation is based on the representation of nested structures by classes and the use of an SQL-like language to define materialized views. We outline the data structures and algorithms used in the implementation and examine performance. This is one of the first pieces of work to explore the applicability of materialized views over complex objects.

1 Introduction

Most past research on materialized views has focused on high level incremental algorithms for updating materialized views efficiently when the base relations are updated [9, 37, 8, 31, 10, 17, 16, 25, 40]. Those studies are in the context of first-normal-form relational databases—materialized views are defined in terms of one or more relations using a relational query language. In this paper, we allow a materialized view to be defined over a nested data model, where a tuple can have arbitrarily deeply nested structures. For the simplicity of our discussion we assume in the rest of paper that all materialized views are *snapshot* views [2], *i.e.*, views that are maintained when an explicit maintenance request is made.

The extension of the relational model to non-first-normal-form goes back to [27], which introduced the concept of nesting. The work of, *e.g.*, [18, 19, 4, 1, 38, 39] further investigated nested properties including the algebra and calculus. Query languages and implementation issues are discussed in, *e.g.*, [5, 15, 30, 24, 33, 34]. The above research aims to extend the relational model to directly represent data that is usually organized hierarchically such as in CAD/CAM and multimedia applications. The idea of having relation names as arguments is presented in [32]. This extension allows relation names to be stored as attributes of other relations (essentially using the name as a pointer), and allows access to one relation or another based on the value of some other attribute. Thus, nested relations can be implemented without directly embedding relations in tuples. Object-oriented databases (OODBs) share this property. An object often has a complex sub-object that is referenced by an object identifier. Further, the nested structures are usually *unnamed* (*i.e.*, the structure has no external name by which it can be referenced; it can be referenced only by navigating through the containing relation/object). In this paper, we consider nesting by reference, as described for the relational and object-oriented models above. We leave the case of embedded nested values within a tuple or object for further work.

We consider the problem of maintaining materialized views over such nested structures. A simple extension of maintenance algorithms for views over normal form relations to views over nested structures yields inefficient algorithms. For example, suppose that p is a binary relation whose second argument is a nested relation with a single attribute. Let q be another binary relation. Let V be a view defined $V(X,Y) \stackrel{def}{=} p(X,Z), Z(W), q(W,Y)$. (in a HiLog style language [11, 32]). Thus, V is a join of p with q on the elements of p's nested attribute. Suppose that $p(a,s)$ are the tuples in the extension of p, and that $\{\langle 1 \rangle, \langle 2 \rangle, \ldots, \langle n \rangle\}$ are the values in the nested relation s. Let us modify s by adding $\langle n+1 \rangle$ to the extension of s. A straightforward application of known view maintenance techniques could "undo" the effect of the whole set $\{\langle 1 \rangle, \langle 2 \rangle, \ldots, \langle n \rangle\}$ and then "redo" the effect of $\{\langle 1 \rangle, \langle 2 \rangle, \ldots, \langle n+1 \rangle\}$. Much of this work is unnecessary— only work corresponding to inserting $\langle n+1 \rangle$ is necessary. We develop auxiliary data structures to find such relevant changes efficiently.

The motivation of this study is the development of the SWORD interface [29] to the Ode OODB [3]. SWORD provides an SQL-like declarative language to define materialized views compositionally and hierarchically on collections of Ode objects. SWORD supports transparent incremental maintenance of those views using the incremental view maintenance algorithm of [17]. The algorithm accumulates the changes made to each base relation of the materialized view in a *log*, a sequential file associated with a base relation. It uses the logs to maintain views. There is only one log for each base relation regardless of the number of the views it derives (*i.e.*, the log is shared by a set of views to be maintained). A log entry holds an *identifier* of the changed tuple (the change may be an insertion, deletion and modification). The data structures used to implement logs are described in [13].

Two problems arise when we enhance the materialized views in SWORD to work with a nested data model. First, how should the log structure be extended? Second, how can one capture the change made in a referenced complex relation? The implementation creates an entry in relation T's log in response to each update to a tuple of T. Suppose that a tuple t of T has a pointer to another relation R whose tuple r is updated. The change to r must be identified both for referring relation T and for referred relation R. How can we identify all such referring tuples t? Recording the change in the log of the referring relation T is not easy since the pointer value in the tuple t will not change unless the whole referred relation R is dropped or newly created. Furthermore, since nested sets are referenced through pointers, the insertion of a single tuple may affect many containing objects—thus, the space required for the log (and, consequently, the time for creating and scanning log records) may balloon. A more subtle problem arises if we consider the efficiency of the maintenance that involves implicit join operations between flat and nested attributes or between nested attributes.

Paper Outline: Section 2 reviews the nested data model [39, 33] used in this paper and then investigates maintaining materialized views over nested data models. The implementation architecture for the non-nested case is reviewed in Section 3; Section 4 presents the necessary extensions for handling nested structures. Section 5 discusses performance results. Related work is discussed in Section 6; Section 7 presents conclusions.

2 Maintaining Materialized Views over Nested Data

2.1 Notation and Definitions

We describe our techniques in the nested relational model context. It should, however, be understood that the techniques developed apply also to OODBs.[4]

---

[4] While we did not discuss the use of our algorithms for OODBs over data with cyclic references, our algorithms extend [17]'s counting algorithms which can incrementally

Following [39], a database scheme is a collection of rules of the form $R = [R_1, ..., R_k]$. Objects $R_1, ..., R_k$ are called *names*. An object is a *higher-order* name if it appears on some rule's left-hand side; else, it is a *zero-order* name. Nested schemes may contain any combination of zero or higher-order attributes on the right-hand side of the rules as long as the scheme remains non-recursive.

An instance of $R = [R_1, ..., R_k]$ is a collection of tuples such that each tuple contains arbitrary combinations of values, or *indirect references* (relation names or pointers to relations) based on the *types* of names $R_1, ..., R_k$. Some object, R_i say, may be a higher-order name, in which case the instance of R_i will be a recursive expansion of the rules in the right-hand side. Hence a tuple of R can be viewed as having arbitrarily deeply nested relation instances. A relation is a stored instance of the database scheme. We call a relation R, defined by schema $R = [R_1, ..., R_k]$, a *nesting relation* if at least one of its attributes $R_1, ..., R_k$, say R_i, is a higher order name. We also call the higher order name, R_i a *nested relation*. A relation that is not defined as a view is called a *base relation*.

Materialized Views: A *view* V is a relation that is defined using a query Q over some set of relations $\{R_1, ..., R_n\}$, denoted as $V \stackrel{def}{=} Q(R_1, ..., R_n)$. The query is said to be defined over relation R_i if R_i appears in the query definition, or if the query follows a reference to a relation of type R_i. $R_1, ..., R_n$ are called the *referenced* relations, and may be base relations or materialized view relations. The referenced relation can be a nesting relation or a nested relation. A *materialized view* is a view whose tuples are physically stored in the database. A *virtual view* is an unmaterialized view; it is computed when it is needed for a query using the R_i. (For brevity, we do not discuss virtual views in the rest of this paper until Section 5 on performance.) □

Log and Delta: For every referenced relation R_i, an additional structure, which we call a *log*, contains the changes made to R_i. Any update to a referenced relation causes a corresponding log entry to be created. The log is used to construct a set of tuples that will be used for the incremental maintenance of view V. We call this set a *delta*, denote as ΔR_i. If multiple views $V_1, ..., V_n$ are defined using relation R_i, the log must be capable of constructing $\Delta R_i(V_j)$ (*i.e.*, a delta of R_i with regard to view V_j), for $1 \leq j \leq n$. □

View-Dependency Graph: The dependency graph G of a view V is a graph with a node for each relation referenced in the view definition, a node labeled V, and a directed edge from the node for each referenced relation to the node for V.

---

maintain recursively defined views over circular data. Thus, we believe our techniques our applicable to arbitrary data in OODBs. Furthermore, our algorithms directly apply to non-recursive view definitions over circular data without extensions.

The dependency graph shows how the view is derived from base relations and/or other views. The view-dependency graph $\mathcal{G}$ of a database schema is the union of the dependency graphs for all the views in the schema. The view-dependency graph shows how all the views in the schema are derived from each other and from base relations. □

2.2 Incremental Change Computation

We consider the counting algorithm of [17] for view maintenance. The counting algorithm keeps a count of the number of derivations for each view tuple. For instance, given a join view $V \overset{def}{=} R_1 \bowtie R_2 \bowtie R_3$, the counting algorithm derives the following algebraic equation to compute the changes ΔV to view V:

$$\Delta V = \Delta R_1 \bowtie R_2^{new} \bowtie R_3^{new} \uplus R_1^{old} \bowtie \Delta R_2 \bowtie R_3^{new} \uplus R_1^{old} \bowtie R_2^{old} \bowtie \Delta R_3$$

where ΔR_i is the set of insertions and/or deletions to relation R_i, R_i^{old} is the old (or pre-update) state of the base relation R_i (before the updates of ΔR_i are applied to R_i), and R_i^{new} is the new (or post-update) state of the base relation R_i (after the updates of ΔR_i are applied to it). The $\uplus$ operator denotes bag union. In the set of changes, insertions (deletions) are represented with positive (negative) counts. Updates are represented by deletions of the before images, and insertions of the new tuples. The count value for each tuple is represented in the materialized view V, and the new materialized view is obtained by combining the changes ΔV with the stored value of view V as follows: Positive counts are added in; negative counts are subtracted. A tuple with a count of zero is deleted.

A view defined over the nested data model can be maintained by the counting algorithm if we can define and identify the nested delta sets correctly. We assume that the view definition language is based on a query language such as HiLog [11].

EXAMPLE 2.1 Consider the schema Emp = [Nm, Dependent], Dependent = [D-Nm, Age], Health-Ins = [D-Nm] with the following database extension: Emp = $\{\langle Fred, D1 \rangle, \langle Mary, D2 \rangle\}$; Health-Ins = $\{\langle Dave \rangle, \langle Jane \rangle\}$; D1 = $\{\langle Dave, 85 \rangle, \langle Bob, 10 \rangle, \langle Jane, 5 \rangle\}$; D2 = $\{\langle Dave, 85 \rangle, \langle Alice, 3 \rangle\}$. (D1 and D2 are ids of otherwise unnamed relations of type Dependent). Consider the view V which contains the employees' dependents who have their own health insurance. V is defined by the following HiLog expression: $V(X, Z) \overset{def}{=}$ Emp$(X, Y), Y(Z, A)$, Health-Ins(Z). The materialization of V is $\{\langle Fred, Dave \rangle, \langle Fred, Jane \rangle, \langle Mary, Dave \rangle\}$. To respond to a change in the relation Health-Ins, we apply the counting algorithm. For this kind of update, we can intuitively express ΔV as $\Delta V(X, Z) \quad =$

$\mathrm{Emp}^{old}(X,Y) \bowtie Y^{old}(Z,A) \bowtie \Delta\mathrm{Heath\text{-}Ins}(Z)$. Note, Y^{old} is not precise since Y is a variable. We discuss what Y^{old} means below. Deleting Jane from Health-Ins (written as $\Delta\mathrm{Heath\text{-}Ins} = \{\langle\mathrm{Jane}\rangle^{-1}\}$) yields $\Delta V = \{\langle\mathrm{Fred}, \mathrm{Jane}\rangle^{-1}\}$. $\quad\Box$

Example 2.1 shows that handling updates to non-nested relations is straightforward. We now consider updates to the nested relations.

Meta-Relation, Extraction Function: Consider a nesting relation $R = [\ldots, S, \ldots]$ where S is a higher-order name. For each such nested S in the database we define a *meta-relation* u_S as follows. $u_S(X)$ is true precisely when X is the id of a nested relation in the database extension, of the same type as S. For each such nested relation S, we define an *extraction function* $e_S(X, A_1, \ldots, A_k)$, where S is defined by the rule $S = [A_1, \ldots, A_k]$. (In other words, $A_1, \ldots, A_k$ are the attributes of relations of type S.)

$$e_S(X, A_1, \ldots, A_k) = u_S(X) \bowtie X(A_1, \ldots, A_k) \qquad\qquad \Box$$

For the nested Dependent tables of Example 2.1, we would have $u_{\mathrm{Dependent}} = \{D1, D2\}$ and $e_{\mathrm{Dependent}} = \{\langle D1, \mathrm{Dave}, 85\rangle, \langle D1, \mathrm{Bob}, 10\rangle, \langle D1, \mathrm{Jane}, 5\rangle, \langle D2, \mathrm{Dave}, 85\rangle, \langle D2, \mathrm{Alice}, 3\rangle\}$.

Consider again a nested relation $R = [\ldots, S, \ldots]$ where S is a higher-order name. Let a view V be defined using R and S, so that $V' = R(\ldots, X, \ldots) \bowtie X(\ldots)$ is a subexpression within V. (Here, X is a variable appearing in the position of the nested attribute of type S.) Rather than doing maintenance on this subexpression directly, we maintain the equivalent subexpression

$$R(\ldots, X, \ldots) \bowtie e_S(X, \ldots). \qquad\qquad (1)$$

The benefit of this transformation is that we no longer have a HiLog variable as a relation name. Treating e_S as a relation, we can express $\Delta V'$ using the counting algorithm as $\Delta R(\ldots, X, \ldots) \bowtie e_S^{new}(X, \ldots) \uplus R^{old}(\ldots, X, \ldots) \bowtie \Delta e_S(X, \ldots)$ In the event that there are multiple levels of nesting, so that S itself contains a nested relation T as an attribute ($S = [\ldots, T, \ldots]$), we can recursively express Δe_S in terms of S and e_T as above.

The expression (1) also gives us a hint about where to keep the delta information for unnamed nested relations. The extraction function can be thought of as a materialized view. However, only the log of the view, not the view's extension, is stored. Conceptually, we should keep the delta information for nested relations of a given type S in a single place associated with S. For the efficient incremental change computation, $\Delta e_S(X, \ldots)$ must be quickly found in the database, so that the system can avoid scanning all tuples in R. In Section 4 we show how this is implemented using "nested descriptors."

EXAMPLE 2.2 The view V in Example 2.1 can be incrementally computed as follows:

$$\Delta V(X, Z) = \Delta \text{Emp}(X, Y) \bowtie e^{new}_{\text{Dependent}}(Y, Z, A) \bowtie \text{Heath-Ins}^{new}(Z)$$
$$\uplus \text{Emp}^{old}(X, Y) \bowtie \Delta e_{\text{Dependent}}(Y, Z, A) \bowtie \text{Heath-Ins}^{new}(Z)$$
$$\uplus \text{Emp}^{old}(X, Y) \bowtie e^{old}_{\text{Dependent}}(Y, Z, A) \bowtie \Delta \text{Heath-Ins}(Z)$$

Suppose Fred changed his name to Greg after V's materialization, and that he no longer has a dependent Dave. So $\Delta \text{Emp} = \{\langle \text{Fred}, D1 \rangle^{-1}, \langle \text{Greg}, D1 \rangle^{+1}\}$ and $\Delta e_{\text{Dependent}} = \{\langle D1, \text{Dave}, 85 \rangle^{-1}\}$. Using the expression above, we compute ΔV as $\{\langle \text{Fred}, \text{Dave} \rangle^{-1}, \langle \text{Fred}, \text{Jane} \rangle^{-1}, \langle \text{Greg}, \text{Jane} \rangle^{+1}\}$. □

Observe that the incremental work needed to maintain a view over nested data is in principle proportional to the *changes* in the contents of the nested relations, and not proportional to the size of the nested relations themselves. In the next two sections we outline how we achieve this performance level *in practice*.

3 Implementation for First Normal Form Relations

This section briefly reviews the implementation of our view maintenance system presented in [13]. The extensions to handle nested data are discussed in Section 4.

A part of the effort in [13] addresses scalability and efficiency concerns since materialized views introduce additional system overheads (*e.g.*, space for storing log, log update time, view maintenance time). Some of the requirements are: (a) The overhead of making log entries must be independent of the number of views. Thus, we rule out a design based on a separate log for each relation-view pair. (b) Time required to compute the delta must be proportional to the size of the relevant log. This prevents us from scanning the entire log to determine the portion of the log's changes. (c) The total space used to store all the logs in the system should be proportional to the number of updates that need to be propagated into materialized views. Thus, log entries should not be replicated, and old log entries must be discarded. (d) Queries over a relation should not be slowed down when views are defined over the relation. (e) Given a view, we should be able to quickly check whether it needs to be refreshed.

A relation (base or materialized view) is implemented as a *collection* class in Ode. A collection has a *materialization* containing tuples and a *descriptor*. A tuple is implemented as an Ode object. The descriptor holds meta-information about the collection, such as the creation date, a pointer to the materialization, and other pointers needed to support materialized views. The collection class provides a number of member functions (methods) such as `insert()`, `remove()`, and `replace()` that can be invoked from the O++ interface to Ode. The `insert()` function creates a new tuple with the given values, and inserts it into the materialization. The `remove()` function removes a tuple from the materialization by marking it as removed, and placing it in a pool of removed tuples. The tuple must stay in this pool until the effects of its removal are propagated to all views defined on the relation, after which point it can be garbage collected. The `replace()` function updates an existing tuple, and stores the pre-update value in a newly created tuple that is placed in the pool of removed tuples. A separate `Iterator` class is provided to iterate over the materialization of any relation.

Extracting Relevant Changes from Logs: The changes made since the last maintenance operation on a view V are the only log entries relevant for a maintenance operation on V. The `DeltaIterator` class is provided to iterate over the relevant changes of a relation R for V. When a `DeltaIterator` object is created for a given relation/view pair, we scan R's log starting from the last maintenance pointer for the view V stored in R's descriptor, and build an in-memory hash table by hashing the *oid* in the log entry. A bucket contains an in-memory copy of the log entry itself. The log is not modified. Hashing is used to compute the net effect of the changes in the log by eliminating and/or collapsing redundant log entries due to insert-remove pairs, replace-remove pairs, replace-replace pairs, and insert-replace pairs [35, 20]. Since the creation of the hash table requires time proportional to the size of the log relevant to the view, and using the hash table requires even less time, we clearly satisfy the efficiency requirement (b).

4   Handling Nested Structures

This section describes key ideas to efficiently capture the incremental changes to nested components. Nested relations in SWORD are defined using an O++ class with an attribute that is an embedded collection class or a pointer to another collection class. We insisted both that view maintenance be transparent to the user and that it not do any (significant amount of) extra work if no views exist. Our algorithms trigger transparent view maintenance work only if the user instantiates a view using the view definition language.

Efficiency Requirements: A major challenge is efficiently detecting changes made to the elements that are in a nested attribute. We must establish associations between such elements and owner tuples. This must be done by the time we construct the extraction function of Section 2.2 for maintenance. In an implementation, a change made to an element of the internally nested relation could be placed in the log of that nested relation. A naive approach is to propagate this change to the log of every *nesting* relation whose tuples reference the nesting relation being changed. This approach imposes a heavy burden on the update transaction since the transaction needs to find all owner tuples in order to insert the log entries. If a large number of tuples contain references to the updated relation, or if the nesting level is deep, the log operation can become very expensive. Log space may blow up. Thus, additional requirements imposed on the implementation are to find (1) an efficient way to collect and store the changes made to the nested elements, (2) an efficient way to establish nesting-nested associations, and (3) the smallest possible update transaction overhead. Section 3's requirements apply as well.

4.1 Capturing Changes in Nested Tables

To meet requirement (1), we create a system collection descriptor that owns a log for *all* nested relations of the same scheme (or class) definition. The descriptor is created when a view involving these nested relations is initially materialized. We call this descriptor a *nested descriptor*. Each SWORD view definition is inspected to find any nested relations (SWORD, like HiLog, requires specifying a variable that ranges over nested relations with the same scheme type). The tuples in the set of individual nested relations are of the same type. Thus, all log entries in the nested descriptor's log are of the same type. After creating a nested descriptor D, every update to a corresponding nested relation N is recorded in D's log (instead of in N's log). When the update transaction calls the `insert()`, `remove()` or `replace()` method of N, the method checks if a nested descriptor, D, of the same relation type exists. If so, it inserts a log entry into D's log. The insertion is done only once. This check is the only overhead to the update transaction, and this overhead is negligible. Thus, requirement (3) is met.

Consider a database scheme defined by the following collection of rules. $R = [T, \ldots], S = [U, \ldots], T = [U, \ldots], U = [\ldots]$. Figure 1 illustrates the structure of the relations (R, S, T_1, T_2, U_1, U_2) and the associated logs (disregard the indices for now). According to the figure, tuples of the relation R have pointers to T_1 and T_2, the tuple of S has a pointer to U_1, and so on. Boxes labeled R, T_1, T_2, ... in the figure represent *relation descriptors* since they contain control information about relations (*e.g.*, information about each relation's indices/views).

Suppose also that two views V_1 and V_2 are defined over R, T, and U (S is not used for the view definition). For example, V_1 is defined as a query of

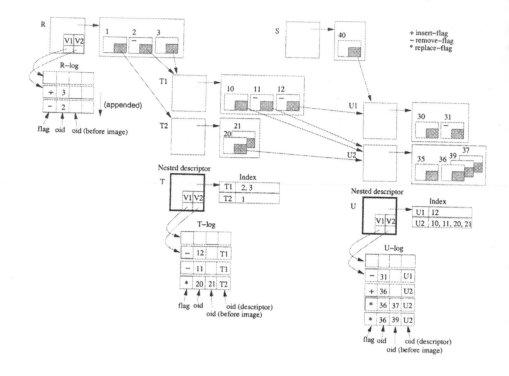

Fig. 1. Log Structure for Nested Tables

$V_1 \overset{def}{=} R(X, \ldots) \bowtie X(Y, \ldots) \bowtie Y(\ldots)$, where a variable X is in the position of the nested attribute T and a variable Y is in the position of the nested attribute of U. In Figure 1, the relation descriptor for R has pointers (labeled V_1 and V_2) into the log. The pointer for V_1 (V_2) points to the last log entry that has been applied to view V_1 (V_2) to have brought it up to date. R contains two current tuples with $oid = 1, 3$ which we will refer to as t_1 and t_3 ($oid = 2$ is a deleted tuple that must be kept around for view maintenance purposes for the time being). t_1 references the nested set T_2. T_2 contains a single active tuple with $oid = 20$, t_{20}. (Tuple t_{20} originally had the same contents as the tuple with $oid = 21$, t_{21}. When t_{20} was modified, a copy, t_{21} was made first for view maintenance. The last log entry for T's nested descriptor indicates that.) Notice that the log entry includes the oid of the relation descriptor. The principles of [13] are used to extract relevant changes from the log for views V_1 and V_2. For example, the maintenance of V_1 and V_2 requires computing the extraction function using t_1.

Note that t_1 is not found in the log of R since the changes were made to T_2 and U_2. Such changes are efficiently found in the logs of nested descriptors T and U. The details will be discussed in Section 4.3.

4.2 Nested-Nesting Associations

To meet requirement (2), we consider an index structure that is associated with each nested descriptor. The reason to have this index is to efficiently expand all changes (particularly those that have occurred in deeply nested elements) into the extraction function of Section 2.2 for maintenance. The index will be created at the same time as the corresponding descriptor. Subsequent view maintenance operations will maintain the index entries. The query transactions never use this index. This structure is similar to those used in nested indices and a path indices [7], but the motivation is quite different since those indices are used to answer queries.

Each key in the index is the *oid* of a relation descriptor (*e.g.*, T_1, T_2) that is directly referenced by some tuple in a nesting relation. This allows the *oid* of each tuple that is directly *nesting* another relation to be found (*e.g.*, it allows us to find that t_1 contains T_2). During the first view materialization operation, the index entries are initialized using mappings from the *oid* of an owned relation descriptor (*e.g.*, T_2) to the *oids* of each tuple that directly owns this relation descriptor (*e.g.*, t_1). Every tuple in the nesting relation must be inserted into this index, whether or not it contributes to the current instance of the materialized view.[5] After the index is created, new nesting tuples may be inserted into a relation relevant to a view. The *oids* of these new tuples will not appear in the nested descriptor's index until view maintenance occurs. Thus, during the subsequent view maintenance, mappings for recently inserted tuples must be inserted into the index (*e.g.*, the pair mapping T_1 to t_3 was added to the T index when the log entry for the insertion of t_3 was processed during the previous maintenance operation on view V_2). Garbage collection sweeps every removed *oid* in the index that is no longer used for any view maintenance. Since this index never adds overhead to update transactions, we satisfy requirement (3). Similarly, log entries may indicate that a nesting tuple has been deleted, in which case its index entry must be removed (*e.g.*, the mapping from T_1 to $oid = 2$ must be removed

---

[5] This is because we scan each relevant log only once to maintain views. If a tuple that previously did not participate in the view was modified so that it could contribute to the join and it was not already in the index, we would have to add it in an initial pass over the relevant logs and then use it in a second pass over the logs.

when the log record for the deletion of $oid = 2$ is processed). A modification is treated like a deletion followed by an insertion. (Note, the implementation actually optimizes the conceptual index described above by storing a pointer to a list of backpointers in the nested descriptor itself to reduce index lookup time—e.g., T1 contains a pointer to a list containing 2 and 3.)

In Figure 1, two indices for T and U are shown. Currently both indices have sufficient information to locate which tuple directly owns the oid of the relation descriptor. Suppose that a new tuple is inserted in R. Then the view maintenance process finds it in the log of R and inserts into the index of T (it may also add its nested set's contents to the index for U). Notice that tuples of S do not participate to the index since S is not defined in any view.

4.3 Incremental Computation

We use a hashing method similar to [35] to quickly compute the net effect of the changes in the log. We create hash buckets by following the nesting levels. Recall from Section 4.1 that the view V_1 in Figure 1 is defined as $V_1 \stackrel{def}{=} R(X, \ldots) \bowtie X(Y, \ldots) \bowtie Y(\ldots)$, where the variables X and Y are respectively bound to T and U. Algorithms of extracting the changes of R and producing the extraction functions of e_T and e_U are highlighted in the following three steps:

1. (Non-nested sets:) For each set mentioned by name in the view definition (*i.e.*, for each non-nested set such as R, scan the corresponding log to create hash buckets in the standard way (see Section 3). Also,
   1-1. If the entry contains the insert flag and the oid o_{new}, add a mapping (if none exists) from each of o_{new}'s nested sets to o_{new} in the indices of the corresponding nested descriptors. If no mappings from the nested set previously appeared in the index, continue this recursively for nested sets of the nested set.
2. (Nested sets:) For each nested set mentioned at the next nesting level in the view definition (*e.g.*, T bound by X), scan the nested descriptor's log to create hash buckets similarly. Furthermore, the descriptor oid (*e.g.*, T_1 and T_2) stored in each scanned log entry L is used to probe the contents of the index in order to determine if L affects the tuple that owns this nested set:
   2-1. L's oid o is used to probe the nested descriptor index. The $oids$ of all tuples mapped to by o that do not yet appear in the hash table are added to the hash buckets as in step 1 (except for those that are marked as deleted or which are used as old versions of tuples). If o is contained in a nested set, recursively probe the nested descriptor of its containing set

and add the containing tuples to the hash table if they are not already there. Continue doing this until no such containing tuples exist or they are all in the hash relation already.

3. Recursively apply step 2 to each of the relations at the next level of nesting (*e.g.*, U bound by Y).

Consider maintenance of V_1. The incremental computation scans the logs of R, T and U to build the net effect of the changes made to them. In step 1, the log of the non-nested set R is hashed, and $oid = 2, 3$ are added to the hash table.

In step 2, the log of the nested descriptor T is scanned, and $oid = 11, 12, 20$ are added to the bucket. Also, step 2-1 adds $oid = 1$ to the hash table created for R in step 1 ($oid = 2, 3$ are already there. $oid = 1$ is identified by probing the index with T_2's descriptor oid—R's tuple t_1 is not updated itself but its nested set T_2 is updated). In step 3, the log of U is scanned to create hash buckets. (This is the recursive step of 2.) $oid = 31, 36$ are inserted into U's hash table. In step 2-1, $oid = 10$ is added to the hash table created for T because $oid = 10$ does not appear there yet. $oid = 20, 11$ are in the bucket already; $oid = 21$ is an old version and so is excluded.

In the end, the hash tables of R, T, and U contain the $oids$ $\{1, 2, 3\}$, $\{10, 11, 12, 20\}$, and $\{31, 36\}$, respectively. The extraction functions then produce descriptor oid/tuple oid pairs by looking into these hash tables. For example, $\Delta e_T = \{(T_1, 10), (T_1, 11), (T_1, 12), (T_2, 20)\}$. The incremental join computation of ΔV_1 uses these descriptor $oids$ to find matching pointer values bound to X (the joined values from the nested set can be obtained by the tuple $oids$). These hash tables are also used to compute pre-update states of the database during the incremental view maintenance [13].

5 Performance Study

This section describes an experimental performance study on top of the disk-based Ode<EOS> database system. The experiments compare the performance of maintaining snapshot views over data that is naturally represented using nesting/nested relationships. All experiments were run in single user mode on a 128 MB, 200 MHz, UltraSparc II station (running Solaris Sun OS5.5.1 operating system). The database was kept on the local disc attachment to eliminate NFS delays.

Experimental Setup: We build databases containing base tables and snapshot materialized views, run 1,000 transactions against each database, and gather various statistics for the set of 1,000 transactions.

Databases: Our experiments use materialized views of the following form:

$$\text{Nest}(A, C) \stackrel{def}{=} \text{base1}(A, N), N(B, C), pred(B)$$

$$\text{Flat}(A, C) \stackrel{def}{=} \text{base2}(A, X), \text{base3}(X, B, C), pred(B)$$

All the non-view tuples (*e.g.*, base1–base3, N) are 300 bytes long. A, B, C, and X are integer fields. There is the natural one-to-one mapping between tuples of base1 and base2 (the nested sets and base3) that one would expect—the X field of base2/base3 contains the values 1–|base2| which correspond to the order in which the base1/base2 tuples were generated. B+tree indices are built on the following attributes: A and C for Nest and Flat; A for base1; A and X for base2; and X for base3. These indices improve both query and incremental view maintenance performance.

Before each experiment, each base table is initialized with tuples of uniformly-distributed, randomly generated data, and each view is materialized. The fields B and C were randomly filled with values in the range [1, |base3|] (A from the range [1, |base1|]). In all experiments, base3 contains 200,000 tuples.

Comparisons: We compared only incremental maintenance techniques. Full refresh of views with the associated indices takes about twenty minutes—far longer than incremental refresh. Since an approach to maintaining views over nested data without back pointers would require something similar to full refresh—each outer tuple examining its inner set for changes—we ignored this possibility.

Transactions: A program produces a stream of transactions, each of which either queries or updates the database. A *query transaction* contains only display operations on a randomly chosen view, while an *update transaction* contains either insert, remove, or replace operations on a randomly chosen base table. The replace operation updates the C field of a nested/base3 tuple. The *update ratio* of the transaction stream is the number of update transactions divided by the total number of transactions in the stream. For instance, if the stream contains 750 updates and 250 queries, then the update ratio is 0.75.

Each transaction contains 1–8 (an average of 4.5) operations over the same table (in Section 5.3, it is 1–4). Thus, for example, a query transaction reads 1–8 tuples matching randomly chosen values from a single view table.

5.1 Comparison between Flat and Nested Representation

Purpose: Our first experiments compare the cost of incrementally maintaining snapshot views over nested and non-nested versions of data. Given the complexity of Section 4's algorithm, *NestMat*, we wanted to verify that it was competitive with maintenance over non-nested data. Since nesting offers superior ease of data modeling, competitive performance is good enough to argue for nesting support. (Since *Nest* and *Flat* have identical contents, the read performance should be identical, so we will only consider update performance—the total time to update base tables and maintain views.)

Method: In our first experiment, base1 (base2) has 2,000 tuples; each base1 tuple has its own non-shared nested set containing approximately 100 tuples. (There are 200,000 nested tuples randomly assigned to nesting tuples.) We call this the *Small Family* data distribution. $pred(B)$ had a 50% selectivity, so the materialized view contained 100,000 tuples. Figure 2(a) contains the results for various snapshot frequencies. In our second experiment, base1 (base2) has 200 tuples; each base1 tuple has its own non-shared nested set containing (approximately) 1,000 tuples. We call this the *Large Family* data distribution. Other factors remain the same as in the previous experiment. Figure 2(b) contains the results.

Analysis: We note first that replaces are more expensive than inserts/deletes because they must copy the old value of a tuple into a newly created tuple used by the log. We note also that *NestMat* is superior to the algorithm over flat data. In large part, this is because insertions/deletions into base3 must modify the X index, while corresponding insertions/deletions of nested tuples do not modify an index—the representation eliminates the need for this index. Another important factor appears to be that it is cheaper to follow a pointer to a list of containing objects than to traverse a B+-tree on base2's X field. We note in Figure 2 that (b) has considerably better performance in the flat case than (a), while the nested performance is about the same. This is because the nested case must do about the same amount of work traversing a list of backpointers in both cases. However, in the flat case, base2's X index in (a) is ten times bigger than in (b), so more CPU and I/O costs are occurred using the index.

5.2 Skewed Access

Purpose: Our previous work [14] showed that incrementally maintaining a view over flat relations is considerably cheaper if the distribution of updates is highly skewed. Log trimming converts several updates to the same tuple into a single update which must be considered by the maintenance algorithm. We wanted to see if the same effect held in the nested case.

Method: In picking the tuples to modify, we picked a parent tuple initially, and then modified its children. 80% of our picks went to 20% of the base1/base2 tuples. Figure 2(c) compares the effect of skew in flat/nested relations. The graph

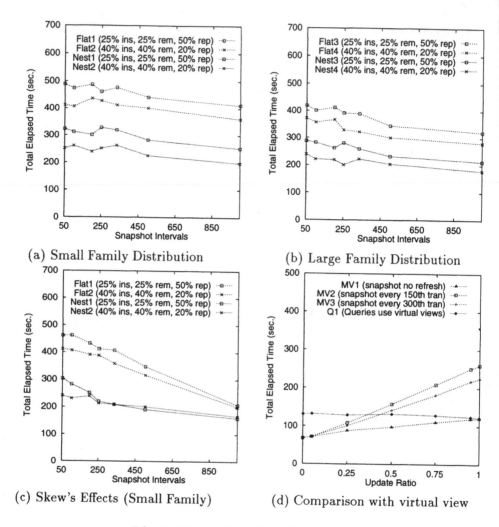

(a) Small Family Distribution

(b) Large Family Distribution

(c) Skew's Effects (Small Family)

(d) Comparison with virtual view

Fig. 2. Materialized View Comparisons

to compare it to is (a), since they use the same initial base data, just different update patterns. Both graphs contain update and maintenance time.

Analysis: The nested performance did not change very much in the presence of skew unlike the flat case. The flat case improves significantly as fewer snapshots are produced since a longer refresh cycle means more log trimming, and hence fewer modifications to the materialized view. However, increased trimming had only minor impact in the nested case.

5.3   Comparison with Virtual Views

Purpose: Under heavy update loads, materialized views become too expensive to maintain, and it is better to use virtual views. We wished to determine at roughly what point this occurs in our system.

Method: We sent 1–4 updates/reads in each transaction, and varied the update ratio. We used the Small Family data distribution and the 40% insert / 40% delete / 20% replace update mix. Given an A value in the view, our queries find the corresponding C values. We compare the total costs of all transactions and view maintenance for snapshots with different snapshot periods and for virtual views (with no view maintenance). Note that with virtual views, the data is fresh. It is somewhat stale with snapshots. However, we are comparing costs when some staleness can be permitted. See Figure 2(d) for the results.

Analysis: MV1 (snapshot with no refresh) shows that it is more expensive to update a base tuple than to read a snapshot tuple. That is why, even with no refresh, the cost increases when the update ratio increases. MV2 and MV3 show the additional overhead of view maintenance on top of the raw base table update costs of MV1. Q1, which uses virtual views, has roughly constant performance across the update range. This is because the computation of a tuple of the virtual view required many I/Os to find base3 tuples that match a given base2 tuple—to check the B/C values. Consequently, computing a virtual view tuple and modifying a base3 tuple (and the associated indices) had comparable cost. In our experiments, using virtual views proved superior to using materialized views once the update ratio reached 30%—40%.

6   Related Work

A preliminary version of this work was presented at a workshop [22]. That version describes earlier versions of the algorithms contained in this paper and contains more details on topics like garbage collection and log trimming. This paper extends that work with performance results.

This paper describes a nested data model based on prior work [39, 33, 32]. Various query languages and implementation frameworks for the nested relation model have been studied (*e.g.*, [5, 15, 30, 24, 33, 34]). These papers do not explicitly mention view definition/maintenance.

Our view definition language in SWORD is based on Noodle [28], and is similar to HiLog [11, 32], where relation names or references may appear as arguments of other relations. We described how [17]'s view maintenance algorithms for flat data models can be extended to handle a nested data model. We then described an implementation based on this extension.

This paper assumes that all materialized views are snapshot views (*i.e.*, views that are maintained when an explicit maintenance request is made). Snapshots were first proposed in [2]. Snapshot view implementation techniques are described in [23, 20, 35]. These papers consider only SP (select-project) views. [23] focuses on detecting relevant changes to snapshots using update tags on base relations. [20, 35] present techniques for maintaining logs and computing the net update to a view. Our log structures are based on the ideas in [35]. However, since [35]'s techniques are limited to SP views, they are not concerned with providing efficient access to past states of relations. Oracle supports snapshot views. However, Oracle only incrementally maintains SP views—using full recomputation on join and aggregate views. In [14], a model that allows multiple views to be maintained with different policies (immediate, deferred and snapshot) is studied, and an experimental performance comparison is made.

Concurrency control algorithms and a serializability model to guarantee serializability in the presence of deferred views are discussed in [21]. The focus of that paper is on doing concurrency control when multiple transactions reading and updating relations are executing concurrently in the system.

Our nested descriptor indices are similar to structures used to maintain join indices (*e.g.*, [26, 7]) and for field replication [36]. All these techniques are based on creating index structures that invert access paths specified by users to allow efficient maintenance of the desired access path (which can be considered as a materialized view of sorts). The nested descriptor indices presented in this paper can be implemented with structures similar to the modified B-tree structures used to model nested indices and path indices [7, 6].

7 Conclusion

This paper describes implementation techniques for maintaining materialized views over a nested data model. We showed that such views can be maintained by simple extensions to the counting algorithm [17]. For efficient computation, we keep track of changes within nested relations by transparently creating a structure that flattens nested log records. We then outlined the data structures/algorithms for the implementation. The implementation was guided by specific goals to minimize view maintenance overhead. The techniques described allow these goals to be achieved. We also measured the performance of our techniques, demonstrating that our algorithm's view maintenance performance over nested data is superior to that of [17]'s counting algorithm over a normalized representation of the data. This is one of the first pieces of work to explore the applicability of materialized views over complex objects.

Currently, we only consider nested objects where an attribute of a tuple can be a reference (*i.e.*, a pointer) to a nested relation. We plan to extend out model to allow an attribute to be a nested relation, without the need to have pointers. Our implementation supports relational style SP and SPJ views over nested data. We plan to support aggregate views over nested data, based on the ideas in this paper. We also plan to improve the maintenance algorithms. For instance, the time for view maintenance can be further improved by having a separate asynchronous process that computes the incremental changes to the view and holds them in view differential files [12]. These view differential files would be updated periodically and be used to update the view relation when it is maintained. We are also investigating more efficient creation/maintenance of the index for nested-nesting associations.

References

1. S. Abiteboul and N. Bidoit. Non first normal form relations to represent hierarchically organized data. In *Proc. PODS*, 1984.
2. M. E. Adiba and Bruce Lindsay. Database snapshots. In *Proc. VLDB*, 1980.
3. R. Agrawal and N. Gehani. Ode (object database and environment): the language and the data model. In *Proc. SIGMOD*, 1989.
4. H. Arisawa, K. Moriya, and T. Miura. Properties on non-first-normal-form relational databases. In *Proc. VLDB*, 1983.
5. F. Bancilhon, P. Richard, and M. Scholl. On line processing of compacted relations. In *Proc. VLDB*, 1982.
6. E. Bertino. *Query Processing for Advanced Database Systems*, chapter A survey of indexing techniques for object-oriented databases. Morgan Kaufmann, 1994.
7. E. Bertino and W. Kim. Indexing techniques for queries on nested objects. *IEEE TKDE*, pages 196–214, June 1989.
8. J. A. Blakeley, P. Larson, and F. W. Tompa. Efficiently Updating Materialized Views. In *Proc. SIGMOD*, May 1986.
9. Peter O. Buneman and Eric K. Clemons. Efficiently monitoring relational databases. *ACM TODS*, 4(3):368–382, September 1979.
10. S. Ceri and J. Widom. Deriving production rules for incremental view maintenance. In *Proc. VLDB*, pages 108–119, 1991.
11. W. Chen, M. Kifer, and D. Warren. HiLog: A first order semantics for higher-order logic programming constructs. In *Proc. N. American Logic Prog. Conf.*, June 1989.
12. L. Colby, T. Griffin, L. Libkin, I. Mumick, and H. Trickey. Algorithms for deferred view maintenance. In *Proc. SIGMOD*, 1996.
13. L. Colby, A. Kawaguchi, D. Lieuwen, I. Mumick, and K. Ross. Implementing materialized views, 1996. Unpublished manuscript.
14. L. Colby, A. Kawaguchi, D. Lieuwen, I. Mumick, and K. Ross. Supporting multiple view maintenance policies. In *Proc. SIGMOD*, May 1997.
15. P. Dadam, K. Kuespert, F. Andersen, H. Blanken, R. Erbe, J. Guenauer, V. Lum, P. Pistor, and G. Walch. A DBMS prototype to support extended NF^2 relations: An integrated view on flat tables and hierarchies. In *Proc. VLDB*, 1986.

16. T. Griffin and L. Libkin. Incremental maintenance of views with duplicates. In *Proc. SIGMOD*, 1995.

17. A. Gupta, I. Mumick, and V. S. Subrahmanian. Maintaining views incrementally. In *Proc. SIGMOD*, 1993.

18. R. Haskin and R. Lorie. On extending the functions of a relational database system. In *Proc. SIGMOD*, 1982.

19. G. Jaeshke and H. Sheck. Remarks on the algebra of non-first-normal-form relational database. In *Proc. PODS*, 1982.

20. B. Kähler and O. Risnes. Extended logging for database snapshots. In *Proc. VLDB*, pages 389–398, 1987.

21. A. Kawaguchi, D. Lieuwen, I. Mumick, D. Quass, and K. Ross. Concurrency control theory for deferred materialized views. In *Proc. ICDT*, January 1997.

22. A. Kawaguchi, D. Lieuwen, I. Mumick, and K. Ross. View maintenance in nested data models. In *Proc. Worshop on Materialized Views: Techniques and Applications (associated with SIGMOD96)*, June 1996.

23. B. Lindsay, L. Haas, C. Mohan, H. Pirahesh, and P. Wilms. A snapshot differential refresh algorithm. In *Proc. SIGMOD*, 1986.

24. V. Linnemann. Non first normal relations and recursive queries: An SQL-based approach. In *Proc. Data. Eng.*, 1987.

25. J. Lu, G. Moerkotte, J. Schu, and V. S. Subrahmanian. Efficient maintenance of materialized mediated views. In *Proc. SIGMOD*, 1995.

26. D. Maier and J. Stein. Indexing in an object-oriented DBMS. In *Workshop on OODB Sys.*, 1986.

27. A. Makinouch. A consideration of normal form of non-necessarily normalized relations in the relational data model. In *Proc. VLDB*, 1977.

28. I. Mumick and K. Ross. **Noodle**: A language for declarative querying in an object-oriented database. In *Proc. DOOD*, 1993.

29. I. Mumick, K. Ross, and S. Sudarshan. Design and implementation of the **SWORD** declarative object-oriented database system, 1993. Unpublished Manuscript.

30. P. Pistor and F. Andersen. Designing a generalized NF2 model with an SQL-type language interface. In *Proc. VLDB*, 1986.

31. Xiaolei Qian and Gio Wiederhold. Incremental recomputation of active relational expressions. *IEEE TKDE*, 3(3):337–341, 1991.

32. K. Ross. Relations with relation names as arguments: Algebra and calculus. In *Proc. PODS*, 1992.

33. M. Roth, H. Korth, and D Batory. SQL/NF: A query language for ¬1NF relational databases. *Information Systems*, 12(1):99–114, 1987.

34. M. Scholl, H. Paul, and H. Schek. Supporting flat relations by a nested relational kernel. In *Proc. VLDB*, 1987.

35. A. Segev and J. Park. Updating distributed materialized views. *IEEE TKDE*, 1(2):173–184, June 1989.

36. E. Shekita and M. Carey. Performance enhancement through replication in an object-oriented DBMS. In *Proc. SIGMOD*, 1989.

37. Oded Shmueli and A. Itai. Maintenance of Views. In *Proc. SIGMOD*, 1984.

38. L. Sterling and E. Shapiro. *The Art of Prolog. Advanced Programming Techniques*. MIT Press, Cambridge, MA, 1986.

39. S. Thomas and P. Fischer. Nested relational structures. In P. Kanellakis, editor, *The Theory of Databases*. JAI Press, 1986.

40. Y. Zhuge, H. Garcia-Molina, J. Hammer, and J. Widom. View maintenance in a warehousing environment. In *Proc. SIGMOD*, 1995.

Incremental Recomputation of Recursive Queries with Nested Sets and Aggregate Functions*

Leonid Libkin[1]   Limsoon Wong[2]

[1] Bell Laboratories/Lucent Technologies, 600 Mountain Avenue, Murray Hill, NJ 07974, USA, Email: libkin@research.bell-labs.com
[2] BioInformatics Center & Institute of Systems Science, Singapore 119597, Email: limsoon@iss.nus.sg

Abstract. We examine the power of incremental evaluation systems that use an SQL-like language for maintaining recursively-defined views. We show that recursive queries such as transitive closure, and "alternating paths" can be incrementally maintained in a nested relational language, when some auxiliary relations are allowed. In the presence of aggregate functions, even more queries can be maintained, for example, the "same generation" query. In contrast, it is still an open problem whether such queries are maintainable in relational calculus. We then restrict the language so that no nested relations are involved (but we keep the aggregate functions). Such a language captures the capability of most practical relational database systems. We prove that this restriction does not reduce the incremental computational power; that is, any query that can be maintained in a *nested* language with aggregates, is still maintainable using only *flat* relations. We also show that one does not need auxiliary relations of arity more than 2. In particular, this implies that the recursive queries maintainable in the nested language with aggregates, can be also maintained in a practical relational database systems using auxiliary tables of arity at most 2. This is again in sharp contrast to maintenance in relational calculus, which admits a strict arity-based hierarchy.

1 Introduction

It is common knowledge that the expressiveness of relational calculus is limited. For example, recursive queries such as the transitive closure cannot be defined [3]. However, in a real database system, one can try to overcome this problem by storing both the relation and its transitive closure and updating the latter whenever edges are added to or removed from the former. In other words, the recursive queries are evaluated and maintained incrementally. One can think of the result of such a recursive query as a view of the database and the incremental evaluation of the query as view maintenance.

---

* Part of this work was done when Wong was visiting Bell Labs and when Libkin was visiting Institute of Systems Science.

The above leads us to the concept of an *incremental evaluation system*, or IES. An IES($\mathcal{L}$) is a system consisting of a finite set of "update" functions expressible in the language $\mathcal{L}$, where each of these functions takes as input the old database, the old answer, the old auxiliary database, and the update. We require the update to be *permissible* according to certain criteria specified for the IES($\mathcal{L}$). In this report, the criteria for permissible update is restricted to insertion and deletion of a single tuple. For each permissible update that is coming in, the system uses its update functions to compute the new answer to the query and the new auxiliary database. A restriction is also imposed so that the constants that appear in auxiliary database must also appear in the database or in the answer or in some fixed set. In this report, this fixed set is $\mathbb{Q}$, the set of rational numbers.

We use the first-order incremental evaluation system, IES($\mathcal{FO}$)(called FOIES in [10]), to illustrate the concept. IES($\mathcal{FO}$) uses first-order logic to express update functions [9, 12]. The permissible updates are tuples to be inserted or deleted from the input relations. For each relation symbol R, we use R^o to refer to the instance of R *before* an update, and R^n the instance of R *after* the update (here 'o' stands for old and 'n' for new). Consider the view $EVEN$ that is defined to be $\{1\}$ if the relation R has even cardinality and $\{\}$ if R has odd cardinality. While $EVEN$ is well known to be inexpressible in first-order logic [1], it can be expressed in IES($\mathcal{FO}$). The update function when a tuple o is deleted from R is given by

$$EVEN^n(1) \quad \text{iff} \quad (R(o) \wedge \neg EVEN^o(1)) \vee (\neg R(o) \wedge EVEN^o(1)).$$

The update function when a tuple o is inserted into R is given by

$$EVEN^n(1) \quad \text{iff} \quad (R(o) \wedge EVEN^o(1)) \vee (\neg R(o) \wedge \neg EVEN^o(1)).$$

The IES($\mathcal{FO}$) that we used to maintain $EVEN$ as above is also called a space-free IES($\mathcal{FO}$), because it does not make use of any auxiliary relations. The transitive closure of acyclic graphs is another view that can be maintained by a space-free IES($\mathcal{FO}$) [9]. However, the transitive closure of general graphs cannot be maintained using space-free IES($\mathcal{FO}$)[10, 7]. Thus, it is sometimes necessary to use auxiliary relations. We write IES($\mathcal{FO}$)$_k$ to mean the subclass of IES($\mathcal{FO}$) where auxiliary relations of arities up to k can be used. Observe that, with maximal arity k, the auxiliary relations can hold at most $O(n^k)$ tuples, where n is the number of constants in the input database.

There are some interesting queries that can be maintained by IES($\mathcal{FO}$) with some auxiliary relations. For the transitive closure of undirected graphs, it can be maintained in IES($\mathcal{FO}$)$_3$ [20] and even in IES($\mathcal{FO}$)$_2$ [10]. But it is open if there is a IES($\mathcal{FO}$) for transitive closure of general directed graphs. Also, Dong and Su [10] showed that the IES($\mathcal{FO}$)$_k$ hierarchy is strict for $k \leq 2$. More recently, using a result of Cai [6], Dong and Su showed in the journal version of their paper [10] that the IES($\mathcal{FO}$)$_k$ hierarchy is strict for every k. However, their example query that proved the strict inclusion of IES($\mathcal{FO}$)$_k$ in IES($\mathcal{FO}$)$_{k+1}$ had input arity much greater than k. It is open whether the IES($\mathcal{FO}$)$_k$ hierarchy remains strict if we restrict to queries having fixed input arity.

The two open questions above render IES($\mathcal{FO}$) a little unsatisfactory. IES($\mathcal{FO}$) uses first-order logic as its ambient language. First-order logic or relational algebra does not properly reflect the power of practical relational systems. One wonders if transitive closure can be maintained in a *real* relational database. Such databases use SQL as their query language. May be transitive closure can be maintained using SQL after all? One also wonders if strictness of the IES($\mathcal{FO}$)$_k$ hierarchy is natural. Maybe such a hierarchy will collapse if the ambient language is SQL?

So we study the incremental evaluation system whose ambient language is $\mathcal{NRC}^{\mathrm{aggr}}$, our reconstruction of SQL based on a nested relational calculus. We use the notation IES($\mathcal{NRC}^{\mathrm{aggr}}$) to denote the incremental evaluation system where both the input database and answer are flat relations, but the auxiliary database can be nested relations. We use the notation IES($\mathcal{SQL}$) when the auxiliary database is restricted to flat relations. The rationale for the IES($\mathcal{SQL}$) is that it more closely approximates what could be done in a relational database, which can store only flat tables. With features such as nesting of intermediate data (as in GROUPBY) and aggregates, the ambient language has essentially the power of SQL, hence the notation. As $\mathcal{NRC}^{\mathrm{aggr}}$ is more expressive than first-order logic, both IES($\mathcal{NRC}^{\mathrm{aggr}}$) and IES($\mathcal{SQL}$) are more powerful than IES($\mathcal{FO}$). So we will concentrate on queries that are not known to be expressible in IES($\mathcal{FO}$).

Our results are organized as follows. In Section 2, we describe $\mathcal{NRC}^{\mathrm{aggr}}$, our reconstruction of SQL. In Section 3, we give a formal definition of IES($\mathcal{L}$). In Section 4, we show that transitive closure of arbitrary graphs, "alternating paths" of arbitrary (and-or) graphs, and "same generation" of acyclic graphs can be maintained in IES($\mathcal{NRC}^{\mathrm{aggr}}$) using some auxiliary space. In addition, we also show that any query that can be implemented using a single application of structural recursion [5] can be maintained in IES($\mathcal{NRC}^{\mathrm{aggr}}$) using some auxiliary space. In fact, some of these do not even require the power of counting.

In Section 5, we consider IES($\mathcal{NRC}^{\mathrm{aggr}}$) where the auxiliary relations are restricted to be flat; that is, we consider IES($\mathcal{SQL}$). We show that a linear order on data can be generated in the context of IES($\mathcal{SQL}$). We then use this order to encode IES($\mathcal{NRC}^{\mathrm{aggr}}$) into IES($\mathcal{SQL}$), demonstrating that storing flat tables is sufficient. This result says in essence that queries that can be maintained by IES($\mathcal{NRC}^{\mathrm{aggr}}$) are precisely those that can be maintained by a practical relational system.

In Section 6, we consider the effect that restriction on the arity of auxiliary relations can have on IES($\mathcal{SQL}$). We prove that a hierarchy does not form under the arity restriction on auxiliary relations. In fact, it does not form even when an arity restriction is imposed on input data as well. This result points out that a hierarchy based on arity restriction (such as the IES($\mathcal{FO}$)$_k$ hierarchy) is not robust.

In Section 7, we discuss the physical costs of maintaining queries in IES($\mathcal{SQL}$). The total overall cost may be unacceptably high, but each incremental step is always guaranteed to be tractable.

Complete proofs are given in the full report[18].

2 Nested Relational Calculus with Aggregates

Let us start by describing our ambient query language. We want this language to be more powerful than the relational calculus in two ways: it will deal with nested relations, and will use aggregate functions. There are many choices for such a language. We use the language similar to those considered in [5, 15, 17, 8]. These languages have been extensively studied and they are easier to work with than most other nested formalisms. However, we would like to emphasize the the choice of a particular language is not central to our problems. In particular, our results extend to any language with the same power as the language $\mathcal{NRC}^{\mathbf{aggr}}$ presented below.

The language $\mathcal{NRC}^{\mathbf{aggr}}$ is obtained by extending the nested relational calculus $\mathcal{NRC}(=)$ of [5, 23] by arithmetics and aggregate functions. The motivation for considering $\mathcal{NRC}^{\mathbf{aggr}}$ is that it is a much more realistic query language than relational algebra. Indeed, as explained later, one can consider $\mathcal{NRC}^{\mathbf{aggr}}$ to be a theoretical reconstruction of SQL, the de facto relational query language of the commercial world.

We present the language incrementally. We start from $\mathcal{NRC}(=)$, which is equivalent to the usual nested relational algebra [2, 5]. The data types that can be manipulated are:

$$s ::= b \mid s_1 \times \cdots \times s_n \mid \{s\}$$

The symbol b ranges over base types like Booleans $\mathbb{B}$, rational numbers $\mathbb{Q}$, etc. The type $s_1 \times \cdots \times s_n$ contains n-ary tuples whose components have types s_1, ..., s_n respectively. The objects of type $\{s\}$ are sets of finite cardinality whose elements are objects of type s.

As can be seen from the data types, $\mathcal{NRC}(=)$ is a language for arbitrarily nested relations. The syntax and typing rules of $\mathcal{NRC}$ are given below.

$$\frac{}{x^s : s} \qquad \frac{}{c : b} \qquad \frac{e : s_1 \times \cdots \times s_n}{\pi_i\, e : s_i} \qquad \frac{e_1 : s_1 \quad \cdots \quad e_n : s_n}{(e_1, \ldots, e_n) : s_1 \times \cdots \times s_n}$$

$$\frac{}{\{\}^s : \{s\}} \qquad \frac{e : s}{\{e\} : \{s\}} \qquad \frac{e_1 : \{s\} \quad e_2 : \{s\}}{e_1 \cup e_2 : \{s\}} \qquad \frac{e_1 : \{t\} \quad e_2 : \{s\}}{\bigcup\{e_1 \mid x^s \in e_2\} : \{t\}}$$

$$\frac{e_1 : s \quad e_2 : s}{e_1 = e_2 : \mathbb{B}} \qquad \frac{}{true : \mathbb{B}} \qquad \frac{}{false : \mathbb{B}} \qquad \frac{e_1 : \mathbb{B} \quad e_2 : s \quad e_3 : s}{if\ e_1\ then\ e_2\ else\ e_3 : s}$$

We often omit the type superscripts as they can be inferred. An expression e having free variables $\vec{x}$ is interpreted as a function $f(\vec{x}) = e$, which given input $\vec{O}$, of the same arity as $\vec{x}$, produces $e[\vec{O}/\vec{x}]$ as its output. Here $[\vec{O}/\vec{x}]$ is the substitution replacing the ith component of $\vec{x}$ by the ith component of $\vec{O}$. An expression e with no free variable can be regarded as a constant function $f \equiv e$.

Let us briefly recall the semantics; see also [5]. Variables x^s are available for each type s. Every constant c of base type b is available. The operations for tuples are standard. Namely, $(e_1, \ldots, e_n)$ forms an n-tuple whose i component is e_i and $\pi_i\ e$ returns the i component of the n-tuple e.

$\{\}$ forms the empty set. $\{e\}$ forms the singleton set containing e. $e_1 \cup e_2$ unions the two sets e_1 and e_2. $\bigcup\{e_1 \mid x \in e_2\}$ maps the function $f(x) = e_1$ over all elements in e_2 and then returns their union; thus if e_2 is the set $\{o_1, \ldots, o_n\}$, the result of this operation would be $f(o_1) \cup \cdots \cup f(o_n)$. For example, $\bigcup\{\{(x, x)\} \mid x \in \{1, 2\}\}$ evaluates to $\{(1, 1), (2, 2)\}$.

The operations for Booleans are also quite typical, with *true* and *false* denoting the two Boolean values. $e_1 = e_2$ returns *true* if e_1 and e_2 have the same value and returns *false* otherwise. Finally, *if* e_1 *then* e_2 *else* e_3 evaluates to e_2 if e_1 is *true* and evaluates to e_3 if e_1 is *false*. We provided equality test on every type s. However, this is equivalent to having equality test restricted to base types together with emptiness test for set of base types [22].

$\mathcal{NRC}$ possesses the so-called conservative extension property [23]: if a function $f : s_1 \to s_2$ is expressible in $\mathcal{NRC}$, then it can be expressed using an expression of height no more than that of s_1 and s_2. The height of a type is defined as its depth of nesting of set brackets. The height of an expression is defined as the maximum height of all types that appear in its typing derivation. More specifically, if $f : s_1 \to s_2$ takes flat relations to flat relations and is expressible in $\mathcal{NRC}$, then it is also expressible in the standard flat relational algebra [19, 5].

It is a common misconception that the relational algebra is the same as SQL. The truth is that all versions of SQL come with three features that have no equivalence in relational algebra: SQL extends the relational calculus by having arithmetic operations, a group-by operation, and various aggregate functions such as AVG, COUNT, SUM, MIN, and MAX.

It is known [5] that the group-by operator can already be simulated in $\mathcal{NRC}(=)$. The others need to be added. The arithmetic operators are the standard ones: $+$, $-$, $\cdot$, and $\div$ of type $\mathbb{Q} \times \mathbb{Q} \to \mathbb{Q}$. We also add the order on the rationals: $\leq_{\mathbb{Q}}: \mathbb{Q} \times \mathbb{Q} \to \mathbb{B}$. As to aggregate functions, we add just the following construct

$$\frac{e_1 : \mathbb{Q} \qquad e_2 : \{s\}}{\sum\{\!|e_1 \mid x^s \in e_2|\!\} : \mathbb{Q}}$$

The semantics is this: map the function $f(x) = e_1$ over all elements of e_2 and then add up the results. Thus, if e_2 is the set $\{o_1, \ldots, o_n\}$, it returns $f(o_1) + \cdots + f(o_n)$. For example, $\sum\{\!|1 \mid x \in X|\!\}$ returns the cardinality of X. Note that this is different from adding up the values in $\{f(o_1), \ldots, f(o_n)\}$; in the example above, doing so yields 1 as no duplicates are kept. To emphasize that duplicate values of f are being added up, we use bag (multiset) brackets $\{\!| \,|\!\}$ in this construct.

We denote this theoretical reconstruction of SQL by $\mathcal{NRC}^{\mathrm{aggr}}$. That is, $\mathcal{NRC}^{\mathrm{aggr}}$ has all the constructs of $\mathcal{NRC}(=)$, the arithmetic operations $+, -, \cdot$ and $\div$, the summation construct $\sum$ and the linear order on the rationals. It was shown in [15, 17] that all SQL aggregate functions mentioned above can be implemented in $\mathcal{NRC}^{\mathrm{aggr}}$. It is also known [15, 17] that $\mathcal{NRC}^{\mathrm{aggr}}$ has the conservative extension property and thus its expressive power depends only on the height of input and output and is independent of the height of intermediate data. So to conform to SQL, it suffices to restrict our input and output to height at most one, that is, to the usual flat relational databases.

Before we begin studying $\mathcal{NRC}^{\text{aggr}}$ in the setting of an incremental evaluation system, let us briefly introduce a nice shorthand, based on the comprehension notation [21, 4], for writing $\mathcal{NRC}^{\text{aggr}}$ queries. Recall from [4, 5, 23] that the comprehension $\{e \mid A_1, \ldots, A_n\}$, where each A_i either has the form $x_i \in e_i$ or is an expression e_i of type $\mathbb{B}$, has a direct correspondent in $\mathcal{NRC}$ that is given by recursively applying the following equations:

- $\{e \mid x_i \in e_i, \ldots\} = \bigcup \{\{e \mid \ldots\} \mid x_i \in e_i\}$
- $\{e \mid e_i, \ldots\} = \textit{if } e_i \textit{ then } \{e \mid \ldots\} \textit{ else } \{\}$

The comprehension notation is more user-friendly than the syntax of $\mathcal{NRC}^{\text{aggr}}$. For example, it allows us to write $\{(x, y) \mid x \in e_1, y \in e_2\}$ for the cartesian product of e_1 and e_2 instead of the clumsier $\bigcup \{\bigcup \{\{(x, y)\} \mid y \in e_2\} \mid x \in e_1\}$.

In addition to comprehension, we also find it convenient to use a little bit of pattern matching, which can be removed in a straightforward manner. For example, we write $\{(x, z) \mid (x, y) \in e_1, (y', z) \in e_2, y = y'\}$ for relational composition instead of the more official $\{(\pi_1 X, \pi_2 Y) \mid X \in e_1, Y \in e_2, \pi_2 X = \pi_1 Y\}$ or the much clumsier $\bigcup \{\bigcup \{\textit{if } \pi_2 X = \pi_1 Y \textit{ then } \{(\pi_1 X, \pi_2 Y)\} \textit{ else } \{\} \mid Y \in e_2\} \mid X \in e_1\}$. Here X and Y denote edges $((x, y)$ and (y, z) respectively), whose components, x, y and z, are obtained by applying projections π_1 and π_2.

3 Formal Definition of IES($\mathcal{L}$)

The definition of IES($\mathcal{L}$) is very similar to the definitions of Dong-Su's FOIES [10] and Immerman-Patnaik's Dyn-$\mathcal{C}$ [20]. The idea is that, in order to incrementally maintain a query Q, we do the following. At the first step, we initialize auxiliary data and compute Q assuming that the input is empty. Then we provide functions that, upon each insertion or deletion, correctly update both the answer to Q and the auxiliary data. If the initializing and the updating functions are definable in $\mathcal{L}$, we say that Q is expressible in IES($\mathcal{L}$). If all auxiliary data are flat relations of arity not exceeding k, we say that Q is expressible in IES($\mathcal{L}$)$_k$.

While this informal definition is sufficient for understanding the results of the paper, we give a formal definition of IES($\mathcal{L}$) for the sake of completeness. Suppose we are given a type $S = \{s_1\} \times \ldots \times \{s_m\}$, where $s_1, \ldots, s_m$ are record types. We consider elementary updates of the form $ins_i(x)$ and $del_i(x)$, where x is of type s_i. Given an object X of type S, applying such an update results in inserting x into or deleting x from the ith set in X, that is, the set of type $\{s_i\}$. Given a sequence $\mathcal{U}$ of updates, $\mathcal{U}(X)$ denotes the result of applying the sequence $\mathcal{U}$ to an object X of type S.

Given a query Q of type $S \to T$, and a type T_{aux} (of auxiliary data), consider a collection of $\mathcal{F}_Q$ functions:

$$f_{\text{init}} : S \to T \qquad\qquad f_{\text{init}}^{\text{aux}} : S \to T_{\text{aux}}$$
$$f_{\text{del}}^i : s_i \times S \times T \times T_{\text{aux}} \to T \quad f_{\text{del}}^{\text{aux}} : s_i \times S \times T \times T_{\text{aux}} \to T_{\text{aux}}$$
$$f_{\text{ins}}^i : s_i \times S \times T \times T_{\text{aux}} \to T \quad f_{\text{ins}}^{\text{aux}} : s_i \times S \times T \times T_{\text{aux}} \to T_{\text{aux}}$$

Given an elementary update u, we associate two functions with it. The function $f_u : S \times T \times T_{\text{aux}} \to T$ is defined as $\lambda(X,Y,Z).f_{\text{del}}^i(a,X,Y,Z)$ if u is $del_i(a)$, and as $\lambda(X,Y,Z).f_{\text{ins}}^i(a,X,Y,Z)$ if u is $ins_i(a)$. We similarly define $f_u^{\text{aux}} : S \times T \times T_{\text{aux}} \to T_{\text{aux}}$.

Given a sequence of updates $\mathcal{U} = \{u_1, \ldots, u_l\}$, define inductively the collection of objects: $X_0 = \emptyset : S, RES_0 = f_{\text{init}}(X_0), AUX_0 = f_{\text{init}}^{\text{aux}}(X_0)$ (where $\emptyset$ of type S is a product of m empty sets), and

$$X_{i+1} = u_{i+1}(X_i)$$
$$RES_{i+1} = f_{u_{i+1}}(X_i, RES_i, AUX_i)$$
$$AUX_{i+1} = f_{u_{i+1}}^{\text{aux}}(X_i, RES_i, AUX_i)$$

Finally, we define $\mathcal{F}_Q(\mathcal{U})$ as RES_l.

We now say that there exists an *incremental evaluation system* for Q in $\mathcal{L}$ if there is a type T_{aux} and a collection $\mathcal{F}_Q$ of functions, typed as above, such that, for any sequence $\mathcal{U}$ of updates, $\mathcal{F}_Q(\mathcal{U}) = Q(\mathcal{U}(\emptyset))$. We also say then that Q is expressible in IES($\mathcal{L}$). If T_{aux} is a product of flat relational types, none of arity more than k, we say that Q is in IES($\mathcal{L}$)$_k$.

Since every expression in $\mathcal{NRC}$ or $\mathcal{NRC}^{\text{aggr}}$ has a well-typed function associated with it, the definition above applies to these languages.

4 Power of IES($\mathcal{NRC}$) and IES($\mathcal{NRC}^{\text{aggr}}$)

It is known [7] that recursive queries such as transitive closure cannot be expressed in space-free IES($\mathcal{NRC}$) and space-free IES($\mathcal{NRC}^{\text{aggr}}$). In this section, we focus on the power of IES($\mathcal{NRC}$) and IES($\mathcal{NRC}^{\text{aggr}}$) in the presence of auxiliary data. We prove four expressibility results. We first show that transitive closure and the "alternating path" query are expressible in IES($\mathcal{NRC}$) (and hence in IES($\mathcal{NRC}^{\text{aggr}}$)). Furthermore, any query expressed using one application of structural recursion (with parameter functions defined in $\mathcal{NRC}$) can be expressed in IES($\mathcal{NRC}$). If the parameter functions are defined in $\mathcal{NRC}^{\text{aggr}}$, then such a query is expressible in IES($\mathcal{NRC}^{\text{aggr}}$). Finally, we show that the "same-generation" query is expressible in IES($\mathcal{NRC}^{\text{aggr}}$), although it is not expressible in space-free IES($\mathcal{NRC}^{\text{aggr}}$).

Proposition 1. *Transitive closure of arbitrary graphs is expressible in* IES($\mathcal{NRC}$). $\qquad\qquad\square$

The idea of the proof is to use an auxiliary nested relation $R : \{b \times b \times \{b \times b\}\}$ such that $(x, y, P) \in R$ iff P represents a path from x to y. (This basic idea is used in most of our results in this section.) The transitive closure of a graph can be straightforwardly generated from this auxiliary nested relation. It is also quite straightforward to maintain this auxiliary relation when edges are added to or deleted from the graph. Its ability to store every paths appears to be vital for transitive closure to be maintained when edges are deleted. In IES($\mathcal{NRC}$) we are able to use a set of edges to represent a path and a nested set of sets to represent all the paths. Such a representation is not possible in IES($\mathcal{FO}$) which allows only flat auxiliary relations. Later, we shall see how IES($\mathcal{SQL}$) gets around this problem by using the summation operation to create new identifiers—essentially each path P_i is assigned an identifier i and each edge (x, y) in P_i can be recorded in the auxiliary flat relation of all paths as (i, x, y).

We also consider a generalization of the transitive closure query, namely the "alternating paths" query, cf. [14]. This query is complete with respect to first-order reductions for PTIME. Since transitive closure is complete for NLOGSPACE, it is likely that the "alternating paths" is harder than the transitive closure.

Suppose we are given a graph G and a subset U of the nodes in G (U is for "universal"). Nodes not in the set U are "existential." Intuitively, an alternating path between two nodes must go through every descendant of a universal node, and through just one descendant of an existential node; thus, one can think of the transitive closure query as a special case of this one when $U = \emptyset$. More formally, we define $apath(x, y)$ to be the smallest relation such that: (1) $apath(x, x)$ holds for each node x, and (2) if $x \in U$ and there is an edge leaving x, and for all edges (x, z) it is the case that $apath(z, y)$, then $apath(x, y)$, and (3) if $x \notin U$, and for some edge (x, z), $apath(z, y)$ holds, then $apath(x, y)$. The "alternating paths" query is simply this: given a graph, compute the $apath$ relation.

Proposition 2. *"Alternating paths" of arbitrary graphs can be expressed in* IES($\mathcal{NRC}$). $\qquad\square$

Corollary 3. *Transitive closure and "alternating path" are expressible in* IES($\mathcal{NRC}^{\text{aggr}}$). $\qquad\square$

The "same generation" query is another recursive query that often serves as one of canonical examples of queries definable in datalog but not in relational calculus. Two nodes x and y of a graph G are in the same generation if and only if there is a node z in G such that there is a walk (an edge sequence, possibly repeated) that goes from z to x and a walk of the same length that goes from z to y. It is known from [7] that this query cannot be maintained in IES($\mathcal{NRC}^{\text{aggr}}$) without using auxiliary space. It turns out that it can be maintained in IES($\mathcal{NRC}^{\text{aggr}}$) with some auxiliary space, if the graph is acyclic. Note that we do need the counting power of $\mathcal{NRC}^{\text{aggr}}$. However, the case of arbitrary graphs remains open.

Proposition 4. *"Same generation" of acyclic graphs can be expressed in* IES($\mathcal{NRC}^{\text{aggr}}$). $\qquad\square$

In general, IES($\mathcal{NRC}$) can express queries specified by a single application of the structural recursion operator of [5]. Let us first define this operator. Let

$f : s \times t \rightarrow t$ be a function expressible in $\mathcal{NRC}$. Let $i : t$ be an object expressible in $\mathcal{NRC}$ (that is, the constant function returning this object is definable). Furthermore, we assume that $f(x, f(x, y)) = f(x, y)$ and $f(x, f(y, z)) = f(y, f(x, z))$ hold. Then the structural recursion operator $sri(f, i) : \{s\} \rightarrow t$ is given by the equations: $sri(f, i)(\{\}) = i$, $sri(f, i)(\{x\} \cup Y) = f(x, sri(f, i)(Y))$. This operator is very powerful. It can generate powersets. It can also produce all three example queries considered above: transitive closure, "alternating paths," and "same generation." Thus these previous results are really corollaries of the next theorem. However, it is possible to find more intuitive incremental evaluation systems for the queries from Propositions 1, 2 and 4. Those are given in the full report [18].

Theorem 5. *Any query expressible as $sri(f, i) : \{s\} \rightarrow \{t\}$, where $\{s\}$ and $\{t\}$ are flat relation types, and f and i are definable in $\mathcal{NRC}$, can be maintained in* $\mathsf{IES}(\mathcal{NRC})$.

Proof sketch: We set up the $\mathsf{IES}(\mathcal{NRC}^{\mathrm{aggr}})$ corresponding to $sri(f, i)$ as follows. Let the input relation be $I : \{s\}$. Let the answer relation be $A : \{t\}$. That is, we want to maintain $A = sri(f, i)(I)$. We use an auxiliary relation $R : \{\{t\} \times \{s\}\}$. We arrange it so that $(X, O) \in R$ iff $O \subseteq I$ and $X = sri(f, i)(O)$. We initialize R to $\{i, \{\}\}$. We show how to maintain A and R when elements are added to or removed from I.

Let the update be the insertion of an object x into I. Then the update to R is $R^n = R^o \cup \{(f(x, X), O \cup \{x\}) \mid (X, O) \in R^o\}$. Then the update to A is simple: $A^n = \{u \mid (X, O) \in R^n, O = I^n, u \in X\}$.

Let the update be the deletion of an object x from I. Then the update to R is $R^n = \{(X, O) \mid (X, O) \in R^o, x \notin O\}$. Then the update to A is again: $A^n = \{u \mid (X, O) \in R^n, O = I^n, u \in X\}$. □

The same argument applies to $\mathcal{NRC}^{\mathrm{aggr}}$:

Corollary 6. *Any query expressible as $sri(f, i) : \{s\} \rightarrow \{t\}$, where $\{s\}$ and $\{t\}$ are flat relation types, and f and i are definable in $\mathcal{NRC}^{\mathrm{aggr}}$, can be maintained in* $\mathsf{IES}(\mathcal{NRC}^{\mathrm{aggr}})$. □

An $\mathsf{IES}(\mathcal{NRC}^{\mathrm{aggr}})$ or $\mathsf{IES}(\mathcal{NRC})$ having input relations $\vec{I}$, answer relation A, and auxiliary relations $\vec{R}$ is said to be *deterministic* if there is a function f such that $f(\vec{I}) = (\vec{R}, A)$. (Note that f needs not be expressible within $\mathcal{NRC}^{\mathrm{aggr}}$.) That is, the values of the auxiliary relations in a deterministic $\mathsf{IES}(\mathcal{NRC}^{\mathrm{aggr}})$ do not depend on the history of updates. Deterministic incremental evaluation systems are interesting in their own right [11]. While we do not examine them further in this paper, it is worth pointing out the following result, follows from the proofs of other results in this section.

Corollary 7. *Transitive closure of arbitrary graphs, "alternating paths" of arbitrary graphs, "same generation" of acyclic graphs, as well as any query expressible as $sri(f, i) : \{s\} \rightarrow \{t\}$, where $\{s\}$ and $\{t\}$ are flat relation types, can be expressed in deterministic $\mathsf{IES}(\mathcal{NRC}^{\mathrm{aggr}})$.* □

5 Power of IES($\mathcal{SQL}$)

We now focus on the power of IES($\mathcal{SQL}$), the restriction of IES($\mathcal{NRC}^{\mathrm{aggr}}$) to use only flat auxiliary relations. We first show that IES($\mathcal{SQL}$) can generate a linear order on all its data. This result is then used to encode IES($\mathcal{NRC}^{\mathrm{aggr}}$) into IES($\mathcal{SQL}$), showing that the two systems are equivalent. Thus the power of IES($\mathcal{NRC}^{\mathrm{aggr}}$) is undiminished even when it is restricted to flat auxiliary relations. Of course this also means that IES($\mathcal{NRC}^{\mathrm{aggr}}$) can be fully implemented using any real relational database.

5.1 Ordering in IES($\mathcal{SQL}$)

Recall that $\mathcal{NRC}^{\mathrm{aggr}}$ is only equipped with a linear order on $\mathbb{Q}$. Linear orders on any other infinite base types are not expressible in $\mathcal{NRC}^{\mathrm{aggr}}$[15]. In this section, we show that in the context of IES($\mathcal{SQL}$), a linear order on any base type b can be expressed, when restricted to its "active domain." By active domain, we mean those constants that currently appear in the input database.

Proposition 8. *For any base type b, IES($\mathcal{SQL}$) is always able to maintain an auxiliary relation that defines a linear ordering on all the objects of type b in the active domain of a database.* □

Thus, for each type b, a linear order $<^b: b \times b \to \mathbb{B}$ can always be simulated in IES($\mathcal{SQL}$). It is known [15, 16] that if a linear order is available on each base types, then there is enough power in $\mathcal{NRC}^{\mathrm{aggr}}$ to compute a linear order $<: s \times s \to \mathbb{B}$ on every type s. Thus from now on, we assume $<$ is available whenever we are talking about IES($\mathcal{SQL}$) when auxiliary relations of arity at least 2 are allowed.

Thus within an IES($\mathcal{SQL}$), we can implement a ranking function $rank : \{s\} \to \{s \times \mathbb{Q}\}$ on any set O built up from the active domain of the IES($\mathcal{SQL}$): $rank(O) = \{(x, \sum\{\!| if\ y < x\ then\ 1\ else\ 0 \mid y \in O |\!\}) \mid x \in O\}$. Then we can define $rankof : \{s\} \times s \to \mathbb{Q}$ to be a function that given any set O built up from the active domain of the IES($\mathcal{SQL}$) and an o in O, produces the rank of o in O: $rankof(O, o) = \sum\{\!| if\ x = o\ then\ r\ else\ 0 \mid (x, r) \in rank(O) |\!\}$. This result is used in the next section to encode nested relations into flat relations.

5.2 IES($\mathcal{SQL}$) Equals IES($\mathcal{NRC}^{\mathrm{aggr}}$)

Let us begin by comparing the power of IES($\mathcal{SQL}$) and IES($\mathcal{NRC}^{\mathrm{aggr}}$). It is clear that IES($\mathcal{SQL}$) $\subseteq$ IES($\mathcal{NRC}^{\mathrm{aggr}}$). We prove that the converse holds and hence the two incremental evaluation systems are equivalent.

Theorem 9. IES($\mathcal{NRC}^{\mathrm{aggr}}$) = IES($\mathcal{SQL}$).

The idea of the proof is that, using $rank$, objects of any type can be encoded with natural numbers. Using this, we manage to encode any auxiliary database in IES($\mathcal{NRC}^{\text{aggr}}$) into a product of flat relations, so that it can be used by IES($\mathcal{SQL}$). Using *rankof*, we can decode the result, and simulate IES($\mathcal{NRC}^{\text{aggr}}$) in IES($\mathcal{SQL}$). All the details can be found at the end of this section.

Corollary 10. IES($\mathcal{NRC}$) $\subseteq$ IES($\mathcal{SQL}$). □

We can conclude that IES($\mathcal{SQL}$) can maintain transitive closure of arbitrary graphs and can maintain queries expressed using a single application of *sri*. In the rest of this report, we concentrate on IES($\mathcal{SQL}$), because it precisely models real relational databases. However, for convenience and clarity, we give proofs using IES($\mathcal{NRC}^{\text{aggr}}$).

It is worth pointing out that previous results on the conservative extension of $\mathcal{NRC}$[19, 23] and $\mathcal{NRC}^{\text{aggr}}$[22, 15] do not imply the collapse of IES($\mathcal{NRC}^{\text{aggr}}$) to IES($\mathcal{SQL}$). The conservative extension property[23] implies that if the input and output of a (update) function are flat, then the function can be implemented using only flat intermediate data. In a IES($\mathcal{NRC}^{\text{aggr}}$) having a non-flat auxiliary relation of nesting depth k, its update functions necessarily have non-flat input of nesting depth k. Thus the conservative extension result on $\mathcal{NRC}$ only guarantees that these update functions will not use intermediate data of nesting depth exceeding k. In other words, in order to guarantee that update functions uses only flat data, it is necessary to guarantee that their input auxiliary relations are also flat. This must be accomplished using means other than the conservative extension property of $\mathcal{NRC}$. This is the significance of the equivalence result above.

Proof Sketch of Theorem 9

The first thing we need to do is to encode the auxiliary database in a IES($\mathcal{NRC}^{\text{aggr}}$) into flat relations so that they can be stored in a IES($\mathcal{SQL}$). Let us first define s', the type of height 1 to which the type s is encoded.

- $b' = \{b\}$
- $(s_1 \times \cdots \times s_n)' = \{t_1 \times \cdots \times t_n\}$, where $s'_i = \{t_i\}$.
- $\{s\}' = \{\mathbb{Q} \times \mathbb{Q} \times t\}$, where $s' = \{t\}$.

We assume that for each base type b, there is a default value. For example, we can take the default value for $\mathbb{B}$ to be *true*, that for $\mathbb{Q}$ to be 0, and so on. Then in what follows, we write $\vec{0}$ to stand for a tuple of default values of the appropriate types. For example, the $\vec{0}$ for the type $\mathbb{Q} \times \mathbb{Q} \times \mathbb{B}$ would be $(0, 0, true)$.

Then the encoding function $p_s : s \to s'$ is defined by induction on s. A set is coded by tagging each element by 1 and by a unique identifier if the set is nonempty and is coded by $\vec{0}$ if it empty. More precisely,

- $p_b(o) = \{o\}$
- $p_{s_1 \times \ldots \times s_n}((o_1, \ldots, o_n)) = \{(x_1, \ldots, x_n) \mid x_1 \in p_{s_1}(o_1),\ \ldots,\ x_n \in p_{s_n}(o_n)\}$
- $p_{\{s\}}(O) = \{(0, 0, \vec{0})\}$, if O is empty. Otherwise, $p_{\{s\}}(O) = \{(1, rankof(o, O), x) \mid o \in O,\ x \in p_s(o)\}$.

It is clear that p_s is expressible in $\mathcal{NRC}^{\mathbf{aggr}}$ as long as the base types can be linearly ordered. Since we will be building a $\mathsf{IES}(\mathcal{SQL})$, we conclude that p_s is expressible.

Now we provide the decoding function $q_s : s' \to s$, which strips tags and identifiers introduced by p_s.

- $q_b(O) = o$, if $O = \{o\}$.
- $q_{s_1 \times \cdots \times s_n}(O) = (o_1, \ldots, o_n)$, if $o_i = q_{s_i}(\{x_i \mid (x_1, \ldots, x_n) \in O\})$.
- $q_{\{s\}}(O) = \{q_s(\{y \mid (1, j, y) \in O, \ i = j\}) \mid (1, i, x) \in O\}$

We note that q_b is not expressible in $\mathcal{NRC}^{\mathbf{aggr}}$ for every base type b. Nevertheless, it is expressible when b is $\mathbb{B}$ and $\mathbb{Q}$ because $q_{\mathbb{B}}(O) = (O = \{true\})$ and $q_{\mathbb{Q}}(O) = \sum \{x \mid x \in O\}$. However, for any type s of the form $\{t\}$, q_s is always expressible in $\mathcal{NRC}^{\mathbf{aggr}}$. The formal proof can be found in [22]. We give an example to illustrate how this can be done. Let $s = \{\{b \times b\} \times b \times b\}$. Let $O : s$ and $O' : s'$, with $O' = p_s(O)$. We temporarily replace q_b by the identity function and this induces a new definition of q_s. To avoid confusion, we call this new version r_s. Then $r_s(O')$ will have type $\{\{\{b\} \times \{b\}\} \times \{b\} \times \{b\}\}$. Moreover, those subobjects in $r_s(O')$ having type $\{b\}$ are always singleton sets. Then it is clear that $q_s(O') = \{(\{(u, v) \mid (U, V) \in X, u \in U, v \in V\}, y, z) \mid (X, Y, Z) \in r_s(O'), y \in Y, z \in Z\}$.

Thus when s is a set type, both p_s and q_s can be expressed in $\mathcal{NRC}^{\mathbf{aggr}}$. In addition, using the fact that $p_s(O)$ is never empty and by induction on the structure of s, we can show that q_s is inverse of p_s

Proposition 11. *Suppose s is a set type. Then $q_s \circ p_s = id$.* $\qquad\square$

We are now ready to embed any $\mathsf{IES}(\mathcal{NRC}^{\mathbf{aggr}})$ into a $\mathsf{IES}(\mathcal{SQL})$. To simplify notations, we drop the type subscripts from p_s and q_s.

Let a family of functions forming a $\mathsf{IES}(\mathcal{NRC}^{\mathbf{aggr}})$ be given. Let its flat input relations be $\vec{I}$. Let its flat answer relation be A. Let its auxiliary data be $\vec{R}$, which we assume all of these are sets of height at least 1. Let $\vec{f}$ be its update functions.

We define the corresponding $\mathsf{IES}(\mathcal{SQL})$ as follows. The input relation is $\vec{I}$, as before. The answer relation is A as before. The auxiliary relations are $\vec{R}'$, where R'_i is the encoded version of the corresponding R_i; that is, $R'_i = p(R_i)$. The update functions are $\vec{f}'$ defined according to cases below. We need some notations. Let $p(\vec{R})$ be the tuple obtained by applying the appropriate p to each component of $\vec{R}$. Let $q(\vec{R}')$ be the tuple obtained by applying the appropriate q to each component of $\vec{R}'$. Let u denote the update made to the input relations $\vec{I}$. There are two cases. If $f_i(u, \vec{I}, A, \vec{R})$ updates the answer relation A, we need an f'_i so that $A^n = f'_i(u, \vec{I}, A, p(\vec{R})) = f_i(u, \vec{I}, A, \vec{R})$. If $f_i(u, \vec{I}, A, \vec{R})$ updates the auxiliary data R_j, we need an f'_i so that $q(f'_i(u, \vec{I}, A, p(\vec{R}))) = f_i(u, \vec{I}, A, \vec{R}) = R^n_j$.

For the case when $f_i(u, \vec{I}, A, \vec{R})$ updates the answer relation A, we set $f'_i(u, \vec{I}, A, \vec{R}') = f_i(u, \vec{I}, A, q(\vec{R}'))$. Now we argue that this is correct. By definition, we have $f'_i(u, \vec{I}, A, p(\vec{R})) = f_i(u, \vec{I}, A, q(p(\vec{R})))$. Since $q \circ p = id$, we have $f_i(u, \vec{I}, A, \vec{R}) = f'_i(u, \vec{I}, A, p(\vec{R}))$ as desired.

For the case when $f_i(u, \vec{I}, A, \vec{R})$ updates the auxiliary data R_j, we set $f'_i(u, \vec{I}, A, \vec{R}') = p(f_i(u, \vec{I}, A, q(\vec{R}')))$. Now we argue that this is correct. By definition, $f'_i(u, \vec{I}, A, p(\vec{R})) = p(f_i(u, \vec{I}, A, q(p(\vec{R}))))$. Since $q \circ p = id$, we have $p(f_i(u, \vec{I}, A, \vec{R})) = f'_i(u, \vec{I}, A, p(\vec{R}))$. Applying q to both sides, we have $q(p(f_i(u, \vec{I}, A, \vec{R}))) = q(f'_i(u, \vec{I}, A, p(\vec{R})))$. Since $q \circ p = id$, we have $f_i(u, \vec{I}, A, \vec{R}) = q(f'_i(u, \vec{I}, A, p(\vec{R})))$ as desired. Finally, the functions f'_i can be implemented so that no nested intermediate data is used – this follows from the conservativity of $\mathcal{NRC}^{\text{aggr}}$ [15]. This completes the proof. $\quad\square$

6 Arity in IES($\mathcal{SQL}$)

We write IES($\mathcal{SQL}$)$_k$ to mean the subclass of IES($\mathcal{SQL}$) that uses auxiliary relations up to arity k. As mentioned earlier, IES($\mathcal{FO}$)$_k$ $\subset$ IES($\mathcal{FO}$)$_{k+1}$ for all $k > 1$, forming a noncollapsing hierarchy for IES($\mathcal{FO}$) based on arity of auxiliary relations. We consider the analogous question on IES($\mathcal{SQL}$)$_k$ and show that the hierarchy collapses for $k > 1$. The proof uses a coding method that could also be used to prove that it is possible to maintain the equi-cardinality view of two k-ary relations in IES($\mathcal{FO}$)$_2$ [13]. After that, we prove that the two levels below IES($\mathcal{SQL}$)$_2$ are strict; thus the IES($\mathcal{SQL}$)$_k$ hierarchy has only three levels.

Proposition 12. IES($\mathcal{SQL}$)$_2$ = IES($\mathcal{SQL}$)$_k$ *for all $k > 1$.*

Proof sketch: We show how a k-ary auxiliary relation $R : \{s_1 \times \cdots \times s_k\}$ can be coded using binary auxiliary relations $B_1 : \{\mathbb{Q} \times s_1\}$, ..., $B_k : \{\mathbb{Q} \times s_k\}$. Recall that in IES($\mathcal{SQL}$)$_2$ every base type can be assigned a linear order and that these linear orders can be used to define a lexicographic linear order on $s_1 \times \cdots \times s_k$. Thus each tuple in R can be assigned a rank r based on the linear order. Then $\vec{B}$ can be defined so that $(r, o_1) \in B_1$, ..., and $(r, o_k) \in B_k$ iff $((o_1, \ldots, o_k), r) \in rank(R)$. This encoding is straightforward to express in $\mathcal{NRC}^{\text{aggr}}$. $\quad\square$

Proposition 13. IES($\mathcal{SQL}$)$_1$ *is strictly less powerful than* IES($\mathcal{SQL}$)$_2$.

Proof sketch: We show that IES($\mathcal{SQL}$)$_1$ cannot maintain transitive closure of arbitrary graphs. Suppose otherwise. Let the unary auxiliary relations used be R_1, ..., R_n. Let the input graph be I. Let the answer be A. Let u be the deletion to be performed on I. We assume there is an update function f in $\mathcal{NRC}^{\text{aggr}}$ for deleting an edge u from I so that $A^n = f(A^o, I^o, u, \vec{R}^o)$. Suppose I^o, the current state of I, is a single cycle and we want to delete an edge u from it. Since I^o is a single cycle, we know that A^o is a complete graph. Therefore A^o can be generated on-the-fly in $\mathcal{NRC}^{\text{aggr}}$ given I^o. In particular, there is a function g in $\mathcal{NRC}^{\text{aggr}}$ so that $A^n = g(I^o, u, \vec{R}^o) = f(\{(x, y) \mid (x, u) \in I^o, (y, v) \in I^o\}, I^o, u, \vec{R}^o)$. Notice that A^o does not appear in the input to g. Now it can be shown that this function g is not definable in $\mathcal{NRC}^{\text{aggr}}$ – this follows from the bounded degree property of

$\mathcal{NRC}^{\text{aggr}}$ [8] which says that on inputs of small degree, any $\mathcal{NRC}^{\text{aggr}}$ query can only produce outputs that realize a small (not depending on the input) number of distinct degrees, provided those outputs do not contain numbers. Consequently, f cannot be defined in $\mathcal{NRC}^{\text{aggr}}$, and thus $\text{IES}(\mathcal{SQL})_1$ cannot maintain transitive closure of arbitrary graphs. Hence, $\text{IES}(\mathcal{SQL})_1 \subset \text{IES}(\mathcal{SQL})_2$. □

Proposition 14. *Space-free* $\text{IES}(\mathcal{SQL})$ *is strictly less powerful than* $\text{IES}(\mathcal{SQL})_1$.

Proof sketch: Let b be a infinite base type that is unordered. Consider the function $f : \{b \times b\} \rightarrow \{\mathbb{Q}\}$ such that $f(X) = \{1\}$ if the number of nodes in the graph X having the maximum out-degree is odd, and $f(X) = \{\}$ otherwise. We show that f is not in space-free $\text{IES}(\mathcal{SQL})$ but is in $\text{IES}(\mathcal{SQL})_1$.

To prove that f cannot be maintained by any space-free $\text{IES}(\mathcal{SQL})$, we recall from [16, 17] that $\mathcal{NRC}^{\text{aggr}}$ cannot test if the cardinality of a chain graph is odd. Now suppose f can be maintained in a space-free $\text{IES}(\mathcal{SQL})$. Consider the input I to be a chain graph $\{(a_0, a_1), \dots, (a_{n-1}, a_n)\}$ with all a_is distinct. Then $f(I) = \{1\}$ iff n is odd. Since f is maintainable in space-free $\text{IES}(\mathcal{SQL})$, let g be the update function of this $\text{IES}(\mathcal{SQL})$ so that $g(A^\circ, I^\circ, u) = A^n$; that is g maintains A when an edge u is deleted from I.

If I is a chain, the graph $I' = I \cup \{(a_0, a_n)\}$, as well as the singleton $x = \{(a_0, a_n)\}$, are definable in $\mathcal{NRC}^{\text{aggr}}$. Note that $f(I') = \{1\}$, because exactly one node has out-degree 2. Thus, $\{g(\{1\}, I', u) \mid u \in x\}$ evaluates to $\{\{1\}\}$ if n is odd, and to $\{\{\}\}$ otherwise, giving us an $\mathcal{NRC}^{\text{aggr}}$-definable test for parity of the cardinality of a chain, which is impossible. Thus, f is not expressible in space-free $\text{IES}(\mathcal{SQL})$.

It remains to show that f can be maintained in $\text{IES}(\mathcal{SQL})_1$. Observe that the out-degree of a node is definable in $\mathcal{NRC}^{\text{aggr}}$; we denote it by $outdeg(x, I)$. Observe also that the maximum out-degree of a graph I, $maxout(I)$, is also expressible in $\mathcal{NRC}^{\text{aggr}}$.

We can now construct the $\text{IES}(\mathcal{SQL})$ as follows. Let $I : \{b \times b\}$ be the input relation. Let $A : \{\mathbb{Q}\}$ be the output relation. Let $R : \{b\}$ be the auxiliary relation so that $o \in R$ iff the number of nodes having the same out-degree as o in I is odd. We show how to maintain A and R under updates to I.

Let the update be the insertion of a new edge (x, y) into I. Let $LESS = \{u \mid (u, v) \in I^\circ, outdeg(u, I^\circ) < outdeg(x, I^\circ)\}$, which are those nodes currently having out-degree less than that of x. The membership of these nodes in R therefore does not change. Let $MORE = \{u \mid (u, v) \in I^\circ, outdeg(u, I^\circ) > outdeg(x, I^n)\}$, which are those nodes currently having out-degree at least 2 more than that of x. The membership of these nodes in R therefore does not change. Let $SAMEBEFORE = \{u \mid (u, v) \in I^\circ, outdeg(u, I^\circ) = outdeg(x, I^\circ)\}$, which are those nodes currently having the same out-degree as x. The membership of these nodes in R is toggled by the update. Let $SAMEAFTER = \{u \mid (u, v) \in I^\circ, outdeg(u, I^\circ) = outdeg(x, I^n)\}$, which are those nodes currently having out-degree one more than that of x. The membership of these nodes in R is toggled by the update. We can now define the update to R as $R^n = (R^\circ \cap LESS) \cup (R^\circ \cap MORE) \cup (\text{if } SAMEBEFORE \neq \{\} \wedge SAMEBEFORE \subseteq R^\circ \text{ then } \{\} \text{ else } SAMEBEFORE - \{x\}) \cup$

$(if\ SAMEAFTER \neq \{\} \wedge SAMEAFTER \subseteq R^\circ\ then\ \{\}\ else\ (SAMEAFTER\ \cup \{x\}))$. Then $A^n = if\ \{u \mid (u,v) \in I^n,\ outdeg(u, I^n) = maxout(I^n)\} \neq \{\} \wedge \{u \mid (u,v) \in I^n,\ outdeg(u, I^n) = maxout(I^n)\} \subseteq R^n\ then\ \{1\}\ else\ \{\}$.

The case when the update is the deletion of an existing edge (x, y) from I is similar, and can be found in the full report [18]. □

Putting all three propositions above together, we conclude that

Theorem 15. *Space-free* $IES(\mathcal{SQL}) \subset IES(\mathcal{SQL})_1 \subset IES(\mathcal{SQL})_2 = IES(\mathcal{SQL})_{k>2}$. □

This result contrasts sharply with the situation of $IES(\mathcal{FO})_k$, which is a strict hierarchy. The strictness of the $IES(\mathcal{FO})_k$ hierarchy were obtained using a result of Cai [6]; it uses queries with input relations of greater and greater arities to separate higher and higher layers of the $IES(\mathcal{FO})_k$ hierarchy. It is not known if $IES(\mathcal{FO})_k$ remains strict if we further impose a restriction on arities of input relations. Since the arity hierarchy collapses in the presence of simple extensions such as aggregate functions as in $IES(\mathcal{SQL})_k$, we feel that a hierarchy based on arities is not robust and not natural for incremental evaluation systems. However, it is still an interesting problem to work out a general hierarchy for incremental evaluation systems.

7 Conclusion

We focused on incremental evaluation systems that use the SQL-like language $\mathcal{NRC}^{\mathrm{aggr}}$. In particular, we examined their power in the presence of auxiliary (nested) relations. With respect to $IES(\mathcal{NRC}^{\mathrm{aggr}})$, we proved that they can maintain transitive closure, "alternating paths," and "same generation." These results are in contrast to earlier ones [9, etc.] on $IES(\mathcal{FO})$, where expressibility of these queries remains unsolved (and the negative results are conjectured). They are also in contrast to earlier results [7] on space-free $IES(\mathcal{NRC}^{\mathrm{aggr}})$, where these queries were shown to be inexpressible.

Then we considered the restriction of $IES(\mathcal{NRC}^{\mathrm{aggr}})$ to $IES(\mathcal{SQL})$, which are allowed to use only flat auxiliary relations. $IES(\mathcal{SQL})$ is an interesting and important subclass because it naturally reflects the capability of commercial relational database systems which use SQL and store flat tables. We showed that $IES(\mathcal{NRC}^{\mathrm{aggr}})$ and $IES(\mathcal{SQL})$ have the same power. Thus all queries that can be expressed in $IES(\mathcal{NRC}^{\mathrm{aggr}})$ can also be maintained using a standard relational database system. We further proved that every $IES(\mathcal{SQL})$ can be replaced by one that uses auxiliary relations of arity at most 2. That means arity restriction on auxiliary relations does not lead to a hierarchy in $IES(\mathcal{SQL})$. This contrasts with [10] showing that arity restriction on auxiliary relations leads to a strict hierarchy in $IES(\mathcal{FO})$.

In some of our proofs, it can be observed that the amount of auxiliary data involved could be exponential with respect to the size of the history of updates. (The size of the history of updates to a $IES(\mathcal{NRC}^{\mathrm{aggr}})$ is defined as the sum of the size of all the tuples that were inserted to or deleted from the IES($\mathcal{NRC}^{aggr}$) up to that point in time.) However, at each update, the size of auxiliary data is changed only a polynomial amount from its current size. Nevertheless, we do not know of a method for maintaining recursive views such as transitive closure of arbitrary graphs in IES($\mathcal{NRC}^{aggr}$) that uses only a polynomial amount of space. We leave the search for such a method or the disprove of its existence for future work.

Acknowledgements. We thank Michael Benedikt, Ke Wang, and especially Guozhu Dong for numerous discussions and valuable inputs, and anonymous referees for their helpful comments on an earlier draft.

References

1. S. Abiteboul, R. Hull and V. Vianu. *Foundations of Databases.* Addison Wesley, 1995.
2. S. Abiteboul and P. Kanellakis. Query languages for complex object databases. *SIGACT News*, 21(3):9–18, 1990.
3. A. Aho and J. Ullman. Universality of data retrieval languages. In *Proceedings 6th Symposium on Principles of Programming Languages, Texas, January 1979*, pages 110–120, 1979.
4. P. Buneman, L. Libkin, D. Suciu, V. Tannen, and L. Wong. Comprehension syntax. *SIGMOD Record*, 23(1):87–96, March 1994.
5. P. Buneman, S. Naqvi, V. Tannen, and L. Wong. Principles of programming with complex objects and collection types. *Theoretical Computer Science*, 149(1):3–48, September 1995.
6. J.-Y. Cai. Lower bound for constant-depth circuits in the presence of help bits. *Information Processing Letters*, 36:79–83, 1990.
7. G. Dong, L. Libkin, and L. Wong. On impossibility of decremental recomputation of recursive queries in relational calculus and SQL. In *Proceedings of 5th International Workshop on Database Programming Languages, Gubbio, Italy, September 1995*, Springer Electronic Workshops in Computing, 1996. Available at http: //www.springer.co.uk /eWiC /Workshops /DBPL5.html.
8. G. Dong, L. Libkin, and L. Wong. Local properties of query languages. In *Proceedings of 6th International Conference on Database Theory*, pages 140–154, Delphi, Greece, January 1997.
9. G. Dong and J. Su. Incremental and decremental evaluation of transitive closure by first-order queries. *Information and Computation*, 120(1):101–106, July 1995.
10. G. Dong and J. Su. Space-bounded FOIES. In *Proceedings of 14th ACM Symposium on Principles of Database Systems, San Jose, California*, pages 139–150, May 1995.
11. G. Dong and J. Su. Deterministic FOIES are strictly weaker. *Annals of Mathematics and Artificial Intelligence* 19(1):127–146, 1997.
12. G. Dong, J. Su, and R. Topor. Nonrecursive incremental evaluation of Datalog queries. *Annals of Mathematics and Artificial Intelligence*, 14:187–223, 1995.
13. G. Dong and L. Wong. Some relationships between FOIES and Σ_1^1 arity hierarchies. *Bulletin of EATCS*, 61:72–79, 1997.
14. N. Immerman. Languages that capture complexity classes. *SIAM Journal of Computing*, 16:760–778, 1987.

15. L. Libkin and L. Wong. Aggregate functions, conservative extension, and linear orders. In C. Beeri, A. Ohori, and D. Shasha, editors, *Proceedings of 4th International Workshop on Database Programming Languages, New York, August 1993*, pages 282–294. Springer-Verlag, January 1994.

16. L. Libkin and L. Wong. Conservativity of nested relational calculi with internal generic functions. *Information Processing Letters*, 49(6):273–280, March 1994.

17. L. Libkin and L. Wong. Query languages for bags and aggregate functions. *Journal of Computer and System Sciences*, 55 (1997), 241–272.

18. L. Libkin and L. Wong. Incremental recomputation of recursive queries with nested sets and aggregate functions. Technical Report 97-224-0, Institute of Systems Science, Heng Mui Keng Terrace, Singapore 119597, April 1997.

19. J. Paredaens and D. Van Gucht. Converting nested relational algebra expressions into flat algebra expressions. *ACM Transaction on Database Systems*, 17(1):65–93, March 1992.

20. S. Patnaik and N. Immerman. Dyn-FO: A parallel dynamic complexity class. In *Proceedings of 13th ACM Symposium on Principles of Database Systems*, pages 210–221, Minneapolis, Minnesota, May 1994.

21. P. Wadler. Comprehending monads. *Mathematical Structures in Computer Science*, 2:461–493, 1992.

22. L. Wong. *Querying Nested Collections*. PhD thesis, Department of Computer and Information Science, University of Pennsylvania, Philadelphia, PA 19104, August 1994. Available as University of Pennsylvania IRCS Report 94-09.

23. L. Wong. Normal forms and conservative extension properties for query languages over collection types. *Journal of Computer and System Sciences*, 52(3):495–505, June 1996.

Towards a Language for the Fully Generic Queries *

Catriel Beeri[1], Tova Milo[2] and Paula Ta-Shma[1]

[1] Institute of Computer Science, Hebrew University
Jerusalem, 91904, Israel
{beeri,paula}@cs.huji.ac.il
[2] Department of Computer Science, Tel-Aviv University
Tel-Aviv, Israel
milo@math.tau.ac.il

1 Introduction

Database queries differ in one fundamental aspect from regular functions — they are generic, that is invariant under database isomorphisms. This property was first discussed in [AU79]. At about the same time, [CH80] posed the problem whether there is a complete query language, that is a language that expresses precisely the computable generic database functions, and presented an affirmative answer.

Over the years, the notion of genericity has been refined. Clearly, if a constant is used in a query, the query cannot be expected to be invariant under renamings that do not preserve it. Consequently, Hull and Yap [HY84] introduced the idea of invariance under isomorphisms that preserve some constants. Their notion of C-genericity, where C is a finite set of constants, is essential to capture functions such as $\sigma_{A=3}(R)$ as queries. But now, if we consider the query $\sigma_{prime(A)}(R)$, we see that the same argument holds: If a renaming does not preserve the primality of numbers, then the query will not be invariant under it. Thus, one must in the general case consider mappings that preserve some set of domain constants, functions and predicates (often referred to as built-in functions/predicates.) Typically, if a query does not use a built-in function/predicate, it should be invariant under mappings that do not preserve it.

Generalizing further, genericity is invariance under some class of mappings [BMT96]. The larger this class of mappings, the smaller the resulting class of queries. The class can be defined by a set of constants and functions that need to be preserved, or by some other means. For example, in recent work on spatial query languages [PVV94, PSV96], genericity is considered w.r.t. translations, similarities and homeomorphisms of the plane, and each defines a different class of queries. In [BMT96], we defined the class of *fully generic* queries as those queries that are invariant under the largest class of mappings. Being the smallest possible class of queries, this class is contained in all other genericity classes, and is in this sense fundamental. This class can be characterized as those queries that

---

* This work was supported in part by grants from the **Israeli Science Foundation**.

are invariant also under mappings that do not preserve equality. Indeed, equality is also a built-in predicate of a domain. When a query uses equality, it is invariant only under mappings that preserve it, i.e. one-to-one mappings; but if it does not use it, it should also be invariant under mappings that are not one-to-one. Thus, the fully generic queries, embodying the "pure" notion of genericity, are invariant under arbitrary mappings on the domain, many-to-many in the general case. Following the view that genericity is a fundamental property of database query languages, one can say that the class of fully-generic queries is the class of quintessential database functions.

In this paper we investigate the existence of a complete language for the fully generic queries:

Open Problem 1.1 *Does there exist a query language $\mathcal{L}$ such that for all queries Q, Q is fully generic iff Q is expressible in $\mathcal{L}$?*

We settle this question in the affirmative for relational databases. We also study queries over complex values and settle the question in the affirmative at certain types, and in particular for all flat or boolean output queries over nested input types, and for queries whose input and output are doubly nested sets. The novel proof technique we use is interesting in itself, and is constructive, in that we construct all possible fully generic queries at these types.

Our investigation continues a long line of research of genericity in database theory. In particular, a solution of our problem may shed some light on the nature of complete languages for other genericity classes, although certainly the nature of the specific class of mappings used to define a genericity class plays an important role as well. Our investigation is also potentially relevant to practical issues. For example, in heterogeneous databases, and data on the Web, equality is often not available. For example, in the databases and logic programming bibliography server [Ley], there are currently separate entries for authors "Ross Paterson" and "Ross A. Paterson". Are these really two distinct authors? While heuristics can be used to guess the answer, there is no computationally feasible way to provide a certain answer. It follows that, for example, if we have lists of accepted papers for DBPL and for VLDB, "Ross Paterson" is in the first list, and "Ross A. Paterson" in the second, then we cannot answer the query which asks for authors that have papers in both conferences; intersection uses equality hence is not fully generic. On the other hand, the ∪, × and π of the relational algebra are fully generic. Our study could therefore delineate theoretical bounds on queries on the Web.

The fully generic queries are also interesting because they are, in a sense, the most optimizable. The invariance of a query under a mapping can be restated as an algebraic equivalence. Invariance under more mappings directly implies more applicable equivalences. For example, projection is a (non-injective) mapping, therefore, fully generic queries, which commute with all mappings, commute with projection. Such equivalences are typically used for query optimization, and in this sense the fully generic queries are the most amenable to algebraic optimization.

We feel that genericity can be profitably used as a tool for language design, and for the study of language properties in general. The fully generic queries can be viewed as the pure restructuring queries, which do not use any domain specific information whatsoever. Our candidate for a complete fully generic language presented in Section 2 is closely related to the elegant core nested relational algebra presented in [BBW92]. As shown in [BBW92], adding equality to this core language gives precisely the nested relational algebra. We feel that, in [BBW92], a key behind the elegant language design is the separation of the fully generic restructuring queries from the domain specific operations (such as equality, orderings etc.) which are added as needed. Although language design is a matter of taste, we point out that the language of [BBW92] was successfully used as a vehicle for proving numerous properties of the nested relational algebra, such as conservative extension [Won93], which were significant improvements on previous results. This is despite the fact that other presentations of the nested relational algebra had been studied for some time.

Finally, we point out that our conjecture and the results we have obtained are of independent interest. For example, if our conjecture about the complete language is true [1], then all fully generic queries are computable. This contrasts with all other genericity classes studied to date, which contain non-computable queries. More importantly, it may be possible, using our methods, to attain a *complete understanding* of the fully generic queries. For example, equivalence of fully generic queries may be decidable, which would again be in contrast with most generic database languages such as the relational algebra.

Section 2 presents the definitions of full genericity and queries, and the candidate language. In Section 3, we show that complex values of a given type can be partitioned into finitely many disjoint classes, such that the behavior of a fully generic query on inputs of this type is determined independently for each class. This allows us to prove the main result for each class separately. Full genericity implies that inputs and outputs of queries are related by patterns. We define these in Section 4, and present closure properties for the set of patterns of a query. In Section 5 we prove our conjecture for the (simple) case of queries with relational output. Section 6 deals with the much more difficult case of input and output with double set nesting. Here we make full use of the closure properties.

2 The Problem and Our Approach

2.1 Complex values

We adopt the complex value model here. A complex value is a generalized nested relation, where set and tuple constructors can be arbitrarily interleaved [AHV95]. Atomic values come from an infinite domain, denoted D.

Definition 2.1 (complex value type) *Complex value types are defined recursively as $t := d \mid [] \mid t \times \ldots \times t \mid \{t\}$, where d denotes the domain D, and $[]$ is the type of 0-ary tuples (there is only one such tuple, which is also denoted $[]$).*

---

[1] As indicated above, we have proofs for some but not for all complex value types.

Each complex value type τ is associated with a domain of complex values, $dom(\tau)$, as follows.

$$dom(d) = D \qquad dom([]) = \{[]\} \qquad dom(\{t\}) = \mathcal{P}^{fin}(dom(t))$$
$$dom(t_1 \times \ldots t_n) = dom(t_1) \times \ldots \times dom(t_n)$$

$\mathcal{P}^{fin}$ denotes finite powerset. Following [CH80, BNTW95], we denote the type $\{[]\}$ as bool, and use $\{\}$ for *false* and $\{[]\}$ for *true*. Complex values can also be viewed as trees, where internal nodes are labeled with the type constructors, and the leaves are labeled with atomic values, $[]$ and $\{\}$.

2.2 Mappings and genericity

We now define mappings on complex values, and then define genericity as invariance under such mappings. A mapping on complex values is obtained by taking some mapping on atoms and extending it. For example, classical genericity considers one-to-one mappings on atoms, which are uniquely extended to one-to-one mappings on complex values. A mapping which maps 1 to a and 2 to b, when extended to complex values, maps $\{[1,2],[2,2]\}$ to $\{[a,b],[b,b]\}$. Our mappings, however, are many-to-many in the general case. [2] For such mappings there is a unique natural extension to tuples, component-wise. However there is more than one candidate extension to sets, hence to complex values, each giving rise to a different notion of genericity [BMT96]. We use the *rel* extension mode of [BMT96], since it is the one that does not preserve equality in any way. [3]

Mappings on complex value types are defined inductively, starting from a mapping on atoms. We associate the two type constructors $\times, \{\}$ with mapping constructors, also denoted $\times, \{\}$:

Definition 2.2 (mappings) *A mapping H on type τ is some subset of $dom(\tau) \times dom(\tau)$. As a special case, a mapping on atoms is some subset of $D \times D$. We write $H(x,y)$ if the pair (x,y) belongs to this subset. Let $H, H_1, \ldots, H_n$ be given mappings on types $\tau, \tau_1, \ldots, \tau_n$.*

tuples: $H_1 \times \ldots \times H_n$ *is the mapping on $\tau_1 \times \ldots \times \tau_n$ such that:*
$$(H_1 \times \ldots \times H_n)([x_1,\ldots,x_n],[y_1,\ldots,y_n]) \iff H_i(x_i,y_i), (1 \le i \le n).$$
sets: $\{H\}$ *is the mapping on $\{\tau\}$ such that:*
$$\{H\}(S_1,S_2) \iff \forall x_1 \in S_1 \exists x_2 \in S_2 \text{ such that } H(x_1,x_2),$$
$$\text{and } \forall x_2 \in S_2 \exists x_1 \in S_1 \text{ such that } H(x_1,x_2).$$

Now, given a mapping H on atoms, it can be extended inductively to each complex value type. We denote by H_τ the mapping obtained by lifting H to type τ. In most of the paper we abuse the notation and simply write $H(t,t')$, for two values of type τ.

---

[2] Many-to-many mappings are commonly referred to as *relations*, although this term is overloaded in our context.

[3] This extension mode has also been used to lift partial orders (as opposed to general relations) to sets, in work on querying incomplete information. There it is known as the Plotkin ordering [LW93].

Example 2.3 Firstly, we extend the mapping $H_d = \{(1, a), (1, b), (2, b)\}$, which is not functional in either direction, to sets, to obtain $H_{\{d\}} = \{(\{1\}, \{a\}), (\{1\}, \{b\}), (\{1\}, \{a, b\}), (\{2\}, \{b\}), (\{1, 2\}, \{a, b\}), (\{1, 2\}, \{b\})\}$.

As a second example, consider the mapping $H_d = \{(e, a)(i, a)(f, b)(j, b)(g, c)\}$ and the two binary relations $r_1 = \{[e, f], [i, f], [e, j], [i, j], [f, g], [j, g]\}$, $r_2 = \{[a, b], [b, c]\}$. H_d can be extended (as explained above) to a mapping over 2-ary tuples, and then further extended to a mapping over sets of 2-ary tuples. It is easy to verify that in this extended mapping, $H_{\{d \times d\}}(r_1, r_2)$ holds. □

We note that for any type τ, $H_\tau(\{\}, S)$ holds for S of type τ if and only if $S = \{\}$. (We overload notation and use $\{\}$ for empty sets of all types). Moreover, extensions of many-to-many mappings do not preserve cardinality of sets (except for cardinality 0, as just noted).

Since databases can be viewed as tuples of complex values, queries are functions from complex values to complex values. Such a function is fully generic if it is invariant under *all* mappings:

Definition 2.4 *A total function $Q : \tau_1 \rightarrow \tau_2$ is **fully generic** if for all mappings H on atomic domains, and for all $S, S' \in dom(\tau_1)$, whenever $H(S, S')$ holds, so does $H(Q(S), Q(S'))$.* [4] *A **query** $Q : \tau_1 \rightarrow \tau_2$ is a total fully-generic function from $dom(\tau_1)$ to $dom(\tau_2)$.*

Note that we require queries to be typed, total and fully generic, but not necessarily to be computable. In [BMT96] we also considered restricting the mappings H above to be *functional*, and showed that the resulting notion of full genericity coincides with this one.

2.3 A fully generic language

We search for a query language that expresses exactly all fully generic queries. Our candidate language $\mathcal{L}$ is the fully generic component of the complex value algebra, and a new operator we call *one-each*, see Figure 1. $\mathcal{L}$ is (essentially) the same language as $\mathcal{M}_\cup(cond)$ from [BNTW95] plus *one-each*. *one-each* can be used in $\mathcal{L}$ to express *powerset* (hence the latter is not included in $\mathcal{L}$), but we do not know how to express *one-each* using the remaining operators of $\mathcal{L}$ and *powerset*. This is why we include it. We note that as soon as equality is added to $\mathcal{L}$ we get the full nested relational algebra plus *powerset* [BNTW95]. [5]

It is not hard to show (proof omitted) that

Proposition 2.5 *All queries expressible in $\mathcal{L}$ are fully generic.*

2.4 The problem and our approach

The rest of this paper deals with the question whether all fully generic queries can be expressed in $\mathcal{L}$. As we mentioned in the introduction, an affirmative

---

[4] This corresponds to rel-fully generic from [BMT96].
[5] Note that *powerset* plus equality can express *one-each*.

Query	Meaning
id	the identity function : $id(S) = S$
$\circ$	function composition
$[f_1, \ldots, f_n]$	takes n functions and creates a new function. On input v, $[f_1, \ldots, f_n](v) = [f_1(v), \ldots, f_n(v)]$.
$\$i$	selects the ith column of an n-tuple
$map(f)$	applies f to each element of a set
$single$	creates a singleton set
$flatten$	flattens a set of sets into a set
$\times$	cartesian product
$\cup$	set union
$powerset$	(finitary) powerset
$one\text{-}each$	accepts a set of sets $S = \{s_1, \ldots, s_n\}$, and returns the set of all sets (whose elements are taken from S) having at least one element from each one of the s_i. For example $one\text{-}each(\{\{1\}, \{2, 3\}, \{3, 5\}\}) = \{\{1, 2, 3\}, \{1, 2, 5\}, \{1, 2, 3, 5\}, \{1, 3\}, \{1, 3, 5\}\}$.
$\{\}_\sigma$	always returns the empty set (of type $\{\sigma\}$)
$[\,]_\sigma$	maps all elements of type σ to the empty tuple, the single element of type $unit$
$cond$	a conditional (if then else) : it returns its second argument if its first is non-empty, and otherwise it returns its third argument.

Fig. 1. Candidate language $\mathcal{L}$

answer would imply, for example, that all fully generic queries are computable. In contrast, queries which are generic in the classical sense are not necessarily so. For example, any query from flat sets to bool that depends only on the input size must be generic w.r.t. all injective mappings, and it is easy to show that there are non-computable such queries. Thus, non-computable generic queries exist. The reason this might be different for fully generic queries is that they must act uniformly across inputs of different sizes, because a many-to-many mapping can relate *any* non-empty flat set to any other.

It is easy to verify that there are four fully generic queries from flat sets to bool, because such a query must choose either *true* or *false* for all non-empty inputs, and similarly for empty inputs. For non boolean output types, there are many more fully generic queries, since there are many ways to permute and combine the elements in the input to produce the output. Allowing flat inputs and outputs, we get, for example, $\cup$, π and $\times$, three out of five of the relational algebra operators. Moving to nested inputs and outputs we have *single, powerset, flatten* etc. Indeed the class of fully generic queries is by no means trivial—adding equality to $\mathcal{L}$ gives the entire nested relational algebra, *powerset* included [BNTW95]. Our experience is that as the inputs and outputs become more deeply nested, solving the problem we posed becomes considerably more difficult. Intuitively, this is because deeply nested inputs can contain many patterns which can be exploited by fully generic queries—if the output is also deeply nested, the query can restructure these patterns in many ways. As the nesting gets deeper, there are just so many more possibilities.

Here is a brief outline of our approach to the solution of the problem. We observe that the inputs and outputs to fully generic queries are related by patterns; full genericity implies there are many such patterns. Descriptors are introduced to formally describe a query's patterns. A query is completely characterized by the set of its descriptors, which typically is infinite. For our purpose, we need a finite representation of this set, which is obtained as follows. We point out that a descriptor d_1 may dominate another descriptor d_2, meaning that whenever d_1 describes a fully generic query, then so does d_2. Therefore, for each fully generic query we search for a finite number of dominating descriptors (this is the most difficult part). Once that is achieved, we find a query in $\mathcal{L}$ corresponding to each dominating descriptor, and take the (finite) union, thus obtaining a query in $\mathcal{L}$.

In this paper we motivate and describe the central constructs and ideas behind the proof. A complete account can be found in [Ta-97].

3 Canonical Forms

Since full genericity deals with mappings between values, we need to understand when it is possible to map one complex value to another. For that we introduce the notion of *canonical form*.

Definition 3.1 *A canonical form (for type τ) is a complex value (of this type) containing at most one atomic value z.*

For example $\{\}$, $\{\{\}\}$, $\{\{[z, z]\}\}$, and $\{\{\}, \{[z, z]\}\}$ are canonical forms.

Definition 3.2 *We say that a complex value S has canonical form c, denoted $cf(S)$, if c is obtained from S by replacing all atomic values in S (if any) by z.*

For instance, both values $\{\{\}, \{[a, b]\}\}$ and $\{\{\}, \{[a, b]\}, \{[c, d], [e, f]\}\}$ have the canonical form $\{\{\}\{[z, z]\}\}$. Think of this canonical form as representing all depth two sets that contain the empty set, and some nonempty sets of pairs.

Note that the number of canonical forms for each type τ is finite, and they can all be constructed inductively from the type definition. (Proof omitted). For example, the type $\{\{b \times b\}\}$ has exactly the 4 canonical forms listed above $\{\}$, $\{\{\}\}$, $\{\{[z, z]\}\}$, and $\{\{\}, \{[z, z]\}\}$.

An important observation, that is used extensively in the proofs in this paper, is that the language $\mathcal{L}$ can distinguish between inputs of different canonical forms.

Claim 3.3 *For each type τ and each canonical form c of type τ, the function $c(x) : dom(\tau) \to \mathtt{bool}$ that returns true iff $cf(x) = c$ is expressible in $\mathcal{L}$.*

The significance of canonical forms for the study of genericity is in the fact they determine whether values can be mapped to each other :

Claim 3.4 *For any two values S_1, S_2 of the same type, there exists some H such that $H(S_1, S_2)$ if and only if $cf(S_1) = cf(S_2)$.*

Basically this means the following: Full genericity means uniformity of behavior, but this uniformity applies only to values of the same canonical form. There is no relationship between the outputs of a query for values with distinct canonical forms. This, with the fact that the language $\mathcal{L}$ can distinguish between canonical forms, implies that to prove our conjecture it suffices to consider a query's behavior separately on values of each canonical form. Another implication concerns partial queries. If for such queries full genericity means that a query is defined on a value if and only if it is defined on each value related to it by a mapping, then a query is fully defined or fully undefined on classes of values defined by canonical forms. Since canonical forms can be computed, each computable partial fully generic query can be 'completed' to a total computable fully generic query. This justifies our choice to study only total queries.

An important observation, that is used in the sequel, is that just 'having the same canonical form' may not suffice to understand the interaction between queries and mappings. Consider for example the nested set $\{\{\}, \{a\}\}, \{\{b\}\}\}$. The elements a and b in it have the same canonical form, and so do the sets $\{a\}$ and $\{b\}$. Still they can be distinguished from each other – the first appears in a nested set containing the empty set, while the other does not, that is, their parents in the input have different canonical forms. Indeed, there is a fully generic query that returns a value where a occurs but b does not.[6] To fully characterize a sub-value of the input, one must consider both its canonical form, and those of its ancestors in the input tree.

4 Query Descriptors

We expect fully generic queries to behave *uniformly* across inputs of the same canonical form. Informally, this means that for a query there are some fixed patterns that relate inputs (having a certain canonical form) to the outputs. *Query descriptors* are intended to capture such patterns.

We first show that a fully generic query is completely characterized by its behavior on what we will call completely disjoint values. We then define the notion of descriptor, which describes the essential patterns which hold between a query output and a completely disjoint query input.

4.1 Completely disjoint values

To study fully generic queries we need to understand their behavior on various inputs. We now justify studying this behavior only w.r.t a subset of all possible inputs—the *completely disjoint* values. These are the values where no atomic value occurs more than once as a leaf in the value tree.

Claim 4.1 *If fully generic queries Q_1, Q_2 agree on all completely disjoint inputs, then they agree on all inputs.*

Hence, in most of this paper we deal only with such input values.

---

[6] For example, the query $Q(s) = \{s'' \mid s'' \in s', s' \in s, \emptyset \notin s\}$.

4.2 Descriptors

Let S and T be values. We want to describe the pattern that relates S as an input to a query, and T as a potential sub-value [7] of the output. (We do not assume that there actually is such a query.) We include the following components: First, T itself (in its tree form). Second, for every atom that appears in T (as a leaf), we record its origin in S. This is well-defined, assuming S is completely disjoint. This component can be visualized as pointers going from T's leaves to S's leaves. Since we want to record only the essential patterns between T and S, and since these should be independent of the actual atomic values involved, we now omit the actual values of the atoms. Moreover, if we can leave out more information (while still retaining the essential patterns), these patterns would become more widely applicable. We note that only a part of S is directly relevant to T: the atomic leaves that occur in T, and their positions in S's structure. We can expect T to be similarly related to other values that have these components of S, but differ from S in other parts. Therefore, we omit all parts of S, except for the leaves of S that have incoming pointers from T, and their ancestors up to the root.

This pruning of S's structure is, however, a bit too drastic. There are two pieces of information that are needed for the patterns to faithfully describe the input-output relations in queries, that cannot be derived without considering all of S. Therefore, these are included as node labels. First, as we noted before, we need to know the canonical forms of all nodes and their ancestors. Therefore we include the canonical form of each node. Second, consider a set node n, and assume it has in S a set of children of canonical form c, and some of them contribute to T. It turns out to be important to know whether all these children contribute to T, hence all are left in the descriptor, or some do not contribute to T, hence are removed. In the first case, we add to n's label the pair $(c, =)$, meaning that the set of such children in S is the same as those represented. In the second case , we add to n's label the pair $(c, <)$, meaning that the set represented is a subset of the set in S. Since n may have children of several canonical forms, its label will contain, in addition to its own canonical form, several such pairs.

Definition 4.2 *Let S be a completely disjoint complex value, and T any value, such that $adom(T) \subseteq adom(S)$. The descriptor of T w.r.t. S is the triple $d = \langle in(d), out(d), map(d) \rangle$, defined as follows:*

- *$in(d)$ is the minimal subtree of S that contains its root, and each leaf that occurs in T, with the atomic values that label the leaves removed, and with each node labeled with its canonical form.*
- *Additionally, internal set constructor nodes are labeled as follows: if a node has in S children of canonical form c, and all of them are in $in(d)$, then its*

---

[7] A sub-value is the value corresponding to a full subtree of a given complex value. For example $\{1, 2, 3\}$ is a sub-value of $\{\{1, 2, 3\}, \{4\}\}$ but $\{1, 2\}$ and $\{\{1, 2, 3\}\}$ are not.

label contains $(c, =)$; *if some of them but not all are in* $in(d)$ *then the label contains* $(c, <)$.

— *The children of tuple constructor nodes are labeled with their component number.*

— $out(d)$ *is* T, *with the atomic values at the leaves omitted.*

— $map(d)$ *is a mapping from the leaves of* $out(d)$ *to the leaves of* $in(d)$, *that maps each node to its unique source in* $in(d)$.[8]

Example 4.3 *Let* $S = \{\{b, c\}, \{d\}\}$ *and* $T = \{\{b, c\}, \{b\}\}$. *The descriptor of* T *w.r.t* S *is described graphically below. The leftmost leaf in* $in(d)$ *corresponds to the value* b, *the rightmost to* c. S *contains two sets of the same canonical form, namely two nonempty sets. Since only one of them contributes values to* T, *only one is represented. Therefore the root of* $in(d)$ *is labeled, in addition to* S's *canonical form, with* $(\{z\}, <)$, *where* $\{z\}$ *is* $cf(\{b, c\}) = cf(\{d\})$. *On the next level down, since both members of* $\{b, c\}$ *occur in* T, *the label contains* $(\{z\}, =)$.

in(d)   out(d)

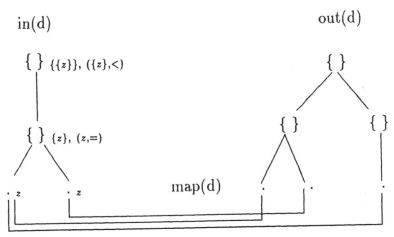

Note that if T is one of $\{\}, [\,], \{[\,]\}$, or any tree without atomic leaves, then its descriptor w.r.t a set S is $(\langle cf(S) \rangle, T, \emptyset)$. Also note that the descriptor is independent of specific atomic values appearing in the input and output. Only the relationship between them is being recorded.

The following claim shows that a descriptor successfully captures the patterns between input and output.

Claim 4.4 *Let* Q *be a fully generic query, and assume that* d *describes* T_1 *w.r.t.* S_1 *and* T_2 *w.r.t.* S_2. *Then* T_1 *is a sub-value of* $Q(S_1)$ *if and only if* T_2 *is a sub-value of* $Q(S_2)$.

This claim would not hold if we did not record the $<, =$ labels of a descriptor. For example, let $Q = id$, $S_1 = T = \{1, 2\}$, $S_2 = \{1, 2, 3\}$. Then a descriptor d which

---

[8] $map(d)$ is defined with respect to the trees before the atomic values are removed.

describes T w.r.t. S_1 has one set node with label $(\{z\}, =)$, and 2 children. The descriptor d' which describes it w.r.t. S_2 has exactly the same structure, except that the $=$ is replaced by $<$. If this information was not present, then since T is a sub-value of $id(S_1) = S_1$ the claim would imply that T is a sub-value of $id(S_2) = S_2$, which is not true (note that subsets are not necessarily sub-values).

For nested outputs, we can consider sub-values T at various levels. In the rest of this paper we are mainly interested in queries whose output is a set, and the sub-values that are considered are the members of these output sets. This together with the above claim justifies the following definition.

Definition 4.5 d **describes a query** Q *(of output type $\{\tau\}$) if there exist S, T such that $T \in Q(S)$ and d describes T w.r.t. S. The* **set of descriptors of** Q, *denoted D_Q is $\{d \mid d$ describes $Q\}$.*

Descriptors describe *members* of query output w.r.t. their input. Since Q above has output type $\{\tau\}$, T has type τ. This is also the type of $out(d)$.

A fully generic query is completely determined by its set of descriptors:

Claim 4.6 *If Q, Q' are fully generic and $D_Q = D_{Q'}$ then $Q = Q'$.*

4.3 Dominance

Our technique for showing that all fully generic queries (of certain types) are expressible in $\mathcal{L}$ works as follows. If D_Q is finite, then we consider each descriptor separately, and find a query in the language for it, then take their union. However, for some queries, (in particular queries with non-relational output type), the set of descriptors is infinite. For this case, think of the space of descriptors as a geometric space, and of D_Q as a subspace. We show that this subspace has a nice geometry, that allows us to infer a division into a *finite* number of subspaces. Then we present a query for each subspace, and take their union.

The observation that we use in this analysis is that some query descriptors are related in the sense that whenever a query has some descriptor, it also has some other descriptors.

Definition 4.7 *We say that d **dominates** d', denoted $d \to d'$, if for all fully generic queries Q, if d describes Q then also d' describes Q. For a descriptor d, $closure(d) = \{d' \mid d \to d'\}$.*

Note that the dominance relation is reflexive and transitive, and $d \to d' \iff closure(d') \subseteq closure(d)$.

The definition of the dominance relation is semantic. Some results concerning it used in our proofs, that use the form of descriptors, are presented below. Additional results that are also used in the proofs are omitted, for lack of space. For details, see [Ta-97].

Claim 4.8 (<-to-= Property) *Assume d' is obtained from d by replacing some $(c, <)$ by $(c, =)$ in the label of a set constructor node. Then $d \to d'$.*

For example, the descriptor described in Example 4.3 dominates the descriptor that has the same components, except that the label of $in(d)$'s root now contains $=$ instead of $<$.

For descriptors whose *out* component has no set constructors, i.e., those that describe atomic values or tuples of such values, the converse holds as well.

Claim 4.9 (=-to-< property) *Assume $out(d)$ has no set constructors, and d' is obtained from d by replacing some $(c,=)$ by $(c,<)$ in the label of a set constructor node. Then $d \to d'$.*

Combining the two results, we have that in descriptors whose *out* component has no set constructors, the components (c,p) in labels can be omitted.

We use other dominance properties which involve a descriptor's structure and not just its labels. Most importantly, the Merge Lemma [Ta-97] shows how a descriptor dominates the result of merging two siblings in its *in* component. We present special cases of the Merge Lemma in section 6.

5 Queries from nested types to flat output

We are now ready to tackle the question whether all fully generic queries can be expressed in the language $\mathcal{L}$. We first consider queries from arbitrary nested input to *flat output*, that is, to sets of tuples, or sets of atoms. The proof technique we use here is specific and does not work for nested outputs, hence the separation.

Theorem 5.1 *All fully generic queries from arbitrary nested types to flat output are expressible in $\mathcal{L}$ (without one-each).*

In particular, all fully generic queries with relational input/output are expressible, and so are all fully generic boolean queries from arbitrary nested types (since the output is a 0-ary relation).

Proof. (sketch) We present below the major ideas behind the proof and the queries that result, for the case that Q is a query with relational output. (The case for output being a set of atoms is similar).

We first argue that for queries Q with fixed input type and relational output, the set D_Q of descriptors is **finite** because

1. Each descriptor d describes a tuple in the output of Q. The number of leaves of such a tuple is the relation arity. Thus the number of leaves in $in(d)$ is bounded by the relation arity.
2. The number of canonical forms for any given type is finite.

Now, assume $D_Q = \{d_1, ..., d_k\}$, for some finite k. We construct a query q_i (of the same type as Q) for each d_i, such that $D_Q = D_{q_1} \cup ... \cup D_{q_k}$, and therefore, $Q = q_1 \cup ... \cup q_k$. Each q_i is expressed in $\mathcal{L}$, (without *one-each*), and the Theorem follows. A brief description of the construction of the q_i's appears in Appendix A. The dominance results of Section 4.3 are used to show that indeed $D_Q = D_{q_1} \cup ... \cup D_{q_k}$.

Corollary 5.2 *All fully generic queries with relational output are computable.*

6   Queries to sets of sets

For queries with nested output, the sizes of the sets in the output is not bounded, hence there is no bound on the sizes of descriptors. It follows that the number of descriptors for a given query may be infinite, hence the case here is considerably more difficult than that for flat output. We did manage to handle certain cases. Specifically, we consider here fully generic queries whose output is a set of sets, and whose input is a set or a set of sets. This section is dedicated to proving the following theorem.

Theorem 6.1 *All fully generic queries from sets (resp. sets of sets) to sets of sets are expressible in $\mathcal{L}$. When the input is a flat set, this can be done without using one-each.*

Corollary 6.2 *All fully generic queries from sets or sets of sets to sets of sets are computable.*

6.1   Descriptors and meta-descriptors

For each canonical form, it is easy to find an expression in $\mathcal{L}$ for a query that gives an empty output ($\{\}$ or $\{\{\}\}$) on inputs of that form. Hence, from now we consider non-empty output. Two ideas facilitate our proof: a *simplification* of the representation of descriptors for the cases under consideration, and a generalization to *meta-descriptors*, that can be used to represent possibly infinite sets of descriptors.

Simplification of descriptors: Since the output is a set of flat sets, each descriptor in D_Q describes a flat set w.r.t. some input. That is, the $out(d)$ component of each descriptor is a flat set. $map(d)$ maps the members of this flat set *onto* the leaves of $in(d)$, the tree representing the input. Moreover, by the semantics of sets, no two members of $out(d)$ could be mapped to the same node of $in(d)$, that is, $map(d)$ is one-to-one. Clearly, given $in(d)$, it is possible to re-construct $out(d)$ and $map(d)$, hence they are superfluous, and are omitted from now.

Assume below that T is a flat non-empty set, S is a set or a set of sets, $T \in Q(S)$, and d ($\equiv in(d)$) describes T w.r.t. S.

First, consider the case that S is a set. For a non-empty T, d is a tree consisting of a root labeled with S's canonical form and a pair (z, p) (where p is $<$ or $=$) and with children that are leaves, all labeled with z. Thus, the only factors that distinguish such a descriptor from others are p and the number k of leaves. Each descriptor can therefore be represented by (p, k).

If S is a set of sets, and T is non-empty, then d is a tree whose root is labeled with S's canonical form c and a pair $(\{z\}, p)$, and with children whose structure is that of a descriptor of a flat set, as considered above. Here also, the component $\{z\}$ in the root's label is redundant. Since the order of the children of the root is immaterial, and repetitions may occur, a descriptor can be represented as $\langle c; p; b \rangle$, where b is a bag of descriptors, each of the previous kind, namely pairs (p', k).

Example 6.3 If $S = \{a, b\}$, and $T = \{a\}$, then the representation of the descriptor of T w.r.t S is $(<, 1)$, meaning that T has one element from S, and S contains additional elements. If $S = \{\{a, b\}, \{c, d, e\}, \{\}\}$, and $T = \{a, b, c\}$, then the representation of the descriptor of T w.r.t S is $\langle c, =, \{\!\{(=, 2), (<, 1)\}\!\} \rangle$, where $c = cf(S) = \{\{z\}, \{\}\}$. Here, the first $=$ indicates that all non empty member sets of S participate in T. The pair $(=, 2)$ in the bag indicates that T contains all elements of a member set of S, that has two elements. The other pair indicates that T contains one element of another set in S, that contains additional elements. □

Dominance for simplified descriptors: Aside from the $<$-to-$=$ Property, there are other dominance properties that we use in our proofs. We now present a couple, as they apply to simplified descriptors.

downwards closedness: *A descriptor dominates all descriptors obtained by replacing (p, k) by (p, k'), $1 \leq k' \leq k$.*
sum property: *A descriptor of the form $\langle c; p; b \rangle$ dominates all descriptors $\langle c; p; b' \rangle$, where b' is obtained from b by replacing elements $(<, k_1)$ and $(<, k_2)$ by $(<, k_1 + k_2)$.*

Note that downwards closedness applies to simplified descriptors of depths 1 and 2, whereas the sum property only applies to those of depth 2. The sum property is a special case of the Merge Lemma [Ta-97].

Generalizing descriptors to meta-descriptors: The observation here is that sets of descriptors describing a query often contain repetitions of similar components, which can be described compactly. By downwards closedness, (p, k) dominates (p, k') if $1 \leq k' < k$. Thus, we take (p, k) to represent the set $\{(p, k') \mid k' \leq k\}$; similarly, we take (p, ∞) to represent $\{(p, k) \mid 1 \leq k\}$. Finally, we take $(p, u)^+$ to represent an arbitrary (but positive) number of occurrences of (p, u) in a bag.

Definition 6.4 *A meta-descriptor of depth 1 is a pair (p, u) where p is $=$ or $<$, and u is either some finite number k, or ∞.*
A meta-descriptor of depth 2 is $\langle c; p; b \rangle$ where c is a canonical form, p is either $<$ or $=$, and b is a bag whose elements are of the form l or l^+, where l is a meta-descriptor of depth 1.

Note that, in particular, each regular descriptor is also a meta-descriptor. We use $d, d_1, \ldots$ for descriptors, and $\hat{d}, \hat{d}_1, \ldots$ for meta-descriptors. Capital letters are used for sets.

Definition 6.5 *We say that a meta-descriptor $\hat{d}$ denotes the set of descriptors that can be obtained from it by performing the following, in any order: (1) Replace each l^+ by a positive number of occurrences of l. (2) Replace each ∞ by some positive finite number. We write denotes$(\hat{d})$ for the set of descriptors denoted by $\hat{d}$. For a set of meta-descriptors $\hat{D}$, denotes$(\hat{D}) = \bigcup\{denotes(\hat{d}) \mid \hat{d} \in \hat{D}\}$.*

Note that the replacement order can be, w.l.o.g. from the top down. As an example of the above definition, $denotes((<, \infty)) = \{(<, 1), (<, 2), (<, 3), \ldots\}$, an infinite set of descriptors.

Definition 6.6 *The **closure** of a set of meta-descriptors $\hat{D}$ is closure$(\hat{D}) = $ closure$(denotes(\hat{D}))$. We say $\hat{D}$ **describes** a query Q if closure$(\hat{D}) \subseteq D_Q$, and that it **defines** a query Q if closure$(\hat{D}) = D_Q$. If $\hat{D} = \{\hat{d}\}$, we also say that $\hat{d}$ describes, respectively defines, Q.*

Claim 6.7 *closure$(\bigcup \hat{D}_i) = \bigcup$ closure$(\hat{D}_i)$, hence closure$(\hat{D}) = \bigcup_{\hat{d} \in \hat{D}}$ closure$(\hat{d})$. It follows that if $\hat{D}_1$ defines Q_1 and $\hat{D}_2$ defines Q_2, then $\hat{D}_1 \cup \hat{D}_2$ defines $Q_1 \cup Q_2$.*

In the proofs below, we consider a query Q, and try to show that D_Q can be described by a finite union of (not necessarily disjoint) sets of descriptors, say $D_1, \ldots, D_n$, and each of these can be associated with a meta-descriptor. Specifically, for each D_i, we show the existence of some meta descriptor $\hat{d}_i$ such that $denotes(\hat{d}_i) \subseteq D_i$ and $D_i \subseteq$ closure$(\hat{d}_i)$. It follows that $denotes(\bigcup\{\hat{d}_i\}) \subseteq D_Q$ and closure$(D_Q) \subseteq$ closure$(\bigcup\{\hat{d}_i\})$. But for any fully generic query Q, D_Q is closed, hence it contains the closure of any subset. Thus, closure$(D_Q) =$ closure$(\bigcup\{\hat{d}_i\})$. Clearly if we find queries $Q_1, \ldots, Q_n$ for the meta-descriptors, we are done. Thus, to prove theorem 6.1 it suffices to show:

Claim 6.8 *Let Q be a fully generic query whose input is a set (set of sets) and output is sets of sets. Then there exist (a) a finite set of meta descriptors $\{\hat{d}_1, \ldots, \hat{d}_k\}$ which defines Q, and (b) fully generic queries $Q_1, \ldots, Q_k$ expressible in $\mathcal{L}$ such that $\hat{d}_i$ defines Q_i.*

It is important to note that many meta-descriptors do not **define** any (fully generic) query, even if they do describe certain queries. For example, this is the case for all descriptors of the form $(=, k)$, k finite (proof omitted). In our search for a finite set of meta-descriptors, since we give each a corresponding query, we must avoid those that do not define queries.

The rest of this section is dedicated to the proof of the above claim. We consider the cases for the two input types separately. In each case the proof has two parts: (a) finding the finite set of descriptors, and (b) presenting a query for each of the descriptors found in step (a). We sketch the (a) parts; the (b) parts are described in appendix B.1, B.2, respectively.

6.2 Set inputs

(a): Finding a finite set of meta-descriptors.

We express D_Q (without empty descriptors) as a union $C_< \cup C_=$, where $C_<$ contains all descriptors of the form $(<,k)$ in D_Q, and $C_=$ contains those of the form $(=,k)$. If $\{k \mid (<,k) \in C_<\}$ is bounded by say k_0, let $\hat{d}_< = (<,k_0)$. Otherwise, let $\hat{d}_< = (<,\infty)$. In either case, $denotes(\hat{d}_<) = C_< \subseteq closure(\hat{d}_<)$, where the latter containment follows from our downwards closedness results. The same analysis applies to $C_=$, giving two possibilities for a $\hat{d}_=$ for it. Now $(=,k)$ does not define a query, for any finite k. However, we show that if $\hat{d}_=$ is $(=,k)$, then $C_= \subseteq closure(C_<)$, hence we do not need to find a meta-descriptor for $C_=$, since we have one for $C_<$. In summary, we need to find queries for at most 2 meta-descriptors.

6.3 Set of sets inputs

(a): Finding a finite set of meta-descriptors.

A descriptor now is $\langle c; p; b \rangle$. The proof here is considerably more difficult than that above, although the main ideas used there still apply. Intuitively, we confront two problems that didn't previously exist. Firstly, the size of descriptors (i.e. the size of bags b) can be arbitrarily large. We need to show that a finite number of meta-descriptors suffice to capture this infinite collection. Secondly, even if the size of bags is bounded, there could still conceivably be infinitely many "independent" descriptors, where no one dominates the other.

Recall that the canonical form c is fixed. Now, we also fix p, and until further notice, c, p are fixed, so we identify a descriptor with its bag b. The descriptors can be further divided into those in which b contains only inequalities, called *pure inequality* descriptors, denoted $D_<$, and those that have at least one equality denoted $D_=$. For each of these, we ask whether the number of inequalities is bounded or not, giving rise to four cases to consider. Let us call the number of inequalities in a bag its *inequality size*.

(1) Pure inequalities, unbounded inequality size: Using the sum property, we show that if the inequality size of bags in $D_<$ is unbounded, then the *values* in the pairs in them are also unbounded. That is, $D_<$ contains **all** bags with any positive inequality size and any values in the pairs. Since inequalities dominate equalities, by the $<$-to-$=$ Property, we get that $D_<$ contains **all** possible bags, with both equalities and inequalities. Also, it is denoted by the meta-descriptor $\{\!\{(<,\infty)^+\}\!\}$.

(2) With equalities, unbounded inequality size: By a similar analysis we obtain that if the inequality size in the subclass of $D_=$ of bags with *precisely one* equality is unbounded, then it contains **all** bags with one equality and any positive inequality size, with any values in the pairs, and therefore the meta-descriptor $\{\!\{(=,\infty),(<,\infty)^+\}\!\}$ denotes it. Furthermore, using the $<$-to-$=$ Property, its closure contains all of $D_=$. Finally (using the sum property and more) we show that if the inequality size of $D_=$ is unbounded, then it is unbounded for this subclass as well. Thus, in summary, for this case it suffices to find a query for the single meta-descriptor above.

(3) Pure inequalities, bounded inequality size: If the inequality size of $D_<$ is bounded, treat each size separately. For a size m, sort the elements of each bag in non-decreasing order. Now, if the numbers in the first positions of all bags are unbounded, then so are the numbers in all remaining positions. The meta-descriptor is $(<, \infty)^m$, where l^m is shorthand for l repeated m times. If the numbers in the first position are bounded by k, we have one pair for the meta-descriptor: $(<, k)$. Now split the bags into a different class for each value in $[1..k]$, and continue inductively to the remaining positions. This gives us a finite number of meta-descriptors, each of the form $\{(<, k_1), \ldots, (<, k_j), (<, \infty)^l\}$, where $m = j + l$.

(4) With equalities, bounded inequality size: The last case, by far the most complex, is when the inequality size of $D_=$ is bounded. Note that the number of *equalities* may still be unbounded. The proof can be summarized as follows (for the full proof see [Ta-97]): Divide $D_=$ into subclasses $D_=^i$ according to the number i of equalities. We show that for each i some descriptors are contained in $closure(D_=^{i-1})$, hence can be removed. The remaining subclass, say $\bar{D}_=^i$, has the property that it is the bag cross product of a set of inequality bags W_i and a set of equality bags of size i. The latter turns out to be the set of **all** equality bags of size i, and can therefore be represented by $(=, \infty)^i$. It remains to find meta-descriptors for W_i. Since W_i has bounded inequality size, the results above imply that there is a finite set of meta-descriptors $\hat{D}_i$ for it. However, this does not suffice, since we have an infinite sequence $W_1, W_2, W_3, \ldots$ corresponding to $\bar{D}_=^1, \bar{D}_=^2, \bar{D}_=^3, \ldots$. We first point out that $W_1 \supseteq W_2 \supseteq \ldots$. The descriptors in these sets are all of bounded size. We then define a relation $\succeq$ on the corresponding finite sets of meta-descriptors, and we show that $\hat{D}_1 \succeq \hat{D}_2 \succeq \ldots$. The crux of the proof is to show that $\succeq$ is well-founded, using König's Lemma.[9] Hence in the sequence there is only a finite number of *distinct* sets, and therefore the same holds for the sequence of the W_i's. It follows that we can construct a finite set of meta-descriptors for the class $D_=$ as a whole. The meta descriptors obtained take the form $\{(<, k_1), \ldots, (<, k_j), (<, \infty)^l, (=, \infty)^m\}$, where l is finite, and m can be finite or $+$. (The $+$ is needed in the representation of the tail of the sequence, where the size of the equality bags for the smallest W_i is between i and ∞.)

This covers the analysis for all cases for fixed c, p. Note that unlike the case for flat input, even though we do guarantee a finite number of meta-descriptors for every query of a given type, there is no bound on their number. Similarly to the case for flat input, if p is $=$, some of the meta-descriptors obtained do not define queries, and as we did there, we show that the corresponding classes of descriptors are included in the closures of classes where p is $<$ and therefore are already covered.

---

[9] A finitely branching tree with no infinite branch is finite.

7 Conclusions

We have shown that when queries are invariant under all (many-to-many) mappings, there is a strong relationship between their inputs and outputs, that can be captured by patterns. The set of patterns of a query enjoys many elegant structural closure properties, some of which we presented (one in a simplified form). We are working towards a full understanding of the structure of the sets of patterns of fully generic queries. For the special cases treated here, the patterns can be represented very succinctly; our success in proving our conjecture for these cases is partially due to this representation.

For the types we considered, all fully generic queries at these types are computable. The same will hold for all types if our conjecture turns out to hold for them, in contrast to the case for all other known cases of genericity.

Finally, we note that for the case of set of sets inputs, we seem to need the operation *one-each* (see Appendix B.2), which to our knowledge has not been considered in the literature on complex object languages so far. Whether this is the only operation needed to obtain a complete language for all types still remains open. Also, while we have not been able to express it using the other operations of $\mathcal{L}$, we have no proof of its independence.

References

[AHV95]   S. Abiteboul, R. Hull, and V. Vianu. *Foundations of Databases*. Addison-Wesley, 1995.

[AU79]   A. V. Aho and J. D. Ullman. Universality of data retrieval languages. In *ACM Symposium on Principles of Programming Languages*, pages 110 – 120, 1979.

[BBW92]   V. Breazu-Tannen, P. Buneman, and L. Wong. Naturally embedded query languages. In Biskup and Hull, editors, *International Conference on Database Theory*, Berlin, Germany, October 1992. Springer-Verlag. LNCS 646.

[BMT96]   C. Beeri, T. Milo, and P. Ta-Shma. On genericity and parametricity. In *ACM Symposium on Principles of Database Systems*, Montreal, Canada, June 1996.

[BNTW95] P. Buneman, S. Naqvi, V. Tannen, and L. Wong. Principles of programming with complex objects and collection types. *Theoretical Computer Science*, 149(1):3–48, 1995.

[CH80]   A. Chandra and D. Harel. Computable queries for relational data bases. *Journal of Computer and System Sciences*, 21(2):156 – 178, 1980.

[HY84]   R. Hull and C. K. Yap. The format model : a theory of database organization. *Journal of the ACM*, 31(3):518 – 537, 1984.

[Ley]   Michael Ley. Databases and logic programming, a bibliography server:. http://www.informatik.uni-trier.de/~ley/db/index.html.

[LW93]   Leonid Libkin and Limsoon Wong. Semantic representations and query languages for or-sets. In *ACM Symposium on Principles of Database Systems*, Washington DC, 1993.

[PSV96] C.H. Papadimitriou, D. Suciu, and V. Vianu. Topological queries in spatial databases. In *ACM Symposium on Principles of Database Systems*, pages 81 – 92, Montreal, Canada, 1996.

[PVV94] J. Paredaens, J. Van den Bussche, and D. Van Gucht. Towards a theory of spatial database queries. In *ACM Symposium on Principles of Database Systems*, pages 279 – 288, 1994.

[Ta-97] Paula Ta-Shma. *Genericity in Database Query Languages*. PhD thesis, The Hebrew University of Jerusalem, 1997.

[Won93] Limsoon Wong. Normal forms and conservative properties for query languages over collection types. In *ACM Symposium on Principles of Database Systems*, pages 26 – 36, Washington, DC, 1993.

A Construction of queries from nested input to flat output

Let $D_Q = \{d_1,...,d_k\}$ be the set of descriptors for Q, where the descriptor $d_i = \langle in(d_i), out(d_i), map(d_i)\rangle$. We construct a query q_i (of the same type as Q) for each d_i, s.t. $D_Q = D_{q_1} \cup ... \cup D_{q_k}$, and therefore, $Q = q_1 \cup ... \cup q_k$.

Given d_i, $q_i = q_i^{out} \circ q_i^{in}$, where q_i^{in}, q_i^{out} deal with $in(d)$ and $out(d)$ respectively. q_i^{in} is constructed inductively on the structure of $in(d)$ as follows, and returns tuples whose arity is the number of leaves of $in(d)$. Let q^n be the query associated with node n.

Node type	Children	Query
Leaf m		$q^m(x) = single([x])$
Tuple m	$m_1,...,m_j$ (in that order)	$q^m(x) = q^{m_1}(\$1(x)) \times ... \times q^{m_j}(\$j(x))$
Set m	$m_1,...,m_j$ of canonical form $c_1,...,c_j$	$q^m(x) =$ $flatten(map(cond(c_1,q^{m_1},\{\}))(x)) \times ...$ $\times flatten(map(cond(c_j,q^{m_j},\{\}))(x))$

$cond(c,q,\{\})$ here is a shorthand for $\lambda y.cond(cf(y) = c, q(y), \{\})$. [10]

q_i^{out} has the form $map(f_i)$, where f_i is a function on tuples which possibly changes column order and duplicates certain columns (also expressible in $\mathcal{L}$), according to the relationship between $in(d), out(d)$, as expressed in $map(d)$.

Example A.1 Suppose d_i describes the tuple $t = [a,b,a]$ w.r.t. a set $S = \{\{\{a\},\{b\}\},\{\{c\}\},\{\{\},\{d\}\}\}$. The *in* part of d_i is shown in figure 2. Let c_1,c_2,c_3 denote the canonical forms $\{\{\{z\}\},\{\{\},\{z\}\}\}$, $\{\{z\}\}$, $\{z\}$ resp. Using the above construction,

$q_i^{in} = flatten(map(cond(c_1, q_{temp} \times q_{temp}, \{\})))$,
where

$q_{temp} = flatten(map(cond(c_2, flatten(map(cond(c_3, single([x]), \{\}))), \{\})))$.
For example $q_i^{in}(S) = \{[a,b],[b,a],[b,b],[a,a],[c,c]\}$.

The *out* part of d_i is a 3-tuple where first and third columns point to the left branch, and second column points to the right branch. Therefore, we need

---
[10] $\mathcal{L}$ is variable free, although we use variables for readability.

258

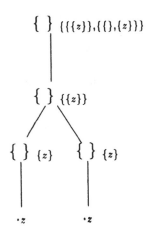

Fig. 2. The *in* component of descriptor d_i

to duplicate the first column of the above query into the third column : $q_i^{out} = map([\$1, \$2, \$1])(x)$.

For example $q_i(S) = q_i^{out}(q_i^{in}(S)) = \{[a, b, a], [b, a, b], [b, b, b], [a, a, a], [c, c, c]\}$.

Note that q_i produces the desired tuple $[a, b, a]$ but additional ones as well. We show in the full paper that the descriptors for all other tuples produced by a query q_i are dominated by d_i, thus belong to D_Q anyhow. So no new descriptors are added in the construction. □

B   Queries for meta-descriptors

For each meta-descriptor $\hat{d}_i$ which arose in section 6, we now present a query Q_i such that $closure(\hat{d}_i) = D_{Q_i}$. For each case (output being a set or set of sets) the resulting query has the form $Q_1 \cup \ldots \cup Q_k$.

B.1   Set inputs

The appropriate queries appear in the following table.

Meta-descriptor	Query
$(<, \infty)$	*powerset* $\setminus \emptyset$
$(<, k)$	$\mathcal{P}^k \setminus \emptyset$
$(=, \infty)$	*single*
c	if $cf(x) = c$ then $\{\{\}\}$ else $\{\}$

$\mathcal{P}^k(S)$ returns all subsets of S of size at most k.

Claim B.1 *Each of the above queries can be expressed in $\mathcal{L}$, without one-each.*

B.2 Set of set inputs

First, we show how to compose queries for more complicated meta-descriptors from those for simpler ones. Given queries defined by two meta-descriptors $\langle c; <; b_1 \rangle$ and $\langle c; <; b_2 \rangle$, we compose the query defined by $\langle c; <; b_1 \uplus b_2 \rangle$, where $\uplus$ denotes bag union.

Claim B.2 *If* $closure(\langle c; <; b_1 \rangle) = D_{Q_1}$ *and* $closure(\langle c; <; b_2 \rangle) = D_{Q_2}$ *then* $closure(\langle c; <; b_1 \uplus b_2 \rangle) = D_Q$, *where* $Q(S) = map(\$1 \cup \$2)(Q_1(S) \times Q_2(S))$.

Therefore, meta-descriptors with root $<$ of finite size can be constructed from meta-descriptors of size 1, and we only present these. For root $<$ we also present the possible meta-descriptors of infinite size (i.e. with $+$). In the second part of the table, we present queries for all meta-descriptors which arise for root $=$.

In the queries below, for readability, we allow queries to use variables, even though formally $\mathcal{L}$ is variable free. It should be clear that this is only syntactic sugar. We assume variable S denotes the query input.

Meta-descriptor	Query		
$\langle c \rangle$	if cf(S) = c then $\{\{\}\}$		else $\emptyset$
$\langle c, <, \{\!\{(<, k)\}\!\} \rangle$	"	$flatten \circ map(\mathcal{P}^k \setminus \emptyset)$	"
$\langle c, <, \{\!\{(<, \infty)\}\!\} \rangle$	"	$flatten \circ map(powerset \setminus \emptyset)$	"
$\langle c, <, \{\!\{(=, \infty)\}\!\} \rangle$	"	id	"
$\langle c, <, \{\!\{(<, \infty)^+\}\!\} \rangle$	"	$(powerset \setminus \emptyset) \circ flatten$	"
$\langle c, <, \{\!\{(=, \infty)^+\}\!\} \rangle$	"	$map(flatten) \circ (powerset \setminus \emptyset)$	"
$\langle c, =, \{\!\{(<, \infty)^+\}\!\} \rangle$	"	$one\text{-}each$	"
$\langle c, =, \{\!\{(=, \infty)^+\}\!\} \rangle$	"	$single \circ flatten$	"
$\langle c, =, \{\!\{(=, \infty), (<, \infty)^+\}\!\} \rangle$	"	$map(\$1 \cup \$2)(one\text{-}each(S) \times S)$	"

Claim B.3 *Each of the above queries can be expressed in* $\mathcal{L}$.

Unlike for the flat input case, *one-each* is necessary here.

On the Power of Aggregation in Relational Query Languages*

Leonid Libkin[1]   Limsoon Wong[2]

[1] Bell Laboratories/Lucent Technologies, 600 Mountain Avenue, Murray Hill, NJ
07974, USA, Email: libkin@research.bell-labs.com
[2] BioInformatics Center & Institute of Systems Science, Singapore 119597, Email:
limsoon@iss.nus.sg

1 Summary

It is a folk result that relational algebra or calculus extended with aggregate
functions cannot compute the transitive closure. However, proving folk results
is sometimes a nontrivial task. In this paper, we tell the story of the work
on expressive power of relational languages with aggregate functions. We also
prove by far the most powerful result that describes the expressiveness of such
languages. There are four main features of our result that distinguish it from
previous ones:

1. It does not rely on any unproven assumptions, such as separation of complexity classes.
2. It establishes a general property of queries definable with the help of aggregate functions. This property can easily be applied to prove many expressiveness bounds.
3. The class of aggregate functions is much larger than any previously considered.
4. The proof is "non-syntactic." That is, it does not depend on a specific syntax
   chosen for the language with aggregates.

Furthermore, our result gives a very general condition that implies inexpressibility of recursive queries such as the transitive closure in an extension
of relational calculus with grouping and aggregation. This extension allows us
to use rational arithmetic and operations such as summation and product over
a column. So, aggregation that exceeds what is allowed by most commercial
systems is still not powerful enough to encode recursion mechanisms.

2 Expressive power of aggregation – brief history

It is a well-known result in database theory that the transitive closure query is
not expressible in relational algebra and calculus [1]. This was proved by Aho

---

* Part of this work was done while the first author was visiting Institute of Systems
  Science.

and Ullman in [2]. A much simpler proof, in the presence of an order relation, was given by Gurevich [13]. Without the order relation, this result follows from many results on the expressive power of first-order logic [7, 9, 10, 11, 17].

Traditional query languages like SQL extend relational algebra by grouping and aggregation. It was widely believed that such plain SQL cannot express recursive queries like the transitive closure query. However, proving this "folk result" turned out to be quite difficult.

Consens and Mendelzon [5] were the first to provide formal evidence for the "folk theorem." In their ICDT'90 paper, they showed that DLOGSPACE $\neq$ NLOGSPACE would imply that the transitive closure is not definable in an aggregate extension of relational algebra. This follows from DLOGSPACE data complexity of their language, and NLOGSPACE-completeness of the transitive closure. Notably, their result cannot say anything about nontrivial recursive queries complete for DLOGSPACE, such as *deterministic* transitive closure [14]. This perhaps can be remedied by reducing the data complexity to, say, NC^1, and making a different assumption like $NC^1 \neq$ DLOGSPACE. Nevertheless, their result does demonstrate that the assumed expressivity bounds on languages with aggregates are likely to be true.

It remained open though whether expressivity bounds for languages with aggregates can be proved without assuming separation of complexity classes, until 1994. In that year, we proved that the transitive closure is not definable in a language with aggregates [17], not assuming any unproven hypotheses from complexity theory. Since the two main distinguishing features of plain SQL are grouping and aggregation, we defined our theoretical reconstruction of SQL as the nested relational algebra [4] augmented with rational arithmetic and a general summation operator. This language can model the GROUPBY construct of SQL and can define familiar aggregate functions such as TOTAL, AVG, STDEV.

The proof of [17] established the folk result above. However, it was far from ideal. It relied on proving a complicated normal form for queries that can only be achieved on a very special class of inputs. From that normal form, we derived results about the behavior of plain SQL on these inputs. That turned out to be enough to confirm the main conjecture. The proof of the normal form result relied on rewrite systems for nested relational languages developed earlier [18, 19, 22]. In particular, it made the proof very "syntactic." A change in syntax would require a new proof, although it is intuitively clear that the choice of a syntax for the language should be irrelevant.

Another problem with the proof of [17] is that, instead of establishing a *general principle* that implies expressiveness bounds, it only implied the desired result for a small number of queries. There was an attempt in [17] to find such a general principle. We introduced the notion of the *bounded degree property*, or BDP. Loosely speaking, a query has the BDP if its outputs are "simple" as long as their inputs are. We showed that (nested) relational algebra queries have the BDP. We also showed that for most recursive queries it is very easy to show how the BDP is violated, thus giving expressiveness bounds. We conjectured that plain SQL has the BDP, but we did not prove it in [17].

We returned to the problem a few years later and proved, via a similar normal form argument, that plain SQL indeed has the BDP [6]. However, the normal form result is more complicated than that of [17] and the proof is also dependent on a particular syntax. In the same paper [6], we introduced a notion more general than the BDP. We defined *local* queries as those whose result on a given tuple can be computed by looking at a neighborhood of this tuple of a predetermined size. This notion is inspired by the classical locality theorem for first-order logic proved by Gaifman [11]. We showed in [6] that locality implies the BDP. However, continuing the pattern of setting our goals too high, we failed to prove locality of plain SQL queries, although we succeeded in proving the BDP for plain SQL queries.

The main problem in proving those results was the lack of techniques and results in finite-model theory for proving "local properties," with the exception of Gaifman's theorem and a result by Fagin, Stockmeyer, and Vardi [10] that only applied to first-order logic. This changed when Nurmonen [21] showed that an analog of the result of [10] holds for first-order logic with counting quantifiers, $\mathcal{FO} + COUNT$ (as defined in [3, 8, 15]). Using Nurmonen's result, the first author proved that $\mathcal{FO} + COUNT$ is local [16] and has the BDP. As an application of these results, it was shown that a large class of queries defined in a sublanguage of plain SQL is local and has the BDP. This sublanguage was obtained by restricting the rational arithmetic of plain SQL to arithmetic of natural numbers: for example, aggregates TOTAL and COUNT were definable, but aggregates AVG, STDEV, and the likes were not.

The technique of [16] was the following: it was shown that for each query Q from a given class, another query Q' can be found such that it shares most nice properties with Q (e.g., locality and the BDP) and can be expressed in $\mathcal{FO}+COUNT$. This suffices to conclude that many queries, such as the transitive closure, are not expressible.

This technique eliminates the complicated syntactic argument entirely. The differences in syntax do affect the encoding, but it is really the semantics of queries that makes the encoding possible.

In this paper, we show that the idea behind the proof in [16] can be extended to capture a much larger class of queries with aggregation. That is, we allow rational arithmetic and products over columns. Consequently, aggregates such as AVG, STDEV and many others are definable. This does complicate the proof quite a bit, but it is still much more intuitive than the syntactic one, because the overall structure of the proof remains quite straightforward, and all tedious details requiring a lot of work happen in the process of the encoding of queries in first-order logic with counting.

3 Defining the language

The goal of this section is to define a theoretical language that has the power of a relational language extended with aggregates. Following our previous approaches to dealing with aggregation, we define this language to be an extension of *nested*

$$\overline{+,*,-,\div,exp,root : \mathbb{Q} \times \mathbb{Q} \to \mathbb{Q}} \qquad \overline{K0, K1 : t \to \mathbb{Q}}$$

$$\overline{=: t \times t \to \{\mathbb{Q}\}} \qquad \overline{<: \mathbb{Q} \times \mathbb{Q} \to \{\mathbb{Q}\}}$$

$$\overline{id : t \to t} \qquad \frac{f : u \to t \quad g : s \to u}{f \circ g : s \to t}$$

$$\frac{f_i : t \to t_i, i = 1, \ldots, n}{(f_1, \ldots, f_n) : t \to t_1 \times \ldots \times t_n} \qquad \frac{i \leq n}{\pi_{i,n} : t_1 \times \ldots \times t_n \to t_i}$$

$$\overline{K\{\} : t \to \{s\}} \qquad \overline{empty : \{t\} \to \{\mathbb{Q}\}} \qquad \overline{\eta : t \to \{t\}}$$

$$\overline{\cup : \{t\} \times \{t\} \to \{t\}} \qquad \frac{f : s \to \{t\}}{ext[f] : \{s\} \to \{t\}}$$

$$\frac{i \leq n}{\rho_{i,n} : t_1 \times \ldots \times \{t_i\} \times \ldots \times t_n \to \{t_1 \times \ldots \times t_n\}}$$

$$\frac{f : s \to \mathbb{Q}}{\sum[f] : \{s\} \to \mathbb{Q}} \qquad \frac{f : s \to \mathbb{Q}}{\prod[f] : \{s\} \to \mathbb{Q}}$$

Fig. 1. Expressions of AGGR

relational algebra with arithmetic operators. Nesting accounts for grouping, as in GROUPBY, and arithmetic gives us the computing power for aggregates themselves. The difference between this paper and previous ones is that the arithmetic is *a lot* richer!

We define the language below. Assume the existence of two base types: type $\mathbb{Q}$ of rational numbers, and an unspecified base type **b** whose domain is a countably infinite set D. Types of the language are given by the grammar

$$t \quad ::= \quad \mathbf{b} \mid \mathbb{Q} \mid t \times \ldots \times t \mid \{t\}.$$

The semantics of type $t_1 \times \ldots \times t_n$ are n-tuples such that the ith component is of type t_i. Objects of type $\{t\}$ are finite sets of objects of type t. Expressions of AGGR are defined in Figure 1.

The semantics follows that of [4, 12, 17]. We use $+$, $-$, $*$, $\div$ to denote the standard operations on rational numbers. The constant functions $K0$ and $K1$

return 0 and 1 respectively, and $=$ is the equality test, where true is represented by $\{0\}$ and false by $\{\}$. With the same representation of true and false, $<$ defines the usual order on rational numbers. We use $exp(x, y)$ for x^y which is only defined if y is a natural number; and $root(x, y)$ for $\sqrt[x]{y}$ which again is undefined if x is not a natural number. These may seem a bit strange, but it does not hurt to *add* primitives if we want to prove *in*expressibility results.

The semantics for identity id, composition $\circ$, tupling, and projections π_i is standard. The result of $K\{\}$ is always the empty set; the function *empty* tests if a set is empty; η forms singleton sets; $\cup$ is set union; and ρ_i is the "pair-with" operation. Given a function $f : s \to \{t\}$ and a set X of type $\{s\}$, $ext[f](X)$ evaluates to $\bigcup_{x \in X} f(x)$.

For the summation and product operators and $f : s \to \mathbb{Q}$, $\sum[f](X)$ is $\sum_{x \in X} f(x)$ and $\prod[f](X)$ is $\prod_{x \in X} f(x)$. For example, $\sum[K1]$ is the cardinality function, and $\prod[K1 + K1](X)$ returns $2^{card(X)}$. (Strictly speaking, $K1 + K1$ should be written as $+(K1, K1)$ but we shall often simplify notation when it does not lead to confusion.)

It is known that, without the type of natural numbers, this language is equivalent to the standard nested relational algebra [4]. Furthermore, when input and output are usual flat relations (sets of atomic tuples), it expresses precisely the first-order queries. Summation, product, and arithmetic give it the power of aggregate functions. For example, the aggregate TOTAL is given by $\sum[id]$ and AVG is given by $\sum[id] \div \sum[K1]$.

Abbreviate $\mathbf{b} \times \ldots \times \mathbf{b}$, m times, as $\mathbf{b}^m$. A standard relational database is represented as an object of type $\{\mathbf{b}^{n_1}\} \times \ldots \times \{\mathbf{b}^{n_k}\}$. In other words, a relational database that consists of k relations, the ith one having arity n_i, is represented as an object of the above type. Types of this form are called *relational*. A query in AGGR is *relational* if both its input and output types are.

For example, a query that takes a graph whose nodes are in D and returns another graph is of type $\{\mathbf{b} \times \mathbf{b}\} \to \{\mathbf{b} \times \mathbf{b}\}$; that is, it is a relational query. If the transitive closure were definable in AGGR, it would have the type above. Thus, we concentrate on expressiveness of relational queries in AGGR. Note that for a relational query, types of its intermediate results need not be relational.

4 Local queries and the main theorem

Structures and neighborhoods A relational signature σ is a set of relation symbols $\{R_1, \ldots, R_l\}$, with an associated arity function. In what follows, $p_i(> 0)$ denotes the arity of R_i. We write σ_n for σ extended with n new constant symbols.

A σ-structure is $\mathcal{A} = \langle A, \overline{R}_1, \ldots, \overline{R}_l \rangle$, where A is a finite set, and $\overline{R}_i \subseteq A^{p_i}$ interprets R_i. The class of finite σ-structures is denoted by STRUCT$[\sigma]$. We adopt the convention that the carrier of a structure $\mathcal{A}$ is always denoted by A.

Given a structure $\mathcal{A}$, its *Gaifman graph* [7, 10, 11] $\mathcal{G}(\mathcal{A})$ is defined as $\langle A, E \rangle$ where (a, b) is in E if there is a tuple $\vec{t} \in \overline{R}_i$ for some i such that both a and b are in $\vec{t}$. The distance $d(a, b)$ is defined as the length of the shortest path from a to b in $\mathcal{G}(\mathcal{A})$; we assume $d(a, a) = 0$. Given $a \in A$, its r-*sphere* $S_r^{\mathcal{A}}(a)$ is $\{b \in A \mid d(a, b) \leq r\}$. For a tuple $\vec{t}$, define $S_r^{\mathcal{A}}(\vec{t})$ as $\bigcup_{a \in \vec{t}} S_r^{\mathcal{A}}(a)$.

Given a tuple $\vec{t} = (t_1, \ldots, t_n)$, its r-*neighborhood* $N_r^{\mathcal{A}}(\vec{t})$ is defined as a σ_n structure

$$\langle S_r^{\mathcal{A}}(\vec{t}), \overline{R}_1 \cap S_r^{\mathcal{A}}(\vec{t})^{p_1}, \ldots, \overline{R}_k \cap S_r^{\mathcal{A}}(\vec{t})^{p_k}, t_1, \ldots, t_n \rangle.$$

That is, the carrier of $N_r^{\mathcal{A}}(\vec{t})$ is $S_r^{\mathcal{A}}(\vec{t})$, the interpretation of the σ-relations is obtained by restricting them from $\mathcal{A}$ to the carrier, and the n extra constants are the elements of $\vec{t}$. If the structure $\mathcal{A}$ is understood, we shall write $S_r(\vec{t})$ and $N_r(\vec{t})$.

Given a structure $\mathcal{A}$ and two m-ary vectors $\vec{a}$ and $\vec{b}$ of elements of A, we write $\vec{a} \approx_r^{\mathcal{A}} \vec{b}$ if $N_r^{\mathcal{A}}(\vec{a})$ and $N_r^{\mathcal{A}}(\vec{b})$ are isomorphic. That is, $\vec{a}$ and $\vec{b}$ are indistinguishable in $\mathcal{A}$ if we can only "see" up to radius r.

Local queries Assume that we have a formula in some logic, which comes with the associated notion of $\models$ between structures and formulae. Following [6, 16], we say that a formula $\psi(x_1, \ldots, x_m)$, in the logical language whose symbols are in σ, is *local* if there exists $r > 0$ such that for every $\mathcal{A} \in \mathrm{STRUCT}[\sigma]$ and for every two m-ary vectors $\vec{a}$, $\vec{b}$ of elements of A, $\vec{a} \approx_r^{\mathcal{A}} \vec{b}$ implies $\mathcal{A} \models \psi(\vec{a})$ if and only if $\mathcal{A} \models \psi(\vec{b})$. The minimum r for which this is true is called the *locality rank* of ψ.

It can be readily verified that transitive closure and deterministic transitive closure are *not* local [6, 16]. There are bounds on the expressive power of local queries that can be easily verified [6, 16]. Thus, it is rather simple to check if a query is local or not. It is particularly easy to verify that locality fails for most familiar recursive queries.

As noted above, we can represent a σ-structure as an object of type $\{b^{p_1}\} \times \cdots \times \{b^{p_l}\}$, where σ has l relations of arities $p_1, \ldots, p_l$. We denote this type by σ_b.

We assume without loss of generality that the output of a relational query is one set of m-tuples. Then such a query is a mapping from σ-structures over D into finite subsets of D^m. It can be easily seen that for any such query Q definable in AGGR, an element $d \in D$ occurs in a tuple in $Q(\mathcal{A})$ for some structure $\mathcal{A}$ with carrier A only if $d \in A$. Thus, we define $\psi_Q(x_1, \ldots, x_m)$ by letting

$$\mathcal{A} \models \psi_Q(\vec{a}) \text{ if and only if } \vec{a} \in Q(\mathcal{A}).$$

Then $Q(\mathcal{A}) = \{\vec{a} \in A^m \mid \mathcal{A} \models \psi_Q(\vec{a})\}$.

We say that Q is *local* if so is the associated formula ψ_Q. Our main result is the following.

Theorem 1. *Every relational query in* AGGR *is local.*

Since the transitive closure query (or deterministic transitive closure) is not local, we obtain the following.

Corollary 2. *Transitive closure is not expressible in* AGGR. $\qquad\qquad$ $\square$

266

This was proved before for a language weaker than AGGR [6, 17]. In fact, the language of [6, 17] is AGGR without the product operator and with less arithmetic.

References [17, 6, 16] also discuss a closely related property, called the bounded degree property, or BDP. When specialized to graphs, it says that for any query q from graphs to graphs, there exists a function $f_q : \mathbb{N} \to \mathbb{N}$ such that, whenever all degrees of nodes in a graph G do not exceed k, the number of distinct in- and out-degrees in $q(G)$ does not exceed $f_q(k)$. This property is particularly easy to use to obtain expressiveness bounds, see [6, 16, 17]. According to [6], locality implies the BDP. Hence,

Corollary 3. *Every relational query in AGGR has the bounded degree property.*
□

5 Flattening the language

Proving inexpressibility results for a language with nesting is hard because nesting essentially corresponds to second-order constructs. Fortunately, we can find a *flat* language AGGR$_{flat}$, that does not use nested sets, such that every relational query definable in AGGR is also definable in AGGR$_{flat}$. Furthermore, AGGR$_{flat}$ uses natural numbers instead of rationals, which makes it easier to encode its queries in an extension of first-order logic with counting.

The expressions of AGGR$_{flat}$ are given in Figure 2. There are a number of differences between AGGR and AGGR$_{flat}$. First, AGGR$_{flat}$'s types are $\mathbf{b}$, $\mathbb{N}$, record types of the form $s_1 \times \ldots \times s_k$ where each s_i is either $\mathbf{b}$ or $\mathbb{N}$, and set types $\{t\}$ where t is a record type. That is, no nested sets are allowed.

In the expressions in Figure 2, s, t, and t_i's range over record types, and S and T range over both record and set types. The operator *cartprod* is the usual cartesian product of sets; it is definable in AGGR using *ext* and ρ. Given a function $f : S \times s \to \{t\}$ and a pair (X, Y), where X is of type S and Y is a set of type $\{s\}$, $ext_2[f](X, Y)$ evaluates to $\bigcup_{y \in Y} f(X, y)$. $ext_2[f](X, Y)$ in AGGR$_{flat}$ can be implemented in AGGR as $ext[f](cartprod(\eta(X), Y))$, which involves a nested set. The extra parameter of $ext_2[f]$ allows us to avoid the construction of a nested set. Note that we do not need to introduce the similar $\sum_2[f]$ or $\prod_2[f]$, because $\sum_2[f] = \sum[\pi_2] \circ ext_2[\eta \circ (\pi_2, f)]$, and similarly for $\prod_2[f]$. On the natural numbers, $root(n, m)$ evaluates to k if $k^n = m$; otherwise *root* evaluates to *zero*. $repr(n, m)$ gives the canonical representation of the rational number $\frac{n}{m}$; that is, $repr(n, m) = (n', m')$ iff $\frac{n}{m} = \frac{n'}{m'}$ and n', m' have no common divisors. This function is undefined if $m = 0$, and is identity if $n = 0$. Note that $n \dot- m$ is the subtraction on natural numbers: $n \dot- m = \max(0, n - m)$.

We now have:

Proposition 4. *Every relational query definable in AGGR is also definable in* AGGR$_{flat}$.

Proof sketch. We first define a language AGGR$^{\mathbf{N}}$ as AGGR$_{flat}$ without restriction to flat types (that is, all the operations are the same, and the type

$$+, *, \div, exp, root : \mathbb{N} \times \mathbb{N} \to \mathbb{N} \quad K0, K1 : T \to \mathbb{N} \quad repr : \mathbb{N} \times \mathbb{N} \to \mathbb{N} \times \mathbb{N}$$

$$=_b: b \times b \to \{\mathbb{N}\} \quad =_N: \mathbb{N} \times \mathbb{N} \to \{\mathbb{N}\} \quad empty : \{t\} \to \{\mathbb{N}\}$$

$$\frac{}{id : T \to T} \qquad \frac{f : u \to t \quad g : s \to u}{f \circ g : s \to t}$$

$$\frac{f_i : t \to t_i, i = 1, \dots, n}{(f_1, \dots, f_n) : t \to t_1 \times \dots \times t_n} \qquad \frac{i \le n}{\pi_{i,n} : t_1 \times \dots \times t_n \to t_i}$$

$$\frac{}{K\{\} : T \to \{s\}} \quad \frac{}{\eta : t \to \{t\}} \quad \frac{}{\cup : \{t\} \times \{t\} \to \{t\}} \quad \frac{f : S \times s \to \{t\}}{ext_2[f] : S \times \{s\} \to \{t\}}$$

$$\frac{}{cartprod : \{t_1\} \times \dots \times \{t_n\} \to \{t_1 \times \dots \times t_n\}}$$

$$\frac{f : s \to \mathbb{N}}{\sum[f] : \{s\} \to \mathbb{N}} \qquad \frac{f : s \to \mathbb{N}}{\prod[f] : \{s\} \to \mathbb{N}}$$

Fig. 2. Expressions of AGGR$_{flat}$

system is $t ::= b \mid \mathbb{N} \mid t \times \dots \times t \mid \{t\}$. We show that every relational AGGR-query is definable in AGGR$^\mathbb{N}$. For that, we model every rational number r by a triple (s, n, m) of natural numbers such that $|r| = \frac{n}{m}$, $s = 0$ if $r < 0$ and $s = 1$ if $r \ge 0$, and n, m have no common divisors. Then it is easy to see that all rational arithmetic can be simulated with natural arithmetic, since we have *repr* in the language. Note that we need $\prod$ over natural numbers in order to simulate both $\sum$ and $\prod$ over the rationals. It further follows that AGGR$^\mathbb{N}$ has the conservative extension property (cf. [18, 19, 22]). Since every relational query has flat input and output, it can be expressed in the flat fragment of AGGR$^\mathbb{N}$, which is precisely AGGR$_{flat}$. □

6 Proof sketch of the main theorem

In view of Proposition 4, we now have to show

Proposition 5. *Every relational query in* AGGR$_{flat}$ *is local.*

We start by defining $\mathcal{FO} + COUNT$, the first-order logic with counting of [8]. The logic has two sorts: the domain for the first sort is D, and the domain for the second is $\mathbb{N}$. Over the first sort, we have the usual first-order logic. The following are available for the second sort: constants 1 and max, where the meaning of max is the size of the finite model; the usual ordering $<$; and the BIT predicate. Second-sort quantifiers $\forall i$ and $\exists i$ are bounded, meaning for all (exists) i between 1 and max. The counting quantifier $\exists i x.\varphi(x)$ means that φ has at least i satisfiers, and again $1 \leq i \leq$ max. This binds x but not i; for example,

$$\exists i.\mathrm{BIT}(1, i) \wedge [\exists i x.\varphi(x) \wedge (\forall j \exists j x.\varphi(x) \to j \leq i)]$$

tests if the number of satisfiers of φ is nonzero and even. We use $\exists ! i x.\varphi(x)$ for $\exists i x.\varphi(x) \wedge (\forall j \exists j x.\varphi(x) \to j \leq i)$; that is, that there exists exactly i satisfiers.

Now suppose we have a relational type σ_b, corresponding to some relational signature σ, and a relational query of type $\sigma_b \to \{b^m\}$. Next, consider the type

$$(\sigma, S)_b = \sigma_b \times \{b \times b\}.$$

Its objects are finite structure of the signature $\sigma \cup \{S\}$, where S is a binary relational symbol not in σ. If $\mathcal{A}$ is a σ-structure and S is a binary relation, we denote the corresponding $\sigma \cup \{S\}$ structure by $\mathcal{A}_S$. We use S for both relational symbol and its interpretation. Such structures are represented as AGGR-objects of type $(\sigma, S)_b$.

In what follows, we use the convention that C stands for the set of elements of S, that is, the union of the two projections of S. Given a function $g : \mathbb{N} \to \mathbb{N}$, we define the following condition $(\star_g[\mathcal{A}_S])$ on a structure $\mathcal{A}_S$:

$$(\star_g[\mathcal{A}_S]) \quad (A \cap C = \emptyset) \wedge (S \text{ is a linear order}) \wedge (card(C) > g(card(A)))$$

We also define a new query Q_g of type $(\sigma, S)_b \to \{b^m\}$ as

$$Q_g(\mathcal{A}_S) = \begin{cases} Q(\mathcal{A}) & \text{if } (\star_g[\mathcal{A}_S]) \text{ holds;} \\ \emptyset & \text{otherwise.} \end{cases}$$

We start with three propositions.

Proposition 6. *All formulae in $\mathcal{FO} + COUNT$ with no free variable of the second sort are local.* $\qquad\square$

Proposition 7. *Let Q be any relational query in $\mathrm{AGGR_{flat}}$. Then for every g, it is the case that Q is local iff Q_g is local.* $\qquad\square$

Proposition 8. *Let Q be any relational query in $\mathrm{AGGR_{flat}}$. Then there is a function g such that ψ_{Q_g} is definable in $\mathcal{FO} + COUNT$.* $\qquad\square$

Now the main theorem can be obtained as follows. We consider a relational query Q of $\mathrm{AGGR_{flat}}$ and use Proposition 8 to find g such that ψ_{Q_g} is definable in $\mathcal{FO} + COUNT$. By Proposition 6, ψ_{Q_g} is local; hence Q_g is local. From Proposition 7 we conclude that Q is local as desired.

To complete the argument, we need to furnish proofs of the three propositions above. The proof of Proposition 6 can be found in [16]. The proof of Proposition 8 is in the appendix. The proof of Proposition 7 is as follows:

Let Q_g be local. Let r be its locality rank. Let the input structure to Q be $\mathcal{A}$. Let $\vec{a} \approx_r^{\mathcal{A}} \vec{b}$, where $\vec{a}$ and $\vec{b}$ are m-vectors of elements of A. Let $n = card(A)$ and let C be a subset of D such that $C \cap A = \emptyset$ and $card(C) > g(n)$. Let S be an arbitrary linear ordering on C. We define $\mathcal{A}_S$ as $\mathcal{A}$ extended with the binary relation S. Since $S_{\vec{a}}^{\mathcal{A}_S}(\vec{a})$ does not contain any element of C, and neither does $S_{\vec{d}}^{\mathcal{A}_S}(\vec{b})$ for any d, we obtain $\vec{a} \approx_r^{\mathcal{A}_S} \vec{b}$. Thus by the locality of Q_g, $\vec{a} \in Q_g(\mathcal{A}_S)$ iff $\vec{b} \in Q_g(\mathcal{A}_S)$. Since all the conditions in $(\star_g[\mathcal{A}_S])$ hold, we have $Q_g(\mathcal{A}_S) = Q(\mathcal{A})$. Hence, $\vec{a} \in Q(\mathcal{A})$ iff $\vec{b} \in Q(\mathcal{A})$, which proves that Q is local, and its locality rank is at most r. □

7 Conclusion

We have proved the most powerful result so far that gives us expressiveness bounds for relational queries with aggregation. In particular, recursive queries such as transitive closure are not definable with the help of grouping, summation, and product over columns, and standard rational arithmetic.

After our PODS'94 paper in which inexpressibility of transitive closure in a weaker language was proved, there was a renewed activity in the area that resulted in 3 papers, improving both results and techniques: [6], presented at ICDT'97, [16], presented at LICS'97 paper, and this paper. So one may ask if this is the end of the story.

We believe that, to the contrary, this work is very far from being completed. Until very recently, it was widely believed that counting formalisms developed in finite-model theory are a *wrong* way to approach the problem of aggregation. We hope to have convinced the reader that this is not necessarily the case, and logics with counting *are* useful. The connection though is not lying on the very surface, as the encoding is not completely trivial. A possible reason why it took a number of years to apply logics with counting to the study of query languages is that, until recently, very few tools for $\mathcal{FO} + COUNT$ were available. The games of Immerman and Lander [15] were essentially the only such tool, and these are *not* convenient to use. The best known separation result proved via games was the one from the conference version of Etessami's paper [8]. It required a complicated combinatorial argument, even though the structures are extremely simple. Tools like those suggested in [16, 21] simplify the proofs considerably, as was demonstrated in [8, 16]. This makes first-order logic with counting much more attractive as a tool for studying aggregation.

But there is still a long way to go. For example, it seems likely that the class of allowed arithmetic functions and predicates should not affect the expressibility of, say, transitive closure. However, first-order logic with counting, which we used for encoding, limits the arithmetic operations. We finish the paper with two main *challenges* that we believe must be addressed to develop a good finite-model theory counterpart for languages with aggregation.

CHALLENGE 1 Find an extension of first-order logic with a counting mechanism that is a *natural* analog of relational languages with aggregation. Furthermore, such an extension must possess nice model-theoretic properties as to be applicable to the study of expressiveness of languages with aggregation. Note that $\mathcal{FO} + COUNT$ is not a good candidate. We have seen that the encoding in $\mathcal{FO} + COUNT$ is quite an unpleasant one, but we had to use $\mathcal{FO} + COUNT$ because of its nice known properties.

CHALLENGE 2 Find techniques that extend the results to *ordered* databases. By this, we mean having an order relation on the elements of the base type, not only on rational (or natural) numbers.

The results on expressive power of relational calculus extend to the ordered setting. To be able to state results about *real* languages with aggregates, we must deal with the ordered case. However, none of the tools developed for logics such as $\mathcal{FO} + COUNT$ gives us any hints as to how to approach the ordered case.

Acknowledgement We thank anonymous referees and Rick Hull for their comments, and Marc Gyssens for suggesting numerous improvements.

References

1. S. Abiteboul, R. Hull, V. Vianu, *Foundations of Databases*, Addison Wesley, 1995.
2. A. V. Aho and J. D. Ullman. Universality of data retrieval languages. In *Proceedings of 6th Symposium on Principles of Programming Languages, Texas*, pages 110–120, January 1979.
3. D.A. Barrington, N. Immerman, H. Straubing. On uniformity within NC^1. *JCSS*, 41:274–306,1990.
4. P. Buneman, S. Naqvi, V. Tannen, L. Wong. Principles of programming with complex objects and collection types. *Theoretical Computer Science*, 149(1):3–48, September 1995.
5. M. Consens and A. Mendelzon. Low complexity aggregation in GraphLog and Datalog, *Theoretical Computer Science* 116 (1993), 95–116. Extended abstract in *ICDT'90*.
6. G. Dong, L. Libkin, L. Wong. Local properties of query languages. *Proc. Int. Conf. on Database Theory*, Springer LNCS 1186, 1997, pages 140–154.
7. H.-D. Ebbinghaus and J. Flum. *Finite Model Theory*. Springer Verlag, 1995.
8. K. Etessami. Counting quantifiers, successor relations, and logarithmic space, *Journal of Computer and System Sciences* 54 (1996), 400–411. Extended abstract in *Structure in Complexity'95*.
9. R. Fagin. Easier ways to win logical games. In *Proc. DIMACS Workshop on Finite Model Theory and Descriptive Complexity*, 1996.
10. R. Fagin, L. Stockmeyer, M. Vardi, On monadic NP vs monadic co-NP, *Information and Computation*, 120 (1994), 78–92.
11. H. Gaifman, On local and non-local properties, *in* "Proceedings of the Herbrand Symposium, Logic Colloquium '81," North Holland, 1982.
12. S. Grumbach, L. Libkin, T. Milo and L. Wong. Query languages for bags: expressive power and complexity. *SIGACT News*, 27 (1996), 30–37.
13. Y. Gurevich. Toward logic tailored for computational complexity. In *Proceedings of Computation and Proof Theory*, Springer Lecture Notes in Mathematics, vol. 1104, 1984, pages 175–216.

14. N. Immerman. Languages that capture complexity classes. *SIAM Journal of Computing*, 16:760–778, 1987.

15. N. Immerman and E. Lander. Describing graphs: A first order approach to graph canonization. In *"Complexity Theory Retrospective"*, Springer Verlag, Berlin, 1990.

16. L. Libkin. On the forms of locality over finite models. In *LICS'97*, pages 204–215.

17. L. Libkin and L. Wong. Query languages for bags and aggregate functions. *JCSS*, 55 (1997), 241–272.

18. L. Libkin and L. Wong. Aggregate functions, conservative extension, and linear orders, *in* "Proceedings of 4th International Workshop on Database Programming Languages," Manhattan, New York, August 1993.

19. L. Libkin and L. Wong. Conservativity of nested relational calculi with internal generic functions. *Information Processing Letters*, 49 (1994), 273–280.

20. I. Niven and H.S. Zuckerman. *Introduction to the Theory of Numbers*. Wiley, 1980.

21. J. Nurmonen. On winning strategies with unary quantifiers. *J. Logic and Computation*, 6 (1996), 779–798.

22. L. Wong. Normal forms and conservative properties for query languages over collection types. *JCSS* 52(1):495–505, June 1996.

Appendix: Proof of Proposition 8

Preliminaries

We start with a few definitions. Given an object x, $\mathsf{adom_b}(x)$ and $\mathsf{adom_N}(x)$ stand for the active domains of type $\mathbf{b}$ and $\mathbb{N}$ of x, respectively. That is, $\mathsf{adom_b}(x)$ is the set of all elements of D (the domain of type $\mathbf{b}$) that occur in x; and $\mathsf{adom_N}(x)$ is the set of all natural numbers that occur in x. We use $\mathsf{adom}(x)$ for $\mathsf{adom_b}(x) \cup \mathsf{adom_N}(x)$. We also assume that D and $\mathbb{N}$ are disjoint. The cardinalities of $\mathsf{adom_b}(x)$, $\mathsf{adom_N}(x)$, and $\mathsf{adom}(x)$ are denoted by $\mathsf{size_b}(x)$, $\mathsf{size_N}(x)$, and $\mathsf{size}(x)$ respectively.

Given an $\mathrm{AGGR_{flat}}$ function f and an object x, we define the set $\mathsf{Int\_res}(f, x)$ of intermediate results of evaluation of f on x as

$$
\begin{array}{ll}
\mathsf{Int\_res}(g, h(x)) \cup \mathsf{Int\_res}(h, x) & \text{if } f = g \circ h; \\
\mathsf{Int\_res}(f_1, x) \cup \ldots \cup \mathsf{Int\_res}(f_n, x) & \text{if } f = (f_1, \ldots, f_n); \\
\{x\} \cup \{f(x)\} \cup \bigcup_{y \in x} \mathsf{Int\_res}(g, y) & \text{if } f = \sum[g] \text{ or } f = \prod[g]; \\
\{(X, Y)\} \cup \{f(X, Y)\} \cup \bigcup_{y \in Y} \mathsf{Int\_res}(g, (X, y)) & \text{if } f = ext_2[g] \text{ and } x = (X, Y); \\
\{x, f(x)\} & \text{otherwise.}
\end{array}
$$

Intuitively, $\mathsf{Int\_res}(f, x)$ contains all intermediate results obtained in the process of evaluating f on x.

We now define

$$
\mathsf{adom_b}(f, x) = \bigcup_{y \in \mathsf{Int\_res}(f,x)} \mathsf{adom_b}(y).
$$

$$
\mathsf{adom_N}(f, x) = \bigcup_{y \in \mathsf{Int\_res}(f,x)} \mathsf{adom_N}(y),
$$

$$
\mathsf{adom}(f, x) = \mathsf{adom_b}(f, x) \cup \mathsf{adom_N}(f, x),
$$

and $\mathsf{size}_b(f, x)$, $\mathsf{size}_N(f, x)$, and $\mathsf{size}(f, x)$ as their cardinalities. That is, $\mathsf{adom}_b(f, x)$ is the set of all elements of D that occur in the process of evaluating of f on x, and $\mathsf{adom}_N(f, x)$ is the set of all natural numbers that occur in this process.

Since all operations in AGGR_{flat} except exp, $root$, and $\prod[f]$ can be evaluated in polynomial time (cf. [4, 12, 17]), and those that cannot be evaluated in polynomial time produce a single number, we obtain:

Lemma 9. *For any AGGR_{flat} expression f, there exists a constant k_f such that for any object x with $\mathsf{size}(x) = n > 1$, on which f is defined,*

$$\mathsf{size}(f, x) < n^{k_f}.$$

From this lemma, by a simple structural induction on AGGR_{flat} expressions, we prove the following.

Lemma 10. *For any AGGR_{flat} expression f, there exists a constant C_f such that for any object x with $\mathsf{size}(x) = n > 1$, on which f is defined, and for every $m \in \mathsf{adom}_N(f, x)$, it is the case that*

$$m < n^{n^{C_f}}.$$

In particular, if f is a relational query, we obtain $m < n^{n^{C_f}}$ for any $m \in \mathsf{adom}_N(f, x)$, where $n = \mathsf{size}_b(x)$. This gives us an upper bound on any natural number that can be encountered in the process of evaluating f on x.

For the rest of the proof, we assume that any input to a relational query has size at least 2. At the end of the proof we shall explain how to deal with empty and one-element active domains.

Given a number $N > 1$, we call a function $enc_m(a_1, \ldots, a_m)$ an *encoding relative to N* if it uniquely encodes m-tuples of natural numbers less than N; that is, $\vec{a} \neq \vec{b}$ implies $enc_m(\vec{a}) \neq enc_m(\vec{b})$, whenever all components of $\vec{a}$ and $\vec{b}$ are below N. Such a function can be chosen so that it is a polynomial in $a_1, \ldots, a_m, N$ and its values are less than N^l for some l. For example, enc_2 can be defined as $enc_2(a, b) = aN + b$; thus, its values do not exceed $N^2 + N$ and are thus less than N^3. To encode m-tuples, we just apply enc_2 to the first component and an encoding of the remaining $m - 1$-tuple.

According to [8], the predicates $+(i, j, k)$ and $*(i, j, k)$ meaning $i + j = k$ and $i * j = k$ are definable in $\mathcal{FO} + COUNT$, as long as i, j, k are elements of the second sort under max. Thus, we shall use polynomial (in)equalities in $\mathcal{FO} + COUNT$ formulae. For example, the parity test can be rewritten as

$$\exists k \exists i.k + k = i \wedge \exists! ix.\varphi(x).$$

The encoding

Let Q be a relational query in AGGR_{flat}. We define g as

$$g(n) = n^{n^{n^c}}$$

where c is a constant to be determined later. We claim that there exists a constant c such that Q_g is definable in $\mathcal{FO} + COUNT$.

The idea of the encoding is that a number n is represented by the element $c_n \in C$ such that the cardinality of $\{x \mid S(x, c_n)\}$ is n. Then the counting power of $\mathcal{FO} + COUNT$ is applied to the relation S. The size of C, given by g, turns out to be sufficient to model all arithmetic that is needed in order to evaluate Q.

Given a $\sigma \cup \{S\}$-structure $\mathcal{A}_S$ (where S is the extra binary relation) and a number k, it is possible to write an $\mathcal{FO} + COUNT$ formula that checks if $(*_g[\mathcal{A}_S])$ holds where g is of the form above. Indeed, we first notice that there are first-order formulae $\mathsf{adom}_\mathcal{A}(x)$ and $\mathsf{adom}_S(x)$ that test if x is in the carrier of $\mathcal{A}$ (that is, $x \in A$), or x is a node in the binary relation S (that is, $x \in C$). For example, $\mathsf{adom}_S(x) = \exists y.S(y, x) \vee S(x, y)$. Also, there exists a first-order formula $LIN(S)$ stating that S is a linear order.

We next claim that there is an $\mathcal{FO} + COUNT$ definable predicate $exp(x, y, z)$ that holds iff $x, y, z \in C$ and $x^y = z$; that is, exp represents the graph of exponentiation, where n is encoded by $c_n \in C$ such that the cardinality of $\{x \mid S(x, c_n)\}$ is n. We use the notation $x^y = z$, but strictly speaking we mean that for numbers i, j, k represented by x, y, z we have $i^j = k$; in what follows we shall often write arithmetic formulae on the elements of C, to keep the notation simpler. We use the shorthand $\mathsf{is}(x, i)$ for $\exists!iy.S(y, x)$; that is, $\mathsf{is}(x, i)$ means that x represents the number i.

To show that exp is definable, first notice that there is a formula $pow(x, y)$ stating that x is a power of y, provided c_y is prime:

$$pow(x, y) = \exists i \exists j.[\mathsf{is}(x, i) \wedge \mathsf{is}(y, j) \wedge (\forall k \forall l.k * l = i \rightarrow (k = 1 \vee (\exists k'.k' * j = k)))]$$

Now $exp_{pr}(x, y, z)$ defined as

$$exp_{pr}(x, y, z) = pow(z, y) \wedge \exists i \exists j.[\mathsf{is}(y, i) \wedge (j = i + 1) \wedge \exists!jv.(pow(x, v) \wedge S(v, z))]$$

states that $x^y = z$ for y prime. That is, $exp_{pr}(x, y, z)$ if z is a power fo x, and the number of powers of x that do not exceed z is $y + 1$.

Now we define two new formulae:

$$div(a, b) = \exists i, j, k \exists u.\mathsf{is}(a, i) \wedge \mathsf{is}(b, j) \wedge \mathsf{is}(u, k) \wedge i = j * k$$

$$prime(p) = \forall u \forall i.(S(u, p) \wedge \mathsf{is}(u, i)) \rightarrow (i = 1 \vee \neg div(p, u))$$

That is, $div(a, b)$ says that a is divisible by b, and $prime(p)$ says that p is prime. Next, we define $factor(p, a, x)$ meaning that p is prime, p^a divides x, but p^{a+1} does not divide x:

$$factor(p, a, x) = prime(p) \wedge \exists v.\ [S(v, x) \wedge exp_{pr}(p, a, v) \wedge div(x, v) \wedge$$
$$\forall w \forall i, j, k.(\mathsf{is}(w, i) \wedge \mathsf{is}(v, j) \wedge \mathsf{is}(p, k) \wedge i = j * k \rightarrow \neg div(x, w))]$$

With this, we finally define $exp(x, y, z)$ as $exp_1(x, y, z) \wedge exp_2(x, y, z)$ where

$$exp_1(x, y, z) = \forall p \forall a.factor(p, a, x) \rightarrow$$
$$(\exists b \exists i, j, k.\text{is}(b, i) \wedge \text{is}(y, j) \wedge \text{is}(a, k) \wedge i = j * k \wedge factor(p, b, z))$$

$$exp_2(x, y, z) = \forall p \forall a.factor(p, a, z) \rightarrow \exists b.factor(p, b, x)$$

With this formula exp, we can define the condition that $card(C) > g(card(A))$ as

$$\chi_g = \exists x \exists y.[(\text{adom}_S(x) \wedge (\exists i.\text{is}(x, i) \wedge \exists! iv.\text{adom}_A(v))) \wedge (\exists v.S(y, v)) \wedge \chi'(x, y)],$$

where $\chi'(x, y)$ expresses the condition that $card(C) > g(card(A))$ as the conjunction of first-order formula stating that C has at least c elements, and for the cth element, denoted by x_c, the following holds:

$$\exists v_1 \exists v_2.(\text{adom}_S(v_1) \wedge \text{adom}_S(v_2)) \wedge (exp(x, x_c, v_1) \wedge exp(x, v_1, v_2) \wedge exp(x, v_2, y))$$

That is, y represents the value of g on x (which is the cardinality of A), and there is an element S-bigger than y, that ensures strict inequality.

Finally, we use

$$test_* = LIN(S) \wedge (\forall x.\text{adom}_A(x) \rightarrow \neg\text{adom}_S(x)) \wedge \chi_g$$

to test for $(\star_g[A_S])$.

Thus, for the rest of the proof, we assume that the input structure satisfies $(\star_g[A_S])$. If we produce ab $\mathcal{FO} + COUNT$ formula ψ that defines Q_g on such structures, the formula that defines Q on all structures is simply $\psi \wedge test_*$.

We now explain the encoding of objects and AGGR$_{\text{flat}}$ functions. The encoding is relative to the input structure A_S. We assume that the first sort is the carrier of the finite structure (A_S in our case); thus, elements of type $\mathbf{b}$ are encoded by themselves. Each element of type $\mathbb{N}$, that is, a natural number n, is encoded by $c_n \in C$ such that $card(\{x \mid S(x, c_n)\}) = n$. Note that we do not use the second sort in the encoding; natural numbers are still encoded as elements of the first sort, and the counting power of $\mathcal{FO} + COUNT$ is only used in simulation of functions.

Suppose we have a function f of type $s \rightarrow t$. Then s is a product of record types and types of the form $\{s'\}$ where s' is a record type. Without loss of generality (and keeping the notation simple) we list types not under the set brackets first; that is, s is

$$\mathbf{b}^l \times \mathbb{N}^k \times \{t_1\} \times \ldots \times \{t_m\}$$

where $t_1, \ldots, t_m$ are record types, t_i being the product of w_i base types. We also assume that t is either $\mathbf{b}$, or $\mathbb{N}$, or $\{u\}$, where u is a record type, since functions into product of types will be modeled by tuples of formulae.

Let x be an arbitrary object. We say that x is A_S-compatible if $\text{adom}_b(x) \subseteq A$ and $i < card(C)$ for any $i \in \text{adom}_\mathbb{N}(x)$. If this is the case, by x_{A_S} we denote an object obtained from x by replacing each natural number n that occurs in x with c_n; its type is then obtained from the type of x by replacing each $\mathbb{N}$ with $\mathbf{b}$.

With each sequence $\mathcal{T} = (\{t_1\}, \ldots, \{t_m\})$, where t_is are record types, we associate a signature $\mathcal{T}_{\text{sig}}$ that consists of m relational symbols $S^1, \ldots, S^m$, with S^i having arity w_i. (At each step of the process of encoding, we shall assume a fresh collection of relation symbols.) By $\sigma(\mathcal{T})$ we denote the disjoint union of σ, $\{S\}$, and $\mathcal{T}_{\text{sig}}$.

Now we consider two cases.

Case 1: t is **b** or $\mathbb{N}$. Then f is encoded as a formula $\psi_f(\vec{x}, \vec{y}, z)$ in the language $\sigma(\mathcal{T})$, where $\vec{x}$ has l elements and $\vec{y}$ has k elements. The condition on ψ_f is the following.

Assume that $\mathcal{B}$ is an object of type $\{t_1\} \times \ldots \times \{t_m\}$ that is $\mathcal{A}_S$-compatible. Let $\mathcal{B}'$ be the $\sigma(\mathcal{T})$ structure that consists of $\mathcal{A}_S$ and $\mathcal{B}_{\mathcal{A}_S}$ (interpreting symbols in $\mathcal{T}_{\text{sig}}$). Let $\vec{x}$ and $\vec{y}$ be $\mathcal{A}_S$-compatible. Then, for every $\mathcal{A}_S$-compatible z, it is the case that

$$z = f(\vec{x}, \vec{y}, \mathcal{B}) \quad \text{if and only if} \quad \mathcal{B}' \models \psi_f(\vec{x}, \vec{y}_{\mathcal{A}_S}, z_{\mathcal{A}_S})$$

Case 2: t is $\{u\}$ where u is a record type with arity w. Then f is encoded as a formula $\psi_f(\vec{x}, \vec{y}, \vec{z})$ in the language $\sigma(\mathcal{T})$, where $\vec{x}$ and $\vec{y}$ are as before, and $\vec{z}$ is a w-vector of variables of the first sort. The condition is that, for every $\mathcal{A}_S$-compatible $\vec{x}$, $\vec{y}$ and $\mathcal{B}$ as above, the set

$$Z = f(\vec{x}, \vec{y}, \mathcal{B})$$

is $\mathcal{A}_S$-compatible, and

$$\{\vec{z} \in (A \cup S)^w \mid \mathcal{B}' \models \psi_f(\vec{x}, \vec{y}_{\mathcal{A}_S}, \vec{z})\} = Z_{\mathcal{A}_S}.$$

If t is a product of types, we encode f as the tuple of encodings of all projections.

We now show how to encode $\text{AGGR}_{\text{flat}}$ expressions so that the conditions 1 and 2 above are satisfied. First, note that composition is rather straightforward and essentially corresponds to substitution. Next, consider natural arithmetic.

The function $K0$ is encoded as

$$\psi_{K0}(\_, x) = \text{adom}_S(x) \wedge \neg \exists y. S(y, x);$$

that is, x is the smallest element of S. Similarly,

$$\psi_{K1}(\_, x) = \text{adom}_S(x) \wedge \exists! y. S(y, x)$$

The encoding of operations on $\mathbb{N}$ is straightforward:

$$\psi_+(x, y, z) = \begin{aligned}&\text{adom}_S(x) \wedge \text{adom}_S(y) \wedge \text{adom}_S(z)\\&\wedge \exists i \exists j \exists k. (\text{is}(x, i) \wedge \text{is}(y, j) \wedge \text{is}(z, k)) \wedge (i + j = k),\end{aligned}$$

and similarly for other $*$, $\dot{-}$ and exp (since we know how to define exp). For *root*, we use

$$\psi_{root}(x, y, z) = exp(z, y, x) \vee (\neg exp(z, y, x) \wedge \neg \exists v. S(v, z))$$

That is, if the root does not exists, we return 0. For *repr* we use

$$\begin{aligned}
&\psi_{repr}(x, y, x', y') \\
&= (\exists i, i', j, j', l. \mathsf{is}(x, i) \wedge \mathsf{is}(x', i') \wedge \mathsf{is}(y, j) \wedge \mathsf{is}(y', j') \wedge l = i * j' \wedge l = j * i') \\
&\quad \wedge \forall z. \neg(div(x', z) \leftrightarrow div(y', z)).
\end{aligned}$$

Note that we have to compute the product of two numbers; thus, the size of S must be at least the square of maximum possible number that can be encountered in evaluating Q. We shall see later when we determine the function g that this is the case, and thus we can use the formula above.

The order on $\mathbb{N}$ is given by

$$\psi_<(x, y, z) = \mathsf{adom}_S(x) \wedge \mathsf{adom}_S(y) \wedge S(x, y) \wedge \neg \exists v. S(v, z)$$

The equality test is similarly defined:

$$\psi_=(x, y, z) = (x = y) \wedge \mathsf{adom}_S(z) \wedge \neg \exists y. S(y, x).$$

The operations on sets are very simple: for example, union is encoded as $\psi_\cup(\vec{z}) = S^1(\vec{z}) \vee S^2(\vec{z})$ (recall that S^1 and S^2 are symbols in the signature $\mathcal{T}$);

$$\psi_{empty}(z) = \neg \exists \vec{x}. S^1(\vec{x}) \wedge \mathsf{adom}_S(z) \wedge \neg \exists y. S(y, x).$$

For the singleton, we have $\psi_\eta(x, y) = (x = y)$. The encoding of *cartprod* depends on the arities of types involved and their number. In general, we define

$$\psi_{cartprod_n}(\vec{x}) = \exists \vec{x}_1 \ldots \exists \vec{x}_n. S^1(\vec{x}_1) \wedge \ldots \wedge S^n(\vec{x}_n) \wedge \chi(\vec{x}_1, \ldots, \vec{x}_n, \vec{x})$$

where $\chi(\vec{x}_1, \ldots, \vec{x}_n, \vec{x})$ is a formula in the language of equality stating that $\vec{x}$ is concatenation of $\vec{x}_1, \ldots, \vec{x}_n$.

The encoding of $K\{\}$ is simply *false*.

To encode $ext_2[f]$, we use ψ_f encoding f and obtain

$$\psi_{ext_2[f]}(\vec{x}, \vec{z}) = \exists \vec{y}. S^1(\vec{y}) \wedge \psi_f(\vec{x}, \vec{y}, \vec{z})$$

in the case when the first argument of f is a record type, and

$$\psi_{ext_2[f]}(\vec{z}) = \exists \vec{y}. S^1(\vec{y}) \wedge \psi_f(\vec{y}, \vec{z})$$

in the case when the first argument is a set; then the formula ψ_f encoding f uses the symbol S^2 for that set.

Below we treat the two most complex cases: $\sum[f]$ and $\prod[f]$.

Encoding $\sum[f]$

Now we consider the case of the summation operator. Assume for the moment that we can write a formula $\exists i\vec{x}.\varphi(\vec{x})$ meaning there are at least i vectors satisfying φ. Then we can also define $\exists!i\vec{x}.\varphi(\vec{x})$, which gives us the encoding of $\varphi_{\sum[f]}$ as follows:

$$\psi_{\sum[f]}(z) \;=\; \exists i.(\exists!i(\vec{x},y,v).S^1(\vec{x}) \wedge \psi_f(\vec{x},y) \wedge S(v,y)) \;\wedge\; \exists!iv.S(v,z).$$

This formula is saying that z is the ith element in S, where i is the number of tuples $(\vec{x},y,v)$ such that $\vec{x}$ is in the input relation S^1, y is the jth element of S where $j = f(\vec{x})$ and v is under y in S. It is easy to see that the number of such tuples is exactly $\sum[f](S^1)$.

Thus, it remains to show how to count tuples, provided that the number of such tuples does not exceed max. Note that for the summation, we need to count tuples of arity up to $m+2$, where m is the maximum arity of a record that can occur in the process of evaluating Q. We show below how to count pairs; counting tuples is similar (only the encoding scheme changes).

To define $\chi(i) = \exists i(x,y).\varphi(x,y)$, we first define

$$\alpha(x,x_0) \;=\; \exists k.[\exists!ky.\varphi(x,y) \wedge \mathrm{adom}_S(x_0) \wedge \exists!kv.S(v,x_0)].$$

Thus, $\alpha(x,x_0)$ holds iff x_0 represents the number of y such that $\varphi(x,y)$ holds. Next, define

$$\beta(x_0,y_0) \;=\; \exists j.[\exists!jz.\alpha(z,x_0) \wedge \mathrm{adom}_S(y_0) \wedge \exists!jv.S(v,y_0)].$$

Now we see that $\chi(i)$ holds iff

$$i \leq \sum(k*j \mid \beta(x_0,y_0) \text{ holds},\ x_0 \text{ represents } k,\ y_0 \text{ represents } j) = G(i).$$

Thus, if we have a formula $enc_4(x_1,x_2,x_3,x_4,N,z)$ that encodes 4-tuples (x_1,x_2,x_3,x_4) of numbers under N (that is, z is the encoding), where N is $n^{n^{c_f}}$ (the maximal number that can occur in the process of evaluating Q), define

$$\chi(i) \;=\; \exists iz.\exists x_0\exists y_0\exists x'\exists y'.enc_4(x_0,y_0,x',y',N,z)\wedge\beta(x_0,y_0)\wedge S(x',x_0)\wedge S(y',y_0).$$

(Note that N is definable.) That is, we count the number of elements that code 4-tuples (x_0,y_0,x',y') such that $\beta(x_0,y_0)$ holds, x' is under x_0 in S and y' is under y_0 in S. It is easy to see that the number of such zs is precisely $G(i)$.

It is easy to extend this technique to counting m-tuples by counting $m-1$-tuples (by α) first; in particular, one can see that in such a counting one never needs enc_m for $m > 4$.

Encoding $\prod[f]$

The final case is that of $\prod[f]$. Before explaining a rather complex encoding scheme, we present it informally.

Assume that we have a set $X = \{\vec{x}_1, \ldots, \vec{x}_K\}$, and let $n_i = f(\vec{x}_i)$. Let $M = \prod[f](X)$. Then M is the number of k-element bags $B = \{n'_1, \ldots, n'_K\}$ such that $1 \le n'_i \le n_i$ for all i.

To find the number of such bags, we have to find their set representation first. Represent the bag $\{n_1, \ldots, n_k\}$ as a set of pairs $X_0 = \{(N_1, m_1), \ldots, (N_s, m_s)\}$ where N_is are among n_js and m_is are their multiplicities. Assume that $N_1 < \ldots < N_s$.

Then the number of bags $B = \{n'_1, \ldots, n'_K\}$ with $1 \le n'_i \le n_i$ is

$$M = \prod_{i=1}^{s} N_i^{m_i}.$$

We next consider sets of the form

$$\bigcup_{i=1}^{s} \bigcup_{j=1}^{m_i} \{(N_i, j, k) \mid 1 \le k \le N_i\}.$$

Such a set can be visualized as

$$\left\{ \begin{array}{cccc} (N_1, 1, c_{11}), & (N_1, 2, c_{12}), & \ldots, & (N_1, m_1, c_{1m_1}) \\ \cdots & \cdots & \cdots & \cdots \\ (N_s, 1, c_{s1}), & (N_s, 2, c_{s2}), & \ldots, & (N_s, m_s, c_{sm_s}) \end{array} \right\}$$

where $1 \le c_{ij} \le N_i$. It can be easily seen that the number of such sets is M. Thus, we have to count to the number of sets above.

Suppose we can write a formula that says that a given set Y is of the form above. Next step is to transform Y into a set $Y' = \{e_1, \ldots, e_t\}$ where each e_i is an encoding (as in the summation case) of a triple (N_i, l, c_{il}). As before, the encoding is relative to N, where N is given by Lemma 10, and is definable in $\mathcal{FO} + \mathcal{COUNT}$. Given such a set, we define its Gödel encoding, to represent it as a number. Finally, M is the number of numbers (represented as elements of S) that are Gödel encodings of such sets.

We now describe the formula that defines M. By now, the reader must be convinced that any arithmetic on numbers can be transferred to the elements of S, so we shall now use those elements of S instead of second-sort variables. This will make the notation somewhat more bearable. The reader should be able to see easily how to do everything rigorously by using counting quantifiers and formulae $\mathrm{is}(x, i)$.

We define

$$\psi_{\prod[f]}(x) = \exists i. \mathrm{is}(x, i) \wedge \exists! iv. encodes\_good\_set(v),$$

where $encodes\_good\_set(v)$ means that v is a Gödel encoding of a set of the form shown above. To define this, we assume four other formulae: $is\_enc(v)$ means that

v is an encoding of some set, *in_set(m,v)* means that m is in the set given by its encoding v, *good(m)* means that m is the encoding of a valid triple (N_i, l, c_{il}), and *nothing_missed(v)* meaning that when v is decoded all the way to the set of the form above, there is a triple $(N_i, j, \cdot)$ for each N_i and each $1 \le j \le m_i$.

With this, we define *encodes_good_set(v)* as

$$is\_enc(v) \;\wedge\; nothing\_missed(v) \;\wedge\; \forall m.in\_set(m,v) \rightarrow good(m).$$

The Gödel encoding of a set $\{k_1, \ldots, k_r\}$ with $k_1 < \ldots < k_r$ is $2^{k_1} \cdot 3^{k_2} \cdot \ldots \cdot p_r^{k_r}$ where p_r is the rth prime. Thus, a number V is an encoding if, whenever divisible by a prime p, is divisible by any other prime $p' < p$, and for m', m which are the largest numbers such that V is divisible by $(p')^{m'}$ and p^m, it holds that $m' < m$. This is clearly definable in $\mathcal{FO} + COUNT$, using the formula *factor* produced earlier.

To check if m is in the set encoded by v we therefore look for a prime p such that v is divisible by p^m but not by p^{m+1}. Assuming formulae *prime* testing for prime and $div(x,y)$ as a an abbreviation for $\exists z.z * y = x$, we write *in_set(m,v)* as

$$\exists p \exists z.prime(p) \wedge div(v,z) \wedge exp(p,m,z) \wedge (\forall z'.z' = z * p \rightarrow \neg div(v,z')).$$

To define *good(m)*, we must check the existence of (n,j,k) such that m encodes (n,j,k) with respect to the same base as in the case of summation, and such

1. that n is a value of f on X (that is, $\exists \vec{x}.R(\vec{x}) \wedge \psi_f(\vec{x}, n)$), and
2. that the number of $\vec{x} \in X$ such that $\psi_f(\vec{x}, n)$ holds is at least j (this can done in $\mathcal{FO} + COUNT$ by counting tuples in exactly the same way we did it in the case of summation), and
3. that $k \le n$.

Finally, to express *nothing_missed(v)*, we have to check that for every n which is a value of f on some $\vec{x} \in X$ and which has multiplicity m in X_0, it is the case that all triples $(n,j,\cdot)$ for $1 \le j \le m$ are present; that is, for each n and each m as above, and each $1 \le j \le m$, there exists a number that codes (n,j,k) for some k. Using the fact the we can count tuples, we conclude that *nothing_missed(v)* can be expressed in $\mathcal{FO} + COUNT$. This completes the encoding of $\prod[f]$.

This completes the description of the encoding of AGGR_{flat} primitives. To encode a query Q, we assume that at the first step, when the function operates on the input structure $\mathcal{A}$, we use the symbols of σ instead of S_is. Then, for each composition, we generate a fresh set of relation symbols. Thus, the encoding of Q is an $\mathcal{FO} + COUNT$ formula in the language $\sigma \cup \{S\}$.

Given a relational query Q in AGGR_{flat}, the function g, and the encoding ψ_Q of Q, we encode Q_g as $\Psi(Q,g) = \psi_Q \wedge test_*$.

Now a straightforward proof by induction on the structure of Q shows that $\Psi(Q,g)$, when given an input $\mathcal{A}_S$ satisfying $(\star_g[\mathcal{A}_S])$ for an appropriately chosen constant c, and having at least two elements in A, defines $Q(\mathcal{A})$. This is because

$\mathrm{adom}_b(Q(\mathcal{A})) \subseteq A$ and, furthermore, all numbers produced by the counting formulae in the encoding are below max.

The latter requires verification in the case of summation and product operations. We know that any number produced in the process of evaluation of Q on $\mathcal{A}$ is at most $N = n^{n^{C_f}}$ for appropriately chosen C_f. Thus, the encodings of fixed length tuples of such elements are bounded by a value of some polynomial in N, that is, by $n^{n^{C'}}$ for some C'. For the Gödel encoding, we need upper bound on the values $P = 2^{k_1} \cdot \ldots \cdot p_r^{k_r}$ where p_r is the rth prime, and both k_r and r are at most N. Thus, P is at most $p_N^{N^2}$. Since there exists a constant d such that $p_k \leq dk \log k$ [20], we obtain

$$P \leq (dN^2)^{N^2} < d(n^{n^{C_f}})^{2n^{2n^{C_f}}} = dn^{2n^{c_f + n^{C_f}}}$$

which shows that there exists a constant such that $P < n^{n^{n^c}}$. This completes the proof that there exists a function g such that $\Psi(Q, g)$ defines $Q(\mathcal{A})$ on inputs satisfying $(\star_g[\mathcal{A}_S])$. Since $test_\star$ is a conjunct of $\Psi(Q, g)$, on inputs not satisfying $(\star_g[\mathcal{A}_S])$, $\Psi(Q, g)$ produces the empty set.

This completes the proof that Q_g is definable by an $\mathcal{FO} + COUNT$ formula $\Psi(Q, g)$ if the active domain of $\mathcal{A}$ has at least two elements.

Finally, we consider the case when the active domain of $\mathcal{A}$ is empty or has one element. In the first case the output is empty as well (we do not have access to the individual constants in D), and in the second case it is either (a) empty, or (b) has a single tuple $(a, \ldots, a)$ where a is the unique element of the active domain. Thus, in the case (a) the formula $\psi(\bar{z})$ encoding Q_g for arbitrary $\mathcal{A}$ is defined by

$$[\exists x \exists y.\mathrm{adom}_\mathcal{A}(x) \wedge \mathrm{adom}_\mathcal{A}(y) \wedge \neg(x = y)] \wedge \Psi(Q, g)(\bar{z})$$

and in the case (b), $\psi(z_1, \ldots, z_m)$ is given by

$$\begin{aligned} &(\exists x.\mathrm{adom}_\mathcal{A}(x)) \\ \wedge\ [\ &(\exists! x.\mathrm{adom}_\mathcal{A}(x) \wedge \bigwedge_{i=1}^{m}(z_i = x)) \\ \vee\ &(\exists x \exists y.\mathrm{adom}_\mathcal{A}(x) \wedge \mathrm{adom}_\mathcal{A}(y) \wedge \neg(x = y) \wedge \Psi(Q, g)(\bar{z}))\ ]. \end{aligned}$$

This completes the proof of Proposition 8. $\square$

Datalog and Description Logics: Expressive Power

Marco Cadoli[1] and Luigi Palopoli[2] and Maurizio Lenzerini[1]

[1] Dipartimento di Informatica e Sistemistica
Università di Roma "La Sapienza"
Via Salaria 113, I-00198 Roma, Italy
e-mail: <lastname>@dis.uniroma1.it
[2] Dipartimento di Elettronica Informatica e Sistemistica
Università della Calabria
I-87036 Rende (CS), Italy
e-mail: palopoli@unical.it

Abstract. Recently there was some attention on integration of description logics of the $\mathcal{AL}$-family with rule-based languages for querying relational databases such as Datalog, so as to achieve the best characteristics of both kinds of formalisms in a common framework. Formal analysis on such hybrid languages has been limited to computational complexity: i.e., how much time/space it is needed to answer to a specific query? This paper carries out a different formal analysis, the one dealing with expressiveness, which gives precise characterization of the concepts definable as queries. We first analyze the applicability to hybrid languages of formal tools developed for characterizing the expressive power of relational query languages. We then present some preliminary results on the expressiveness of hybrid languages. In particular, we show that relatively simple hybrid languages are able to define all finite structures expressed by skolemized universally quantified second-order formulae with some constraints on the quantified predicates.

1 Introduction

Recently there was some attention on integration of description logics of the $\mathcal{AL}$-family with rule-based languages for querying relational databases such as Datalog. The two classes of languages exhibit different properties.

- Description logics are good at structuring knowledge in terms of classes and relationships, but are not suitable for expressing complex queries.
- Datalog is good at formulating deductive queries, but uses a flat data model, namely, the relational model, for representing the knowledge base.

Therefore, it is reasonable to investigate knowledge representation systems, hereafter called hybrid languages, integrating the two paradigms so as to achieve the best characteristics of both kinds of formalisms in a common framework. Notable attempts of this sort are [DLNS91,LR96b,LR96a,DLNS97].

The formal analysis reported in such papers is limited to *computational complexity*: i.e., how much time/space is needed to answer to a specific query? This paper carries out a different formal analysis, the one dealing with *expressiveness* of such hybrid languages. Intuitively, the expressiveness, or expressive power, of a query language tells us what "properties" can be extracted from a knowledge base. Thus, the notion of expressive power complements that of computational complexity of a knowledge representation formalism, because the latter tells us how difficult it is to answer a query, while the former gives precise characterization of the concepts that it is possible to define as queries.

Formal studies of expressive power of description logics have been recently pursued. In particular, [Bor96] shows that description logics built using constructors usually considered in the literature are characterized by subsets of first-order logic allowing only three variable symbols. [Baa96] gives a methodological contribution, pointing out that expressiveness must be defined within a precise formal framework, and proposes the model-theoretic approach for the characterization of expressive power. Interestingly, he shows that the complexity of inference of two equally expressive languages may be different.

Since we are dealing with a framework comprising Datalog, specifically designed for querying relational databases, it seems natural to look at the formal tools and methods developed in the database field to investigate the expressiveness of query languages. The importance of formal analysis of expressive power of query languages is acknowledged in the database community [Kan90]. However, the exploitation of such formal tools in our context is not straightforward, as they have been devised to handle a case where, from the logical point of view, the knowledge base has a single model over a fixed domain — this not being the case for $\mathcal{AL}$-languages. In fact, description logics permit the specification (in the TBox) of incomplete information about the world, i.e., they permit the specification of a set of possible worlds. As we will see in the paper, this is a fundamental reason for the increased expressive power of hybrid languages.

The goal of this paper is twofold:

1. To carry out an analysis of the adequacy of the above mentioned formal tools.
2. To perform some considerations and give preliminary results on the expressiveness of hybrid languages.

With regard to the first goal, we observe that the expressive power of query languages has been measured in at least three different ways:

1. With respect to a specific property, such as transitive closure. For example, it is well-known that there is no fixed query in relational calculus that, for any graph G encoded as a relation *edge*/2 in the obvious way, determines whether the transitive closure of G contains a specific edge or not. Vice-versa, such a query does exist in Datalog.
2. With respect to a set of logical formulae, such as first- or second-order logic. For instance, "while queries" [AV92] can express exactly the set of second-order properties over ordered finite structures.

3. With respect to a complexity class, such as P, NP, coNP, PSPACE, etc. As an example, Datalog with stable negation can express all NP properties of finite structures [Sch95], e.g., whether a graph is 3-colorable or not.

According to the above classification, [Bor96] gives a contribution in the context of the second measure, whereas the so-called "Fagin's theorem" [Fag74], provides the basis for unifying the second and the third modalities. This theorem, which is one of the major results in this field, says that the set of NP properties coincides with the set of properties expressed by existentially quantified second-order formulae. This result has been generalized to other complexity classes and sets of logical formulae. In this work, we are going to use both the second and the third modality.

With regard to the second goal, let us discuss an example to help clarify the issue. Suppose we want to check the 3-colorability of a graph $G = \langle V, A \rangle$ encoded as a set of facts $\Delta_\mathcal{E} = \{edge(a, b) \mid (a, b) \in A\}$. In the hybrid languages we are considering, this can be done by means of a 2-components query:

TBox ($\Delta_\mathcal{T}$):

$$\top \sqsubseteq red \sqcup green \sqcup blue$$
$$red \sqsubseteq \neg green$$
$$green \sqsubseteq \neg blue$$
$$red \sqsubseteq \neg blue$$

Datalog rules ($\Delta_\mathcal{R}$):

$$non\_3\_col \leftarrow edge(X, Y), red(X), red(Y).$$
$$non\_3\_col \leftarrow edge(X, Y), blue(X), blue(Y).$$
$$non\_3\_col \leftarrow edge(X, Y), green(X), green(Y).$$

where the axioms in the TBox (called inclusion axioms) impose that the three colors actually partition the domain, and the Datalog rules are used to define the concept of non-3-colorability (a more formal introduction to the syntax and semantics of description logics will be presented in Section 2). Indeed, one can verify that $\Delta_\mathcal{T} \cup \Delta_\mathcal{R} \cup \Delta_\mathcal{E} \models non\_3\_col$ iff G is not 3-colorable (where $\models$ denotes the usual logical consequence operator, i.e., validity in all models). In the terminology of [LR96b], $\Delta_\mathcal{T}$ is "acyclic", and $\Delta_\mathcal{R}$ is "non-recursive". Moreover $\Delta_\mathcal{T}$ belongs to the class CARIN-MARC of "maximal (decidable) $\mathcal{ALCNR}$ recursive CARIN", which includes the constructors $\sqcup, \sqcap, (\geq n\ R), \exists R.C$, and negation on primitive concepts. $\Delta_\mathcal{R}$ is "role-safe", i.e., each of its rules is such that for every atom of the form $R(x, y)$ in the antecedent, where R is a role, then either x or y appear in an ordinary atom of the antecedent. In fact, the TBox is a set of *inclusion axioms* [BDS93], and concept constructors used in the TBox are just propositional. Actually, this is an $\mathcal{AL}$-log program [DLNS91]. From the point of view of expressiveness, we can conclude that Datalog, when augmented with inclusion axioms typical of description logics, is able to capture some coNP-complete queries.

The above example just proves that the *data complexity* (i.e., complexity considering the extensional component as the input and the intensional component –the query– $\Delta_T \cup \Delta_R$ not part of the input) of $\mathcal{AL}$-log is coNP-hard, but it does not imply that either $\mathcal{AL}$-log or CARIN are able to express *all* queries in coNP. Such a distinction is important since the expressive power of a language is not necessarily the same as its complexity (it is always less than or equal to). Several languages with bounding complexity class properly containing their expressiveness are known, cf. e.g., [AV92,EGM97]. In the present paper we show that relatively simple hybrid languages are able to define all finite structures expressed by skolemized universally quantified second-order formulae with some constraints on the quantified predicates.

The paper is organized as follows. In Section 2 we recall the definition of hybrid knowledge bases and of expressiveness of a query language. In Section 3 we show various options for setting up a framework for expressive power in hybrid languages. In Section 4 we give results about expressiveness of two hybrid languages. In Section 5 we discuss an extension of our framework obtained by allowing stratified negation in the bodies of rules. In Section 6 we present conclusions and some open problems.

2 Preliminaries

In this section we give some preliminary notions on description logics, hybrid systems, and queries.

2.1 Description logics

From the syntactic point of view, the language of description logics contains unary relations representing classes of objects and referred to as *concepts* and binary relations, called *roles*, by which relationships between concepts can be established. Complex knowledge is defined by means of descriptions built from a set of given constructors. In this paper, we shall deal with hybrid languages whose descriptive component is a subset of $\mathcal{ALCNR}$ descriptors, which are reported next (A represents a primitive concept, and $P_1, \ldots, P_m$ represent primitive roles; C, D represent complex concepts, and R represents a complex role).

$$
\begin{array}{lll}
C, D \rightarrow & A \mid & \text{(primitive concept)} \\
& \top \mid & \text{(universal concept)} \\
& \bot \mid & \text{(empty concept)} \\
& C \sqcap D \mid & \text{(conjunction)} \\
& C \sqcup D \mid & \text{(disjunction)} \\
& \neg C \mid & \text{(complement)} \\
& \forall R.C \mid & \text{(universal quantification)} \\
& \exists R.C \mid & \text{(existential quantification)} \\
& (\geq n\, R) \mid (\leq n\, R) & \text{(number restrictions)} \\
R \rightarrow & P_1 \sqcap \cdots \sqcap P_m & \text{(role conjunction)}
\end{array}
$$

As an example, the following complex concept

$$(\exists \text{friend.tall}) \sqcap \forall \text{friend.}(\forall \text{friend.doctor}),$$

where doctor and tall are primitive concepts and friend is a primitive role, denotes the set of the individuals having at least one tall friend and such that for each of their friends, each of his or her friends is a doctor.

Description logic knowledge bases contain two parts: a terminological component Δ_T, often called TBox, and an assertional component Δ_A, also called ABox. The TBox contains sentences of the form $C \sqsubseteq D$, telling that every instance of the concept C must be also an instance of the concept D.

As an example, the following sentence states that all parents whose children are either doctors or lawyers are happy.

$$\text{happy\_parent} \sqsubseteq (\exists \text{child.}\top) \sqcap \forall \text{child.}(\text{doctor} \sqcup \text{lawyer}).$$

Concepts can be named by declaring that both $C \sqsubseteq D$ and $D \sqsubseteq C$ hold, often abbreviated $C := D$, where C is a concept name and D is an arbitrary description.

The ABox of a knowledge base includes sentences of the form $C(a)$ and $R(a, b)$, where C is a concept, R is a role and a and b are individual objects.

As an example, the sentence $(\exists \text{friend.tall})(marco)$ stored in the ABox tells that the individual $marco$ has at least one tall friend. Similarly, the sentence $\text{friend}(luigi, marco)$ tells that the individuals $luigi$ and $marco$ are friends.

In general, whereas the TBox contain descriptions predicating general properties of the structured domain, the ABox serves the purpose of expressing (possibly complex) properties characterizing individual domain objects.

A description logic knowledge base Δ is given semantics through *interpretations*. An interpretation I is associated with a domain of constants $\mathcal{D}^I$, which can be finite or infinite. Actually $\mathcal{ALCNR}$ has the so-called *finite model property* [CL94], i.e., if a knowledge base has a model, then it has a finite one. As a consequence, inference in all models is equivalent to inference in finite ones, and we can restrict to finite domains. We note that some concept description languages do not have the finite model property [Cal96]. Any interpretation is supposed to:

1. map each individual object a from Δ onto an element a^I of $\mathcal{D}^I$ and each concept C (resp., role R) onto a unary (resp., binary) relation C^I (resp., R^I) over $\mathcal{D}^I$, and

2. satisfy the following equations:

$$
\begin{aligned}
\top^I & = \mathcal{D}^I \\
\bot^I & = \emptyset \\
(C \sqcap D)^I & = C^I \cap D^I \\
(C \sqcup D)^I & = C^I \cup D^I \\
(\neg C)^I & = \mathcal{D}^I \setminus C^I \\
(\forall R.C)^I & = \{a \in \mathcal{D}^I \mid \forall b : (a,b) \in R^I \to b \in C^I\} \\
(\exists R.C)^I & = \{a \in \mathcal{D}^I \mid \exists b : (a,b) \in R^I \wedge b \in C^I\} \\
(\geq n\, R)^I & = \{a \in \mathcal{D}^I \mid \#\{b \mid (a,b) \in R^I\} \geq n\} \\
(\leq n\, R)^I & = \{a \in \mathcal{D}^I \mid \#\{b \mid (a,b) \in R^I\} \leq n\} \\
(P_1 \sqcap \cdots \sqcap P_m)^I & = P_1^I \cap \cdots \cap P_m^I
\end{aligned}
$$

where $\#S$ denotes the cardinality of the set S.

Following conventions, the Unique Name Assumption is assumed, whereby interpretations map distinct individual objects from the knowledge base into distinct elements of $\mathcal{D}^I$.

An interpretation I of a knowledge base Δ is a *model* for Δ if for each inclusion $C \sqsubseteq D$ defined in its TBox, $C^I \subseteq D^I$ and, furthermore, for each assertion $C(a)$ (resp., $R(a,b)$) $a^I \in C^I$ (resp., $(a^I, b^I) \in R^I$). Finally, Δ logically implies a sentence γ if γ is true in every model of Δ.

Note that, since the Unique Name Assumption holds, we can limit ourselves to consider interpretations mapping individual elements to themselves. In the following, we shall implicitly assume such interpretations.

2.2 Horn rules

Syntactically, a Horn rule has the form

$$p(\mathbf{X}) \leftarrow p_1(\mathbf{X}_1), \ldots, p_k(\mathbf{X}_k)$$

where $\mathbf{X}$, $\mathbf{X}_i$ are lists of variables or constants. We require that every variable appearing in $\mathbf{X}$ also appears in $\mathbf{X}_1 \cup \cdots \cup \mathbf{X}_n$. The part on the left of the implication sign is usually referred to as the *head* of the rule, whereas that on the right is its *body*. A rule with an empty body and where no variables appear is called a *fact*. Sets of facts can be thought of as tuples stored in relational tables separate from the Horn rules. So, in our framework, $\Delta_{\mathcal{R}}$ is assumed not to contain facts. Also, as most often assumed, predicates occurring in rule heads in $\Delta_{\mathcal{R}}$ do not occur in facts.

2.3 Hybrid knowledge bases

A hybrid knowledge base Δ is obtained by coupling a description logic knowledge base with a set of Horn rules and a relational database. For any hybrid knowledge base Δ, $\Delta_{\mathcal{R}}$ denotes its rule component, $\Delta_{\mathcal{E}}$ denotes its relational database, Δ_T is its TBox and, finally $\Delta_{\mathcal{A}}$ is its ABox. Predicates appearing in $\Delta_{\mathcal{R}} \cup \Delta_{\mathcal{E}}$ but not belonging to the description logic component of Δ are called *ordinary* predicates. For any hybrid knowledge base Δ we require that Horn rule heads in $\Delta_{\mathcal{R}}$ always contain ordinary predicates. However, descriptive predicates can occur in facts encoded in relational tables of $\Delta_\mathcal{E}$. The conceptual assumption here is that the terminological and assertional components of the hybrid knowledge base completely capture the structuring of the application domain objects, whereas Horn rules are used to describe inference processes to be carried out during query answering.

The semantics of a hybrid knowledge base is obtained by extending that of its description logic component to Horn rules and relational databases. Thus, models of a hybrid knowledge base Δ are models of $\Delta_\mathcal{T} \cup \Delta_\mathcal{A}$ which satisfy each rule in $\Delta_\mathcal{R}$ and each fact in $\Delta_\mathcal{E}$. A rule

$$p(\mathbf{X}) \leftarrow p_1(\mathbf{X}_1), \ldots, p_k(\mathbf{X}_k)$$

is satisfied by an interpretation I if for each mapping α from variables to $\mathcal{D}^I$ such that $\alpha(\mathbf{X}_i) \in p_i^I$, for each i $(1 \leq i \leq k)$, then $\alpha(\mathbf{X}) \in p^I$, where p^I, p_i^I are the extensions assigned by I to p, p_i, respectively. A fact $p(\mathbf{a})$ is satisfied by I if $\mathbf{a}^I \in p^I$. Note that we are not assuming the Closed World Assumption to hold over $\Delta_\mathcal{E}$.

In order to clarify what kind of queries hybrid knowledge bases allow to express, we report next an example, taken from [LR96a].

comp, am_co, and am_ass_co are symbols for concepts denoting companies, American companies, and companies having at least one associate company which is American, respectively. asso is a symbol for a role denoting association between companies. Consider the knowledge base Δ consisting of the following components:

1. The TBox $\Delta_\mathcal{T}$ contains the following sentences:
   comp $\sqsubseteq$ ∃asso.comp
   am_ass_co $\sqsubseteq$ comp $\sqcap$ ∃asso.am_co
   For instance, the second sentence tells that American associate companies are those companies that have at least one American associate.
2. The ABox $\Delta_\mathcal{A}$ contains the assertion am_ass_co(b)
3. The rule set $\Delta_\mathcal{R}$ consists of the following rule:

$$price(X, usa, high) \leftarrow made\_by(X, Y), \mathsf{comp}(Y), \mathsf{asso}(Y, Z), \mathsf{am\_co}(Z),$$
$$monopoly(Y, X, usa)$$

4. Finally, the relational database $\Delta_\mathcal{E}$ contains the facts $made\_by(a, b)$ and $monopoly(b, a, usa)$.

Then, we can infer $\Delta \models price(a, usa, high)$. Indeed, from am_ass_co(b) we deduce that b has at least one American associate company. That is, there exist a c such that am_co(c) which is associate with b. Therefore, from the rule, we infer that $price(a, usa, high)$ is entailed, even if the body of the rule is not "immediately" instantiated by $\Delta_\mathcal{A} \cup \Delta_\mathcal{E}$.

2.4 Measuring expressive power

Given a language L for transforming information from a designated input knowledge repository (e.g., a relational database or a description logic knowledge base) to a designated output information, by the expressive power of L we mean the set of all transformations between its input and its output that L can express. For instance, if L is the language of Turing machines, we know that L can express any computable transformation from an input string into an output string. An important body of work done on this subject has been developed in the realm of relational database query languages. Next, we survey the main formal tools used in that realm.

As in most of the papers discussing the expressive power of query languages, in this paper we focus on Boolean queries, which are Boolean transformations defined on relational databases. D is a finite set of domain constants.

Definition 1 (From [CH80]). A *(Boolean) query* is a mapping from relational databases onto $\{True, False\}$ satisfying the following constraints:

1. Q is partial recursive;
2. Q is generic, i.e., for each bijection ρ over D, $\rho(Q(D)) = Q(\rho(D))$.

Thus a query is a computable, generic (in other words, constants are uninterpreted), and well-typed mapping that takes a relational database as the input and returns a Boolean value as the output.

As we have pointed out in Section 1, expressive power of query languages has been measured in at least three different ways. For the sake of completeness, with reference to the third measure, we explain how a query language expressing boolean queries can be related to a complexity class. Each query Q defines a family of databases DB_Q as follows:

$$DB_Q = \{D \mid Q(D) = True\}.$$

Let $\mathbf{D}$ be a collection of databases. Let C be a Turing complexity class (e.g., NP). Then the family $\mathbf{D}$ is said to be C-*recognizable* if the problem of deciding if a given database D belongs to $\mathbf{D}$ is in C. Then we say that a query language L *expresses* a database complexity class C if for each C-recognizable database family $\mathbf{D}$ there is an expression e of L which defines $\mathbf{D}$.

Fagin's theorem [Fag74], cited in Section 1, states that a query language expresses NP iff it has the same expressive power of the language of existentially quantified second-order formulae $(\exists \mathbf{S})\phi$, where $\mathbf{S}$ is a tuple of predicate names and ϕ is a first-order formula. Subsequently, many other similar results relative to other complexity classes have been proved. In our framework, since TBoxes are assumed to contain predicates (concepts, roles) with fixed arity, we will refer in the following to fragments of universal second-order logic with fixed arity [Fag75]. The class NP_k, $k \geq 1$, includes all collections which can be expressed by second-order formulae $(\exists \mathbf{S})\phi$ where each predicate in $\mathbf{S}$ has arity less than or equal to k. Classes NP_k form a proper hierarchy within NP, in that each class NP_k is strictly contained in NP_{k+1} [Fag93]. This hierarchy does not immediately relate to computational complexity: In fact, the smallest class in the hierarchy (NP_1) contains NP complete collections (e.g., the collection of

3-colorable graphs). Nevertheless there are polynomial collections of databases (e.g., the collection of dyadic relations with even number of tuples) that are not in NP_1 [Fag93]. The class NP_1 has interesting properties: as an example, in [Cos93] it is proven that NP_1 differs from $coNP_1$, while this is a long-standing open question for unbounded NP and coNP.

In the following, we shall show some expressive power results for hybrid languages by relating them to subsets of NP_k, $k \geq 1$, including only those collections expressed by skolemized NP_k formulae $\exists S \forall X \exists Y \phi(X, Y)$ where $\phi(X, Y)$ is a quantifier-free first-order formula[1].

It is not known whether imposing skolemization actually excludes some collections from NP_k or not.

3 Which definition of expressiveness for hybrid languages?

Most of the work on expressiveness of query languages assume that the input to the query answering process is a relational database. From the logical point of view, a relational database is a first-order finite interpretation that satisfies the properties expressed in the relational schema (the database is indeed seen as a model of the schema, see [Rei84]). Thus, a query is actually a function over the collection of all possible finite models of the relational schema.

In hybrid languages, the situation is more complicated. Indeed, we have four components involved in query processing, namely, the TBox, the ABox, the set of Horn rules, and the relational database, and we have to decide which are the components that form the input to a query, as opposed to the ones that form the query itself. Moreover, knowledge bases expressed in hybrid languages generally admit several models, in particular when the description logic employs disjunction and/or existential quantification. It follows that a query cannot in general be considered as a computation over a single first-order structure.

The above observations show that we have different options for setting up a formal framework for expressiveness in hybrid languages. The goal of this section is to present some basic considerations about such options.

3.1 Query structure

Let Δ be a hybrid knowledge base, and let Δ_R, $\Delta_\mathcal{E}$, Δ_T, and Δ_A be defined as in Section 2. The components Δ_A and $\Delta_\mathcal{E}$ express properties of individuals, in particular, about their membership in concepts, and their mutual relationships (roles and relations). In other words, Δ_A and $\Delta_\mathcal{E}$ deal with the extensional level of the knowledge base Δ, and, as such, will be considered as parts of the input to the queries.

On the other hand, Δ_T and Δ_R deal with the intensional level of the knowledge base. The former expresses general knowledge about the concepts of the

---

[1] Formulae of this kind are said to be in *doubly prenex normal form* [MP96].

description logic part, whereas the latter is used to define intensional predicates in terms of concepts, roles, and relations.

Following the spirit of deductive databases, it is reasonable to conceive $\Delta_{\mathcal{R}}$ as specifying the computation needed to extract information from the knowledge base. This leads to consider $\Delta_{\mathcal{R}}$ as part of the query. As for $\Delta_{\mathcal{T}}$, we have two possibilities:

- To consider it as a set of integrity constraints over the extensional part of the knowledge base. In this case, $\Delta_{\mathcal{T}}$ is used to specify which are the interpretation structures that are legal with respect to the application, and, therefore, is considered as part of the input to query processing.
- To consider it as part of the specification of the computation to be carried out in the process of query answering, and therefore as part of the query. We note that this option was implicitly used in the example of Section 1, where trying the color of the nodes of the graph was done during query evaluation. An interesting generalization of this idea to other coNP queries leads to viewing $\Delta_{\mathcal{T}}$ as playing its role in the guessing stage, and $\Delta_{\mathcal{R}}$ as specifying the computation to be performed in the checking stage.

We observe that the framework for expressiveness in databases corresponds to the special case where both $\Delta_{\mathcal{A}}$ and $\Delta_{\mathcal{T}}$ are empty, and, therefore, $\Delta_{\mathcal{R}}$ is the query, and $\Delta_{\mathcal{E}}$ is the input.

3.2 Semantical issues

As pointed out before, a query in relational databases is considered as a function applied to a single first-order model in order to compute the desired result. This idea is not directly applicable for devising a formal setting for expressiveness of hybrid knowledge bases. Indeed, we can single out at least three interesting cases of increasing difficulty:

1. The query extracts information from a single finite first-order structure.
2. The output of the query depends on a bounded number of finite structures over a single finite domain.
3. The output of the query depends on an arbitrary collection of structures over a (finite or infinite) domain.

Case (a) occurs when the TBox is seen as part of the query and the ABox is empty, or when both the TBox and the ABox are empty, and is the one where the formal tools developed in relational theory are satisfactory. We note that the example of Section 1 falls under this category.

Case (b) occurs when the ABox and the TBox have a finite Herbrand Universe, which can be considered as the domain of interpretation. The multiplicity of models in this setting is due to the use of disjunction or existential quantification in the description logic component. More generally, whenever the ABox and the TBox use only propositional connectives, i.e., neither quantifications nor number restrictions, we are in case (b).

Another way to achieve the conditions of case (b) is to impose the Unique Domain Assumption, for example by adding a special axiom to the knowledge base, called the Domain Closure Axiom (DCA). The DCA is the formula

$$\forall X \ (X = t_1 \vee \cdots \vee X = t_n),$$

where $t_1, \ldots, t_n$ are all constant symbols occurring in the knowledge base. To see the role of this assumption in query answering, consider the following example:

TBox (Δ_T): $\top \sqsubseteq \exists q. \top$
Datalog rules (Δ_R): $r_1(X, Y) \leftarrow q(X, Y), r_2(a).$
Relational database ($\Delta_\mathcal{E}$): $r_2(a)$

It is easy to see that, under the DCA, $r_1(a, a)$ is implied by the knowledge base, whereas this is not the case without such an assumption.

Case (c) is the one when no special assumption holds. It is therefore very complex, and seems to be basically unexplored in the literature. Indeed, a precise definition of expressiveness of queries posed to knowledge bases with arbitrary models is missing. Preliminary attempts to deal with this problem are [Var86,BE96]. However, these works adopt various simplifying assumptions, that are not suited to this framework.

4 The expressive power of CARIN knowledge bases

In this section, we present some results about the expressive power of hybrid languages. The framework used in the analysis can be described as follows:

- We assume that the relational database is the input to the query, whereas the TBox and the Horn rules form the query expression.
- We assume that the ABox is empty, and that the TBox uses only propositional connectives. In other words, we are in case (a) according to the classification illustrated in Section 3.2.

In [LR96b] it is proved that the data complexity (the input being the ABox and the relational database) of logical inference in both CARIN-MARC and ROLE-SAFE CARIN is coNP-complete, and we showed in Section 1 that coNP-complete problems are indeed expressed by very simple CARIN knowledge bases, where the Horn component is non-recursive. In this section we prove two results:

1. That ROLE-SAFE CARIN-MARC$^{=,\neq}$ with a non-recursive Horn component expresses all queries that are defined by formulae of the kind $\neg\exists S \forall X \exists Y \phi(\mathbf{X}, \mathbf{Y})$, where S is a list of monadic predicates, ϕ is a quantifier-free first-order formula, and $\mathbf{X}$, $\mathbf{Y}$ are lists of variables, provided that the input finite structure is given in suitable form, as specified below. The superscript $=,\neq$ denotes availability of pre-interpreted symbols for equality and inequality to be used in Datalog rules. Formulae $\neg\exists S \forall X \exists Y \phi(\mathbf{X}, \mathbf{Y})$ define queries that form a subset of monadic coNP queries (hereafter, called coNP$_1$ cf.

[Fag75,Fag93,Cos93]), which contains several coNP complete queries (e.g., the complement of 3-colorability of a graph). At the moment, we do not know whether this result can be generalized to the entire set of monadic coNP queries.

2. That CARIN-MARC= with a non-recursive Horn component enriched with propositional inclusion axioms on primitive roles expresses all queries that are defined by formulae of the kind $\neg \exists \mathbf{S}' \forall \mathbf{X} \exists \mathbf{Y} \phi'(\mathbf{X}, \mathbf{Y})$, where $\mathbf{S}'$ is a list of predicates with arity at most 2 and ϕ' is a quantifier-free first-order formula, provided that the input finite structure is given in suitable form, as specified below. Analogously to the previous case, such formulae define queries that form a subset of dyadic coNP (coNP_2), and we do not know whether this result can be generalized to the entire set of dyadic coNP queries.

The coNP-completeness of querying the classes of CARIN-MARC and ROLE-SAFE CARIN knowledge bases, whose definition has been recalled in Section 1, established in [LR96b] serves also as an upper bound to the expressiveness when the ABox is empty. In other words we know that no CARIN-MARC or ROLE-SAFE CARIN knowledge base can express queries which are not in coNP.

In the following, σ denotes a fixed set of relational symbols not including equality "=" and $\mathbf{S}$ denotes a list of variables ranging over monadic relational symbols distinct from those in σ. By Fagin's theorem [Fag74], any NP-recognizable collection $\mathbf{D}$ of finite structures over σ is defined by a second-order existentially quantified formula. In particular, NP-recognizable collections $\mathbf{D}$ of finite structures, defined by formulas where all existentially quantified relational symbols are 1-ary, form the set of NP_1 collections.

In the following, we deal with skolemized second-order formulae of the following kind:

$$\phi = (\exists \mathbf{S})(\forall \mathbf{X})(\exists \mathbf{Y})(\theta_1(\mathbf{X}, \mathbf{Y}) \vee \cdots \vee \theta_k(\mathbf{X}, \mathbf{Y})), \tag{1}$$

where $\theta_1, \ldots, \theta_k$ are conjunctions of literals involving relational symbols in σ and $\mathbf{S}$, plus relational symbol "=", and all relational symbols in $\mathbf{S}$ are constrained to be monadic. The set of variable occurrences in θ_i is contained in $\mathbf{X} \cup \mathbf{Y}$. As usual, "=" is always interpreted as "equality". The set of uninterpreted relational symbols occurring in formula (1) –i.e., $\sigma \cup \mathbf{S}$– will be denoted either by $\mathcal{L}$ or by $\{a_1, \ldots, a_l\}$. In the following art(a) denotes the arity of a predicate a.

We illustrate a method that transforms a formula ϕ of the kind (1) and a finite structure D into a ROLE-SAFE CARIN-MARC knowledge base $\Delta(\phi, D)$ and a query γ. Both $\Delta(\phi, D)$ and γ use an enlarged set of relational symbols $\mathcal{L}'$ which is built as follows:

1. each relational symbol $a \in \mathcal{L}$ is in $\mathcal{L}'$;
2. for each relational symbol $a \in \mathcal{L}$ there is one relational symbol $\bar{a}$ with the same arity as a in $\mathcal{L}'$;
3. there are relational symbols t and U' with the same arity as $\mathbf{X}$, U'' with the same arity as $\mathbf{Y}$, and U with arity 1;
4. there are two binary "built-in" relational symbols eq and $\overline{eq}$ denoting equality and inequality, respectively.

The ROLE-SAFE CARIN-MARC knowledge base $\Delta(\phi, D) = \Delta_{\mathcal{T}}(\phi) \cup \Delta_{\mathcal{R}}(\phi) \cup \Delta_{\mathcal{E}}(\phi, D)$ is built as follows:

1. For each relational symbol $s \in \mathbf{S}$, the following axioms are in $\Delta_{\mathcal{T}}(\phi)$:

$$\top \sqsubseteq s \sqcup \bar{s}, \qquad s \sqsubseteq \neg\bar{s}$$

2. For each relational symbol $a \in \sigma$, the following $art(a)$ rules are in $\Delta_{\mathcal{R}}(\phi)$;

$$U(X) \leftarrow a(X, Y_1, \ldots, Y_{art(a)-1})$$

$$\cdots$$

$$U(X) \leftarrow a(Y_1, \ldots, Y_{art(a)-1}, X)$$

3. the following rules are also in $\Delta_{\mathcal{R}}(\phi)$:

$$U'(X_1, \ldots, X_n) \leftarrow U(X_1), \ldots, U(X_n)$$
$$U''(Y_1, \ldots, Y_m) \leftarrow U(Y_1), \ldots, U(Y_m)$$

where n and m are the number of variables occurring in $\mathbf{X}$ and $\mathbf{Y}$, respectively.

4. For each conjunct

$$\theta_i(\mathbf{X}, \mathbf{Y}) = \neg w_1(\mathbf{X}, \mathbf{Y}) \wedge \cdots \wedge \neg w_n(\mathbf{X}, \mathbf{Y}) \wedge$$
$$w_{n+1}(\mathbf{X}, \mathbf{Y}) \wedge \cdots \wedge w_{n+m}(\mathbf{X}, \mathbf{Y})$$

$(1 \leq i \leq k)$ in ϕ, the rule

$$t(\mathbf{X}) \leftarrow \overline{v_1}(\mathbf{X}, \mathbf{Y}), \ldots, \overline{v_n}(\mathbf{X}, \mathbf{Y}),$$
$$v_{n+1}(\mathbf{X}, \mathbf{Y}), \ldots, v_{n+m}(\mathbf{X}, \mathbf{Y}), U'(\mathbf{X}), U''(\mathbf{Y})$$

is in $\Delta_{\mathcal{R}}(\phi)$, where:
- $\overline{v_i}$ $(1 \leq i \leq n)$ is:
  - $\overline{eq}$, if w_i is "=" (this is just used here to make the syntax used for equality uniform to that used for predicates in $\mathbf{S}$),
  - $\overline{w_i}$, otherwise;
- v_{n+i} $(1 \leq i \leq m)$ is:
  - eq, if w_{n+i} is "=",
  - w_{n+i}, otherwise.

Furthermore, the query γ is

$$(\exists X_1, \ldots, X_{art(t)}) \, \neg t(X_1, \ldots, X_{art(t)}), U'(X_1, \ldots, X_{art(t)}).$$

We remark that $\Delta_{\mathcal{T}}(\phi) \cup \Delta_{\mathcal{R}}(\phi)$ is a ROLE-SAFE CARIN-MARC knowledge base.

Now, given a finite structure D, we define the complementary structure $\overline{D}$ as follows. For each relational symbol $r \in D$ there is a relational symbol $\bar{r}$ in $\overline{D}$ with the same arity as r. Then, for each relational symbol $\bar{r}$ in $\overline{D}$ and for each tuple $\mathbf{t}$ of constants from D, it holds that $\overline{D} \models \bar{r}(\mathbf{t})$ iff $D \not\models r(\mathbf{t})$. Thus, finally, let $\Delta_{\mathcal{E}}(\phi, D) = D \cup \overline{D}$, and $\Delta(\phi, D) = \Delta_{\mathcal{T}}(\phi) \cup \Delta_{\mathcal{R}}(\phi) \cup \Delta_{\mathcal{E}}(\phi, D)$. We are now ready for the first main result about expressive power of ROLE-SAFE CARIN-MARC.

Theorem 2. *For any skolemized NP_1 collection* **D** *of finite structures over σ –characterized by a formula ϕ of the kind (1)– and for any finite structure D, the* ROLE-SAFE CARIN-MARC *knowledge base $\Delta(\phi, D)$ built according to the above rules is such that D is in* **D** *if and only if $\Delta(\phi, D) \not\models \gamma$.*

In other words, the theorem says that each collection of finite structures in skolemized coNP$_1$ is definable by a ROLE-SAFE CARIN-MARC knowledge base $\Delta(\phi, D)$ and query γ.

To allow role axioms to occur in $\Delta_T(\phi)$ enhances the expressive power of the language. Indeed, consider formulae of the form:

$$\phi' = (\exists \mathbf{S}')(\forall \mathbf{X})(\exists \mathbf{Y})(\theta_1(\mathbf{X}, \mathbf{Y}) \vee \cdots \vee \theta_k(\mathbf{X}, \mathbf{Y})), \qquad (2)$$

where $\theta_1, \ldots, \theta_k$ are conjunctions of literals involving relational symbols in σ and $\mathbf{S}'$, plus relational symbol "=", and all relational symbols in $\mathbf{S}'$ are constrained to be either monadic or dyadic. Such formulae define a subset of NP$_2$ that contains NP-complete problems. We note that there are collections of polynomial-time recognizable databases (e.g., the collection of ternary relations with even number of tuples) that are not in NP$_2$ [Fag93], and that NP$_2$ strictly contains NP$_1$ (e.g., the collection of dyadic relations with even number of tuples is in NP$_2$).

In this case, we do assume the language includes built-in predicate for equality only (denoted also eq by analogy to the previous theorem). Inequality will be derived. To illustrate the transformation of a formula ϕ' of the kind (2) into a CARIN-MARC$^=$ knowledge base $\Delta'(\phi', D) = \Delta'_T(\phi') \cup \Delta_R(\phi') \cup \Delta_E(\phi', D)$ with axioms on roles and a query $\gamma' = \gamma$, we modify the translation provided for the monadic case. $\Delta'(\phi', D)$ is equal to $\Delta(\phi, D)$ except that for each dyadic relational symbol $s' \in \mathbf{S}'$, the following role axioms are in $\Delta'_T(\phi')$:

$$\top \times \top \sqsubseteq s' \sqcup \overline{s'} \qquad\qquad s' \sqsubseteq \neg \overline{s'}$$
$$\top \times \top \sqsubseteq eq \sqcup \overline{eq} \qquad\qquad eq \sqsubseteq \neg \overline{eq}$$

We are now ready for our second result about expressive power of CARIN languages.

Theorem 3. *For any skolemized NP_2 collection* **D** *of finite structures over σ –characterized by a formula ϕ' of the kind (2)– and for any finite structure D, the* CARIN-MARC$^=$ *knowledge base $\Delta'(\phi', D)$ built according to the above rules is such that D is in* **D** *if and only if $\Delta'(\phi', D) \not\models \gamma'$.*

5   Current work on negation

In this section, we overview some current research we are conducting which focuses on extending our hybrid languages by adding stratified negation in its rule component. In particular, in the following we shall define the semantics of such extended languages and show that their data complexity is still within coNP.

We begin with syntax. A stratified Datalog$^\neg$ program is a set of rules of the form:

$$p(\mathbf{X}) \leftarrow p_1(\mathbf{X_1}), \dots p_k(\mathbf{X_k}), \neg q_1(\mathbf{Y_1}), \dots, \neg q_n(\mathbf{Y_n})$$

such that it is possible to assign a level $lev(p)$ to each predicate symbol p and for each rule of the form above, $lev(p) > lev(q_i)$, $1 \leq i \leq n$, and $lev(p) \geq lev(p_i)$, $1 \leq i \leq k$. Then, the program can be partitioned into strata $\{S_i\}$, each stratum S_i containing all the rules whose head predicate symbol has been assigned the level i.

The semantics of a Datalog$^\neg$ program on their own is given by its *stratified* or *perfect* model, which is constructed by evaluating the program a stratum at a time, beginning from the lowest stratum. Because of stratification, each time a stratum is evaluated, the negative literals in the bodies of its rules have already been computed, so that they can be treated as base predicates.

Define now a stratified hybrid knowledge base Δ to be a knowledge base having a stratified Datalog$^\neg$ program as its rule component $\Delta_\mathcal{R}$.

To define the semantics of stratified hybrid knowledge bases, we proceed as follows. Consider $\Delta_{nR} = \Delta \backslash \Delta_\mathcal{R}$. Δ_{nR} has in general a set of models $\{M_i\}$. In our assumptions, each of these models can be looked at as an extensional relational database. Then, the semantics of Δ is given by the set of perfect models obtained by union of $\Delta_\mathcal{R}$ with each one such M_i. More formally, let γ be a query and Δ be a stratified hybrid knowledge base. Then, $\Delta \models \gamma$ iff for each perfect model M of $\Delta_\mathcal{R} \cup N$, it holds that $M \models \gamma$, where N is a model of Δ_{nR}.

Using stratified rule components probably enhances the expressive power of hybrid knowledge bases, even if we do not have a formal proof yet. However, it clearly improves their amenability at expressing interesting queries in a simple way, as the one presented below.

Datalog rules ($\Delta'_\mathcal{R}$):

$$non\_red\_path(X, Y) \leftarrow edge(X, Y), \neg red(X), \neg red(Y).$$
$$non\_red\_path(X, Y) \leftarrow non\_red\_path(X, Z), edge(Z, Y), \neg red(Y).$$
$$non\_red \leftarrow \neg non\_red\_path(a, b).$$
$$non\_red \leftarrow non\_3\_col.$$

The rules above, when added to the 3-coloring example given in Section 1, with the query $\gamma = non\_red$ solve the following problem.

Does there exists a 3-coloring of G such that there is at least one path between nodes a and b which does not use red-colored nodes?

But what is the computational cost of adding stratified negation to hybrid knowledge bases? We can prove that the data complexity (i.e., the complexity of query answering measured as the size of $\Delta_\mathcal{E} \cup \Delta_\mathcal{A}$ varies while the size of the rest of the knowledge base remains fixed) for hybrid knowledge bases remains unchanged when stratified negation is added.

Indeed, to show that a query γ is not entailed by a knowledge base Δ it is sufficient to show a perfect model M of Δ which does not entail γ. To this end, we do the following: (1) guess an interpretation M of Δ; (2) verify that M is a perfect model of Δ; (3) verify that M does not entail γ. Clearly, step (3) can be done in polynomial time. As for step (2), it can be carried out into two substeps: (2.1) verify that M is a model of Δ_{nR}; (2.2) verify that it is a perfect model of $\Delta_R \cup M_{nR}$, where M_{nR} is the projection of M on predicate symbols occurring in Δ_{nR} (recall that such a set is disjoint from the set of predicate symbols occurring in the rule component of the knowledge base). Both step (2.1) and step (2.2) are carried out in polynomial time. The result follows considering that the size of M is polynomial in the size of $\Delta_{\mathcal{E}} \cup \Delta_{\mathcal{A}}$

Current research we are conducting focuses on establishing the expressive power of stratified hybrid knowledge bases as well as of other variants, where more involved form of negation is allowed (e.g., stable negation).

6   Conclusions

In the present paper we discussed the possibility of exploiting the formal analysis tools developed in the database field within the context of description logics augmented with rules. Also, we proved some results on the expressive power of two hybrid languages, in particular obtaining two lower bounds on their expressiveness (Theorems 2 and 3). Upper bound for the expressiveness of the former language follows from the results of [LR96b]. We still have to investigate the upper bound of expressiveness of the latter language.

In this work we assumed empty ABoxes. Nevertheless the results we presented are valid also if the ABox contains positive atomic assertions such as $red(node1)$. Furthermore, it is important to stress that by allowing predicates with any arity to appear in a propositional TBox, we obtain languages capturing all coNP properties.

Several questions are still open. Regarding the two languages we have analyzed in this paper, (1) determine whether there are queries in $coNP_2$ which cannot be expressed by the former language, and (2) determine whether the languages express all (even non-skolemized) queries in $coNP_1$, resp. $coNP_2$. More generally, how to define the expressive power over finite formulae possibly denoting infinitely many models?

Acknowledgements

The authors would like to thank Alon Levy and Rick Hull for their useful comments. Thanks are also due to the anonymous referees for their precious suggestions.

This work has been supported by ASI (Italian Space Agency), MURST (Italian Ministry for University and Scientific and Technological Research), CNR (Italian Research Council), and the European Community under the Esprit Project 22469 - DWQ.

References

[AV92]   S. Abiteboul and V. Vianu. Expressive power of query languages. In J. D. Ullman, editor, *Theoretical Studies in Computer Science*. Academic Press, 1992.

[Baa96]   Franz Baader. A formal definition for the expressive power of terminological knowledge representation languages. *Journal of Logic and Computation*, 6:33–54, 1996.

[BDS93]   Martin Buchheit, Francesco M. Donini, and Andrea Schaerf. Decidable reasoning in terminological knowledge representation systems. *Journal of Artificial Intelligence Research*, 1:109–138, 1993.

[BE96]   P. Bonatti and T. Eiter. Querying disjunctive databases through nonmonotonic logics. *Theoretical Computer Science*, 160:321–363, 1996.

[Bor96]   Alexander Borgida. On the relative expressiveness of description logics and predicate logics. *Artificial Intelligence Journal*, 82:353–367, 1996.

[Cal96]   Diego Calvanese. Finite model reasoning in description logics. In Luigia C. Aiello, John Doyle, and Stuart C. Shapiro, editors, *Proceedings of the Fifth International Conference on the Principles of Knowledge Representation and Reasoning (KR-96)*, pages 292–303. Morgan Kaufmann, Los Altos, 1996.

[CH80]   A. Chandra and D. Harel. Computable queries for relational databases. *Journal of Computer and System Sciences*, 21:156–178, 1980.

[CL94]   Diego Calvanese and Maurizio Lenzerini. Making object-oriented schemas more expressive. In *Proceedings of the Thirteenth ACM SIGACT SIGMOD SIGART Symposium on Principles of Database Systems (PODS-94)*, pages 243–254, Minneapolis, 1994. ACM Press and Addison Wesley.

[Cos93]   S. S. Cosmadakis. Logical reducibility and monadic NP. In *Proceedings of the Thirtyfourth Annual Symposium on the Foundations of Computer Science (FOCS-93)*, 1993.

[DLNS91]   Francesco M. Donini, Maurizio Lenzerini, Daniele Nardi, and Andrea Schaerf. A hybrid system integrating Datalog and concept languages. In *Proceedings of the Second Conference of the Italian Association for Artificial Intelligence (AI*IA-91)*, number 549 in Lecture Notes In Artificial Intelligence. Springer-Verlag, 1991.

[DLNS97]   Francesco M. Donini, Maurizio Lenzerini, Daniele Nardi, and Andrea Schaerf. $\mathcal{AL}$-log: Integrating Datalog and description logics. *Journal of Intelligent Information Systems*, 1997. To appear.

[EGM97]   T. Eiter, G. Gottlob, and H. Mannila. Disjunctive Datalog. *ACM Transactions on Database Systems*, 22:364–418, 1997.

[Fag74]   R. Fagin. Generalized First-Order Spectra and Polynomial-Time Recognizable Sets. In R. M. Karp, editor, *Complexity of Computation*, pages 43–74. AMS, 1974.

[Fag75]   Ronald Fagin. Monadic generalized spectra. *Zeitschrift für mathematische Logik und Grundlagen der Mathematik*, 21:89–96, 1975.

[Fag93]   Ronald Fagin. Finite-model theory – a personal perspective. *Theoretical Computer Science*, 116:3–31, 1993.

[Kan90]   P. Kanellakis. Elements of relational database theory. In J. van Leeuwen, editor, *Handbook of Theoretical Computer Science*, volume B, chapter 17. Elsevier Science Publishers (North-Holland), Amsterdam, 1990.

[LR96a]   Alon Y. Levy and Marie-Christine Rousset. CARIN: A representation language combining Horn rules and description logics. In *Proceedings of the*

Twelfth European Conference on Artificial Intelligence (ECAI-96), pages 323–327, 1996.

[LR96b]   Alon Y. Levy and Marie-Christine Rousset. The limits on combining recursive Horn rules with description logics. In *Proceedings of the Thirteenth National Conference on Artificial Intelligence (AAAI-96)*, pages 577–584, 1996.

[MP96]   J.A. Makowsky and Y.B. Pnueli. Arity and alternation in second-order logic. *Annals of Pure and Applied Logics*, 78:189–202, 1996.

[Rei84]   Raymond Reiter. Towards a logical reconstruction of relational database theory. In M. L. Brodie, J. Mylopoulos, and J. W. Schmidt, editors, *On Conceptual Modelling*. Springer-Verlag, 1984.

[Sch95]   J. S. Schlipf. The expressive powers of the logic programming semantics. *Journal of Computer and System Sciences*, 51:64–86, 1995.

[Var86]   M. Y. Vardi. Querying logical databases. *Journal of Computer and System Sciences*, 33:142–160, 1986.

Formal Foundations for Optimising Aggregation Functions in Database Programming Languages

Alexandra Poulovassilis[†] and Carol Small[‡]

[†]Dept. of Computer Science, King's College London
Strand, London WC2R 2LS
alex@dcs.kcl.ac.uk

[‡]Autosimulations Ltd.
2 Millbanke Court, Millbanke Way, Bracknell, Berkshire, U.K.
carols@autosim.com

Abstract. This paper investigates the optimisation of aggregation functions in the context of computationally complete database programming languages and aims to generalise and provide a unifying formal foundation for previous work. We define a 'fold' operator ϕ over collection types in terms of which operations such as selection, projection, join and group-by can be defined, as well as aggregation functions such as sum, max and min. We introduce two equivalences for ϕ which respectively govern the commuting and coalescing of applications of ϕ. From these two equivalences we then formally derive equivalences governing the commuting and coalescing of iteration operations over collections, the mapping of aggregation functions over grouped collections, the introduction and elimination of aggregation functions, and the promotion of aggregation functions through iteration operations. We also show how some of these equivalences can be used to optimise comprehensions, a high-level query construct supported by many database languages.

1   Introduction

The optimisation of aggregation functions has been the subject of much recent research, prompted by the emergence of new application areas such as data warehousing. This paper contributes to this area by: generalising many previously proposed equivalences and showing that they follow from a very small set of initial equivalences; providing a framework for formally proving existing and new equivalences; and extending previous work to computationally complete database programming languages (DBPLs), in which issues of non-termination, infinite data structures and user-defined data types arise.

This introductory section begins with a summary of the DBPL that we will be considering here in Sections 1.1 and 1.2, including its syntax, semantics and type system, In Section 1.3 we define the notion of a collection type and a generic 'fold' operator, ϕ, over collection types. In Section 1.4 we give an overview of the equivalences that we will be considering, including two equivalences for ϕ from which all the others are derived. We discuss the proof framework for proving these equivalences. Our motivation for starting out with ϕ and two top-level equivalences is that many aggregation functions can be defined in terms of ϕ — and in sections 1.5 and 1.6 we show how several iteration, grouping and clustering operations can be so defined. The equivalences for ϕ then yield equivalences for these operations which need simpler or, in some cases, no provisos. Such equivalences can then be used for practical query optimisation.

Sections 2, 3, 4 and 5 form the core of the paper. In these sections we respectively introduce equivalences governing the mapping of aggregation functions over grouped collections, the introduction and elimination of aggregation functions, the promotion of aggregation functions through iteration operations, and the commuting and coalescing of iteration operations over collections. These kinds of optimisations are important because coalescing two operations into a single one can eliminate the computation of, potentially large, intermediate data structures, while commuting two operations can reduce the size of such structures.

In Section 6 we show how some of the equivalences we derive here can be applied to the optimisation of comprehensions. This is important because comprehensions provide a unifying high-level query formalism for many languages. For example, monoid comprehensions have been used to define the main features of OQL [7], and thus our work can contribute towards practical query optimisers for OQL. In Section 7 we briefly review related work. We give our concluding remarks in Section 8.

1.1   The Language

Following on from our recent work [11, 12], the language that we consider is the λ-calculus extended with constructors, pattern-matching λ-abstractions and *let* expressions. Here we give a necessarily brief description of its syntax and semantics, and full details can be found in [11, 12].

Expressions in the language have the following syntax:

$$
\begin{aligned}
expr \quad &= var \mid constructor \mid builtin \mid \text{``}\lambda\text{''} pattern \text{``.''} expr \mid expr_1\ expr_2 \mid \\
&\quad \text{``}let\text{''}\ var_1 \text{`` = ''} expr_1 \text{``;''}\ \ldots\ \text{``;''}\ var_n \text{`` = ''} expr_n\ \text{``}in\text{''}\ expr \mid \\
&\quad \text{``(''} expr \text{``)''} \\
pattern &= var \mid constructor\ pattern_1\ \ldots\ pattern_n
\end{aligned}
$$

Tuples, $(e_1, \ldots, e_n)$, are regarded as syntactic sugar for applications of the n-ary tuple constructor $Tuple_n$ to n arguments, $e_1, \ldots, e_n$. Functions are defined by equations of the form $f = e$, where f is a variable and e an expression.

An occurrence of a variable x in an expression e is said to be *bound* if it occurs in a sub-expression of e of the form $\lambda p.e'$ or *let* $x_1 = e'_1;\ \ldots; x_n = e'_n$ *in* e', and x also occurs in p or $\{x_1, \ldots, x_n\}$, respectively; otherwise the occurrence of x is *free*. $FV(e)$ denotes the set of variables with at least one free occurrence in e.

The semantics of functional languages are typically specified denotationally [13], whereby each expression is denoted by some member of a semantic domain — this is the *value* of the expression. The semantic domain contains for each type t an element $\perp_t$ which denotes any expression of type t whose evaluation fails to terminate and outputs no information (below, we omit the type subscript to $\bot$ unless there is a risk of ambiguity). Our language is *lazy* in that it ensures termination whenever possible by only evaluating the arguments to functions if needed by the function to return a result. An n-ary function f is *strict* in its ith argument if that argument must be evaluated in order for the function to return a result i.e. if the value of $f \; e_1 \; \ldots \; e_n$ is $\bot$ whenever the value of e_i is $\bot$.

The usual arithmetic and comparison operators are built into our language and a detailed discussion of their semantics can be found in [11]. The 3-argument conditional function *if* is built-in and has the following semantics:

$$if \; \bot_{Bool} \; x \; y = \bot$$
$$if \; True \; x \; y \; = x$$
$$if \; False \; x \; y = y$$

We should note that here, as in all our definitions of built-in functions, the constants $\bot_{Bool}$, $True$ and $False$ refer to members of the semantic domain, in this case to possible values of expressions of type $Bool$. We should also note that the first equation implies that *if* is strict in its first argument.

We sometimes use $if \; e_1 \; then \; e_2 \; else \; e_3$ as syntactic sugar for $if \; e_1 \; e_2 \; e_3$. Negation can be defined in terms of if, as can conjunction and disjunction:

$$not \; = \lambda x.if \; x \; then \; False \; else \; True$$
$$and = \lambda x.\lambda y.if \; x \; then \; y \; else \; False$$
$$or \; \; = \lambda x.\lambda y.if \; x \; then \; True \; else \; y$$

However, *and* and *or* are not commutative; in particular *and* $\bot$ *False* $\neq$ *and False* $\bot$ and *or* $\bot$ *True* $\neq$ *or True* $\bot$. So we also assume as built-in commutative operators $\vee$ and $\wedge$ with the following semantics:

$True$	$\vee \; y$	$= True$	$False$	$\wedge \; y$	$= False$
x	$\vee \; True$	$= True$	x	$\wedge \; False$	$= False$
$False$	$\vee \; y$	$= y$	$True$	$\wedge \; y$	$= y$
x	$\vee \; False$	$= x$	x	$\wedge \; True$	$= x$
$\bot$	$\vee \; \bot$	$= \bot$	$\bot$	$\wedge \; \bot$	$= \bot$

1.2   The type system

Our language is strongly, statically typed and supports a number of primitive types, such as booleans, strings and numbers. Also, $(t_1, \ldots, t_n)$ is an n-product type for any types $t_1, \ldots, t_n$, $List \; t$ is a list type for any type t, and $t_1 \rightarrow t_2$ is the type of functions from t_1 to t_2. The function type constructor $\rightarrow$ is right-associative, so that $t_1 \rightarrow t_2 \rightarrow t_3$ and $t_1 \rightarrow (t_2 \rightarrow t_3)$ are synonymous.

Analogously to the unary type constructor, $List$, we also assume as built-in the set and bag type constructors Set and Bag. Enumerated sets, bags and lists are delimited by $\{\ldots\}$, $\langle\ldots\rangle$ and $[\ldots]$ brackets, respectively. The set-union, bag-union and list-append operators are $\cup$, $\cup_B$ and $++$. We note here that the list, bag and set types are *lazy* in the sense that the result of a computation may be an infinite list, bag or set, which can be incrementally computed and output.

The denotation of such infinite structures in the semantic domain contains the $\bot$ element since their computation does not terminate.

We use the notation $e :: t$ to indicate that an expression e has type t. We use letters from the start of the alphabet to indicate type variables in type expressions. For example, the infix 'compose' function, $\circ$, defined by $(f \circ g)\ x = f\ (g\ x)$ is of type $(b \to c) \to (a \to b) \to (a \to c)$, where the type variables a, b and c can be instantiated to any type.

1.3 Collection types

A *collection type* is one constructed by a unary type name, T, for which there exist a constant $Empty :: T\ a$ and two functions

$$single :: a \to T\ a$$
$$\_ \oplus \_ :: T\ a \to T\ a \to T\ a$$

such that $\oplus$ has $Empty$ as a left and right identity. We can define an operator, $\phi :: (a \to b) \to (b \to b \to b) \to b \to T\ a \to b$, which 'folds' a binary function op into a collection as follows:

$coll/1$	$\phi\ f\ op\ e\ \bot$	$= \bot$
$coll/2$	$\phi\ f\ op\ e\ Empty$	$= e$
$coll/3$	$\phi\ f\ op\ e\ (single\ e')$	$= f\ e'$
$coll/4$	$\phi\ f\ op\ e\ (s \oplus s')$	$= op\ (\phi\ f\ op\ e\ s)\ (\phi\ f\ op\ e\ s')$

There is of course a different set of functions $single$, $\oplus$ and ϕ for each collection type, T. If there is a risk of ambiguity, we explicitly indicate which particular function is meant by subscripting it with its collection type.

'fold' operators and their equivalences have been the subject of much work in the functional programming and database communities, This is work too numerous to fully list here and we refer to [1, 2, 3, 4, 5] as a representative sample. Collection types were first defined by Wadler [18] where their relationship with comprehensions was explored. Our ϕ is an elaboration of the structural recursion over the union presentation (SRU) of [4, 5] to allow for non-terminating computations and infinite collections. Hence the need for $coll/1$ above which ensures that ϕ is monotonic (since $\bot \sqsubseteq Empty$, we need $\phi\ f\ op\ e\ \bot \sqsubseteq \phi\ f\ op\ e\ Empty$, i.e. $\phi\ f\ op\ e\ \bot \sqsubseteq e$, for all e; so $\phi\ f\ op\ e\ \bot$ must be equal to $\bot$).

The set, bag and list types of our language all satisfy the above definition of a collection type, with the same provisos on op and e as for SRU. For sets, $T = Set$, $Empty = \{\}$, $\oplus = \cup$ and $single = \lambda x.\{x\}$; in order for an application $\phi\ f\ op\ e\ s$ to be well-defined for any set s, op must be commutative, associative and idempotent, and must have e as a left and right identity. For bags, $T = Bag$, $Empty = \langle\rangle$, $\oplus = \cup_B$ and $single = \lambda x.\langle x\rangle$; in order for $\phi\ f\ op\ e\ b$ to be well-defined for any bag b, op must be commutative and associative, and must have e as a left and right identity. For lists, $T = List$, $Empty = []$, $\oplus = ++$ and $single = \lambda x.[x]$; in order for $\phi\ f\ op\ e\ l$ to be well-defined for any list l, op must be associative, and must have e as a left and right identity.

1.4   The Proof Framework

We now define two equivalences over expressions involving the ϕ operator from which all the remaining equivalences in the paper can be derived. Two assumptions that we make for all the equivalences that we state are that all expressions are well-typed and all applications of ϕ are well-defined. Figures 1 and 2 show a 'route-map' through the entire set of equivalences that we explore. For example, Figure 2 indicates that equivalence $ag/3$ is a special case of equivalence $\phi/3$, which is in turn a special case of $\phi/2$.

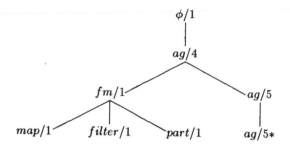

Fig. 1. Equivalences derived from $\phi/1$

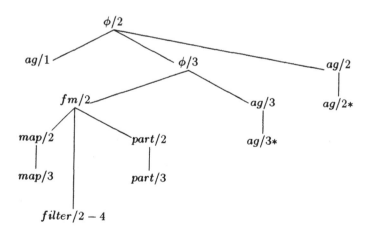

Fig. 2. Equivalences derived from $\phi/2$

The top-level equivalence of Figure 1 governs the commutativity of ϕ:

$$\phi/1 \quad g\ (h\ s) = h\ (g\ s) \quad where \quad g = \phi\ f\ op\ e \quad and \quad h = \phi\ f'\ op'\ e'$$

We note that in order for this equivalence to be well-typed, the instances of ϕ in g and h must both have type $(a \to T\ a) \to (T\ a \to T\ a \to T\ a) \to T\ a \to$

$T\ a \to T\ a$ for some collection type T. Clearly $\phi/1$ does not hold in general. In fact, in the Appendix we prove that it holds subject to the following provisos:

Provisos for $\phi/1$: $g\ e' = h\ e$, $g \circ f' = h \circ f$, and $g\ ((h\ s_1)\ op'\ (h\ s_2)) = h\ ((g\ s_1)\ op\ (g\ s_2))$.

Moving now to the top-level equivalence of Figure 2, this governs the replacement of two applications of ϕ by one:

$$\phi/2 \quad \phi\ f\ op\ e\ (\phi\ f'\ op'\ e'\ s) = \phi\ ((\phi\ f\ op\ e) \circ f')\ op''\ (\phi\ f\ op\ e')\ s$$

Here op'' is an arbitrary operation satisfying the proviso stated below. In order for this equivalence to be well-typed, the inner instance of ϕ on the LHS must have type $(a \to T\ b) \to (T\ b \to T\ b \to T\ b) \to T\ b \to T\ a \to T\ b$ for some T, the outer instance of ϕ on the LHS have type $(b \to c) \to (c \to c \to c) \to c \to T\ b \to c$ and the outer instance on the RHS have type $(a \to c) \to (c \to c \to c) \to c \to T\ a \to c$. This equivalence also does not hold in general and has the following associated proviso:

Proviso for $\phi/2$: $(\phi\ f\ op\ e\ s)\ op''\ (\phi\ f\ op\ e\ s') = \phi\ f\ op\ e\ (s\ op'\ s')$.

A useful consequence of $\phi/2$ from which a number of further equivalences follow is $\phi/3$ which concerns the *fusion* of two applications of ϕ into one. $\phi/3$ is obtained by setting $op'' = op'$ in $\phi/2$ (giving $c = T\ b$ in the above type signatures):

$$\phi/3 \quad \phi\ f\ op\ e\ (\phi\ f'\ op'\ e'\ s) = \phi\ ((\phi\ f\ op\ e) \circ f')\ op'\ (\phi\ f\ op\ e')\ s$$

Proviso for $\phi/3$: $\phi\ f\ op\ e$ distributes over op'.

In the Appendix we give proofs that $\phi/1$, $\phi/2$ and $\phi/3$ hold subject to their stated provisos. Each lower-level equivalence of Figures 1 and 2 can then be shown by substituting the more general functions in its parent equivalence by the more specific functions of the child equivalence and simplifying the associated provisos. The Appendix gives a representative sample of proofs.

1.5 Iteration operations

Using ϕ, the maximum and minimum element of a collection s can be found, where id is the identity function $\lambda x.x$:

$$max\ s = \phi\ id\ (\lambda x.\lambda y.if\ (x > y)\ x\ y)\ minNum\ s$$
$$min\ s = \phi\ id\ (\lambda x.\lambda y.if\ (x < y)\ x\ y)\ maxNum\ s$$

Cardinality and summation functions can be defined over bags and lists (but not sets since $+$ is not idempotent):

$$count\ s = \phi\ (\lambda x.1)\ (+)\ 0\ s$$
$$sum\ s = \phi\ id\ (+)\ 0\ s$$

We note that all these functions return $\bot$ for infinite collections. Finite, first-order sets can be counted or summed by converting them to sorted lists and then applying *count* or *sum* (see [11] for details).

Existential and universal quantifiers can be defined over collections, where p is a predicate:

$$some \ p \ s = \phi \ p \ (\vee) \ False \ s$$
$$all \ p \ s \quad = \phi \ p \ (\wedge) \ True \ s$$

We note that $some \ p \ s$ can return $True$ if s is infinite, but not $False$. Similarly $all \ p \ s$ can return $False$ if s is infinite but not $True$.

ϕ_T can be used to define a function $flatmap_T$ that applies a function of type $a \rightarrow T \ b$ to each element of a collection of type $T \ a$ and merges the results using $\oplus_T$:

$$flatmap_T \quad :: (a \rightarrow T \ b) \rightarrow T \ a \rightarrow T \ b$$
$$flatmap_T \ f \ s = \phi_T \ f \ \oplus_T \ Empty_T \ s$$

We note that $flatmap_T \ f$ is the $ext(f)$ operation of [4]. Using $flatmap_T$, functions map_T, $filter_T$ and $join_T$ can be defined which generalise relational projection, selection and join operations, respectively:

$$map_T \quad :: (a \rightarrow b) \rightarrow T \ a \rightarrow T \ b$$
$$map_T \ f \ s \quad = flatmap_T \ (single_T \circ f) \ s$$

$$filter_T \quad :: (a \rightarrow Bool) \rightarrow T \ a \rightarrow T \ a$$
$$filter_T \ f \ s = flatmap_T \ (\lambda x.if \ (f \ x) \ (single_T \ x) \ Empty_T) \ s$$

$$join_T \quad :: (a \rightarrow b \rightarrow c) \rightarrow T \ a \rightarrow T \ b \rightarrow T \ c$$
$$join_T \ f \ r \ s = flatmap_T \ (\lambda x.flatmap_T \ (\lambda y.f \ x \ y) \ s) \ r$$

Henceforth we will omit the subscripts to $flatmap$, map, $filter$ and $join$ unless there is a risk of ambiguity. Due to $coll/1$, if s is infinite then so is result of $flatmap \ f \ s$. The map, $filter$ and $join$ operations can similarly operate on infinite collections. [1]

1.6 Grouping and clustering operations

We now see how grouping and clustering operations can be defined in terms of ϕ, leading the way to identifying equivalences for grouping and clustering in

---

[1] Given that we are exploring equivalences derived from $\phi/1$ and $\phi/2$, and that these equivalences involve iteration over a single collection type, the above definitions of $flatmap$, map, $filter$ and $join$ suffice for the purposes of this paper. In fact, a more general function, $flatmap_{T,T'} :: (a \rightarrow T' \ b) \rightarrow T \ a \rightarrow T' \ b$, can be defined for a pair of collection types T and T': $flatmap_{T,T'} \ f \ s \ = \ \phi_T \ f \ \oplus_{T'} \ Empty_{T'} \ s$.

From the restrictions on op and e discussed in Section 1.3, in order for $flatmap_{T,T'}$ to be well-defined if $T = List$ then T' can be $List$, Bag or Set, if $T = Bag$ then T' can be Bag or Set, and if $T = Set$ then T' can only be Set. Fegaras and Maier [7] also identify these restrictions on comprehensions over multiple collection types. Functions $map_{T,T'} :: (a \rightarrow b) \rightarrow T \ a \rightarrow T' \ b$, $filter_{T,T'} :: (a \rightarrow Bool) \rightarrow T \ a \rightarrow T' \ a$ and $join_{T,T',T''} :: (a \rightarrow b \rightarrow c) \rightarrow T \ a \rightarrow T' \ b \rightarrow T'' \ c$ can be defined using $flatmap_{T,T'}$, with similar restrictions on possible combinations of T, T' and T''.

subsequent sections of the paper. We first define an operation $group_{T,T'}$ which takes a collection of type T (t, t') and returns a collection of type T $(t, T'\ t')$, for some T and T', by grouping together all pairs with the same first component. We next define a clustering operation, $partition_T$, which takes a collection $xs :: T\ t$ and a function g and returns a partition of xs, $xss :: T\ (T\ t)$, such that: (i) for each collection $xs_i \in xss$ and each pair of elements $x, y \in xs_i$, $g\ x = g\ y$, and (ii) for each distinct pair of collections $xs_i, xs_j \in xss$ and each pair of elements $x \in xs_i, y \in xs_j$, $g\ x \neq g\ y$.

$group$ and $partition$ are both defined in terms of a binary operator, m, which merges two collections into one by applying a predicate p to pairs of elements x and y drawn from each collection and, if $p\ x\ y$ holds, replacing x and y by $f\ x\ y$ for a given function f:

$$
\begin{aligned}
m \quad &:: (a \to a \to Bool) \to (a \to a \to T\ a) \to T\ a \to T\ a \\
m\ p\ f\ Empty\ s &= s \\
m\ p\ f\ (single\ x)\ Empty &= single\ x \\
m\ p\ f\ (single\ x)\ (single\ y) &= if\ (p\ x\ y) \\
&\quad then\ (f\ x\ y) \\
&\quad else\ (single\ x) \oplus (single\ y) \\
m\ p\ f\ (single\ x)\ (s \oplus s') &= if\ (some\ (p\ x)\ s) \\
&\quad then\ (m\ p\ f\ (single\ x)\ s) \oplus s' \\
&\quad else\ if\ (some\ (p\ x)\ s') \\
&\quad\quad then\ s \oplus (m\ p\ f\ (single\ x)\ s') \\
&\quad\quad else\ (single\ x) \oplus (s \oplus s') \\
m\ p\ f\ (s \oplus s')\ s'' &= m\ p\ f\ s\ (m\ p\ f\ s'\ s'')
\end{aligned}
$$

We observe from the fourth equation above that the two arguments to m are assumed to be already "merged" in the sense that, for either argument, if the argument is of the form $s \oplus s'$ then $m\ p\ f\ s\ s' = s \oplus s'$. Subject to this assumption, m has $Empty$ as a left and right identity.

$group_{T,T'}$ is then defined as follows:

$$
\begin{aligned}
group_{T,T'} \quad &:: T\ (a, a') \to T\ (a, T'\ a') \\
group_{T,T'}\ s &= \phi_T\ nest\ merge\ Empty_T\ s
\end{aligned}
$$

where:

$$
\begin{aligned}
nest\ (x, y) &= single_T\ (x, single_{T'}\ y) \\
merge\ s\ s' &= m\ sameFirst\ mergeSecond\ s\ s' \\
sameFirst\ (x, ys)\ (x', ys') &= x = x' \\
mergeSecond\ (x, ys)\ (x', ys') &= single_T\ (x, ys \oplus_{T'} ys')
\end{aligned}
$$

Similar grouping operations can be defined which operate on n-tuples or records, and which group over arbitrary combinations of their components, not just the first component. However, for ease of exposition, we confine ourselves to grouping over collections of pairs. The equivalences that we develop for $group$ would hold also for grouping operations over collections of n-tuples or records.

Finally, $partition_T$ is defined as follows:

$$partition_T \quad :: (a \to b) \to T\ a \to T\ (T\ a)$$
$$partition_T\ g\ s = \phi\ nestP\ (mergeP\ g)\ Empty\ s$$

where:

$$nestP\ x \qquad = single\ (single\ x)$$
$$mergeP\ g\ s\ s' = m\ (\lambda s.\lambda s'.allSame\ g\ (s \oplus s'))\ mergeNest\ s\ s'$$
$$allSame\ g\ s \qquad = (join\ (\lambda x.\lambda y.if\ (g\ x \neq g\ y)\ (single\ (x,y))\ Empty)\ s\ s)$$
$$= Empty$$
$$mergeNest\ s\ s' = single\ (s \oplus s')$$

The comprehension notation discussed in Section 6 below gives a perhaps clearer definition of $allSame$: $allSame\ g\ s = [(x,y)\ |\ x \leftarrow s;\ y \leftarrow s;\ g\ x \neq g\ y] = Empty$.

Henceforth we will omit the subscripts to $group$ and $partition$, unless there is a risk of ambiguity. We note that in order for $m\ p\ f\ s$ not to lose information, $p\ x\ y$ must terminate for all pairs of elements x and y of s. In the case of $group\ s$, this means that $sameFirst$ must terminate for all arguments, which requires the first component of each tuple in s to be terminating and first-order (its second component need not be). In the case of $partition\ g\ s$, $allSame\ g\ s'$ must terminate for all finite subcollections s' of s, which requires $g\ x$ to terminate for all elements of s. Subject to these provisos, $merge$ and $mergeP\ g$ have the same idempotence, commutatitivy and associativity properties as $\oplus$.

2 Mapping aggregation functions over grouped collections

The application of $group$ to a collection of pairs followed by the mapping of an aggregation function $aggr$ over the second component of each resulting pair can be optimised into a single application of ϕ. In particular, let $nest$, $merge$ and $group$ be as defined in Section 1.6 and $aggr$, h and $merge'$ be defined as follows for some op and e:

$$aggr \qquad = \phi\ id\ op\ e$$
$$h \qquad = map\ (\lambda(x,ys).(x,aggr\ ys))$$
$$merge'\ s\ s' = merge\ (flatmap\ nest\ s)\ (flatmap\ nest\ s')$$

Then the following equivalence holds:

$$ag/1 \qquad h\ (group\ s) = \phi\ (h \circ nest)\ (h \circ merge')\ Empty\ s$$

For example, a function $groupSum$ can be defined which performs a group operation, followed by a summation operation:

$$groupSum\ s = h\ (group\ s)$$
$$where\ h = map\ (\lambda(x,ys).(x,sum\ ys))$$

However, this definition undertakes two applications of ϕ and can be optimised to the following definition which undertakes only one application of ϕ:

$$groupSum\ s = \phi\ (h \circ nest)\ (h \circ merge')\ Empty\ s$$
$$where\ h\ =\ map\ (\lambda(x, ys).(x, sum\ ys))$$

More generally, a generic 'group-and-compute' function, gc, that takes an aggregation function, $aggr = \phi\ id\ op\ e$, as an argument can be defined:

$$gc\ aggr\ s = h\ (group\ s)$$
$$where\ h\ =\ map\ (\lambda(x, ys).(x, aggr\ ys))$$

and this definition can be optimised to the following definition which undertakes a single application of ϕ:

$$gc\ aggr\ s = \phi\ (h \circ nest)\ (h \circ merge')\ Empty\ s$$
$$where\ h\ =\ map\ (\lambda(x, ys).(x, aggr\ ys))$$

3 Introducing/eliminating aggregation functions

The following equivalence can be shown for any function j and collection s of the appropriate type by appealing to $\phi/2$, where $f\ =\ \phi\ f_1\ op\ (f_1\ e)$ and $g\ =\ \phi\ f_2\ op\ e$:

$$ag/2 \quad f\ (map\ (g \circ j)\ s) = f_1 \circ g\ (flatmap\ j\ s)$$

Provisos for $ag/2$: f_1 is strict and distributes over op.
   The following equivalences are instances of $ag/2$ (and all have $f_1 = j = id$):

$ag/21$	$max\ (map\ max\ xss)$	$= max\ (flatmap\ id\ xss)$
$ag/22$	$min\ (map\ min\ xss)$	$= min\ (flatmap\ id\ xss)$
$ag/23$	$sum\ (map\ sum\ xss)$	$= sum\ (flatmap\ id\ xss)$
$ag/24$	$sum\ (map\ count\ xss)$	$= count\ (flatmap\ id\ xss)$
$ag/25$	$some\ id\ (map\ (some\ p)\ xss)$	$= some\ p\ (flatmap\ id\ xss)$
$ag/26$	$all\ id\ (map\ (all\ p)\ xss)$	$= all\ p\ (flatmap\ id\ xss)$

The following equivalence follows from $\phi/3$ and concerns the idempotence of group-and-compute operations:

$$ag/3 \quad (gc\ aggr) \circ (gc\ aggr') = gc\ aggr'$$

where $aggr\ =\ \phi\ id\ op\ e$ and $aggr'\ =\ \phi\ f\ op\ e$ for some f, op and e. Instances of $ag/3$ are:

$ag/31$	$(gc\ max) \circ (gc\ max)$	$= gc\ max$
$ag/32$	$(gc\ min) \circ (gc\ min)$	$= gc\ min$
$ag/33$	$(gc\ sum) \circ (gc\ sum)$	$= gc\ sum$
$ag/34$	$(gc\ sum) \circ (gc\ count)$	$= gc\ count$

4 Promoting aggregation functions

The following equivalence governs the promotion of a function $g = \phi\ f\ op\ e$ through an iteration over a collection s:

$ag/4 \quad g\ (flatmap\ j\ s) = flatmap\ j\ (g\ s)$

j can be any function of the appropriate type, subject to the following.

Provisos for $ag/4$: $flatmap\ j\ e = e$, $g \circ j = (flatmap\ j) \circ f$, and $flatmap\ j$ distributes over op.

A useful instance of $ag/4$ is $ag/5$ which governs the promotion of a group-and-compute operation $gc\ aggr$, where $aggr = \phi\ id\ op\ e$:

$ag/5 \quad gc\ aggr\ (flatmap\ j\ s) = flatmap\ j\ (gc\ aggr\ s)$

Provisos for $ag/5$: $(gc\ aggr) \circ j = j$ and $flatmap\ j$ distributes over $h \circ merge'$ where $h = map\ (\lambda(x, ys).(x, aggr\ ys))$.

For example, the following instances of $ag/5$ govern the promotion of a gc operation through a product, a selection and an equijoin, respectively:

$ag/51 \quad gc\ aggr\ (join\ f\ r\ s) = join\ f\ (gc\ aggr\ r)\ s$
$\qquad where\ f = \lambda(a, c).\lambda b.single\ ((a, b), c)$
$ag/52 \quad gc\ aggr\ (filter\ (\lambda(a, b).f\ a)\ r) = filter\ (\lambda(a, b).f\ a)\ (gc\ aggr\ r)$
$ag/53 \quad gc\ aggr\ (join\ f\ r\ s) = join\ f\ (gc\ aggr\ r)\ s$
$\qquad where\ f = \lambda(b, c).\lambda(a, b').if\ (b = b')\ (single\ ((a, b), c))\ Empty$

We note that for $ag/51$ and $ag/53$ the first of the two provisos associated with $ag/5$ holds only if there are no duplicates in the collection s e.g. if s is a set or is a bag or list without duplicates.

5 Commuting and coalescing applications of *flatmap*

$fm/1$ governs the commuting of two applications of *flatmap* and holds subject to the stated proviso while equivalence $fm/2$ states that two successive applications of *flatmap* can always be coalesced into one application with a second nested within it:

$fm/1 \quad flatmap\ f\ (flatmap\ g\ s) = flatmap\ g\ (flatmap\ f\ s)$
$fm/2 \quad flatmap\ f\ (flatmap\ g\ s) = flatmap\ ((flatmap\ f) \circ g)\ s$

Proviso for $fm/1$: $(flatmap\ f) \circ g = (flatmap\ g) \circ f$.

The following equivalences are instances of $fm/1$ and respectively state that two applications of *map*, *filter* and *partition* commute:

$map/1 \quad map\ f\ (map\ g\ s) = map\ g\ (map\ f\ s)$
$filter/1 \quad filter\ f\ (filter\ g\ s) = filter\ g\ (filter\ f\ s)$
$part/1 \quad flatmap\ (partition\ g)\ (flatmap\ (partition\ g')\ xss) = flatmap\ (partition\ g')\ (flatmap\ (partition\ g)\ xss)$

They have the following provisos associated with them:

Proviso for $map/1$: $f \circ g = g \circ f$.
Proviso for $filter/1$: For all x, $f\ x = \bot \iff g\ x = \bot$.
Proviso for $part/1$: $\oplus$ is commutative.

Two equivalences derived from $fm/2$ are:

$part/2$ $flatmap\ (partition\ g)\ (flatmap\ (partition\ g')\ xss) =$
         $flatmap\ ((flatmap\ (partition\ g)) \circ (partition\ g'))\ xss$
$part/3$ $flatmap\ (partition\ g)\ (flatmap\ (partition\ g')\ xss) =$
         $flatmap\ (partition\ (\lambda x.(g\ x, g'x))\ xss$

$part/2$ is an instance of $fm/2$. $part/3$ follows from $part/2$ by showing that $(flatmap\ (partition\ g)) \circ (partition\ g') = partition\ (\lambda x.(g\ x, g'x))$ and has the same proviso as $part/1$. Other equivalences that can be derived from $fm/2$ include $map/2$ and $map/3$ which govern the combining of two successive applications of map into one (c.f. combining cascades of projections), $filter/2$ which is a generalised cascade of selections, and $filter/3$ and $filter/4$ which combine successive applications of $filter$ and $flatmap$ into a single $flatmap$:

$map/2$	$map\ f\ (map\ g\ s)$	$= map\ (f \circ g)\ s$
$map/3$	$map\ (\lambda p'.e)\ (map\ (\lambda p.p')\ s)$	$= map\ (\lambda p.e)\ s$
$filter/2$	$filter\ f\ (filter\ g\ s)$	$= filter\ (\lambda x.(g\ x)\ and\ (f\ x))\ s$
$filter/3$	$flatmap\ f\ (filter\ g\ s)$	$= flatmap\ (\lambda x.if\ (g\ x)\ (f\ x)\ Empty)\ s$
$filter/4$	$filter\ f\ (flatmap\ g\ s)$	$= flatmap\ (\lambda x.filter\ f\ (g\ x))\ s$

In [11] we have already explored some of the above equivalences for sets, namely $fm/2$, $map/2 - 3$, and $filter/2 - 4$, and in an extended version of that paper [12] we extended the treatment to bags. In those papers we also explored several equivalences that do not slot into the framework of Figures 1 and 2, for example equivalences governing iteration over more than one collection (we note that our top-level equivalences here, $\phi/1$ and $\phi/2$, are concerned with iteration over a single collection).

6 Optimising comprehensions

We now consider how the equivalences developed above can be used to optimise comprehensions. We recall that the syntax of comprehensions is $[e \mid Q_1; \ldots; Q_n]$. e is an expression, termed the *head* of the comprehension, and Q_1 to Q_n are *qualifiers*, where $n \geq 0$. Each qualifier is either a *filter* or a *generator*. A filter is a boolean-valued expression. A generator has syntax $p \leftarrow s$, where p is a pattern and s is a collection-valued expression. For the purposes of this paper we assume that all the generators in a comprehension iterate over collections of the same collection type, T. Overall, a comprehension returns a collection of type $T\ t$, where t is the type of its head expression.

Developing optimisation techniques for comprehensions is important because comprehensions provide a unifying query formalism for functional, relational and object-oriented languages. Wadler [18] defines many equivalences for comprehensions. Paton and Gray [10] translate DAPLEX queries into set comprehensions and discuss their optimisation. Trinder [16, 17] gives a translation of the relational calculus into list comprehensions. Buneman *et al.* [4] discuss expressing SQL in the comprehension language CL and review previous work on the expressiveness of the comprehension syntax. Fegaras and Maier [7] define a calculus based on monoid comprehensions and use it to model the essential features of OQL (monoid comprehensions are more general than conventional comprehensions in that they can iterate over multiple collection types). Grust *et al.* [8] discuss optimisation of this calculus and propose a method whereby subqueries expressed in the calculus are translated into algebraic expressions for more efficient evaluation.

Comprehensions add no extra expressiveness to our language and they translate into the syntax of Section 1.1 as follows [2]:

$$[e \mid p \leftarrow s; Q] \equiv flatmap_T \ (\lambda p.[e \mid Q]) \ s$$
$$[e \mid e'; Q] \quad \equiv if \ e' \ then \ [e \mid Q] \ else \ Empty_T$$
$$[e \mid] \quad \equiv single_T \ e$$

In [11, 12] we explored three categories of equivalences for comprehensions, in the context of our computationally complete DBPL: those for interchanging pairs of qualifiers, for introducing/eliminating a qualifier, and for moving qualifiers into/out of nested comprehensions. Some of these equivalences could slot into the framework of Figures 1 and 2 while others do not, for example those governing iteration over multiple collections. Here, we will be needing two of the equivalences from [11, 12], $c/1$ and $c/2$ below, and also $c/3$ which follows from the fact that *flatmap single s = s*:

$c/1$ $\quad [e \mid Q; \ f; \ g; \ Q'] \qquad = [e \mid Q; \ g; \ f; \ Q']$
$\qquad\qquad\qquad\qquad\qquad\qquad\quad$ provided $f = \bot \iff g = \bot$
$c/2$ $\quad [e \mid Q; \ p \leftarrow [p \mid Q']; \ f; \ Q''] = [e \mid Q; \ p \leftarrow [p \mid Q'; \ f]; \ Q'']$
$\qquad\qquad\qquad\qquad\qquad\qquad\quad$ provided $FV(f) \subseteq FV(p)$
$c/3$ $\quad [p \mid p \leftarrow s] \qquad\qquad = s$

---

[2] For the purposes of this paper we assume all patterns p in generators $p \leftarrow s$ are *irrefutable* i.e. consist of tuple constructors and variables only, so that $(\lambda p.[e \mid Q]) \ e'$ does return not *Fail* for any element e' of s. If this were not the case, then the RHS of the first equation would be:

$$flatmap_T \ (\lambda x.if \ ((\lambda p.[e \mid Q]) \ x) \ \neq Fail \ then \ ((\lambda p.[e \mid Q]) \ x) \ else \ Empty_T) \ s$$

We also note that it is the use of $flatmap_T$ in the translation scheme that restricts comprehensions to iterate over a single collection type. If $flatmap_{T,T'}$ were used this restriction could be relaxed, subject to the restrictions on possible combinations of T and T' stated in Footnote 1. Fegaras and Maier [7] also identify these restrictions on comprehensions over multiple collection types.

Several of the equivalences that we have stated in this paper, namely $ag/2$, $ag/4$ and their descendants, can be directly reformulated for comprehensions, with the same associated provisos:

$ag/2$ $f \; [g \; (j \; x)|x \leftarrow s]$ $= f_1 \circ g \; [y|x \leftarrow s; y \leftarrow j \; x]$

$ag/21$ $max \; [max \; xs|xs \leftarrow xss]$ $= max \; [x|xs \leftarrow xss; xs \leftarrow xss]$

$ag/22$ $min \; [min \; xs|xs \leftarrow xss]$ $= min \; [x|xs \leftarrow xss; xs \leftarrow xss]$

$ag/23$ $sum \; [sum \; xs|xs \leftarrow xss]$ $= sum \; [x|xs \leftarrow xss; xs \leftarrow xss]$

$ag/24$ $sum \; [count \; xs|xs \leftarrow xss]$ $= count \; [x|xs \leftarrow xss; xs \leftarrow xss]$

$ag/25$ $some \; id \; [some \; p \; xs|xs \leftarrow xss]$ $= some \; p \; [x|xs \leftarrow xss; xs \leftarrow xss]$

$ag/26$ $all \; id \; [all \; p \; xs|xs \leftarrow xss]$ $= all \; p \; [x|xs \leftarrow xss; xs \leftarrow xss]$

$ag/4$ $g \; [y|x \leftarrow s; y \leftarrow j \; x]$ $= [y|x \leftarrow g \; s; y \leftarrow j \; x]$

$ag/5$ $gc \; aggr \; [y|x \leftarrow s; y \leftarrow j \; x]$ $= [y|x \leftarrow gc \; aggr \; s; y \leftarrow j \; x]$

$ag/51$ $gc \; aggr \; [((a,b),c)|(a,c) \leftarrow r; b \leftarrow s] =$
         $[((a,b),c)|(a,c) \leftarrow gc \; aggr \; r; b \leftarrow s]$

$ag/52$ $gc \; aggr \; [(a,b)|(a,b) \leftarrow s; f \; a]$ $= [(a,b)|(a,b) \leftarrow gc \; aggr \; s; f \; a]$

$ag/53$ $gc \; aggr \; [((a,b),c)|(b,c) \leftarrow r; (a,b') \leftarrow s; b = b'] =$
         $[((a,b),c)|(b,c) \leftarrow gc \; aggr \; r; (a,b') \leftarrow s; b = b']$

We illustrate the practical use of some of these equivalences by means of an example query over a database containing information about music sales. The following extensionally-defined collections are maintained in the database:

$categories \; :: \; Bag \; (Category, Group)$
$recordings \; :: \; Bag \; (RecNo, Group, Margin, Sales)$

These detail for each group with whom the company has a contract the category (e.g. Folk, Rock, Jazz) of the group, and for each recording a recording number, the group that made the recording, the profit margin and the total sales.

Our example query involves finding the total sales per category and group, for those categories which satisfy a stated predicate, p. A naive formulation of this query is to project the group and sales attributes from $recordings$, join the result with $categories$, select the tuples which satisfy p, and then perform a $gc \; sum$:

$let \; r1 \; = \; [(g,s) \; | \; (r,g,m,s) \leftarrow recordings];$
    $r2 \; = \; [((c,g),s) \; | \; (g,s) \leftarrow r1; (c,g') \leftarrow categories; g = g']$
$in \; gc \; sum \; [((c,g),s) \; | \; ((c,g),s) \leftarrow r2; p \; c]$

Using $ag/52$ we can push $gc \; sum$ before the selection $p \; c$:

$let \; r1 \; = \; [(g,s) \; | \; (r,g,m,s) \leftarrow recordings];$
    $r2 \; = \; [((c,g),s) \; | \; (g,s) \leftarrow r1; (c,g') \leftarrow categories; g = g']$
$in \; [((c,g),s) \; | \; ((c,g),s) \leftarrow gc \; sum \; r2; p \; c]$

Using $ag/53$ we can then push $gc \; sum$ into the join, to obtain an expression which projects the group and sales attributes from $recordings$, computes for each group their total sales, joins the result with $categories$, and finally selects the tuples which satisfy p:

$let\ r1\ =\ [(g,s)\mid (r,g,m,s)\leftarrow recordings];$
$\quad r2\ =\ [((c,g),s)\mid (g,s)\leftarrow gc\ sum\ r1;\ (c,g')\leftarrow categories;\ g=g']$
$in\ [((c,g),s)\mid ((c,g),s)\leftarrow r2;\ p\ c]$

Using $c/2$ and then $c/1$ we can push the filter $(p\ c)$ into the second comprehension and then promote it past $g=g'$:

$let\ r1\ =\ [(g,s)\mid (r,g,m,s)\leftarrow recordings];$
$\quad r2\ =\ [((c,g),s)\mid (g,s)\leftarrow gc\ sum\ r1;\ (c,g')\leftarrow categories;\ p\ c;\ g=g']$
$in\ [((c,g),s)\mid ((c,g),s)\leftarrow r2]$

Finally, using $c/3$ we can eliminate the third comprehension:

$let\ r1\ =\ [(g,s)\mid (r,g,m,s)\leftarrow recordings];$
$\quad r2\ =\ [((c,g),s)\mid (g,s)\leftarrow gc\ sum\ r1;\ (c,g')\leftarrow categories;\ p\ c;\ g=g']$
$in\ r2$

7 Related Work

Sheard and Fegaras [14] investigate the optimisation of a fold operator over types that are sums-of-products (e.g. lists and trees) drawing together and generalising previous work in this area in the context of functional programming languages. They state and prove a *Fold Promotion Theorem* which is the analogue of our equivalence $\phi/3$.

Steenhagen *et al.* [15] use the following instance of $fm/2$ to replace the nested selection expression on the RHS by the *nestjoin* expression on the LHS:

$$[f\ x\mid (x,ys)\leftarrow [(x,[g\ x\ y\mid y\leftarrow s';\ q\ x\ y])\mid x\leftarrow s];\ p\ x\ ys]\ =$$
$$[f\ x\mid x\leftarrow s;\ p\ x\ [g\ x\ y\mid y\leftarrow s';\ q\ x\ y]]$$

Chaudhuri and Shim [6] investigate the optimisation of queries containing group-and-compute operations. They give three equivalences: $ag/53$, $eq/1$ below which introduces/eliminates a redundant group-and-compute operation, and $eq/2$ below which allows a group of tuples to be coalesced into a single tuple together with a count of the number of tuples which were coalesced:

$eq/1 \quad gc\ aggr\ (flatmap\ f\ s)\ =\ gc\ aggr\ (flatmap\ f\ (gc\ aggr\ s))$
$eq/2 \quad gc\ aggr\ [(a,(n,c))\mid (a,n)\leftarrow gc\ count\ s;\ (a',c)\leftarrow s';\ a=a']\ =$
$\quad\quad\quad gc\ aggr'\ [(a,c)\mid (a,b)\leftarrow s;\ (a',c)\leftarrow s';\ a=a']$

$eq/1$ has $aggr\ =\ \phi\ id\ op\ e$ and holds provided $(gc\ aggr)\circ(flatmap\ f)$ distributes over $h\circ merge'$, where $h\ =\ map\ (\lambda(x,ys).(x,aggr\ ys))$. Superficially, $eq/1$ would seem to be captured by applying $ag/3$ followed by $ag/5$ to the left-hand-side. However, the latter step generates the proviso $(gc\ aggr)\circ f\ =\ f$, which is not needed due to the retention of the outer $gc\ aggr$ operation on the right-hand-side. In fact, $eq/1$ can be accommodated by a third top-level equivalence governing the replacement of three applications of ϕ by two. $eq/2$ has $aggr\ =\ \phi\ f\ op\ e$ and $aggr'\ =\ \phi\ f'\ op\ e$, and holds provided

$aggr'$ $(replicate\ n\ x)$ $=$ $aggr$ $(single\ (n, x))$, where $replicate\ n\ x$ returns a collection containing n instances of x. This too cannot be derived from $\phi/1$ and $\phi/2$ but would be accommodated by the same top-level equivalence as required for $eq/1$.

Gupta et al. [9] examine the optimisation of SQL query trees built from selection, product and 'generalised projection' nodes. They consider aggregation where the aggregate over a set s can be computed from aggregates over subsets of s and identify $ag/21 - 3$. Other equivalences they develop allow a group-and-compute to be promoted through a product and a selection i.e. $ag/51$ and $ag/52$. A further equivalence they give governs the removal of redundant group-by operations:

$$gc\ aggr\ [(a, b)\ |\ (c, d) \leftarrow gc\ aggr\ s] = gc\ aggr\ [(a, b)\ |\ (c, d) \leftarrow s]$$

provided $FV(a, b) \subseteq FV(c)$ and $\oplus$ is idempotent. This can be shown to be an instance of $eq/1$ above.

Yan and Larson [19] examine the optimisation of decomposable aggregation functions over bags, where an aggregation function f is *decomposable* if there exist functions f_1 and f_2 such that $f\ (s_1 \oplus s_2) = f_2\ (f_1\ s_1)\ (f_1\ s_2)$. They identify *sum*, *max*, *min* and *count* as decomposable and use combinations of $eq/1$ and $eq/2$ to push/pull group-and-compute operations through one or both branches of a join.

8   Conclusion

We have defined a 'fold' operator ϕ over collection types such as lists, bags and sets, and have investigated the optimisation of aggregation functions defined in terms of ϕ. We defined two equivalences for ϕ. The first, $\phi/1$, governs the commutativity of ϕ, and the second, $\phi/2$, governs the coalescing of two applications of ϕ into one. Many of the equivalences proposed by other researchers turn out to be special cases of $\phi/1$ and $\phi/2$. Conversely, we have discovered new equivalences such as $ag/25$, $ag/26$ and $part/1 - 3$, and we conjecture that many other new equivalences based upon $\phi/1$ and $\phi/2$ remain to be discovered. We are currently exploring equivalences such as $eq/1$ and $eq/2$ above that can be derived from a third top-level equivalence which governs the replacement of three applications of ϕ by two.

We see our work as having application in two main areas. Firstly, it provides a rich, yet simple, theoretical framework for exploring and formally proving new equivalences for aggregation functions. Secondly, the equivalences that we derive for our functional DBPL clearly also hold for less expressive sub-languages, for example the monoid comprehension calculus, OQL and SRU, and could thus be used in practical query optimisers for such languages, as well as for our own DBPL.

Acknowledgements

This work has been supported by the U.K. Engineering and Physical Sciences Research Council (grant no. GR/L 26872). We thank the referees for their helpful comments on earlier versions of this paper.

Appendix - Proofs of the key equivalences

We give proofs of $\phi/1, \phi/2, \phi/3, ag/1$ and $ag/2$. The remaining equivalences of Figures 1 and 2 follow straight-forwardly from their parent equivalence.

(a) Proof of $\phi/1$

$\phi/1$ states that for all collections s, $g\,(h\,(s)) = h\,(g\,(s))$, where $g = \phi\,f\,op\,e$ and $h = \phi\,f'\,op'\,e'$, provided that:

(1) $g\,e' = h\,e$,
(2) $g \circ f' = h \circ f$,
(3) $g\,((h\,s_1)\,op'\,(h\,s_2)) = h\,((g\,s_1)\,op\,(g\,s_2))$.

We show this equivalence by structural induction over s (this is a valid proof technique even for infinite s because all functions in our language are continuous — see [13]):
If $s = Empty$ then

$LHS\ Empty = g\,(h\ Empty) = g\,e'$
$RHS\ Empty = h\,(g\ Empty) = h\,e$

and these are equal by (1).
If $s = \bot$ then $LHS \perp = RHS \perp = \perp$ by $coll/1$.
If $s = single\ a$ for some expression a, then

$LHS\ s = g\,(h\,(single\ a)) = g\,(f'\ a)$
$RHS\ s = h\,(g\,(single\ a)) = h\,(f\ a)$

and these are equal by (2).
If $s = s_1 \oplus s_2$ then

$$
\begin{aligned}
LHS\ s &= g\,(h\,(s_1 \oplus s_2)) \\
&= g\,((h\ s_1)\,op'\,(h\ s_2)) \quad \text{by } coll/4 \\
&= h\,((g\ s_1)\,op\,(g\ s_2)) \quad \text{by (3)} \\
&= h\,((g\,(s_1 \oplus s_2)) \quad \text{by } coll/4 \\
&= RHS\ s
\end{aligned}
$$

(b) Proof of $\phi/2$

$\phi/2$ states that $\phi\,f\,op\,e\,(\phi\,f'\,op'\,e'\,s) = \phi\,((\phi\,f\,op\,e) \circ f')\,op''\,(\phi\,f\,op\,e\,e')\,s$ provided that:

(1) $(\phi\ f\ op\ e\ s)\ op''\ (\phi\ f\ op\ e\ s') = \phi\ f\ op\ e\ (s\ op'\ s')$

We show this equivalence by structural induction over s:

If $s = Empty$ then $LHS\ Empty = RHS\ Empty = \phi\ f\ op\ e\ e'$.

If $s = \bot$ then $LHS\ \bot = RHS\ \bot = \bot$ by $coll/1$.

If $s = single\ a$ for some expression a, then

$$LHS\ s = \phi\ f\ op\ e\ (\phi\ f'\ op'\ e'\ (single\ a))$$
$$= \phi\ f\ op\ e\ (f'\ a)$$
$$= RHS\ s$$

If $s = s_1 \oplus s_2$ then

$$LHS\ s = \phi\ f\ op\ e\ (\phi\ f'\ op'\ e'\ (s_1 \oplus s_2))$$
$$= \phi\ f\ op\ e\ ((\phi\ f'\ op'\ e'\ s_1)\ op'\ (\phi\ f'\ op'\ e'\ s_2))\ \ \text{by } coll/4$$

while

$$RHS\ s = \phi\ ((\phi\ f\ op\ e)\circ f')\ op''\ (\phi\ f\ op\ e\ e')\ (s_1 \oplus s_2)$$
$$= (\phi\ ((\phi\ f\ op\ e)\circ f')\ op''\ (\phi\ f\ op\ e\ e')\ s_1))\ op''$$
$$(\phi\ ((\phi\ f\ op\ e)\circ f')\ op''\ (\phi\ f\ op\ e\ e')\ s_2))\ \ \text{by } coll/4$$
$$= (\phi\ f\ op\ e\ ((\phi\ f'\ op'\ e'\ s_1))\ op''$$
$$(\phi\ f\ op\ e\ ((\phi\ f'\ op'\ e'\ s_2))\ \ \text{by the induction hypothesis}$$
$$= LHS\ s\ \ \text{by (1)}$$

(c) Proof of $\phi/3$

Substituting op' for op'' in $\phi/2$ transforms the proviso stated for $\phi/2$ into the proviso stated for $\phi/3$.

(d) Proof of $ag/1$

The equivalence is easily seen to be an instance of $\phi/2$: substitute $\phi\ f\ op\ e$ in $\phi/2$ by h, $\phi\ f'\ op'\ e'$ by $group$ and op'' by $h \circ merge'$. It therefore only remains to show that the proviso holds i.e. that $h\ (merge'\ (h\ s)\ (h\ s')) = h\ (merge\ s\ s')$ or, substituting for the definition of $merge'$, that

$$h\ (merge\ (flatmap\ nest\ (h\ s))\ (flatmap\ nest\ (h\ s'))) = h\ (merge\ s\ s')$$

Now every tuple (x, ys) of s or s' results in a tuple $(x, aggr\ ys)$ when h is applied to s and s' in the LHS of this equivalence. This tuple in turn results in a tuple $(x, single\ (aggr\ ys))$ when $flatmap\ nest$ is applied to $h\ s$ and $h\ s'$. Since $merge$ depends on the first components of tuples only, the collections $merge\ s\ s'$ and $merge\ (flatmap\ nest\ (h\ s))\ (flatmap\ nest\ (h\ s'))$ are thus identical, except that every tuple (x, ys) in the former corresponds to a tuple $(x, single\ (aggr\ ys))$ in the latter. Applying h to these two collections transforms (x, ys) to $(x, aggr\ ys)$ and $(x, single\ (aggr\ ys))$ to $(x, aggr\ (single\ (aggr\ ys)))$. Since first argument to ϕ in the definition of $aggr$ is id, $aggr \circ single = id$. The second tuple thus simplifies to $(x, aggr\ ys)$, and the two tuples are identical.

(e) Proof of $ag/2$

$ag/2$ states that $f\ (map\ (g \circ j)\ s) = f_1 \circ g\ (flatmap\ j\ s)$, where $f = \phi\ f_1\ op\ (f_1\ e)$ and $g = \phi\ f_2\ op\ e$, provided that:

(1) f_1 is strict.
(2) f_1 distributes over op.

To show this, we first apply $\phi/2$ to the LHS of $ag/2$, setting op'' in $\phi/2$ to be op above, and obtaining:

$$\phi\ (f_1 \circ g \circ j)\ op\ (f_1\ e)\ s$$

We need to check that the proviso to $\phi/2$ holds i.e. that $(f\ s)\ op\ (f\ s') = f\ (s \oplus s')$, which is indeed the case, by $coll/4$.

We next apply $\phi/2$ to the RHS of $ag/2$, again setting op'' in $\phi/2$ to be op above, and obtaining:

$$f_1(\phi\ (g \circ j)\ op\ e\ s)$$

We again need to check that the proviso to $\phi/2$ holds i.e. that $(g\ s)\ op\ (g\ s') = g\ (s \oplus s')$, which again is the case, by $coll/4$.

$ag/2$ has thus been simplified to

$$\phi\ (f_1 \circ g \circ j)\ op\ (f_1\ e)\ s = f_1(\phi\ (g \circ j)\ op\ e\ s)$$

This can now be shown by structural induction on s:
If $\underline{s = Empty}$ then $LHS\ Empty = RHS\ Empty = f_1\ e$.
If $\underline{s = \bot}$ then $LHS\ \bot = \bot$ and $RHS\ \bot = f_1\ \bot = \bot$ by (1).
If $\underline{s = single\ a}$ then $LHS\ s = RHS\ s = f_1(g(j\ a))$.
If $\underline{s = s_1 \oplus s_2}$ then

$$
\begin{aligned}
LHS\ s &= \phi\ (f_1 \circ g \circ j)\ op\ (f_1\ e)\ (s_1 \oplus s_2)) \\
&= (\phi\ (f_1 \circ g \circ j)\ op\ (f_1\ e)\ s_1)\ op\ (\phi\ (f_1 \circ g \circ j)\ op\ (f_1\ e)\ s_2) \\
&= (f_1(\phi\ (g \circ j)\ op\ e\ s_1))\ op\ (f_1(\phi\ (g \circ j)\ op\ e\ s_2)) \\
&\quad \text{by the induction hypothesis} \\
&= f_1((\phi\ (g \circ j)\ op\ e\ s_1)\ op\ (\phi\ (g \circ j)\ op\ e\ s_2))\ \text{by (2)} \\
&= f_1(\phi\ (g \circ j)\ op\ e\ (s_1 \oplus s_2)) \\
&= RHS\ s
\end{aligned}
$$

References

1. F.Bancilhon, T.Briggs, S.Khoshafian and P.Valduriez, FAD, a powerful and simple database language, *Proc. 13th VLDB Conference*, Brighton, September 1987, pp 97-106.

2. C.Beeri and Y.Kornatzky, Algebraic optimization of object-oriented query languages, *Proc. 3rd ICDT*, Paris, December 1990, pp 72-88. Springer-Verlag LNCS 470.
3. R.Bird and P.Wadler, *Introduction to functional programming*, Prentice-Hall, 1988.
4. P.Buneman, L.Libkin, D.Suciu, V.Tannen and L.Wong, Comprehension Syntax, *ACM SIGMOD Record*, 23(1), pp 87-96, 1994.
5. P.Buneman, S.Naqvi,V.Tannen and L.Wong, Principles of programming with complex objects and collection types, *Theoretical Computer Science*, 149(1), pp 3-48, 1995.
6. S.Chaudhuri and K.Shim, Including group-by in query optimisation, *Proc. 20th VLDB Conference*, Santiago, September 1994, pp 354-366.
7. L.Fegaras and D.Maier, Towards an effective calculus for Object Query Languages, *Proc. ACM SIGMOD Conference*, May 1995, pp 47-58.
8. T.Grust, J.Kroger, D.Gluche, A.Heuer and M.Scholl, Query evaluation in CROQUE - Calculus and Algebra coincide, *Proc. 15th British National Conference on Databases*, London, July 1997, pp 84-100. Springer-Verlag LNCS 1271.
9. A.Gupta, V.Harinarayan and D.Quass, Aggregate query-processing in Data Warehousing Environments, *Proc. 21st VLDB Conference*, Zurich, 1995, pp 358-369.
10. N.W.Paton and P.M.D.Gray, Optimising and executing DAPLEX queries using Prolog, *The Computer Journal*, 33(6), pp 547-555, 1990.
11. A.Poulovassilis and C.Small, Investigation of algebraic query optimisation for database programming languages, *Proc. 20th VLDB Conference*, Santiago, 1994, pp 415-426.
12. A.Poulovassilis and C.Small, Algebraic query optimisation for database programming languages, *The VLDB Journal*, 5(2), pp 119-132, 1996.
13. D.A.Schmidt, *Denotational Semantics*, Allyn and Bacon, 1986.
14. T.Sheard and L.Fegaras, A fold for all seasons. *Proc. ACM Conference on Functional Programming and Computer Architectures (FPCA)*, 1993, pp 233-242.
15. H.J.Steenhagen, P.M.G.Apers, H.M.Blanken and R.A.de By, From nested-loop to join queries in OODB, *Proc. 20th VLDB Conference*, Santiago, 1994, pp 618-629.
16. P.Trinder, *A functional database*, D.Phil Thesis, Oxford University, 1989.
17. P.Trinder, Comprehensions: a query notation for DBPLs. *Proc. 3rd Int. Workshop on Database Programming Languages*, Nafplion, August 1991, pp 55-68.
18. P.Wadler, Comprehending Monads, *Proc. ACM Conference on Lisp and Functional Programming*, Nice, June 1990, pp 61-78.
19. W.Yan and P.Larson, Eager aggregation and lazy aggregation, *Proc. 21st VLDB Conference*, Zurich, 1995, pp 345-357.

Querying Multidimensional Databases*

Luca Cabibbo and Riccardo Torlone

Dipartimento di Informatica e Automazione
Università di Roma Tre
Via della Vasca Navale, 79 — I-00146 Roma, Italy
E-mail: {cabibbo,torlone}@inf.uniroma3.it

Abstract. Multidimensional databases are large collections of data, often historical, used for sophisticated analysis oriented to decision making. This activity is supported by an emerging category of software technology, called On-Line Analytical Processing (OLAP). In spite of a lot of commercial tools already available, a fundamental study for OLAP systems is still lacking. In this paper we introduce a model and a query language to establish a theoretical basis for multi-dimensional data. The model is based on the notions of dimension and f-table. Dimensions are linguistic categories corresponding to different ways of looking at the information. F-tables are the constructs used to represent factual data, and are the logical counterpart of multi-dimensional arrays, the way in which current analytical tools store data. The query language is a calculus for f-tables, and as such it offers a high-level support to multi-dimensional data analysis. Scalar and aggregate functions can be embedded in calculus expressions in a natural way. We discuss on conceptual problems related with the design of multidimensional query languages, and compare our model and language with other approaches.

1 Introduction

The integration of database management systems with on-line analytical processing (OLAP) technology is a challenging goal of recent years [8]. In fact, while the former provide solid and efficient tools for on-line *transaction* processing, OLAP systems can support knowledge workers and decision makers in the sophisticated analysis of enterprise data. The effectiveness of this analysis is related to the ability to describe and manipulate data according to different and often independent perspectives or "dimensions." For instance, single sales of items provide much more information to business analysis when organized into, e.g., number of items sold by category of product, geographical location, and time. Thus, we can say that OLAP technology complements database technology, in providing a multi-dimensional view of raw data and suitable tools for its analysis. Generally, these tools enable the users to: (i) define analytical equations across multiple data dimensions, possibly involving complex calculations, to represent numerous, speculative enterprise model scenarios; (ii) summarize data sets, aggregating

---

* This work was partially supported by *Consiglio Nazionale delle Ricerche* and by *MURST*.

and disaggregating over the various dimensions; and (iii) evaluate and view the outcomes of the analysis. To understand the effect of changes in environmental factors, this process is often iterated by changing equations and parameters.

Current technology provides both OLAP data servers and front-end analysis tools. The former can be either relational systems (ROLAP) or proprietary multi-dimensional database systems (MOLAP) [9]. The latter offer interactive graphical user interfaces, usually similar to spreadsheets. While this allows the user to easily summarize and view data, spreadsheet-like environments suffer from several limitations in constructing and maintaining analytical models over the enterprise data. The main point is that these models rely an a logic that is often left implicit, leading to several problems, including redundancy and inconsistency [15]. Moreover, the integration with database technology is based on ad-hoc techniques, rather than any systematic approach. As others [12], we believe that the problem is the lack of a formal theoretical foundation.

In this paper, we propose the MultiDimensional data model and query language, as a new basis for OLAP systems. The model allows to describe the logical structure of the enterprise data according to multiple perspectives, by providing an explicit notion of *dimension*. Dimensions are the linguistic categories used to characterize the structure of data, according to a conceptual business perspective. They are organized into hierarchies of levels, corresponding to possible granularities of data. Factual data are then represented by *f-tables*, the logical counterpart of "multi-dimensional arrays" (the way in which OLAP systems store values). Values in f-tables are accessed through symbolic coordinates. The query language enables the user to express cross-dimensional analytical equations, based on logical expressions over f-tables, in a simple and declarative way. Queries make use of interpreted functions, but the language is parametric with respect to the ones chosen. A distinctive feature of our model is the use of *roll-up functions*, which describe how data are related within hierarchies of levels. Roll-up functions provide the query language with a simple and powerful mechanism to join data at different levels of aggregation.

The main contributions of the paper are the following. The presentation of a multi-dimensional database model, which provides a first step towards a logical foundation of OLAP systems. The development of a calculus-like query language, which offers a high-level support to multi-dimensional data analysis. The study of the expressiveness of the model and the query language, based on a comparison with other related approaches in the literature. In particular, we show that our model subsumes the relational data model. We then prove that our query language, with a suitable collection of functions, expresses the relational algebra, eventually extended with aggregate functions [16]. We also show that, with a limited set of interpreted functions, the query language is able to express a broad class of queries.

Related work. The term OLAP has been recently introduced by Codd et al. [8] to characterize the category of analytical processing over large, historical databases (data warehouses) oriented to decision making. Further discussion on OLAP, multi-dimensional analysis, and data warehousing can be found in [6,14,22,24].

A comparison between OLAP concepts and the area of statistical databases is given in [20].

An important OLAP operation is summarization of data over one or more dimensions. Klug [16] provided a first theoretical basis in this respect, by extending the relational algebra and calculus with aggregate functions, that is, interpreted functions taking a set of tuples as argument and producing a single value as result. Our approach is more general than Klug's one, since the MultiDimensional model subsumes the relational one. Furthermore we consider, in addition to aggregate functions, also scalar functions.

Many authors [5,11,19,23] claim that SQL is unsuited to data-analysis applications, since some aggregate and grouping queries are difficult to express and optimize. They thus consider the problem of extending SQL with aggregation and analysis-oriented operators that are more powerful, but also specific to particular application domains. Gray et al. [11] propose cube as an operator generalizing group by. Chatziantoniou and Ross [5] extend both SQL and the relational algebra with an operator, dealing with "aggregation variables", to succinctly express common queries, providing also a basis for improved query optimization. Rao et al. [19] consider the issue of supporting quantified queries, a class of queries that is difficult to deal with in SQL; they introduce a number of "generalized quantifiers", that is, aggregate set-predicates such as some, all, and at-least. Many of the features considered in such proposals can be easily expressed in our language using a limited collections of scalar and aggregate interpreted functions.

Agrawal at al. [4] have proposed a simple hypercube-based data model, and a few algebraic operators for it. This framework shares a number of characteristics and goals with ours. However, the approach is rather pragmatic, mainly oriented towards a direct SQL implementation into a relational database. Conversely, we have followed a more systematic approach. Moreover, our notion of roll-up function let us capture and describe hierarchies of levels within dimensions in a neater way, and allows us to express more easily complex aggregations in queries.

Libkin et al. [17] have defined a language for querying data organized in multi-dimensional arrays, to support the scientific computing community with database technology. The MultiDimensional model is at a different, and perhaps higher, abstraction level; our notion of f-table is indeed a "logical" counterpart of a "physical" multi-dimensional array. It should also be noted that our approach is motivated by a business context.

Gyssens et al. [12] have proposed the tabular database model, together with a complete algebraic language for querying and restructuring, as a first theoretical foundation for OLAP systems. A main difference with respect to their approach is that we introduce an explicit logical notion of dimension, allowing for multi-dimensional structures, whereas their tables are bidimensional. Their query language covers only the aspect of restructuring, whereas we allow complex computations based on formulas and functions.

Organization. The paper is organized as follows. The MultiDimensional data model is presented in Section 2. The associated query language is introduced informally, by means of examples, in Section 3, and described formally in Section 4. Section 5 presents expressiveness results. Finally, Section 6 discusses further research topics.

2 The MultiDimensional Data Model

This section introduces the MultiDimensional data model (MD for short). The model is based on the notion of *dimension* that allows to specify multiple "ways" to look at information, according to natural business perspectives under which its analysis can be performed. Each dimension is organized in a hierarchy of *levels*, corresponding to data domains at different granularities. A MultiDimensional *scheme* consists of a set of *f-tables* that are defined with respect to particular combinations of levels. A MultiDimensional *instance* associates *measures*, which correspond to data being tracked, with *symbolic coordinates* over f-tables.[1] Finally, within a dimension, values of a finer granularity can *roll up* to (that is, can be grouped into) values of a coarser one.

Example 1. A marketing analyst of a chain of toy stores may organize its business data along dimensions like time, product, and location. The time dimension may be organized in levels day, quarter, week, and year, and Feb 19, 97 is an element of the day level. The elements of this level roll up to elements of levels week and quarter. Similarly, both weeks and quarters roll up to years. Note however that weeks do not roll up to months, since months do not divide evenly into weeks. In this framework, a measure can be the number of items sold by the chain. This measure could be represented by means of an f-table SALES, having symbolic coordinates on the levels day, item, and store: an instance of SALES might state the fact that on Feb 19, 97 the store Colosseum has sold 11 pieces of Lego.

2.1 MultiDimensional Schemes

Let us fix two disjoint countable sets of *names* and *values*. We denote by $\mathcal{L}$ a set of names called *levels* such that: (i) each level $l \in \mathcal{L}$ is associated with a countable set of values $\text{DOM}(l)$, called the *domain of l*; and (ii) the various domains associated with different levels are pairwise disjoint.

Definition 2 (Dimension). A *dimension* d is a triple $(L, \preceq, \text{R-UP})$, where:

- $L \subseteq \mathcal{L}$ is a finite set of levels;
- $\preceq$ is a partial order defined among the levels of d. Whenever $l_1 \preceq l_2$ we say that l_1 *rolls up to* l_2 or that l_2 *drills down to* l_1;

---

[1] Actually, the 'f' in the term 'f-table' has a double meaning. On one hand, it stands for 'function', because each f-table is indeed a function, from coordinates to measures. On the other hand, it stands also for 'fact', since f-tables represent a form of information that practitioners implement by means of the so-called 'fact tables'.

- R-UP is a family of functions, called *roll-up functions*, satisfying the following conditions:
  - for each pair of levels l_1, l_2 such that $l_1 \preceq l_2$, the roll-up function $\text{R-UP}_{l_1}^{l_2}$ maps each element of $\text{DOM}(l_1)$ to an element of $\text{DOM}(l_2)$. Whenever $\text{R-UP}_{l_1}^{l_2}(o_1) = o_2$ we say that o_1 *rolls up to* o_2, or that o_2 *drills down to* o_1;
  - given levels l_1, l', and l_2 such that $l_1 \preceq l' \preceq l_2$, (and thus, $l_1 \preceq l_2$) the function $\text{R-UP}_{l_1}^{l_2}$ equals the composition $\text{R-UP}_{l'}^{l_2} \circ \text{R-UP}_{l_1}^{l'}$. This implies that: (i) for each level l, the function R-UP_{l}^{l} is the identity on $\text{DOM}(l)$; and (ii) whenever a level l_1 rolls up to l_2 in different ways (e.g., rolling up through either l' or l'') then the elements of l_1 roll up to elements of l_2 in a consistent way.

Example 3. Consider Example 1. The relevant information is organized along dimensions time, product, and location, and involves numeric data describing sales and prices. The dimension hierarchies are depicted on top of Figure 1; note that each dimension takes the name from one of its levels (often the least upper bound of its lattice). The figure shows that, e.g., level item rolls up to both category and brand; because of reflexivity, item rolls up also to itself and, because of transitivity, it rolls up to product. The domain associated with the level day contains, among others, values Jan 5, 97, Feb 19, 97, and Mar 10, 97, all of which roll up to the element 1Q-97 of the level quarter. The level store contains values Colosseum and Navona, both of them rolling up to Rome (in level city) and Italy (in level area). The level numeric is a built-in level type, having as domain the rational numbers.

Definition 4 (Scheme). A *MultiDimensional scheme* is a pair (D, F), where:

- D is a finite set of *dimensions*;
- F is a finite set of *f-table schemes* of the form $f[A_1 : l_1, \ldots, A_n : l_n] : l_0$, where f is a name (with the condition that different f-table schemes have distinct names), each A_i, for $1 \leq i \leq n$, is a distinct name (called an *attribute of f*), and each l_i, for $0 \leq i \leq n$, is a level of some dimension in D.

Example 5. Figure 1 shows the MD scheme Toys, having two f-tables, named SALES and PRICE-LIST. Intuitively, the f-table SALES represents summary data for the sales of the chain in terms of pieces sold (dimension numeric), organized along dimensions time (at day level), location (at store level), and product (at item level). F-table PRICE-LIST is instead used to price the various items, assuming that prices may vary from month-to-month, and that different stores sell each item at the same price.

2.2 MultiDimensional Instances

Definition 6 (Coordinate). Let $\mathcal{S} = (D, F)$ be a MultiDimensional scheme and $f[A_1 : l_1, \ldots, A_n : l_n] : l_0$ be an f-table scheme in F. A *(symbolic) coordinate*

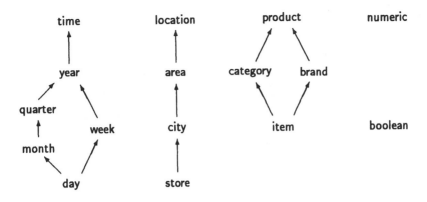

SALES [*day* : day, *item* : item, *store* : store] : numeric
PRICE-LIST [*item* : item, *month* : month] : numeric

Fig. 1. The sample **Toys** scheme.

γ *over* f is a function mapping each attribute name A_i (with $1 \leq i \leq n$) to an element $o_i \in \text{DOM}(l_i)$. If γ is a coordinate over f such that $\gamma(A_i) = o_i$, for $1 \leq i \leq n$, we denote γ by $[A_1 : o_1, \ldots, A_n : o_n]$.

Definition 7 (Instance). Let $S = (D, F)$ be a MultiDimensional scheme and $f[A_1 : l_1, \ldots, A_n : l_n] : l_0$ be an f-table scheme in F. An *instance over* f is a function from coordinates over f to $\text{DOM}(l_0)$, which is defined over a finite set of coordinates. An *instance over* S is a function mapping each f-table f in F to an instance over f.

An *entry* of an f-table instance f is a coordinate over which f is defined. The actual value that f associates with an entry is called a *measure*. Note that measures and attributes are both defined with respect to levels of dimensions, and thus the distinction between them is terminological and not conceptual. In other words, our model does allow a symmetric treatment of measures and components of coordinates.

It is apparent that our notion of "symbolic coordinate" is related with that of "tuple" in the relational model. This is motivated by the intuition that an f-table is a "logical" counterpart of the "physical" notion of a multi-dimensional array. It can also be noted that the notation we use for symbolic coordinates resembles subscripting into a multi-dimensional array (although in a non-positional way). There is however an important difference between f-tables and multi-dimensional arrays. Specifically, in arrays, "physical" coordinates vary over intervals within linearly-ordered domains (in particular, over initial segments of natural numbers), whereas we do not pose any restrictive hypothesis on the domains over which coordinates range. In this sense, our notion of coordinate is "symbolic."

Example 8. A possible instance for the sample scheme **Toys** defined in Example 5 is shown in Figure 2. Note that two different (graphical) representations for f-tables are used in the figure. A symbolic coordinate over the f-table SALES is [day : Jan 5, 97, item : Scrabble, store : Navona]. The actual instance associates the measure 32 with this entry.

day	item	store	SALES
Jan 5, 97	Scrabble	Navona	32
Jan 5, 97	Risiko	Navona	27
Jan 5, 97	Lego	Sun City	42
Jan 5, 97	Risiko	Sun City	22
Feb 19, 97	Scrabble	Navona	32
Feb 19, 97	Lego	Navona	25
Feb 19, 97	Lego	Colosseum	11
Mar 10, 97	Risiko	Navona	5
Mar 10, 97	Lego	Sun City	6

PRICE-LIST	Jan-97	Feb-97	Mar-97
Lego	$12.^{99}$	$9.^{99}$	$9.^{99}$
Risiko	$14.^{99}$	$12.^{99}$	$12.^{99}$
Scrabble	$12.^{99}$	$12.^{99}$	$12.^{49}$
Trivia		$18.^{99}$	$17.^{99}$

Fig. 2. A sample instance over the Toys scheme.

Figure 2 suggests that several different representations of a same f-table are possible. A tabular representation for an f-table f (like the one used for SALES) consists of a relation over the attributes of f, plus a further column for the measures provided by the instance; this representation suggests a way to implement f-tables with the relational model. If an f-table has n attributes, it can be also represented as a n-dimensional array (like the one used for PRICE-LIST) in which an entry corresponds to a measure of the instance. This representation recalls the way in which multidimensional systems usually store data.

3 The MultiDimensional Calculus by Examples

In this section, we present MD-CAL, a query language for the MD model. This language is a calculus for f-tables, and allows the analyst to express analytical queries in a declarative way.

Interpreted scalar and aggregate functions can be used in queries, but the semantics of the language is parametric with respect to them. This gives us the freedom of choosing the most suitable collection of functions, according to the specific application domain. Then, given a collection $\mathcal{G}$ of interpreted functions, we denote by MD-CAL($\mathcal{G}$) the MD query calculus that allows to use the functions in the collection $\mathcal{G}$.

The presentation is mainly based on examples that refer to the Toys sample scheme introduced in the previous section.

3.1 Basic Queries

Intuitively, a *MultiDimensional query* is a mapping from instances over an input MD scheme to instances over an output MD scheme. The input and output schemes are defined over the same dimensions but distinct f-tables. For the sake of simplicity, we shall assume that the output scheme of a query contains just a single f-table, called the *output f-table* of the query.

If the output f-table of a query has scheme $f[A_1 : l_1, \ldots, A_n : l_n] : l$, then an MD-CAL *query* is specified by means of an expression of the following form.

$$\{x_1, \ldots, x_n : x \mid \psi(x, x_1, \ldots, x_n)\}$$

In the first part of the query, called the *target list*, $x, x_1, \ldots, x_n$ are distinct *variables*; the distinguished variable x is called the *result variable*. Furthermore, $\psi(x, x_1, \ldots, x_n)$ is a first-order formula in which $x, x_1, \ldots, x_n$ are the only free variables. The formula ψ is composed by equality atoms involving f-tables, roll-up functions, and interpreted scalar and aggregate functions.

Intuitively, the result of the query is an instance over the output f-table, associating a measure m to the entry $[A_1 : c_1, \ldots, A_n : c_n]$ for those values $m, c_1, \ldots, c_n$ that, respectively substituted to $x, x_1, \ldots, x_n$, satisfy the formula.

An important aspect in MD-CAL is what we call "definiteness" of queries. Intuitively, this property guarantees that queries define indeed f-tables, which, by definition, must be finite and satisfy a sort of functional dependency from coordinates to measures. We shall discuss on this issue in Section 4.3; for the time being, we present only examples that obviously satisfy this property.

As a first example, the following query is used to define an f-table

ROME-SALES $[day : \mathsf{day}, item : \mathsf{item}, store : \mathsf{store}] : \mathsf{numeric}$

to represent the same information as SALES, but limited to the stores in Rome.

$$\{x_1, x_2, x_3 : x \mid$$
$$x = \text{SALES}[day : x_1, item : x_2, store : x_3] \land \text{Rome} = \text{R-UP}^{\mathsf{city}}_{\mathsf{store}}(x_3)\}$$

3.2 Scalar Functions

As we have said, an atom in the formula of a query can use a predefined set $\mathcal{G}$ of interpreted functions. This set can include system-defined or user-defined *scalar* functions, that is, functions that use only atomic values as inputs and outputs (e.g., all the standard mathematical operators, such as $+$ and $*$). Special care must be devoted in defining the semantics of a scalar function when one or more of its arguments is undefined. In what follows, unless otherwise stated, we will assume that the result of a function is undefined whenever one of its argument is undefined.

The following query defines the f-table with scheme

DAILY-REVENUES $[day : \mathsf{day}, item : \mathsf{item}, store : \mathsf{store}] : \mathsf{numeric}$

that represents the daily revenues, for each store and item. A measure for a certain item is obtained by multiplying the number of pieces sold in a day, by the price of the item in that month.

$$\{x_1, x_2, x_3 : x \mid$$
$$\exists x_4 \Big(x_4 = \text{R-UP}_{\text{day}}^{\text{month}}(x_1) \wedge$$
$$x = \text{SALES}[day : x_1, item : x_2, store : x_3] * \text{PRICE-LIST}[item : x_2, month : x_4] \Big) \}$$

3.3 Aggregate Functions

The set $\mathcal{G}$ can also include *aggregate* functions, that is, functions that applied to a collection of values yield an atomic value; these are of special interest in OLAP systems. Typical aggregate functions are those of SQL, that is, `min`, `max`, `count`, `sum`, and `avg`, which apply to expressions over columns.

For instance, the following query defines the f-table having scheme

SUMMARY-SALES[*week* : week, *item* : item, *area* : area] : numeric,

which represents summary data of sales, detailed by week, item, and area.

$$\{x_1, x_2, x_3 : x \mid$$
$$x = \text{sum}\Big(y_1, y_2 : y \mid y = \text{SALES}[day : y_1, item : x_2, store : y_2] \wedge$$
$$x_1 = \text{R-UP}_{\text{day}}^{\text{week}}(y_1) \wedge x_3 = \text{R-UP}_{\text{store}}^{\text{area}}(y_2) \Big) \}$$

The argument of the operator `sum` in the above query is a query q itself. The target list of q specifies "local" variables, and the result variable is used for the aggregation. Intuitively, the result of the whole query is as follows. For a week w, an item i, and an area a, let $S_{w,i,a}$ be the result of the query obtained from q by substituting w, i, a for x_1, x_2, x_3, respectively. It is easy to see that $S_{w,i,a}$ represents the number of sales of the item i in the days of the week w, in the stores of a. Now, let m the total sum of the sales in $S_{w,i,a}$. Then, the result of the whole query associates m with the coordinate w, i, a.

Note that, similarly to SQL, only entries of f-tables (which are non-null by definition) take part of the computation of the sum.

Assume now that we want to compute the f-table having scheme

WEEKLY-REVENUES[*week* : week, *item* : item, *store* : store] : numeric,

which represents the weekly revenues, detailed by item and store. To do so, we can make use of the previously defined f-table DAILY-REVENUES, summarizing by weeks, as follows.

$$\{x_1, x_2, x_3 : x \mid$$
$$x = \text{sum}\Big(y_1 : y \mid y = \text{DAILY-REVENUES}[day : y_1, item : x_2, store : x_3] \wedge$$
$$x_1 = \text{R-UP}_{\text{day}}^{\text{week}}(y_1) \Big) \}$$

However, we can also write the following query, which does not require the definition of DAILY-REVENUES.

$$\{x_1, x_2, x_3 : x \mid x = \text{sum}\Big(y_1 : y \mid$$
$$\exists y_2 \Big(x_1 = \text{R-UP}_{\text{day}}^{\text{week}}(y_1) \wedge y_2 = \text{R-UP}_{\text{day}}^{\text{month}}(y_1) \wedge$$
$$y = \text{SALES}[day : y_1, item : x_2, store : x_3] * \text{PRICE-LIST}[item : x_2, month : y_2] \Big) \Big) \}$$

3.4   Abstraction Queries

In the context of multi-dimensional data, it is often useful to transform measures
into components of coordinates of f-tables, and vice versa. We call *abstractions*
such transformations. The following example shows how to perform an abstraction in MD-CAL. The query generates the boolean f-table

TOTAL-SALES[*item* : item, *store* : store, *year* : year, *items-sold* : numeric] : boolean

by summarizing on the number of sales and using the result as an element of a
symbolic coordinate.

$$\{x_1, x_2, x_3, x_4 : x \mid x = \text{true} \wedge$$
$$x_4 = \textbf{sum}\big(y_1 : y \mid y = \text{SALES}[day : y_1, item : x_1, store : x_2] \wedge x_3 = \text{R-UP}_{\textbf{day}}^{\textbf{year}}(y_1)\big)\}$$

Intuitively, the effect of this query is the following. For each triple c_1, c_2, c_3 of
values over the variables x_1, x_2, x_3, the two formulas in the body are evaluated,
using x_4 and x to hold the respective results, say, c_4 and m. Then m (that
is, true) is assigned to the entry having coordinate $[c_1, c_2, c_3, c_4]$. Note that the
f-table we obtain represents, in every respect, a relation of the relational model.

4   The MultiDimensional Calculus

In this section we formally introduce the MultiDimensional query calculus
MD-CAL.

In what follows we fix a MultiDimensional scheme S and an instance $\mathcal{I}$ over
S. We also fix a collection $\mathcal{G}$ of scalar and aggregate interpreted functions. Each
function in $\mathcal{G}$ is characterized by a *signature* and an *interpretation*. For a *scalar
function* $g \in \mathcal{G}$, the signature has the form $g : l_1 \times \ldots \times l_n \rightarrow l$, where $l, l_1, \ldots, l_n$
are levels; an interpretation for g is a function from $\text{DOM}(l_1) \times \ldots \times \text{DOM}(l_n)$ to
$\text{DOM}(l)$. For an *aggregate function* $h \in \mathcal{G}$, the signature has the form $h : 2^{l'} \rightarrow l$,
where l and l' are levels; an interpretation for h is a function from finite *multi*-sets
of elements in $\text{DOM}(l')$ to elements of $\text{DOM}(l)$.

4.1   Syntax

For each level l, assume the existence of a countable set of *variables of type l*.

The *terms* (over S and $\mathcal{G}$) and their respective types are recursively defined
as follows.

- A variable of type l is a term of type l;
- a value in $\text{DOM}(l)$ is a term of type l;
- if t is a term of type l and l rolls up to a level l', then $\text{R-UP}_l^{l'}(t)$ is a term of
  type l';
- if $f[A_1 : l_1, \ldots, A_n : l_n] : l$ is an f-table scheme and $t_1, \ldots, t_n$ are terms of
  type $l_1, \ldots, l_n$, respectively, then $f[A_1 : t_1, \ldots, A_n : t_n]$ is a term of type l;

- if $g : l_1 \times \ldots \times l_n \to l$ is a scalar function and $t_1, \ldots, t_n$ are terms of type $l_1, \ldots, l_n$, respectively, then $g(t_1, \ldots, t_n)$ is a term of type l;
- if $h : 2^{l'} \to l$ is an aggregate function, and $\tau \mid \psi$ is a query (defined below) whose result variable is of type l', then $h(\tau \mid \psi)$ is a term of type l.

An *atom* (over S and $\mathcal{G}$) is an expression of the form $t = t'$, where t and t' are terms (over S and $\mathcal{G}$) of the same type. The *formulas* (over S and $\mathcal{G}$) are defined as follows.

- An atom is a formula;
- if ψ_1 and ψ_2 are formulas, then $\psi_1 \wedge \psi_2$, $\psi_1 \vee \psi_2$, and $\neg\psi_2$ are formulas;
- if ψ is a formula and x is a variable, then $\exists x(\psi)$ and $\forall x(\psi)$ are formulas.

The notions of *free* and *bound* occurrences of variables are as usual, with the following additional consideration: the variables in the target list of an aggregation term are bound outside the term.

An MD-CAL *query* is an expression of the form

$$\{x_1, \ldots, x_n : x \mid \psi(x, x_1, \ldots, x_n)\},$$

where $\psi(x, x_1, \ldots, x_n)$ is a formula having $x, x_1, \ldots, x_n$ as distinct free variables. The expression $x_1, \ldots, x_n : x$ is called the *target list*, and x the *result variable*.

4.2 Semantics

Let q be an MD query of the form $\{x_1, \ldots, x_n : x \mid \psi(x, x_1, \ldots, x_n)\}$. The *pre-result* of q on $\mathcal{I}$, denoted by $\mathrm{PRE}(q(\mathcal{I}))$, is the set of tuples of values $c, c_1, \ldots, c_n$ that, respectively, substituted to $x, x_1, \ldots, x_n$, satisfy the formula ψ with respect to $\mathcal{I}$. In such tuples, the first component c is called the *result value*.

The notion of *satisfaction* of a formula with respect to a substitution θ and an instance $\mathcal{I}$ is defined in the usual way, with the following considerations.

- The substitutions are typed, so that variables vary over values of the corresponding types. For the time being, we assume that values are chosen from the domain $\mathrm{DOM}(S)$, that is, the union of the domains of the levels occurring in S.
- Consider an atom of the form $t = h(\tau \mid \psi)$, where h is an aggregate function, and a substitution θ over the free variables of the atom. Let T be the pre-result of the query $\{\tau \mid \theta(\psi)\}$ over $\mathcal{I}$ and let M be the multi-set containing the result values of T, with the respective multiplicity. Then, the atom is satisfied if $\theta(t) = h(M)$.

Thus, the pre-result of an MD-CAL query is a set of tuples, to be used as coordinates and measures of the result f-table. This is however not always possible, since there are pre-results that do not correspond to f-table instances. We say that the pre-result of a query over an instance is *functional* if it does not contain a pair of different tuples that coincide on all values, but the result value.

Let q be a query having $f[A_1 : l_1, \ldots, A_n : l_n] : l$ as output scheme. If the pre-result $F = \text{PRE}(q(\mathcal{I}))$ of q is functional, then we can build in the natural way an f-table instance $\text{FT}(F)$ from it, as follows. For each tuple $c, c_1, \ldots, c_n$ in F, $\text{FT}(F)$ associates the result value c to the symbolic coordinate $[A_1 : c_1, \ldots, A_n : c_n]$. Then, the *result* of q over $\mathcal{I}$, denoted by $q(\mathcal{I})$ is defined as $\text{FT}(\text{PRE}(q(\mathcal{I})))$.

4.3 Definiteness

Apart from functionality, the result of a query should satisfy another important property: the finiteness of the result. Actually, in the context of the relational calculus, a more general notion, the *domain independence*, has been defined to capture the finiteness of queries. In this section, we introduce and discuss the issue of *definiteness* as a desirable property for MD-CAL queries: intuitively, this notion combines the properties of domain independence (in the context of the MD model) and functionality.

Indeed, the notion of domain independence has been further generalized for queries involving interpreted functions, in particular, to *bounded depth domain independence* [1]. Now, it is straightforward to define the result of an MD-CAL query relativized to a domain D rather than to the domain $\text{DOM}(\mathcal{S})$. Then, we can say that, intuitively, an MD-CAL query q (using functions from a collection $\mathcal{G}$) is bounded depth domain independent if, for any instance $\mathcal{I}$, its result depends only on a domain including the active domain $\text{ADOM}(q, \mathcal{I})$ of $\mathcal{I}$ and of q, plus a further small set of values obtained by applying a bounded number of times the roll-up functions and the functions in $\mathcal{G}$ to $\text{ADOM}(q, \mathcal{I})$.

We say that an MD-CAL query q is *definite* if, for any input instance $\mathcal{I}$, it is bounded depth domain independent and functional.

Syntactic characterizations that ensure bounded depth domain independence have been proposed, for instance, *embedded allowedness* [10]. On the other hand, the property of functionality can be reduced to a problem of implication of *functional dependencies* for the MD-CAL language.

Example 9. Let us consider the query in Section 3.2 defining the f-table DAILY-REVENUES. Intuitively, this query is bounded depth domain independent since: (i) the variables x_1, x_2, x_3, x_4 are bounded to values occurring in the input instance (note that the variable x_4 is bounded also because its values can be obtained by applying a roll-up function to a bounded variable); and (ii) the variable x is bounded to values that can be obtained by a single application of the scalar function $*$. Moreover, the query is functional since the functional dependency $x_1, x_2, x_3 \rightarrow x$ is implicated by the following facts: (i) x_4 functionally depends on x_1, because of the roll-up function; and (ii) x functionally depends on x_1, x_2, x_3, x_4, because of the application of a scalar function to two measures that functionally depends on x_1, x_2, x_3 and x_2, x_4, respectively. Hence, the query is definite.

If we restrict MD-CAL to queries involving no functions (neither roll-up nor interpreted ones), definiteness of MD-CAL queries corresponds to domain independence and functionality in the context of the relational model. It is well-know that both properties are undecidable, but become decidable if the language is restricted to *positive existential* calculus queries [2]. It is also clear that definiteness is undecidable in MD-CAL, but decidable in positive existential MD-CAL without functions. We can show that definiteness is decidable for positive existential MD-CAL queries involving roll-up functions.

5   Expressive Power

In this section we study expressiveness of the MultiDimensional model and the MD-CAL query language. We show that the MD model subsumes the relational data model. We also show that, with suitable choices of interpreted functions, the conjunctive MD-CAL expresses the relational calculus (Section 5.1) and Klug's query languages with aggregate functions [16] (Section 5.2). In doing so, we show that a restricted number of functions suffices to express SQL with aggregation operators, and some of its extensions in the context of data analysis.

In what follows, given a data model m, we denote by $\text{REP}_m(S)$ ($\text{REP}_m(I)$, respectively), the representation, in the MultiDimensional model, of the scheme S (instance I) of the model m. Then, we say that an MD-CAL query q *expresses* a query q' in a language L for a model m if, for any instance I of m it is the case that $\text{REP}_m(q'(I))$ equals $q(\text{REP}_m(I))$. We also say that an MD query language *expresses* another query language L if it expresses all the queries that are expressible in L.

5.1   MD and Relational Databases

Let S be a relational database scheme, that is, a set of relational schemes of the form $R(A_1 : d_1, \ldots, A_k : d_k)$, where each A_i (with $1 \le i \le k$) is an attribute name and each d_i is an associated domain. The *representation* $\text{REP}_{rel}(S)$ of the scheme S is the MD scheme containing: (i) a dimension (consisting of a single level) for each distinct domain of S; and (ii) an f-table scheme $R[A_1 : l_1, \ldots, A_k : l_k] : \mathsf{T}$ for each relation scheme $R(A_1 : d_1, \ldots, A_k : d_k)$, where each l_i is the level associated to the domain d_i, and T is a level whose domain contains only the boolean value "true."

Then, the *representation* $\text{REP}_{rel}(I)$ contains, for each relation $R \in S$, an f-table instance R such that $R[t] = \text{true}$ if and only if the tuple t belongs to R in the instance I.

Clearly, MD-CAL expresses the relational calculus and, therefore, the relational algebra. However, an interesting result is that the *conjunctive* MD-CAL language (involving only $\exists$ and $\wedge$) plus two simple interpreted functions is as expressive as the relational algebra. These functions are: (i) the aggregate function $\varPhi$, which tests whether its argument is not empty; (ii) the scalar function **if**, to compose terms of the form **if** C **then** E **else** E', whose first argument C is a conjunction of boolean terms, that returns the second argument E if C evaluates to "true," and the third argument E' if C evaluates to "false" or it is undefined.

Theorem 10. *Conjunctive* MD-CAL(Φ, if) *expresses the relational algebra.*

Proof: (*Sketch*) All the operators of the relational algebra, but the projection, the union, and the difference, can be easily implemented in conjunctive MD-CAL without interpreted functions. We then use the following expression to compute the result of a projection $R = \pi_{A_1,...,A_k}(S)$.

$$\{x_1, \ldots, x_k : x \mid$$
$$x = \Phi\big(y_{k+1}, \ldots, y_n : y \mid y = S[A_1 : x_1, \ldots, A_k : x_k, A_{k+1} : y_{k+1}, \ldots, A_n : y_n]\big)\}$$

The difference of two relations R and S is expressed by:

$$\{x_1, \ldots, x_n : x \mid$$
$$x = \text{if } R[A_1 : x_1, \ldots, A_n : x_n] \wedge S[A_1 : x_1, \ldots, A_n : x_n]$$
$$\text{then } \perp \text{ else } R[A_1 : x_1, \ldots, A_n : x_n]\},$$

where the symbol $\perp$ stands for 'undefined.'

Finally, the union of two relations R and S is expressed by:

$$\{x_1, \ldots, x_n : x \mid$$
$$x = \text{if } R[A_1 : x_1, \ldots, A_n : x_n]$$
$$\text{then } R[A_1 : x_1, \ldots, A_n : x_n] \text{ else } S[A_1 : x_1, \ldots, A_n : x_n]\}$$

□

5.2 MD and Aggregate Functions

We now compare the expressive power of MD-CAL with the languages (an algebra and a calculus) having aggregate functions proposed by Klug [16]. In particular, Klug's algebra, denoted by RA^{Agg}, is a standard relational algebra extended with an *aggregate formation* operator and a family Agg of aggregate functions. Intuitively, the aggregate formation operator partitions its argument according to a group-by list, and then applies an aggregate function h to each partition, to yield a tuple in the result. We assume that any aggregate function in Agg has a natural counterpart in the MD setting.

Theorem 11. *Conjunctive* MD-CAL$(\Phi, \text{if}, \text{Agg})$ *expresses* RA^{Agg}.

Interestingly, there is a trade-off between scalar functions and the more complex aggregate functions. In particular, it turns out that any traditional aggregate function is subsumed by **sum** together with suitable scalar functions.

Theorem 12. *Conjunctive* MD-CAL$(\text{sum}, \text{if}, \geq)$ *expresses* MD-CAL$()$.

Let $\mathcal{G}_{sql}$ be the set of SQL aggregation operators, that is, **sum**, **count**, **avg**, **min**, and **max**. We also have the following result.

Theorem 13. *Conjunctive* MD-CAL$(\text{sum}, \text{if}, +, *, /, \geq)$ *expresses* MD-CAL$(\mathcal{G}_{sql})$.

The intuition behind this result is that many statistical computations on numeric series are essentially based on the evaluation of the "expected value" of some scalar functions, defined as the mean of the function applied to the elements of the series. A similar result has been obtained in the context of a nested relational language [18].

Actually, we can show that conjunctive MD-CAL(sum, if, +, *, /, $\geq$) expresses other aggregate functions, including the *generalized quantifiers* (set predicates such as **some**, **all**, and **at-least**) introduced in [19], and special operators (like **rank**, **ratio-to-report**, and **n-tile**) introduced in some SQL's extensions in the context of data analysis [23].

Example 14. Let S[A : d] : numeric be an f-table that associates a numeric measure to elements of a dimension d. The following query defines the f-table S-RANK[A : d] : numeric that associates a rank with S. Specifically, if there are n distinct values that occur in the measure of S, then S-RANK associates a natural number with each entry of S: n with the entry having the highest value, and 1 with the entry having the lowest.

$$\{x_1 : x \mid x = \mathbf{sum}(y_1 : y \mid y = \mathbf{if}\ S[A : x_1] \geq S[A : y_1]\ \mathbf{then}\ 1\ \mathbf{else}\ 0)\}$$

6 Conclusion

In this paper we have proposed a model and a calculus-based query language to establish a theoretical basis for multidimensional data.

Practical OLAP systems require a number of query languages, at different abstraction levels. On one hand, the final user should be enabled to perform point-and-click operations by means of graphical metaphors. Typical ways of manipulating a multi-dimensional data collection are: roll up (summarize data), drill down (go to more detailed data), slice and dice (select and project on a bidimensional view), pivot (reorient a data cube, projecting on different dimensions). On the other hand, the sophisticated user that needs to express more complex queries should be allowed to use a declarative, high-level language. Note that a practical language of this kind can be easily drawn from MD-CAL by adding some syntactical sugar. Finally, query optimization can be effectively performed by referring to a procedural, algebraic language. Thus, a family of different languages should by adopted by an OLAP system, and mapping between them should be defined.

Further current research topics in the context of OLAP systems are modeling and optimization. Dimensional modeling focuses on how information can be organized according to natural business concepts, i.e., the way decision-makers look at their business data, to enable decision support. Optimization concerns the ways in which factual data can be efficiently stored and manipulated. There are two main approaches to this problem in the context of decision-support applications: materialization of pre-computed summary data [13,21] and query optimization [3,7].

The formal nature of the model proposed here is well-suited for an investigation of the above problems. In particular, we are currently developing an algebra for the MultiDimensional model, for studying the efficient evaluation of multidimensional queries.

Acknowledments

We would like to thank Sophie Cluet and the anonymous referees for helpful suggestions.

References

1. S. Abiteboul and C. Beeri. On the power of languages for the manipulation of complex objects. Technical Report 846, INRIA, 1988.
2. S. Abiteboul, R. Hull, and V. Vianu. *Foundations of Databases*. Addison-Wesley, 1995.
3. S. Agarwal et al. On the computation of multidimensional aggregates. In *Twenty-second Int. Conf. on Very Large Data Bases, Bombay*, pages 506–521, 1996.
4. R. Agrawal, A. Gupta, and S. Sarawagi. Modeling multidimensional databases. In *Thirteenth IEEE International Conference on Data Engineering*, pages 232–243, 1997.
5. D. Chatziantoniou and K. Ross. Querying multiple features of groups in relational databases. In *Twenty-second Int. Conf. on Very Large Data Bases, Bombay*, pages 295–306, 1996.
6. S. Chaudhuri and U. Dayal. Decision support, Data Warehousing, and OLAP. In *Tutorials of the Twenty-second Int. Conf. on Very Large Data Bases*, 1996.
7. S. Chaudhuri and K. Shim. Optimization of queries with user-defined predicates. In *Twenty-second Int. Conf. on Very Large Data Bases, Bombay*, pages 87–98, 1996.
8. E.F. Codd, S.B. Codd, and C.T. Salley. Providing OLAP (On Line Analytical Processing) to user-analysts: An IT mandate. Arbor Software White Paper, *http://www.arborsoft.com*.
9. G. Colliat. OLAP, relational, and multidimensional database systems. *ACM SIGMOD Record*, 25(3):64–69, September 1996.
10. M. Escobar-Molano, R. Hull, and D. Jacobs. Safety and translation of calculus queries with scalar functions. In *Twelfth ACM SIGACT SIGMOD SIGART Symp. on Principles of Database Systems*, pages 253–264, 1993.
11. J. Gray, A. Bosworth, A. Layman, and H. Pirahesh. Data Cube: a relational aggregation operator generalizing group-by, cross-tab, and sub-totals. In *Twelfth IEEE International Conference on Data Engineering*, pages 152–159, 1996.
12. M. Gyssens, L.V.S. Lakshmanan, and I.N. Subramanian. Tables as a paradigm for querying and restructuring. In *Fifteenth ACM SIGACT SIGMOD SIGART Symp. on Principles of Database Systems*, pages 93–103, 1996.
13. V. Harinarayan, A. Rajaraman, and J. Ullman. Implementing data cubes efficiently. In *ACM SIGMOD International Conf. on Management of Data*, pages 205–216, 1996.
14. W.H. Inmon. *Building the Data Warehouse*. John Wiley, second edition, 1996.
15. T. Isakowitz, S. Schocken, and H.C. Lucas. Toward a logical/physical theory of spreadsheet modeling. *ACM Trans. on Inf. Syst.*, 13(1):1–37, January 1995.

16. A. Klug. Equivalence of relational algebra and relational calculus query languages having aggregate functions. *Journal of the ACM*, 29(3):699–717, 1982.

17. L. Libkin, R. Machlin, and L. Wong. A query language for multidimensional arrays: Design, implementation, and optimization techniques. In *ACM SIGMOD International Conf. on Management of Data*, pages 228–239, 1996.

18. L. Libkin and L. Wong. Aggregate functions, conservative extension, and linear orders. In *Workshop on Database Programming Languages*, pages 282–294, 1993.

19. S. Rao, A. Badia, and D. Van Gucht. Providing better support for a class of decision support queries. In *ACM SIGMOD International Conf. on Management of Data*, pages 217–227, 1996.

20. A. Shoshani. OLAP and statistical databases: Similarities and differences. In *Sixteenth ACM SIGACT SIGMOD SIGART Symp. on Principles of Database Systems*, pages 185–196, 1997.

21. D. Srivastava, S. Dar, H.V. Jagadish, and A. Levy. Answering queries with aggregation using views. In *Twenty-second Int. Conf. on Very Large Data Bases, Bombay*, pages 318–329, 1996.

22. Stanford Technology Group, Inc. Designing the data warehouse on relational databases, 1995. Unpublished manuscript.

23. Red Brick Systems. Decision-makers, business data, and RISQL, 1995. White Paper, *http://www.redbrick.com*.

24. J.L. Weldon. Managing multidimensional data: Harnessing the power. *Database Programming & Design*, 8(8):24–33, August 1995.

Integrating Organisational and Transactional Aspects of Cooperative Activities*

Frans J. Faase[1], Susan J. Even[1], Rolf A. de By[2], Peter M. G. Apers[1]

[1] University of Twente, Enschede, The Netherlands
E-mail: {faase,seven,apers}@cs.utwente.nl
[2] International Institute for Aerospace Survey & Earth Sciences ITC,
Enschede, The Netherlands
E-mail: deby@itc.nl

Abstract. This paper introduces the specification language CoCoA. The features of CoCoA are designed for the specification of both organisational and transactional aspects of cooperative activities, based on the CoAct cooperative transaction model. The novelty of the language lies in its ability to deal with a broad spectrum of cooperative applications, ranging from cooperative document authoring to workflow applications.

1   Introduction

CoCoA is a specification language for cooperative activities [20]. The novelty of the language lies in its ability to deal with a broad spectrum of cooperative applications, ranging from cooperative document authoring to workflow applications. CoCoA is unique in that it deals with both organisational and transactional aspects of cooperation in a single language, but without coupling them as is done in *transactional workflows* [27], which assign transactional properties to the organisational steps of a workflow. In CoCoA, the organisational aspects of a cooperative activity are specified by means of a procedure definition mechanism, which is based on a formal state transition model. Transactional aspects are specified by means of execution order rules. Termination constraints link the state of the execution order rules to the transitions in the procedure definition. The language features in CoCoA are used to extend an existing database schema for cooperative work.

CoCoA has a rich set of primitives for specifying the organisational aspects of a cooperative activity. A procedure definition specifies which operations are enabled at each stage of an activity by means of *steps*. The CoCoA concept of a step is much broader than that found in traditional workflow systems. A single step can deal with more than one user, and each user can be involved in more than one step at the same time. A step can allow a user to execute many different operations, without prescribing a fixed order. Also, CoCoA allows

---

* This research was supported by the ESPRIT BRA project TRANSCOOP (8012). TRANSCOOP was funded by the Commission of the European Communities. The partners in the TRANSCOOP project were GMD (Germany), Universiteit Twente (The Netherlands), and VTT (Finland).

the specification of the dynamic instantiation of a single step with different parameters. This makes $CoCoA$ suitable for specifying free forms of cooperation, such as those found in cooperative document authoring, while still being able to specify the more restricted forms of cooperation found in workflow applications. Details of the procedure definition mechanism are given in Section 3.

$CoCoA$ specifies dynamic consistency requirements on data operation invocations. To do this, *execution order rules* are used to specify the allowed orderings of invocations by means of an extended form of regular expression with operation invocation patterns. Each execution order rule applies to a parameterised subset of the invoked data operations. Details of the execution order rules mechanism of the language are given in Section 4.1.

The underlying transaction model of $CoCoA$ is the CoAct transaction model [20], which is based on the idea of exchanging partial results between the users involved in a cooperative activity. In addition to a centralised database, each user has a workspace, in which private copies of the data reside. Users can exchange partial results with each other, or via the central database. After the completion of the cooperative activity, which can be considered as a long-lived transaction, the result of the activity is found in the shared central database. In the CoAct model, the operations performed on the data are exchanged, instead of the data itself. CoAct uses a merge algorithm [24], which exploits the commutativity properties of database operations, to allow the users in the cooperative activity to work in parallel. We refer to [13] for a discussion on the need for operation-based merging in the CAMERA system. Because operation-based merging permits a larger number of histories to be merged than state-based merging, more work can be done in parallel.

Both the specification language $CoCoA$ [7] and the transaction model CoAct were designed during the ESPRIT TransCoop project. $CoCoA$ is based on the object-oriented, functional database specification language TM [2, 3]. The semantics of $CoCoA$ has been defined by mappings to the language LOTOS/TM [6], which is based on TM and the process-algebraic language LOTOS [5], both of which have well-defined semantics. A tool set for $CoCoA$ has been implemented within the TransCoop project; it includes a graphical scenario editor, a simulation environment (based on the TM Abstract Machine [8]), and a compiler to a run-time environment, which consists of a CoAct transaction manager and a cooperation manager running on top of the VODAK object-oriented database system [10]. This environment is being studied in the context of the SEPIA cooperative document authoring system [22]. Proving the correctness of commutativity relationships is the subject of further research.

The different aspects of the $CoCoA$ language are illustrated in this paper by means of a cooperative document authoring (CDA) example, to which workflow aspects have been added. For the sake of compactness, the details of this example are presented as the various aspects of the language are explained. Section 2 gives an introduction to the CDA example, and shows the general parts of a $CoCoA$ specification by means of the example. Section 3 explains how the procedure of a scenario is specified in $CoCoA$. The subsequent sections deal with the transactional consistency rules. Section 4.1 explains the execution order rules, and Section 4.2 discusses the commutativity rules that are needed for the CoAct transaction model. Section 5 looks at the integration of the organisational and transactional consistency rules. Section 6 outlines how properties of the organisational aspects can be verified. Our conclusions are given in Section 8.

2   An Example CDA Scenario

The example cooperative scenario that we use throughout this paper describes an editor who, with the help of some co-authors, must write a document that is reviewed by a referee. The document consists of a number of chapters with text, which can be spell-checked and annotated. The example has been constructed such that it demonstrates sequencing, parallelism, choice, repeated activation and dynamic step activation. It also illustrates a break-point condition that enforces that all annotations are processed, and a termination condition that guarantees that the final version of the document is spell-checked.

The organisation of the cooperative scenario consists of three steps: a *preparation step* (in which the editor writes a title page and an introduction), a *writing step* (in which the editor assigns the writing tasks to groups of authors that perform the actual writing), and a *review step* (in which the referee reviews the document).

Figure 1 provides the first part of the example scenario specification. Only the *signatures* of the data(base) operations are required, as they are defined in a separate database schema. Chapters can be added, edited, removed and spell-checked; annotations can be added to or removed from a chapter text. Type definitions also originate from the database schema, and only their names need to be mentioned.

CoCoA allows the specification of *user roles*. The actual users are determined at execution time (i.e., when the scenario is instantiated). A user role is identified by means of a user type in CoCoA, and is assigned a workspace type. Workspace types restrict the data operations that can be recorded in the private workspace of a user. In our example, only one workspace type is defined, and it allows all data operations. Three user types are defined: referee, editor, and author.

Users can exhibit other activities besides data operations. Through so-called *communications*, a user may initiate a state transition in the scenario. State transitions influence the set of allowed data operations of other users in the scenario. (By including a 'system' user, issuing certain communications at regular intervals, reactive applications can be specified.) In Figure 1 only the names and parameter types of the communications are provided. They are used in the procedure definition, as illustrated in the next section.

The underlying CoAct transaction model uses history merging as the principle for its operation. Each user workspace maintains a history of data operations that have been performed since the start of the scenario. A user can import or export data, and this exchange is achieved by re-executing a relevant sequence of data operations from one workspace in another workspace. To allow the user

```
scenario write_document
data types   chapter, text, annotation

database operations
  addChapter(chapter)   remChapter(chapter)
  editChapter(chapter, text)   spellCheck(chapter)
  addAnnotation(chapter, annotation)   remAnnotation(chapter, annotation)

workspace types
  cda = { addChapter, editChapter, remChapter, spellCheck,
          addAnnotation, remAnnotation }

user types
  referee using cda,   editor using cda,   author using cda

communications
  introWritten(),
  startTask(chapter, P author), completeTask(chapter),
  readyWriting(), documentOkay(), reviseDocument(), abortWriting()

data exchange operations
  Annotations(c : chapter)
  = select addAnnotation(c,_), remAnnotation(c, _)
  Chapter(c : chapter)
  = select addChapter(c), editChapter(c,_), remChapter(c)
```

Fig. 1. Interface specification of scenario

this data exchange, the specifier needs to indicate those data operations from the history that are relevant to a particular piece of data. The **select** construct can be used for this. Two data exchange operations are defined in Figure 1. One allows exchange of annotations, the other allows the exchange of text changes. Selection clauses use invocation patterns of the data operations, in which the symbol '_' is used to indicate a *don't-care* value of a parameter.

When exchanging data, consistency needs to be preserved, which means that additional, logically dependent data operations should also be selected from the workspace history. The rules for selecting these operations are described in Section 4.2. They are implemented in CoAct's merge algorithm, which takes two histories and tries to combine them into a consistent one.

3   Organisation of a Cooperative Activity

3.1   Procedure Definition

A CoCoA procedure serves to define the organisation of activities within a scenario. It lists a number of steps and a number of transition rules. The latter define how the former are chained together, and define, so to say, the **coarse-grain** control flow of the procedure. Each step definition defines its *entry, interrupt, signal* and *exit interaction points*, at which interaction events with other steps can take place. This form of interaction is mandatory: the initiators of such an event forces the receivers to follow. The allowed interactions are defined in the transition rules. Entry interactions activate the step; exit interactions deactivate it. There may be several of each of them. Interrupts are received while the step is active; signals are sent when it is active.

As an illustration, consider the partial specification provided in Figure 2. It defines a **preparation** step and a **writing** step, amongst others. The first has an exit (interaction point) **done**, the second has an entry point **start**. The two interaction points are made to coincide in the second transition rule, i.e., the second line with the 'on ... do' syntax. This example shows a standard sequence of two steps, but more elaborate control flow can be built. As an aside, we mention that these definitions can be carried out in a graphic interface, which makes it less cumbersome.

The procedure itself also has entry and exit interaction points, and these are declared between square brackets on the header line. They signal start and end of the procedure, and are used to declare interaction with the procedure's step interaction points. In addition, the procedure header also the defines the different user roles of users in the scenario.

In some transactional workflow techniques, step-like structures serve also to define transactional boundaries. This is not the case in *CoCoA*, where steps only help to organise the work in smaller units of activity.

3.2 Inside Steps

A step definition defines which data operations, data exchange operations, and communications can be enabled for the users of the scenario inside the step. This is free-form usage: enabled operations can be invoked any number of times, and in any given order. The enabling takes place only when the required communication takes place, as defined in the step. There exists no explicit disabling in the language: when a step terminates all permissions issued from it are automatically withdrawn. Only by invoking (enabled) communications, can one or more other steps be activated or deactivated.

Data operations and data exchange operations are enabled inside a step for a specific user role, using the following construct:

on $\langle$intpoint$\rangle$ **enable** $\langle$userrole$\rangle$: $\langle$operationlist$\rangle$ **endon**

This indicates that whenever the interaction at **intpoint** occurs, the user in the role of **userrole** is allowed to perform the listed operations, (at least) up to the point where the step terminates. Figure 3 shows examples in the context of the **preparation** step. In these examples, a literal argument value for an operation indicates that the user is allowed to invoke an operation only with that value.

```
procedure (ref : referee, ed : editor,
           authors : P author)[in start out cancel, done]
begin workspace  document : cda

  step preparation[in start  out done] ...

  step writing[in start  out done]
  begin
    parallel(ch : chapter)
      step task[in start(P author)  out compl] ...
    endpar

    on start enable
      when ed issues startTask(c, tas) iff
                 (tas subset authors) do task(c).start(tas),
      when ed issues readyWriting() do done
    endon
  end

  step review[in start  out accept, reject, revise] ...

  on start do preparation.start
  on preparation.done do writing.start
  on writing.done do review.start
  on review.accept do done
  on review.revise do writing.start
  on review.reject do cancel
end
```

Fig. 2. Procedural specification of a scenario. Ellipses indicate omitted text.

The enabling of communications (also illustrated in the figure) requires slightly more involved syntax:

when ⟨userrole⟩ **issues** ⟨communication⟩ **do** ⟨intpoint⟩

This construct enables the user in the given user role to submit the indicated communication. The **do**-part identifies which interaction will occur.

The enabling of communications can sometimes be conditional. In such cases, a statement of the form **iff** ⟨condition⟩ is added to the communication enabling statement. Figure 2 has an example that indicates that a writing task should only be started if the involved authors are known to the overall procedure.

3.3 Dynamic Step Activation

A special form of step definition is *dynamic step activation*, of which the task step inside the writing step of Figure 2 is an example. It defines an *a priori*

```
step preparation[in start  out done]
begin
  on start enable
    ed : addChapter("title"), editChapter("title", _),
         addChapter("intro"), editChapter("intro", _),
         export Chapter("title") to document,
         export Chapter("intro") to document
    when ed issues introWritten() do done
  endon
end
```

Fig. 3. The enabling of operations and communications inside a step

unlimited number of similar tasks, which can be active in parallel. To identify them, they should be parameterised with appropriate parameters, either users or data sources, for instance. In the case of our example, the chapter serves as the identification. In this example, the editor can only issue a **startTask** communication if the prospective set of authors **tas** is a subset of the set of known **authors**. The set **tas** is transferred to the **task** step via an additional parameter associated with the interaction point **start**.

3.4 Informal Interaction Point Semantics

Interaction points identify the interaction possibilities between steps, and between a step and its substeps. If an interaction takes place, the involved steps coincide at the interaction point. We assume synchronous communication, and thus abstract away from the asynchronous communication characteristics of a possible implementation. An interaction at an entry point brings a step to life; an interaction at an exit point terminates a step. Interactions cannot be ignored, i.e., they are mandatory. A step can be defined to have several entry and exit interaction points. In addition, there can be interrupt interaction points, at which interrupts will be received and handled by the step only if it is active. These interrupts can be subject to synchronisation with interactions at points internal to the step. An active step can also submit interactions, known as signals (at signal interaction points), but the step will remain active after doing so. There is a natural relationship between all these types of interaction and the primitives of a process specification language like LOTOS [5], and we refer to [7] for a detailed discussion.

4 Transaction Consistency Rules of a Cooperative Activity

Whenever two users want to exchange information, they will perceive it as data-based exchange: the receiving user obtains a new version of the entity of interest. The preservation of *data consistency* in a workspace, however, should not be data-based, but rather operation-based, as this has a far bigger potential for conflict-resolution. To this end, each workspace maintains a history of invoked operations. When an entity is selected for data export, the system will determine the *relevant* (not necessarily contiguous) *operation subsequence* of the workspace's history, and export this subsequence. Then, an attempt is made to merge this subsequence with the history of the receiving workspace.

The definition of workspace consistency is based on these ideas, and takes shape through two types of rules: *execution order rules* and *history merge rules*. The first type restricts the allowed sequences of operations in a workspace; the second type defines what constitutes the relevant operation subsequence, and allows to identify potential conflict situations.

4.1 Execution Order Rules

The *execution order rules* restrict the order of invoked data operations in the workspace history. A history contains both data operations executed by its owner, and imported data operations from other workspaces. The ordering constraints are expressed through extended regular expressions, the elements of which are data operation patterns. These patterns may include values and variables for the operation parameters. A history is *order correct with respect to an execution order rule*, if and only if it is a prefix of one of the filtered histories described by the rule's regular expression. A *filtered history* is obtained from the real history by removing all data operation invocations that do not match any pattern in the rule. This includes proper treatment of parameter instantiations. A history is *order correct* if it is order correct for all execution order rules.

The following execution order rule is defined for the given editing example:

```
data operation order
  chapter_rule :
    forall c : chapter
    order addChapter(c) "edited";
          (editChapter(c,_) "edited" | spellCheck(c))*;
          remChapter(c)
```

The rule states that a chapter can only be edited, spell-checked, or removed after it has been added to the document, and that a chapter cannot be edited or spell-checked after it is removed. This rule does not restrict how often a chapter can be edited or spell-checked. The string `"edited"` following the `addChapter(c)` and `editChapter(c,_)` operation patterns indicates that the chapter is in the edited state, directly after these data operations are carried out. Section 5 explains how these state tags are used to integrate the transactional aspects and the organisational aspects of a CoCoA scenario.

The following order rule places restrictions on the occurrence of operations on annotations:

```
annotation_rule :
  forall c : chapter, an : annotation
```

```
order addChapter(c);
        (addAnnotation(c,an) "added"; remAnnotation(c,an))*;
        remChapter(c)
```

The rule states that annotations can only be made to a chapter after it has been added to the document, and that all annotations have to be removed before a chapter is removed.

In [9], regular expressions are used to specify the external behaviour of objects in an object database. This approach can be compared to the execution order rules of CoCoA when the database itself is considered as a single, complex object. Nodine [17] describes *transaction groups* as a formal notation for the specification of cooperative transactions. An LR(0) grammar is used to describe a transaction group's correctness criteria in terms of valid histories. Neither of these approaches deals with organisational aspects or history merging. Furthermore, they do not consider constraints that depend on the state tags of the execution order rules.

4.2 History Merge Rules

Consistent operation history merging is implemented via the merging algorithm of the CoAct transaction model, which needs information about the commutativity of data operations. The first requirement for performing a consistent merge is that the relevant operation subsequence is correctly determined. In our example, we cannot select an editChapter operation without its corresponding addChapter operation. The notion of *backward commutativity*, as defined in [25], is used to determine which operations depend on each other, but it is the specifier who has to indicate which pairs of operations backward commute. Given an initial set of operations selected by the user who invokes a data exchange operation, the first part of the merge algorithm calculates the minimal transitive closure of this set with respect to the defined backward commutativity conflicts.

The second part of the merging algorithm determines how the extended set of selected operations can be merged with receiving history such that a consistent result is produced. The notion of *forward commutativity*, also defined in [25], is used to detect conflicts between operations of the relevant operation subsequence and operations in the receiving history. If no conflicts are present, the two histories can be merged. In case there are conflicts, the user is given the option to either choose a smaller set of operations to be merged, or to undo operations present in the receiving history. For details about the history merging algorithm of CoAct, we refer to [24].

In CoCoA, commutativity relations are specified by enumerating pairs of conflicting operation patterns. For each pair, a predicate expression over the parameters of the operations identifies when a forward and/or backward commutativity conflict exists. When the conditions for forward and backward commutativity are the same, which is often the case, syntax allows to provide the predicative only once. Below, an example for the editChapter and spellCheck operations is given. Because these operations do not, in general, commute (neither forward nor backward), we specify their non-commutativity using history merge rules, as follows:

history rules
  forall c : chapter
  non-commutative editChapter(c,_) **and** editChapter(c,_),
  non-commutative editChapter(c,_) **and** spellCheck(c),
  non-commutative spellCheck(c) **and** spellCheck(c)

In the CDA example, we have assumed that there are no commutativity conflicts between the data operations that edit the text of a chapter and the data operations that add or remove its annotations. However, to capture the application semantics that an edit operation incorporates prior annotations that were removed since the last edit, a backwards commutativity rule can be specified to enforce that remAnnotation operations should always be exchanged with a subsequent editChapter operation. This application semantics requirement can be specified using the following history rule:

  forall c : chapter
  non-commutative remAnnotation(c,_) **and** editChapter(c,_)
  backward true **forward false**

Because the backward commutativity relationship of CoAct is symmetric, the above conflict also implies that remAnnotation operations depend on previously issued editChapter operations. This unwanted side effect could be avoided, if the CoAct transaction model supported an asymmetric relationship, such as the *right backwards commutativity* relationship introduced in [26].

Relationship with the Execution Order Rules Both the execution order rules and the history merge rules are based on the semantics of the operations. For this reason, it is not surprising that they enforce overlapping constraints. The execution order rule chapter_rule, for example, specifies that the operation addChapter can only occur once in each history for each chapter. This allows the situation where two users issue this operation independently for the same chapter. Any attempt to merge these two operations into a single history will fail because of chapter_rule. Such a merge also fails if the following forward commutativity conflict is specified:

  forall c : chapter
  non-commutative addChapter(c) **and** addChapter(c)
  backward false **forward true**

The reverse, however, is not true. Specifying the above conflict does not state that a single user can execute the operation addChapter more than once for the same chapter. In case an execution order rule enforces that an operation pattern can only occur once in a history, then this, in a certain sense, implies a forward commutativity conflict.

In our example, the chapter_rule enforces that the addChapter operation for a certain chapter always occurs before any of the other operations on that chapter. This means a user cannot import an editChapter operation without importing also the related addChapter operation. To ensure that the addChapter operation is included, a backward commutativity conflict has to be specified.

Again, we could conclude that an execution order rule implies a certain commutativity conflict.

Unfortunately, not all commutativity conflicts are 'implied' by execution order rules. The conflicts between the `editChapter` and `spellCheck` operations, for example, are not implied by any of the given execution order rules. Because it lies in the intention that these operations can be executed in any order, it is not possible to add execution order rules that would imply the existing conflicts.

It is also clear that not all order constraints as specified by the execution order rules could be enforced by the commutativity rules. A merging algorithm based on execution order rules seems to be an interesting research direction.

5   Integrating Organisation and Transaction Consistency

In the previous sections, we explained how organisational and transactional aspects of a cooperative activity are specified in isolation. Both the operation/communication enabling statements and ordering constraints are descriptive, not prescriptive: they express what *may* happen, not what *must* happen. *Termination constraints* are used for the latter purpose. They can be added to the communication enabling statements in the form of a predicate. Such a predicate is allowed to query rule states, i.e. check the current state value of a rule. If the enabling concerns an exit point, we have defined a condition that must be satisfied before the step can finish. This approach allows the formulation of break-point and termination conditions.

To express the condition that the editor can only terminate the writing step when all the chapters in the shared workspace are spell-checked, the following condition is added:

```
step write[in start, revise   out done]
begin   ....
  on start enable   .....
    when ed issues readyWriting()
    iff forall ch : chapter
        |(query document on chapter_rule(ch) <> "edited")
    do done
  endon
  step
```

Here, the predicate checks the status of the execution order rule with respect to all chapters. If the condition is not met, the `readyWriting` communication is not enabled, and the step cannot exit. The parameter list attached to the rule name serves to uniquely identify the rule instantiation, and for `chapter_rule` we need one such parameter. In case the current state of the execution order rule is not tagged with a string, the query expression returns an empty string value.

If we would like to state that a task for writing can be completed only if all the annotations are removed from the chapter (and hopefully processed as well), this can be done by adding the following condition to the transition:

```
when a issues completeTask(ch)
iff forall an : annotation
    |(query document on annotation_rule(ch, an) <> "added")
do compl
```

6 Properties of Scenarios

A major reason to use a formal specification technique is to find design flaws at an early stage of the application development process. This section discusses checking run-time properties at design time. The run-time properties can be divided into generic properties, such as termination, and user-defined ones, like post-state requirements. An example is the question of whether all chapters will be spell-checked at the end of the scenario. To a certain degree the generic properties can be checked by means of static analysis of the scenario specification, by analysing how steps are activated through transitions, ignoring the conditions on the execution order rules, which may be set on the various communication operations.

A more accurate analysis can be performed by generating the state space of the organisation of the scenario. In practical examples, generating a complete state space may be both impossible and undesirable. There are, however, some-times possibilities for finitely representing an infinite state space. Other, more pragmatic approaches may yield still interesting analysis results by limiting the maximum number of step instantiations and data items to a fixed number. If those limits are set appropriately, one may hope to generalise the results to arbitrary numbers.

To perform such analyses, we have to provide the formal semantics of the language first. Section 6.1 below indicates how procedure specifications are mapped to a state transition system. This mapping has been automated in one of the tools developed by the TRANSCOOP project.

When organisational characteristics are analysed in isolation, the blocking conditions of termination and break points are ignored. It may be useful to check if such conditions can be met, using the properties of the execution order rules. These rules are (tagged) regular expressions that define a language, i.e. a set of sentences, and some of the blocking conditions can be rephrased as quantified logical expressions over this set. In a similar way, some of the user-defined statements about the result of a scenario can be investigated. We discuss this in greater detail in Section 6.2.

6.1 Formalisation of the Organisational Aspects

The organisation of a scenario can be represented as a state transition system. Such a system is defined by a set of state representations, and a state transition function. In our case, the first represents the status of the scenario instance, and the second represents the behaviour of the defined procedure, i.e., how instances change from one to the other.

A state of a scenario instance S consists of four parts, U, A, E and T:

- U: The assignment of users to user parameters, i.e., the set of actual users and their roles. These parameters are assigned a value when the scenario is instantiated, and this assignment does not change during the execution of the scenario instance.
- A: The set of steps currently active in the scenario. Each active step is represented as a structure a, of which the first component is a list of step names identifying the hierarchical position of the step in the procedure definition, and the second component is a (possibly empty) list of values for the parallel clause parameters that enclose the step.
- E: The set of enabled interaction points that have operation enabling statements attached. Each point is represented as a structure with four components. The first two components are the same as for a step. The third component is the name of the interaction point, and the fourth component is a list of values for the point parameters.
- T: The terminations state set. This is a possibly empty set of names of exit points of the scenario. This set is empty if and only if it represents a running scenario instance.

From any scenario state, its set of enabled operations can be inferred. The initial state of a scenario instance is determined from the scenario's entry points. Communications semantically are state transitions, and each communication is defined precisely once in the procedure definition. This allows us to construct a complete state transition function from the communications. An entry signal is interpreted as an insertion of the step into the set A of active steps. An exit signal from a step is interpreted as removal of the step from the set A of active steps. At the same time, any steps that were activated from that now deactivated step are automatically also deactivated, i.e., they are removed from A. Interrupt signals do not affect the set A, and therefore steps that are not active cannot become active because of them. Bellow we give a pseudo-code algorithm which, for a given state S and signal s, calculates the effects on the A and E components of state S:

```
P := points_of_communication(s);
while not_empty(P)
{
    for all p in interrupt_points_in(P)
    {   if step_of(p) in A
        {   E := E ∪ p; }}
    for all p in entry_points_in(P)
    {   A := A ∪ step_of(p);
        E := E ∪ p; }
    for all p in exit_points_in(P)
    {   A := A - step_and_sub_steps_of(p);
        E := E - points_of(step_and_sub_steps_of(p)); }
    P := points_reached_by_transitions_from(P);
}
```

Once the state transition model is established, it can be used to perform a state space analysis, to find out if the scenario terminates, and whether there are no blocking states. It is also useful for checking whether the specified behaviour matches the behaviour the specifier had in mind. As the mapping does not take into account the state of the workspaces, it does not match with the run-time behaviour. The next section describes how reasoning about the execution order rules can give a more accurate analysis of run-time behaviour.

6.2 Including Transactional Aspects

The mapping described in the previous section does not take into account transactional aspects. This means that scenario instances may not terminate when the above analysis would conclude that they likely do. Also, questions like whether the last version of the chapters are always spell-checked, cannot be answered.

To make such additional claims, we can analyse the conditions under which the communications occur, and compare these with the execution order rules. In our example, the communication readyWriting inside the writing step has a condition attached to it, which queries the chapter_rule. An analysis of this rule reveals that this condition is violated by the addChapter and editChapter operation, and made valid again by the spellCheck and remChapter operations. By querying which operations are enabled at the various paths reaching the state in which the readyWriting communication is enabled, we can verify that the condition can be met.

Likewise, if we would want to verify if indeed all chapters are spell-checked when the scenario terminates successfully, we have to check if this condition is valid when the scenario terminates at the done exit. Analysis shows this condition is enforced when the writing step is deactivated through the readyWriting communication, and that step review is activated next, which can lead to a successful termination of the scenario. We know that in the reviewer is only allowed to make annotations in the review step, which means that the operations addChapter and editChapter are not enabled. From this, we may conclude that all the chapters will be spell-checked when the scenario terminates at the done exit.

7 Related Work

Several extended transaction models have been designed to deal with the relaxed correctness requirements found in cooperative systems. See, for example, the open nested transaction model [29, 10], transaction groups [17], and the ConTract model [19, 21]. Although these transaction models support long-lived, multi-participant transactions, they are limited in their support for the organisational aspects of cooperation. In contrast, workflow applications typically offer plenty of support for the organisation of activities. During the past decade, several workflow systems have been extended with transactional abilities. See, for example, the TriGS system [12], and the Exotica system [1]. However, the extension of workflow systems with transactional properties is not sufficient to model cooperation: the tight coupling of the control-flow and transactional behaviour in these systems limits the types of behaviour that can be modelled. In addition to workflow, there are other domains for which cooperative applications have been developed, such as software engineering and cooperative document authoring [11, 18]. Although these applications have good support for various forms of cooperation, they typically do not offer transaction support.

The transactional features of CoCoA are based on the CoAct transaction model [20]. The CoAct model assumes that each scenario instance is an ACID transaction. All data operations are considered to be ACID subtransactions within a scenario execution. In the CoAct model, there are no 'transactional' conflicts between operations executed in different workspaces; conflicts can only arise during an attempt to merge operations from different workspaces [24]. For this reason, the CoAct model does not describe a *transactional workflow*, as defined in [27]. The transaction model by which the data operations are executed in CoAct is the *open nested transaction* model [28], which is a *semantic transaction model* [27]. The semantics of the CoAct model has played an important role in the design of CoCoA.

The history merging mechanism provided by the CoAct transaction model has allowed us to take advantage of high-level system primitives in the definition and implementation of the CoCoA language. In related work, the ASSET transaction framework [4] has identified a number of system-level primitives to support the definition of application-specific transaction models. It is shown how to use the primitives to model the relaxed correctness requirements found in cooperating transactions and workflows. It is assumed that the primitives are used in the code generated by a compiler; the issue of mapping a high-level specification language to these primitives is not addressed. In contrast, in the TransCoop Project, we have concentrated on the development of high-level language features to describe cooperation in the context of a specific cooperative transaction model.

The ASSET primitives have recently been used in [15] to synthesise delegation and the resulting history rewriting found in advanced transaction models. Our work also involves delegation, but we take a more fine-grained view with respect to the operations that are delegated. Delegations (exchanges) in the TransCoop model are made by users (specified in terms of user roles) rather than by transactions as they are in ASSET. User-directed delegation provides more flexibility for the support of cooperative activities: multiple users can participate in a transaction, and a transaction boundary is not tied to a particular user. Another difference between our work and the ASSET approach is that delegation in the TransCoop model is semantics-based, whereas in [15] delegation is described in terms of a *generic update operation* on database objects.

During the first year of the TransCoop Project, we investigated the use of the process algebraic specification language LOTOS [5] to specify cooperative activities [6]. A drawback of this approach was the fact that distinct scenario concepts were all described by events. This lack of a linguistic distinction between different concepts proved difficult for the typical scenario specifier to understand and use. It was for this reason that we opted to design the more conceptual language CoCoA. Other formal techniques have been used to specify the semantics of workflows: Aalst [23] shows how Petri-nets can be used to verify properties of workflows, whereas [16] is an example of a communication constraint formalism based on Propositional Temporal Logic [14]. With these formalisms, we see the potential for the same drawbacks that we experienced with LOTOS. It is also the case that some semantics issues are abstracted away in these approaches. For example, [23] abstracts away from the computations done by the tasks in a workflow.

The MENTOR Project [31, 30] looks at the specification and execution of distributed workflows. The formalism is based on state and activity charts, which share similarities with the step definition facilities of CoCoA. A notable difference is that an activity in MENTOR is 'an arbitrary piece of C code' [31]. The main contribution of [30] is a method for the behaviour-preserving transformation of a centralised workflow specification into a distributed workflow specification. The MENTOR transformation assumes that the centralised state and activity chart is defined in such a way that *orthogonal business units* can be identified by the partitioning. The main distinction between the MENTOR approach and the model underlying the CoCoA language is that CoCoA addresses cooperation inside what would be a *single* business unit in the MENTOR approach. In contrast to our work, the formal model described in [30] does not address the kinds of complex values found in object-oriented databases. In a distributed MENTOR workflow, variable updates done in different activities must be detected and collected (apparently as part of the C code) for communication to other activities to keep shared data consistent [31].

8 Conclusions

In this paper we describe CoCoA, a specification language for data-intensive co-operative applications; the language is based on the CoAct cooperative transaction model. Compared to other advanced transaction model work, CoCoA takes an alternative approach in combining organisational aspects and transactional aspects of cooperative activities.

During the design of CoCoA, special attention has been paid in defining the semantics of the language through mappings to two well-defined formal languages: the process-algebraic language LOTOS, and the database specification language TM. Within the ESPRIT TransCoop project, prototype implementations of a cooperation manager that implements the organisational aspects of CoCoA specifications, and of the CoAct transaction model have been made. These were tested with a demonstrator application based on the SEPIA cooperative hypertext authoring system.

Language features for cooperative decisions could be improved upon. CoCoA lacks an 'and'-join possibility in the organisational rules of the language. The reason for this lies in the fact that different semantics can be assigned to 'and'-joins, all of them adding additional state variables. [7] suggests an extension of the language which allows groups of users to execute a communication according a specified protocol.

The usefulness of execution order rules as a specification mechanism needs further investigation. The current implementation of the CoAct transaction model does not check execution order rules. Imposing execution order rules as a post-condition on the result histories of the current merging algorithm seems to be too restrictive an approach. Alternative merging algorithms which do take into account the execution order rules during the merge would allow more histories to be merged. On the other hand, it is not clear whether the proposed execution order rules are powerful enough to specify all possible ordering constraints.

We have observed that operation-based merging does not always result in the most intuitive semantics from the perspective of the end-users. For example, when a user wants to import a certain data item, which happens to be an older version than the one the user has, the merging algorithm is such that nothing is changed in the user's workspace, because there is nothing new to be imported. This is logically correct, but confusing to the users who are not always able to keep track of object versions. Going back to an older version can only be achieved by undoing operations.

A language to support the specification of cooperative systems must provide many diverse features. Within the TRANSCOOP project, we designed CoCoA in such a way that it could be used to specify information needed by the CoAct cooperative transaction model, as well as information helpful in structuring the activities of a cooperative scenario. The combination of features in CoCoA has been interesting to study. The experience we have gained in using the language to describe a real system has revealed that some features are easier to use than others (as described above). The ability to specify different aspects of a cooperative system in an orthogonal manner is pleasing to us. However, the interactions of these orthogonal components requires more study. This also holds for the interaction of the merge algorithm and the execution rules of the transaction model.

References

1. G. Alonso, D. Agrawal, A. El-Abbadi, M. Kamath, R. Günthör, and C. Mohan. Advanced transaction models in workflow contexts. In *Proceedings of the 12th International Conference on Data Engineering*, pages 574–583, New Orleans, Louisiana, March 1996. IEEE Computer Society Press.
2. René Bal, Herman Balsters, Rolf A. de By, Alexander Bosschaart, Jan Flokstra, Maurice van Keulen, Jacek Skowronek, and Bart Termorshuizen. The TM Manual, version 2.0, revision f. Technical Report IMPRESS/UT-TECH-T79-001-R2, Universiteit Twente, The Netherlands, Enschede, The Netherlands, February 1996.
3. H. Balsters, R. A. de By, and R. Zicari. Typed sets as a basis for object-oriented database schemas. In Oscar M. Nierstrasz, editor, *Proceedings of the Seventh European Conference on Object-Oriented Programming*, volume 707 of *Lecture Notes in Computer Science*, pages 161–184, Kaiserslautern, Germany, 1993. Springer-Verlag.

4. A. Biliris, S. Dar, N. Gehani, H. V. Jagadish, and K. Ramamritham. ASSET: A System for Supporting Extended Transactions. In *Proceedings of the ACM SIG-MOD Conference on Management of Data*, pages 44–54, Minneapolis, Minnesota, May 1994.

5. Tommaso Bolognesi and Ed Brinksma. Introduction to the ISO Specification Language LOTOS. *Computer Networks and ISDN Systems*, 14:25–59, 1987.

6. Susan J. Even, Frans J. Faase, and Rolf A. de By. Language features for cooperation in an object-oriented database environment. *International Journal of Cooperative Information Systems, Special Issue on Formal Methods*, 5(4):469–500, December 1996.

7. Frans J. Faase, Susan J. Even, and Rolf A. de By. An Introduction to CoCoA. Technical Report INF-96-10, University of Twente, Enschede, The Netherlands, September 1996.

8. Jan Flokstra and Reinier Boon. The TM Abstract Machine (TAM). Internal working document, University of Twente, Enschede, The Netherlands, February 1996.

9. Nicoletta De Francesco and Gigliola Vaglini. Concurrent Behavior: A Construct to Specify the External Behavior of Objects in Object Databases. *Distributed and Parallel Databases*, 2(1):33–58, January 1994.

10. GMD-IPSI. VODAK V4.0 User Manual. Arbeitspapiere der GMD 910, Technical Report, GMD, April 1995.

11. Philip M. Johnson. Experiences with EGRET: An exploratory group work environment. *Collaborative Computing*, 1(1), January 1994.

12. G. Kappel, B. Pröll, S. Rausch-Schott, and W. Retschitzegger. TriGS$_{flow}$—Active Object-oriented Workflow Management. In *Proceedings of the 28th International Conference on System Sciences*, 1995.

13. Ernst Lippe and Norbert van Oosterom. Operation-based merging. In *Proceedings of the Fifth Symposium on Software Development Environments*, volume 17 of *ACM SIGSOFT Software Engineering Notes*, pages 78–77, Tyson's Corner, Virginia, December 1992.

14. Z. Manna and A. Pnueli. Verification of temporal programs: the temporal framework. In R. S. Boyer and J. S. Moore, editors, *The Correctness Problem in Computer Science*. Academic Press, New York, 1981.

15. C. P. Martin and K. Ramamritham. Delegation: Efficiently Rewriting History. In *Proceedings of the Thirteenth International Conference on Data Engineering*, Birmingham, U.K., April 1997.

16. A. H. H. Ngu, R. Meersman, and H. Weigand. Specification and verification of communication constraints for interoperable transactions. *International Journal of Cooperative Information Systems*, 3(1), 1994.

17. H. M. Nodine, S. Ramaswamy, and S. B. Zdonik. A cooperative transaction model for design databases. In Ahmed K. Elmagarmid, editor, *Database Transaction Models for Advanced Applications*, chapter 3, pages 53–85. Morgan Kaufmann Publishers, Inc., 1992.

18. Atul Prakash and Hyong Sop Shim. DistView: Support for building efficient collaborative applications using replicated objects. In *Proceedings of the Fifth Conference on Computer-Supported Cooperative Work*, Chapel Hill, North Carolina, October 1994.

19. Andreas Reuter and Helmut Wächter. The ConTract Model. *IEEE Data Engineering Bulletin*, 14(1):39–43, March 1991.

20. Marek Rusinkiewicz, Wolfgang Klas, Thomas Tesch, Jürgen Wäsch, and Peter Muth. Towards a Cooperative Transaction Model—The Cooperative Activity Model. In *Proceedings of the 21st VLDB Conference*, Zurich, Switzerland, September 1995.

21. F. Schwenkreis. APRICOTS—A Prototype Implementation of a ConTract System—Management of the Control Flow and the Communication System. In *Proceedings of the 12th Symposium on Reliable Distributed Systems*, Princeton, New Jersey, 1993. IEEE Computer Society Press.

22. N. Streitz, J. Haake, J. Hannemann, W. Schuler A. Lemke, H. Schuett, and M. Thuering. SEPIA: A Cooperative Hypermedia Authoring Environment. In *Proceedings of the ACM Conference on Hypertext*, pages 11–22, Milano, Italy, 1992.

23. W. M. P. van der Aalst. Verification of workflow nets. In P. Azema and G. Balbo, editors, *Application and Theory of Petri Nets*, Lecture Notes in Computer Science. Springer-Verlag, Berlin, 1997.

24. Jürgen Wäsch and Wolfgang Klas. History merging as a mechanism for concurrency control in cooperative environments. In *Proceedings of the 6th International Workshop on Research Issues in Data Engineering: Interoperability on Nontraditional Database Systems (RIDE-NDS'96)*, pages 76–85, February 1996.

25. W. E. Weihl. Commutativity-based concurrency control for abstract data types. *IEEE Transactions on Computers*, 37(12):1488–1505, 1988.

26. William E. Weihl. The impact of recovery on concurrency control. *Journal of Computer and System Sciences*, 47:157–184, 1993.

27. Gerhard Weikum. Extending transaction management to capture more consistency with better performance. In *Proceedings of the 9th French Database Conference*, Toulouse, France, September 1993. Invited Paper.

28. Gerhard Weikum and Hans-Jörg Scheck. Multi-level transactions and open nested transactions. *IEEE Data Engineering Bulletin*, 14(1), 1991.

29. Gerhard Weikum and Hans-Jörg Scheck. Concepts and applications of multilevel transactions and open nested transactions. In Ahmed K. Elmagarmid, editor, *Database Transaction Models for Advanced Applications*, chapter 13. Morgan Kaufmann Publishers, Inc., 1992.

30. Dirk Wodtke and Gerhard Weikum. A formal foundation for distributed workflow execution based on state charts. In *Proceedings of the Sixth International Conference on Database Theory (ICDT'97)*, volume 1186 of *Lecture Notes in Computer Science*, Delphi, Greece, January 1997. Springer-Verlag.

31. Dirk Wodtke, Jeanine Weissenfels, Gerhard Weikum, and Angelika Kotz Dittrich. The MENTOR Project: Steps towards Enterprise-Wide Workflow Management. In *Proceedings of the 12th International Conference on Data Engineering*, February 1996.

Business Conversations:
A High-Level System Model for Agent
Coordination

Florian Matthes

AB 4-022 Softwaresysteme
Technical University Hamburg-Harburg
D-21071 Hamburg, Germany
f.matthes@tu-harburg.de

Abstract. In this paper we introduce Business Conversations as a high-level software structuring concept for distributed systems where multiple autonomous agents (possibly in different organizational units) have to coordinate their long-term activities towards the fulfillment of a cooperative task. We first motivate Business Conversations as a system model suitable for the description of human-human, human-software as well as software-software cooperation. We then explain why we consider this model be more suitable for the description o organizational cooperative work than software-centered object models. The core concepts of the Business Conversation model are described using an object-oriented model. Finally, we report on our experience gained building a prototypical agent programming framework with Business Conversations for agent coordination based on mobile and persistent threads as provided by the persistent programming language Tycoon.

1   Motivation and Background

Following [De Michelis et al. 97] a cooperative information system (COOPIS) can be described using three complementary facets: A system integration facet which addresses data transfer as well as semantic and control integration, a group collaboration facet which is concerned with how people working on a common business process can coordinate their activities, and an organizational facet which views cooperation from a formal organizational perspective, regardless by whom or with what technology it is carried out.

In this paper we propose a high-level system model for the system integration facet where distributed autonomous (human or software) agents coordinate their long-term activities towards the fulfillment of a cooperative task via structured Business Conversations. In our prototypical implementation of this model agents and conversations are treated as first-class entities: They can be named, classified, specialized, made persistent and they can migrate across heterogeneous execution and communication platforms.

As should become clear in the remainder of this paper, this system integration model fits well with modern models for the group collaboration facet (business process modeling, workflow management, groupware support systems) and the organizational facet (virtual enterprises, electronic commerce, radically decentralized information processing). Our model therefore has the potential to simplify the central task of *change propagation* between the facets of a larger-scale COOPIS.

To our understanding, any model developed for the system facet should allow system builders to abstract from the details of

1. cooperation over **time**: Agents and artifacts should exist as long as required by the business processes they support, independently of the underlying language and system concepts, e.g. the lifetime of operating system processes or of database schema revisions.
2. cooperation within **space**: Agents and artifacts should be able to migrate freely within a physically distributed environment, independently of the particular system platforms or organizational structures (e.g. business units) involved in the cooperative work.
3. cooperation in multiple **modalities**: Artifacts should be accessible uniformly for agents that cooperate in different modalities (simple overnight batch processing, online transaction processing, direct manipulation by human agents via form-based or graphical user interfaces, computer-supported cooperative work by humans, computer-assisted workflow management, automatic information processing by mobile software agents) and using different media (email messages, EDI-messages, HTTP requests, CORBA object requests, RPC invocations).

As a consequence, a system builder can focus on the "what" and "how" of the particular problem at hand (e.g. compilation of an insurance offer) without worrying about the "when" (batch processing, interactive session, long-term conversation with a human customer), the "where" (on a centralized host, on a server within sales department, on a mobile laptop of a salesperson) and the "who" (customer via letter, salesperson, workflow management system, visit of an Internet agent). Moreover, applications are not cluttered with unnecessary data movement, synchronization and conversion details and can absorb much better changes in time, platform and modality than it is the case today.

Our research work of the past three years has focused on the issues (1) and (2) by providing full **persistence** and **mobility** abstraction in the platform-independent Tycoon system [Matthes, Schmidt 94; Mathiske et al. 95] culminating in the development of persistent migrating threads [Mathiske et al. 96] which can be used to implement software agents similar to Telescript agents [Mathiske 96; Johannisson 97]. In this paper, we describe Business Conversations as a contribution to the third issue, cooperation in multiple modalities. Even though Business Conversations are implemented in the Tycoon environment, this high-level system model has a much wider applicability since it makes little assumptions about the underlying agent infrastructure and (persistent) programming model.

This paper is organized as follows: In Section 2 we position our activity-oriented approach to system cooperation relative to other, more traditional, data-oriented and object-oriented models. In Section 3 we give a high-level overview of our Business Conversation model using examples from the insurance sector. Details of this model are then given in Section 3 which also discusses our prototypical implementation of the model. The paper ends with a comparison with related work and an outlook on future work.

2 System Models for Cooperative Business Applications

In this section we motivate the need for a high-level, activity-oriented agent coordination model and also relate our work to other models for cooperative business applications.

At a certain level of abstraction, the evolution of system models for cooperative business applications can be classified roughly into three stages. Within each of these "historic" stages, the primary focus of research and development has been on a certain aspect of business applications, namely data, behavior and activity. As a consequence, one can distinguish roughly between data-oriented, object-oriented and agent-oriented approaches for the construction of distributed business applications.

2.1 Distributed Business Data

The sharing of business data between multiple applications of an enterprises has been the first approach to the construction of large cooperative information systems (banking systems, airline reservation systems, management information systems, CIM systems). A cooperation of multiple applications is supported by persistence and distribution abstraction as provided, for example, by modern relational database systems. Due to the failure of distributed database technology, most existing cooperative IS are based on centralized data servers, as exemplified by integrated business application systems like SAP R/3, Baan or Oracle Financials.

In a nutshell, such cooperative information systems are viewed as collections of shared database servers and distributed database clients (application programs or ad-hoc human users).

2.2 Distributed Business Objects

The promise of distributed object management is to arrive at more flexible, scaleable and maintainable system architectures by building cooperative information systems using distributed business objects [Orfali et al. 96]. A business object encapsulates business data and achieves a higher degree of autonomy by restricting access to the business data through well-defined method interfaces. Clients of a business object not only can abstract from the internal representation of the business information but they can also rely on an open communication platform (middleware) that achieves full distribution and platform transparency, possibly also across organizational boundaries. Moreover, it is expected that there exists a refinement relationship between business objects (e.g., a car insurance contract is a refinement of a general insurance contract which is in turn a refinement of a generic customer contract) which can be exploited to develop generic domain-specific application models or to define standardizable business APIs.

In the Distributed Business Object model, a cooperative information system is viewed as a collection of distributed objects which exchange messages that are dispatched by an "ubiquitous" object request broker infrastructure.

In our view, Distributed Business Objects are a promising software structuring concept for rather tightly integrated business applications, e.g. in-house desktop clients accessing corporate business object servers. However, we believe that it does not scale well for more advanced patterns of cooperative work involving truly autonomous "profit centers" within an organization or involving several departments of independent enterprises which are unlikely to agree on a common business object model and a shared object infrastructure which may be expensive to maintain.

The interaction between business objects and the coordination of their behavior is "hard-coded" and often distributed in a complex way over the methods of multiple objects. This is to be seen in contrast with the need for multiple modalities for cooperative work quoted in the introduction of this paper and the flexibility requirements imposed by business process reengineering [De Michelis et al. 97].

2.3 Distributed Business Agents

In recent years, activity-oriented models centered around the notion of "agents" have attracted a lot of interest in the research community. Despite significant differences in detail, all of these models suggest to view cooperative systems as being composed of largely autonomous agents, each with a well-defined "responsibility", "independent activity", private "knowledge", "memory" and "capabilities". Moreover, agents are to be regarded as a unit of persistence and mobility.

Agents provide a system structuring concept appropriate for the decomposition of cooperative systems into smaller subsystems responsible for well-defined short-term or long-term tasks (claims processing, order management, shopping, information retrieval) which can be carried out either by a human or a software agent (demon, robot, script invocation, etc.) at a single site or involving a migration from site to site.

In order to avoid the deficiencies of business objects described at the end of the previous section, the notion of a business agent should not simply expand the notion of a business object (consisting of encapsulated state and behavior) by adding autonomous activity (active objects) and platform-independent mobility as suggested by some software agent models.

Instead of this, our proposal de-emphasizes the importance of agents themselves (how they are created, classified, duplicated, etc.) and concentrates on their externally observable behavior, namely their ability to sustain long-term, goal-directed conversations with other agents which is also an important mechanism to *coordinate* agents (synchronization, delegation, replication, ...).

Another view on the evolution of cooperation models is to regard it as a gradual generalization process, since each of the newer models subsumes concepts of its predecessors and puts them into a larger context which tends to be more stable over the lifetime of a cooperative information systems.

- Data-centered modeling: Which data structures are maintained by the system? What are their attributes and relationships? Which integrity constraints exist on these data structures?
- Object-centered modeling: Which operations can be applied to these data structures? What are legal state transitions on these objects?
- Activity-centered modeling: How does the system interact with its environment over time? Are there subsystems with restricted communication links to other subsystems? What is the long-term goal to be achieved by a sequence of communication steps between subsystems?

3 Concepts of the Business Conversation Model

The leitmotiv of the Business Conversation model are speech acts between customers and performers. The model is inspired by the work of Terry Winograd and Fernando Flores in the domain of computer-supported cooperative work [Winograd 87; Flores et al. 88; Medina-Mora et al. 92] which introduce the concept of "conversations for action" based on linguistic studies and the speech act theory developed by Austin and Searle [Austin 62; Searle 69]. However, our goals are different from the more descriptive work of Winograd and Flores in that we intend to develop a *system model* and system design techniques which can be used during system analysis, system design and system implementation (similar to the work on distributed object models).

3.1 Business Conversations of an Enterprise

In the Business Conversation model, an enterprise or a business unit is viewed as an agent that is involved in a number of (long-term) business conversations with other agents like customers, suppliers or government agencies. Within each of these conversations, each agent has a fixed role (either customer or performer). For example, an insurance broker is a performer for its customers and at the same time a customer for several insurance agencies.

The main purpose of a business conversation is to coordinate the otherwise autonomous activities of both agents towards a common goal which is typically specified in the course of the conversation. A business conversation can be decomposed into an ordered sequence of speech acts which can be classified into four phases that occur in the following order (see also Figure 1):

- Request Phase: During this conversation phase, the customer identifies himself to the performer and states its (business) goal to be achieved during the

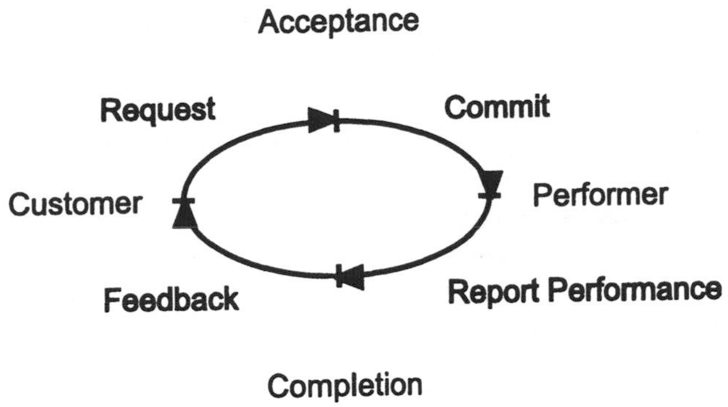

Acceptance

Request   Commit

Customer   Performer

Feedback   Report Performance

Completion

Fig. 1. The four phases of a Business Converation

conversation. The main purpose with respect to the customer is to check whether the performer is ready to start such a conversation or not. ("I want to insure my car").

- Negotiation Phase: A sequence of negotiation speech acts may be necessary to align the specific customer needs and the available performer services. Only if both partners (as autonomous agents) agree on the (refined) common goal, a commit of the performer is reached which can be understood as a "promise" about its future activity. During the negotiation phase, exception handling and recovery policies (or more general "quality of service" parameters) for the remainder of the conversation can be specified. ("Here are our insurance policies", "Your insurance contract number is 12345").
- Performance Phase: The performer reports on the progress of and/or the completion of the requested activity to the customer. This may also involve requests for additional information or actions from the customer to take place under the already committed QoS conditions. ("'We covered your last accident", ...)
- Feedback Phase: This phase gives the customer the opportunity to declare its satisfaction with the service provided and may comprise the obligation for payment. During the feedback phase, no further services have to be provided by the performer.

If required by a specific real-world cooperative activity, some of these phases may be skipped. For example, a simple atomic client/server transaction (money bank transfer) involves neither a negotiation nor a feedback phase.

3.2 Cooperation in Multiple Modalities

The utterances of customers and performers quoted in the preceding section are deliberately chosen to resemble natural language statements of human actors. However the Business Conversation model and the system infrastructure described in Section 3 are intended to cover uniformly human as well as software agents. Given a formal conversation specification for a specific business task such as claims handling, it can be utilized directly to support agent cooperation in four modalities

Application Linking: Customer and performer are realized as two autonomous applications that synchronize via asynchronous message exchange.

GUI Management: A human user interacts with a software system. Legal interaction patterns are described by the Business Conversation specification which are interpreted by a software system called "generic customer".

Workflow Management: A software system (as a customer) requests actions from a human user who is guided by a software system called "generic performer".

Structured Message Handling: The cooperative work of two human users can also profit from tool-supported message handling ensuring the adherence to pre-defined business rules.

An interesting technical implication of this unification of human and software agents is the ability to first develop a stand-alone information system based on its externally observable interaction patterns (similar to Visual Basic or Visual Age) and then to scale this application to a richer distributed environment where it is necessary to cooperate with other information systems without modifying the application logic of the individual systems.

Moreover, we are currently building generic application wrappers for legacy applications (Windows-95 applications and SAP R/3) which translate automatically conversation specifications and dialog steps to support the integration of such applications (without access to their source code) as agents into an open cooperation environment.

Finally, it should be noted that the modality may change dynamically during an ongoing conversation. For example, similar to an automated telephone call center, standard requests could be handled by a software agent which transfers its conversation (i.e. a simple trace of past communication steps) to a human performer as soon as more complex or exceptional requests occur.

3.3   Refinement and Abstraction

An externally observable "customer-oriented" business conversation (primary business conversation) of an enterprise may lead to other internal business conversations (secondary business conversations) between autonomous business units of an enterprise.

A secondary business conversation follows the same communication pattern described for primary conversations. For example, a performer in a primary conversation may become a customer in multiple secondary conversations to coordinate the cooperative work of multiple subordinate agents towards the common goal requested by the external customer in the primary conversation.

Such a situation is displayed in the upper part of Figure 2, where the external customer establishes a conversation with a performer which delegates the

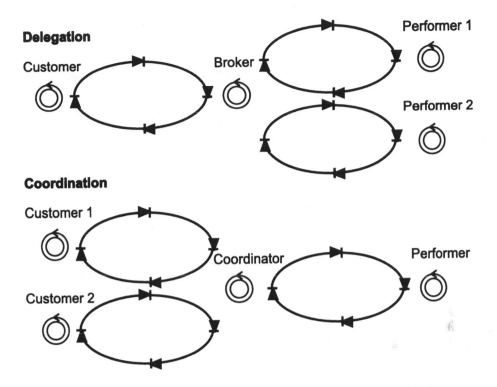

Fig. 2. Interactions between conversations: delegation and coordination

customers requests transparently to the respective subordinate performer specialized on this particular kind of task (claims processing, assessment of damage) and reports their utterances back to the customer of the primary conversation.

An agent can also take the performer role in multiple conversations simultaneously (see the lower part of Figure 2), hiding coordination details (planning, prioritizing, ...) in cases where the customers request activities on shared resources.

Similarly, an "external" customer may consist of a collection of cooperating subordinate agents (secretary, deputy) which cooperate through (externally invisible) means like peer to peer business conversations or simple authority chains (from boss to employee).[1]

To summarize, the iterated decomposition of a binary customer/performer conversation into secondary conversations or subordinate agents ultimately terminates with a collection of human or software agents which carry out their work tasks in total autonomy but which are linked by a tree of speech acts (requests, commitments and task completion dependencies) and by an authority hierarchy.

---

[1] In the remainder of this paper we ignore the implications of the concept of subordinate agents which participate in business conversations on behalf of their authority (security, addressing, mobility, ...).

3.4 Structured Dialogs and Conversation Specifications

In our model, the speech acts (protocols) between customer and performer are constrained to be *structured dialogs* and they have to adhere to explicit *conversation specifications*.

Two adjacent speech acts of a business conversation are grouped together and form a dialog step which involves the exchange of a dialog understood as a document with a hierarchically structured content according to the following basic pattern: The performer sends a dialog with an initial content, for example, a list of insurance offers with a partially filled-out contract that contains placeholders to prompt the customer for additional information. (3.) The customer updates its copy of the dialog (i.e., "fills out the form") and returns it to the performer with a request from a set of possible requests available in this particular dialog step (e.g. "Please revise the offer" or "I accept the offer").

A conversation is initiated by the customer with an initial request consisting of a description of the conversation specification (protocol) the customer will utilize for the remainder of the conversation. This description is represented as a structured dialog itself.

The conversation terminates successfully only when both agents agree that the conversation is completed. In each dialog step, a time-out can be regarded as an implicit request (of the customer) or as an implicit reply (of the performer), respectively.

Each structured document exchanged between customer and performer is required to contain a document header that permits the receiving agent to uniquely identify the context of the dialog (i.e. the enclosing conversation). As a consequence, the very first request in a conversation uttered by the customer ("I want to start a new conversation conforming to specification X") has to be different from all its subsequent requests which are shipped together with the revised content of its previous dialog step and a reference to an already existing conversation.

The advantage of imposing additional structure onto conversations and of constraining conversations by structured meta data (conversation specifications) can be best understood by the analogy with the concept of data and object types which also provide a stable basis for formal reasoning, for tool support (consistency checking) and for system analysis (classification, generalization, parameterization).

Moreover, this meta information (protocol information) is readily available (business rules, workflow specifications, object interaction diagrams) at system design time and is essential for the understanding of large reactive agent systems. [2]

---

[2] "An object-oriented program's run-time structure often bears little resemblance to its code structure. The code is frozen at compile-time, it consists of classes of fixed inheritance relationships. A program's run-time structure consists of rapidly changing networks of communicating objects. Trying to understand one from the other is like trying to understand the dynamism of living ecosystems from the static taxonomy of plants and animals, and vice versa". [Gamma et al. 95]

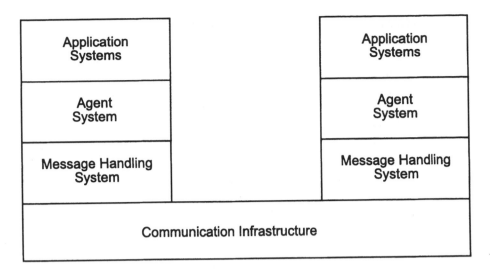

Fig. 3. Layers of the Business Conversations library framework

4 Implementing Business Conversations

This section gives an overview of our prototypical implementation of the business conversation model sketched in the previous section. This implementation consists of a polymorphically-typed framework written in the Tycoon persistent and distributed programming environment [Matthes et al. 97], exploiting mobile persistent threads described in [Mathiske et al. 96]. The framework components are replicated at each agent-enabled network site and are therefore viewed as an "ubiquitous" infrastructure.

The three layers of this library framework are depicted in Figure 3:

Application system layer: This layer contains the application-specific agent definitions ("domain-specific business logic") consisting of Business Conversation specifications with attached event specifications which in turn are bound to statically scoped and typed Tycoon application code.

Agent system layer: The API provided by the agent system layer is used by the agents to interact with their environment. This layer is responsible for the coordination of concurrent conversations and the tracing of conversation instances. Furthermore, agent mobility and persistence services are localized in this layer.

Message handling layer: This layer provides a programming abstraction from local and remote communication implementing a store-and-forward messaging scheme. Message queues ensure the correct transmission of a message even in cases where the receiver is temporarily unavailable [MSMQ95 95].

All interactions between agents at higher layers are carried out via this component. Furthermore, the message handling system provides an abstraction of the underlying communication infrastructure. As of today, simple (secure) Internet socket connections are used to transfer linearized typed Tycoon objects. We are currently experimenting with software components for automatic forms processing (FAX communication channel) and with SGML (in particular HTML) converters as commercially-relevant alternatives for communication in open networks with legacy applications.

In the following sections we focus on the object types and services provided by the agent system layer to the application systems.

4.1 Conversation Specifications as First-Class Objects

A conversation specification is a contract between two agents since it constrains the behavior of the performer and provides a promise to the customer. A conversation specification can express type constraints (the structure of the documents sent and received) but also as state-dependent constraints on the conversation history (e.g., claims can only be settled after a contract has been signed and the first payment has been received). A more software-oriented example is the state-dependent specification that a customer will never execute a *pop* operation on an empty stack.

In contrast to earlier models based on the speech act model like the Coordinator Tool [Flores et al. 88], a conversation specification is not given as part of the business conversations model. Instead of this, a conversation specification is a dynamically-created structured object which describes the set of all possible conversations between a customer and a performer in a given application domain expressed in the syntax of the business conversation model.

The object model in Figure 4 defines the abstract elements of conversation specifications using the Mainstream Objects Model as a meta model notation [?] (IH = inheritance, A = aggregation. Circle = cardinality zero, double line = optional, crow foot = cardinality n).

Technically speaking, conversation specifications are typed, persistent and mobile objects that are created bottom up using constructors of their respective classes (compare Figure 4), for example:

```
let contract = RecordContentSpec.new()
 .add("name" AtomicContentSpec.new(String))
 .add("first" AtomicContentSpec.new(String))
 .add("birthday" AtomicContentSpec.new(Date))
 .add("method of payment" MultipleChoiceSpec.new().add( ... ) )
let contractDialog = DialogSpec.new(contract)
 .addPossibleRequest("Accept" #(confirmationDialog))
 .addPossibleRequest("Reject" #(negotiationSubConversation, noAgreementDialog
let carInsuranceConversationSpec = ConversationSpec.new("carInsurance")
 .add("Welcome" welcomeDialog)
 .add("Contract" contractDialog)
 ...
```

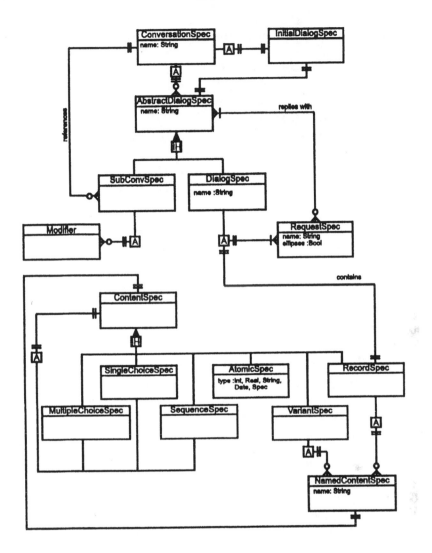

Fig. 4. Class diagram for content, dialog and conversation specifications

It is also possible to generate a conversation specification from a textual or graphical representation of the dialog graph or to receive it from a remote agent, for example, a "conversation broker".

A conversation specification ("car insurance") is a dictionary of named dialog specifications with a distinguished initial dialog specification which describes the initial state for both communication partners. A dialog specification can be are either a concrete dialog specification ("contract") or a subconversation specification ("negotiation on contract details"). The latter is obtained by an incremental modification of an existing conversation specification. This incremental modification concept is intended to generalize the concept of inheritance on object classes to conversation specifications.

A concrete dialog specification consists of a record dialog content specification and a (possibly empty) set of request specifications available for this dialog. A record dialog content specification aggregates named content specifications ("name", "birthday", "method of payment") which in turn (and recursively) can be either atomic (integer, string, ...), record, variant, sequence, single choice and multiple choice content specifications. In this way, content specifications define a simple monomorphic type system. More details on the Tycoon implementation can be found in [Johannisson 97].

A dialog specification can be understood as a labeled state of a non-deterministic finite automaton. The states of a conversation are connected by directed edges, each labeled by a request (uttered by the customer, e.g. "reject contract"). In a given dialog, there may be multiple outgoing edges with the same label. This nondeterminism makes it possible for the performer to choose between multiple follow states ("no agreement possible", "start with negotiation").

4.2 Event-Based Software Agent Programming

Once a Business Conversation specification object has been created, performer and customer agents which adhere to this specification can be defined by rules consisting of an event and a piece of code. This code typically triggers state transitions, initiates secondary conversations or performs actions through effectors attached to the agent. The code is parameterized by a conversation descriptor which holds conversation-specific data (identity of the conversation partner, contents and requests of all preceding dialog steps, etc.). This descriptor can be expanded by agent-specific data (invisible to other agents) and greatly simplifies the management of concurrent conversations with multiple customers and performers, respectively. On termination, the code attached to an event has to return an object that matches the constraints expressed in the corresponding conversation specification which is then transferred back to the customer.

An agent can support multiple customer and performer roles (e.g. performer for car insurance, performer for freight insurance). For each of these roles there exists a set of customer and performer rules, respectively.

A performer rule is defined for a particular request of a particular dialog specification (contract.accept, to be issued by a an agent in a customer role) and has to return an object of class dialog while a customer role is defined for a particular dialog specification (e.g., contract, to be generated by an agent in the performer role) and has to return an object of class request which has to be one of the requests admissible in this dialog step (e.g., accept, reject, explain).

The matching between dialog and dialog specification is checked by the agent system which gives a special treatment to the distinguished initial request of a conversation ("I want to start a new conversation of type X") and a predefined "breakdown" request which is allowed to occur in any state of the conversation.

An active conversation links exactly one customer role and one performer role of an agent. It also implements exactly one conversation specification and aggregates an ordered list of history elements which record the past dialog steps and requests of this conversation.

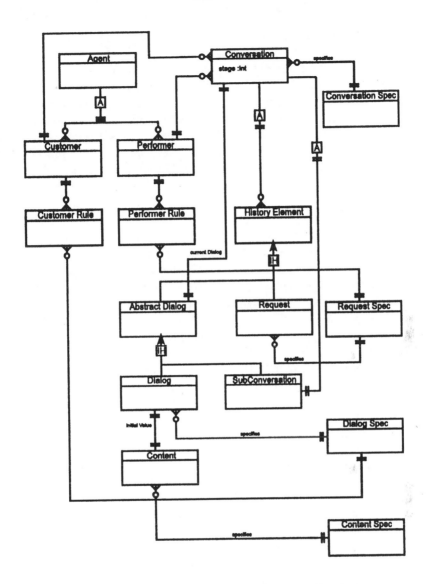

Fig. 5. Class diagram for agents, roles and conversation instances

Figure 5 summarizes the semantic relationships between the relevant classes, some of which have already been introduced in Figure 4.

Customer and performer neither share data nor code or thread state. In particular, the conversation specification and the conversation trace are duplicated in the address spaces of both communication partners which ensures a high degree of agent autonomy and mobility.

The generic customer and performer described in Section 3.3 are also implemented using this event-based execution model and simply transfer incoming and outgoing information to a human agent via a (HTML-based) user interface.

369

4.3 Agents, Places and Place Guards

Our prototypical execution environment for Business Conversation agents incorporates a rich spatial world metaphor for the "agent world" which is similar to the one of Telescript based on the concepts of *domain* and *place* (see Figure 6). A domain is associated with a node in a network and has its own communication end point on the network. A domain is uniquely addressable in the network and consists of at least one place which constitutes the root of the local place hierarchy of this domain. A place can host an arbitrary number of other places and agents for which it provides a dynamic name space. Each place is represented by a specialized agent, a so-called place guard. This guard can selectively grant access to agents which request to enter its place through agent migration.

An agent can establish conversations with agents at its own place. A place (resp. its place guard) can be accessed from within its place as well as from other places and it is therefore positioned on the borderline of its place in Figure 6. Agent migration is controlled by a path consisting of the network domain of the destination domain and of the names of all places on the way to the target place. Local migration can be controlled by relative path names.

By treating agents and places (via their place guards) uniformly, both utilize the business conversation model for cooperative work. In particular, a migration conversation consists of a migration request of an agent, followed by a negotiation with its place guard, a subconversation with the target place guard(s) carried out by the place guard, a completion report and finally a declaration of satisfaction of the agent as soon as it resumes execution at the receiver side.

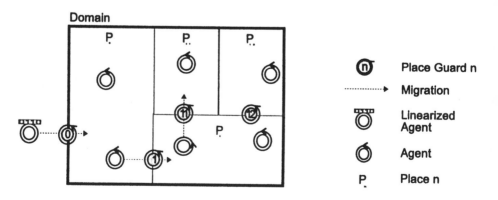

Fig. 6. Logical structure of the agent world

Similarly, the core model makes very little assumptions about the mechanisms through which a customer localizes a matching performer in a wide-area network. This well-known problem of *trading* or *brokering* in client/server programming can be solved above the core agent system layer by transmitting conversation specifications as part of ordinary trading conversations.

4.4 Comparison with Related Work

Dialog-oriented cooperation based on the Business Conversation model has several advantages over cooperation based on direct object interaction (message passing) which underlies popular agent system like Telescript [General Magic 95], Mole [Hohl 95], Facile [Knabe 95], COSY [Haddadi 95], Tcl/MIME agents [Rose 93] and Obliq [Cardelli 94]:

- Conversations do not impair agent autonomy. By exchanging well-defined dialog content with copy semantics only, no private object bindings become available to the communication partner. Therefore, it is not necessary to introduce new binding mechanisms like the ill-defined concept of "object references" described in [White 94; GMI95 95] which attempts to distinguish objects belonging to the customer and the performer, respectively.
- Conversations do not restrict agent mobility since local and remote agents are treated uniformly. Therefore, it is possible for an agent to migrate between address spaces while sustaining long-term conversations, e.g. with its human "owner".
- The agent system already provides a well-defined concurrent execution model. Contrary to direct object interactions, the coordination of multiple agents and conversations is encapsulated in the agent system layer and there is no necessity for application-level synchronization in cases where shared resources are manipulated. The application programmer is thus shielded from much of the complexity that arises in highly concurrent agent systems
- The details of the information exchange between agents are to a large degree independent of the underlying communication infrastructure. In particular, it is possible to translate existing object-based distribution mechanisms (e.g., CORBA [Otte et al. 96]) systematically into Business Conversations.
- Conversations are based on static process descriptions (conversation specifications) which are first-class run-time objects available to both communication partners as soon as a conversation is initiated. This makes it possible to detect mismatches between the customer and performer view early.

4.5 Concluding Remarks

We have presented a high-level coordination model for autonomous agents which is tailored to the needs of (cross-enterprise) business information systems and which is excelled by its uniform treatment of human and software agents. The model exhibits several advantages over other agent models and can be implemented with limited effort in modern platform-independent, distributed and persistent programming languages like Tycoon, Napier and P-Java.

Open issues include a formalization of the refinement relationship between conversation specifications (subtyping) and of their incremental modification by overriding (inheritance). Moreover, we plan to investigate whether it is possible to build a static type checker that guarantees that a software agent generates (at run-time) only conversation traces which conform to a given static conversation specification.

References

[Austin 62] Austin, J. *How to do things with words*. Technical report, Oxford University Press, Oxford, 1962.

[Cardelli 94] Cardelli, L. *Obliq: A Language with Distributed Scope*. Technical report, Digital Equipment Corporation, Systems Research Center, Palo Alto, California, Juni 1994.

[De Michelis et al. 97] De Michelis, Giorgio, Dubois, Eric, Jarke, Matthias, Matthes, Florian, Mylopoulos, John, Papazoglou, Mike, Pohl, Klaus, Schmidt, Joachim, Woo, Carson, and Yu, Eric. *Cooperative Information Systems: A Manifesto*. In: Papazoglou, Mike P. and Schlageter, Gunther (Eds.). *Cooperative Information System: Trends and Directions*. Academic Press, 1997.

[Flores et al. 88] Flores, F., Graves, M., Hartfield, B., and Winograd, T. *Computer Systems and the Design of Organizational Interaction*. ACM Transactions on Office Information Systems, Jg. 6, 1988, Nr. 2, S. 153–172.

[Gamma et al. 95] Gamma, E., Helm, R., Johnson, R., and Vlissades, J. *Design Patterns: Elements of Reusable Object-Oriented Software*. Addison-Wesley Publishing Company, 1995.

[General Magic 95] *General Magic's Telescript home page* . http://www.genmagic.com/Telescript/, 1995.

[GMI95 95] General Magic, Inc. *Telescript Developer Environment, Version 1.0 alpha*, Oktober 1995. Internet WordWideWeb, see General Magic homepage.

[Haddadi 95] Haddadi, Afsaneh. *Communication and Cooperation in Agent Systems*. Springer-Verlag, 1995.

[Hohl 95] Hohl, Fritz. *Konzeption eines einfachen Agentensystems und Implementation eines Prototyps*. Diplomarbeit, Universitaet Stuttgart, Abteilung Verteilte Systeme, August 1995.

[Johannisson 97] Johannisson, Nico. *An environment for mobile agents: agent-oriented distributed databases*. Diplomarbeit, Fachbereich Informatik, Universität Hamburg, Germany, April 1997. (In German).

[Knabe 95] Knabe, Frederick Colville. *Language Support for Mobile Agents*. Dissertation, Carnegie Mellon University, Pittsburgh, PA 15213, Oktober 1995.

[Mathiske et al. 95] Mathiske, B., Matthes, F., and Schmidt, J.W. *Scaling Database Languages to Higher-Order Distributed Programming*. In: *Proceedings of the Fifth International Workshop on Database Programming Languages, Gubbio, Italy*. Springer-Verlag, September 1995. (Also appeared as TR FIDE/95/137).

[Mathiske et al. 96] Mathiske, B., Matthes, F., and Schmidt, J.W. *On Migrating Threads*. Jg. 8, 1996, Nr. 2. Journal of Intelligent Information Systems.

[Mathiske 96] Mathiske, B. *Mobility in Persistent Object Systems*. Dissertation, Fachbereich Informatik, Universität Hamburg, Germany, Mai 1996. (in German).

[Matthes et al. 97] Matthes, F., Schröder, G., and Schmidt, J.W. *Tycoon: A Scalable and Interoperable Persistent System Environment*. In: Atkinson, M.P. (Ed.). *Fully Integrated Data Environments*. Springer-Verlag (to appear), 1997.

[Matthes, Schmidt 94] Matthes, F. and Schmidt, J.W. *Persistent Threads*. In: *Proceedings of the Twentieth International Conference on Very Large Data Bases, VLDB*, Santiago, Chile, September 1994, S. 403–414.

[Medina-Mora et al. 92] Medina-Mora, R., Winograd, T., Flores, R., and Flores, F. *The Action Workflow Approach to Workflow Management Technology*. In: Turner, J. and Kraut, R. (Eds.). *Proceedings of the Fourth Conference on Computer-Supported Cooperative Work*. ACM Press, 1992, S. 281–288.

[MSMQ95 95] *Microsoft Message Queue Server (MSMQ). A White Paper from the Business Systems Technologie Series.* Technical report, Microsoft Corporation, 1995. http://www.microsoft.com/msmq/overview.htm.

[Orfali et al. 96] Orfali, Robert, Harkey, Dan, and Edwards, Jeri. *The Essential Distributed Objects Survival Guide.* John Wiley & Sons, 1996.

[Otte et al. 96] Otte, R., Patrick, P., and Roy, M. *Understanding CORBA: the Common Object Request Broker Architecture.* Prentice Hall, Englewood Cliffs, New Jersey, 1996.

[Rose 93] Rose, Marshall T. *MIME Extensions for Mail-Enabled Applications: application/Safe-Tcl and multipart/enabled-mail .* Internet WWW, 1993. working draft.

[Searle 69] Searle, J. *Speech Acts.* Technical report, Cambridge University Press, Cambridge, 1969.

[White 94] White, J.E. *Telescript Technology: The Foundation for the Electronic Marketplace.* White paper, General Magic Inc., Mountain View, California, USA, 1994.

[Winograd 87] Winograd, T.A. *A Language/Action Perspective on the Design of Cooperative Work.* Technical Report Report No. STAN-CS-87-1158, Stanford University, Mai 1987.

Transaction Datalog: A Compositional Language for Transaction Programming

Anthony J. Bonner

University of Toronto, Department of Computer Science,
Toronto, Ontario, Canada M5S 1A4
www.cs.toronto.edu/~bonner

Abstract. In the classical model of database transactions, large transactions cannot be built out of smaller ones. Instead, transactions are modelled as atomic and isolated units of work. This model has been widely successful in traditional database applications, in which transactions perform only a few simple operations on small amounts of simply-structured data. Unfortunately, this model is inappropriate for more complex applications in which transactions must be combined and coordinated to achieve a larger goal. Examples include CAD, office automation, collaborative work, manufacturing control, and workflow management. These applications require new transaction models, new methods of transaction management, and new transaction languages. This paper focuses on the latter issue: languages for specifying non-classical transactions, and combining them into complex processes. In particular, we develop *Transaction Datalog*, a deductive language that integrates queries, updates, and transaction composition in a simple logical framework. This integration extends the deductive-database paradigm with several new capabilities. For instance, Transaction Datalog supports all the properties of classical transactions, such as persistence, atomicity, isolation, abort and rollback. It also supports properties found in many new transaction models, such as subtransaction hierarchies, concurrency within individual transactions, cooperation between concurrent activities, a separation of atomicity and isolation, and fine-grained control over abort and rollback. These capabilities are all provided within a purely logical framework, including a natural model theory and a sound-and-complete proof theory. This paper outlines the problems of developing a compositional transaction language, illustrates our solution (Transaction Datalog) through a series of examples, and develops its formal semantics in terms of a logical inference system.

1   Introduction

Database transactions were originally modeled as atomic and isolated units of work, with no internal structure and no external connections [4]. This "classical" transaction model has been widely successful for applications like banking, airline reservations, and inventory control, where transactions perform only a few simple operations on small amounts of simply-structured data. Unfortunately, this model is inappropriate for more complex applications in which transactions must be combined and coordinated to achieve a larger goal. This need is typical of new database applications involving distributed systems, complex data structures, and cooperation between multiple users or multiple concurrent processes. Examples include CAD, office automation, collaborative work, manufacturing control, and workflow management. Such applications combine database transactions, application programs, and other activities into larger information systems and business processes [15, 18, 19, 21]. These applications require new transaction models, new methods of transaction management, and new transaction languages [14, 15, 18, 19].

This paper focuses on the latter issue: languages for specifying non-classical transactions, and for combining them into complex processes. In particular, we argue that logic provides a natural basis for such languages. The main contribution is a new deductive language called *Transaction Datalog* (abbreviated $\mathcal{TD}$). $\mathcal{TD}$ has a natural model theory and a sound-and-complete proof theory, and it extends the paradigm of deductive databases with several new capabilities. For instance, in addition to declarative queries and views, $\mathcal{TD}$ provides (*i*) updates and nested transactions, (*ii*) composition of transaction programs, and (*iii*) concurrency and communication. In addition, it provides a smooth integration of procedural and declarative programming, and in the absence of updates, it reduces to classical Datalog.

Transaction Datalog is derived from a general logic of state change called *Transaction Logic* [8, 9, 10, 11]. Transaction Logic allows users to express properties of transaction programs and to reason about them [7]. For instance, one can reason about when a program will commit or abort, and about whether a program preserves integrity constraints. In addition, like classical logic, Transaction Logic has a "Horn" fragment with both a procedural and declarative semantics. This fragment provides a logic programming language in which users can specify and execute database transactions. Transaction Datalog is derived from this Horn fragment by restricting it to relational databases and to rules without function symbols (*i.e.*, just as classical Datalog is derived from classical Horn logic). Transaction Datalog thus inherits the semantics of the full logic, which has been published elsewhere [8, 9, 11]. However, because Transaction Datalog is a specialized system, it has a specialized semantics, which is simpler than the more-general semantics of the full logic. This paper develops the simplified semantics in terms of a logical inference system. The paper also illustrates the properties of $\mathcal{TD}$ through a series of examples. The examples show how logical formulas in $\mathcal{TD}$ can be interpreted both procedurally and declaratively. They also show how the logical structure of $\mathcal{TD}$ naturally captures many basic properties of non-classical transactions.

Related papers on Transaction Logic, a prototype implementation, and the results of benchmark tests are available at the Transaction Logic web-page: http://www.cs.toronto.edu/~bonner/transaction-logic.html

1.1 Background

The limitations of the classical transaction model are well-documented in the literature (*e.g.*, [15, 18, 19, 27]). One important limitation is that this model does not support the composition of transaction programs. For instance, database transactions are usually defined by embedding SQL commands within a host programming language. Unfortunately, there are severe restrictions on the ability of embedded SQL to combine simple transaction programs into larger ones, regardless of the host language. These restrictions greatly hinder the modular development of large transaction programs. This problem is not limited to embedded SQL, but is shared by almost all application programming languages for commercial database systems, since these systems are based on the classical transaction model.

The first attempt to address this problem lead to the nested transaction model, in which a transaction can be composed of subtransactions [19, 27]. As a simple example, suppose we have a transaction program for withdrawing money from a bank account, and another for depositing money. We would like to compose these two programs into a third program for transferring money from one account to another, and we would like this third program to execute as a transaction, *i.e.*, as an atomic and isolated unit of work. Of course, we could write a money-transfer program from scratch in embedded SQL, but that is not the point. The point is to reuse and combine existing transaction programs. In particular, we would like to execute the withdraw and deposit programs concurrently; and if one fails, we would like them both to abort, and their effects on the database to be undone. This requirement poses several serious problems for the classical transaction model, and for transaction management systems based on it. First, the withdraw and deposit transactions are not independent. In particular, the failure of one implies the failure of the other, even if the other has successfully completed its execution and has committed. Second, we now need serializability *within* transactions, not just between them. In particular, the withdraw and deposit transactions must be executed serializably within the transfer transaction. Third, composite transactions can now behave like atomic and isolated units of work. In particular, the transfer program must execute to completion or not at all (atomicity), and its execution with other transactions must be serializable (isolation). These requirements are not supported by most commercial products. In particular, they cannot be met by having application programmers specify transactions in a conventional programming language on top of a conventional DBMS (*e.g.*, by using SQL embedded in C, or even concurrent C).

As another example, consider the following abstract process, taken from [35]:

Run Transaction T1. Then execute transactions T2, T3, and T4 in parallel. Immediately after their successful completion, start T5. But, if one of T2, T3, or T4 fails, then abort the other two. In this case, the effects of T1 have to be cancelled as well.

This process is a composition of five transactions, *T1–T5*. As in the previous example, the transactions are not independent, and the failure of one can require that others be undone, even if they have already completed and committed. This dependence conflicts with the classical transaction model, which assumes that separate transactions are unrelated units of work. Such dependencies are typical of many new database applications, in which transactions participate in a complex web of relations. These new applications require the development of new transaction models. This need has been eloquently expressed by Jim Gray [15, page xvii]:

> *The transaction concept has emerged as the key structuring technique for distributed data and distributed computations. Originally developed and applied to database applications, the transaction model is now being used in new application areas ranging from process control to cooperative work. Not surprisingly, these more sophisticated applications require a refined and generalized transaction model. The concept must be made recursive, it must deal with concurrency within a transaction, it must relax the strict isolation among transactions, and it must deal more gracefully with failures.*

Many new transaction models have been proposed in the literature. Nested Transactions were the first [19, 27]. More recent models include Sagas [17], Con-Tracts [35], Flex Transactions [16], Cooperative Transactions [29], Multi-Level Transactions and Open Nested Transactions [36], among others [15]. Much of the research on these models emphasizes transaction *management*. The focus has therefore been on systems issues such as concurrency control and recovery, locking protocols, distributed commit and abort, fault tolerance, scheduling, implementation and performance.

In addition to new methods of transaction management, new transaction *languages* are also needed [14]. These languages must deal *both* with conventional programming issues *and* with transactional issues. For instance, they must allow transaction programs to be combined sequentially, concurrently, and hierarchically. In addition, they must deal with persistent data and with transaction abort, rollback, atomicity, and isolation. Moreover, they must deal with these issues both for elementary transactions and for composite transactions. For example, suppose that a number of small transaction programs are combined into a larger program. Numerous questions about the larger program immediately arise. Does it execute as a transaction? Does it execute atomically? Does it execute in isolation? If some of the small transaction programs abort, does the larger program abort as well? If so, is it aborted completely or partially? What effect does this have on the database? What effect does this have on the program's execution state? These questions must be addressed by any language that supports the composition of transaction programs.

The database systems community has begun to address these questions. For instance, some transaction programming languages offer save points, which support a limited form of nested transactions and partial rollback. In addition, *Transactional-C* is a commercial programming language for the Encina TP monitor, which provides full support for nested transactions [33]. Likewise, a number of research projects have developed programming languages for nested transactions and other non-classical transaction models.

Unfortunately, although some programming languages have been implemented and others have been proposed, their theoretical foundations are incomplete. In general, the theory of non-classical transactions has focussed on transaction management, not on transaction languages. For instance, there has been no attempt to integrate relational algebra and relational updates into a language for transaction composition. Likewise, issues such as declarative semantics, data complexity, and transaction expressibility have been completely ignored. These issues have been studied extensively in the context of classical transactions and database queries (*e.g.*, [1, 2, 12]). The challenge is to extend this theory to non-classical transactions. This paper takes a first step.

1.2 Transaction Datalog

In this paper, we propose a logic-based approach to the problems of specifying non-classical transactions. In particular, we develop *Transaction Datalog* (or $\mathcal{TD}$), a deductive database language for specifying transactions and combining simple transactions into complex ones. Like classical Datalog, $\mathcal{TD}$ has *both* a declarative semantics *and* an equivalent operational semantics. The declarative semantics includes a logical model theory and a sound-and-complete inference system. The operational semantics includes an SLD-style proof procedure in the logic-programming tradition [8, 9, 10, 11]. This procedure executes transactions and updates the database as it proves theorems. Transaction Datalog is a minimal language based on a few simple operations. However, these operations lead directly to a wide range of transactional and programming capabilities. For instance, $\mathcal{TD}$ supports all the properties of classical transactions, such as persistence, atomicity, isolation, abort and rollback. It also supports many properties found in non-classical transaction models, such as subtransaction hierarchies, concurrency within individual transactions, cooperation between concurrent activities, a separation of atomicity and isolation, and fine-grained control over abort and rollback. Moreover, these features are seamlessly integrated with the traditional features of classical deductive databases, namely declarative queries and views. In fact, in the absence of updates, Transaction Datalog reduces to classical Datalog. It therefore represents a conservative extension of the deductive-database paradigm.

This extension is possible because, unlike ordinary programs, transactions either commit (succeed) or abort (fail). We can therefore associate a truth value with each execution of a transaction program, where *true* corresponds to commit, and *false* corresponds to abort. Based on this idea, we develop a logical calculus for combining transaction programs, including connectives for sequential and concurrent composition, and a modality for specifying isolation. All formulas in the calculus represent transaction programs. In the declarative semantics, a formula specifies a program's legal execution traces (Section 3). In the operational semantics, the formula is evaluated as the program executes; if at any point the formula evaluates to false, then the execution is aborted and the database is rolled back to an earlier state (Section 2). In $\mathcal{TD}$, calculus formulas are used as rule bodies. In this way, users can define named procedures (such as views and subroutines), exactly as in deductive databases and logic programming.

Like classical Datalog, Transaction Datalog can be embellished with negation-as-failure. When this is done, $\mathcal{TD}$ can simulate a number of different transaction models. For simplicity, though, this paper focuses on the negation-free version of the language, which is well-suited to specifying nested transactions [19, 27]. In this model, a transaction may be decomposed into subtransactions. These subtransactions may execute serially or concurrently, and their effects are undone if the parent transaction aborts, even if the subtransactions have already committed. "Nested transactions provide a powerful mechanism for fine-tuning the scope of rollback in applications with a complex structure" [19]. Moreover, "there is a strong relationship between the concept of modularization in software engineering and the nested transaction mechanism" [19]. These properties make nested transactions ideal for distributed applications, object-oriented databases, and layered software systems. Numerous examples in this paper deal with nested transactions.

In addition to transactional features, Transaction Datalog provides all the functionality of a declarative query language and a procedural programming language, seamlessly integrated. To see this, it is instructive to compare and contrast Transaction Datalog with embedded SQL (*e.g.*, SQL embedded in C). Like embedded SQL, Transaction Datalog is a database programming language for defining queries, updates and transactions. Both languages integrate programming constructs with database access. However, unlike embedded SQL, Transaction Datalog is a single, unified formalism, not an amalgamation of two formalisms (SQL and C). In particular, Transaction Datalog does not make a sharp distinction between declarative programming (SQL) and procedural programming (C). In fact, because it has a logic-programming foundation, Transaction Datalog provides a seamless integration of procedural and declarative programming styles. For instance, users can write classical Datalog queries, and they can write sequential and concurrent algorithms, and they can write programs that are neither procedural nor declarative, but somewhere in between. The result is that Transaction Datalog avoids many of the problems of embedded SQL, such as the infamous "impedance mismatch" problem. Of course, Transaction Datalog can also *compose* transactions and define *nested* transactions, which goes well beyond the capabilities of embedded SQL.

2   Overview of Transaction Datalog

This section introduces Transaction Datalog informally through a series of simple examples. The examples show how logical formulas in $\mathcal{TD}$ can be interpreted procedurally and declaratively, and how they lead quickly to the basic properties of nested transactions. More-involved examples are given in the long version of this paper [6].

As in any programming language, programs in Transaction Datalog are ultimately built from a set of elementary operations. In the case of *database* programming languages (like $\mathcal{TD}$), these operations are elementary database transactions. The precise set of elementary operations is somewhat arbitrary, and in this paper, four are provided. These operations are simple, they can be efficiently implemented, and they lead to expressive completeness [5]. They are also minimal, since removing any one of them causes a loss of expressive completeness [5]. To represent these four operations, we use four types of expression: q, $r.empty$, $ins.q$, $del.q$. The first two expressions are yes/no queries. Intuitively, q means "*Is atom q in the database*," and $r.empty$ means "*Is relation r empty*." The other two expressions are updates. Intuitively, $ins.q$ means "*Insert atom q into the database*," and $del.q$ means "*Delete atom q from the database*." These four elementary operations are transactions. The two updates are transactions that always succeed; and the two queries are transactions that succeed if they return "yes," and fail if they return "no." We shall see that the queries can be used as tests and conditions to force larger, composite transactions to fail. In the examples below, we adopt the Prolog convention that variables begin in upper case, and constants begin in lower case.

2.1 Sequential Transactions

To combine transaction programs sequentially, $\mathcal{TD}$ includes a logical connective called *serial conjunction*, denoted $\otimes$. Intuitively, if formulas ϕ_1 and ϕ_2 represent transaction programs, then the formula $\phi_1 \otimes \phi_2$ represents their sequential composition, that is, program ϕ_1 followed by program ϕ_2. Thus, the formula $del.q(a) \otimes ins.r(a)$ deletes the atom $q(a)$ from the database, and then inserts the atom $r(a)$. Formulas of the form $\phi_1 \otimes \phi_2 \otimes \cdots \otimes \phi_n$ are called *serial programs*.

To assign a name to a program, $\mathcal{TD}$ uses Horn-like rules. Intuitively, if p is an atomic formula, and ϕ is a program, then the rule $p \leftarrow \phi$ is a procedure definition, where p is the procedure name and ϕ is the procedure body. Thus, the formula $p(X) \leftarrow del.q(X) \otimes ins.r(X)$ defines $p(X)$ to be the program $del.q(X) \otimes ins.r(X)$. The variable X is a parameter of the procedure, and is bound to a constant symbol at run time. Rules may be recursive.

Example 1. (**Financial Transactions: I**) Suppose the balance of a bank account is given by the relation $balance(Acct, Amt)$. The rules below define four transaction programs: $change(Acct, Bal_1, Bal_2)$, which changes the balance of account $Acct$ from Bal_1 to Bal_2; $withdraw(Amt, Acct)$, which withdraws an amount from an account; $deposit(Amt, Acct)$, which deposits an amount into an account; and $transfer(Amt, Acct_1, Acct_2)$, which transfers an amount from account $Acct_1$ to account $Acct_2$.

$$transfer(Amt, Acct_1, Acct_2) \leftarrow withdraw(Amt, Acct_1) \otimes deposit(Amt, Acct_2)$$

$$withdraw(Amt, Acct) \leftarrow$$
$$balance(Acct, Bal) \otimes Bal > Amt \otimes change(Acct, Bal, Bal - Amt)$$

$$deposit(Amt, Acct) \leftarrow balance(Acct, Bal) \otimes change(Acct, Bal, Bal + Amt)$$

$$change(Acct, Bal_1, Bal_2) \leftarrow del.balance(Acct, Bal_1) \otimes ins.balance(Acct, Bal_2)$$

In each rule, the premises are evaluated from left to right. For instance, the first rule says: to transfer an amount, Amt, from $Acct_1$ to $Acct_2$, first withdraw Amt from $Acct_1$; and then, if the withdrawal succeeds, deposit Amt in $Acct_2$. Likewise, the second rule says, to withdraw Amt from an account $Acct$, first retrieve the balance of the account; then check that the account will not be overdrawn by the transaction; then, if all is well, change the balance from Bal to $Bal - Amt$. Notice that the atom $balance(Acct, Bal)$ is a query that retrieves the balance of the specified account, and $Bal > Amt$ is a test. All other atoms in this example are updates. The last rule changes the balance of an account by deleting the old balance and then inserting the new one.

A transaction defined by serial conjunction succeeds if and only if each of its subtransactions succeed. More formally, the transaction $\phi_1 \otimes \phi_2$ succeeds if and only if both ϕ_1 and ϕ_2 succeed (which is why $\otimes$ is called serial *conjunction*). This implies that the failure of a subtransaction can cause the failure of its parent transaction. For instance, in Example 1, the *transfer* transaction fails if either of the subtransactions *withdraw* and *deposit* fail. Likewise, the *withdraw* transaction fails if the test $Bal > Amt$ fails. In the terminology of nested transactions, ϕ_1 and ϕ_2 are *vital* subtransactions of $\phi_1 \otimes \phi_2$, since both are crucial to its success.

Serial conjunction leads immediately to a basic property of nested transactions — *relative commit*. For instance, in the transaction $\phi_1 \otimes \phi_2$, if subtransaction ϕ_2 fails, then the whole transaction fails and must be undone. In particular, subtransaction ϕ_1 must be undone, even though it has already succeeded (and committed). Thus, subtransaction commits are not irrevocable, and can be undone if the parent transaction fails. The following is a more concrete illustration of this phenomenon.

Example 2. (**Relative Commit**) Consider a transaction involving two transfers, defined as follows:

$$transfer(fee, client, broker) \otimes transfer(cost, client, seller) \qquad (1)$$

This transaction transfers a fee from a client to a broker, and then transfers a cost from the client to a seller. The transaction succeeds if and only if both transfers succeed. In a successful execution, the first transfer succeeds (and commits), and then the second transfer succeeds (and commits). However, suppose that the first transfer succeeds, and then the second transfer fails (due to lack of funds). In this case, the whole transaction fails, and is undone. In particular, even though the first transfer has already committed, its effects are undone, and the database is restored to its initial state. Thus, the commit of the first transfer was not absolute, but was relative to the overall transaction. In this way, the whole transaction (like the individual transfers) behaves like an atomic operation, which executes to completion or not at all.

A transaction defined by a rule succeeds if the rule body succeeds. More formally, given the rule $p \leftarrow \phi$, then p succeeds if ϕ succeeds. This leads immediately to non-determinism. For instance, suppose we are given the rules $p \leftarrow \phi_1$, $p \leftarrow \phi_2, \ldots p \leftarrow \phi_n$. Then, p succeeds if ϕ_1 succeeds, and p succeeds if ϕ_2 succeeds, and p succeeds if ϕ_3 succeeds, etc. Thus, p succeeds if *some* ϕ_i succeeds. Intuitively, each ϕ_i represents an alternative execution of p. Because of these alternatives, no ϕ_i by itself is crucial to the success of p. In the terminology of nested transactions, each ϕ_i is a *non-vital* subtransaction of p.

As with nested transactions, the presence of alternative subtransactions allows transaction failure and rollback to be localized. This is possible because the effects of failure can be limited to a single subtransaction: if a subtransaction fails because of a logical error, then it can be undone and an alternative subtransaction can be executed.[1] In this way, we can undo the effects of a small part of a transaction without undoing the entire transaction (which is the normal procedure for classical transactions). This ability, known as *partial failure* or *partial rollback*, is particularly important for long-running transactions, since the likelihood of failure is high, and we do not want to undo a large quantity of work.

Example 3. (**Save Points and Partial Rollback**) Consider the following three rules:

$$parent \leftarrow task_1 \otimes choose \qquad choose \leftarrow task_2 \qquad choose \leftarrow task_3$$

These rules define a *parent* transaction having three subtransactions, $task_1$, $task_2$ and $task_3$, and a non-deterministic choice. The *parent* transaction commits if both $task_1$ and *choose* commit, and *choose* commits if $task_2$ or $task_3$ commit. Because *choose* has more than one possible execution, the point between $task_1$ and *choose* acts as both a choice point and a save point. That is, if an execution of *choose* aborts, then the state of the system can be rolled back to the choice point, from which a different execution of *choose* can be attempted.

As an example, consider a specific execution of the *parent* transaction. When *parent* is invoked, $task_1$ is immediately executed. If $task_1$ commits, then *choose* is invoked, which causes either $task_2$ or $task_3$ to be chosen non-deterministically. Suppose $task_2$ is chosen. If $task_2$ eventually aborts, then its effects must be undone; so, the database state and the program state are rolled back to the choice point. After rollback, $task_3$ is executed. If $task_3$ eventually commits, then *choose* commits, and the *parent* transaction commits. In this case, therefore, a local abort (of $task_2$) does not cause a global abort (of *parent*). Moreover, the

---

[1] Even without alternatives, if a subtransaction fails because of a system error (*e.g.*, deadlock), then it can be undone and restarted by the transaction manager.

choice point acts as a save point, so the effects of the abort are localized (to within the *choose* transaction).

2.2 Concurrent Transactions

To combine transaction programs concurrently, $\mathcal{TD}$ includes a logical connective called *concurrent conjunction*, denoted |. Intuitively, if formulas ϕ_1 and ϕ_2 represent transaction programs, then the formula $\phi_1 \mid \phi_2$ represents their concurrent composition, that is, a program in which ϕ_1 and ϕ_2 execute concurrently in an interleaved fashion. As in most concurrent programming languages, programs in Transaction Datalog may communicate and synchronize themselves. This is possible because one program can read what another program writes. The database thus acts as the medium of communication.[2] Of course, when programs are executed in isolation (Section 2.3), communication can take place freely *within* individual programs, but not *between* them.

A transaction defined by concurrent conjunction succeeds if and only if each of its subtransactions succeed. More formally, the transaction $\phi_1 \mid \phi_2$ succeeds if and only if both ϕ_1 and ϕ_2 succeed (which is why | is called concurrent *conjunction*). Like serial conjunction, concurrent conjunction leads immediately to relative commit. For instance, in the transaction $\phi_1 \mid \phi_2$, if subtransaction ϕ_1 fails, then the entire transaction fails, and subtransaction ϕ_2 is undone, even though it may have already succeeded (and committed). Thus, when a subtransaction commits, it only commits relative to its parent transaction. As a more concrete example, consider the following program:

$$transfer(fee, client, broker) \mid transfer(cost, client, seller) \qquad (2)$$

This is a concurrent version of Example 2, involving two money transfers. As in the sequential version, if either transfer fails, then both transfers are undone, and the database is restored to its initial state. Unlike the sequential version, either transfer can now start first, and neither is delayed by an artificially-imposed execution order. In particular, each transfer can execute as soon as the data items it needs are available (*i.e.*, not locked by other transactions). As another example, consider the composition of five transactions described in the third paragraph of Section 1.1. This composition is easily specified in Transaction Datalog by the following formula: $t_1 \otimes (t_2 \mid t_3 \mid t_4) \otimes t_5$. In this case, if one of transactions t_2, t_3 or t_4 fails, then the other two are aborted, and the effects of t_1 are also undone. Transaction t_5 is unaffected, since it had not been started when the failure occurred.

Concurrent programs in $\mathcal{TD}$ can cooperate by using the database to communicate and synchronize themselves. This idea is illustrated in Example 4 below.

---

[2] Here, we are using the term "database" is a general sense that includes any kind of shared memory, as long as the information in it can be viewed as a set of tuples. In particular, the database can contain structures and access methods designed for efficient communication. For instance, some relations in the database could be a view of a set of message queues or communication channels, as described in [11].

To convey the right intuition, we refer to formulas of the form $q_1 \otimes q_2 \otimes \cdots \otimes q_n$ as *sequential processes*, or simply as *processes*. The example also illustrates how concurrency in $\mathcal{TD}$ can be interpreted both procedurally and declaratively. The declarative semantics involves checking all possible interleavings of several processes, as described in Section 3. In contrast, the procedural semantics involves one process waiting for another process to perform an update, as described in Example 4. A more-involved example of cooperation between processes in $\mathcal{TD}$ is given in the long version of this paper [6], where concurrent transactions are combined into a workflow.

Example 4. (**Communication and Synchronization**) The rules below define a process and two subprocesses. The subprocesses communicate with each other and synchronize the execution of several tasks.

$$process \leftarrow processA \mid processB$$
$$processA \leftarrow taskA_1 \otimes ins.startB_2 \otimes taskA_2 \otimes startA_3 \otimes taskA_3$$
$$processB \leftarrow taskB_1 \otimes startB_2 \otimes taskB_2 \otimes ins.startA_3 \otimes taskB_3$$

The first rule defines the top-level process, which immediately splits into two subprocesses, called $processA$ and $processB$. The two subprocesses execute concurrently, but not independently. In particular, each subprocess executes three tasks, where $taskB_2$ cannot start until $taskA_1$ is finished, and $taskA_3$ cannot start until $taskB_2$ is finished. To see this, observe that while executing $taskA_1$ and $taskB_1$, the two subprocesses run concurrently without interacting with each other. However, when $processB$ completes $taskB_1$, it cannot start $taskB_2$ until the atom $startB_2$ is in the database, which only happens after $processA$ has executed $taskA_1$. In this way, the two subprocesses communicate, and $processB$ is synchronized with $processA$. Likewise, on completing $taskA_2$, $processA$ cannot start $taskA_3$ until the atom $startA_3$ is in the database, which only happens after $processB$ has executed $taskB_2$. In this way, the two subprocesses again communicate (in the reverse direction), and $processA$ is synchronized with $processB$. Observe that if $process$ is executed in isolation, then it is a transaction. However, because the two subprocesses communicate in both directions, they cannot be isolated from each other, so they are not subtransactions.

Queries are transactions that do not update the database (*i.e.*, read-only transactions). Thus, in the absence of updates, transaction composition reduces to query composition, *i.e.*, the composition of simple queries into complex queries. In this case, serial and concurrent conjunction both reduce to classical conjunction, and Transaction Datalog reduces to classical Datalog. Formally, in the absence of updates, $\alpha \otimes \beta \equiv \alpha \mid \beta \equiv \alpha \wedge \beta$. This reduction leads to a seamless integration of procedural and declarative programming in $\mathcal{TD}$. Programs involving only queries are purely declarative. But, as updates are gradually introduced, programs gradually become procedural. In particular, conjunctive queries become sequential or concurrent programs, and union queries become non-deterministic programs.

Example 5. (**Declarative Queries**) The following rules of classical Datalog express the transitive closure of a binary relation, r:

$$tr(X,Y) \leftarrow r(X,Y) \qquad tr(X,Y) \leftarrow r(X,Z) \wedge tr(Z,Y)$$

These rules translate directly into Transaction Datalog in two ways.

Translation 1: $\quad tr(X,Y) \leftarrow r(X,Y) \qquad tr(X,Y) \leftarrow r(X,Z) \otimes tr(Z,Y)$

Translation 2: $\quad tr(X,Y) \leftarrow r(X,Y) \qquad tr(X,Y) \leftarrow r(X,Z) \mid tr(Z,Y)$

2.3   Isolation and Nested Transactions

As described above, concurrent programs in Transaction Datalog can interact and communicate with each other. Because communication can be two-way, executions of such programs need not be serializable [4], so $\mathcal{TD}$ programs need not be isolated transactions. To specify isolation, $\mathcal{TD}$ includes a logical modality called the *modality of isolation*, denoted $\odot$. Intuitively, the formula $\odot\phi$ means that program ϕ executes in isolation from all other concurrent programs. For instance, in the program $\phi_1 \mid (\odot\phi_2) \mid \phi_3$, the subprograms ϕ_1 and ϕ_3 may communicate with each other, but not with ϕ_2, which is an isolated transaction. As a special case, in the program $(\odot\phi_1) \mid (\odot\phi_2)$, the subprograms ϕ_1 and ϕ_2 execute in isolation from each other, and do not communicate. They must therefore execute as serializable transactions. In $\mathcal{TD}$, isolated transactions may be nested within other isolated transactions to arbitrary depth. For example, the program $\phi_1 \mid \odot(\phi_2 \mid \odot\phi_3)$ contains an isolated transaction, which in turn contains an isolated subtransaction. The transaction $\phi_2 \mid \odot\phi_3$ executes concurrently with, but in isolation from ϕ_1. Likewise, within this transaction, the subtransaction ϕ_3 executes concurrently with, but in isolation from ϕ_2.

As described earlier, logical rules are used to define named procedures and subroutines. In general, the body of a rule may use the three connectives $\otimes, \mid$ and $\odot$ in any combination. For instance, the formula $p \leftarrow (q_1 \otimes q_2) \mid \odot(r_1 \otimes r_2)$ is a legal rule. Intuitively, this rule says, "To execute procedure p, concurrently execute the programs $q_1 \otimes q_2$ and $r_1 \otimes r_2$, where the latter program must execute in isolation."

Example 6. (**Financial Transactions: II**) Consider the banking programs of Example 1, which transfer money between accounts. In the presence of concurrency, these programs must be modified to ensure that they execute as transactions. For instance, as is, there is nothing to prevent non-serializable behavior during two concurrent money transfers, as in program (2). We can use the modality of isolation to ensure serializability. We can also use concurrent conjunction to exploit intra-transaction concurrency, and increase the throughput of the transaction system. Here are the modified rules:

$$sell(Brkr, Client, Seller, Cost, Fee) \leftarrow$$
$$\odot[transfer(Fee, Client, Brkr) \mid transfer(Cost, Client, Seller)]$$

$$transfer(Amt, Acct_1, Acct_2) \leftarrow \odot[withdraw(Amt, Acct_1) \mid deposit(Amt, Acct_2)]$$

$$withdraw(Amt, Acct) \leftarrow$$
$$\odot[balance(Acct, Bal) \otimes Bal > Amt \otimes change(Acct, Bal, Bal - Amt)]$$

$$deposit(Amt, Acct) \leftarrow \odot[balance(Acct, Bal) \otimes change(Acct, Bal, Bal + Amt)]$$

$$change(Acct, Bal_1, Bal_2) \leftarrow del.balance(Acct, Bal_1) \mid ins.balance(Acct, Bal_2)$$

These rules define four isolated transactions — *sell*, *transfer*, *withdraw* and *deposit* — and one subroutine — *change*. Observe that *withdraw* and *deposit* are nested within *transfer*, and two instances of *transfer* are nested within *sell*. In these rules, we have used concurrent composition where possible, although in some cases, we have used sequential composition because of dataflow within a rule. For instance, in the rule for *withdraw*, the account balance is retrieved and tested before it is updated. Note that the rule for *sell* simply turns program (2) into a named transaction.

The depth of nesting in Transaction Datalog is not always static, as in Example 6, but can depend on the database. Dynamic nesting arises from recursion through isolation. Such recursions add no complications to the logical semantics of Transaction Datalog.

Example 7. **(Dynamic Nesting)** Suppose that r is a database relation with n tuples. Then, the rules below define a transaction *trans* that spawns n concurrent instances of $task(x)$, one instance for each tuple x in relation r. Moreover, as they are spawned, successive tasks are nested more and more deeply within *trans*, so that the final task is nested $n - 1$ levels deep.

$$trans \leftarrow r(X) \otimes del.r(X) \otimes [task(X) \mid \odot trans]$$
$$trans \leftarrow r.empty$$

The first rule is recursive. At each level of recursion, it non-deterministically chooses a tuple X from relation r, deletes it from the database, and then applies the task to the tuple by spawning $task(X)$ as a concurrent process. In addition, the rule calls itself recursively and in isolation; so, each recursive call to *trans* is nested one level deeper than the previous call. The second rule halts the recursion after all the tuples have been deleted from relation r, *i.e.*, after $n - 1$ recursive calls

3 Syntax and Semantics

Recall that Transaction Datalog is a fragment of Transaction Logic, which is a general logic of state change [8, 9, 10, 11]. Transaction Datalog therefore inherits the semantics of Transaction Logic, including its model theory and proof procedures, which have been published elsewhere [8, 9, 11]. For convenience, this section develops a simplified version of that semantics, specialized for Transaction Datalog. The simplification comes from restricting Transaction Logic to relational databases and Horn-like rules without function symbols (in much the same way that classical Datalog is a restriction of classical logic). The simplified semantics is based on a logical inference system that describes the legal execution traces of a $\mathcal{TD}$ program.

It should also be mentioned that Transaction Logic (and thus Transaction Datalog) has an operational semantics based on a proof procedure with unification [11, 10, 8]. This procedure executes transactions, updates the database, and generates query answers, all as a result of proving theorems. Transactional features such as abort, rollback, and save-points are also handled by the proof procedure. This procedure is the foundation of our implementation [22].

3.1 Syntax

The language of Transaction Datalog includes three infinite enumerable sets of symbols: constant symbols $(a, b, c, ...)$, variables $(X, Y, Z, ...)$, and predicate symbols $(p, q, r, ...)$. We adopt the Prolog convention that variables begin in upper case, and constant symbols begin in lower case. As in classical Datalog, there are two sorts of predicate symbol: base and derived. In addition, for each base predicate, p, there are three special predicate symbols, denoted $p.empty$, $ins.p$ and $del.p$. The first has arity zero, and the other two have the same arity as p. We define a *database state* to be a finite set of ground atomic formulas with base predicate symbols. We sometimes refer to a database state simply as a *database* or a *state*.

Definition 1. (Goals and Rules) A *goal* is a formula of the following form:

- an atomic formula;
- $(\phi_1 \otimes \phi_2 \otimes \cdots \otimes \phi_k)$ where $k \geq 0$ and each ϕ_i is a goal; or
- $(\phi_1 \mid \phi_2 \mid \cdots \mid \phi_k)$ where $k \geq 0$ and each ϕ_i is a goal; or
- $\odot\phi$ where ϕ is a goal.

A *rule* is a formula of the form $p \leftarrow \phi$, where ϕ is a goal, and p is an atomic formula with a derived predicate symbol.

A *transaction base* is a set of rules. A *program* is a transaction base together with a goal. Intuitively, the goal defines the main procedure, and each rule in the transaction base defines a subroutine. When the transaction base is implicit, we sometimes refer to the goal as a program. A *transaction program* is a program whose main procedure executes in isolation, *i.e.*, has the form $\odot\phi$. In the literature [4, 19], a *transaction* is a particular execution of a transaction program. This paper uses the same definition, but when there is no confusion, we sometimes use "transaction" as an abbreviation for "transaction program."

3.2 Execution Traces

Concurrency in Transaction Datalog has an interleaving semantics. Intuitively, a $\mathcal{TD}$ program consists of a number of concurrent processes, where each process generates a sequence of elementary database operations. By interleaving these sequences, we obtain a new sequence of operations, which can then be executed. The set of legal interleavings is determined partly by the need for subtransactions to execute in isolation, and partly by the need for other activities to execute cooperatively. As an example of the latter, suppose that one process writes data that another process must read; then the write operation must come *before* the read operation in the interleaved sequence. These needs are specified by $\mathcal{TD}$ programs.

In an interleaving semantics, only one program executes at a time, while all concurrent programs are suspended. To model this behavior, $\mathcal{TD}$ records the state of the database whenever a program is suspended or awakened. Formally, an execution of a program, ϕ, is represented as a finite sequence of pairs, $\mathbf{D_1 D_2}, \mathbf{D_3 D_4}, \mathbf{D_5 D_6}, ..., \mathbf{D_{n-1} D_n}$, which we call an *execution trace*, or simply an *execution* or a *trace*. In this sequence, each pair $\mathbf{D_i D_{i+1}}$ represents a period of uninterrupted execution of program ϕ during which ϕ changes the database from state $\mathbf{D_i}$ to $\mathbf{D_{i+1}}$. Between adjacent pairs, ϕ is suspended and other programs execute. Thus, initially ϕ changes the database from state $\mathbf{D_1}$ to $\mathbf{D_2}$. Then, ϕ is suspended, while other programs change the database from state $\mathbf{D_2}$ to $\mathbf{D_3}$. Then, ϕ is awakened and changes the database from $\mathbf{D_3}$ to $\mathbf{D_4}$. Then, ϕ is suspended again, while other programs change the database from $\mathbf{D_4}$ to $\mathbf{D_5}$. This process of execution and suspension continues until ϕ terminates, leaving the database in state $\mathbf{D_n}$. For example, the sequence $\{a\}\{ab\}, \{d\}\{cd\}$ is an execution trace of the program $ins.b \otimes ins.c$. That is, starting from state $\{a\}$, the program first inserts b, changing the database to state $\{ab\}$. Then, the program is suspended, and other programs change the database to state $\{d\}$. Finally, the original program is re-awakened, and it inserts the atom c, leaving the database in state $\{cd\}$.

If a program is isolated, then its execution is not interleaved with that of any other programs. It should therefore execute continuously, without interruption or suspension. An execution trace of an isolated program thus consists of a single database pair, $\mathbf{D_1 D_2}$. For example, the pair $\{a\}\{abc\}$ is an execution trace of the program $\odot(ins.b \otimes ins.c)$. That is, starting from state $\{a\}$, the program inserts the atoms b and c, leaving the database in state $\{abc\}$. Transactions always execute in isolation, so in $\mathcal{TD}$, each execution of a transaction is represented by a single database pair. One consequence of this idea is that a concurrent execution of several transactions is equivalent to a serial execution. For instance, if ϕ_1 and ϕ_2 are $\mathcal{TD}$ programs, then a correct execution of $(\odot\phi_1) \mid (\odot\phi_2)$ is equivalent to an execution of $\phi_1 \otimes \phi_2$ or $\phi_2 \otimes \phi_1$.

We are *not* saying here that to achieve isolation, transactions must be executed serially. Rather, a program that executes in isolation must behave *as if* it were not interleaved with any other programs. As a special case, a concurrent execution of transactions must have the same effect as a serial execution;

i.e., transactions must be serializable, which is the normal understanding in database concurrency control [4]. Our semantics therefore specifies the *effects* of a $\mathcal{TD}$ program, but not its actual execution inside a DBMS. In fact, inside a DBMS, concurrent programs may be executed in parallel, rather than in an interleaved fashion. For instance, suppose that predicates p and q are stored on different disks. Then, when the transaction $ins.p(a) \mid ins.q(b)$ is executed, the elementary updates $ins.p(a)$ and $ins.q(b)$ can be executed *simultaneously*. On the other hand, if p and q are stored on the same disk, then $ins.p(a)$ and $ins.q(b)$ must be executed serially, in some order. In either case, the effect is the same: to insert the atoms $p(a)$ and $q(b)$ into the database. The details of how and when concurrent operations are actually executed is an implementation issue, and is beyond the scope of this paper.

With the above model of execution, we can develop a simple semantics for the three logical connectives $\otimes$, $\mid$ and $\odot$. The semantics is defined in terms of three operations on execution traces: *concatenation, interleaving* and *reduction*. The first two are familiar list operations. For example, the concatenation of lists $[a, b, c]$ and $[x, y, z]$ is the list $[a, b, c, x, y, z]$. An interleaving of two lists, L_1 and L_2, is any list composed of the elements of L_1 and L_2 that preserves the relative order of the elements in each list. For example, the two lists $[a, b]$ and $[x, y]$ have six interleavings:

$$[a, b, x, y] \qquad [a, x, b, y] \qquad [a, x, y, b] \qquad [x, a, b, y] \qquad [x, a, y, b] \qquad [x, y, a, b]$$

We use concatenation and interleaving to model serial and concurrent conjunction, respectively. Intuitively, suppose that $\overline{\mathbf{D}}_1$ is an execution of ϕ_1, and $\overline{\mathbf{D}}_2$ is an execution of ϕ_2. Then, the concatenation of $\overline{\mathbf{D}}_1$ and $\overline{\mathbf{D}}_2$ is an execution of $\phi_1 \otimes \phi_2$, and any interleaving of $\overline{\mathbf{D}}_1$ and $\overline{\mathbf{D}}_2$ is an execution of $\phi_1 \mid \phi_2$.

Unlike concatenation and interleaving, which are general list operations, reduction is specific to execution traces.

Definition 2. (Reduction) The execution trace $[\mathbf{D}_1\mathbf{D}'_1, \mathbf{D}_2\mathbf{D}'_2, ...\mathbf{D}_n\mathbf{D}'_n]$ is *reducible* if $\mathbf{D}'_i = \mathbf{D}_{i+1}$ for $1 \leq i \leq n$. In this case, $[\mathbf{D}_1\mathbf{D}'_n]$ is the *reduction* of the trace.

Thus $[\mathbf{D}_1\mathbf{D}_2, \mathbf{D}_2\mathbf{D}_3, \mathbf{D}_3\mathbf{D}_4]$ is reducible, and its reduction is $[\mathbf{D}_1\mathbf{D}_4]$. Intuitively, if a program has a reducible execution trace, then the database does not change when the program is suspended. The suspensions are therefore unnecessary, and the program could execute continuously, without interruption. The reduced trace therefore represents another possible execution of the program. In fact, it represents an *isolated* execution, *i.e.*, an execution that is not interleaved with the executions of other programs. Intuitively, if $[\mathbf{D}_1\mathbf{D}_2, \mathbf{D}_2\mathbf{D}_3, \mathbf{D}_3\mathbf{D}_4]$ is an execution of ϕ, then $[\mathbf{D}_1\mathbf{D}_4]$ is an execution of $\odot\phi$.

3.3 Logical Inference

This section develops a declarative semantics for $\mathcal{TD}$. The development is based on a logical inference system that specifies the legal execution traces of a $\mathcal{TD}$

program. In [11], an equivalent, model-theoretic semantics is developed, along with a practical proof procedure based on unification.

The inference system below manipulates expressions of the form $\mathbf{P} : \overline{\mathbf{D}} \vdash \phi$, called *sequents*. Here, $\mathbf{P}$ is a transaction base, ϕ is a ground goal, and $\overline{\mathbf{D}}$ is an execution trace. This sequent means that $\overline{\mathbf{D}}$ is an execution trace of program ϕ. The inference system itself is a collection of axioms and inference rules. Each inference rule consists of several sequents, and has the following interpretation: if the sequent(s) above the horizontal line can be derived, then the sequent below the line can also be derived. Based on the axiom sequents, the system uses the inference rules to derive more-and-more sequents. Observe that the inference system guarantees safety, since the data domain is fixed.

Definition 3. (Inference System) Let *dom* be a finite set of constant symbols, called the *data domain*. Then $\Im(dom)$ is the system of axioms and inference rules below, where each sequent contains only those constants in *dom*. Here, $\mathbf{P}$ is a transaction base, $\mathbf{D}$ is a database, $\overline{\mathbf{D}}$ is an execution trace, q is a ground atomic formula, and ϕ is a ground goal.

Axioms:

1. *Elementary Queries:*

   $\mathbf{P} : \mathbf{DD} \vdash ()$

   $\mathbf{P} : \mathbf{DD} \vdash q$ *if* $q \in \mathbf{D}$

   $\mathbf{P} : \mathbf{DD} \vdash r.empty$ *if* $\mathbf{D}$ *contains no atoms with predicate symbol* r

2. *Elementary Updates:*

   $\mathbf{P} : \mathbf{D}_1 \mathbf{D}_2 \vdash ins.q$ *if* $\mathbf{D}_2 = \mathbf{D}_1 + \{q\}$

   $\mathbf{P} : \mathbf{D}_1 \mathbf{D}_2 \vdash del.q$ *if* $\mathbf{D}_2 = \mathbf{D}_1 - \{q\}$

Inference Rules:

3. *Subroutines: if* $q \leftarrow \phi$ *is a ground instantiation of a rule in* $\mathbf{P}$, *then*

$$\frac{\mathbf{P} : \overline{\mathbf{D}} \vdash \phi}{\mathbf{P} : \overline{\mathbf{D}} \vdash q}$$

4. *Sequential Composition: if* $\overline{\mathbf{D}}_3$ *is the concatenation of* $\overline{\mathbf{D}}_1$ *and* $\overline{\mathbf{D}}_2$, *then*

$$\frac{\mathbf{P} : \overline{\mathbf{D}}_1 \vdash \phi_1 \qquad \mathbf{P} : \overline{\mathbf{D}}_2 \vdash \phi_2}{\mathbf{P} : \overline{\mathbf{D}}_3 \vdash \phi_1 \otimes \phi_2}$$

5. *Concurrent Composition: if* $\overline{\mathbf{D}}_3$ *is an interleaving of* $\overline{\mathbf{D}}_1$ *and* $\overline{\mathbf{D}}_2$, *then*

$$\frac{\mathbf{P} : \overline{\mathbf{D}}_1 \vdash \phi_1 \qquad \mathbf{P} : \overline{\mathbf{D}}_2 \vdash \phi_2}{\mathbf{P} : \overline{\mathbf{D}}_3 \vdash \phi_1 \mid \phi_2}$$

6. *Isolation: if* $\overline{\mathbf{D}}_1$ *reduces to* $\overline{\mathbf{D}}_2$, *then*

$$\frac{\mathbf{P} : \overline{\mathbf{D}}_1 \vdash \phi}{\mathbf{P} : \overline{\mathbf{D}}_2 \vdash \odot \phi}$$

Each axiom and inference rule in Definition 3 has a simple, intuitive interpretation. For instance, axioms of type 1 all have the form $\mathbf{P} : \mathbf{DD} \vdash \phi$. Here, the execution trace is a single database pair, $\mathbf{DD}$, in which the initial and final states are the same, $\mathbf{D}$, which means that ϕ is a read-only transaction (*i.e.*, a query). The first axiom defines the empty goal ( ), which is a transaction that does nothing and always succeeds. The second axiom defines simple queries that ask whether a given atom, q, is in the database. The third axiom defines queries that ask whether a given relation, r, is empty.

Axioms of type 2 all have the form $\mathbf{P} : \mathbf{D_1 D_2} \vdash \phi$. Here, the execution trace is a single database pair, $\mathbf{D_1 D_2}$, in which the initial and final states of the database may be different. This means that ϕ is an updating transaction that changes the database from state $\mathbf{D_1}$ to $\mathbf{D_2}$. The first axiom says that transaction *ins.q* changes the database from state $\mathbf{D}$ to state $\mathbf{D} + \{q\}$. Likewise, the second axiom says that transaction *del.q* changes the database from state $\mathbf{D}$ to state $\mathbf{D} - \{q\}$. The following sequents are instances of these two axioms:

$$\mathbf{P} : \{p\} \{pq\} \vdash ins.q \qquad\qquad \mathbf{P} : \{pq\} \{q\} \vdash del.p \qquad (3)$$

The four inference rules are also straightforward. For instance, suppose that $\overline{\mathbf{D}}_1$ is an execution of ϕ_1, and $\overline{\mathbf{D}}_2$ is an execution of ϕ_2. Then, rule 4 says that the concatenation of $\overline{\mathbf{D}}_1$ and $\overline{\mathbf{D}}_2$ is an execution of $\phi_1 \otimes \phi_2$. Likewise, rule 5 says that any interleaving of $\overline{\mathbf{D}}_1$ and $\overline{\mathbf{D}}_2$ is an execution of $\phi_1 \mid \phi_2$. Thus, the following sequent can be derived from sequents (3) using inference rule 4:

$$\mathbf{P} : \{p\} \{pq\}, \{pq\} \{q\} \vdash ins.q \otimes del.p \qquad (4)$$

Rule 6 says that if $\overline{\mathbf{D}}$ is an execution of ϕ, then the reduction of $\overline{\mathbf{D}}$ is an execution of $\odot\phi$, assuming that $\overline{\mathbf{D}}$ is reducible. Thus, the following sequent can be derived from sequent (4) using inference rule 6:

$$\mathbf{P} : \{p\} \{q\} \vdash \; \odot (ins.q \otimes del.p) \qquad (5)$$

Inference rule 3 uses the rules in the transaction base, $\mathbf{P}$. Recall that each rule represents a procedure, where the rule head is the procedure name, and the rule body is the procedure definition. Variables in the rule represent parameters of the procedure, and are instantiated at run time. Intuitively, inference rule 3 says that if $\overline{\mathbf{D}}$ is an execution of an instantiated procedure body, ϕ, then it is also an execution of the instantiated procedure name, q. For instance, if $r \leftarrow \odot(ins.q \otimes del.p)$ is a ground instantiation of a rule in $\mathbf{P}$, then the sequent $\mathbf{P} : \{p\} \{q\} \vdash r$ can be derived from sequent (5) using inference rule 3.

A more-involved example of logical inference is given in the long version of this paper [6].

4 Related Work

This section compares and contrasts Transaction Datalog with other languages in the literature. We have divided the comparison into several broad areas. Due to space limitations, we have limited most of the comparisons to formalisms involving concurrency. In addition, $\mathcal{TD}$ can be compared to the numerous logics for representing action. These include dynamic logic, process logic, action logic, algorithmic logic, procedural logic, the event calculus, the situation calculus, and many others. However, none of these formalisms provide concurrency and communication, none provide composition of transaction programs, and none can model nested transactions. In addition, many have no notion of database state or declarative query, many are propositional, and many are simply inappropriate for database applications. An extensive comparison of these formalisms with the sequential version of Transaction Logic can be found in [9, 10].

Transaction Languages: Broadly speaking, the theoretical literature has explored two kinds of transaction language, in order to address two different problems. In the first approach, the user specifies the effects of individual transactions; and in the second approach, he coordinates the execution of a set of transactions. We shall refer to these two approaches as *specification* and *coordination*, respectively. In software-engineering terms, these two approaches correspond to "programming in the small" and "programming in the large," respectively [14].

The specification approach implicitly focuses on classical transactions. The problem is to develop a high-level language for specifying database queries and updates, and to establish its theoretical properties, such as formal semantics, data complexity, and expressive power. Numerous languages with logical, algebraic and procedural semantics have been developed. Like SQL and relational algebra, these languages are often related to first-order predicate logic. Typical results are, "Language L1 expresses more transactions than language L2," and "The data complexity of language L1 is complete for PSPACE." Relationships between transactions are not an issue here; so concurrency, communication, isolation, abort and rollback are not addressed. Formally, these issues are abstracted away, and only the effects of transactions are considered. These languages therefore model a transaction as a mapping from databases to databases. Developments in this area include the procedural and declarative transaction languages of Abiteboul and Vianu [1, 2], the procedural language QL of Chandra and Harel [12],[3] Dynamic Prolog [24], LDL [28], and numerous other languages. A detailed discussion of these works can be found in [9, 10].

The coordination approach focuses on non-classical transactions. The problem is to develop a high-level language for combining a set of tasks into a larger application or software system. The focus is on relationships between tasks. Typical problems are to specify intertask dependencies, including data-flow and control flow, and to schedule and coordinate the execution of tasks. A typical control dependency is, "Task T2 cannot start until task T1 has committed;" and a typical data dependency is, "Task T2 can start if task T1 returns a value greater than 25" [30]. Specifying database updates and queries is not an issue here. Formally, the effects of tasks are abstracted away, and only the relation-

---

[3] Although presented as a query language, QL is even more natural as an update language.

ships between tasks are considered. Typically, these languages model a classical transaction as a finite automaton with a small number of states such as "start," "commit" and "abort." Temporal constraints between the states of different automata are then specified in a propositional logic. Developments in this area include ACTA [13], proposals for Third Generation TP Monitors [14], approaches based on temporal logic [3] and event algebras [32], and numerous other works.

In this paper, we addressed both issues, and integrated them into a single language. Specifically, Transaction Datalog can specify the effects of classical and non-classical transactions, and it can compose simple transaction programs into complex ones. For instance, $\mathcal{TD}$ can specify queries (Example 5), updates (Example 1), and nested transactions (Example 6). Given a set of transaction programs, $\mathcal{TD}$ can impose a control structure on them (Examples 2), co-ordinate their execution (Example 4), and nest them to arbitrary depth (Example 7). The programs themselves can execute sequentially, concurrently and non-deterministically, they can execute in isolation, and they can cooperate with each other by communicating and synchronizing.

Concurrent Logic Programming: There has been considerable research on concurrency in the logic programming community. However, this work has focussed on the implementation of concurrency and on communication via shared variables. In particular, there has been no emphasis on logical semantics, database updates, or database transactions. Transaction Datalog and Transaction Logic therefore make a two-fold contribution to logic programming. First, they extend the logic programming paradigm with a host of transactional notions, including atomicity, isolation, rollback, and subtransaction hierarchies. Second, they integrate concurrency, communication and updates into a purely logical framework, including a natural model theory and a sound-and-complete proof theory [11].

This integration presents interesting possibilities for concurrent logic programming (CLP). For instance, concurrent processes can now communicate via the database, since one process can read what another process writes. This form of communication leads to a programming style that is very different from that of existing CLP languages [31]. In such languages, concurrent processes communicate via shared variables and unification. This kind of communication is orthogonal to communication via the database. Both are possible in $\mathcal{TD}$. Implementations of $\mathcal{TD}$ may therefore adopt many of the techniques of shared-variable communication developed for CLP. However, this possibility is *not* the focus of our work. Instead, we focus on concurrent processes that interact and communicate via the database. Indeed, one of the novelties of $\mathcal{TD}$ is that it provides a logical foundation for exactly this kind of interaction.

Process Algebras: These are a family of algebraic systems for modeling concurrent communicating processes. They include Milner's *Calculus of Communicating Systems* (CCS) [25], and Hoare's *Communicating Sequential Processes* (CSP) [20], among others. Transaction Datalog and process algebras use very different formal frameworks. This difference is most easily seen in terms of COSY [23], an early algebraic approach to modeling concurrent processes. COSY is an extension of regular expressions, while Transaction Datalog is an extension of deductive databases. Process algebras have since developed into equational theories, but the formal differences with $\mathcal{TD}$ remain the same.

The main conceptual difference between process algebras and Transaction Datalog is that process algebras are high-level models of shared-nothing systems, while Transaction Datalog is a high-level model of shared-memory systems, especially database systems with transaction processing. For instance, process algebras explicitly reject the notion of processes interacting via shared memory (such as a database) [26]. Instead, each process has its own local memory, and it interacts with other processes via synchronized communication. In contrast, Transaction Datalog is explicitly intended for database transactions, *i.e.*, processes that interact with a shared database. As such, it provides high-level primitives for database functions such as declarative queries, subtransaction hierarchies, serializable execution, transaction abort and rollback, etc. This difference in intent is reflected by differences in semantics: process algebras emphasis synchronized communication, while Transaction Datalog emphasizes database states.

Transaction Datalog integrates processes and data. It therefore unifies two previously disparate views of information systems and workflow management: the process-oriented view, and the data-oriented view. The former view is embodied in business processes and process algebras, while the latter view is embodied in database systems and query languages. As the examples in this paper illustrate, programs in Transaction Datalog can take either point of view, or a combination of both.

Acknowledgements: Transaction Logic was developed in collaboration with Michael Kifer [8, 9, 10, 11]. Thanks go to David Toman and Michael Kifer for their comments and suggestions on this paper. This work was supported in part by a Research Grant from the Natural Sciences and Engineering Research Council of Canada (NSERC).

References

1. S. Abiteboul and V. Vianu. Procedural languages for database queries and updates. *Journal of Computer and System Sciences*, 41:181–229, 1990.
2. S. Abiteboul and V. Vianu. Datalog extensions for database queries and updates. *Journal of Computer and System Sciences*, 43:62–124, 1991.
3. P. Attie, M. Singh, A. Sheth, and M. Rusinkiewicz. Specifying and enforcing inter-task dependencies. In *Intl. Conference on Very Large Data Bases*, Dublin, Ireland, August 1993.
4. P.A. Bernstein, V. Hadzilacos, and N. Goodman. *Concurrency Control and Recovery in Databases*. Addison Wesley, 1987.
5. A.J. Bonner. The power of cooperating transactions. Manuscript, 1997.
6. A.J. Bonner. Transaction Datalog: a compositional language for transaction programming. In *Proceedings of the International Workshop on Database Programming Languages*, Estes Park, Colorado, August 1997. Springer Verlag. Long version available at http://www.cs.toronto.edu/~bonner/papers.html #transaction-logic.

7. A.J. Bonner and M. Kifer. Results on reasoning about action in transaction logic. 1998. Submitted for publication.

8. A.J. Bonner and M. Kifer. Transaction logic programming. In *Intl. Conference on Logic Programming*, pages 257–282, Budapest, Hungary, June 1993. MIT Press.

9. A.J. Bonner and M. Kifer. An overview of transaction logic. *Theoretical Computer Science*, 133:205–265, October 1994.

10. A.J. Bonner and M. Kifer. Transaction logic programming (or a logic of declarative and procedural knowledge). Technical Report CSRI-323, University of Toronto, November 1995. http://www.cs.toronto.edu/~bonner/transaction-logic.html.

11. A.J. Bonner and M. Kifer. Concurrency and communication in transaction logic. In *Joint Intl. Conference and Symposium on Logic Programming*, pages 142–156, Bonn, Germany, September 1996. MIT Press.

12. A.K. Chandra and D. Harel. Computable queries for relational databases. *Journal of Computer and System Sciences*, 21(2):156–178, 1980.

13. P.K. Chrysanthis and K. Ramamritham. Synthesis of extended transaction models using ACTA. *ACM Transactions on Database Systems*, 19(3):450–491, Sept. 1994.

14. U. Dayal, H. Garcia-Molina, M. Hsu, B. Kao, and M.-C. Shan. Third generation TP monitors: A database challenge. In *ACM SIGMOD Conference on Management of Data*, pages 393–397, Washington, DD, May 1993.

15. A.K. Elmagarmid, editor. *Database Transaction Models for Advanced Applications*. Morgan-Kaufmann, San Mateo, CA, 1992.

16. A.K. Elmagarmid, Y. Leu, W. Litwin, and M. Rusinkiewcz. A multidatabase transaction model for interbase. In *Intl. Conference on Very Large Data Bases*, pages 507–518, Brisbane, Australia, August 13–16 1990.

17. H. Garcia-Molina and K. Salem. Sagas. In *Intl. Conference on Very Large Data Bases*, pages 249–259, May 1987.

18. J. Gray. The transaction concept: Virtues and limitations. In *Intl. Conference on Very Large Data Bases*, pages 144–154, Cannes, France, September 1981.

19. J. Gray and A. Reuter. *Transaction Processing: Concepts and Techniques*. Morgan Kaufmann, San Mateo, CA, 1993.

20. C.A.R. Hoare. *Communicating Sequential Processes*. Prentice Hall, Englewood Cliffs, NJ, 1985.

21. M. Hsu, Ed. Special issue on workflow and extended transaction systems. *Bulletin of the Technical Committee on Data Engineering (IEEE Computer Society)*, 16(2), June 1993.

22. Samuel Y.K. Hung. Implementation and Performance of Transaction Logic in Prolog. Master's thesis, Department of Computer Science, University of Toronto, 1996. http://www.cs.toronto.edu/~bonner/transaction-logic.html.

23. P.E. Lauer and R.H. Campbell. Formal semantics of a class of high-level primitives for co-ordinating concurrent processes. *Acta Informatica*, 5:297–332, 1975.

24. S. Manchanda and D.S. Warren. A logic-based language for database updates. In J. Minker, editor, *Foundations of Deductive Databases and Logic Programming*, pages 363–394. Morgan-Kaufmann, Los Altos, CA, 1988.

25. R. Milner. *Communication and Concurrency*. Prentice Hall, 1989.

26. R. Milner. Operational and algebraic semantics of concurrent processes. In [34], chapter 19, pages 1201–1242. 1990.

27. J. E. B. Moss. *Nested Transactions: An Approach to Reliable Distributed Computing*. Series in Information Systems. MIT Press, Cambridge, MA, 1985.

28. S. Naqvi and R. Krishnamurthy. Database updates in logic programming. In *ACM Symposium on Principles of Database Systems*, pages 251–262, New York, March 1988. ACM.

29. M. H. Nodine, S. Ramaswamy, and S. B. Zdonik. A cooperative transaction model for design databases. In [15], chapter 3, pages 53–85. 1992.

30. M. Rusinkiewicz and A. Sheth. Specification and execution of transactional workflows. In W. Kim, editor, *Modern Database Systems: The Object Model, Interoperability, and Beyond*. Addison-Wesley, 1994.

31. E. Shapiro. A family of concurrent logic programming languages. *ACM Computing Surveys*, 21(3), 1989.

32. M.P. Singh. Semantical considerations on workflows: An algebra for intertask dependencies. In *Proceedings of the International Workshop on Database Programming Languages*, Gubbio, Umbria, Italy, September 6–8 1995.

33. Transarc-Encina. *Encina Transactional Processing System: Transactional-C Programmers Guide and Reference, TP-00-D347*. Transarc Corp., Pittsburg, PA, 1991.

34. J. van Leeuwen, editor. *Handbook of Theoretical Computer Science, Volume B, Formal Methods and Semantics*. Elsevier, Amsterdam, 1990.

35. H. Wachter and A. Reuter. The ConTract model. In [15], chapter 7, pages 220–263. 1992.

36. G. Weikum and H.-J. Schek. Concepts and applications of multilevel transactions and open nested transactions. In [15], chapter 13, pages 515–553. 1992.

Automatic Verification of Transactions on an Object-Oriented Database[*]

David Spelt[1], Herman Balsters[2]

University of Twente, Enschede, The Netherlands

Abstract. In the context of the object-oriented data model, a compile-time approach is given that provides for a significant reduction of the amount of run-time transaction overhead due to integrity constraint checking. The higher-order logic Isabelle theorem prover is used to automatically prove which constraints might, or might not be violated by a given transaction in a manner analogous to the one used by Sheard and Stemple (1989) for the relational data model. A prototype transaction verification tool has been implemented, which automates the semantic mappings and generates proof goals for Isabelle. Test results are discussed to illustrate the effectiveness of our approach.

Keywords: object-oriented databases, transaction semantics, transaction verification

1 Introduction

Static integrity constraints are essential in mission-critical application domains, where one wants to offer integrity preserving update operations to clients. One way to enforce database integrity is by testing at run-time those constraints that are possibly violated by a transaction before allowing the transaction to commit. Various techniques, surveyed in [1], have been proposed to optimize such a test for a limited class of simple constraints, such as key and referential integrity. But commiting complex transactions on large amounts of data becomes increasingly difficult if the constraint language is extended to include full first-order logic formula with bounded quantifications over arbitrary collection types.

A second approach towards integrity maintenance aims at a compile-time reduction of the amount of run-time transaction overhead due to integrity constraint checking. This approach was first introduced by Sheard & Stemple ([2]) for the relational data model. It uses a theorem prover to verify that a transaction will never raise an integrity conflict, provided that the database was in a consistent state before the transaction was executed. Transactions are complex updates involving multiple relations, whereas the constraint language includes quantifications and aggregate constructs. These are related to expressions in higher-order logic for automatic proof assistance.

Another related compile-time approach is proposed in [3,4]. It exploits several techniques of *abstract interpretation* for the task of compile-time transaction verification in an O2 database system extended with a notion of declarative integrity

---

[*] Our e-mail addresses are: [spelt,balsters]@cs.utwente.nl

constraints. Their analysis starts with a simple compilation technique. It identifies those constraints that will certainly not be affected by a transaction because different attributes or even different class extents are accessed. For instance, a transaction that only changes the age of a person can never violate a constraint that does not access this field. Recently, in [5], this approach was augmented with a second, more powerful analysis. For each combination of transaction and constraint that could not be proved safe in the first step, it applies Dijkstra's concept of *predicate transformer*. This yields a simple first-order logic formula which is automatically verified by a theorem prover. A major difference between this approach and the one presented in [2] is that the latter fully exploits the (denotational) semantics of a database specification, whereas the former only takes some global abstract properties of the semantics into account.

The above compile-time strategies supplement the existing run-time techniques: they can filter out the set of relevant constraint checks, thus allowing the run-time optimizer to focus on a restricted set of constraint predicates that could not be proved safe at compile-time.

Our work extends the work of [2]. Rather than a relational model, it uses a powerful specification and verification environment for object-oriented databases with transactions and integrity constraints. The specification framework uses TM [6,7], a typed formal specification language based on the well-known ideas of Cardelli [8], extended with logic formalism and sets [9]. The declarative flavour of this language permits compile-time transaction verification using a theorem prover, while retaining ODMG compliancy [10].

The verification framework uses higher-order logic. Specifications in TM are automatically mapped to expressions in higher-order logic (HOL), such that the consistency requirements can be given as input to the higher-order logic Isabelle theorem prover [11] for automatic proof assistance.

The rest of this paper is organized as follows. Section 2 introduces the TM data model and gives an example of a job agency service. This example was also studied by [2]. In Section 3, the Isabelle theorem prover is introduced, along with a motivation for why the HOL theory is used. We then proceed with a sketch of how TM database schemas are represented in HOL. Section 5, discusses transaction verification using the Isabelle theorem prover and shows how standard Isabelle tactics can be used to implement a transaction verifier in HOL. In Section 6, we then compare our work to several related compile-time approaches. We finish by stating our conclusions and give directions for future work.

2 Database Definition in TM

This section introduces the TM data model, using the job agency service example [2], which is re-engineered to the object-oriented data model. Objects in the database include people who apply for, and are placed with certain jobs. A job can be shared by multiple employees. Skills are required to execute jobs, and people should have abilities that satisfy these requirements. TM extends the ODMG interface definitions with formal specifications of methods, transactions and integrity constraints. The non-procedural declarative characteristic of these additional features enable compile-time verification by a theorem prover.

```
interface Skill
(   extent SKILL)
{
    attribute String description;
};
interface Job
(   extent JOB)
{
    attribute String description;
    attribute Set<Skill> req_skills;
    attribute Boolean placed;
};
interface Person
(   extent PERS
    key ssn)
{
    attribute String ssn;
    attribute Int age;
    attribute Set<Job> applications;
    attribute Set<Struct(job:Job,sal:Int)> placements;
    attribute Set<Skill> abilities;
    Person allocate(in Job j, in Int salary) =
            self except (placements = placements + set struct(job : j, sal : salary),
                         applications = applications − set j)
};
```

2.1   Methods

Methods are specified using OQL, augmented with an additional **except**-construct that enables modification of an object (a mutable and shared value) or record (a non-mutable and non-shared value). The `allocate` method in the Person interface allocates a job to a person. It does so by "moving" the job argument from the `applications` set to the `placements` set, where it is paired with a salary value. The method returns the modified Person-object (**self**).

2.2   Transactions

Transactions in our framework are specified using a high-level declarative update language. An **update**-construct provides for the declarative update of arbitrary collections of objects. It takes a sequence of OQL query blocks and commits to the database all (possibly) modified and newly created mutable objects as indicated by these blocks. Below, the reader finds several examples of complex transactions using this construct. Actually, these are the same — but reengineered — ones that also appear in the Sheard & Stemple paper.

The following transaction subscribes a new person to the job agency service. The transaction takes as input parameters a person-**ssn** and an initial set of skills; the **applications** and the **placements**-attributes are initialized with the empty set value.

> **Transaction** *Subscribe*(**in String** *pssn*, **in Set** < Skill > *pskills*)
> **Preconditions**
>   **forall** *p* **in** PERS : *p* · ssn ≠ *pssn*
> **Begin**
>   **update** Person(ssn : *pssn*, **applications** : set(), **placements** : set(),
>   abilities : *pskills*)
> **End**;

Observe that it is necessary to add the precondition, for otherwise the key-constraint might be violated. Our transaction verification system would actually report a potential conflict on this constraint, if the condition was omitted.

> **Transaction** *Hire*(**in String** *assn*, **in** Job *j*, **in Int** *salary*)
> **Preconditions**
>   **exists** *p* **in** PERS : *p* · ssn = *assn*
> **Begin**
>   **update** (*j* **except** (placed = **true**), **select** *p* · allocate(*j*, *salary*)
>   **from** PERS *p*
>   **where** *p* · ssn = *assn*)
> **End**;

The *Hire* transaction places an applicant on a particular job: observe that two query blocks are supplied to the update construct. The first block sets the **placed** field of the job object to true, while the second block applies the **allocate** method to the Person-object that matches the **ssn** supplied as an input parameter to the transaction. There is no ordering imposed on the execution of these blocks and parallelisation is allowed provided that there are no conflicts of multiple incompatible parallel updates applied to the same object.

Finally, the *Fire* transaction removes a job from the **placements**-attribute. It also sets the **placed**-field in the Job-object to **false** if there is no other person placed in that same job:

> **Transaction** *Fire*(**in String** *assn*, **in** Job *j*)
> **Preconditions**
>   **exists** *p* **in** PERS : *p* · ssn = *assn*
> **Begin**
>   **update** (*j* **except** (placed = **exists** *x* **in** PERS : **exists** *y* **in** *x* · **placements** :
>   *y* · job = *j* **and** *x* · ssn ≠ *assn*),
>   **select** *p* **except** (placements = **select** *x* **from** *p* · **placements** *x*
>   **where** *x* · job ≠ *j*)
>   **from** PERS *p*
>   **where** *p* · ssn = *assn*)
> **End**;

2.3 Integrity Constraints

TM extends the ODMG data model with integrity constraints, which can be arbitrary well-typed boolean-valued OQL expressions, ranging over the extents of the database. This generalizes the notion of key constraints in the ODMG data model, which in fact are simple first-order formulae on a single class extent. Although the Object Database Management Group has the provision to also include a more general notion of integrity constraints in a future language release [10], constraint specification remains limited at present. The use of OQL as a constraint definition language is fairly straightforward, as illustrated by the examples below. In addition to the key constraint that was already part of the schema definition, we add the following constraints to our job agency service specification; these constraints will be the subject of transaction verification in Section 5

Example 1. All persons applying for a job should have the required skills to execute those jobs:

$$C_1 : \textbf{forall } x \textbf{ in PERS } : \textbf{ forall } j \textbf{ in } x \cdot \textbf{applications} : j \cdot \textbf{req\_skills} \leq x \cdot \textbf{abilities}$$

Example 2. The **placed**-field in the Job-class is a redundant field.

$$C_2 : \textbf{forall } x \textbf{ in JOB } : x \cdot \textbf{placed} = \textbf{exists } y \textbf{ in PERS } :$$
$$\textbf{exists } z \textbf{ in } y \cdot \textbf{placements} : z \cdot \textbf{job} = x$$

Example 3. A person can never simultanously apply for and be placed in one and the same job:

$$C_3 : \textbf{forall } x \textbf{ in PERS } : \textbf{ forall } y \textbf{ in } x \cdot \textbf{placements} : \textbf{not}(y \cdot \textbf{job in } x \cdot \textbf{applications})$$

Example 4. All persons in the database are younger than 65:

$$C_4 : \textbf{forall } x \textbf{ in PERS } : x \cdot \textbf{age} \leq 65$$

3 Introduction to Isabelle/HOL

Isabelle/HOL is a general-purpose higher-order logic-based theorem proof system. Using the system's built-in deductive system, mechanical reasoning is supported for the most commonly used data types in programming languages, such as booleans, integers, characters, strings, tuples, lists and sets. Isabelle provides an OQL-like functional language interface, supporting complex values nested up to arbitrary depth. From a database perspective, the Isabelle/HOL specification language relates to the NF2 data model, extended in the sense that attributes may be arbitrary collections and tuples, rather than relations. This makes the HOL-language particularly suitable for representing object-oriented database schemas.

Isabelle specifications are called *theories*. A theory consists of a collection of axioms and definitions. Our system generates an Isabelle theory file from a TM database specification. The definitions of this newly added theory being the definitions of methods, transactions, and constraints. Properties can be asserted and proved about these definitions by calling *tactics*, which are implementations of individual proof steps. The Isabelle/HOL package provides powerful tactics that can automate seemingly highly complex proofs. Predefined automatic tactics are available for simplification — term-rewriting with an arbitrary set of (conditional) term-rewriting lemmas is supported — and a natural deduction solver. The *Simplifier* performs term-rewriting with an arbitrary set of theorems of the form

$$H \Rightarrow LHS = RHS$$

Such rules read in the obvious straightforward manner: a term unifying with the expression on the left-hand side of the equation (LHS) is rewritten to the term that appears on the right-hand side (RHS) provided that the hypothesis (H) holds. The default Isabelle/HOL simplifier already installs a large collection of standard reduction rules for HOL, but new rules can be easily added to customize the Simplifier to a particular domain.

The *Natural Deduction Solver* uses a set of introduction and elimination properties for higher-order logic to automate natural deduction inferences. The tool implements a depth-first search strategy. It systematically breaks up the goals that are left after simplification in a number of smaller sub-goals. Variables, introduced by the use of quantifiers, can be automatically instantiated, allowing backtracking between different alternative unifiers. Before each inference step, the solver will call the Simplifier to allow further syntactic reductions to take place. Usually, this amounts to a highly complex proof structure and even seemingly simple proofs may take hundreds (but small, easy to automate) steps. It is not necessary, however, to understand the full details of the algorithms that are used, and the interested reader is further referred to [11].

In Section 5 we discuss how these tools can be used for the task of verifying transaction safety. First we do the representation of OO database schema's in HOL and show how (parts of) the example specification are translated. For the target language, a simply typed lambda calculus is used with OQL, rather than specific Isabelle syntax style, to slightly simplify the presentation. Thus we abstract from certain pecularities of the Isabelle/HOL system. For instance, the Isabelle system uses non-labeled tuples instead of labeled records, but a standard encoding can be used where (1) the order in which the labels occur is fixed and (2) projections are replaced by the typical operations `fst` and `snd`.

4 Mapping OO Language Features to Isabelle/HOL

We first define a structural mapping of the class structures of the ODMG data model to HOL records as a means of implementing these structures. An additional `id`-field of type integer is used to represent an object's identity. At the same time, class references in compound object types are replaced by pointer (oid) references in the form of integer-values, instead of copies of the objects themselves. The database itself is also represented as a record structure, called object store (OS), which holds entries for each extent of the database. The associated object store of our example specification becomes a record structure:

$$OS = \textbf{struct}(\texttt{SKILL} : \textbf{Set} < \textbf{struct}(\,\texttt{id} : \textbf{Int}, \texttt{description} : \textbf{String}) >$$
$$\texttt{JOB} : \textbf{Set} < \textbf{struct}(\,\texttt{id} : \textbf{Int}, \texttt{description} : \textbf{String},$$
$$\texttt{req\_skills} : \textbf{Set} < \textbf{Int} >,$$
$$\texttt{placed} : \textbf{Boolean}) >,$$
$$\texttt{PERS} : \textbf{Set} < \textbf{struct}(\,\texttt{id} : \textbf{Int}, \texttt{ssn} : \textbf{String}, \texttt{age} : \textbf{Int},$$
$$\texttt{applications} : \textbf{Set} < \textbf{Int} >,$$
$$\texttt{placements} : \textbf{Set} < \textbf{struct}(\texttt{job} : \textbf{Int}, \texttt{sal} : \textbf{Int}) >$$
$$\texttt{abilities} : \textbf{Set} < \textbf{Int} >) >,$$

Integrity constraints are represented as functions of type $OS \rightarrow Bool$ in the HOL framework. By the introduction of object identifiers, however, we have created some form of indirection which slightly complicates such a translation. For instance, a constraint expression of the form

$$\lambda\, os : OS \bullet \textbf{forall}\, x \,\textbf{in}\, os \cdot \texttt{PERS} :$$
$$\textbf{forall}\, j \,\textbf{in}\, x \cdot \texttt{applications} : j \cdot \texttt{req\_skills} \leq x \cdot \texttt{abilities}$$

can no longer be maintained in a context where the variable j is an object reference of type **Int**. To select the $\texttt{req\_skills}$-attribute of j we now first need to query the Job-extent. This form of indirection is provided for in the translation; i.e., functions like

$$get\_Job \equiv \lambda\, os : OS \bullet o : \textbf{Int} \bullet \textbf{elmt}(\,\textbf{select}\, x$$
$$\textbf{from}\, os \cdot \texttt{JOB}\, x$$
$$\textbf{where}\, x \cdot \texttt{id} = o)$$

will be automatically inserted at appropriate places. Note that the above function is generated for each class C. The function takes an object reference o and retrieves the corresponding full object representation from the associated class extent.

Example 5. The following Isabelle/HOL function representation is generated for the constraint C_1

$$C_1 \equiv \lambda\, os : OS \bullet \textbf{forall}\, x \,\textbf{in}\, os \cdot \texttt{PERS} : \textbf{forall}\, j \,\textbf{in}\, x \cdot \texttt{applications} :$$
$$(get\_Job\, os\, j) \cdot \texttt{req\_skills} \leq x \cdot \texttt{abilities}$$

Aside from the user-defined *explicit constraints*, the schema also has a number of *implicit constraints*. Implicit schema constraints include constraints for referential integrity and object identity. These will be automatically generated during the translation to HOL.

Example 6. The id-field acts as a key to the PERS-extent.

$$C_5 \equiv \lambda\, os : OS \bullet \textbf{forall } x \textbf{ in } os \cdot \textbf{PERS :}$$
$$\textbf{forall } y \textbf{ in PERS : } x \cdot \textbf{id} = y \cdot \textbf{id implies } x = y$$

Example 7. The oid's in the applications-field refer to items in the JOB-table.

$$C_6 \equiv \lambda\, os : OS \bullet \textbf{forall } x \textbf{ in } os \cdot \textbf{PERS : forall } y \textbf{ in } x \cdot \textbf{applications :}$$
$$\textbf{: exists } z \textbf{ in } os \cdot \textbf{JOB : } y = z \cdot \textbf{id}$$

The semantics of transactions is functional: transactions are formally represented as functions of type $OS \to t_1 \to \cdots \to t_k \to OS$ in the Isabelle framework, where the types $t_1 \cdots t_k$ represent the types of optional input parameters. At the semantical level, the **update** primitive constructs a new object store value, where all possibly modified object representations resulting from the functional evaluation of the OQL sub-expressions are unioned with the unmodified objects for each extension. The collection of objects that are not modified is easily obtained by inspecting the id-field. Furthermore, method calls are replaced by substituting the TM-OQL expressions defining their functionality. At present, our prototype does not support recursive method calls.

Example 8. The following Isabelle representation function is generated for the *Hire* transaction:

$$Hire \equiv \lambda\, os : OS \bullet \lambda\, assn : \textbf{String} \bullet \lambda\, j : \textbf{Int} \bullet \lambda\, salary : \textbf{Int}\bullet$$
$$\textbf{struct}(\textbf{SKILL} : os \cdot \textbf{SKILL},$$
$$\textbf{JOB} : \{(get\_Job\ os\ j)\,\textbf{except}\,(\textbf{placed} = \textbf{true})\} + \textbf{select } x$$
$$\textbf{from } os \cdot \textbf{JOB } x$$
$$\textbf{where } x \cdot \textbf{id} \notin \{j\}$$
$$\textbf{PERS} : (\textbf{select } p\,\textbf{except}\,(\textbf{placements} = p \cdot \textbf{placements}+$$
$$\textbf{set}(\textbf{struct}(\textbf{job} : j, \textbf{sal} : salary)),$$
$$\textbf{applications} = \textbf{applications} - \textbf{set } j)$$
$$\textbf{from } os \cdot \textbf{PERS } p$$
$$\textbf{where } p \cdot \textbf{ssn} = assn) + (\textbf{select } p$$
$$\textbf{from } os \cdot \textbf{PERS } p$$
$$\textbf{where } p \cdot \textbf{ssn} \neq assn)$$

The above function generates modifications to the JOB as well as the PERS-extent, while the SKILL-extent is not modified. Note that the job-object j is expanded to allow the placed field to be changed. The expression on the left-hand side of the union (+) denotes the collection of modified objects, while the collection of objects that are not updated appears on the right-hand side. The precondition of the transaction is stored in a seperate definition and can be treated as an ordinary constraint.

Example 9. The pre-condition of the *Hire*-transaction is represented as a function:

$$Pre\_Hire \equiv \lambda\, os : OS \bullet \lambda\, assn : \textbf{String} \bullet \lambda\, j : \textbf{Int} \bullet \lambda\, salary : \textbf{Int}\bullet$$
$$\textbf{exists } p \textbf{ in PERS : } p \cdot \textbf{ssn} = assn$$

5 Automatic Transaction Verification in Isabelle/HOL

Once the schema has been translated to Isabelle, its automatic proof tactics as mentioned in Section 3 can be used to statically identify the integrity constraints that are possibly violated by a transaction and the ones that are not. Transaction verification starts by asserting as a *proof goal* the fact that a constraint will never be violated by the execution of a transaction. Given an Isabelle transaction representation function T, an associated pre-condition representation Pre_T, and a constraint representation function C, the following goal needs to be verified:

$$C\,(os) \wedge (Pre\_T\ os\ p_1 \cdots p_k) \Rightarrow C\,(T\ os\ p_1 \cdots p_k)$$

for arbitrary object store os and input parameters $p_1 \cdots p_k$. With slight syntactic modifications — into ASCII — theorems of the above form can be given as input and mechanically verified by the Isabelle theorem prover. In our analysis, we use both the Simplifier and the Natural Deduction Solver — the basic tools (tactics) for automatic proof in Isabelle, as introduced in Section 3.

The rest of this section discusses in some more detail how these tools can be used for the task of compile-time transaction verification. In the next paragraph, we demonstrate how the term-rewriting tool applies to implement a simple, fairly rough analysis, analogous to the *path analysis* presented in [3–5]. The harder cases are then further processed by the natural deduction solver for a more detailed analysis, which is the subject of Section 5.2.

5.1 A Simple Analysis using the Simplifier

When starting an automatic proof, Isabelle first tries to simplify the initial proof goal as much as possible. This is done by term-rewriting with the Simplifier tool. The default Isabelle/HOL Simplifier, however, is not directly suitable to enable verification of a robust class of transactions over arbitrary database schemas, thus requiring some extensions. Extensions to the Simplifier will be made by adding some new rewrite-rules, such that at least the trivial cases — of a transaction and constraint operating on different parts of the database — can be identified. The following example illustrates how the Isabelle Simplifier can be used for verifying transaction safety, and which extensions have been made.

$$C_4(\text{Hire}\ os\ ssn\ j) \tag{1}$$

$$= \textbf{forall } x \textbf{ in} \qquad (2)$$
$$\textbf{struct}(\text{SKILL} : os \cdot \text{SKILL},$$
$$\text{JOB} : \{(get\_Job\ os\ j)\ \textbf{except}\ (\text{placed} = \text{true})\} + \textbf{select } x$$
$$\textbf{from } os \cdot \text{JOB } x$$
$$\textbf{where } x \cdot \text{id} \notin \{j\}$$
$$\text{PERS} : (\textbf{select} p\ \textbf{except}\ (\text{placements} = p \cdot \text{placements} +$$
$$\textbf{set}(\textbf{struct}(\text{job} : j, \text{sal} : salary)),$$
$$\text{applications} = \text{applications} - \textbf{set} j)$$
$$\textbf{from } os \cdot \text{PERS } p$$
$$\textbf{where } p \cdot \text{ssn} = assn) + \textbf{select } p$$
$$\textbf{from } os \cdot \text{PERS } p$$
$$\textbf{where } p \cdot \text{ssn} \neq assn$$
$$) \cdot \text{PERS} : x \cdot \textbf{age} \leq 65$$

$$= \textbf{forall } x \textbf{ in} ((\textbf{select } p\ \textbf{except}\ (\text{placements} = p \cdot \text{placements} + \qquad (3)$$
$$\textbf{set}(\textbf{struct}(\text{job} : j, \text{sal} : salary)),$$
$$\text{applications} = \text{applications} - \textbf{set} j)$$
$$\textbf{from } os \cdot \text{PERS } p$$
$$\textbf{where } p \cdot \text{ssn} = assn) + \textbf{select } p$$
$$\textbf{from } os \cdot \text{PERS } p$$
$$\textbf{where } p \cdot \text{ssn} \neq assn) : x \cdot \textbf{age} \leq 65$$

$$= (\textbf{forall } x \textbf{ in } (\textbf{select } p\ \textbf{except}\ (\text{placements} = p \cdot \text{placements} + \qquad (4)$$
$$\textbf{set}(\textbf{struct}(\text{job} : j, \text{sal} : salary)),$$
$$\text{applications} = \text{applications} - \textbf{set} j)$$
$$\textbf{from } os \cdot \text{PERS } p$$
$$\textbf{where } p \cdot \text{ssn} = assn) : x \cdot \textbf{age} \leq 65) \textbf{ and}$$
$$(\textbf{forall } x \textbf{ in } (\textbf{select } p$$
$$\textbf{from } os \cdot \text{PERS } p$$
$$\textbf{where } p \cdot \text{ssn} \neq assn) : x \cdot \textbf{age} \leq 65)$$

$$= (\textbf{forall } p \textbf{ in } os \cdot \text{PERS} : (p \cdot \text{ssn} = assn)\ \textbf{implies} \qquad (5)$$
$$p\ \textbf{except}\ (\text{placements} = p \cdot \text{placements} +$$
$$\textbf{set}(\textbf{struct}(\text{job} : j, \text{sal} : salary)),$$
$$\text{applications} = p \cdot \text{applications} - \textbf{set} j) \cdot \textbf{age} \leq 65) \textbf{ and}$$
$$(\textbf{forall } p \textbf{ in } os \cdot \text{PERS} : (p \cdot \text{ssn} \neq assn)\ \textbf{implies}\ (p \cdot \textbf{age} \leq 65)$$

$$= (\textbf{forall } p \textbf{ in } os \cdot \text{PERS} : (p \cdot \text{ssn} = assn)\ \textbf{implies}\ (p \cdot \textbf{age} \leq 65) \textbf{ and} \qquad (6)$$
$$(\textbf{forall } p \textbf{ in } os \cdot \text{PERS} : (p \cdot \text{ssn} \neq assn)\ \textbf{implies}\ (p \cdot \textbf{age} \leq 65)$$

The above example traces the systematic reduction of the consequent of the goal that is generated for verifying that the *Hire*-transaction preserves integrity of constraint C_4. The proof starts by substituting the transaction in the constraint predicate (1) and unfolding the database specific definitions of the transaction and constraint (2). In general, this results in a highly complex proof term. Fortunately, as already suggested by [2], many of the complex terms can be easily reduced using standard[2] reduction rules for the tuple datatype:

---

[2] In Isabelle/HOL syntax these rules are actually encoded at a much lower level. As was already mentioned in Section 3, Isabelle uses non-labeled tuples instead of labeled records, and the reductions are realized by using standard rules involving the typical operations fst and snd.

[REC1]	$\mathbf{struct}(a_1 : e_1, \cdots, a_n : e_n) \cdot a_i = e_i$
[REC2]	$i \in n \Rightarrow e\,\mathbf{except}(a_1 : e_1, \cdots, a_n : e_n) \cdot a_i = e_i$
[REC3]	$i \notin n \Rightarrow e\,\mathbf{except}(a_1 : e_1, \cdots, a_n : e_n) \cdot a_i = e \cdot a_i$

The above rules allow the Simplifier to identify those cases of a transaction and constraint operating on different class extents such that integrity is trivially preserved. For instance, application of the first rule [REC1] to (2), discards the update operation on the Job-extent. Note that such an update is 'irrelevant' in the presence of the current constraint predicate, since the constraint only takes the Person-extent into account. At this point, simplification with the default Simplifier stops : none of the standard rewrite-rules matches with the remaining proof term (3) and additional knowledge about the general structure of the proof goals that are generated is needed, to proceed with simplification.

By studying the cases where the Simplifier got stuck during a transaction safety proof, several recurring patterns could be identified. For instance, in Section 4, we defined the contents of the extent of a class after an update operation occurs as the union (+) of the set of objects that got changed and the set of objects that did not change. Combining this with the assumption that many constraint predicates quantify over class extents, we will be frequently left with terms that match with one of the following rules

[UN_ALL]	$(\mathbf{forall}\ x\ \mathbf{in}\ (A + B)\ :\ \phi(x)) = (\mathbf{forall}\ x\ \mathbf{in}\ A\ :\ \phi(x))\,\mathbf{and}$
	$(\mathbf{forall}\ x\ \mathbf{in}\ B\ :\ \phi(x))$
[UN_EX]	$(\mathbf{exists}\ x\ \mathbf{in}\ (A + B)\ :\ \phi(x)) = (\mathbf{exists}\ x\ \mathbf{in}\ A\ :\ \phi(x))\,\mathbf{or}$
	$(\mathbf{exists}\ x\ \mathbf{in}\ B\ :\ \phi(x))$

The above rules will split universal and existential quantifications so that is discriminated between the 'modified' and the 'unmodified' case. For instance, the first rule [UN_ALL] matches with term (3) of the example proof, and the Simplifier splits the quantification resulting in (4). Note that the proposition on the left-hand side of the conjunction quantifies over the collection of modified objects, while the quantification over the collection of objects that is not modified is on the right-hand side.

At this point, the general structure of the goal gradually seems to disappear. Transactions and constraints can be expressed in many ways, and general patterns can hardly be identified. Transaction definitions, however, frequently use a select-from-where clause, making it useful to add the following reduction rules

[DIS1]	$\mathbf{forall}\ y\ \mathbf{in}\ (\mathbf{select}\ e\ (x)$
	$\qquad \mathbf{from}\ x\ \mathbf{in}\ A$
	$\qquad \mathbf{where}\ p(x))\ :\ \phi(y) = \mathbf{forall}\ x\ \mathbf{in}\ A\ :\ p(x)\,\mathbf{implies}\,\phi(e(x))$
[DIS2]	$\mathbf{exists}\ y\ \mathbf{in}\ (\mathbf{select}\ e\ (x)$
	$\qquad \mathbf{from}\ x\ \mathbf{in}\ A$
	$\qquad \mathbf{where}\ p(x))\ :\ \phi(y) = \mathbf{exists}\ x\ \mathbf{in}\ A\ :\ p(x)\,\mathbf{and}\,\phi(e(x))$

The above rules will distribute functional replacements over quantifier bodies. This enables the Simplifier to also identify combinations of transactions and constraints where — although the same class extents are involved — integrity is trivially preserved because different attributes of the objects are accessed. For instance, application of the first rule [DIS1] to (4), will distribute the functional replacement over the quantifier body, thus resulting in (5). Now, simplification can proceed using standard reduction rules. Using [REC3], the Simplifier destroys the remaining record-update operation, and we are left with a formula that closely matches the original assumption (6). The remaining term will be solved since the Simplifier automatically asserts the original assumption

forall x **in** $os \cdot$ PERS : $x \cdot$ **age** ≤ 65

as an additional rewrite rule while simplifying the consequent. □

5.2   A Detailed Analysis using the ND-Solver

Unfortunately, not all goals are as easily solved as the one that is discussed in the previous example. Often, when a transaction and constraint operate on the same parts of the database, it becomes difficult to completely solve the goal by simplification. There are many possibilities of how the final proof term may look like and there hardly seems to be a general pattern that would allow further simplification. For instance, the *Hire* transaction updates the **applications**-field from the PERS-table, which is exactly the same field that is also accessed by the integrity constraint oc_3. In this case, simplification alone cannot prove the entire goal and the following goal is left after simplification:

(**forall** x **in** PERS :
  forall y **in** $x \cdot$ **applications** : $get\_Job(os\ y) \cdot$ **req_skills** $\leq x \cdot$ **abilities**)
    $\Rightarrow$ (**forall** x **in** PERS : **forall** y **in** $x \cdot$ **applications** $-$ **set**(j) :
            $get\_Job(os\ y) \cdot$ **req_skills** $\leq x \cdot$ **abilities**)   (7)

Do we need to derive another rewrite-lemma that will allow further simplification of this term? In the approach taken by Sheard & Stemple [2], further simplification would be employed by adding the following rule

(**forall** x **in** A : $\phi(x)$) $\Rightarrow$ (**forall** x **in** $(A - B)$: $\phi(x)$)

to their knowledge base. Indeed, by adding the above rule to the Isabelle Simplifier we could also solve the remaining proof goal. However, many of such rules can be added and one may doubt whether they would apply more frequently in other proofs. This is one of the shortcommings of their approach as mentioned in [2].

Fortunately, Isabelle largely eliminates the need for adding an extensive amount of knowledge to the Simplifier. The simplifications discussed in the previous section are usually sufficient to already yield a proof goal that can be further processed by the Natural Deduction Solver, which only employs standard lemmas by means of introduction and elimination properties for HOL. In the case of formula (7), Isabelle will invoke the introduction and elimination properties of

universal quantification and set-membership, eventually proving the validity of
(7). By interleaving the slightly customized Isabelle Simplifier with the Natural
Deduction Solver, a powerful transaction verifier is provided for: most of the
examples can be solved in just a few seconds time.

	C_1	C_2	C_3	C_4	C_5	C_6	C_7	C_8	C_9	C_{10}	C_{11}
Hire	10.4	7.7	3.9	2.4	4.9	5.4	3.2	2.1	2.3	2.6	2.5
Fire	10.3		3.5	2.5	4.5	2.7	3.7	1.6	2.3	5.5	2.4
Subsribe	5.9	2.7	1.0	1.1	3.4	1.4	1.7	1.6	1.5	1.5	2.9

Table 1. Proof Timings for the Job Specification (in seconds)

Table 5.2 shows the proof-times for our example specification. All timings are
obtained running Isabelle on an ordinary SPARC-5 workstation with 80MB of
internal memory. Horizontally alligned are the constraints, while the transactions
are vertically alligned. Including the implicit schema constraints for referential
integrity and object identity a total of 11 constraints is listed. This generates a
total of 33 proof goals, one for each combination of transaction and constraint.
These are put in a ML-text file and on loading the specification, the file will be
automatically processed by the Isabelle theorem prover. Only one of the goals
(for C_2 and *Fire*) could not be solved automatically; constraint C_2 should be
tested at run-time after the *Fire*-transaction commits.

6 Comparison with Related Work

Our work follows the line of research set out by Sheard & Stemple ([2]). In this
approach, the Boyer-Moore theorem prover is used to implement a compile-time
mechanism to verify constraint invariance with respect to update operations on
a relational database. The initial database specifications are given in a language
called ADABTPL, which are then mapped to the Boyer-Moore theorem prover
for automatic proof assistance. To that end, the Boyer-Moore theorem prover
is enriched with higher-order functions, and a basic theory about tuples, finite
sets and natural numbers is defined, in which databases can be represented.
The actual transaction safety verifier component is implemented using a *term-rewriting* system. The term-rewriter uses a large knowledge base, which stores
general knowledge about the transaction and constraint language. This includes
basic theorems, such as a rule asserting the commutativity of the set-union operation. Much of the power of the Sheard & Stemple system derives from adding
more problem-specific rules (so-called meta-lemmas) which enable the simplification of terms that frequently appear during transaction safety analysis. Our
approach using Isabelle/HOL differs in that it uses the object-oriented rather

than the relational framework. Also, we employ a novel more general verification strategy that uses *natural deduction* in addition to *term-rewriting*. This has the benefit of offering a more general proof strategy for transaction verification. Initially, we tried to follow the approach of [2], but we soon ended up adding many new non-standard rewrite-rules to the Simplifier. Often, it was doubtful if they were relevant in the context of other database specifications; the knowledge base approach of Sheard & Stemple [2] tends to tune the transaction verifier to specific example databases, rather than offering a verifier which is more broadly applicable.

In [12] another related approach is described, as employed in the DAIDA-project, which also allows for proof assistance in demonstrating constraint invariance with respect to operations on a database. The main topic of [12] did not concern constraint invariance, but incremental refinement of initial database specifications to actual database programs; the work on proof asssitance for constraint invariance is more or less a spinn-off of the actual topic of the DAIDA-project. The initial database specification is given in a language called TDL, and the TDL specification is then mapped to Abrial's language of Abstract Machines. By employing the B-tool, interactive proof assistance is offered for checking constraint invariance. The most notable difference with our approach employing Isabelle/HOL is that our system offers automatic, rather than an interactive, proof assistance. Another difference is that TM/ODMG employs an object-oriented style and is purely functional, whereas TDL has less object-oriented features and uses an explicit pre-/post-conditional style based on predicates and sets.

The later work of [3–5] follows a different approach. It exploits several techniques related to *abstract interpretation* for the task of compile-time transaction verification in an O2 database system. Their analysis starts with a simple compilation technique to identify those combinations of transaction and constraint that are certainly not in conflict because the transaction and constraint access different attributes or class extents. The same analysis is actually implemented in our system using term-rewriting with the Isabelle Simplifier tool. For those combinations of transaction and constraint that could not be proved safe in the first step, Benzaken *et al* use a second more detailed analysis. This analysis takes some details of the semantics into account. It can, for instance, prove that deletion of an object from a set does not affect a constraint that universally quantifies over it. It is not clear, however, what the exact limitations are of taking only small portions of the semantics of the application into account. In principle, the line of research set out by Sheard & Stemple [2] (and our extension of it) offers more potential: since the full semantics of the application is taken into account, we should eventually increase the amount of proofs that can be performed. Furthermore, we use a functional rather than an imperative programming language for transaction specification. It is well-known that functional languages offer a relatively clean logical structure which is more suitable for verification; in imperative languages the simple structure is destroyed by constructions such as assignment and aliasing.

7   Conclusions & Future Work

In this paper, we have outlined a framework for compile-time verification of transaction safety in an object-oriented database. It is a first attempt at generalizing the ideas of Sheard & Stemple as presented in [2] to the object-oriented data model, using modern theorem proving technology. The higher-order logic Isabelle theorem prover is used to automatically verify which constraints might, or might not be violated by a given transaction. An improved verification strategy is presented, that involves *natural deduction* in addition to *term-rewriting*. This eliminates the need for extensive customized proof strategies, and our system largely builds on general purpose proof algorithms supplied by the Isabelle/HOL package.

Tests have been done using a prototype system for a realistically large example specification, which we believe is representative of many real-world OO database applications. The example includes several complex transactions and constraints which are potentially in conflict because the same extensions, or often even the same attributes, are accessed. For instance, the constraint C_2 mentions the **placed**-field from the JOB-table, and the **placements**-field from the PERS-table. Although the same fields are updated by the *Hire* transaction, the system proves that there is actually no conflict. Such a proof can only be done using a sophisticated *semantic* analysis. Typically, these are the harder cases where our approach should offer more potential than an analysis based on an *abstract interpretation* as outlined in [3–5] which only takes some very global properties of the semantics into account.

In this paper we have highlighted some of the difficulties found in the mapping of an object-oriented database schema to HOL, but many issues remain open and full ODMG is not yet supported by our first prototype. For instance, our system does not yet support the concept of relationships, nor do we fully support the important notions of polymorphic sets and late-binding. Embedding of these language features – whose semantics is known to be difficult [13–15] — in the HOL framework remains a future challenge, but is a topic of ongoing research. At present we are experimenting using disjoint sum-types to represent polymorphic sets in the HOL-setting. Obviously, this will further complicate the proofs as additional case-splits are needed.

On the other hand, it seems that there are some ways that reasoning about the OO case is easier than for the relational case. The relational data model does not provide support of nested-sets and other complex (nested) data structures as already available in HOL. As a consequence, when mapping a relational database language to HOL, we do not fully benefit from the power of the HOL language and rather inefficient input is generated for the theorem prover.

An interesting feature of our system is that it is more broadly applicable than transaction verification; since it largely builds on standard Isabelle proof algorithms, the system should be fairly easily customized to different domains. Preliminary test results using the bank-account example of [16,17] have shown that the same proof algorithms are applicable to several forms of transaction commutativity analysis as well.

A topic that was not discussed in this paper is the generation of feedback to database designers. At present, the system only reports a 'yes', could prove, or 'no', could not prove, but eventually we would like to support some more advanced modes of feedback to database designers. For instance, designers would typically like to know why a proof actually failed or how a transaction might be corrected such that integrity will be preserved. An overview of the different modes of feedback can be found in [18] and we plan to study the implementation of a similar feedback component for our system.

References

[1] Piero Fraternali & Stefano Paraboschi, "A Review of Repairing Techniques for Integrity Maintenance," in *Proceedings First International Workshop on Rules in Database Systems, Edinburgh, Scotland, 30 August–1 September, 1993*, Norman W. Paton & M. Howard Williams, eds., Springer-Verlag, New York–Heidelberg–Berlin, 1994, 333–346.

[2] Tim Sheard & David Stemple, "Automatic verification of database transaction safety," *ACM Trans. Database Syst.* 14 (Sept., 1989), 322–368.

[3] Veronique Benzaken & Doucet, "Themis: a database programming language with integrity constraints," in *Database programming languages (DBPL-4): Proceedings of the 4th International Workshop on Database Programming Languages, Object Models and languages*, Springer-Verlag, 1994, 243–262.

[4] Veronique Benzaken & Doucet, "Themis: a Database Programming Language Handling Integrity Constraints," *VLDB Journal* 4 (1995).

[5] Veronique Benzaken & Xavier Schaefer, "Ensuring efficiently the integrity of a persistent object store via abstract interpretation," in *Proceedings of the 7th International Workshop on Persistent Object Systems*, Morgan Kaufmann, May, 1996.

[6] H. Balsters, R. A. de By & R. Zicari, "Typed sets as a basis for object-oriented database schemas," in *ECOOP 1993 Kaiserslautern*, 1993.

[7] René Bal, Herman Balsters, Rolf A. de By, Alexander Bosschaart, Jan Flokstra, Maurice van Keulen, Jacek Skowronek & Bart Termorshuizen, "The TM Manual; version 2.0, revision e," Universiteit Twente, Technical report IMPRESS / UT-TECH-T79-001-R2, Enschede, The Netherlands, June 1995.

[8] Luca Cardelli, "A semantics of multiple inheritance," *Inf. and Comput.* 76 (1988), 138–164.

[9] Herman Balsters & Chris C. de Vreeze, "A semantics of object-oriented sets," in *The Third International Workshop on Database Programming Languages: Bulk Types & Persistent Data (DBPL–3), Aug. 27–30, 1991, Nafplion, Greece*, Paris Kanellakis & Joachim W. Schmidt, eds., Morgan Kaufmann Publishers, San Mateo, CA, 1991, 201–217.

[10] R. G. G. Cattell, *The Object Database Standard: ODMG–93*, Morgan Kaufmann Publishers, San Mateo, CA, 1994.

[11] Lawrence C. Paulson, *Isabelle: A Generic Theorem Prover*, Lecture Notes in Computer Science #828, Springer-Verlag, Berlin, 1994.

[12] Alexander Borgida, John Mylopoulos & Joachim W. Schmidt, *Database Programming by Formal Refinement of Conceptual Designs*, IEEE Data Engineering, Sept., 1989.

[13] Luca Cardelli, "Amber," *Combinators and Functional Programming*, New York–Heidelberg–Berlin (1986).

[14] G. Castagna, "Object-Oriented Programming: A Unified Foundation," *Progress in Theoretical Computer Science* (1996,).

[15] Peter Buneman & Atsushi Ohori, "A Type System that Reconciles Classes and Extents," in *The Third International Workshop on Database Programming Languages: Bulk Types & Persistent Data (DBPL–3), Aug. 27–30, 1991, Nafplion, Greece,* Paris Kanellakis & Joachim W. Schmidt, eds., Morgan Kaufmann Publishers, San Mateo, CA, 1991, 191–202.

[16] Man Hon Wong & Divyakant Agrawal, "Context-specific synchronization for atomic data types in object-oriented databases," *TCS* (1995).

[17] William E. Weihl, "The Impact of Recovery on Concurrency Control," *Journal of Computer and System Sciences* (1993).

[18] David Stemple, Subhasish Mazumdar & Tim Sheard, "On the modes and meaning of feedback to transaction designers," in *Proceedings of ACM-SIGMOD 1987 International Conference on Management of Data, San Francisco, CA, May 27–29, 1987,* Umeshwar Dayal & Irv Traiger, eds., ACM Press, New York, NY, 1987, 374–386, (also appeared as ACM SIGMOD Record 16, 3, Dec., 1987).

Static Analysis of Transactions for Conservative Multigranularity Locking[1]

G. Amato, F. Giannotti, G. Mainetto

CNUCE–CNR, Via S. Maria 36, 56126 Pisa

This paper shows a concrete example in which a technique of static analysis, mainly used in the programming language area, can be successfully applied to a database problem. The database problem is the automatic (i.e., without a transaction programmer's intervention) realization of a new concurrency control protocol called conservative multiple granularity locking. Being conservative, the scheduler of this protocol ensures that the database resources needed from a transaction are granted before such a transaction begins its execution. Being multigranular, this protocol deals with an hierarchical organization of database resources and it allows to strike a balance between locking overhead and degree of concurrency allowed from one transaction. The analysis we present allows to automatically infer from the text of a transaction a safe approximation of the set of hierarchical database resources needed from the transaction. The analysis gives particular attention to the management of sets of resources to statically foresee if a transaction will access most of the resources in the set. The proposed technique, which can take advantage of statistical information on database resources, infers an approximation close to the actual resources that the transaction is going to use at run time.

1   Introduction

In our opinion if database programming languages (DBPLs – [Atkinson 1987]) and persistent programming languages (PPLs - [Atkinson 1995]) aspire to become an effective technology, then the research for these languages should concentrate on the solutions of problems typical of databases, that are, mainly, optimisation problems. In dealing with optimising techniques for DBPLs, the ideal should be that of providing systems that combine the high expressiveness of languages with the efficiency of databases. Several reasons suggest the use of techniques of static analysis for this purpose. In fact, they can safely optimise and transform programs, they can take advantage of the high level semantics of the language for the sake of optimization, optimisation problems of database should be faced at compile-time because of the unmanageable amount of data involved at run-time, etc.

This paper shows a concrete example in which a technique of static analysis, mainly used in the programming language area, is applied to a database problem. The database problem is the automatic (i.e., without a transaction programmer's intervention) realization of a new concurrency control protocol called conservative multiple granularity locking. Being conservative, the scheduler of this protocol ensures that the database resources needed from a transaction are granted before such transaction begins its execution. Being multigranular, this protocol deals with an hierarchical organization of database resources and it allows to strike a balance between locking overhead and degree of concurrency allowed from one transaction. The analysis we present allows to automatically infer from the text of a transaction a safe approximation of the set of hierarchical database resources needed from the transaction. The analysis gives a particular attention to the management of sets of resources to statically foresee if a transaction will access most of the resources in the set. The

[1] This work was partly funded by the ESPRIT Project No. 22552 – Pastel (Persistent Application Systems, Technologies, Environments and Languages).

proposed technique, which can take advantage of statistical information on database resources, infers an approximation close to the actual resources that the transaction is going to use at run time.

We emphasize that in this context the transaction programmer is completely relieved from the burden of explicitly programming a complex concurrency control protocol such as conservative multigranularity locking. In this way the expressiveness of the language is not changed although the accesses of the transactions are optimised.

The static analysis is applied to implicit transactions written in an object–oriented PPL, called Abstract Persistent Programming Language (APPL), which is a subset of Galileo [Albano 1985]. The technique of static analysis used belongs to the *abstract interpretation* framework [Cousot 1977] [Jones 1995].

The paper is organised as follows. Section 2 briefly introduces some preliminary notions such as the main features of APPL language and the multigranularity locking protocol; Section 3 gives an overview of the approach by informally describing the analyses and the transformations of a transaction and discussing some technical problems that have been solved; Section 4 is the central part of the paper that describes the formal framework on which is based the static analysis; Section 5 presents the application of the analysis to simple APPL transactions and Section 6 concludes.

2 Preliminaries

2.1 The APPL Language

APPL is a version of Galileo tailored to keep the most relevant database programming language constructs provided by the original language [Albano 1985]. APPL has OO features: *classes* with inheritance that, for simplicity reasons of this paper, is single and *objects* with methods are the most important persistent values. Also *individual objects* can populate an APPL database (e.g. integers, functions, records).

A class is a "bulk" type constructor, like *set_of* or *list*, characterised by two facts: an *instance_of* relation exists between a class and the set of actual objects belonging to it (this set of objects is called the *extension* of the class); a subset relation exists between the extensions of two classes that are in an *is_a* relation. Classes have a *unique class identifier*. Objects are instances of record types and every object has a *unique object identifier*. The same object can simultaneously belong to several classes, those that are in an *is_a* relation. Equality on objects means *sameness*: two objects are equal if and only if they have the same object identifier. The identity of an object is used for modelling its association with other objects. Objects can have values of any type as components, as for example functions used to model methods of classical OO languages.

APPL is an expression language. As in every non–purely functional language, the term expression denotes also statements. The following conventions will be used:

$e \in$ Exp	generic values	$b \in$ Exp	boolean values
$c \in$ Con	constants	$f \in$ Exp	functional values
$p \in$ Prim	primitives	$l \in$ Exp	reference values
$x \in$ Ide	identifiers	$o \in$ Exp	object values
$lb \in$ Lab	labels of fields	$r \in$ Exp	record values

APPL language assumes that a user–defined function has a single argument, and only sequential declarations of (recursive) values are allowed.

An APPL transaction is a block containing an optional sequence of declarations, that (recursively) bind an identifier to a value, followed by a sequence of expressions:

$$transaction ::= trans\ (d_1, ..., d_n, e_1, ..., e_n)\ |\ trans\ (e_1, ..., e_n)$$
$$d ::= let\ (x,e)\ |\ letrec\ (x,e)$$

During the execution an APPL transaction acceses a global shared environment and a global shared store[2]. The environment component constitutes the database schema; this information is frozen after being defined. The global shared store represents the database and its state can change during the execution of APPL transactions.

An APPL expression can be a constant, an identifier, the application of a user defined function and the application of a language primitive:

$$e ::= c\ |\ x\ |\ e\ (e_1)\ |\ p\ (e_1, ..., e_n)$$

Important primitives are those defined on references:

$ref\ (e)$	creates and returns a reference to the value of e
$deref\ (l)$	dereferences l i.e. returns the value referenced by l
$assign\ (l, e)$	assigns the value of e to the reference l

APPL primitives on classes are: insertion of an object in a base class; specialisation of an object from a superclass to a subclass; test of the membership of an object to a class extension; removal of an object from all the classes to which it belongs; query on all objects belonging to the extension of a class.

$insert\ (x, r)$	creates an object and inserts it in the class x
$specialise\ (x, r, o)$	specialises o with r and inserts o in the class x
$is\_in\ (x, o)$	tests whether the object o belongs to the class x
$remove\ (o)$	removes the object o from all classes
$for\_class\ (x, f)$	f function is applied to all objects of class x

The query primitive for_class is semantically equivalent to the *mapcar* construct of Lisp [McCarthy 1962]: the function is successively applied to one object of the extension at a time, and the results are collected into a sequence. The query primitive is computationally complete and thus it is more powerful than the traditional query constructs with associative retrieval.

Classes, objects and references are the only modifiable values of the language, the ones on which side-effects can be performed. Other important primitives are:

$same\ (o_1, o_2)$	test for object equivalence
$obj\_of\ (o, lb)$	selection of field lb from object o
$ite\ (b, e_1, e_2)$	if_then_else conditional primitive
$func\ (x,e)$	function constructor

Since inheritance is single, in this paper we will use the version of the MGL protocol that works on *tree* of data items.

---

[2] A mapping from names of variables to object identities and a mapping from object identities to object states, respectively.

	NL	IS	IX	S	SIX	X
NL	√	√	√	√	√	√
IS	√	√	√	√	√	No
IX	√	√	√	No	No	No
S	√	√	No	√	No	No
SIX	√	√	No	No	No	No
X	√	No	No	No	No	No

Fig. 1. Compatibility matrix for Multiple Granularity Locking protocol

2.2 Conservative Multiple Granularity Locking Protocol

The most interesting feature of MGL is that for every transaction it is possible to strike a balance between locking overhead and degree of concurrency allowed from the transaction in the system [Gray 1975] [Gray 1978]. In fact, in a tree data structure the greatest degree of concurrency could be obtained by a transaction if it locks individually the leaves just needed from the computation, but this behaviour implies a great cost of locking because the transaction has to request several locks. Viceversa, if a transaction locks a non-leaf node, then such transaction saves locking overhead time because it requests only one lock, but at the same time this reduces concurrency in the system because the transaction probably locks more resources than those effectively needed from computation.

The protocol allows to lock *granules* (i.e., nodes of the tree) in five different modes. An *exclusive* (X) lock excludes any other transaction from accessing (reading or writing) that granule. A *shared* (S) lock permits other transactions to read the same granule concurrently but inhibits any updating. A nonleaf granule is locked in *intention–shared* (IS) mode to specify that descendant granules will be explicitly locked in S mode. Similarly, an *intention–exclusive* (IX) lock implies that explicit locking is being done on a descendant in X mode. A *shared and intention–exclusive* (SIX) lock on a nonleaf granule implies that the whole subtree rooted at the granule is locked in S mode and that explicit X locking will be done at a lower level. Notice that an explict lock on a leaf granule can only be either X or S. **Fig.** 1 shows the compatibility matrix for the five kinds of locks; in the figure, *null* (NL) mode represents the absence of a lock request.

The Lock Manager of a DBMS records the locks on granules in a hierarchical data structure called Lock Instance Graph (LIG). The design of an appropriate LIG for a DBPL is a non trivial task [Amato 1996]. The LIG of APPL is a tree, with a granule representing the whole database as root. The granules for *class extensions* represent sets of object identities. The granules for *class hierarchies* represent sets of object states. Class extensions are separate sets with no explicit subset relationship: for example, if an object at the same time belongs to the class A and to the subclass B then its identity is replicated in the extensions of A and B. In an APPL LIG the granules for class extensions contain smaller granules for extension elements. The granules for class hierarchies contain smaller granules for object states. In an APPL LIG a superclass S is directly related to its subclasses and to those object states having S as the most specific class. **Fig.** 2 shows a simple example of APPL LIG (**nl-ee** stands for null extension element).

The standard MGL protocol requires that locks are requested in top-down order and released bottom-up. The Conservative MGL protocol requires that locks of the appropriate mode on all non-leaf granules of the LIG are requested before a transaction

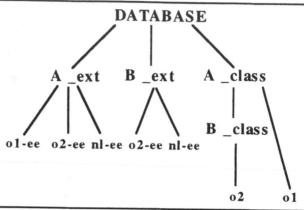

Fig. 2. Example of Lock Instance Graph for APPL

begins its execution. Until all these locks have not been granted, the transaction cannot start. Once started, the transaction could dynamically need to require a lock on some leaf granules. Notice that Conservative MGL protocol is not deadlock free.

3. An Informal Overview of the approach

Having clarified the organization of the LIG for the APPL language and the functioning of Conservative MGL protocol, the functioning of the system and the role of static analysis should be much clearer. The static analysis of APPL transactions allows the deduction of a safe approximation of the set of non-leaf granules accessed from the transaction and the way in which these granules should be locked. Once this information is deduced, a step of transaction transformation is necessary. This step inserts explicit lock primitives in the code of a transaction before an object access primitive only if the object is not implicitly locked from locks on non-leaf granules. The information on non-leaf granules is obtained by the combination of the results of two analyses that we call the *conservative locking analysis* and the *multigranular locking analysis*.

In the rest of this paper, transactions of the examples will access a database with the following Galileo schema. In this schema there are two classes which are in

```
use    Employees class
             employee <->
                    ( I name: string;
                    and code: string
                    and salary: ref int ... I )
             key (code)

and    Managers subset of Employees class
             manager <->
                    ( I is employee
                    and groupname: string
                    and group: ref seq employee      % 1-N association
             and ... I );
```

Fig. 3. Database schema in Galileo for transactions in the examples

an *is_a* relationship: Managers is a subclass of Employees. Every manager object is associated with the set of employees that constitute his group and the attribute code is a primary key of these classes. Only these two class names are defined in the global shared environment.

Env
Employees
Managers

3.1 Conservative Locking Analysis for Object-Oriented Accesses

The conservative locking analysis that we summarize here is a simple variant of that presented in [Amato 1993]. This analysis provides enough insight about navigation in the database. This information is sufficient to statically set *intention* locks on class extensions and on the class hierarchy. The conservative locking analysis implicitly assumes that navigational accesses deal only with a subset of the objects of a class. This is a safe assumption that usually corresponds to the real situation.

The analysis is automatically performed by running an interpreter that executes the transaction on an "abstract" global environment and an "abstract" global store. During the execution of the transaction, the interpreter records accesses to "abstract" storable values and this is all that is needed for inferring information about intention locks.

The particular global environment is isomorphic to the real shared global environment: there are all the names of both classes and individual objects of the real database[3]. From a technical point of view, the only problem is how to represent the abstract store to ensure that the interpreter terminates for every transaction and that the collected information is significant.

In the abstract store, the individual objects do not represent a problem because they are frozen: every individual persistent object is represented by exactly one abstract individual object. Furthermore, if the abstract individual object represents a modifiable value, then a pair of flags is used to record abstract read/write accesses. These two flags are present in the abstract store for every object that represents a modifiable value.

The main problem is to make finite the abstract domains for the data structures whose cardinality cannot be statically determined: class extensions and sequences. A class extension is abstracted by a sequence of exactly two object identifiers: the first object identifier relates the class extension to one abstract object representing all the objects existing in the database *before* transaction execution, the second object identifier relates the class extension to all the *new* objects potentially created by the transaction. In this way the analysis can distinguish new objects from old ones. Sequences are abstracted in the same way of class extensions.

Another problem to solve is how to render finite the number of new values generated from the analysed transaction. Indeed a real execution of a transaction could loop for ever and it could for example generate an infinite number of new persistent values and repeatedly assign it to the same field of the same class object. The solution is to bind statically the occurrence of every value constructor in a transaction's text to

---

[3] We remind that the environment of the database is shared among transactions and, once defined, it is frozen for the rest of the life of the database.

419

trans (	*let*	(EmpCode,inputstring()),
	let	(GroupName,*inputstring*()),
	let	(FindManager,*func*(ManObj,
	ite	(*stringeq*(*obj_of*(ManObj, 'code'),EmpCode),

$\qquad$ *specialise* (Managers,   % *a class extension*

$\qquad\qquad$ *record* ('groupname', GroupName,

$\qquad\qquad\qquad$ 'group', **ref** (**emptyseq**()))),

$\qquad\qquad$ ManObj),

$\qquad$ *skip*))),

$\quad$ *for_class* (Employees, FindManager))   % *a class extension*

Fig. 4. APPL transaction T1

just one abstract location. In this way every time a value constructor occurs during an abstract execution, it evaluates to the same abstract location and one abstract stored value plays the rôle of a set of concrete values.

Following the previous suggestions, the reader can verify that a textual analysis of the transaction T1 can easily be used to discover which are the class extensions and the class hierarchies accessed during the execution and in which way (see **Fig. 4**). The transaction promotes an employee to a manager. It accesses with the intention of reading the Employees class hierarchy and extension, and with the intention of writing the Managers granule in the class hierarchy and the Managers extension.

3.2 Multigranular Locking Analysis for Set-Oriented Accesses

The multigranular locking analysis is the central issue of this paper, described in detail in the next section. Multigranular locking analysis provides information for setting shared, exclusive and shared intention exclusive locks on the class hierarchy of APPL LIG. Furthermore it gives information about shared locks on class extensions.

The central point of the multigranular locking analysis is the query primitive. The query primitive is the unique primitive that deals with a class extension as a whole. It is quite simple to statically determine a superset of the class extensions that will be accessed during a transaction execution. Multigranular analysis infers this information just looking for every occurrence of a query primitive in the text of a transaction (and in the text of involved methods). These class extensions will be locked in S mode.

Starting from the occurrence of a query primitive in the text of the transaction, a control-flow analysis is performed that verifies if along an execution path there is a primitive that accesses the state of an object belonging to the extension of the class. An execution path is thus a chain in an execution tree whose nodes represent APPL primitives. The head of the chain and the root of the execution tree is the query primitive. The object access primitive has a variable weight that depends on the probability that the execution path is effectively executed. This probability depends only on the conditional expressions encountered in the path and on the distribution of the probability that regards the condition of the conditional. Intuitively, with uniform distribution of probability, if an access primitive to an object state is applied in a branch of a conditional then its execution probability is half of the conditional execution's probability. Using simple probabilistic theory and standard statistical

	Extension	Ext_element	Class	Object
insert (x,r)	IX x	X nl_ee	NL	NL
specialise (x,r,o)	IX x	X nl_ee	IX x, o's classes	X o
is_in (x,o)	S x	NL	NL	NL
remove (o)	IX o's exts	X o's ee	IX o's classes	X o
for_class (x,f)	S x	NL	NL	NL
obj_of (o,lb)	NL	NL	IS o's classes	S o

Fig. 5. Lock modes of primitives in APPL Lock Instance Graph

information on the database state, it is possible to compute the weight of an object access primitive. The MGL analysis computes all possible weights and combines them in an consistent way. The analysis stops to gather useful information in two cases: when the transaction performs a navigation, that is when the execution flows to another class or to an individual object; or when the weight of an execution path drops to insignificant values. We notice that in case of navigation between classes it could be possible to provide a clever analysis if statistical information about association were available. This kind of information is used for example by OO query language optimisers (see [Graefe 1993] for a comprehensive survey).

    Fig. 5 shows the standard lock modes set from a transaction that consists of a single primitive. With this information it is possible to statically analyse the text of T1 for collecting information about lock modes appropriate for the transaction. An immediate decision is for locking in S mode the Employees extension. Then, the second decision is for putting an S lock on the Employees class hierarchy because the object access primitive *obj_of* is found on the unique execution path that starts from the query primitive. Finally, a decision about the *specialise* primitive has to be taken. This primitive is part of the 'then' branch of a conditional expression *ite*, and thus it is placed on an execution path that involves the probability of the condition. If statistical information are available, a statistical approximation of the probability that all employees are going to become a managers can be computed. For example, if the statistical information ensures that the n employees in the database have different values for the field 'code' (it is a primary key), then it is possible to infer that only one employee out of n is going to become a manager and hence to decide to lock in IX mode the Employees class hierarchy.

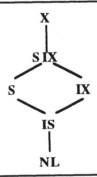

Fig. 6. Domain of lock modes for MGL protocol

3.3 Conservative Multigranular Locking Analysis

When the multigranular locking analysis finishes, the results of the two analyses are put together. Given two LIGs with non-leaf nodes labelled by a lock mode, the combination of the two LIGs consists in performing a set of *join* diadic operations, one for every pair of lock modes of the same non-leaf node. The *join* operation is defined on the domain shown in **Fig. 6**, which reflects the rules of compatibility between lock modes defined for MGL protocol. Finally, some simple computations are necessary to complete the LIG for conservative multigranular locking. In this final step, new intention locks can be inserted for topmost nodes and redundant locks can be eliminated for nodes close to the leaves.

4. Formal Framework

The chosen formal framework prescribes the following steps. Firstly, an exact "non–standard" semantics of APPL transactions is defined. It behaves as the standard one, moreover it collects information on the dynamic behaviour of a transaction. Notice that an exact non-standard interpretation of an APPL transaction may not terminate as the standard one. Secondly, an abstract version of the exact non–standard semantics is defined, aimed to deduce information about how many objects of a class are manipulated and in which way. Finally, results of abstract semantics have to be proven correct with respect to exact ones and it must be formally proven that abstract semantics terminates for every possible input APPL transaction. It should be noted that in practice only the abstract version of the semantics needs to be implemented.

4.1 Exact Non–standard Semantics

This semantics is *exact* because it behaves exactly as the standard one, and it is *non-standard* because it computes something different from the "standard" function computed from a transaction. In fact, this semantics keeps track of the accesses to modifiable persistent values. We remind that in APPL language, these values are references, object states and class extensions. The non-standard behaviour is obtained by associating two flags with every storage location that stores a persistent modifiable value. During the exact non–standard execution of a transaction the flags of a location are set to record if such a location has been accessed for reading and/or updating its content. Flags are set when one of the following primitives is executed in a non-standard way:

i) A reference is read when a dereference primitive *deref* is executed, and it is updated when an assignment *assign* is performed;

ii) An object state is read when the *object access primitive obj_of* selects a field of the object, and it is updated when a specialisation primitive *specialise* is performed;

iii) A class extension is read from a query primitive *for_class* and from the membership primitive *is_in*, a base class extension is updated from the insertion primitive *insert*, a subclass extension is updated from the specialisation primitive *specialise*.

4.2 Abstract Non–standard Semantics

The goal of the analysis is to detect the probability that a transaction accesses all objects of a class in the class hierarchy. In APPL, *for_class* is the unique primitive that always involves a computation on every object of a class. A *for_class* construct takes a class identifier x and a function f as arguments and it applies f to all object identifiers belonging to the extension of x one at a time. During its execution, f may ormay not access the object state. The useful information to discover is the probability that such object state is accessed. To obtain this information, we analyse the text of the function f to verify if all possible execution paths have an object access primitive and the probability of the execution of every execution path.

We would like to have an abstract semantics that expresses a notion of *probability about the execution* of constructs that compose APPL transactions. Intuitively, if an object access primitive is present in the text of a conditional branch, then its execution probability depends on the probability that the conditional is satisfied. Furthermore, *then* and *else* branches have an execution probability whose sum is equal to the execution probability of the whole conditional statement. The abstract semantics will be constructed on the following notions:

i)   *condition probability*: the probability that a conditional holds;
ii)   *execution probability*: the probability that an expression of a transaction is executed;
iii)   *access probability*: the probability that all object states of a class are accessed.

4.2.1   Abstract domains

The previous notions of probabilities are summarized by an abstract domain that contains the non negative integer values in the range $0..max$. The constant max is a predefined positive integer that represents, in terms of the usual representation of probability on the real closed domain $[0..1]$, the value 1, that means the certainty of occurrence of an event. Pragmatically, the values in this range are used to give a different weight to the primitives found in the different execution paths. In Sect. 4.3, there is A slightly deeper discussion on the choice of a significant value for max .

$$\begin{array}{ll}
\text{Aenv} = \text{Ide} \rightarrow \text{Val} + \text{Class} & \text{\% environment} \\
\text{Val} = \text{Aval} + \text{Aobj} + \text{Afun} & \text{\% individual values} \\
\text{Aval} = \{none\} & \\
\text{Aobj} = \{1 .. class\_no\} & \text{\% object identifiers} \\
\text{Class} = \{1 .. class\_no\} & \text{\% class identifiers} \\
\text{AFun} = \text{Val} \rightarrow \text{Ast} \rightarrow \text{Aeprob} \rightarrow (\text{Val x Lock}) & \\
\text{Ast} = \text{Class} \rightarrow \text{Aobj} & \text{\% store} \\
\text{Lock} = \text{Aobj} \rightarrow (\text{X x S x SIX}) & \text{\% locks i.e. stored values} \\
\text{X} = \text{S} = \text{SIX} = \text{Aaprob} = \text{Aeprob} = \text{Acprob} = \{0, 1, 2, ..., max\} &
\end{array}$$

An abstract environment maps identifiers into individual values or classes. Val represents the domain of all abstract individual values. Aval represent those individual values that are abstracted by the singleton {*none*} (basic values, references, records, object states and sequences). In this way, we model the fact that the analysis is not interested in the behaviour of a transaction on individual values. It is important to notice that the extension of every class is represented by exactly one abstract object. *class_no* is both the number of abstract classes and abstract objects. This number represents the number of classes declared in the schema of the real database.

Lock is the most interesting domain. It is used to record the *abstract access probability* of an object by associating an abstract object identifier with a triple <X,S,SIX>. The corresponding X, S, and SIX domains have 0 as bottom, max as top, and the ordering of the other elements is the usual natural ordering. We will indicate the bottom of the Lock domain with NL, i.e. NL=λo.<0,0,0>. The elements of the Aaprob, Aeprob, Acprob domains represent respectively *abstract access probability*, *abstract execution probability*, *abstract condition probability*. Finally, the Afun domain is used for functions: given its argument, a store and an *abstract execution probability*, a function returns a value and a lock.

4.2.2 Semantic equations

The *abstract access probability* is the probability we are interested in. Its computation depends on the computation of the abstract execution probability which is performed according to the rules that follow. The rules are recursively defined on the structure of the sentence representing an APPL transaction:

i) Let *e* be transaction. Its abstract execution probability is *max* (i.e., the initial value).

ii) Let *e* be a conditional expression *ite(b,e1,e2)* with abstract execution probability *aep*, and let *acp* the abstract condition probability of *b*. The abstract execution probability of then-branch depends on the joint probability representing both the execution probability of the conditional and the condition probability. *e1* should have as abstract execution probability computed in the usual way: $(aep/max)*(acp/max)$; but reminding that values of the Aeprob domain represent rational fractions with *max* as implicit denominator, we will use the following: $\lceil (aep*acp)/max \rceil$. *e2* will have the probability of the complementary event: $\lfloor (aep*(max-acp))/max \rfloor$. Note that both formulas evaluates to an element of the Aeprob domain. Finally, *b* will take *aep* as execution probability.

iii) Let *e* be any other expression with execution probability *aep*. All its subexpressions will have the same execution probability *aep*.

The *abstract access probability* is computed in the following way:

i) when an access primitive *p* to the current object *o* is reached in an execution path that starts from a *for_class* primitive, the *abstract access probability* of *o* is the *abstract execution probability* of *p*;

ii) when a conditional is evaluated, the *abstract access probability* of all classes is the least upper bound between the sum of the *abstract access probabilities* collected in else and then branches, and the *abstract access probability* of the condition;

iii) when any other expression is evaluated the *abstract access probability* of all classes is the least upper bound of the *abstract access probabilities* computed while executing the subexpressions.

The semantic functions have the following signatures:

AL: Exp → Aenv → Ast → Aeprob → (Val x Lock)
AD: Dec → Aenv → Ast → Aeprob → (Val x Lock x Aenv)
AP: Exp → Aenv → Ast → Acprob

AL and **AD** evaluate respectively an expression and a declaration given an environment, a store and an *abstract execution probability*. **AL** returns a value and a lock, **AD** returns a value, a lock and a modified environment. Finally, given a condition, an environment and a store, **AP** computes the *abstract condition probability* .

We will briefly comment on **AP** function in the conclusions. As far as the analysis is concerned, the unique important point is that this function can be statically computed, and it can be modelled by:

$$\textbf{AP}\,[e]\,\rho\,\sigma = oracle(e, \rho, \sigma)$$

where: $\qquad oracle: (Exp, Aenv, Ast) \rightarrow Acprob$

is a function that computes the *abstract condition probability* given a certain class of boolean expressions, an abstract environment, an abstract store and statistical information on the state of the real database[4].

In the rest of this section only few relevant semantic equations of the abstract semantics are presented. The following variables will be used: $\rho \in \text{Aenv}$, $\sigma \in \text{Ast}$, $\pi \in \text{Aeprob}$.

$$\textbf{AL}\,[c]\,\rho\,\sigma\,\pi = <\{none\},NL>$$
$$\textbf{AL}\,[x]\,\rho\,\sigma\,\pi = <\rho\,(x),NL>$$

The previous equations evaluate respectively a constant and an identifier. No action on the lock domain is taken because no action is performed on class objects. This is expressed through the bottom NL of the Lock domain.

$$\textbf{AL}\,[e(e_1)\,]\,\rho\,\sigma\,\pi = \quad \text{let} \quad \begin{aligned} &<fun, lk_1> = \textbf{AL}\,[e]\,\rho\,\sigma\,\pi \\ &<val, lk_2> = \textbf{AL}\,[e_1]\,\rho\,\sigma\,\pi \\ &<val_1, lk_3> = fun\;val\;\rho\;\sigma\;\pi \end{aligned}$$
$$\text{in} \qquad <val_1, sup\;(lk_1, lk_4, lk_3)>$$

To deal with a user defined function application first the expression that evaluates to the function is computed, then the argument is evaluated, and finally the application takes place. The final result is a pair having as lock component the least upper bound of locks computed in previous steps.

$$\textbf{AL}[\,func\;(x, e)]\,\rho\,\sigma\,\pi = <(\lambda val.\,\lambda\sigma'\,\pi.\,\textbf{AL}[e]\rho\,[val/x]\,\sigma'\pi), NL>$$

The evaluation of the *func* primitive creates a lexically scoped function.

$$\textbf{AL}[\,ite\;(b, e_1, e_2)\,]\,\rho\,\sigma\,\pi = \text{let} \quad \begin{aligned} p &= \textbf{AP}\,[b]\,\rho\,\sigma \\ <-, lk_1> &= \textbf{AL}\,[b]\,\rho\,\sigma\,\pi \\ <-, lk_2> &= \textbf{AL}\,[e_1]\,\rho\,\sigma\lceil(\pi * p)\,/\,max\rceil \\ <-, lk_3> &= \textbf{AL}\,[e_2]\,\rho\,\sigma\lfloor(\pi * (max - p))\,/\,max\rfloor \\ lk_4 &= asum\;(lk_2, lk_3)[5] \end{aligned}$$
$$\text{in} \qquad <none, sup\;(lk_1, lk_4)>$$

---

[4] This implicit parameter is not shown in the semantic equation.

[5] The auxiliary function $asum$: Lock x Lock $\rightarrow$ Lock is defined as follows:

$$asum\;(lk_1, lk_2) = [sm/oid] \quad \textbf{where}\;\forall\;oid \in \text{Dom(Lock)}$$
$$sm = <lk_1(oid)\downarrow1 +^a lk_2(oid)\downarrow1, lk_1(oid)\downarrow2 +^a lk_2(oid)\downarrow2, lk_1(oid)\downarrow3 +^a lk_2(oid)\downarrow3>$$

and $+^a: \{0, ..., max\} \times \{0, ..., max\} \rightarrow \{0, ..., max\}$ is:

$$\begin{aligned} a +^a b \quad &= a + b \quad \textbf{if}\;a + b \leq max \\ &= max \quad \textbf{elsewhere} \end{aligned}$$

The boolean expression b is evaluated at the execution probability of the conditional construct itself. The *then* and the *else* branches are evaluated at the appropriate execution probability as described previously. The global result is the greater of the sum of the locks resulting by the evaluation of the two branches and the locks resulting by the evaluation of the boolean expression.

$$\textbf{AL}[\, \textit{for\_class}\ (x, f)\,]\ \rho\ \sigma\ \pi = \quad \textbf{let} \quad \begin{aligned} &<\!fun, lk_1\!> = \textbf{AL}\ [f]\ \rho\ \sigma\ \pi \\ &cid = \rho\ (x) \\ &oid = \sigma\ (cid) \\ &<\!-, lk_2\!> = fun\ oid\ \sigma\ \pi \end{aligned}$$
$$\textbf{in} \quad <\!none, sup(lk_1, lk_2)\!>$$

for_class primitive applies a function f to the unique class object bound to the class identifier x. The lock of the object changes only if it is accessed during the function application.

$$\textbf{AL}[\, \textit{specialise}\ (x, r, o)\,]\ \rho\ \sigma\ \pi = \quad \textbf{let} \quad \begin{aligned} &<\!oid, lk_1\!> = \textbf{AL}\ [o]\ \rho\ \sigma\ \pi \\ &<\!-, lk_2\!> = \textbf{AL}\ [r]\ \rho\ \sigma\ \pi \\ &lk = \textbf{if}\ (oid \neq none) \\ &\qquad\qquad \textbf{then}\ [<\!\pi, 0, \pi\!>/oid] \\ &\qquad\qquad \textbf{else}\ \text{NL} \end{aligned}$$
$$\textbf{in} \quad <\!oid, sup\ (lk_1, lk_2, lk)\!>$$

specialise primitive modifies an object so its lock is updated in X and SIX mode. Notice that o expression evaluates to *none* if the object has not been reached through a *for_class* primitive: in this case π (execution probability), is not recorded.

$$\textbf{AL}[\, \textit{obj\_of}\ (o, lb)\,]\ \rho\ \sigma\ \pi = \quad \textbf{let} \quad \begin{aligned} &<\!oid, lk_1\!> = \textbf{AL}\ [o]\ \rho\ \sigma\ \pi \\ &lk = \textbf{if}\ (oid \neq none) \\ &\qquad\qquad \textbf{then}\ [<\!0, \pi, \pi\!>/oid] \\ &\qquad\qquad \textbf{else}\ \text{NL} \end{aligned}$$
$$\textbf{in} \quad <\!none, sup\ (lk_1, lk)\!>$$

The *obj_of* primitive reads the object so the object lock is updated in S and SIX mode.

$$\textbf{AL}[\, \textit{remove}\ (o)\,]\ \rho\ \sigma\ \pi = \quad \textbf{let} \quad \begin{aligned} &<\!oid, lk_1\!> = \textbf{AL}\ [o]\ \rho\ \sigma\ \pi \\ &lk = \textbf{if}\ (oid \neq none) \\ &\qquad\qquad \textbf{then}\ [<\!\pi, 0, \pi\!>/oid] \\ &\qquad\qquad \textbf{else}\ \text{NL} \end{aligned}$$
$$\textbf{in} \quad <\!none, sup\ (lk_1, lk)\!>$$

The *remove* primitive modifies the object lock in X and SIX modes.

The last three primitives manipulate objects. The analysis is interested only in these accesses, thus no other action like reading a field, specialising or removing an object is taken into account. *insert* and *is_in* primitives are not particularly interesting.

$$\textbf{AD}[\, \textit{let}\ (x, e)\,]\ \rho\ \sigma\ \pi = \quad \textbf{let} \quad <\!val, lk_1\!> = \textbf{AL}\ [e]\ \rho\ \sigma\ \pi$$
$$\textbf{in} \quad <\!none, lk_1, \rho[\, val\ /x\,]\!>$$

$$\mathbf{AD}[\; letrec\,(x\,,e\,)\,]\,\rho\,\sigma\,\pi = fix \quad (\lambda <val',lk',\rho'>.$$
$$\mathbf{let} \quad <val,lk_1> = \mathbf{AL}\,[\,e\,]\,\rho\,[\rho'\,(x\,)\,/x\,]\sigma\,\pi$$
$$\mathbf{in} \quad <none,lk_1,\rho[val\,/x\,]>)$$

The previous are the semantic equations for recursive and non recursive declarations. Notice that the first argument of the function on which the functional *fix* operates will converge to *none* after the first iteration; the remaining arguments will converge in a finite number of iterations because of the domain's finiteness and the monotonicity of the function.

4.2.3   Correctness and termination

The correctness of the analysis has been proven with respect to the exact non-standard semantics of the language. The intuitive notion of correctness is the following: if after the analysis of a transaction an abstract object o_a contains *max* in X (S) then all the objects of the exact class, that corresponds to the abstract class to which o_a belongs to, will be accessed for updating (reading); if after the analysis of a transaction an abstract object o_a contains *max* in SIX then all the objects of the exact class, that corresponds to the abstract class to which o_a belongs to, will be indifferently accessed for updating or reading.

The termination of the analysis is guaranteed by the finiteness of the abstract domains and by the monotonicity of the functions that perform the analysis on such domains. In fact the termination of the fix–point computation depends on the monotonicity of the function involved in the computation and on the usage of domains with finite ascending chains. The finiteness of the domains is trivially stronger than having finite ascending chains.

4.3   Tuning of the Analysis

The accuracy of the probability computed by the abstract analysis depends on the choice of *max*. The abstract execution probability of expressions decreases every time an occurrence of the conditional construct is evaluated, until it becomes 0. Notice that 0 does not mean that an expression has 0 as execution probability, but it means that the initial choice of *max* has not allowed to consider as significant the computation performed along the execution path that is labelled with a 0 execution probability. If there are further subexpressions to evaluate along that execution path, then their contribution will be ignored even if the real execution will access objects in some classes. Notice that this behaviour affects only the significance of the analysis while the correctness is preserved.

An ideal choice of *max* should ensure that all nested conditionals that can be reached during a real execution should have an abstract execution probability greater than 0. This ideal is not statically decidable because of recursion. Thus an acceptable choice of *max* should allow to maintain a proportion among the abstract probabilities that finitely approximate the probabilities of real execution.

In practice, the choice of *max* should be made in such a way that it allows to give a non null weight to every branch of every conditional that appears in the text of a transaction and of the involved functions. Following a well-known technique of approximation usually used in this kind of static analysis, we suggest the way that follows to "cut" recursion. Starting from the syntax tree of the text of the transaction, recursively build a syntax tree in which every node n representing a function call $g(x)$

Lock	
obj1	$<1/n,max,max>$
obj2	$<0,0,0>$

Lock	
obj1	$<0,max,max>$
obj2	$<0,0,0>$

Lock	
obj1	$<0,0,0>$
obj2	$<0,0,0>$

Fig. 7. Analyses' results for T1, T2, T3.

is replaced by the syntax tree of $g(x)$'s body, unless a function call $g(x)$ has not been previously replaced somewhere in the path from the node n up to the root of the syntax tree. Once this syntax tree has been built, *max* should be chosen as an integer *greater than* the maximum number of nested conditionals that can be found in the tree.

5. Examples of the Analysis

X	*max*	*0*	*>0,<max*	*0*	*>0,<max*	*<max*
S	–	*max*	*<max*	*>0,<max*	*max*	*<max*
SIX	–	–	*<max*	–	–	*max*
Final Lock	X	S	IX	IS	SIX	SIX

The goal of transaction's analysis is to know for each class the approximate access probability in S, X and SIX mode of all objects in its extension. The above table reports the combination of the admissible results of the analysis and the final lock decisions. For example, suppose that the analysis results in a *max* value for the X component of *cl* class's abstract object. Independently from the values of the other two components, we deduce that the greatest part of *cl* objects will be dynamically modified from the transaction so we ask an X lock for *cl* class to lock implicitly all its objects (first column of the table).

The next three examples have the database schema previously shown. In the database there are $n=e+m$ employees and m managers, and thus there is in the average one manager every n/m employees; furthermore all employees have a different value for the attribute 'code'. This statistical information is available to our static analyser. The abstract environment will have two abstract classes with a single abstract object.

Aenv		Ast	
Persons	cl1	cl1	obj1
Employees	cl2	cl2	obj2

The results of the three analyses are shown in **Fig. 7**. Not all results are "normalised" on the domain representing the range $0..max$.

Example T1

Transaction T1 is the example transaction previously shown in **Fig. 4**, the transaction that transforms an employee into a manager. Because statistical information are available, the analyser will know that only one employee out of n will be promoted. This leads to the results shown in the first table of **Fig. 7** and thus the analysis deduces an SIX lock has to be requested for the Employees class. Notice that the analysis does not infer any lock mode for the Managers class: this task is accomplished from the conservative analysis that derives an IX lock for this class. In **Fig. 8** there is the execution tree of the analysis.

428

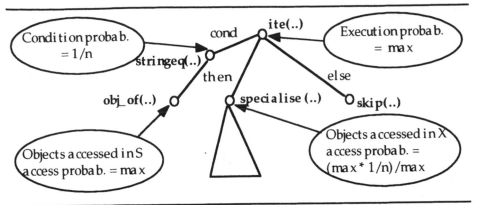

Fig. 8. Tree of abstract execution of Example T1

Example T2

Transaction T2 increases of a fixed amount of money the salary of all employees that are not managers. T2 returns the sequence of the salaries of all employees.

```
trans ( let   (Amount,inputstring ()),
        let   (Pay,func(   Obj,
                    ite       (is _in (Managers, Obj),
                    deref (obj_of (Obj, 'salary')),
                    block (  let (Sal,obj_of (Obj, 'salary')),
                            assign (Sal,+ (deref (Sal),Amount)),
                            deref (Sal))))),
        for_class (Employees,Pay))
```

As shown in the execution tree of **Fig. 9**, the analysis indicates that all the Employee objects are accessed in shared mode because the then branch has m/n access probability in S mode, the else branch has $n-m/n$ value as access probability in S mode, thus the sum of the two access probabilities is n, that is max. The result of the computation of the access probability is trivially correct because in both branches of the conditional there are *obj_of* primitives. This leads to ask for an S lock on the

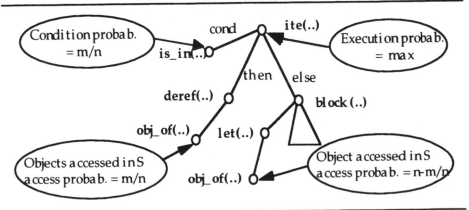

Fig. 9. Tree of abstract execution of Example T2

Employees class, according to the indications contained in the table shown at the beginning of this section.

Example T3

T3 is a transaction that counts the objects of Employees class.

> *trans* (*let* (Counter, *ref* (0)),
>   *let* (Count, *func*(Obj,
>   *ite*   (*is _in* (Managers, Obj),
>   *skip*(),
>   *assign* (Counter,+ (*deref* (Counter),1))))),
>   *for_class* (Employees,Count),
>   *outint* (Counter))

T3 does not access any object state. This means that the class hierarchy in APPL LIG is not involved. The occurrence of the *for_class* primitive in the text of the transaction will only produce an S lock on Employees extension of APPL LIG.

6. Final Remarks

We have presented an approach for dealing with conservative multigranular locking in a DBPL with OO features inspired by Galileo. There are several firm believes that motivate a static analysis of the implicit transactions expressed in this language:

a) the programmer is relieved from the burden of explicitly programming a complex concurrency control protocol;

b) the supporting system knows that the use of concurrency control protocol has been automatically generated and it is safely used, so the system is relieved from the task of controlling the correctness of the implemented concurrency control protocol;

c) the overhead of the static analysis in our client–server architecture completely lies on clients;

d) the use of conservative multigranular locking protocol reduces the run–time overhead of the supporting system while allows a satisfactory concurrency degree.

The result is a programmable system that as a whole represents a compromise between a high level of abstraction during its programming and a satisfactory efficiency at run–time. The efficiency is pursued reducing at a minimum the functionalities provided at run–time by the scheduler in the server, increasing the set of functionalities provided by a client (static analysis and part of the concurrency control functionalities at run–time), transferring in a phase that precedes transaction execution the granting of access to shared resources (conservative protocol).

The significance of the proposed analysis greatly depends on the possibility of static evaluation of the condition probability. This same problem has already been faced in the context of query optimisation and specifically concerns the problem of estimating query result sizes and frequency distribution. In our opinion, the techniques proposed in [Mannino 1988], that uses statistical approximations, should be a good starting point for tackling this problem. Of course, if we want to be sure that the condition probability is statically computable with sufficient approximation, then we should have to choose a limited class of expressions as conditions of conditionals. The problem is furtherly complicated because our language is object-oriented. In general, our opinion is that the transaction programmer should write transactions without any restriction on the use of the language's constructs; if he writes simple transactions, then these transactions can be optimised, otherwise simply they can not be optimised.

7. References

[Albano 1985]
Albano A., L. Cardelli, R. Orsini, "Galileo: A strongly typed interactive conceptual language", *ACM Trans. on Database Systems, Vol. 10(2)*, pp. 230-260.

[Amato 1993]
Amato G., F. Giannotti and G. Mainetto, "Data Sharing Analysis for a Database Programming Language via Abstract Interpretation", *Proc. of the 19th Int. Conf. on VLDB*, Dublin, Ireland, pp. 405–415.

[Amato 1996]
Amato G., M. Biscari, G. Mainetto and F. Rabitti, "Multigranularity Locking with the Use of Semantic Knowledge in a Layered Object Server", *Proc. of the 7th Int. Workshop POS*, Cape May, USA, pp. 151-163.

[Atkinson 1987]
Atkinson M.P. and O.P. Buneman, "Types and Persistence in Database Programming Languages", *ACM Computing Surveys, Vol 19(2)*, pp. 105–190.

[Atkinson 1995]
Atkinson M. P. and R. Morrison, "Orthogonally Persistent Object Systems", *The VLDB Journal, Vol. 4(3)*, pp. 319–401.

[Cousot 1977]
Cousot P. and R. Cousot, "Abstract Interpretation: an unified lattice model for static analysis of programs by construction of approximation of fixpoints", *Proc. 4th Int. Conf. POPL*, pp. 238-252.

[Graefe 1993]
Graefe G., "Query Evaluation Techniques for Large Databases", *ACM Computing Surveys, Vol. 25(2)*, pp. 71-170.

[Gray 1975]
Gray J., R. Lorie and G. Putzolu, "Granularity of locks and degrees of consistency in a shared database", *IBM Res. Rep. RJ1654*, San Jose, CA.

[Gray 1978]
Gray J., "Notes on Database Operating System", *IBM Res. Rep. RJ2188*, IBM Research Laboratory, San Jose, CA also in *Operating Systems – An Advanced Course*, Springer Verlag, *LNCS 60*, 1978.

[Jones 1995]
Jones N. D. and F. Nielson, "Abstract interpretation: a semantics-based tool for program analysis", in *Handbook of Logic in Computer Science. Vol. 4 - Semantic Modelling*, Oxford University Press, Oxford, pp. 527-636.

[Mannino 1988]
Mannino M. V., P. Chu and T. Sager, "Statistical profile estimation in database systems", *ACM Computing Surveys, Vol. 20(3)*, pp. 192–221.

[McCarthy 1962]
McCarthy J., P.W. Abrahams, D.J. Edwards, T.P. Hart and M.I. Levin, *Lisp 1.5 programmers's manual*, MIT Press.

Author Index

Lecture Notes in Computer Science

For information about Vols. 1–1376

please contact your bookseller or Springer-Verlag

Vol. 1414: M. Nielsen, W. Thomas (Eds.), Computer Science Logic. Selected Papers, 1997. VIII, 511 pages. 1998.

Vol. 1415: J. Mira, A.P. del Pobil, M.Ali (Eds.), Methodology and Tools in Knowledge-Based Systems. Vol. I. Proceedings, 1998. XXIV, 887 pages. 1998. (Subseries LNAI).

Vol. 1416: A.P. del Pobil, J. Mira, M.Ali (Eds.), Tasks and Methods in Applied Artificial Intelligence. Vol.II. Proceedings, 1998. XXIII, 943 pages. 1998. (Subseries LNAI).

Vol. 1417: S. Yalamanchili, J. Duato (Eds.), Parallel Computer Routing and Communication. Proceedings, 1997. XII, 309 pages. 1998.

Vol. 1418: R. Mercer, E. Neufeld (Eds.), Advances in Artificial Intelligence. Proceedings, 1998. XII, 467 pages. 1998. (Subseries LNAI).

Vol. 1419: G. Vigna (Ed.), Mobile Agents and Security. XII, 257 pages. 1998.

Vol. 1420: J. Desel, M. Silva (Eds.), Application and Theory of Petri Nets 1998. Proceedings, 1998. VIII, 385 pages. 1998.

Vol. 1421: C. Kirchner, H. Kirchner (Eds.), Automated Deduction – CADE-15. Proceedings, 1998. XIV, 443 pages. 1998. (Subseries LNAI).

Vol. 1422: J. Jeuring (Ed.), Mathematics of Program Construction. Proceedings, 1998. X, 383 pages. 1998.

Vol. 1423: J.P. Buhler (Ed.), Algorithmic Number Theory. Proceedings, 1998. X, 640 pages. 1998.

Vol. 1424: L. Polkowski, A. Skowron (Eds.), Rough Sets and Current Trends in Computing. Proceedings, 1998. XIII, 626 pages. 1998. (Subseries LNAI).

Vol. 1425: D. Hutchison, R. Schäfer (Eds.), Multimedia Applications, Services and Techniques – ECMAST'98. Proceedings, 1998. XVI, 532 pages. 1998.

Vol. 1427: A.J. Hu, M.Y. Vardi (Eds.), Computer Aided Verification. Proceedings, 1998. IX, 552 pages. 1998.

Vol. 1430: S. Trigila, A. Mullery, M. Campolargo, H. Vanderstraeten, M. Mampaey (Eds.), Intelligence in Services and Networks: Technology for Ubiquitous Telecom Services. Proceedings, 1998. XII, 550 pages. 1998.

Vol. 1431: H. Imai, Y. Zheng (Eds.), Public Key Cryptography. Proceedings, 1998. XI, 263 pages. 1998.

Vol. 1432: S. Arnborg, L. Ivansson (Eds.), Algorithm Theory – SWAT '98. Proceedings, 1998. IX, 347 pages. 1998.

Vol. 1433: V. Honavar, G. Slutzki (Eds.), Grammatical Inference. Proceedings, 1998. X, 271 pages. 1998. (Subseries LNAI).

Vol. 1434: J.-C. Heudin (Ed.), Virtual Worlds. Proceedings, 1998. XII, 412 pages. 1998. (Subseries LNAI).

Vol. 1435: M. Klusch, G. Weiß (Eds.), Cooperative Information Agents II. Proceedings, 1998. IX, 307 pages. 1998. (Subseries LNAI).

Vol. 1436: D. Wood, S. Yu (Eds.), Automata Implementation. Proceedings, 1997. VIII, 253 pages. 1998.

Vol. 1437: S. Albayrak, F.J. Garijo (Eds.), Intelligent Agents for Telecommunication Applications. Proceedings, 1998. XII, 251 pages. 1998. (Subseries LNAI).

Vol. 1438: C. Boyd, E. Dawson (Eds.), Information Security and Privacy. Proceedings, 1998. XI, 423 pages. 1998.

Vol. 1439: B. Magnusson (Ed.), System Configuration Management. Proceedings, 1998. X, 207 pages. 1998.

Vol. 1441: W. Wobcke, M. Pagnucco, C. Zhang (Eds.), Agents and Multi-Agent Systems. Proceedings, 1997. XII, 241 pages. 1998. (Subseries LNAI).

Vol. 1443: K.G. Larsen, S. Skyum, G. Winskel (Eds.), Automata, Languages and Programming. Proceedings, 1998. XVI, 932 pages. 1998.

Vol. 1444: K. Jansen, J. Rolim (Eds.), Approximation Algorithms for Combinatorial Optimization. Proceedings, 1998. VIII, 201 pages. 1998.

Vol. 1445: E. Jul (Ed.), ECOOP'98 – Object-Oriented Programming. Proceedings, 1998. XII, 635 pages. 1998.

Vol. 1446: D. Page (Ed.), Inductive Logic Programming. Proceedings, 1998. VIII, 301 pages. 1998. (Subseries LNAI).

Vol. 1447: V.W. Porto, N. Saravanan, D. Waagen, A.E. Eiben (Eds.), Evolutionary Programming VII. Proceedings, 1998. XVI, 840 pages. 1998.

Vol. 1448: M. Farach-Colton (Ed.), Combinatorial Pattern Matching. Proceedings, 1998. VIII, 251 pages. 1998.

Vol. 1449: W.-L. Hsu, M.-Y. Kao (Eds.), Computing and Combinatorics. Proceedings, 1998. XII, 372 pages. 1998.

Vol. 1450: L. Brim, F. Gruska, J. Zlatuška (Eds.), Mathematical Foundations of Computer Science 1998. Proceedings, 1998. XVII, 846 pages. 1998.

Vol. 1451: A. Amin, D. Dori, P. Pudil, H. Freeman (Eds.), Advances in Pattern Recognition. Proceedings, 1998. XXI, 1048 pages. 1998.

Vol. 1452: B.P. Goettl, H.M. Halff, C.L. Redfield, V.J. Shute (Eds.), Intelligent Tutoring Systems. Proceedings, 1998. XIX, 629 pages. 1998.

Vol. 1453: M.-L. Mugnier, M. Chein (Eds.), Conceptual Structures: Theory, Tools and Applications. Proceedings, 1998. XIII, 439 pages. 1998. (Subseries LNAI).

Vol. 1454: I. Smith (Ed.), Artificial Intelligence in Structural Engineering. XI, 497 pages. 1998. (Subseries LNAI).

Vol. 1456: A. Drogoul, M. Tambe, T. Fukuda (Eds.), Collective Robotics. Proceedings, 1998. VII, 161 pages. 1998. (Subseries LNAI).

Vol. 1457: A. Ferreira, J. Rolim, H. Simon, S.-H. Teng (Eds.), Solving Irregularly Structured Problems in Prallel. Proceedings, 1998. X, 408 pages. 1998.

Vol. 1458: V.O. Mittal, H.A. Yanco, J. Aronis, R-. Simpson (Eds.), Assistive Technology in Artificial Intelligence. X, 273 pages. 1998. (Subseries LNAI).

Vol. 1459: D.G. Feitelson, L. Rudolph (Eds.), Job Scheduling Strategies for Parallel Processing. Proceedings, 1998. VII, 257 pages. 1998.

Vol. 1461: G. Bilardi, G.F. Italiano, A. Pietracaprina, G. Pucci (Eds.), Algorithms – ESA'98. Proceedings, 1998. XII, 516 pages. 1998.

Vol. 1464: H.H.S. Ip, A.W.M. Smeulders (Eds.), Multimedia Information Analysis and Retrieval. Proceedings, 1998. VIII, 264 pages. 1998.